Psychometrics

Second Edition

Michael Furr dedicates this book to his Mother and Father.
Verne Bacharach dedicates this book to his children,
Leigh, Sam, and Will, and to their Mothers.

Psychometrics

An Introduction

Second Edition

R. Michael Furr
Wake Forest University

Verne R. Bacharach
Appalachian State University

Los Angeles | London | New Delhi
Singapore | Washington DC

Los Angeles | London | New Delhi
Singapore | Washington DC

FOR INFORMATION:

SAGE Publications, Inc.
2455 Teller Road
Thousand Oaks, California 91320
E-mail: order@sagepub.com

SAGE Publications Ltd.
1 Oliver's Yard
55 City Road
London, EC1Y 1SP
United Kingdom

SAGE Publications India Pvt. Ltd.
B 1/I 1 Mohan Cooperative Industrial Area
Mathura Road, New Delhi 110 044
India

SAGE Publications Asia-Pacific Pte. Ltd.
3 Church Street
#10-04 Samsung Hub
Singapore 049483

Acquisitions Editor: Reid Hester
Associate Editor: Eve Oettinger
Editorial Assistant: Sarita Sarak
Production Editor: Eric Garner
Copy Editor: QuADS Prepress (P) Ltd.
Typesetter: Hurix Systems Pvt. Ltd.
Proofreader: Laura Webb
Indexer: Marilyn Augst
Cover Designer: Edgar Abarca
Marketing Manager: Lisa Sheldon Brown
Permissions Editor: Karen Ehrmann

Printed in the United States of America

A catalog record of this book is available from the Library of Congress.

978-1-4522-5680-1

This book is printed on acid-free paper.

SUSTAINABLE FORESTRY INITIATIVE
Label applies to the text stock
Certified Sourcing
www.sfiprogram.org
SFI-00341

13 14 15 16 17 10 9 8 7 6 5 4 3 2 1

Contents

PART II. RELIABILITY

PART IV. THREATS TO PSYCHOMETRIC QUALITY

PART V. ADVANCED PSYCHOMETRIC APPROACHES

Preface

Measurement is at the heart of all science and of all applications of science. This is true for all areas of science, including the scientific attempt to understand or predict human behavior. Behavioral research, whether done by educators, psychologists, or other social scientists, depends on successful measurement of human behavior or of psychological attributes that are thought to affect that behavior. Likewise, the application of psychological or educational science often rests on successful measurement at a level that is no less important than it is in research. Indeed, scientifically sound clinical or educational programs and interventions require measurement of the behaviors or psychological attributes of the individuals enrolled in these programs.

This book is concerned with methods used to evaluate the quality of measures, such as psychological tests, that are used in research and applied settings by psychologists and others interested in human behavior. The scientific study of the quality of psychological measures is called psychometrics. Psychometrics is an extremely important field of study, and it can be highly technical. In fact, an article published in the *New York Times* (Herszenhorn, 2006) stated that "psychometrics, one of the most obscure, esoteric and cerebral professions in America, is also one of the hottest."

The Conceptual Orientation of This Book, Its Purpose, and the Intended Audience

Despite the potential "esoteric and cerebral" nature of the field, psychometrics does not need to be presented in a highly technical manner. The purpose of our book is to introduce the *fundamentals* of psychometrics to people who need to understand the properties of measures used in psychology and other behavioral sciences. More specifically, our goal is to make these important issues as accessible and as clear as possible, to as many readers as possible—including people who might initially shy away from something that might be seen as "obscure, esoteric, and cerebral."

With these goals in mind, our coverage of psychometrics is intended to be deep but intuitive and relatively nontechnical. We believe that this is a novel approach. On one hand, our treatment is much broader and deeper than the cursory treatment of psychometrics in undergraduate "Tests and Measurement" texts. On the other hand, it is more intuitive and conceptual than the highly technical treatment in books and journal articles intended for use by professionals in the field of psychometrics. We believe that anyone familiar with basic algebra and something equivalent to an undergraduate course in statistics will be comfortable with most of the material in this book. In general, our hope is that readers will attain a solid and intuitive understanding of the importance, meaning, and evaluation of a variety of fundamental psychometric concepts and issues.

This book is highly relevant for a variety of courses, including Psychological Testing, Psychometrics, Educational Measurement, Personality Assessment, Cognitive Assessment, Clinical Assessment, and, frankly, any type of Assessment course. Moreover, it could be an important part of courses with an emphasis on measurement in many areas of basic and applied science—for example, in medical training, sociology, exercise science, and public health.

Thus, this book is intended for use by advanced undergraduates, graduate students, and professionals across a variety of behavioral sciences and related disciplines. It will be of value to those who need a solid foundation in the basic concepts and logic of psychometrics or measurement more generally. Although it was not primarily written for people who are intending to become or already are psychometricians, it can serve as a very useful complement to the more technical texts.

In our attempt to make the topics of psychometrics accessible to our target audience, we constructed illustrative testing situations along with small artificial data sets to demonstrate important features of psychometric concepts. The data sets are used alongside algebraic proofs as a way of underscoring the conceptual meaning of fundamental psychometric concepts. In addition, we have departed from the usual practice of having a separate chapter devoted to statistics. Instead, we introduce statistical concepts throughout the text as needed, and we present them as tools to help solve particular psychometric problems. For example, we discuss factor analysis initially in the context of exploring the dimensionality of a test. Thus, we tie the statistical procedures to a set of important and intuitive conceptual issues. Our experience as classroom instructors has taught us that students benefit when quantitative concepts are linked to problems in this way, as the links seem to reinforce students' understanding of both the statistical procedures and the psychometric concepts.

Organizational Overview

The organization of this book is intended to facilitate the readers' insight into core psychometric concepts and perspectives. In the first chapter, we address the basic importance of psychological measurement and psychometrics. In addition, we examine a few important issues and themes that cut across all remaining chapters. This explicit treatment of these issues and themes should help solidify the concepts that are addressed in the later chapters.

In Chapters 2 through 4, we address important issues in measurement theory and in the statistical basis of psychometric theory. These chapters are fundamental to a full appreciation and understanding of the later chapters that examine psychometric theory in depth. Specifically, these chapters examine issues of scaling in psychological measurement, concepts in the quantification of psychological differences and the quantification of associations among psychological variables, issues in the interpretation of test scores, and concepts in the meaning and evaluation of test dimensionality. Although these topics can be technical, our intention is to focus these chapters at a level that is relatively intuitive and conceptual.

In Chapters 5 through 7, we examine the psychometric concept of reliability. In these chapters, we differentiate three fundamental aspects of reliability. In Chapter 5, we introduce the conceptual basis of reliability, focusing on the perspective of classical test theory. In Chapter 6, we discuss the common methods of estimating and evaluating the reliability of test scores. In Chapter 7, we explore the importance of reliability in terms of applied testing, scientific research, and test development. We believe that differentiating these three aspects of reliability provides readers with an understanding of reliability that is clearer and deeper than what might be obtained from many existing treatments of the topic. In all these chapters, we emphasize the psychological meaning of the concepts and procedures. We hope that this maximizes readers' ability to interpret reliability information meaningfully.

In Chapters 8 and 9, we examine the psychometric concept of validity. In these chapters, we examine the conceptual foundations of this important psychometric issue, we discuss many methods that are used to evaluate validity, and we emphasize the important issues to consider in the evaluation process. In these chapters, we adopt the most contemporary perspective on validity, as articulated by three national organizations involved in psychological testing—the American Psychological Association (APA), the American Educational Research Association (AERA), and the National Council on Measurement in Education (NCME). Although we discuss the traditional "tripartite" model of validity (i.e., content validity, criterion validity, and construct validity), which is emphasized in most existing measurement-oriented texts, our core discussion represents a more modern view of test validity and the evidence relevant to evaluating test validity.

In Chapters 10 and 11, we discuss two important threats to the psychometric quality of tests. We believe that it is vital to acknowledge and understand the challenges faced by those who develop, administer, and interpret psychological tests. Furthermore, we believe that it is crucial to grasp the creative and effective methods that have been developed as ways of coping with many of these challenges to psychometric quality. In Chapter 10, we explore response biases, which obscure the true differences among individuals taking psychological tests. In this chapter (which is unique to this book), we describe several different types of biases, we demonstrate their deleterious effects on psychological measurement, and we examine some methods of preventing or minimizing these effects. In Chapter 11, we examine test bias, which obscures the true differences between groups of people. In this chapter, we describe the importance of test bias, the methods of detecting different forms of test bias, and the important difference between test bias and test fairness.

Finally, in Chapters 12 to 14, we present advanced contemporary approaches to psychometrics. Much of the book reflects the most common psychometric approach in behavioral research and application—classical test theory. In the final three chapters, we provide overviews of approaches that move beyond this traditional approach. In Chapter 12, we present confirmatory factor analysis (CFA), which is a powerful tool that allows test developers and test users to examine important psychometric issues with flexibility and rigor. In Chapter 13, we discuss the basic concepts and purpose of generalizability theory, which can be seen as an expansion of the more traditional approaches to psychometric theory. In Chapter 13, we discuss item response theory (IRT) (aka latent trait theory or modern test theory), which is a very different way of conceptualizing the psychometric quality of tests, although it does have some similarities to classical test theory. In all three chapters, we provide in-depth examples of the applications and interpretations, so that readers can have a deeper understanding of these important advanced approaches. Although a full understanding of these advanced approaches requires greater statistical knowledge than is required for most of the book, our goal is to present these approaches at a level that emphasizes their conceptual basis more than their statistical foundations.

New to This Edition

I (Mike Furr) have made important revisions for the second edition of the book. These revisions reflect, in part, the valuable suggestions made by the reviewers of the first edition. They also reflect my views of the important issues that needed new coverage, greater attention, or better clarity. Considering these significant changes, I believe that the second edition is thus meaningfully improved beyond the first edition—it covers all of the previous content, it includes a great amount of important new content, and it does an even better job of achieving our overarching goal of accessibility and intuitiveness.

General Changes

Some changes are consistent throughout the book, not being limited to particular chapters. I have thought long and hard about all the material in the book, searching for opportunities to make several types of general changes.

1. Many changes were made to increase the clarity and accessibility of the material. I identified sections, paragraphs, sentences, and words that, I felt, could be improved for clarity, and I rewrote and/or reorganized this material.

2. Relatedly, many changes added to the depth of coverage of important material. Sometimes this depth was provided by adding a sentence or two, sometimes it was a new paragraph, sometimes it was a new section, and, in one instance, it was an entirely new chapter.

3. There were also a number of opportunities to be more explicit about the importance and implications of the material. If this book can't convey why readers should care about the material, then why should they spend their valuable time working through any particular concept, why should they bother reading this book, why should they try to remember the material, and why should they believe that psychometrics is, in general, a field with anything to offer society? Although this was a goal in the first edition, there were new opportunities to go even further in the new edition.

4. Largely as a function of other changes, the references were expanded and updated significantly. Specifically, this book has expanded from approximately 170 references to approximately 210. This expansion by nearly 25% provides readers with even more original sources that they can turn to for greater depth, more technical discussions, and useful illustrations.

5. Finally, the clarity of connections among the chapters was enhanced throughout the book. Many chapters now include a greater number of explicit references to other chapters, when discussing concepts that led to (or built on) principles or concepts that appeared in those other chapters. These changes were intended to help readers move back and forth more easily in the book, allowing them to remind themselves of important points when building on those points.

Chapter-Specific Changes

Of course, there are substantial—and often unique—changes to each individual chapter in the book. To be sure, some chapters received more attention than others; however, all chapters, at a minimum, went through changes that improve their content and style.

Chapter 1 (Introduction): The most noticeable revisions to this chapter are in the very beginning. The first several paragraphs have been rewritten to make the relevance and important of psychological testing and psychometrics as clear and robust as possible, as early as possible. This change was made to grab readers' attention immediately and to convey the importance of the material—both personally and societally.

Chapter 2 (Scaling): The changes to this chapter are mostly among the "General Changes" mentioned above. That is, this chapter has received a great deal of attention to its clarity, depth, and importance (e.g., a new brief section on the practical implications of scales of measurement has been introduced). Indeed, this chapter has perhaps benefited from such fundamental changes more than any other chapter in the book.

Chapter 3 (Individual Differences and Correlations): There are three significant changes to this chapter. The discussion of the relevance of "individual differences" in experimental research was expanded to clarify and convey the true scope of importance of the topic. I also presented the logic and structure of variance/covariance matrices, which are the basis of some later concepts/procedures. Finally, the discussion of composite variables was extended to include the covariance between composite variables, which is directly relevant to the discussion of reliability in Chapter 5.

Chapter 4 (Dimensionality and Factor Analysis): There are several important additions and revisions to this chapter. First, the three core dimensionality questions were cast in a more central manner, expanding their role in the conceptual foundations of dimensionality and in factor analysis (e.g., viewing exploratory factor analysis as a tool to answer these questions). Second, and most substantially, the chapter now includes a greatly expanded discussion of the process of conducting an exploratory factor analysis, along with a new flowchart that presents this process in an intuitive and visual way. This discussion expands on the illustration in the previous edition, adding much more depth of discussion regarding topics such as factor rotation, factor loadings, simple structure, and what to do when there are violations of simple structure. These additions should provide a much more robust foundation for readers who are beginning to learn the logic, execution, and interpretation of factor analysis. A third addition is a new brief section that presents an overview of CFA, with reference to Chapter 12, later in the book.

Chapter 5 (Reliability, Conceptual Basis): Changes to this chapter focused mainly on enhancing the clarity of presentation, adding depth in some important places. Even though reviewers' comments about this chapter have been very positive, these improvements should make the chapter even more accessible.

Chapter 6 (Empirical Estimates of Reliability): There are several key additions to this chapter. First, there is added depth to the discussion of standardized alpha—separating it more clearly from raw alpha and explaining when and why it is relevant and appropriate to use. Second, additional discussion and examples (i.e., output) have been provided on how to use statistical software to obtain various estimates of reliability. Third, I acknowledged some criticisms of alpha and the existence of alternative reliability indices based on internal consistency. Fourth, and most substantially, the discussion of the psychometric quality of difference scores was greatly expanded and generalized.

Chapter 7 (The Importance of Reliability): In this revised chapter, extensive text and tables were added to link reliability to effect size and significance testing in a broader range of analytic contexts. This was done via expanded explanations, fundamental equations, and illustrations focusing mainly on a basic independent-groups comparison. This significantly broadens the scope of implications. In addition, the chapter now explicitly discusses the fact that test development procedures (e.g., reliability-oriented item analyses) should be conducted separately for *each* dimension being assessed by the test. This was implicit in the previous edition of the book, but the revision should reduce any relevant confusion about this matter when working with multidimensional tests.

Chapter 8 (Validity, Conceptual Basis): This chapter has been very well received by reviewers, so I chose not to make too many revisions. That said, the chapter was revised for clarity, and the discussion of the importance of validity was moved to a much earlier section, making sure that readers appreciated the value of what they would learn as the chapter unfolded.

Chapter 9 (Estimating and Evaluating Convergent and Discriminant Validity Evidence): This chapter now explicitly discusses the importance of understanding and being attentive to the factors that affect the size of a validity coefficient. It also provides more practical guidelines for using information about the factors affecting a validity coefficient (e.g., what exactly to look for and what to do). In addition, the section on relative proportions was broadened to include skew as a more general concept, of which relative proportions is one intuitive example. Finally, and perhaps most significantly, the chapter now focuses deeply on a debate about the validity of the SAT as a practical example of the interpretation of validity coefficients and related issues.

Chapter 10 (Response Bias): Revisions to this chapter were relatively minimal. However, the chapter does have an enhanced discussion of the implications for applied testing contexts, some new discussion of the literature on "faking good" in employment settings, a new example of "adjusting" for social desirability from a research study of moral behavior, and (again) general revisions for clarity and depth.

Chapter 11 (Test Bias): This chapter benefited from several important changes. First, it has a deepened explanation of several important concepts, along with useful examples. Second, it now notes particular software programs that can be used to conduct relevant analyses. Third, and most substantially, it has an extensive new section that focuses on the 2001 University of California Report on the SAT as a real-life example of an examination of potential predictive bias.

Chapter 12 (Confirmatory Factor Analysis): This chapter is entirely new to this edition. Several reviewers suggested that the book would benefit from discussion of CFA, given its important and growing role in psychometrics. I agreed with this suggestion, and I am happy to offer what's hopefully an accessible and intuitive introduction to the topic. This chapter primarily focuses on the use of CFA to evaluate measurement models, with an in-depth discussion of the logic and interpretation of the process. It also discusses the use of CFA to evaluate reliability and convergent/discriminant validity evidence. As a side note, the chapters' overview of the logic and interpretation of CFA can be extended to other modeling procedures, including path analysis and structural equation modeling.

Chapter 13 (Generalizability Theory): This revised chapter has three main additions. First, it provides much greater discussion of the meaning and interpretation of variance components. Second, it has a much deepened discussion of the difference between random effects and fixed effects, particularly in terms of their estimation and interpretation. Finally, it now explicitly notes that researchers are primarily interested in relative effects rather than absolute effects.

Chapter 14 (Item Response Theory): Several key revisions to this chapter have been made. First, the introductory section has been expanded a bit, to provide greater context for the chapter. Second, it has a new discussion of "guessing" as an item parameter applicable in some testing contexts. Third, and very substantially, it benefits from new and extensive discussion of more advanced IRT models, particularly the graded response model (GRM). In doing this, it includes an in-depth (but hopefully intuitive) coverage of the GRM model's articulation of response probabilities, item characteristic curves, and item information curves. This expansion makes the chapter much more relevant for modern testing practices.

Acknowledgments

Authors' Acknowledgments

In moving toward the second edition, I (M. Furr) relied on the invaluable assistance of several people. At SAGE, Chris Cardone was Senior Acquisitions Editor for Psychology, and she proposed the idea of a second edition to SAGE's Editorial Board. Without her interest and effort in preparing that proposal, the second edition would never have emerged. In addition, I benefited greatly from advice and assistance provided by Astrid Virding, Lisa Shaw, Sarita Sarak, and Reid Hester, all at SAGE. In addition, I thank Wake Forest University, which generously provided a Reynolds leave, during which I was able to produce the second edition. Finally, but most important, I am grateful for the love, support, and encouragement of my wife, Sarah Squire. From one of our first dates, during which she told me that she took an online test "to see what the Big Five was all about" to her celebration of my completion of the second edition of this book, Sarah has been a constant source of joy, validation, and love.

In preparation for the second edition, we (M. Furr and V. Bacharach) relied on many people. Indeed, the prospectus reviewers made many useful suggestions concerning the content of the book. Later in the production process, we had the great fortune to have the comments of the draft reviewers. Their suggestions were instrumental in the development of the second edition of the book. We also deeply appreciated to editors who were involved in the development of the second edition, Jim Brace-Thompson and Cheri Dellelo. Jim encouraged us to write this book and guided us through the prospectus process. Cheri guided us through the manuscript-writing process. We could not have managed the book without her patience and good advice. Finally, Anna Mesick took responsibility for the final production of the book. We turned to her on numerous occasions for technical help with that process. We also appreciated Dr. Paul Fox and the members of the psychology department at Appalachian State University for supporting VB's request for a semester's leave to work on the second edition of this book.

Publisher's Acknowledgments

SAGE Publications gratefully acknowledges the contributions of the following reviewers:

First Edition Reviewers

Rainer Banse, Sozial-und Rechtspsychologie, Institut für Psychologie, Universitat Bonn

Patricia L. Busk, University of San Francisco

Kevin D. Crehan, University of Nevada, Las Vegas

Dennis Doverspike, University of Akron

Barbara A. Fritzsche, University of Central Florida

Jeffrey H. Kahn, Illinois State University

Howard B. Lee, California State University, Northridge

Craig Parks, Washington State University

Steven Pulos, University of Northern Colorado

David Routh, Exeter University and University of Bristol

Aloen L. Townsend, Mandel School of Applied Social Sciences, Case Western Reserve University

Vish C. Viswesvaran, Florida International University

Alfred W. Ward, Pace University

Second Edition Reviewers

Patricia Newcomb, University of Texas at Arlington

Sunny Lu Liu, California State University, Long Beach

Joel T. Nadler, Southern Illinois University Edwardsville

Barbara Fritzsche, University of Central Florida

Keith Kraseski, Touro College

Michael R. Kotowski, University of Tennessee, Knoxville

About the Authors

R. Michael Furr is Professor of Psychology and McCulloch Faculty Fellow at Wake Forest University, where he received the 2012 Award for Excellence in Research. His methodological work focuses on the measurement of similarity between psychological profiles, on the measurement of behavior, and on contrast analysis. His substantive research focuses on personality judgment and on the links between personality, situational forces, and behavior. He is a former associate editor of the *Journal of Research in Personality*, a former executive editor of the *Journal of Social Psychology*, and a consulting editor for several other scholarly journals. He has taught graduate and undergraduate courses in psychometrics, psychological testing, personality psychology, statistics, and research methods at Appalachian State University and Wake Forest University.

Verne R. Bacharach is Professor of Psychology at Appalachian State University. He has held faculty appointments at the University of Alabama, Peabody College of Vanderbilt University, and Acadia University in Nova Scotia and has chaired the departments at Appalachian State and Acadia. He has taught undergraduate and graduate courses in statistics, tests and measurements, and research methods for nearly 40 years. He has a long journal publication history of research and review articles. He obtained a PhD in experimental psychology from the University of Kansas in 1971.

CHAPTER 1

Psychometrics and the Importance of Psychological Measurement

Your life has probably been shaped, in part, by psychological measurement. Whether you are a student, a teacher, a parent, a psychologist, a physician, a nurse, a patient, a lawyer, a police officer, or a business person, you have taken psychological tests, your family members have taken psychological tests, or you have been affected by people who have taken psychological tests. These tests can affect our education, our careers, our family life, our safety, our health, our wealth, and, potentially, our happiness. Indeed, almost every member of an industrialized society is affected by psychological measurement at some point in his or her life—both directly and indirectly.

It is even fair to say that in extreme situations psychological measurement can have life or death consequences. You might think that this suggestion is overly sensational, far-fetched, and perhaps even simply wrong, but it is true. The fact is that in some states and nations prisoners who are mentally retarded cannot receive a death penalty. For example, the North Carolina State General Assembly states that "a mentally retarded person convicted of first degree murder shall not be sentenced to death" (Criminal Procedure Act, 2007); it defines mental retardation, in part, as general intellectual functioning that is "significantly sub-average." But what is significantly subaverage intellectual functioning, and how could we know whether a person's intelligence is indeed significantly subaverage?

These difficult questions are answered in terms of psychological tests. Specifically, the General Assembly states that significantly subaverage intellectual functioning is indicated by a score of 70 or below "on an individually administered, scientifically recognized standardized intelligence quotient test administered by a licensed psychiatrist or psychologist." Put simply, if a person has an intelligence quotient (IQ) score below 70, then he or she might not be sentenced to death by the state of North

Carolina; however, if a person has an IQ score above 70, then he or she can legally be put to death. Thus, though it might seem hard to believe, intelligence testing can affect whether men and women might live or die, quite literally.

Of course, few consequences of psychological measurement are so dramatic, but they can indeed be real, long-lasting, and important. Given the important role of psychological tests in our lives and in society more generally, it is imperative that such tests have extremely high quality. If testing has such robust implications, then it should be conducted with the strongest possible tools and procedures.

This book is about understanding whether such tools and procedures are indeed strong—how to determine whether a test produces scores that are psychologically meaningful and trustworthy. In addition, the principles and concepts discussed in this book are important for creating tests that are psychologically meaningful and trustworthy. These principles and concepts are known as "psychometrics."

Why Psychological Testing Matters to You

Considering the potential impact of psychological testing, we believe that everyone needs to understand the basic principles of psychological measurement. Whether you wish to be a practitioner of behavioral science, a behavioral researcher, or a sophisticated member of modern society, your life is likely to be affected by psychological measurement.

If you are reading this book, then you might be considering a career involving psychological measurement. Some of you might be considering careers in the practice or application of a behavioral science. Whether you are a clinical psychologist, a school psychologist, a human resources director, a university admissions officer, or a teacher, your work might require you to make decisions on the basis of scores obtained from some kind of psychological test. When a patient responds to a psychopathology assessment, when a student completes a test of cognitive ability, or when a job applicant fills out a personality inventory, there is an attempt to measure some type of psychological characteristic.

In such cases, basic measurement information needs to be examined carefully if it is going to be used to make decisions about the lives of people. Without a solid understanding of the basic principles of psychological measurement, test users risk misinterpreting or misusing the information derived from psychological tests. Such misinterpretation or misuse might harm patients, students, clients, employees, and applicants, and it can lead to lawsuits for the test user. Proper test interpretation and use can be extremely valuable for test users and beneficial for test takers.

Some of you might be considering careers in behavioral research. Whether your area is psychology, education, or any other behavioral science, measurement is at the heart of your research process. Whether you conduct experimental research, survey research, or any other kind of quantitative research, measurement is at the heart of your research process. Whether you are interested in differences between individuals, changes in people across time, differences between genders, differences between classrooms, differences between treatment conditions, differences between teachers, or differences between cultures, measurement is at the heart of your research process. If something is not measured or is not measured well, then it cannot be studied with any scientific validity. If you wish to interpret your research findings in a meaningful and accurate manner, then you must evaluate critically the data that you have collected in your research.

As mentioned earlier, even if you do not pursue a career involving psychological measurement, you will almost surely face the consequences of psychological measurement, either directly or indirectly. Applicants to graduate school and various professional schools must take tests of knowledge and achievement. Job applicants might be hired (or not) partially on the basis of scores on personality tests. Employees might be promoted (or passed over for promotion) partially on the basis of supervisor ratings of psychological characteristics such as attitude, competence, or collegiality. Parents must cope with the consequences of their children's educational testing. People seeking psychological services might be diagnosed and treated partially on the basis of their responses to various psychological measures.

Even more broadly, our society receives information and recommendations based on research findings. Whether you are (or will be) an applicant, an employee, a parent, a psychological client, or an informed member of society, the more knowledge you have about psychological measurement, the more discriminating a consumer you will be. You will have a better sense of when to accept or believe test scores, when to question the use and interpretation of test scores, and what you need to know to make such important judgments.

Given the widespread use and importance of psychological measurement, it is crucial to understand the properties affecting the quality of such measurements. This book is about the important *attributes of the instruments* that psychologists use to measure psychological attributes and processes.

We address several fundamental questions related to the logic, development, evaluation, and use of psychological measures. What does it mean to attribute scores to characteristics such as intelligence, memory, self-esteem, shyness, happiness, or executive functioning? How do you know if a particular psychological measure is trustworthy and interpretable? How confident should you be when interpreting an individual's score on a particular psychological test? What kinds of questions should you ask to evaluate the quality of a psychological test? What are some of the different kinds of psychological measures? What are some of the challenges to psychological measurement? How is the measurement of psychological characteristics similar to and different from the measurement of physical characteristics of objects? How should you interpret some of the technical information regarding psychological measurement?

We hope to address these kinds of questions in a way that provides a deep and intuitive understanding of psychometrics. This book is intended to provide you with the knowledge and skills needed to evaluate psychological tests intelligently. Testing plays an important role in our science and in our practice, and it plays an increasingly important role in our society. We hope that this book helps you become a more informed consumer and, possibly, producer of psychological information.

Observable Behavior and Unobservable Psychological Attributes

People use many kinds of instruments to measure the observable properties of the physical world. For example, if a person wants to measure the length of a piece of lumber, then he or she might use a tape measure. People also use various instruments to measure the properties of the physical world that are not directly observable. For example, clocks are used to measure time, and voltmeters are used to measure the change in voltage between two points in an electric circuit.

Similarly, psychologists, educators, and others use psychological tests as instruments to measure observable events in the physical world. In the behavioral sciences, these observable events are typically some kind of behavior, and behavioral measurement is usually conducted for two purposes. Sometimes, psychologists measure a behavior because they are interested in that specific behavior in its own right. For example, some psychologists have studied the way facial expressions affect the perception of emotions. The Facial Action Coding System (FACS; Ekman & Friesen, 1978) was developed to allow researchers to pinpoint movements of very specific facial muscles. Researchers using the FACS can measure precise "facial behavior" to examine which of a person's facial movements affect other people's perceptions of emotions. In such cases, researchers are interested in the specific facial behaviors themselves; they do not interpret them as signals of some underlying psychological process or characteristics.

Much more commonly, however, behavioral scientists observe human behavior as a way of assessing unobservable psychological attributes such as intelligence, depression, knowledge, aptitude, extroversion, or ability. In such cases, they identify some type of observable behavior that they think represents the particular unobservable psychological attribute, state, or process. They then measure the behavior and try to interpret those measurements in terms of the unobservable psychological characteristics that they think are reflected in the behavior. In most, but not all, cases, psychologists develop psychological tests as a way to sample the behavior that they think is sensitive to the underlying psychological attribute.

For example, suppose that we wish to identify which of two students, Sam and William, had greater working memory. To make this identification, we must measure each of their working memories. Unfortunately, there is no known way to observe directly working memory—we cannot directly "see" memory inside a person's head. Therefore, we must develop a task involving observable behavior that would allow us to measure working memory. For example, we might ask the students to repeat a string of digits presented to them one at a time and in rapid succession. If our two students differ in their task performance, then we might assume that they differ in their working memory. If Sam could repeat more of the digits than William, then we might conclude that Sam's working memory is in some way superior to William's. This conclusion requires that we make an inference—that an overt behavior, the number of recalled digits, is systematically related to an unobservable mental attribute, working memory.

There are three things that you should notice about this attempt to measure working memory. First, we made an inference from an observable behavior to an unobservable psychological attribute. That is, we assumed that the particular behavior that we observed was in fact a measure of working memory. If our inference was reasonable, then we would say that our interpretation of the behavior has a degree of *validity*. Although validity is a matter of degree, if the scores from a measure seem to be actually measuring the mental state or mental process that we think they are measuring, we say that our interpretation of scores on the measure is valid.

Second, for our interpretation of digit recall scores to be considered valid, the recall task had to be theoretically linked to working memory. It would not have made theoretical sense, for example, to measure working memory by timing William's and Sam's running speed in the 100-meter dash. In the behavioral sciences, we often make an inference from an observable behavior to an unobservable psychological attribute. Therefore, measurement in psychology often, but not always, involves some type of theory linking psychological characteristics, processes, or states to an observable behavior that is thought to reflect differences in the psychological attribute.

There is a third important feature of our attempt to measure working memory. Working memory is itself a theoretical concept. When measuring working memory, we assume that working memory is more than a figment of our imagination. Psychologists, educators, and other social scientists often turn to theoretical concepts such as working memory to explain differences in people's behavior. Psychologists refer to these theoretical concepts as *hypothetical constructs* or *latent variables*. They are theoretical psychological characteristics, attributes, processes, or states that cannot be directly observed, and they include things such as learning, intelligence, self-esteem, dreams, attitudes, and feelings. The operations or procedures used to measure these hypothetical constructs, or for that matter to measure anything, are called *operational definitions*. In our example, the number of recalled digits was used as an operational definition of some aspect of working memory, which itself is an unobservable hypothetical construct.

You should not be dismayed by the fact that psychologists, educators, and other social scientists rely on unobservable hypothetical constructs to explain human behavior. Measurement in the physical sciences, as well as the behavioral sciences, often involves making inferences about unobservable events, things, and processes based on observable events. As an example, physicists write about four types of "forces" that exist in the universe: (1) the strong force, (2) the electromagnetic force, (3) the weak force, and (4) gravity. Each of these forces is invisible, but their effects on the behavior of visible events can be seen. For example, objects do not float into space off the surface of our planet. Theoretically, the force of gravity is preventing this from happening. Physicists have built huge pieces of equipment to create opportunities to observe the effects of some of these forces on observable phenomena. In effect, the equipment is used to create scenarios in which to measure observable phenomena that are believed to be caused by the unseen forces.

To be sure, the sciences differ in the number and nature of unobservable characteristics, events, or processes that are of concern to them. Some sciences might rely on relatively few, while others might rely on many. Some sciences might have strong empirical bases for their unobservable constructs (e.g., gravity), while others might have weak empirical bases (e.g., penis envy). Nevertheless, all sciences rely on unobservable constructs to some degree, and they all measure those constructs by measuring some observable events or behaviors.

Psychological Tests: Definition and Types

What Is a Psychological Test?

According to Cronbach (1960), a psychological test "is a systematic procedure for comparing the behavior of two or more people" (p. 21). The definition includes three important components: (1) tests involve behavioral samples of some kind, (2) the behavioral samples must be collected in some systematic way, and (3) the purpose of the tests is to compare the behaviors of two or more people. We would modify the third component to include a comparison of performance by the same individuals at different points in time, but otherwise we find the definition appealing.

One of the appealing features of the definition is its generality. The idea of a test is sometimes limited to paper-and-pencil tests. For example, the Beck Depression Inventory (BDI; Beck, Steer, & Brown, 1996) is a 21-item multiple-choice test designed to measure depression. People who take the test read each question and then choose an answer from one of several supplied answers. Degree of depression is evaluated by counting the number of answers of a certain type to each of the questions. The BDI is clearly a test, but other methods of systematically sampling behavior are also tests. For example, in laboratory situations, researchers ask participants to respond in various ways to well-defined stimulus events; participants might be asked to watch for a particular visual event and respond by pressing, as quickly as possible, a response key. In other laboratory situations, participants might be asked to make judgments regarding the intensity of stimuli such as sounds. By Cronbach's definition, these are also tests.

The generality of Cronbach's definition also extends to the type of information produced by tests. Some tests produce numbers that represent the amount of some psychological attribute possessed by a person. For example, the U.S. National Assessment of Education Progress (NAEP; http://nces.ed.gov/nationsreportcard/nde/help/qs/NAEP_Scales.asp) uses statistical procedures to select test items that, at least in theory, produce data that can be interpreted as reflecting the amount of knowledge or skill possessed by children in various academic areas, such as reading. Other tests produce categorical data—people who take the test can be sorted into groups based on their responses to test items. The House-Tree-Person Test (Burns, 1987) is an example of such a test. Children who take the test are asked to draw a house, a tree, and a person. The drawings are evaluated for certain characteristics, and on the basis of these evaluations, children can be sorted into groups (however, this procedure might not be "systematic" in Cronbach's terms). Note that we are not making any claims about the quality of the information obtained from the tests that we are using as examples. In Chapter 2, we will discuss the data produced by psychological tests.

Another extremely important feature of Cronbach's definition concerns the general purpose of psychological tests. Specifically, tests must be capable of comparing the behavior of different people (*interindividual differences*) or the behavior of the same individuals at different points in time or under different circumstances (*intra-individual differences*). The purpose of measurement in psychology is to identify and, if possible, quantify interindividual or intra-individual differences. This is a fundamental theme that runs throughout our book, and we will return to it in every chapter. Inter- and intra-individual differences on test performance contribute to test score variability, a necessary component of any attempt to measure any psychological attribute.

Types of Tests

There are tens of thousands of psychological tests in the public domain (Educational Testing Service, 2011). These tests vary from each other along dozens of different dimensions. For example, tests can vary in content: There are achievement tests, aptitude tests, intelligence tests, personality tests, attitude surveys, and so on. Tests also vary with regard to the type of response required: There are open-ended tests, in which people can answer test questions by saying anything they want in response to the questions on the test, and there are closed-ended tests, which require people to answer questions by choosing among alternative answers provided in the test. Tests also vary according to the methods used to administer them: There are individually administered tests, and there are tests designed to be administered to groups of people.

Another common distinction concerns the intended purpose of test scores. Psychological tests are often categorized as either *criterion referenced* (also called domain referenced) or *norm referenced.* Criterion-referenced tests are most often seen in settings in which a decision must be made about a person's skill level. A fixed, predetermined cutoff test score is established, and it is used to sort people into two groups: (1) those whose performance exceeds the performance criterion and (2) those whose performance does not. In contrast, norm-referenced tests are usually used to compare a person's test score with scores from a *reference sample or a normative sample*, in order to understand how the person compares with other people. Characteristics of the reference sample are thought to be representative of some well-defined population. A person's test score is compared with the expected or average score on the test that would be obtained if the test were to be given to all members of the population. Scores on norm-referenced tests are of little value if the reference sample is not representative of some population of people, if the relevant population is not well-defined, or if there is doubt that the person being tested is a member of the relevant population. In principle, none of these issues arise when evaluating a score on a criterion-referenced test.

In practice, the distinction between norm-referenced tests and criterion-referenced tests is often blurred. Criterion-referenced tests are always "normed" in some sense. That is, criterion cutoff scores are not determined at random. The cutoff score will be associated with a decision criterion based on some standard or expected level of performance of people who might take the test. Most of us have taken written driver's license tests. These are criterion-referenced tests because a person taking the test must obtain a score that exceeds some predetermined cutoff. The questions on these tests were selected to ensure that the average person who is qualified to take the test has a good chance of answering enough of the questions to pass the test. The distinction between criterion- and norm-referenced tests is further blurred when scores from norm-referenced tests are used as cutoff scores. Institutions of higher education might have minimum SAT or American College Testing (ACT) score requirements for admission or for various types of scholarships. Public schools use cutoff scores from intelligence tests to sort children into groups. In some cases, the use of scores from norm-referenced tests can have life or death consequences. Despite the problems with the distinction between criterion-referenced tests and norm-referenced tests, we will see that there are slightly different methods used to assess the quality of criterion-referenced and norm-referenced tests.

Yet another common distinction is between *speeded tests* and *power tests*. Speeded tests are time-limited tests. In general, people who take a speeded test are not expected to complete the entire test in the allotted time. Speeded tests are scored by counting the number of questions answered in the allotted time period. It is assumed that there is a high probability that each question will be answered correctly; each of the questions on a speeded test should be of comparable difficulty. In contrast, power tests are not time limited, in that examinees are expected to answer all the test questions. Often, power tests are scored also by counting the number of correct answers made on the test. Test items must range in difficulty if scores on these tests are to be used to discriminate among people with regard to the psychological attribute of interest. As is the case with the distinction between criterion-referenced tests and norm-referenced tests, slightly different methods are used to assess the quality of speeded and power tests.

A brief note concerning terminology: There are several different terms that are often used as synonyms for the word *test*. The words *measure, instrument, scale, inventory, battery, schedule*, and *assessment* have all been used in different contexts and by different authors as synonyms for the word *test*. We will sometimes refer to tests as instruments and sometimes as measures. The word *battery* will be restricted in use to references to bundled tests; bundled tests are instruments intended to be administered together but are not *necessarily* designed to measure a single psychological attribute. The word *measure* is one of the most confusing words in the psychology testing literature. In Chapter 2, we are going to discuss in detail the use of this word as a verb, as in "The BDI was designed *to measure* depression." The word *measure* also is often used in its noun form, as in "The BDI is a good *measure* of depression." We will use both forms of the term and will rely on the context to clarify its meaning.

Psychometrics

What Is Psychometrics?

We previously defined a test as a procedure for systematically sampling behavior. These behavioral samples are attempts to measure, at least in some sense, psychological attributes of people. The act of giving psychological tests to people is referred to as testing. In this book, we will not be concerned with the process of testing; rather, our concern will focus on psychological tests themselves. We will not, however, be concerned with particular psychological tests, except as a test might illustrate an important principle. In sum, we focus on the *attributes* of tests.

Just as psychological tests are designed to measure psychological attributes of people (e.g., anxiety, intelligence), psychometrics is the science concerned with evaluating the attributes of psychological tests. Three of these attributes will be of particular interest: (1) the type of information (in most cases, scores) generated by the use of psychological tests, (2) the reliability of data from psychological tests, and (3) issues concerning the validity of data obtained from psychological tests. The remaining chapters in this book describe the procedures that psychometricians use to evaluate these attributes of tests.

Note that just as psychological attributes of people (e.g., anxiety) are most often conceptualized as hypothetical constructs (i.e., abstract theoretical attributes of the mind), psychological tests also have attributes that are represented by theoretical concepts such as validity or reliability. The important analogy is that just as psychological tests are about theoretical attributes of people, psychometrics is about theoretical attributes of psychological tests. Just as psychological attributes of people must be measured, so also psychometric attributes of tests must be estimated. Psychometrics is about the procedures used to estimate and evaluate the attributes of tests.

Francis Galton and the Scope of Psychometrics

Francis Galton (1822–1911) seems to have been obsessed with measurement. Among other things, he tried to measure the efficacy of prayer (Galton, 1883), the number of brush stokes needed to complete a painting, and the number of times children fidgeted (i.e., moved around in their seats; Galton, 1885) while in a classroom. He was a meteorologist (Galton, 1863) and a geneticist (Galton, 1869), making important contributions to measurement in both fields. Most important for our purpose, however, was his interest in what he called "anthropometrics," the measurement of human features, such as head size, arm length, and physical strength. For Galton (1879), these features included psychological characteristics. He referred to the measurement of mental features as "psychometry," which he defined as "the art of imposing measurement and number upon operations of the mind" (p. 149). Today, we might refer to this "art" as psychometrics; however, the term has acquired a variety of meanings since it was first coined by Galton.

Galton is considered the founding father of modern psychometrics. He made many conceptual and technical innovations that are the foundations of psychometric theory and practice. In fact, you might already be familiar with some of Galton's innovations. For example, he demonstrated the utility of using the normal distribution (Galton, 1907) to model many human characteristics, he developed the idea of the correlation coefficient (Galton, 1889), and he pioneered the use of sampling for the purpose of identifying and treating measurement error (Galton, 1902; this is a remarkable article, followed by an extensive development by Karl Pearson of Galton's ideas). All these are concepts that we will treat in detail in subsequent sections of this book. Galton also tried to measure mental abilities using mental tests. Although his specific efforts in this regard proved unsuccessful, the idea that a relatively simple, easy to administer test of mental abilities could be developed laid the foundation for the modern intelligence test.

While other early pioneers in psychology pursued general laws or principles of mental phenomena that apply to all people, Galton focused on the variability of human characteristics. That is, Galton was primarily interested in the ways in which people differ from each other. Some people are taller than others, some are smarter than others, some are more attractive than others, and some are more aggressive than others. How large are these differences, what causes such differences, and what are the consequences of such differences?

Galton's approach to psychology became known as differential psychology, the study of individual differences. This is usually seen as contrasting with experimental psychology, which focused mainly on the average person instead of the differences among people. Because Galton is closely associated with both psychometrics and differential psychology, contemporary authors sometimes view psychometrics as an issue that concerns only those who study individual differences. They sometimes seem to believe that psychometrics is not a concern for those who take a more experimental approach to human behavior. We absolutely disagree with this view.

Our view of psychometrics, as well as our use of the term, is not limited to issues in differential psychology. Our view is that all psychologists, whatever their specific area of research or practice, must be concerned with measuring behavior (in this context, we will be concerned only with human behavior) and psychological attributes. Therefore, they should all understand the problems of measuring behavior and psychological attributes, and these problems are the subject matter of psychometrics. Regardless of one's specific interest, all behavioral sciences and all applications of the behavioral sciences depend on the ability to identify and quantify variability in human behavior. We will return to this issue later in the book, with specific examples and principles underscoring the wide relevance of psychometric concepts. Psychometrics is the study of the operations and procedures used to measure variability in behavior and to connect those measurements to psychological phenomena.

Challenges to Measurement in Psychology

We can never be sure that a measurement is perfect. Is your bathroom scale completely accurate? Is the odometer in your car a flawless measure of distance? Is your new tape measure 100% correct? When you visit your physician, is it possible that the nurse's measure of your blood pressure is off a bit? Even the use of highly precise scientific instruments is potentially affected by various errors, not the least of which is human error in reading the instruments. All measurements, and therefore all sciences, are affected by various challenges that can reduce measurement accuracy.

Despite the many similarities among the sciences, measurement in the behavioral sciences has special challenges that do not exist or are greatly reduced in the physical sciences. These challenges affect our confidence in our understanding and interpretation of behavioral observations. We will find that one of these challenges is related to the complexity of psychological phenomena; notions such as intelligence, self-esteem, anxiety, depression, and so on, have many different aspects to them. Thus, one of our challenges is to try to identify and capture the important aspects of these types of human psychological attributes in a single number.

Participant reactivity is another such challenge. Because, in most cases, psychologists are measuring psychological characteristics of people who are conscious and generally know that they are being measured, the act of measurement can itself influence the psychological state or process being measured. For example, suppose we design a questionnaire to determine whether you are a racist. Your responses to the questionnaire might be influenced by your desire not to be thought of as a racist rather than by your true attitudes toward people who belong to ethnic or racial groups other than your own. Therefore, people's knowledge that they are being observed can cause them to react in ways that obscure the interpretation of the behavior that is being observed. This is usually not a problem when measuring features of nonsentient physical objects; the weight of a bunch of grapes is not influenced by the act of weighing them.

Participant reactivity can take many forms. In research situations, some participants may try to figure out the researcher's purpose for a study, changing their behavior to accommodate the researcher (*demand characteristics*). In research and in applied-measurement situations, some people might become apprehensive, others might change their behavior to try to impress the person doing the measurement (*social desirability*), and still others might even change their behavior to convey a poor impression to the person doing the measurement (*malingering*). In each case, the validity of the measure is compromised—the person's "true" psychological characteristic is obscured by a temporary motivation or state that is a reaction to the very act of being measured.

A second challenge to psychological measurement is that, in the behavioral sciences, the people collecting the behavioral data (observing the behavior, scoring a test, interpreting a verbal response, etc.) can bring biases and expectations to their task. Measurement quality is compromised when observers allow these influences to distort their observations. *Expectation* and *bias* effects can be difficult to detect. In most cases, we can trust that people who collect behavioral data are not consciously cheating; however, even subtle, unintended biases can have effects. For example, a researcher might give intelligence tests to young children as part of a study of a program to improve the cognitive development of the children. The researcher might have a vested interest in certain intelligence test score outcomes, and as a result, he or she might allow a bias, perhaps even an unconscious one, to influence the testing procedures. *Observer,* or *scorer, bias* of this type can occur in the physical sciences, but it is less likely to occur because physical scientists rely more heavily than do social scientists on mechanical devices as data collection agents.

The measures used in the behavioral sciences tend to differ from those used by physical scientists in a third important respect. Psychologists tend to rely on *composite scores* when measuring psychological attributes. Many of the tests used by psychologists involve a series of questions, all of which are intended to measure some aspect of a particular psychological attribute or process. For example, a personality test might have 10 questions designed to measure extroversion. Similarly, class examinations that are used to measure learning or knowledge generally include many questions. It is common practice to score each question and then to sum or otherwise combine the items' scores to create a total or composite score. The total score represents the final measure of the relevant construct—for example, an extroversion score or a "knowledge of algebra" score. Although composite scores do have their benefits (as we will discuss in a later chapter), several issues complicate their use and evaluation. In contrast, the physical sciences are less likely to rely on composite scores in their measurement procedures (although there are exceptions to this). When measuring a physical feature of the world, such as the length of a piece of lumber, the weight of a molecule, or the speed of a moving object, scientists can usually rely on a single value obtained from a single type of measurement.

A fourth challenge to psychological measurement is *score sensitivity.* Sensitivity refers to the ability of a measure to discriminate adequately between meaningful amounts or units of the dimension that is being measured. As an example from the physical world, consider someone trying to measure the width of a hair with a standard yardstick. Yardstick units are simply too large to be of any use in this situation. Similarly, a psychologist may find that a procedure for measuring a psychological attribute or process may not be sensitive enough to discriminate between the real differences that exist in the attribute or process.

For example, imagine a clinical psychologist who wishes to track her clients' emotional changes from one therapeutic session to another. If she chooses a measure that is not sufficiently sensitive to pick up small differences, then she might miss small but important differences in mood. For example, she might ask her clients to complete this very straightforward "measure" after each session:

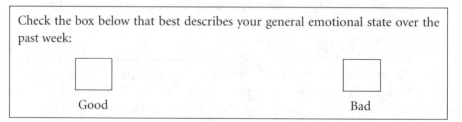

The psychologist might become disheartened by her clients' apparent lack of progress because her clients might rarely, if ever, feel sufficiently happy to checkmark the "Good" box. The key measurement point is that her measure might be masking real improvement by her clients. That is, her clients might be making meaningful improvements—originally feeling extremely anxious and depressed and eventually feeling much less anxious and depressed. However, they might not actually feel "good," even though they feel much better than they did at the beginning of therapy. Unfortunately, her scale is too crude or insensitive, in that it allows only two responses and does not distinguish among important levels of "badness" or among levels of "goodness." A more precise and sensitive scale might look like this:

Choose the number that best describes your general emotional state over the past week:

1   2   3   4   5   6   7   8   9

Extremely Good   Somewhat Good   Somewhat Bad   Extremely Bad

---

A scale of this kind might allow more fine-grained differentiation along the "good versus bad" dimension as compared with the original scale.

For psychologists, the sensitivity problem is exacerbated because we might not anticipate the magnitude of meaningful differences associated with the mental attributes being measured. Although this problem can emerge in the physical sciences, physical scientists are usually aware of it before they do their research. In contrast, social scientists may be unaware of the scale sensitivity issue even after they have collected their measurements.

A final challenge is an apparent lack of awareness of important psychometric information. In the behavioral sciences, particularly in the application of behavioral science, psychological measurement is often a social or cultural activity. Whether it provides information from a client to a therapist regarding psychiatric symptoms, from a student to a teacher regarding the student's level of knowledge, or from a job applicant to a potential employer regarding the applicant's personality traits and skill, applied psychological measurement often is used to facilitate the flow of information among people. Unfortunately, such measurement often seems to be conducted with little or no regard for the psychometric quality of the tests.

For example, most classroom instructors give class examinations. Only on very rare occasions do instructors have any information about the psychometric properties of their examinations. In fact, instructors might not even be able to clearly define the reason for giving the examination. Is the instructor trying to measure knowledge (a latent variable or hypothetical construct), trying to determine which students can answer the most questions, or trying to motivate students to learn relevant information? Thus, some classroom tests might have questionable quality as indicators of differences among students in their knowledge of a particular subject. Even so, the tests might serve the very useful purpose of motivating students to acquire the relevant knowledge.

Although a poorly constructed test might serve a meaningful purpose in some community of people (e.g., motivating students to learn important information), psychometrically well-formed information is better than information that is not well-formed. Furthermore, if a test or measure is intended to reflect the psychological differences among people, then the test must have strong psychometric properties. Knowledge of these properties should inform the development or selection of a test—all else being equal, test users should use psychometrically sound instruments.

In sum, this survey of challenges should indicate that although measurement in the behavioral sciences and measurement in the physical sciences have much in common, there are important differences. These differences should always inform our understanding of data collected from psychological measures. For example, we should be aware that participant reactivity can affect responses to psychological tests. At the same time, we hope to demonstrate that behavioral scientists have significant understanding of these challenges and that they have generated effective methods of minimizing, detecting, and accounting for various problems. Similarly, behavioral scientists have developed methods that reduce the potential impact of experimenter bias in the measurement process. In this book, we discuss methods that psychometricians have developed to handle the challenges associated with the development, evaluation, and process of measurement of psychological attributes and behavioral characteristics.

Theme: The Importance of Individual Differences

A fundamental theme links the following chapters. The theme is related to the fact that our ability to identify and characterize psychological differences is at the heart of all psychological measurement and is the foundation of all methods used to evaluate tests. The purpose of measurement in psychology is to identify and quantify the psychological differences that exist between people, over time or across conditions. These differences contribute to score variability and are the basis of all psychometric information. Even when a practicing psychologist, educator, or consultant makes a decision about a single person based on the person's score on a psychological test, the meaning and quality of the person's score can be understood only in the context of the test's ability to detect differences among people.

All measures in psychology require that we obtain behavioral samples of some kind. Behavioral samples might include scores on a paper-and-pencil test, written or oral responses to questions, or records based on behavioral observations. Useful psychometric information about the samples can be obtained only if people differ with respect to the behavior that we are sampling. If a behavioral sampling procedure produces individual differences, then the psychometric properties of the scores obtained from the sampling procedure can be assessed along a wide variety of dimensions. In this book, we will present the logic and analytic procedures associated with these psychometric properties.

If we think that a particular behavioral sampling procedure is a measure of an unobservable psychological attribute, then we must be able to argue that individual differences on the behavioral sample are indeed related to individual differences on the relevant underlying psychological attribute. For example, a psychologist might be interested in measuring visual attention. Because visual attention is an unobservable hypothetical construct, the psychologist will have to create a behavioral sampling procedure that reflects individual differences in visual attention. Before concluding that the procedure is interpretable as a measure of visual attention, the psychologist must accumulate evidence suggesting that there is an association between individuals' scores on the test and their "true" levels of visual attention. The process by which the psychologist accumulates this evidence is called the validation process; it will be examined in later chapters.

In the following chapters, we will show how individual differences are quantified and how their quantification is the first step in solving many of the challenges to measurement in psychology to which we have already alluded. Individual differences represent the currency of psychometric analysis. In effect, individual differences provide the data for psychometric analyses of tests.

Suggested Readings

For a history of early developments in psychological testing:

DuBois, P. H. (1970). *A history of psychological testing.* Boston, MA: Allyn & Bacon.

For a modern historical and philosophical treatment of the history of measurement in psychology:

Michell, J. (2003). Epistemology of measurement: The relevance of its history for quantification in the social sciences. *Social Science Information, 42,* 515–534.

PART I

Basic Concepts in Measurement

CHAPTER 2

Scaling

If something exists, it must exist in some amount (Thorndike, 1918). Psychologists generally believe that people have psychological attributes, such as thoughts, feelings, emotions, personality characteristics, intelligence, learning styles, and so on. If we believe this, then we must assume that each psychological attribute exists in some quantity. With this in mind, psychological measurement can be seen as a process through which numbers are assigned to represent the quantities of psychological attributes. The measurement process succeeds if the numbers assigned to an attribute reflect the actual amounts of that attribute.

The standard definition of measurement (borrowed from Stevens, 1946) found in most introductory test and measurement texts goes something like this: "Measurement is the assignment of numerals to objects or events according to rules." In the case of psychology, education, and other behavioral sciences, the "events" of interest are generally samples of individuals' behaviors. The "rules" mentioned in this definition usually refer to the scales of measurement proposed by Stevens (1946).

This chapter is about scaling, which concerns the way numerical values are assigned to psychological attributes. Scaling is a fundamental issue in measurement, and a full appreciation of scaling and its implications depends on a variety of abstract issues. In this chapter, we discuss the meaning of numerals, the way in which numerals can be used to represent psychological attributes, and the problems associated with trying to connect psychological attributes with numerals. We emphasize psychological tests that are intended to measure unobservable psychological characteristics, such as attitudes, personality traits, and intelligence. Such characteristics present special problems for measurement, and we will discuss several possible solutions for these problems.

We acknowledge that these issues might not elicit cheers of excitement and enthusiasm among some readers or perhaps among most readers (or perhaps in any reader?); however, these issues are fundamental to psychological measurement, to measurement in general, and to the pursuit and application of science. More specifically, they are important because they help define scales of measurement. That is, they help differentiate the ways in which psychologists apply numerical values in psychological measurement. In turn, these differences have important implications for the use and interpretation of scores from psychological tests. The way scientists and practitioners use and make sense out of tests depends heavily on the scales of measurement being used.

Thus, we encourage you to devote attention to the concepts in this chapter. We believe that your attention will be rewarded with new insights into the foundations of psychological measurement and even into the nature of numbers. Indeed, in preparing this chapter, our own understanding of such issues has grown and evolved.

Fundamental Issues With Numbers

In psychological measurement, numerals are used to represent an individual's level of a psychological attribute. For example, we use your scores on an IQ test to represent your level of intelligence, we might use your scores on the Rosenberg Self-Esteem Inventory to represent your level of self-esteem, and we might even use a zero or one to represent your biological sex (e.g., males might be referred to as "Group Zero" and females as "Group One"). Thus, psychological measurement is heavily oriented toward numbers and quantification.

Given this heavily numerical orientation, it is important to understand that numerals, however, can represent psychological attributes in different ways, depending on the nature of the numeral that is used to represent the attribute. In this section, we describe important properties of numerals, and we show how these properties influence the ways in which numerals represent psychological attributes.

We must understand three important numerical properties, and we must understand the meaning of zero. In essence, the numerical properties of identity, order, and quantity reflect the ways in which numerals represent potential differences in psychological attributes. Furthermore, zero is an interestingly complex number, and this complexity has implications for the meaning of different kinds of test scores. A test score of 0 can have extremely different meanings in different measurement contexts.

The Property of Identity — *categorical*

The most fundamental form of measurement is the ability to reflect "sameness versus differentness." Indeed, the simplest measurements are those that differentiate between categories of people. For example, you might ask first-grade teachers to identify those children in their classrooms who have behavior problems. The children who are classified as having behavior problems should be *similar to* each other with respect to their behavior. In addition, the children with behavior problems should be *different from* the children who are classified as not having behavioral problems. That is, the individuals within a category should be the same as each other in terms of sharing a psychological feature, but they should be different from the individuals in another category. In psychology, this requires that we sort people into at least two categories. The idea is that objects or events can be sorted into categories that are based on similarity of features. In many cases, these features are behavioral characteristics reflecting psychological attributes, such as happy or sad, introverted or extraverted, and so on.

There are certain rules that must be followed when sorting people into categories. The first and most straightforward rule is that, to establish a category, the people within a category must satisfy the property of identity. That is, all people within a particular category must be "identical" with respect to the feature reflected by the category. For example, everyone in the "behavioral problem" group must, in fact, have behavioral problems, and everyone in the "no behavioral problem" group must not have behavioral problems. Second, the categories must be *mutually exclusive*. If a person is classified as having a behavioral problem, then he or she cannot simultaneously be classified as not having a behavioral problem. Third, the categories must be *exhaustive*. If you think that all first-graders can be classified as either having behavioral problems or not having behavioral problems, then these categories would be exhaustive. If, on the other hand, you can imagine someone who cannot be so easily classified, then you would need another category to capture that person's behavior. To summarize the second and third rules, each person should fall into one and only one category.

At this level, numerals serve simply as labels of categories. The categories could be labeled with letters, names, or numerals. We could label the category of children with behavior problems as "Behavior Problem Children," we could refer to the category as "Category B," or we could assign a numeral to the category. For example, we could label the group as "0," "1," or "100." At this level, numerals are generally not thought of as having true mathematical value. For example, if "1" is used to reflect the category of children with behavioral problems and "2" is used to represent the category of children without behavioral problems, then we would not interpret the apparent 1-point difference between the numerical labels as having any form of quantitative significance.

The latter point merits some additional depth. When making categorical differentiations between people, the distinctions between members of different categories represent differences in kind or quality rather than differences in amount. Again returning to the teachers' classifications of children, the difference between the two groups is a difference between *types* of children—those children who have behavioral problems and those who do not. In this example, the classification is not intended to represent the amount of problems (e.g., a lot vs. a little) but rather the presence or absence of problems. In this way, the classification is intended to represent two qualitatively distinct groups of children. Of course, you might object that this is a rather crude and imprecise way of measuring or representing behavioral problems, suggesting that such an attribute is more accurately reflected in some quantity than in a simple presence/absence categorization. This leads to additional properties of numerals.

The Property of Order   — ordinal

Although the property of identity reflects the most fundamental form of measurement, the property of order conveys greater information. As discussed above, when numerals have only the property of identity, they convey information about whether two individuals are similar or different, but nothing more. In contrast, when numerals have the property of order, they convey information about the relative amount of an attribute that people possess.

When numerals have the property of order, they indicate the rank order of people relative to each other along some dimension. In this case, the numeral 1 might be assigned to a person because he or she possesses more of an attribute than anyone else in the group. The numeral 2 might be assigned to the person with the next greatest amount of the attribute, and so on. For example, teachers might be asked to rank children in their classrooms according the children's interest in learning. Teachers might be instructed to assign the numeral 1 to the child who shows the most interest in learning, 2 to the child whose interest in learning is greater than all the other children except the first child, continuing in this way until all the children have been ranked according to their interest in learning.

When numerals are used to indicate order, the numerals again serve essentially as labels. For example, the numeral 1 indicated a person who had more of an attribute than anyone else in the group. The child with the greatest interest in learning was assigned the numeral 1 as a label indicating the child's rank. In fact, we could just as easily assign letters as numerals to indicate the children's ranks. The child with the most (least) interest in learning might have been assigned the letter A to indicate his or her rank. Each person in a group of people receives a numeral (or letter) indicating that person's relative standing within the group with respect to some attribute. For communication purposes, it is essential that the meaning of the symbol used to indicate rank be clearly defined. We simply need to know what 1, or A, means in each context.

Although the property of order conveys more information than the property of identity, it is still quite limited. While it tells us the relative amount of differences between people, it does not tell us about the actual degree of differences in that attribute. For example, we know that the child ranked 1 has more interest in learning than the child ranked 2, but we do not know *how much* more interest he has. The two children could differ only slightly in their amount of interest in learning, or they could differ dramatically. In this way, when numerals have the property of order, they are still a rather imprecise way of representing psychological differences.

The Property of Quantity   — interval / ratio

Although the property of order conveys more information than the property of identity, the property of quantity conveys even greater information. As noted above, numerals that have the property of order convey information about which of two individuals has a higher level of a psychological attribute, but they convey no information about the exact amounts of that attribute. In contrast, when numerals have the property of quantity, they provide information about the magnitude of differences between people.

At this level, numerals reflect *real numbers* or, for our purposes, numbers. The number 1 is used to define the size of the basic *unit* on any particular scale. All other values on the scale are multiples of 1 or fractions of 1. Each numeral (e.g., the numeral 4) represents a count of basic units. Think about a thermometer that you might use to measure temperature. To describe how warm the weather is, your thermometer reflects temperature in terms of "number of degrees" (above or below 0). The degree is the unit of measurement, and temperature is represented in terms of this unit.

Units of measurement are standardized quantities; the size of a unit will be determined by some convention. For example, 1 degree Celsius (1°C) is defined (originally) in terms of 1/100th of the difference between the temperature at which ice melts and the temperature at which water boils. We will expand on this important point shortly.

Real numbers are also said to be continuous. In principle, any real number can be divided into infinitely small parts. In the context of measurement, real numbers are often referred to as *scalar, metric, or cardinal,* or sometimes simply as *quantitative* values.

The power of real numbers derives from the fact that they can be used to measure the quantity of an attribute of a thing, person, or event. When applied to an attribute in an appropriate way, a real number indicates the amount of something. For example, a day that has a temperature of 50°C is not simply warmer than a day that has a temperature of 40°C; it is precisely 10 units (i.e., degrees) warmer.

When psychologists use psychological tests to measure psychological attributes, they often assume that the test scores have the property of quantity. As we will see later, this is seldom a good assumption.

The Number 0

The number 0 is a strange number, with a variety of meanings. In fact, it has only been during the past couple of 100 years that the numeral 0 has been treated effectively as an integer. There are two potential meanings of the number 0. To properly interpret a test score of 0, you must understand which meaning is relevant.

In one possible meaning, zero reflects a state in which an attribute of an object or event has no existence. If you said that an object was 0.0 cm long, you would be claiming that the object has no length, at least in any ordinary sense of the term *length.* Zero in this context is referred to as *absolute zero.* In psychology, the best example of a behavioral measure with an absolute 0 point might be reaction time.

The second possible meaning of zero is to view it as an arbitrary quantity of an attribute. A zero of this type is called a *relative* or *arbitrary zero.* In the physical world, attributes such as time (e.g., calendar, clock) and temperature measured by standard thermometers are examples. In these examples, 0 is simply an arbitrary point on a scale used to measure that feature. For example, a temperature of 0 on the Celsius scale represents the melting point of ice, but it does not represent the "absence" of anything (i.e., it does not represent the absence of temperature or of warmth).

The psychological world is filled, at least potentially, with attributes having a relative 0 point. For example, it is difficult to think that conscious people could truly have no (zero) intelligence, self-esteem, introversion, social skills, attitudes, and so on. Although we might informally say that someone "has no social skill," psychologists would not suggest this formally—indeed, we actually believe that everyone has some level of social skill (and self-esteem, etc.), though some people might have much lower levels than other people.

Despite the fact that most psychological attributes do not have an absolute 0 point, psychological tests of such attributes could produce a score of 0. In such cases, the zero would be considered arbitrary, not truly reflecting an absence of the attribute. Furthermore, we will see that many if not most psychological test scores can be expressed as a type of score called a z score, which will be discussed in Chapter 3. The mean of a distribution of z scores will always be 0. Zero in this case represents an arbitrary or relative zero.

In psychology, there is a serious problem in determining whether zero should be thought of as relative or absolute. The problem concerns the distinction between the features of a test used to measure a psychological attribute and the features of the psychological attribute that is being measured. We will use an example from Thorndike (2005) to illustrate this problem. Thorndike describes a scenario in which sixth-grade children are given a spelling test. He asks us to imagine that one of the children fails to spell correctly any of the words on the test. That is, the child receives a score of 0 on the test. In this case, the spelling test is the instrument used to measure an attribute of the child—the child's spelling ability. The test has an absolute 0 point. That is, a test score of 0 means that the child failed to answer any of the spelling questions correctly. It is difficult, however, to imagine that a sixth-grade child is incapable of spelling; the child's *spelling ability* is probably not zero. The question then becomes how we are going to treat the child's test score. Should we consider it an absolute zero or a relative zero?

Interpretation of psychological test scores will be influenced by the type of zero associated with a test. As a technical matter, if we can assume that a test has an absolute zero, then we can feel comfortable performing the arithmetical operations of multiplication and division on the test scores. On the other hand, if a test has a relative 0 point, we would probably want to restrict arithmetical operations on the scores to addition and subtraction. As a matter of evaluation, it is important to know what zero means—does it mean that a person who scored 0 on a test had none of the attribute that was being measured, or does it mean that the person might not have had a measurable amount of the attribute, at least not measurable with respect to the particular test you used to measure the attribute?

In sum, the three properties of numerals and the meaning of zero are fundamental issues that shape our understanding of psychological test scores. If two people share a psychological feature, then we have established the property of identity. If two people share a common attribute but one person has more of that attribute than the other, we can establish order. If order can be established and if we can determine *how much* more of the attribute one person has compared with others, then we have established the property of quantity. Put another way, identity is the most fundamental level of measurement. To measure anything, the identity of the thing must be established. Once the identity of an attribute is known, then it might be possible to establish order. Furthermore, order is a fundamental characteristic of quantity. As we will see, numbers play a different role in representing psychological attributes depending on their level of measurement.

Most psychological tests are treated as if they provide numerical scores that possess the property of quantity. In the next two sections, we will discuss two fundamental issues regarding the meaning and use of such quantitative test scores. Specifically, we will discuss the meaning of a "unit of measurement," the issues involved with counting those units, and the implications of those counts.

Units of Measurement

The property of quantity requires that units of measurement be clearly defined. As we will discuss in the next section, quantitative measurement depends on our ability to count these units. Before we discuss the process and implications of counting the units of measurement, we must clarify what is meant by a unit of measurement.

In many familiar cases of physical measurement, the units of measurement are readily apparent. If people want to measure the length of a piece of lumber, then they will probably use some type of tape marked off in units of inches or centimeters. The length of the piece of lumber is determined by counting the number of these units from one end of the board to the other end.

In contrast, in many cases of psychological measurement, units of measurement are often less obvious. When we measure a psychological characteristic such as shyness, working memory, attention, or intelligence, what are the units of measurement? Presumably, they are responses of some kind, perhaps to a series of questions or items. But how do we know whether, or to what extent, those responses are related to the psychological attributes themselves? We will return to these questions at a later time, as they represent the most vexing problems in psychometrics. At this point, we simply want to concentrate on the notion of a unit of measurement. Because this notion can be most easily illustrated in the context of the measurement of the length of physical objects (Michell, 1990), we will introduce it in that way.

Imagine that you are building a bookshelf and you need to measure the length of pieces of wood. Unfortunately, you cannot find a tape measure, a yardstick, or a ruler of any kind—how can you precisely quantify the lengths of your various pieces of wood? When push comes to shove, you could create your own unique measurement system. First, you happen to find a long wooden curtain rod left over from a previous project. You cut a small piece of the curtain rod; let us call this an "xrod." Because your pieces of bookshelf wood are longer than your xrod, you will need a number of xrods. Therefore, you can use this original xrod as a template to produce a collection of identical xrods. That is, you can cut additional xrods from the curtain rod, making sure that each xrod is the same, exact length as your original xrod. You can now use your xrods to measure the length of all your pieces of wood. For example, to measure the length of one of your shelves, place one of the xrods at one end of the piece of wood that you will use as a shelf. Next, place xrods end to end in a straight line until you reach the opposite end of the piece of wood. Now count the number of xrods, and you might find that the shelf is "8 xrods long."

You have just measured length in "units of xrods." You can use your set of xrods to measure the length of each and every piece of wood that you need. In fact, you could use your xrods to measure the length of many things, not just pieces of wood. In many ways, your measure is a good as any measure of length (except that you are the only one who knows what an xrod represents!).

Arbitrariness is an important concept in understanding units of measurement, and it distinguishes between different kinds of measurement units. There are three ways in which a measurement unit might be arbitrary. First, the unit size can be arbitrary. That is, the specific size of a unit might be arbitrary. Consider your xrod—the size of your original xrod could have been any length. When you cut that first xrod, your decision about its length could be completely arbitrary—there was no "true" xrod length that you were trying to obtain. You simply chose a length to cut, and that length became the "official" length of an xrod. In this sense, the actual length of our unit of measurement, the xrod, was completely arbitrary. Similarly, the amount of weight that is represented by a "pound" is an arbitrary amount. Although there is now clear consensus regarding the exact amount of weight represented by a pound, we can ask why a pound should reflect that *specific* amount. The choice was likely quite arbitrary.

A second form of arbitrariness is that some units of measurement are not tied to any one type of object. That is, there might be no inherent restriction on the objects to which a unit of measurement might be applied. Our xrods can be used to measure the spatial extent of anything that has spatial extent. For example, they could be used to measure the length of a piece of wood, the length of a table, the distance between two objects, or the depth of water in a swimming pool. Similarly, a pound can be used to measure the weight of many different kinds of objects.

A third form of arbitrariness is that, when they take a physical form, some units of measurement can be used to measure different features of objects. For example, the xrods that we used to measure the length of a piece of lumber could also be used as units of weight. Imagine that you needed to measure the weight of a bag of fruit. If you had a balance scale, you could put the bag in one of the balance's baskets, and you could gradually stack xrods in the other basket. When the two sides of the scale "balance," then you would know that the bag of fruit weighs, say, 4 xrods.

Units of measurement, called *standard measures,* are based on arbitrary units of measurement in all three ways when they take a physical form. In physical measurement, standard units include units such as pounds, liters, and milliseconds. The fact that they are expressed in arbitrary units gives them flexibility and generality. For example, you can use milliseconds to measure anything from a person's reaction time to the presentation of a stimulus to the amount of time it takes a car to travel down the street.

In contrast to many physical measures, most psychological units of measurement (e.g., scores on tests such as mechanical aptitude tests or on intelligence tests) are generally arbitrary only in the first sense of the term *arbitrary* mentioned above. That is, most psychological units of measurement are arbitrary in size, but they are typically tied to specific objects or dimensions. For example, a "unit" of measurement on an IQ test is linked in a nonarbitrary way to intelligence, and it is not applicable to any other dimension. Because of this feature of IQ test scores, we refer to IQ score units as "IQ points"; the points have no referent beyond the test used to measure intelligence. There is one important exception to this observation; standard measures are sometimes used to measure psychological attributes. For example, reaction times are often used to measure various cognitive processes.

Additivity and Counting

The need for counting is central to all attempts at measurement. Whether we are trying to measure a feature of the physical world or of the psychological world, all measurement involves counting. For example, when you used xrods to measure the length of a piece of wood, you placed the xrods end to end, starting from one end of the piece of wood and continuing until you reached the other end. You then counted the xrods to determine the length of the object. The resulting count was a measure of length. Similarly, when you use a behavioral sampling procedure (i.e., a test) to measure a person's self-esteem, you count responses of some kind. For example, you might count the number of test statements that a test respondent marks as "true," and you might interpret the number of "true" marks as indicating the level of the respondent's self-esteem. That is, you count units to obtain a score for your measurement.

Additivity

Importantly, the process of counting as a facet of measurement involves a key assumption that might not be valid in many applications of psychological measurement. The assumption is that the unit size does not change—that all units being counted are identical. In other words, additivity requires unit size to remain constant; a *unit* increase at one point in the measurement process must be the same as a unit increase at any other point.

Recall the xrod example, where you used the original xrod as a guide to cut additional xrods—we encouraged you to make "sure that each xrod is the same exact length as your original xrod." By doing so, you ensured that any time you laid xrods side by side and counted them, you could trust that your count accurately reflected a length. Say that you had cut 10 xrods; if they are all identical, then it does not matter which xrods you used when measuring the length of any piece of wood. That is, a piece of wood that you measured as 5 xrods would be measured as 5 xrods no matter which 5 xrods you used to measure the piece of wood.

Now imagine that instead of having a collection of equal-length xrods, your xrods had various lengths. In that case, if you measured the same piece of wood on two occasions, you might get two different counts, indicating different lengths! That is, if some xrods were longer than the others, then your piece of wood might be 5 xrods when you use the shorter xrods, but it would be only 3 xrods if you happened to use the longer xrods. Because your units were not constant in magnitude, your entire measurement system is flawed—there is no single unit of length that is represented by an xrod. This would prevent you from determining the real length of the lumber.

In addition, the size of a measurement unit should not change as the conditions of measurement change. For example, the size of an xrod should remain constant regardless of the time of day that the xrod is used to measure a piece of wood. In effect, we want our measure to be affected by only one attribute of the thing we are measuring, regardless of the conditions that exist at the time or place of measurement. This condition is referred to as conjoint measurement (Luce & Tukey, 1964) and is a complex issue beyond the scope of this book (but see Green & Rao, 1971, for a clear, nontechnical discussion).

Although these issues might be initially clearest in terms of physical measurements (e.g., xrods), we are most concerned about psychological measurement. So imagine that you are a history teacher who wants to measure a psychological attribute such as "knowledge of American history." Generally, this would be done by asking students a series of questions that you believed were diagnostic of their knowledge, recording their responses to the questions. Let us temporarily differentiate between measurement units and psychological units. That is, each test item represents a measurement unit, and again you count the correctly answered items to obtain a score that you interpret as a student's knowledge of American history. In contrast, we will use the crude and informal idea of psychological units to mean "true" levels of knowledge. Ideally, the measurement units will correspond closely with psychological units. That is, we use test scores to represent levels of psychological attributes. With this in mind, you combine each student's test responses in some way (e.g., by counting the number of questions that each student answered correctly) to create a total score that is interpreted as a measure of knowledge of American history.

Suppose that one of the questions on your test was "Who was the first president of the United States?" and another was "Who was the first European to sail into Puget Sound?" It should be clear that the amount of knowledge of American history you need to answer the first question correctly is considerably less than the amount you need to answer the second question correctly. In terms of psychological units, let's say that you needed only 1 psychological unit of American history knowledge to answer the first question correctly but you needed three times as much knowledge (i.e., 3 psychological units of knowledge) to answer the second question correctly. Consider a student who answered both questions correctly. In terms of amount of true knowledge, that student would have 4 psychological units of history knowledge. However, in terms of measurement, that student would have a score of only 2. That is, if you simply summed the number of correct responses to the questions to get a total score, the student would get a score of 2. This would suggest that the person had 2 units of American history knowledge when in fact he or she had 4 units of knowledge. This discrepancy occurs because the measurement units are not constant in terms of the underlying attribute that they are intended to reflect. That is, the answers to the questions are not a function of equal-sized units of knowledge—it takes less knowledge to answer the first question than it does to answer the second. Thus, the additive count of correct answers is not a good measure of amount of knowledge.

From a psychological perspective, the assumption is often made that a psychological attribute such as knowledge of American history actually exists in some amount. However, unlike a piece of wood, whose "length" can be directly observed, we cannot directly observe "knowledge of American history." As a result, we cannot simply see if a count of American history questions corresponds to the actual amount of American history knowledge possessed by a particular individual. There is a paradox in this: We want to translate the amount of a psychological attribute onto a set of numbers in order to measure the attribute. But it appears that this cannot be done because we do not know how much of the attribute actually exists. In a subsequent section of this chapter, we will suggest ways to get around this problem. Before we do that, we must develop several other measurement themes.

Counts: When Do They Qualify as Measurement?

Although all measurement relies on counting, not all forms of counting qualify as forms of measurement. Indeed, a controversy about the relationship between counting and measurement arises when we count *things* rather than *attributes* (Lord & Novick, 1968; Wright, 1997). For example, if you count the number of forks on a table, are you "measuring" something? Similarly, if you count the number of children in a classroom, are you measuring something?

Some experts argue that simply counting the number of some kind of object does not qualify as a "measurement"; rather, counting qualifies as measurement only when one is counting to reflect the amount of some feature or attribute of an object. For example, if a physical scientist uses a Geiger counter to count radioactive emissions from an object, then he or she is measuring the radioactivity of the object, where "radioactivity" is a feature of the object. Similarly, if a professor counts the number of correct answers given by a student on a multiple-choice mathematics test, then he or she might be measuring the amount of mathematical knowledge of the student, where "amount of mathematical knowledge" is the psychological attribute of the student.

Four Scales of Measurement

As discussed earlier, measurement involves the assignment of numbers to observations in such a way that the numbers reflect the real differences that exist between the levels of a psychological attribute. Scaling is the particular way in which numbers are linked to behavioral observations to create a measure (Allen & Yen, 1979; Crocker & Algina, 1986; Guilford, 1954; Magnusson, 1967).

In actuality, the definition of scaling is itself controversial. On one hand, some experts might find our definition of scaling unacceptably liberal, and they might restrict scaling to the assignment of numbers that, at a minimum, have the property of order (Magnusson, 1967; McDonald, 1999). On the other hand, some experts might prefer an even more restrictive definition that requires the use of scalars (Wright, 1997). This is another controversy in the measurement literature that we are not going to try to resolve. It should be pointed out that for some authors the terms *scaling* and *measurement* are synonymous (Bartholomew, 1996).

In a frequently cited framework, Stevens (1946) identified four levels of measurement. In the standard definition of measurement, the assignment of numbers to observations of behaviors is said to be "rule governed." In most cases, these "rules" refer to the scales of measurement proposed by Stevens (1946, 1951). Stevens's measurement scales are "rules" in that they suggest how certain properties of numerals might be linked to particular types of behavioral observations associated with psychological attributes. Table 2.1 integrates these levels of measurement with the fundamental numerical properties outlined earlier.

Nominal Scales

The most fundamental level of measurement is the nominal scale of measurement. In a nominal scale, numerals that have the property of identity are used to label observations in which behaviors have been sorted into categories according to some psychological attribute. For example, we can "measure" biological sex by sorting people into two categories—males and females, represented as Group 0 and Group 1, respectively. Similarly and as described earlier, children in a classroom might be sorted into groups based on the presence or absence of behavioral problems, with the numeral 1 identifying the children with behavioral problems and the numeral 2 identifying the children without behavioral problems. As long as we can be sure that the groups are mutually exclusive and exhaustive, our only concern will have to do with our ability to correctly sort the children into the groups.

It is important to distinguish nominal scale labels, as used in the above example, from labels used to identify or name individuals. Nominal scale labels are used to identify *groups* of people who share a common attribute that is not shared by people in other groups. In contrast, numerals that are used to identify individuals, such as Social Security numbers, are generally not intended to establish group membership. The distinction can be clouded, however, when numerals are assigned to individuals in some systematic fashion. For example, it is possible to sort people into groups according to their year of birth, and numerals on the jerseys of individual football players might be used to differentiate people who play different positions on a team (see Lord, 1953, for a humorous discussion of this problem). The important point is that when using numerals to identify people, you need to

Table 2.1   Association Between Numerical Principles and Levels of Measurement

Principle	Level of Measurement			
	Nominal	**Ordinal**	**Interval**	**Ratio**
Identity	X	X	X	X
Order		X	X	X
Quantity			X	X
Absolute zero				X
Example	Biological sex	Class rank	Temperature	Distance

be clear about your intent. That is, are you using the numerals to identify group membership (as is the case for the nominal level of measurement) or as labels that essentially serve as names for individuals?

Ordinal Scales

As its name implies, an ordinal scale defines measurement in terms of numerals that have the property of order. That is, ordinal scales produce ranks in which people are ordered according to the amounts of some attribute that they possess. For example, the members of an athletic team might be ranked according to their athleticism. The team's coaches might create the rankings based on their own judgments of the athleticism of each team member. The player judged to have the most athleticism might be assigned the numeral 1, the next most athletic player the numeral 2, and so on.

As described earlier, numerals used in this sense are simply labels indicating the relative position of people with regard to the relative levels of the attribute being measured (e.g., athleticism). However, there is no attempt to determine how *much* of that attribute is actually possessed by each person. The numerals simply indicate that one person has more or less of the attribute than another person.

Though this level of measurement conveys more information than a nominal level of measurement, it is limited. One way to think about its limitation is to imagine two different athletic teams, one team composed of professional athletes and one team of high school athletes. Players on each team are ranked according to athleticism by their respective coaches; each professional player is ranked in comparison with the other professionals, and each high school player is ranked in comparison with the other students. The most athletic professional player and the most athletic high school student are each given a ranking of "1" by their coaches. Their "scores" tell us that these two people are the most athletic members of their teams, but the fact that both of them scored a "1" on the athleticism rankings clearly does not imply that they are equally athletic. Obviously, we should not infer that the most athletic high school player is as athletic as the most athletic professional player. Such quantitative comparisons would require a measurement that has the property of quantity.

Interval Scales

The property of quantity characterizes two remaining scales of measurement. That is, interval scales and ratio scales of measurement are based on numbers that represent quantitative differences between people in terms of the attribute being measured. However, the difference between the two scales rests primarily on the meaning of zero.

Interval scales have an arbitrary zero. As noted earlier, temperature expressed in Celsius (or Fahrenheit) units is a classic example of an attribute (temperature) measured on an interval scale. That is, a temperature of 0 °C (or 0 °F, Fahrenheit) is arbitrary because it does not represent the absence of any attribute. That is, it does not represent the absence of heat.

In interval scales, the size of the unit of measurement is constant and additive, but the scale does not allow multiplicative interpretations. That is, you can add 2°h to 40° and get 42°, or you can add 2°, to 80° and get 82°. In each case, a 2° change in the thermometer represents the same change in the underlying amount of heat. That is, the amount of heat required to change the temperature from 40 to 42°C is the same as the amount of heat required to change it from 80 to 82°C. However, it is not appropriate to interpret a temperature of 80°F as "twice as warm" as 40°F.

As discussed later, many psychological tests are used and interpreted as if they are based on an interval scale of measurement. For example, the vast majority of intelligence tests, personality tests, achievement tests, developmental tests, and many other types of psychological assessments are treated as if they are interval scales. By assuming that a test's scores have the property of quantity and that the units of measurement have a constant magnitude, test users can make many research-based and practice-based applications of test scores.

Unfortunately, according to many measurement experts, there are few psychological tests that can be truly said to yield interval-level scores (Ghiselli, Campbell, & Zedeck, 1981). Scores obtained from some well-known academic assessment tests, such as the SAT and the American College Testing (ACT) program, are probably on an interval scale. However, it has been argued that scores from the vast majority of psychological tests are, in fact, not on an interval scale. We will return to the implications of this issue soon.

Ratio Scales

In contrast to interval scales, with an arbitrary 0 point, ratio scales have an absolute 0 point. For example, measures of physical distance are ratio scales. We might intend to measure the distance between two objects, and we find that the distance is 0. In such a case, the zero indicates a true "absence of distance." That is, the zero indicates an absence of the feature being measured.

Ratio scales are considered a "higher" level of measurement than interval, ordinal, and nominal scales, because they provide more information and allow for more sophisticated inferences. Specifically, ratio scales allow additivity as well as multiplicative interpretations in terms of ratios. For example, it is appropriate to interpret a distance of 80 miles as "twice as far" as a distance of only 40 miles.

This important issue has implications for our interpretations of the differences between objects. In applied settings, a ratio scale would allow a test user to make statements such as "Psychiatric patient A is twice as mentally disturbed as Psychiatric patient B." In research settings, a ratio scale would allow researchers to interpret the results of certain statistical procedures in terms of the underlying attributes being measured.

According to most testing experts, there probably are no psychological tests that yield ratio-level data. This might be surprising because you are probably familiar with attempts to measure psychological attributes using standard measures. For example, reaction times are a common currency of measurement in cognitive psychology and are becoming more popular in personality psychology. Standard measures such as reaction time are ratio-level measures. So why are we claiming that there are no ratio-level psychological tests?

Remember that ratio scales have an absolute 0 point. A moment's reflection, however, will show that it is impossible for a person to respond to anything in 0 seconds (or milliseconds). The measuring device—for example, a stop clock—has an absolute zero, but a person's reaction time can never be zero. We are not claiming that reaction time measures are poor measures of psychological processes. In fact, we agree with Jensen (2005) that reaction times might be the most natural way to measure mental activity. Our point with this example is that test users must distinguish between the zero associated with a measuring device and the zero associated with characteristics of the psychological attribute that we think we are measuring. Although a measuring instrument might have an absolute zero, this does not mean that the psychological attribute being measured has an absolute zero (Blanton & Jaccard, 2006).

Scales of Measurement: Practical Implications

As noted earlier, a test's scale of measurement can have important implications. Among behavioral researchers, it is commonly noted that this issue can have implications for the meaningfulness of specific forms of statistical analysis. That is, it has been argued that some of the most common, fundamental, and familiar statistical procedures should be used only with measurements that are interval or ratio, not with nominal or ordinal measurements. For example, Cohen (2001) states that "parametric statistics are truly valid only when you are dealing with interval/ratio data" (p. 7).

However, there is, in fact, some disagreement about this. For example, Howell (1997) asserts that "the underlying measurement scale is not crucial in our choice of statistical techniques" (p. 8). Reflecting on such disagreements, Maxwell and Delaney (2000) admit that "level of measurement continues to be controversial as a factor that might or might not influence the choice between parametric and nonparametric approaches" (p. 710).

Regardless of ambiguities and disagreements, behavioral researchers generally treat most tests and measures as having an interval level of measurement. Particularly for aggregated scores obtained from multi-item scales, researchers assume that scores are "reasonably" interval level. For very brief or single-item scales, this assumption is more tenuous. In such cases, researchers should either consider alternative analytic strategies or acknowledge the potential problem.

Additional Issues Regarding Scales of Measurement

Stevens's rules for assigning symbols, including numbers, to behavioral observations used as tests should be taken as heuristic devices rather than as definitive and exhaustive. In fact, other authors have proposed additional levels of measurement, with corresponding rules for creating scales. For example, Coombs (1950) argues for a level of measurement between nominal and ordinal levels and another between ordinal and interval levels. Moreover, counting can be considered a level of measurement in its own right, and when used to quantify a psychological attribute, it can be thought of as a measure with an absolute zero and a fixed nonarbitrary unit of measurement (the number 1). Our discussion focused on Stevens's framework because it is the most common such framework and because it provides a reasonable foundation for understanding the key issues as related to psychometrics.

Another point is that, although they are often used to reflect nominal scales, dichotomous variables that have been assigned binary codes (such as 0 and 1) can sometimes be thought of as producing interval-level data. If you have reason to believe that discrete dichotomous categories were created based on some underlying quantitative psychological attribute, then the binary codes possess all of the properties associated with quantity. For example, imagine that you have a measure of depression. You give the test to a large group of people and sort people into two categories based on their scores—those who are depressed and those who are not depressed. If you assigned numerical codes to these categories, then the numbers can be seen as reflecting the differences in the amount of depression in the people in the two categories. In this case, the values could be conceptualized on an interval scale. On the other hand, if a sort into categories is not predicated on a quantitative attribute, then it would not make sense to treat the codes as having quantitative properties. An example might be a case in which people are sorted into categories based on whether they have used an illegal drug.

Summary

This chapter has addressed a variety of important theoretical issues in an attempt to outline the foundations of psychological measurement. The core goal of scaling in the context of this book is to link numerical values to people's psychological attributes. As outlined in this chapter, fundamental issues in scaling concern (a) the connection between the observations of a behavior and numerical symbols and (b) the degree to which this connection is made in such a way that the symbols identify the real differences that exist between the behaviors under observation.

The scaling of people's psychological attributes is faced with challenges that partly arise from the fact that psychological attributes (e.g., traits, abilities, skills, attitudes) are not directly observable. Therefore, in many cases of psychological measurement, psychologists are likely to rely on nonquantitative measures of psychological attributes or simply assume that quantitative measurement models work well enough to approximate quantities of psychological attributes. Nevertheless, all psychological scaling procedures have one feature in common—they are all procedures for representing the differences among people. In the next chapter, we will discuss the statistical procedures that are used to treat and describe these individual differences.

Suggested Readings

This is the classic article on psychological scaling:

Stevens, S. S. (1946). On the theory of scales of measurement. *Science, 1103*, 677–680.

This is an article that discusses many variations on Stevens's scales of measurement:

Coombs, C. H., Raiffa, H., & Thrall, R. M. (1954). Some views on mathematical models and measurement theory. *Psychological Review, 61*, 132–144.

The following is a good recent discussion of one of the most fundamental problems of measurement in psychology:

Blanton, H., & Jaccard, J. (2006). Arbitrary metrics in psychology. *American Psychologist, 61*, 27–41.

CHAPTER 3

Individual Differences and Correlations

This chapter covers three key building blocks of psychological measurement: variability, covariability, and the interpretation of test scores. As we shall see, these three issues are a fundamental part of measurement theory, test evaluation, and test use. Much of the material covered in this chapter will be statistical in nature, and some of the concepts that we discuss might be familiar to many of you. However, these concepts must be very well understood before a coherent perspective on psychometrics and the meaning of psychological test scores is possible.

The current chapter integrates these three key building blocks. We begin with a discussion of variability—the differences within a set of test scores or among the values of a psychological attribute. We first discuss the importance of this concept and then describe the procedures for quantifying the degree of variability within a set of scores. Next, we describe the concept of covariability—the degree to which variability in one set of scores corresponds with variability in another set of scores. We discuss the importance of the concept and detail the statistical procedures for quantifying the covariability between two sets of scores. Finally, we describe the procedures that have been developed to enhance the ability of test users and test takers to interpret test scores. As we will see, these procedures are firmly based on the concept of variability.

The Nature of Variability

As we have mentioned previously, psychological measurement rests on the assumption that people differ (or might differ) with respect to their behavior or other psychological characteristics. This assumption is sometimes explicit, as in research that attempts to explore the source and meaning of psychological differences among people. However, this assumption is sometimes implicit. For example, a test user might wish to understand a single individual, as in making a diagnosis regarding mental retardation. Even in these kinds of "single-case" situations, the measurement process rests on the assumption that differences exist among people and that a diagnostic measure is capable of detecting those differences.

There are at least two kinds of differences that behavioral scientists attempt to measure. *Interindividual differences* are differences that exist between people. For example, when high school students take the SAT, all do not get the same score. The differences among the students' SAT scores represent interindividual differences. Similarly, when a researcher conducts an experiment and measures a dependent variable (DV), the participants do not all have the same score on the DV. The differences among the participants' scores are interindividual differences. Importantly, in an experiment, some of these interindividual differences are between people in the same experimental group, and some are between people who are in different experimental groups. In this way, even strict, heavily controlled experimental research hinges on the measurement and analysis of interindividual differences.

The other kind of differences that behavioral scientists attempt to measure is *intra-individual differences*, which are differences that emerge in one person over time or under different circumstances. For example, intra-individual differences might be seen if we recorded changes in a psychiatric patient's symptom level over the course of therapeutic treatment.

Our ability to create, evaluate, and ultimately use any measure in psychology requires that psychological differences exist and can be quantified. In this chapter, we will primarily focus our attention on interindividual variability, which is consistent with many applications of psychological measurement.

Importance of Individual Differences

It would be nearly impossible to overemphasize the importance of individual differences in psychology. Long ago, the scientist Sir Francis Galton recognized that variability was the currency not only of evolution but also of psychology. Psychology is about variability in the behavior of individual people. Indeed, the behavioral sciences are largely about individual differences, and the measurement of those differences is a necessary component of those sciences.

As we have emphasized, variability is at the heart of research and the application of research in the behavioral sciences. In a research context, behavioral scientists often strive to understand important differences among people (including differences between groups of people). When psychologists and other behavioral scientists conduct studies of aggression, intelligence, psychopathy, happiness, marital satisfaction, or academic aptitude, they are attempting to identify and understand the causes and consequences of differences between people. Why are some people more aggressive than others? Are differences in intelligence associated with differences in biological traits? Does variability in marital satisfaction seem to be related to variability in children's self-esteem? Do differences in medication dosage affect differences in patients' levels of depressive affect? All such questions begin with the assumption that people differ in important ways and that these differences can be measured.

In an applied context, behavioral scientists often assume that psychological characteristics can and do vary. Employers attempt to detect variability in characteristics such as conscientiousness, integrity, and intelligence in order to improve their hiring efficacy. College admissions committees attempt to detect variability in academic aptitude in order to improve their admission choices. Clinicians attempt to detect variability in various psychological disorders in order to identify which clients might benefit from which therapeutic interventions.

Individual differences are also fundamental to psychological measurement. As described earlier, measurement is based on the simple but crucial assumption that psychological differences exist and can be detected through well-designed measurement processes. As we will see later in this book, the existence and detection of individual differences lie at the heart of test construction and test evaluation. More specifically, psychometric concepts such as reliability and validity are entirely dependent on the ability to quantify the differences among people.

Traditionally, individual differences have been considered a subject that concerned only those who construct and use traditional psychological tests. For example, the study of individual differences is often seen as primarily relevant only to researchers who study personality, intelligence, or achievement. This traditional, commonly held view limits the importance or meaning of "individual differences" to only some areas of behavioral science. As such, this view limits the relevance of psychometrics to only a few areas of behavioral science. Although this view is long-standing and common, it is simply incorrect.

In fact, all research in psychology and all scientific applications of psychology depend on the ability to measure individual differences. For example, research in experimental psychology involves exposing people to different experiences and then measuring the effects of these experiences on their behavior. For example, a clinical experimentalist might randomly assign some depressed individuals to receive a new medication and randomly assign other depressed individuals to receive placebo pills, and he or she then measures all the individuals' levels of depressive affect after 2 months of taking their respective "treatments." Of course, the researcher likely expects to find that the differences between the individuals' depression levels are highly related to the type of "treatment" they received—individuals who received the new medication are expected to have lower levels of depression than are individuals who received the placebos. In this way, the experimental psychologist is trying to show that individual differences in a psychological response (i.e., depressive affect) are, in part, a function of the experiences to which the participants were exposed.

Likewise, in all cases, the scientific application of psychology requires at a minimum that individual differences be measured. For example, in clinical settings, diagnosis of psychological pathology rests on a clinician's ability to measure the pathology. This requires that the clinician can show how an individual with the pathology differs from those who do not exhibit the pathology. If the clinician is committed to the science of psychology, the clinician will also try to determine if there is a change in client behavior over time and, if there is a change, try to establish if the change might be attributable to therapy. We believe that it is important to realize that any domain of scientific psychology—experimental or nonexperimental, basic or applied—depends on the existence and quantification of individual differences.

The process of the quantification of psychological differences begins with the recognition that scores on a psychological test or measure will vary from person to person or from time to time. When taken from a group of people or at different points in time from the same individuals, these test scores or measures constitute a *distribution* of scores. The differences among the scores within a distribution are often called *variability*. A key element in most behavioral research is to quantify precisely the amount of variability within a distribution of scores.

Variability and Distributions of Scores

To understand many of the fundamental concepts in psychometrics, it is necessary to understand some basic statistical concepts. In particular, we must understand how variance and covariance are computed and how they are related to each other. We need to compute variance as a way of quantifying variability or individual differences in a distribution or set of scores, and we need to compute covariance as a way to quantify the extent to which variability in one set of scores is related to variability in another set of scores.

Many of the fundamental concepts in psychological measurement are built on our ability to detect and describe distributions of test scores. When a group of people take a psychological test, each person obtains a score. Usually, these scores differ from each other, with some people obtaining high scores, some obtaining low scores, and some scoring in between. The group's set of scores is a distribution of scores. Table 3.1 presents a small example in which six people take an IQ test. As you can see, this small distribution of six scores reflects individual differences—scores range from a high of 130 to a low of 90.

Table 3.1   Example for Describing a Distribution of Scores

IQ (X)	Deviation, (X - X̄)	Squared Deviation, (X - X̄)²
110	0	0
120	10	100
100	−10	100
90	−20	400
130	20	400
110	0	0

NOTE: Sum $\left(\sum (X)\right)$ = 660, SS $\left(\sum (X - \overline{X})^2\right)$ = 1,000, mean $(\overline{X})$ = 110; variance (s^2) = 166.67, standard deviation (s) = 12.91.

One key goal of statistics is to describe a distribution of scores in a meaningful way, and at least three kinds of information can be used to do this. Many of you are probably already familiar with concepts such as central tendency, variability, and shape. We will discuss these concepts in a way that should set the stage for our discussion of psychometric concepts such as reliability and validity.

Central Tendency

Perhaps the most basic facet of a distribution of scores is central tendency: What is the "typical" score in the distribution or what is the score that is most representative of the entire distribution? Although there are several statistical values that can be used as indexes of central tendency (e.g., median and mode), the mean is the most common.

The arithmetic *mean* ($\overline{X}$) is a value that represents the "typical" score in a distribution of scores. Many of you are probably familiar with the equation for the mean:

$$\text{Mean} = \overline{X} = \frac{\sum X}{N}. \tag{3.1}$$

In this equation and those that follow, each individual's score is represented by an "X." Those of you who are familiar with summation notation will recall that the sigma symbol tells us to sum the elements X. In addition, N is used to represent the total number of people in the group (or, more generally, the total number of X values in the distribution). For the data in Table 3.1, the mean IQ is

$$\overline{X} = \frac{100+120+100+90+130+110}{6},$$
$$= \frac{660}{6},$$
$$= 110.$$

Thus, the "average person" in the group has an IQ of 110.

Although the mean of a distribution can be an interesting and useful piece of information, we are much more interested in quantifying the degree to which the people in a group differ from each other. One method of doing this is to quantify the degree to which each person's score deviates from the group mean. We turn to that next.

Variability

As we have emphasized (and as we will continue to emphasize), measurement rests on the concept of variability. If our measures are to be useful, they need to be sensitive to meaningful psychological variability by reflecting the differences in people's psychological attributes. Thus, we must be able to quantify precisely the amount of variability within a distribution of test scores.

Although several statistical values can be used to quantify the variability within a distribution of scores, we will focus on two—the variance and its close relative, the standard deviation. We focus on these because they are the most commonly used indexes of variability in behavioral research in general and because they lie at the heart of psychometric theory in particular.

The variance and the standard deviation reflect variability as the degree to which the scores in a distribution deviate (i.e., differ) from the mean of the distribution. In the data in Table 3.1, we see that the IQ scores do indeed vary. We see that one person scores a full 20 points above the mean, and another scores 10 points above the mean. On the other end of the distribution, one person scores 20 points below the mean, and another scores 10 points below the mean. The variance is computed from these deviations.

Variance is a crucial concept in psychometrics. Therefore, let us think carefully about where it comes from and what it means. Building on the deviations of each score from the mean, the process of computing the variance can be summarized in three steps. First, we find the deviation from the mean for each score in the distribution (note that we must have already computed the mean of the distribution). Formally, the deviation from the mean is $X - \overline{X}$ for each score, as shown in the "Deviation" column of Table 3.1. These values represent the degree to which each score is above or below the mean. Second, we square each deviation $(X - \overline{X})^2$, as shown in the "Squared Deviation" column in Table 3.1. Third, we compute the mean of these squared deviations, resulting in the variance:

$$\text{Variance} = s^2 = \frac{\sum (X - \overline{X})^2}{N}. \tag{3.2}$$

For the data in Table 3.1, the variance is

$$s^2 = \frac{(110-110)^2 + (120-110)^2 + (100-110)^2 + (90-110)^2 + (130-110)^2 + (-110-110)^2}{6},$$

$$= \frac{(0)^2 + (10)^2 + (-10)^2 + (-20)^2 + (20)^2 + (0)^2}{6},$$

$$= \frac{0 + 100 + 100 + 400 + 400 + 0}{6},$$

$$= \frac{1000}{6}$$

$$= 166.67.$$

The numerator of the variance is sometimes called the "sum of squared deviations about the mean," but it is more commonly shortened to the "sum of squares."

In a sense, the variance is itself a type of mean. Specifically, the variance is the mean of squared deviation scores. As mentioned, an individual's squared deviation score $(X - \overline{X})^2$ represents the degree to which the individual differs from the mean. By calculating the mean of these squared deviation scores, we get a number that represents the average degree to which people differ from each other, and as such, it is a measure of variability.

A close relative of the variance, the standard deviation is simply the square root of the variance:

$$\text{Standard deviation} = s = \sqrt{s^2} = \sqrt{\frac{\sum(X - \overline{X})^2}{N}}. \tag{3.3}$$

For the data in Table 3.1, the standard deviation is

$$s = \sqrt{s^2} = \sqrt{166.67} = 12.91.$$

As an index of variability, the standard deviation has the advantage of reflecting variability in terms of the size of raw deviation scores, whereas the variance reflects variability in terms of squared deviation scores. Thus, the standard deviation is sometimes viewed as more intuitive.

Although the variance and standard deviation are fundamental elements of many psychometric concepts, their interpretation is not always clear. The size of the variance (and, consequently, the size of the standard deviation) is determined by two factors. The first and most obvious factor is the degree to which the scores in a distribution differ from each other. In the hypothetical IQ data presented in Table 3.1, the variance is 166.67. However, if we had a distribution of IQ scores with less variability, then we would have a smaller variance. For example, we might have the following distribution of IQ scores: 111, 110, 109, 112, 110, 108. Note that this distribution of scores is very tightly clustered around the mean of 110; at most, the scores differ from the mean by only two points. Consequently, the variance for this distribution is only $s^2 = 1.67$. Thus, all else being equal, a larger variance (and standard deviation) indicates greater variability within a distribution. However, all else is not always equal, which brings us to the second factor that affects the size of the variance.

The second factor that determines the size of a variance is the metric of the scores in the distribution. Consider the difference between IQ scores and grade point average (GPA) values. IQ scores are much larger than GPA scores: IQ scores average near 100, with values such as 130 and 80 not being uncommon, but GPA values range only between 0 and 4.0. Thus, IQ scores and GPA values are measures that are on very different forms of measurement. For example, consider the GPA data in Table 3.2. Note that the mean is 2.7 and that scores range from 1.5 to 3.4, a nearly 2-point range. Clearly, "a 2-point range" means something very different in terms of GPA scores from what it does in terms of IQ scores. Thus, although the variance of the IQ scores is $s^2 = 166.67$ and the variance of the GPA scores is "only" $s^2 = 0.39$, this difference does not mean that people differed more in terms of their IQ scores than in terms of their GPAs. The dramatic difference in the two variances arises largely because of the dramatic difference in the metrics of the two sets of scores.

Considering the nature of variance and the factors that affect its size, there are four factors to consider in interpreting a variance or standard deviation. The first factor is that neither one can ever be less than 0. At a minimum, they can be 0, which indicates that the scores in the distribution do not vary at all. A positive

Table 3.2   Example for Computing Covariance and Correlation

IQ Score (X)	GPA (Y)	IQ Deviation, $(X - \overline{X})$	GPA Deviation, $(Y - \overline{Y})$	Cross-Product, $(X - \overline{X})(Y - \overline{Y})$
110	2.6	0	−0.1	0
120	3	10	0.3	3
100	2.5	−10	−0.2	2
90	1.50	−20	−1.2	24
130	3.2	20	0.5	10
110	3.4	0	0.7	0

NOTE: Mean $(\overline{X})$ = 110, mean $(\overline{Y})$ = 2.70, $\sum (X - \overline{X})(Y - \overline{Y})$ = 39; variance s_x^2 = 166.67, variance (s_Y^2) = 0.39, covariance (c_{xy}) = 6.5; standard deviation (s_x) = 12.91, standard deviation (s_y) = 0.62, correlation (r_{xy}) =.81.

value indicates that there is some amount of variability. Both mathematically and conceptually, it is impossible to have a negative variance or standard deviation.

Second, there is no simple way to interpret a variance or standard deviation as large or small. Imagine that we tell you that the variance of a distribution is 56.23, but we do not tell you what the distribution refers to (i.e., is it SAT scores, is it milliseconds on a decision-making task, is it scores on a self-esteem questionnaire?) or what the "typical" variability might be for whatever scores are in the distribution (i.e., what size variance do we usually find within a distribution of scores on this test?). In such a case, you would have no way of judging whether the s^2 = 56.23 reflects a large amount of variability or a small amount.

Third (and related to the second), the variance of a distribution of scores is most interpretable and meaningful when it is put into some kind of context. For example, a variance of one distribution of scores is potentially meaningful when compared with the variance of another distribution of scores. If two distributions are based on the same measure (i.e., both are based on an IQ test, or both are distributions of GPAs), then the distribution with the larger variance has greater variability than the distribution with the smaller variance. Note that such a comparison is meaningful only when the two distributions are indeed based on the same measure. It would be inappropriate to compare the variance of IQ scores with the variance of GPAs and conclude that people vary more in their IQs than in their GPAs.

Fourth, the importance of variance and standard deviation lies mainly in their effects on other values that are more directly interpretable. The variance and standard deviation are fundamental components of many psychometric concepts and procedures. For example, in this book, we show that the variance and standard deviation are a part of concepts such as the correlation coefficient, the reliability coefficient, confidence intervals, and test bias. Thus, you might not often hear or read interpretations of variances by themselves. However, your understanding of many crucial concepts (e.g., correlations and reliability) depends heavily on understanding that the variance and the standard deviation reflect the degree to which the values in a distribution differ from each other.

At the risk of causing a bit of confusion, we should acknowledge something that some of you might find odd about Equations 3.2 and 3.3. Those of you who have previously taken courses in statistics might notice a subtle discrepancy between the equations that we have presented and the equations for the variance and standard deviation that you might have seen in other courses or other textbooks. Specifically, the variance and standard deviation are often presented with $N-1$ in their denominators, instead of simply N. The "$N-1$" versions of the equations are appropriate when researchers wish to compute inferential statistics (e.g., t tests) regarding properties of populations. However, the issues involved in this book do not require the computation of such inferential statistics, and therefore we use the simpler, and logically appropriate, "N" versions of the equations. This somewhat tangential point does not change the essential interpretation of a variance or a standard deviation as important indicators of the degree of variability within a distribution of scores.

Distribution Shapes and Normal Distributions

The final qualities of a distribution that we will discuss are related to the shape of the distribution. A distribution of scores can be graphically represented by a curve. Figure 3.1 presents a curve for a large distribution of IQ scores. The x-axis presents various values for IQ scores, and the y-axis represents proportions. Thus, the curve represents the proportion of people in a group who have IQ scores at a specific value. Figure 3.1 tells us that the greatest proportion of the sample have IQ scores near 100. It also tells us that very few people have IQ scores that are far above or below 100.

The curve in Figure 3.1 presents a distribution that is symmetric—the shape of the curve is mirrored on both sides of an IQ of 100. One type of distribution of scores that produces a curve with this shape is called a *normal distribution*. The idea of a normal distribution is important, and it is implicit in many statistical procedures and concepts. Indeed, many of the statistical procedures that can be conducted on distributions of scores are based on the assumption that the scores

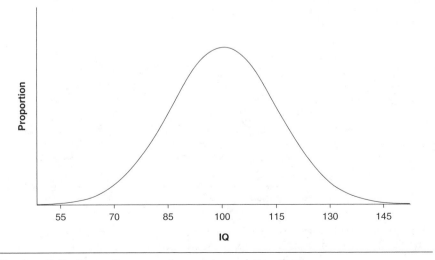

Figure 3.1 Curve Representing a Normal Distribution

are normally distributed (or at least that the scores on the underlying construct are normally distributed). In addition, as we will soon see, the very meaning of test scores sometimes hinges on the assumption that the scores are normally distributed.

Although some of the procedures that we will present are based on the assumption that distributions are normal, in fact normal distribution is a theoretical ideal. When we work with distributions of actual test scores, those distributions are rarely (if ever) perfectly "normal." For example, in one distribution of real IQ scores, there might be a few more people who are on the lower side of the scores (e.g., who have IQ scores less than 100) than on the higher side (see Figure 3.2a). In another distribution of real IQ scores, there might be more people who have high IQ scores than people who have low IQ scores (see Figure 3.2b). Such distributions are skewed, and thus they are not exactly normal (although they might be close to normal). Despite the fact that real data are unlikely to be exactly normally distributed, many times they are close enough so that the normal distribution can be used as a model for interpreting scores in a distribution of scores.

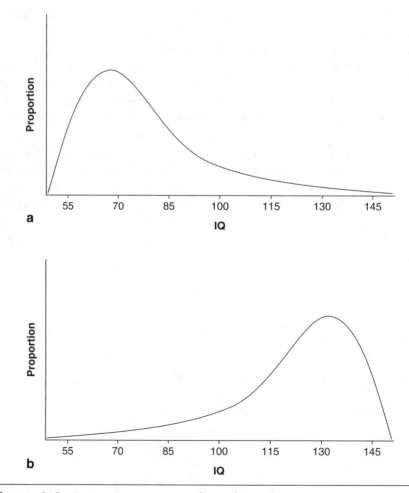

Figure 3.2 Curves Representing Skewed Distributions

Quantifying the Association Between Distributions

Although science and measurement are based on variability, an equally important concept is covariability or association. Covariability is the degree to which two distributions of scores vary in a corresponding manner. For example, we might find that people vary in terms of their IQ scores, and we might find that people vary in their GPAs. These two facts become much more interesting when we examine the possibility that variability in IQ scores is associated with (i.e., covaries with) variability in GPA—do people with relatively high IQ scores tend to earn relatively high GPAs? If so, to what degree? Is there a strong association between IQ and GPA, or is it weak? Such questions are at the heart of most behavioral science and at the heart of psychometric theory.

To examine most questions of covariability, each participant must have scores on at least two variables. For example, if we want to examine the association between IQ and GPA, then we would need to have a sample of participants each of whom has taken an IQ test and has earned a GPA. Thus, we would have a data set in which there are two distributions of scores, with each distribution defined by a different variable. We would then compute statistical values that reflect the degree to which the two variables (as represented by those distributions) are associated with each other.

Interpreting the Association Between Two Variables

There are two types of information that we would like to know about the association between two variables (i.e., between two distributions of scores). First, we would like to know the *direction of the association*. Do people who obtain relatively high scores on one variable tend to obtain relatively high scores on the other? If so, then we say that the two variables have a positive or direct association. It is also possible that people who obtain relatively high scores on one variable tend to obtain relatively low scores on the other. In this case, we say that the two variables have a negative or inverse association.

The second type of information that we would like to know about the association between two variables is the *magnitude of the association*. Are two variables very strongly associated with each other or only weakly? For example, we might wish to know the strength of the association between SAT scores and college GPA. Most colleges and universities place considerable emphasis on SAT scores as a criterion for admission, presumably on the assumption that there is a strong positive association between SAT scores and college GPA. Admissions officers operate under the assumption that people who obtain high SAT scores have a rather strong tendency to earn relatively high GPAs. But just how strong is the actual association between SAT scores and college GPA? All of us probably know at least one person who performed poorly on the SAT but who did well in college, and all of us might know someone who performed well on the SAT but did poorly in college. Clearly, the association between SAT scores and college GPA is not perfect, but is it even as strong as the admissions officers might assume? A great deal of research in behavioral science has been dedicated to understanding the strength of association between important behavioral variables.

Consistency is a useful concept to consider when thinking about the associations between variables. We can interpret a strong association between two variables as showing that individual differences are consistent across the two variables. For example, a strong positive association between SAT scores and GPA would mean that differences in SAT scores are highly consistent with differences in GPA—people with relatively high SAT scores have a strong tendency to earn a relatively high GPA. As a matter of fact, a strong negative association can be interpreted in terms of consistency. For example, a strong negative association between "number of class absences" and GPA would mean that differences in the number of absences are inversely consistent with GPA—people who miss relatively many classes have a strong tendency to earn a relatively low GPA. Whereas strong associations (either positive or negative) indicate a high level of consistency between two variables, weak associations indicate inconsistency. If we find evidence that there is no clear association between two variables, then we know that individual differences in one variable are totally inconsistent with individual differences in the other variable. For example, we might find no association between shoe size and GPA—people who wear relatively large shoes have no consistent tendency to earn higher (or lower) GPAs than people who wear relatively small shoes. In other words, you are as likely to find a person with large shoes and a high GPA as you are to find a person with small shoes and a high GPA. In our discussion of reliability (see Chapter 5), we will rely heavily on the concept of consistency.

In the remainder of this section, we will discuss two statistical terms that can be used to quantify the association, or covariability, between two distributions of scores. In this discussion, we will demonstrate the fact that these two terms—the covariance and the correlation—emerge from statistical concepts that we have already presented. This discussion should help you develop an intuitive and clear sense of what these values mean and where they come from.

Covariance

Covariance begins building a bridge between the concept of variability and an interpretable index of covariability. Recall that variance is computed from a single distribution of scores. In contrast, covariance is computed from the variability among scores in two different distributions. The covariance represents the degree of association between the variability in the two distributions of scores.

As mentioned earlier, indexes of association typically require that each person have at least two scores. That is, each score in one distribution (e.g., IQ scores) is paired with one and only one score in the other distribution (e.g., GPAs). See Table 3.2 for an example that includes six participants who have scores on two variables—IQ and GPA.

Computing the covariance between two distributions of scores can be seen as a three-step process. First, similar to the variance, we compute deviation scores. Specifically, we compute the deviation of each score from the mean of its distribution. In Table 3.2, these values are presented in the columns labeled "IQ Deviation" and "GPA Deviation." If we refer to IQ scores as variable X and to GPAs as variable Y, then these deviation scores can be formally written as $X - \overline{X}$ and $Y - \overline{Y}$, respectively.

In the second step, we compute the "cross-products" of these deviation scores by multiplying each individual's two deviation scores (see the "Cross-Product" column in Table 3.2). Formally, a cross-product is $(X - \overline{X})(Y - \overline{Y})$. Take a moment to think about the meaning of these values. Note that in Table 3.2, several of the cross-products are positive. Why? A positive cross-product is obtained when an individual's scores are consistent with each other: The individual is either above the mean on both variables or below the mean on both variables. Now, think about the meaning of a negative cross-product. A negative cross-product is obtained when an individual's scores are inconsistent with each other: The individual is above the mean on one variable (and thus obtains a positive deviation score for that variable) but below the mean on the other variable (and thus obtains a negative deviation score for that variable).

In the third and final step, we compute the mean of the cross-products. We need to understand the trend in the cross-products across all the people in the sample. In general, do people have positive cross-products or negative cross-products? Or do the cross-products cancel themselves out, equaling 0? In addition, how large are the cross-products? The third step provides the equation for the covariance:

$$\text{Covariance} = c_{xy} = \frac{\sum (X - \overline{X})(Y - \overline{Y})}{N}. \tag{3.4}$$

Putting it all together, the data in Table 3.2 have a covariance of 6.5:

$$
\begin{aligned}
c_{xy} &= \frac{(0)(-0.1)+(10)(0.3)+(-10)(-0.2)+(-20)(-0.2)+(20)(0.5)+(0)(0.7)}{6} \\
&= \frac{0+3+2+24+10+0}{6} \\
&= \frac{39}{6} \\
&= 6.5.
\end{aligned}
$$

As we have discussed, there are two important issues to be considered in interpreting the association between variables—direction and magnitude. The covariance provides clear information about one of these issues but not the other.

The covariance provides clear information about the direction of the association. If a covariance is positive, as it is in our example, then we know that there is a positive or direct association between the two variables. Because we obtained a positive covariance in our example, we know that, to some degree, people who have relatively high IQ scores *tend* to earn relatively high GPAs. If the covariance value is negative, then we would know that there is a negative or inverse association between the two variables.

Unfortunately, the covariance does not provide clear information about the magnitude of the association between two variables. In a sense, the covariance is very similar to the variance, as we discussed earlier. Specifically, there are two factors that affect the magnitude or size of the covariance. First, the strength of association affects the magnitude of the covariance—all else being equal, large values of the covariance (whether large positive values or large negative values) reflect strong associations. So in the examination of the association between IQ and GPA, a covariance of 6.5 indicates a stronger association than a covariance of only 2.3. However, the metrics of the two variables also affects the magnitude of the covariance. That is, the covariance between two "large-scale" variables (e.g., SAT and IQ) is likely to be larger than a covariance that involves one or more "small-scale" variables (e.g., GPA), regardless of the strength of the associations. Therefore, we might find that the covariance between IQ and SAT (say $c_{XY} = 154.32$) is much larger than the covariance between IQ and GPA ($c_{XY} = 6.5$, as in our example), but this does not necessarily mean that IQ is more strongly associated to SAT scores than to GPA.

Thus, covariance is an important statistical concept, but it has limited direct interpretability. It is important because, like variance, it serves as a basis for many other important statistical concepts and procedures. Most immediately, it is important because it begins to bridge the gap between variability and an easily interpretable index of association. Such an index is the correlation coefficient, which we will examine soon.

Before turning to the correlation coefficient, we will take a moment to describe something that will appear later in this book—a variance–covariance matrix. Some psychometric and statistical procedures are based on the analysis of sets of variances and covariances, and these sets of values can be captured efficiently in square matrices of values, such as the one in Table 3.3a. Table 3.3a presents the smallest possible type of variance–covariance matrix—it is based on only two variables, and it includes two variances and one covariance.

A variance–covariance matrix is always organized in a specific way, with several standard properties. First, each variable has a row and a column. For example, the matrix in 3.3a has two rows and two columns, each based on one of the two variables—IQ and GPA. Similarly, Table 3.3b presents the generalized form of a variance–covariance matrix based on four variables, with four rows and four columns.

A second property of a variance–covariance matrix is that the variables' variances are presented "on the diagonal." That is, the variances are presented in a diagonal line going from the upper left to the bottom right of the matrix. In Table 3.3a, we see that IQ's variance ($s_{IQ}^2 = 166.67$) is in the upper left corner and that GPA's variance ($s_{GPA}^2 = 0.39$) is in the lower right. Similarly, Table 3.3b shows the more general form, in which the variance of Variable 1 (s_1^2) is in the uppermost left cell, the variance of Variable 2 (s_2^2) is in the next cell down the diagonal, and so on.

The third property of a variance–covariance matrix is that all other cells present covariances between pairs of variables. For example, in Table 3.3a, the "off-diagonal" cells present the covariance between IQ and GPA ($c_{IQ,GPA} = 6.5$). Similarly, in Table 3.3b, the value in the first column and second row is the covariance between Variable 1 and Variable 2 (c_{12}), the value in the first column and third row is the covariance between Variable 1 and Variable 3 (c_{13}), and so on.

Table 3.3a   Example of a 2 x 2 Variance–Covariance Matrix

	IQ	GPA
IQ	166.67	6.5
GPA	6.5	.39

Table 3.3b   Generalized Form of a 4 x 4 Variance–Covariance Matrix

	Variable 1	Variable 2	Variable 3	Variable 4
Variable 1	s_1^2	c_{12}	c_{13}	c_{14}
Variable 2	c_{12}	s_2^2	c_{23}	c_{24}
Variable 3	c_{13}	c_{23}	s_3^2	c_{34}
Variable 4	c_{14}	c_{24}	c_{34}	s_4^2

The fourth property is that the covariances are "symmetric" in that the values below the diagonal are identical to the values above the diagonal. This is clear in Table 3.3a, with the covariance between IQ and GPA being presented in the lower left of the matrix and in the upper right. This is also apparent in Table 3.3b, in which, for example, the covariance between Variable 1 and Variable 4 would be presented in the lower left cell and in the uppermost right cell.

In sum, covariances reflect the association between two variables. But again, although they clearly reflect the direction of association, they do not clearly reflect the magnitude of association. In contrast, correlation coefficients clearly reflect both qualities.

Correlation

The correlation coefficient is intended to provide an easily interpretable index of linear association. Correlation coefficients are bounded within a very specific range of possible values—they can range only from −1 to +1. Partially because of this "boundedness," correlations are much more easily interpretable than covariances.

Like the covariance, a correlation coefficient reflects the *direction* of the association between two variables. A correlation with a value that lies between 0 and +1 tells us that there is a positive association between the two variables. In contrast, a correlation with a value that lies between 0 and −1 tells us that there is a negative association between the two variables.

The great benefit of a correlation is that it reflects the *magnitude* of the association between two variables much more clearly than does the covariance. A correlation coefficient of a specific absolute value (e.g., $r_{XY} = .30$ or $r_{XY} = −.30$) represents the same magnitude of association, regardless of the variables on which the correlation is based. Regardless of the metrics of the variables, a large correlation (in terms of its absolute value) reflects a strong association, and a small correlation (i.e., a correlation that is close to 0) reflects a weak association. For example, we always know that a correlation of .30 reflects a stronger association than a correlation of .20, but it reflects a weaker association than a correlation of .40. In addition, we know that a correlation of .30 is the same magnitude as a correlation of −.30. Furthermore, the maximum possible correlation is 1.0 (or −1.0), whether we are talking about the association between IQ and GPA or the association between IQ and SAT. As we described earlier, this is not true for a covariance.

The correlation is based on statistical values that we have already discussed. As a measure of association, the correlation between two variables is based partially on the covariance between the variables. However, the correlation obtains its "bounded" quality by dividing the covariance by the standard deviations of the two variables:

$$\text{Correlation} = r_{xy} = \frac{c_{xy}}{s_x s_y}. \tag{3.5}$$

For the two variables in Table 3.2, the correlation is very strong:

$$r_{xy} = \frac{6.5}{(12.91)(0.62)} = \frac{6.5}{8} = .81.$$

The importance of the correlation cannot be overemphasized. From this point forward, nearly every chapter will use the concept of a correlation coefficient in some way. You will find that the correlation coefficient is an important part of reliability theory, the estimation of reliability, the conceptual basis of validity, the estimation of validity, the effect of response biases on test scores, and the idea of test bias.

Again, it is useful to view correlation as an index of the consistency of individual differences. A strong positive correlation indicates a consistent tendency for people who have relatively high scores on one variable to have relatively high scores on the other (and for people who have relatively low scores on one variable to have relatively low scores on the other). A strong negative correlation indicates a consistent inverse tendency for people who have relatively high scores on one variable to have relatively low scores on the other. A weak correlation—a correlation that is very close to 0—indicates no consistency of individual differences. That is, people who have relatively high scores on one variable are as likely to have low scores as they are to have high scores on the other variable.

Variance and Covariance for "Composite Variables"

In many, if not most, cases, scores on psychological tests are determined by asking people a series of questions, or they are based on several behavioral observations. Responses to these questions or observations are usually summed or averaged to form a composite score. For example, the Beck Depression Inventory (BDI; Beck, Ward, Mendelson, Mock, & Erbaugh, 1961) includes 21 items referring to various symptoms related to depression. An individual's response to each item is scored on a scale of 0 to 3. An individual's score on the BDI is the sum of his or her scores across the 21 items. Thus, BDI scale scores can range from 0 to 63.

The variance of composite scores can be computed in the way we outlined previously (see Equation 3.2). However, it is also important to realize that the variance of a composite score is determined by the variability of each item within the composite, along with the correlations among the items. As an example, we will use the simplest case of a composite score—when a composite is created by summing only two items (note that this case is also directly applicable to the concept of reliability as described in Chapter 5). We will call the two items i and j. The variance of the composite will be

$$s^2_{composite} = s_i^2 + s_j^2 + 2r_{ij}s_i s_j, \tag{3.6}$$

where $s^2_{composite}$ is the variance of the composite variable, s_i^2 and s_j^2 are the variances of items i and j respectively, r_{ij} is the correlation between scores on the two items, and s_i and s_j are the standard deviations of the two items. Note that if the two items are uncorrelated with each other, then the variance of the composite simply equals the sum of the two items' variances (i.e., if $r_{ij} = 0$, then $s^2_{composite} = s_i^2 + s_j^2$).

For more than one pair of items, the right-hand term of the expression is expanded, repeating itself for each additional item pair. For our purposes, the important feature of this equation is that it shows that *total test score variance will depend solely on item variability and the correlation between item pairs*. This issue is an important facet of reliability theory, as we will discuss in a later chapter.

Going further, we can consider the association between two composite scores, which again is relevant to our later discussion of the psychometric concept of reliability. Imagine two composite scores, one comprising items i and j and one comprising items k and l. In this case of a pair of two-item composites, the covariance between the composite scores is simply the sum of the cross-composite covariances. That is, it is the sum of covariances between the items from the different composites (i.e., the covariances between the items from composite 1 and the items from composite 2):

$$c_{composite_1 composite_2} = c_{ik} + c_{il} + c_{jk} + c_{jl}. \tag{3.7}$$

To avoid additional complexity, we will not present the equation for the correlation between two composites. However, interested readers can obtain that equation by substituting values in equation 3.7. We will return to Equations 3.6 and 3.7 in Chapter 5, where we discuss the definition of reliability and the concept of parallel tests.

Binary Items

Some psychological tests are based on dichotomous responses to test items or to behavioral observations that have been scored dichotomously. For example, we might ask people to give a "Yes" or "No" answer to questions or ask them if they agree or disagree with statements. Sometimes responses to questions are scored as correct or incorrect, or we might watch for the occurrence of a behavior and record whether it occurred. In cases where we have binary items, only one of two outcomes is available for each observation or for each test item.

As we have been discussing, variance is one of the most important concepts in psychometrics, so it is worth considering the way variance is represented for binary items. Suppose there was a depression test with questions that require a "Yes" or "No" answer. For example, people might be asked simply, "Do you feel depressed?" with a "0" assigned to a no answer and a "1" assigned to a yes answer. It is common to assign codes to binary responses in this fashion, with 0 used as a code for "negatively" valenced answers. Negatively valenced answers would be answers such as "No," "Never," "Don't agree," "False," and "Incorrect." The number 1 is then assigned to positively valenced answers (i.e., answers such as "Yes," "Always," "Agree," "True," or "Correct").

Like other tests, tests based on binary items are scored by summing or averaging responses across items. For example, if our depression test had 10 items, then we would compute a person's score by summing (or averaging) all 10 responses. If we use a 0 and 1 coding scheme, then the sum would range between 0 and 10, representing the number of items to which the person responded "Yes." Alternatively, the average score will range between 0 and 1, representing the proportion of items to which the person responded "Yes."

In this way, tests based on binary items are very similar to other tests; however, binary items have some special properties that we will reference later in this book. To prepare for those later sections, we will outline a few of these special considerations with regard to the mean and variance of such items. Specifically, we will consider the mean and variance of a binary item, based on several test takers who respond to the item.

If responses are coded in this 0 versus 1 manner, then the mean of a binary item is equal to the proportion of positively valenced answers. Let p stand for the proportion of positively valenced responses to the item (e.g., the proportion of people who respond "Yes" to a binary depression item):

$$\overline{X} = p = \frac{\sum X}{N}.$$

(3.8)

This, of course, is also the formula for the mean of any set of quantitative values. Imagine that 10 people take the depression test that consists of one binary question, with 6 responding "Yes" to the item and 4 responding "No." In these data, we find that the proportion of "Yes" responses was

$$\overline{X} = p = \frac{1+0+1+1+1+0+0+1+0+1}{10} = \frac{6}{10} = .60.$$

Once we recognize that p is equivalent to the mean for a binary test item, we can use that information to translate the variance of binary items into the simple terms of proportion. For this, let q stand for the proportion of negatively valenced responses. Because proportions can range only between 0 and 1, we know that $q = 1 - p$. Recall (Equation 3.2) that the formula to compute the variance for a distribution of ordinary scores is

$$s^2 = \frac{\sum(X - \overline{X})^2}{N}.$$

As we have seen, $\overline{X}$ is equal to p for binary items. Therefore, we can substitute p for $\overline{X}$:

$$s^2 = \frac{\sum(X - p)^2}{N}.$$

If we expand this expression, we obtain

$$s^2 = \frac{\sum X^2}{N} + \frac{\sum p^2}{N} - \frac{2p\sum X}{N}.$$

However, because this is a binary item that is scored 0 versus 1, X can only have values of 0 or 1. Since the square of 0 is 0 and the square of 1 is 1, $X = X^2$. Therefore,

$$\frac{\sum X^2}{N} = \frac{\sum X}{N},$$

which equals p (see Equation 3.8). Substituting this into the equation for the variance,

$$s^2 = p + \frac{\sum p^2}{N} - 2p^2.$$

Because p is constant across all respondents,

$$\frac{\sum p^2}{N} = \frac{Np^2}{N} = p^2.$$

Substituting again, we have

$$s^2 = p + p^2 - 2p^2,$$
$$= p - p^2,$$
$$= p(1 - p).$$

Because we defined q as $1 - p$ (the proportion of people given negatively valenced responses), the variance of a binary item can be expressed as

$$s^2 = pq. \tag{3.9}$$

For the sample in which six people responded "Yes" to the one-item depression test, the variance would be

$$s^2 = (.60)(.40),$$
$$= .24.$$

Equation 3.9 is important because it shows that the variance of a binary response item depends simply on p and q. The variance of a binary item is maximized when half of the people provide a positively valenced response and the other half provide a negatively valenced response—that is, when $p = q = .50$. In this case, the item's variance will be $s^2 = pq = (.50)(.50) = .25$. Any other value of p will result in a reduction of variance. If $p = 1.00$ or $.00$, the associated item will have no variance. Returning to our definition of covariance, it should be clear that if tests scores have no variance, then the scores cannot be correlated with any other set of scores. Again, we will return to these ideas later in this book.

Interpreting Test Scores

As we discussed in the opening chapters of this book, many psychological tests are based on scores that are inherently ambiguous. For example, imagine that you take a personality questionnaire that includes agree/disagree questions intended to measure your level of neuroticism, and the test administrator counts the number of times you responded to a question in a way that indicated some level of neuroticism (e.g., the number of times you marked "Agree" to an item like "I tend to get upset easily."). Let' say that the test administrator tells you that you obtained a "raw" score of 34 on the neuroticism scale, how would you interpret your score? What does it mean to have a score of 34? Do you have 34 "units" of neuroticism? Is your score high? Is it low? If your friend took a different personality questionnaire and obtained a score of 98 on a neuroticism scale, does that mean that your friend is much more neurotic than you are? Actually, it could mean that your friend is *less* neurotic than you are.

On most psychological tests, the raw score on the test is not inherently meaningful and thus not easily interpretable. By "raw" scores, we mean scores that are obtained most directly from the responses to test items, such as the number of "Agree" responses on a personality test or the number of correct responses on an achievement test.

There are at least two facets to the "meaning" of test scores in psychological measurement. The first is the basic meaning of a raw test score as being relatively high or low. Perhaps surprisingly, even this basic interpretative issue is obscure for many psychological tests. In the remainder of this chapter, we discuss some of the basic concepts and procedures that have been developed to allow test users to clarify this facet of test interpretation. Many of these procedures emerge from concepts covered in the first part of this chapter—means, standard deviations, and "normally shaped" distributions. The second facet of meaning is more abstract and psychological. Specifically, the second facet concerns the psychological implications of test scores. That is, what does a high score on a particular test actually mean, psychologically? Based on the concepts to be covered in the remainder of this chapter, you might take a test and know that your score is indeed high. However, you might still wonder about the psychological implications of your high score. The test developer or test user might tell you that the test is a measure of neuroticism, but is that really true? Is it possible that the test user is misinterpreting the test scores? If it is indeed a measure of neuroticism, then what does it mean to have a high level of neuroticism? Such questions are answered on the basis of psychological research, theory, and statistical analysis, and they will be covered later in this book, in the chapters on validity.

Thus, the remainder of this chapter will address the fundamental problem of interpreting the magnitude of test scores as low, medium, or high. Solutions to this problem are built on issues we have already discussed in terms of quantifying individual differences within a distribution of scores. That is, to interpret an individual's raw test score, we need to make reference to an entire distribution of scores on the test, and we must identify where the individual falls within that distribution.

When a person takes a psychological test, he or she receives a test score. These scores can be expressed in different forms. For example, when people take a class examination, the instructor has a variety of score-reporting options. The instructor might report the "number correct" (e.g., 40) or the "percent correct" (e.g., 80%). As we have emphasized throughout this book, one of the most serious problems with psychological tests is that raw scores on such tests are often difficult to interpret. For example, what does it mean to take a class examination and get a raw score of 40? Test scores are based on behavioral samples, and they seldom index an *amount* of a psychological characteristic. Therefore, we are left with a number that needs an interpretive frame of reference.

In most applications of psychological testing, the interpretive frame of reference is based on two key pieces of information about a test score in relation to a distribution of test scores. The first key is whether the raw score falls above or below the mean of an entire distribution of test scores (or perhaps exactly at the mean). For example, you might compare your class examination score of 40 with the mean test score in the class. For purposes of illustration, assume that the mean class test score is 36. The class mean provides a frame of reference for interpreting your score. You now know that your test score is above the class's average test score, and this single piece of information provides an important step toward clarity in interpreting your test score.

Knowing that your raw score is above or below the mean tells you something about your performance on the test relative to your classmates, but this information could be enriched if you knew *how far* above or below the mean your test score is. Is 40 a slightly high score, a moderately high score, or a very high score compared with the mean score? That is, if the class mean is 36, then you know that your test score is 4 points above the mean; however, does 4 points represent a small difference or a large difference? Four points on most IQ tests is a relatively small psychological difference, but a difference of 4 points in other types of tests could indicate a dramatic psychological difference.

A solution to this "degree of difference" question involves knowing something about the individual differences that exist in the raw test scores among the people who took the test. If there were large individual differences associated with test scores (i.e., if people have a wide range of scores on the test), then 40 might be interpreted as a *slightly* high score. On the other hand, if most of the students in the class earned scores between 34 and 38 (i.e., if there were only small differences among most individuals), then your score of 40 might seem to be moderately or even *very* high. What we need is a number that provides information about the relative size of the distance between your score and the mean.

Thus, the second key piece of information in interpreting a test score is the variability within a distribution of raw test scores. Most typically, the standard deviation is used to help interpret the distance of a particular score from the mean score. As discussed earlier, the standard deviation tells us the degree to which the raw scores within a distribution differ from each other. Thus, knowing the standard deviation of a distribution can help us calibrate the degree to which an individual score is above or below the mean, which in turn helps us interpret your score as slightly high, moderately high, or very high. The two pieces of information—whether a raw score falls above or below the mean and the distance of the score from the mean—are used to compute z scores (sometimes called standard scores), which we turn to next. After discussing z scores, we turn to two additional ways of representing test scores: (1) converted standard scores (sometimes called standardized scores) and (2) percentile ranks. We will then discuss the process of "normalizing" test scores, which test developers might do in some circumstances.

z Scores (Standard Scores)

In this section, we describe the computation, logic, and interpretation of z scores. In addition, we describe some of their advantages and limitations as ways of expressing scores on psychological tests. Finally, we describe some of their important statistical properties.

An understanding of z scores is important for at least two reasons. First, and by far the most important for our purposes, z scores provide insight into the meaning of test scores as being high, medium, or low. More specifically, they provide fairly precise information about the degree to which an individual's test score is above or below the mean test score. Thus, they are informative in their own right, but they are also the basis of other ways that can be used to represent test scores, as we will discuss later in this chapter. A second reason why z scores are important is that they can be used to conceptualize and compute important statistical values, such as correlation coefficients.

In an attempt to give meaning to test scores, we can transform an individual's raw test score into a z score, which reflects the distance that the score falls above or below the mean. We can transform a raw test score into a z score by computing the difference between the score (X) and the mean of its distribution ($\overline{X}$) and then dividing this difference by the standard deviation (s) of that distribution:

$$z = \frac{X - \overline{X}}{s}. \tag{3.10}$$

For example, to compute the z score for your class examination, let us first imagine that there are large individual differences in the raw test scores. That is, the distribution of raw scores has a relatively large standard deviation, say $s = 8$. Your z score would be

$$z = \frac{40 - 36,}{8} = \frac{4}{8} = 0.5.$$

Z scores have specific, albeit somewhat abstract, interpretations. They can be interpreted in "standard deviation" units. That is, you would interpret your *z* score as indicating that your test score is "0.5 standard deviations above the mean" or "half of a standard deviation above the mean." Because of this close connection to standard deviations, *z* scores are sometimes called "standard scores."

Another way of thinking about *z* scores is that they indicate the extremity of a score. A larger *z* score (in terms of absolute values) indicates a more extreme score. Thus, the fact that your *z* score is only 0.5 indicates that your test score is not particularly extreme. In other words, a score that is only one half of a standard deviation away from the mean is, all things considered, fairly close to the mean. In theory, *z* scores are unbounded—they can be infinitely large. However, in real data that tend to be normally distributed, it is rare to find *z* scores that are greater than 3 or 4 (or that are less than –3 or –4).

Now, let us now imagine that there are small individual differences in the raw test scores. That is, the distribution of test scores has a relatively small standard deviation, indicating that raw scores were clustered tightly about their mean. In such a case, the standard deviation (*s*) might be only 2, rather than 8. If this were the case, your *z* score would be meaningfully larger, at 2:

$$z = \frac{40 - 36}{2} = \frac{4}{2} = 2.$$

You could interpret this as showing that your test score is 2 standard deviations above the mean, which indicates a relatively extreme score (i.e., it is relatively far above the mean).

An important issue in fully understanding and interpreting *z* scores is their unique and important statistical properties. If you take a distribution of test scores and convert each into a *z* score, then your set of *z* scores will have a mean of 0 and a standard deviation of 1.0. This is important because it will affect the permissible values of certain statistical indices, such as correlations.

z scores have several benefits in terms of interpreting test scores. First, they express test scores in a way that bypasses the ambiguity of most psychological measures. By framing the meaning of a score in terms of "distance from the mean," the *z* score frees us from worrying about the units of the original test score.

Second, *z* scores can be used to compare scores across tests that are on different-sized units. For example, two people, Adam and Barbara, might take different neuroticism tests, with Adam getting a score of 34 on one test and Barbara getting a score of 98 on the other test. As described earlier, these scores by themselves simply are not comparable. We can solve this problem by transforming each test score into a *z* score (based on the mean and standard deviation of each distribution) and then comparing the *z* scores. We might find that Adam's score transforms into a *z* score of 1.3 and Barbara's score transforms into a *z* score of –0.4. In this case, we would conclude that, in a sense, Adam has a higher level of neuroticism than Barbara.

The *z* score transformation is even useful when behaviors are measured with instruments that produce well-defined units, such as clocks that record milliseconds. Although we know what a millisecond is and can compare response times between people or across conditions by simple subtraction, we might want to compare response times with other types of measures of behavior that might be recorded with a different measure (e.g., weight) or expressed in units that are not standard (e.g., scores on a test of optimism). These comparisons can be made by transforming milliseconds and the scores from the other measures into *z* scores.

One important additional interpretive fact should be emphasized about *z* scores: They express a score in terms of its relation to an entire distribution of scores. That is, they express scores in relative terms. For example, your *z* score of +2 on the class examination tells us about your performance *in relation to the rest of the class.* Specifically, by framing a score in terms of its distance above or below the mean, a *z* score tells us about how well you did in comparison with the average person. However, a *z* score does not tell us about your overall level of performance in some absolute sense. For example, we might know that you scored 1 standard deviation above the mean on a biology examination (i.e., $z = 1$). This tells us that you seem to know more biology than the average student, but it does not tell us "how much" biology knowledge you actually have, in some absolute sense. Although *z* scores express scores in relative terms and not in absolute terms, this might not be considered a problem. After all, as we have mentioned before, the "absolute" meaning of most psychological tests is ambiguous. *Z* scores are very helpful because they provide a frame of reference that is based on the way scores relate to each other.

As noted earlier, *z* scores not only serve an important interpretive role for test scores, but they also can be used to conceptualize and compute some important statistical values. For example, it is sometimes useful to think of a correlation as the consistency of individual differences expressed in *z* score units. It is often difficult to examine the consistency of raw scores when those scores are values expressed in different metric units. For example, suppose that you have collected the GPAs of 100 students and you want to know if their GPAs are correlated with the number of hours that the students study each week. GPA values will be expressed as relatively small numbers (e.g., 3.2), while hours per week might be expressed by relatively large numbers (e.g., 10). Furthermore, the two variables are measured with different metrics—GPA units and units of hours per week. By transforming each set of values to *z* scores, we express both sets of scores with a common metric, a *z*-score metric. Now, for example, we can ask whether students who study more than the average student have higher GPAs than the average student. We can make this comparison directly by comparing the *z* scores for GPA with the *z* scores for hours of study. If there are consistent differences between individuals, then you would expect to find that each individual would have a pair of *z* scores of roughly the same magnitude (not necessarily with the same sign).

The formula for computing the correlation between variables using *z* scores is

$$r_{xy} = \frac{\sum Z_x Z_y}{N},$$

(3.11)

where $\sum Z_x Z_y$ is the sum of the cross-products of each individual's z scores. It can be shown that Equation 3.11 is algebraically equivalent to Equation 3.5, which expressed the correlation in terms of covariance and standard deviations. Some of you might have encountered Equation 3.11 in other books or classes in which you learned about the correlation coefficient.

Returning to the role that z scores can play when interpreting test scores, they are useful but they might not be ideal for some purposes. That is, despite the advantages of z scores as ways of interpreting test scores, some test users and test takers might find them to be less than intuitive. Indeed, there are at least two potential reasons why test users and test takers might struggle to interpret z scores. First, some respondents' test scores would be expressed as negative numbers. If a respondent's test score is below the mean, then he or she will have a negative z score. For people who are not familiar with concepts such as "standard deviation units" and "distance from the mean," the notion of having a negative level of neuroticism, self-esteem, or intelligence might be difficult to comprehend, and perhaps even objectionable! A second reason why z scores are potentially confusing is that scores are often expressed in fractions or decimals. Some people simply might not find it clear or appealing to be told, "Your IQ test score is 1.24."

To account for some of these nonintuitive aspects of z scores, test developers and test users will sometimes transform scores yet again. These scores, which we will address next, are sometimes called converted standard scores, standardized scores, or derived standard scores.

Converted Standard Scores (Standardized Scores)

Converted standard scores are simply z scores that have been converted into values that people might find easier to understand. This is accomplished by rescaling the scores so that the converted scores have a different mean and standard deviation. For example, scores on the Minnesota Multiphasic Personality Inventory-2 (MMPI-2; Butcher, Dahlstrom, Graham, Tellegen, & Kaemmer, 1989) are often converted so that each of its scales has a mean of 50 and a standard deviation of 10. It is assumed that test takers and test users might be more likely to understand the meaning of a score of 65 or 45 on the Paranoia scale than a score of 1.5 or –0.5.

The conversion can be accomplished through a two-step process in which test users or test developers first select a new mean for the scores ($\overline{X}_{new}$) and a new standard deviation (s_{new}) for the distribution of converted scores. Again, the marketers of the MMPI-2 have elected to have a mean of 50 and a standard deviation of 10.

In the second step, an individual's z score is converted through the following equation:

$$T = Z(s_{new}) + \overline{X}_{new},$$

where T is the converted standard score and z is the individual's original z score. For example, someone with a z score of 1.5 on the MMPI-2 Paranoia scale would have a T score of

$$T = 1.5(10) + 50,$$
$$= 15 + 50,$$
$$= 65.$$

The T score of 65 tells us that the individual is 1.5 standard deviations above the mean on the Paranoia Scale.

Some of you might feel that there is something "fishy" about this process—is it really legitimate for a test user simply to decide that he or she wants scores to have a specific mean or standard deviation? We understand such skepticism, but these types of conversions are, in fact, psychologically valid and meaningful.

The legitimacy of this conversion process goes back to the ambiguity of most psychological measures. As we pointed out earlier, a neuroticism score of 34 has little inherent meaning. For most psychological measures, the meaning of an individual's score arises only in relation to other individuals' scores. The neuroticism score of 34 has no clear meaning until we know whether it is higher or lower than what other people tend to score and until we know *how much* higher or lower most people tend to score. Thus, z scores (standard scores) are informative because they are a pure expression of a score's distance above or below the group mean. By extension, converted standard scores are informative because they simply reexpress z scores in a way that might be more intuitive for more people. The essence and meaning of converted standard scores are the same as for a z score—they tell us how far above or below the mean an individual's score is. The trick to interpreting converted standard scores is that you must know the mean and standard deviation of the converted scores. For example, to know that a score of 65 on the MMPI-2 Paranoia scale is 1 standard deviation above the mean, you must know that the MMPI-2 Paranoia scale has a standard deviation of 15 points. This (or closely related) information should be readily available from test users and test developers.

Whether this conversion process actually improves communication among test users and test takers is an interesting issue, but it is a common practice among those who construct psychological tests. Converted standard scores are the reported scores on many tests with which you are probably familiar, including the SAT, American College Testing (ACT), Graduate Record Examination (GRE), Medical College Admission Test (MCAT), and Law School Admission Test (LSAT) examinations, many personality tests, and many intelligence tests.

Percentile Ranks

Another common way of presenting and interpreting test scores is through percentile ranks, which indicate the percentage of scores that are below a specific test score. For example, if we know that a test taker has scored at the 85th percentile on an achievement test, then we know that the person has a relatively high score. Specifically, we know that he or she scored higher than 85% of the other people who have taken the test. Thus, the percentile rank is yet another way of expressing test scores in relative terms.

There are two ways to determine the percentile rank for an individual's test score. The direct or empirical way is useful if one has access to all the raw scores in a distribution. If so, then an individual's percentile rank can be calculated by identifying the exact number of raw scores in the distribution that are lower than the individual's raw test score and dividing by the total number of scores in the distribution. For example, if 75 people take a test and one of them, Carol, obtains a raw score of 194, we might wish to report her percentile rank. To do this, we first count the number of people who scored below 194 (say, we find that 52 people did so). We then simply divide this number by 75 and multiply by 100 to obtain the percentile rank: $(52/75)(100) = 69\%$. This tells us that Carol scored at the 69th percentile. The direct or empirical way of calculating percentile ranks becomes a bit more complicated if Carol's score is tied with one or more other people, but the general idea and interpretation are the same.

A second way of identifying an individual's percentile rank might be useful if we do not have access to the complete distribution of individual scores. For example, we might have information about only the mean and standard deviation of raw test scores. In such a case, we might be able to compute a standard score (i.e., z score) for the individual and then link it to a percentile. If (and this is an important *if*) we can assume that individual differences on the psychological attribute that underlies the test scores are normally distributed, then we can link standard scores to the *standard normal distribution* (also called the unit normal distribution or the standard normal curve, which some readers might be familiar with). The standard normal distribution, not surprisingly, represents standard scores distributed in a perfectly normal form (see our discussion above regarding "normal" distributions and skew). The standard normal distribution has a special quality, in that it allows us to link specific standard scores to percentiles. This process is a potentially useful way of making z scores more interpretable for some test takers.

There are at least two convenient ways to use the standard normal distribution as a way of linking standard scores to percentiles. First, and the most modern, we can use websites (such as http://davidmlane.com/hyperstat/z_table.html) or computer programs (such as Microsoft Excel) to compute the percentile from a standard score (e.g., using the "NORMSDIST" function in Excel).

Second, and more traditionally, many statistics textbooks provide tables that present the standard normal distribution (see Table 3.4 for an example of part of the distribution). Once we have computed an individual's standard score (e.g., $z = 1.5$), we can turn to this table and begin linking to a percentile. Unfortunately, books differ in the way they present the table for the standard normal distribution, although they will provide sufficient information to interpret the table. Our presentation in Table 3.4 is a fairly common format, including only two columns. One column presents possible z scores, so we simply need to identify the row that includes the z score that we have computed. The second column, as described in its label, presents the proportion of scores that fall between the mean and the score for which we have computed the z score. For example, for an individual with a z score of 1.5, Table 3.4 tells us that .4332 of the scores in the distribution fall between the

Table 3.4   Excerpt From a Table of the Standard Normal Distribution

z Score	Area Between Mean and z Score
1.40	.4192
1.41	.4207
1.42	.4222
1.43	.4236
1.44	.4251
1.45	.4265
1.46	.4279
1.47	.4292
1.48	.4306
1.49	.4319
1.50	.4332
1.51	.4345
1.52	.4357
1.53	.4370
1.54	.4382
1.55	.4394
1.56	.4406
1.57	.4418
1.58	.4429
1.59	.4441
1.60	.4452

mean and that individual's score. To estimate the total percentage of scores that fall below that person's score, we add .50 to the value in Table 3.4 and multiply the sum by 100, for a total of 93.32%. This tells us that if the distribution of scores is normal in shape, then someone with a score of 1.5 has a percentile rank of 93.32%—that is, approximately 93% of the other test takers score below this person.

In short, a table such as Table 3.4 can be used to estimate the percentile rank for any z score, with only one procedural consideration and one theoretical consideration. The procedural consideration refers to the way the table is used. If the z score is positive, we add .50 to the proportion obtained from Table 3.4, as we have illustrated. However, if the z score is negative, we subtract the proportion from .50. For example, if our person had obtained a z score of −1.5, we calculate the percentile as .50 −.4332 = .0668. After multiplying by 100, this would tell us that only 6.68% of the scores in the distribution fall below the person's score. The theoretical consideration refers to the assumption, mentioned earlier, that the underlying distribution is normal. If we can safely assume that the distribution of scores is truly normal, then we can safely use the standard normal distribution to link standard scores to percentiles. However, if there is good reason to suspect that the distribution of scores is *not* normal, then we should not use the standard *normal* distribution to link standard scores to percentiles.

Normalized Scores

For tests that are widely marketed, distributed, and used, test developers might argue that their tests measure a psychological attribute that is normally distributed in the population. For example, many theorists feel comfortable with the assumption that the distribution of intelligence within the general population is fairly normal in shape. Thus, if we create a new intelligence test, we might like to provide a scoring mechanism that produces scores that are normally distributed. We might do this so that we could provide test users with interpretive guides (i.e., "norms") that reflect the assumed normality of the construct.

Unfortunately, we might encounter a problem. Specifically, if the scores that are actually obtained from test takers during the test development process are not distributed normally, then we encounter a discrepancy that complicates our goal of producing a set of "normal" scores. That is, there might be a discrepancy between our theory-based belief about a psychological attribute (e.g., that intelligence is normally distributed) and the actual test data that have been obtained (e.g., IQ test scores are not exactly normally distributed). In such a case, test developers might make two assumptions: (1) their theory is correct (i.e., the attribute is indeed normally distributed) and (2) the actual test data (IQ scores in this example) are imperfect reflections of the distribution of the construct itself.

One way in which test developers have tried to solve this nonnormality problem is by transforming the imperfect (i.e., nonnormal) distribution of test scores into a distribution that more closely approximates a normal distribution. These procedures are sometimes called *normalization transformations* or *area transformations*.

This normalization transformation is a three-step process. The first step is to compute direct or empirical percentile ranks from the raw test scores. That is, we transform each individual's original raw score on the IQ test into a percentile rank, using the first procedure that we described for percentile ranks (i.e., based on having access to all the raw scores in the distribution). The second step in the normalization process is to convert the percentile ranks into standard scores (i.e., *z* scores). To do this, we take a percentile rank (obtained in Step 1), go to the table of the standard normal distribution (see Table 3.4), look in the column that corresponds to percentile ranks, identify the specific rank that we are working with, and then identify the *z* score associated with that percentile rank. Third, we take the *z* score (standard score) and compute a converted standard score onto the metric that we would like (i.e., to fit a specific mean and standard deviation).

For example, we might want our IQ test scores to be reported on a metric with a mean of 100 and a standard deviation of 15, and we might wish to report the converted standard score resulting from the normalization procedure for an original raw test score of 28. We first find the percentile rank associated with a score of 28.

Imagine that a score of 28 is quite high, corresponding to a percentile rank of 92%, based on the entire set of test responses that we have obtained. We take this value and, looking in Table 3.4, we find that a percentile of approximately 92% is linked to a standard score of +1.41 from a normal distribution (i.e., .92 − .50 = .42, which is the proportion associated with a standard score of +1.41 in a normal distribution). Because we want scores to be reported on a metric with a mean of 100 and a standard deviation of 15, we convert this into a standard score (T):

$$T = 1.41(15) + 100,$$
$$= 21.15 + 100,$$
$$= 121.15.$$

Thus, an individual with a raw score of 28 on our test would obtain a "normalized" converted standard score of 121.15. If we, as test developers, wished to make a general interpretive guide for test users, we would conduct this normalization process for all possible original scores on our test. Test users could then use our guide for future measurements to link any individual's original score with the appropriate normalized converted standard score.

The normalization transformation that we have outlined is but one option for handling nonnormal test data. Additional options include the computation of "normal curve equivalents" or "stanines." Details of these procedures are beyond the scope of our current discussion, but they are available in other sources, particularly those that deal with educational measurement.

Test Norms

In psychological measurement, many tests have been *normed* to facilitate their interpretation by test users. Often during a test construction process, test developers administer their new test to a large group of people who are believed to be representative of some relevant population. After this large group has taken the test and their scores have been calculated, test users can use their scores as a frame of reference for interpreting the scores of other people who will eventually take the test. The large group of people used in the construction of a test is referred to as the *reference sample*, and their scores are called the "norms" for the test.

Thus, test developers often use the procedures that we have outlined above to prepare interpretive guides for test users, and test users can use these guides to interpret each new score on the test. For example, test developers will use the reference sample scores to calculate "converted standard scores" for each possible score on the original test. That way, when a test user obtains a test score from a new test taker, he or she can simply use the reference sample norms to automatically link the test taker's original score on the test to a more interpretable T score (i.e., converted standard score) or percentile rank. Because the test developers have already worked through all of the conversions and transformations that we have discussed, the test user does not have to worry about those processes. This norming process makes test use and interpretation much easier and more efficient.

In research settings, test users might not rely heavily on test norms for at least two reasons. First, test norms, standard scores, and percentile ranks might not be available for many tests that researchers use. The norming and standardization processes that we have discussed are often conducted for psychological tests that are widely used in applied areas of behavioral science, such as clinical assessment, achievement testing, intelligence testing, and employee screening. When tests are developed for more specialized research use, test developers are less likely to spend time and effort to develop a set of norms and standardized scores. A second reason why researchers are less likely to use information about test norms and standardized scores is that they are not usually interested in interpreting individual scores. Rather, researchers are usually interested in finding associations among variables—computing correlations and other statistics to understand the way in which important behavioral variables are associated with each other. Because they are not usually interested in focusing on any particular individual's score, there are few reasons to worry about identifying percentile ranks and standardized scores for the participants who happened to volunteer for the research project.

Representativeness of the Reference Sample

As we have just seen, tests are normed to provide information to use as a frame of reference for the interpretation of individual test scores. The value of the normed data, however, depends on the extent to which the reference sample truly represents a relevant population and the extent to which an individual who takes a normed test can be thought of as a member of that population. In both cases, the target population must be well-defined, and we must have confidence that the reference sample is, in fact, representative of that population.

For example, suppose that you want to develop a self-esteem test to use in the counseling center of a university. To interpret clients' test scores, you want to norm the test. The first thing that you would have to do is to define the appropriate target population. In this example, the population *might* include full-time students enrolled in 4-year undergraduate programs in American universities. Because it is unlikely that you could administer your self-esteem test to all of the students in this enormous population, you would need to select a sample of students (i.e., the reference sample) from that target population of students. The reference sample needs to be representative of the population. By "representative," we mean that if the self-esteem test questions were given to everyone in the entire population, the self-esteem scores from the reference sample could be shown to have statistical properties similar to the properties of the scores from that population.

Selecting the individuals for a reference sample that is truly representative of a target population is a very complex issue. There are entire books written on the issue, but for our purposes, we need to discuss only two types of sampling procedures: (1) probability sampling and (2) nonprobability sampling. Probability samples are obtained using procedures that ensure a representative sample. No such assurances can be made if a sample is obtained using a nonprobability sampling procedure. You are probably familiar with the idea of a random sample. If a sample selection procedure produces a selection of people for a sample in a truly random fashion, we can say that the sample is a random sample. Such a sample would be a type of probability sample. Now consider a sampling procedure in which you go to universities in your vicinity and ask for students to volunteer for your reference sample. This procedure would produce a nonprobability sample because students who are willing to volunteer might not be perfectly representative of *all* students. Notice that it is the procedure and not the results of the application of the procedure that defines the type of sample. You can never know for sure if any particular sample is representative of any particular population, but if a reference sample is obtained using a probability sampling procedure, you can be fairly confident of the sample's representativeness.

Summary

Individual differences constitute the basic source of data for all the statistical procedures used to evaluate the psychometric properties of psychological tests. Psychological tests are instruments for identifying individual differences, and we will show that a good psychological test captures these differences accurately.

In this chapter, we showed that individual differences in test scores or trait levels can be quantified by computing the variance and/or the standard deviation. Variance is a value that reflects the average size of (squared) differences among scores in a distribution of scores; each tested individual has a test score that might differ by some amount from the mean of a distribution of test scores. These differences are used to compute variance.

We also demonstrated the importance and meaning of covariability—the degree to which variability within one set of values corresponds with variability within another set of values. Emerging from the logic of variance and covariance, correlation coefficients are values that represent the extent to which variability in one set of scores is systematically related to variability in another set of scores, and they play an extremely important role in psychometric evaluation.

Finally, we discussed some ambiguities in the interpretation of test scores, and we described some ways in which such ambiguities are managed. Specifically, we described standard scores (z scores) and derived standard scores (e.g., T scores). Such scores allow us to compare a person's score on two different tests even if the tests are measured using different metrics. In conjunction with the normal distribution, they can also be used to make predictions from performance in one testing situation to performance in subsequent testing situations, they can be converted to percentile rank scores, and they can be used to make inferences about one person's test performance compared with the test performance of others. Our discussion highlighted the fact that such interpretive values are based on an interpretive framework in which an individual's test score is defined in relation to other individuals' scores. That is, they are based on describing test scores as reflecting individual differences among test takers.

Suggested Readings

Many introductory statistics textbooks provide good treatments of fundamental concepts such as the mean, variance, and standard deviation. One such source is Chapter 2 in

Howell, D. C. (2012). *Statistical methods for psychology* (8th ed.). Belmont, CA: Wadsworth.

There is no better place to start exploring the importance of individual differences than with Darwin and there is no better place to start with Darwin than

Darwin, C. (1859). *On the origin of the species by means of natural selection.* London, England: John Murray.

For those who would like to read a technical account of how individual differences play a role in an important area of experimental cognitive psychology, see

Jensen, A. R. (2006). *Clocking the mind: Mental chronometry and individual differences.* Oxford, England: Elsevier.

Individual differences have always been at the core of personality theory and research. A classic in this area is

Eysenck, H. J., & Eysenck, M. W. (1985). *Personality and individual differences: A natural science approach.* New York, NY: Plenum Press.

For a good overview of participant sampling procedures see Chapter 9 in

Rosenthal, R., & Rosnow, R. L. (2008). *Essentials of behavioral research, methods and data analysis* (3rd ed.). New York, NY: McGraw-Hill.

An algebraically complete but very easy to follow discussion of the Pearson product moment correlation coefficient can be found in a small book, almost a monograph (particularly Chapters 4–8):

Edwards, A. L. (1976). *An introduction to linear regression and correlation.* San Francisco, CA: W. H. Freeman.

An overview of 13 ways of conceptualizing and defining the correlation is available in

Rodgers, J. L., & Nicewander, W. A. (1988). Thirteen ways to look at the correlation coefficient. *The American Statistician, 42,* 59–66.

For a concise but thorough discussion of different types of test norms see Chapter 3 in

Thorndike, R. M. (2005). *Measurement and evaluation in psychology and education.* Upper Saddle River, NJ: Pearson Education.

CHAPTER 4

Test Dimensionality and Factor Analysis

Imagine that a colleague wishes to use a personality inventory that includes the following six adjectives: *talkative, assertive, imaginative, creative, outgoing*, and *intellectual*. For this brief questionnaire, participants are asked to consider the degree to which each adjective describes their personality in general. Your colleague asks for your opinion of this common, adjective-based form of personality assessment. You consider the inventory for a moment, and you begin to wonder—what exactly does this inventory measure? Does it measure six separate facets of personality, with each facet being reflected by a single adjective? Or does it measure a single construct? If so, then what is that construct—what do these six adjectives have in common as a psychological characteristic or dimension? Or are there two or three separate dimensions reflected within these six adjectives? How will this questionnaire be scored?

Take a moment to think about the six adjectives on the short inventory, and group them into clusters that seem to share some common meaning. That is, group them in terms of their similarity to each other. Some people might suggest that the questionnaire includes only two sets of items. For example, some might argue that talkative, assertive, and outgoing are three variations on one attribute (let us call it "extraversion") and that imaginative, creative, and intellectual are three variations on another attribute (let us call it "openness to experience"). From this perspective, responses to these six personality adjectives reflect two basic dimensions: one set of responses that are a function of an extraversion dimension and one set of responses that are the result of an openness-to-experience dimension.

In contrast, some people might suggest that the six adjectives reflect three dimensions, not two. Specifically, "talkative," "assertive," and "outgoing" might go together, and "imaginative" and "creative" might go together, but "intellectual" is importantly different from the other five items. From this perspective, responses to the six items reflect three basic dimensions. Put another way, these six test items essentially reflect three ways in which people differ from each other psychologically.

This example illustrates the issue of test dimensionality, which is a fundamental consideration in test development, evaluation, and use. There are at least three fundamental psychometric questions regarding the dimensionality of a test, and the answers to these questions have important implications for evaluating the psychometric properties of any behavioral test, for appropriately scoring on a test, and for the proper interpretation of test scores.

In this chapter, we discuss the concept of dimensionality, the key questions related to dimensionality, and the implications that dimensionality has for test construction, evaluation, use, and interpretation. Indeed, as shown in Figure 4.1, the answers to the three key questions lead to three main types of tests: (1) unidimensional tests, (2) multidimensional tests with correlated dimensions, and (3) multidimensional tests with uncorrelated dimensions. Test developers and test users must understand which type of test is being developed or used, because these tests have important psychometric differences from each other.

Given the importance of understanding a test's dimensionality, we also describe one way the dimensionality questions can be answered quantitatively. We describe the way in which test developers, test evaluators, and test users identify the number of dimensions reflected by a test, the meaning of those dimensions, and the degree

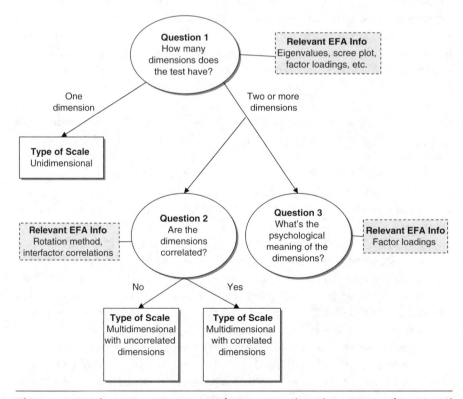

Figure 4.1   Three Core Questions of Dimensionality, Three Types of Tests, and the Relevant Information From Exploratory Factor Analysis (EFA)

to which the dimensions are associated with each other. A statistical procedure called *factor analysis* is an extremely useful tool in the psychometrician's statistical toolbox. Although factor analysis can be a highly technical procedure, we will present its general logic and use in a way that is accessible to those who do not have a great interest or background in advanced statistics. A basic understanding of factor analysis can provide a solid foundation for several important psychometric issues.

Test Dimensionality

If you step on a bathroom scale, the resulting number on the scale is a value that tells you something about one of your physical attributes or features—your weight. As a human being, you have many other physical attributes, including height, skin color, length of hair, and so on. When you weigh yourself, the number that represents your weight should not be influenced by attributes such as your hair color, your height, or your age. The "score" on the bathroom scale should (and does) reflect one and only one physical dimension.

Similarly, if we have a psychological test that yields some kind of number, then we would like to think of the number as a value representing a single psychological feature or attribute. For example, suppose you had a test of courage. If you have a test that produces scores that can be treated as if they are real numbers, then a person's score on the test might indicate the amount of courage that he or she had when taking the test. We could then think of courage as an attribute of that person and the test score as an indication of the amount of the person's courage. The score on the courage test *should* reflect one and only one psychological dimension.

As a general rule (but not always), when we measure a physical or psychological attribute of an object or a person, we intend to measure a *single* attribute of that object or person. In the case of weight, we try to measure weight so that our measurement is not affected by other attributes of the person being measured. Furthermore, it would not be reasonable to measure someone's weight, measure his or her hair length, and then add those two scores together to form a "total" score. Clearly, the total score would be a blend of two physical dimensions that are almost totally unrelated to each other, and the combination of the two scores would have no clear interpretation. That is, the total score would not have clear reference to a single physical attribute and thus would have no clear meaning. Similarly, it would not be reasonable to measure someone's courage, measure his or her verbal skill, and then add those two scores together to form a "total" score. Again, the total score would be a blend of two dimensions that are clearly unrelated to each other (i.e., one's courage is probably unrelated to one's level of verbal skill). Combining test scores from two independent psychological attributes produces a total score that has no clear meaning.

As discussed in our presentation of composite scores, the scores from a wide variety of psychological tests are based on multiple questions or test items. For example, personality tests range in length from 5 or fewer questions to several hundred questions. In scoring such tests, item responses are combined in some way, usually by computing one or more scores of some kind, and these combined scores are used to reflect the psychological attribute(s) of interest. These scores are referred to as composite scores, and ideally, a composite score reflects one and only one dimension. However, a test may include items that reflect more than a single dimension.

Three Dimensionality Questions

As mentioned earlier, there are at least three core questions regarding a test's dimensionality. First, how many dimensions are reflected in the test items? As we shall see, some tests reflect one and only one dimension, while others reflect two or more psychological dimensions. This issue is important because each dimension of a test is likely to be scored separately, with each dimension requiring its own psychometric analysis.

The second core dimensionality question is this: If a test has more than one dimension, then are those dimensions correlated with each other? As we shall see, some tests have several dimensions that are somewhat related to each other, while other tests have several dimensions that are essentially independent. This issue is important, in part, because the nature of the associations among a test's dimensions has implications for the meaningfulness of a "total score" for a test.

Third, if a test has more than one dimension, then what *are* those dimensions? That is, what psychological attributes are reflected by the test dimensions? For example, in the six-adjective personality test described previously, does the first dimension reflect the psychological attribute of extraversion or some other attribute? The importance of this issue should be fairly clear—if we score and interpret a dimension of a test, we must understand the score's psychological meaning.

Figure 4.1 summarizes these questions and illustrates their connections to three different types of tests. These types of tests have different properties, different implications for scoring and for psychometric evaluation, and ultimately different psychological implications.

Unidimensional Tests

The first question regarding test dimensionality concerns the number of dimensions reflected in a set of test items. Some tests include items that reflect a single psychological attribute, and others include items that reflect more than one attribute.

When a psychological test includes items that reflect only a single attribute of a person, this means that responses to those items are driven only by that attribute (and, to some degree, by random measurement error—see Chapters 5–7). In such cases, we say that the test is *unidimensional,* because its items reflect only one psychological dimension.

Consider a multiple-choice geometry exam given in a classroom. Typically, a student takes the exam and receives a score based on the number of questions that he or she answers correctly. The student's score is then interpreted as a measure of the amount of his or her "knowledge of geometry." This interpretation makes sense only if the answers to all the test items truly require knowledge of geometry, and *only* knowledge of geometry. For example, if we can believe that the test does not (mistakenly) include algebra items, calculus items, or vocabulary items in addition to geometry items, then we can indeed have some confidence in interpreting test scores as reflecting knowledge of geometry. That is, we could assume that the answers to each of the questions on the test are affected by that single psychological attribute. Such a test would be thought of as unidimensional. In addition, the test items or questions would have the property of *conceptual homogeneity*—responses to each item would be a function of the same psychological attribute.

The concept of a unidimensional test is illustrated in Figure 4.2. This figure uses formatting that is standard for graphically representing a test's dimensionality (or factorial structure, as we shall describe later). In such figures, a circle or oval represents a hypothetical psychological attribute or latent variable that affects participants' responses to test questions. Returning to the geometry test example, the circle would represent "knowledge of geometry" because it is the psychological property that (supposedly) determines whether a student answers the test items correctly. Correspondingly, in figures like Figure 4.2, squares or rectangles represent responses to each of the test questions. Finally, the arrows' directionality (i.e., they point from the attribute to the responses) represents the idea that the psychological attribute affects responses to test questions. For example, they represent the assumption that knowledge of geometry (as a psychological ability) is what affects students' answers to the test questions. Because it shows a single psychological attribute affecting participants' responses, this figure illustrates a unidimensional test.

As we have mentioned, a test's dimensionality has implications for its scoring, evaluation, and use. For a unidimensional test, only a single score is computed, reflecting the single psychological attribute measured by the test. That is, all the items are combined in some way (usually through averaging, summing, or counting) to form a composite or "total" score. For example, if it is indeed unidimensional, the geometry test produces a single score (e.g., the total count of the number of correctly answered questions) reflecting "knowledge of geometry." In terms of

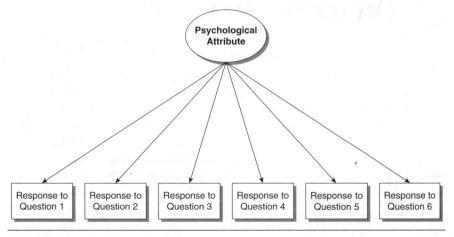

Figure 4.2 Unidimensional Test

psychometric evaluation, psychometric quality is evaluated for the single score that is obtained from a unidimensional test. In later chapters, we shall discuss reliability and validity, which reflect the psychometric quality of test scores. For unidimensional tests, reliability and validity should be estimated and evaluated for the total score produced by the test. In terms of test use, test users compute and interpret the total score produced by a unidimensional test.

Multidimensional Tests With Correlated Dimensions (Tests With Higher-Order Factors)

When a psychological test includes items reflecting more than one psychological attribute, the test is considered multidimensional. In such cases, we confront a second dimensionality question—are the test's dimensions associated with each other? As shown in Figure 4.1, the answer to this question differentiates two types of tests. When a test has multiple dimensions that are correlated with each other, the test can be considered a *multidimensional test with correlated dimensions* (this has also been called a test with higher-order factors).

Intelligence tests such as the Wechsler Intelligence Scale for Children (WISC-IV) (Wechsler, 2003a, 2003b) and the Stanford-Binet (SB5) (Roid, 2003) are examples of multidimensional tests with correlated dimensions. These tests include groups of questions that assess different psychological attributes. The groups of questions are called subtests, and they each reflect a different facet of intelligence. For example, the SB5 has five subtests: (1) one to measure fluid reasoning, (2) one to measure general knowledge, (3) one to measure quantitative processing ability, (4) one to measure visual-spatial processing ability, and (5) one that is thought to measure working memory. Research by test developers and test evaluators has shown that the subtests of the SB5 are correlated with each other. That is, a participant who scores relatively high on one subtest is likely to score relatively high on the other subtests as well.

As we have mentioned, a test's dimensionality has important implications for the scoring, evaluation, and use of the test. Multidimensional tests with correlated dimensions can produce a variety of scores. Typically, each subtest has its own subtest score. In principle, each subtest is, itself, unidimensional, and the questions in each subtest are conceptually homogeneous. For example, the quantitative processing subtest of the SB5 might require a test taker to answer 10 questions. Presumably, responses to each of those 10 questions reflect only quantitative processing and not one of the constructs represented by the other subtests. That is, a person's responses to the 10 questions are affected only by the person's quantitative processing skills and not some other psychological attribute. If a subtest is unidimensional, then the subtest's score is interpretable with regard to a single psychological attribute.

In addition to scores for each subtest, multidimensional tests with correlated dimensions are often scored in a way that produces a total score, combined across several subtests. That is, subtest scores are often combined with each other (again, either through summing or by averaging the scores) to produce a *total test score.* For example, the five subtest scores from the SB5 are combined to form an overall

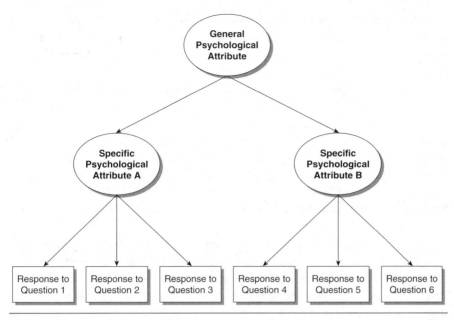

Figure 4.3   Multidimensional Test With Correlated Dimensions (i.e., a Higher-Order Factor Test)

"full-scale" score representing general intelligence, or *g*. We can think of *g* (a general psychological attribute) as affecting a variety of more specific psychological attributes, which in turn affect the way people answer the test questions.

This type of test structure is presented in Figure 4.3. Note that there are two levels of psychological attributes. Responses to each test question are affected by a specific attribute, or factor. For example, an individual's responses to the questions on the quantitative processing subtest of the SB5 are affected by his or her psychological ability to process quantitative information. In contrast, an individual's responses to the questions on the visual–spatial processing subtest of the SB5 are affected by his or her psychological ability to process visual–spatial information. In addition to these specific psychological attributes, there is a general psychological attribute affecting each specific attribute. For example, an individual's abilities to process quantitative information and to process visual–spatial information are partially determined by his or her general cognitive ability, or intelligence. This general attribute is often called a *higher-order factor* because it is at a more general level (or "order") than the specific factors or attributes.

In terms of test evaluation, multidimensional tests are different from unidimensional tests. Recall that a unidimensional test has one and only one score and this score is evaluated with regard to its psychometric quality. In contrast, multidimensional tests have a score for each subtest, and each subtest score is evaluated with regard to its psychometric quality. It is possible that a multidimensional test could have some subtests that have reasonable psychometric quality and other subtests that have poor psychometric quality. Therefore, each subtest requires psychometric examination. For example, the developers and users of the SB5 have examined carefully the reliability and validity of each of its five subtests. In addition, a multidimensional test with correlated dimensions may have a total test score that is computed across its subtests. Thus, this total score also requires psychometric evaluation. For example, the developers and users of the SB5 have examined the reliability and validity of its full-scale score.

In terms of test use, multidimensional tests offer a variety of options. Test users could use any or all of the subtest scores, depending on their relevance to the research or practical context. In addition, test users could use a total test score from a test with correlated dimensions if such a score is computed and has acceptable psychometric properties.

Multidimensional Tests With Uncorrelated Dimensions

As we discussed, the second dimensionality question regards the degree to which a multidimensional test's dimensions are associated with each other (see Figure 4.1). If a test's dimensions are not associated with each other (or are only weakly associated with each other), then the test can be considered a *multidimensional test with uncorrelated dimensions.*

Several personality tests are multidimensional with dimensions that are generally treated as if they are uncorrelated. For example, a test called the NEO Five Factor Inventory (NEO-FFI; Costa & McCrae, 1992) is a 60-item questionnaire reflecting five dimensions, or factors of personality. That is, the NEO-FFI is designed to measure five relatively independent personality attributes, and these five attributes are not typically treated as reflecting any higher-order factors. Test takers receive five scores—one for each dimension—and each one is itself treated as if it were unidimensional. In a sense, such tests could be viewed as a set of unrelated unidimensional tests that are presented with their items mixed together.

With regard to scoring, evaluation, and use, multidimensional tests with uncorrelated dimensions are similar to multidimensional tests with correlated dimensions, with one important exception. For tests with uncorrelated dimensions, no total test score is computed. That is, a score is obtained for each dimension, but the dimensions' scores are not combined to compute a total test score. Furthermore, each of the dimension scores is evaluated in terms of psychometric quality, and each is potentially used by researchers and practicing psychologists. For example, the NEO-FFI produces only five scores—one for each of the five factors or dimensions; however, no total test score is computed for the NEO-FFI.

This type of test structure is presented in Figure 4.4. Similar to the multidimensional test presented in Figure 4.3, there are two psychological attributes, each one affecting responses to a set of questions. However, in this figure, the two attributes are not linked together in any way. This implies that the attributes are uncorrelated with each other.

The Psychological Meaning of Test Dimensions

After the first two dimensionality issues are addressed (the number of dimensions reflected in a test's items and the association among multiple dimensions), a third important dimensionality issue needs examination. Specifically, test

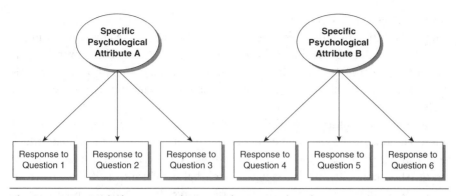

Figure 4.4 Multidimensional Test With Uncorrelated Dimensions

developers, evaluators, and users must understand the psychological meaning of each test dimension. For a test's dimensions to be used and interpreted accurately, test developers and evaluators must conduct research that reveals the psychological attribute that is represented by each test dimension.

In the next section, we discuss a common way in which such research is conducted. We present the basics of a statistical procedure called factor analysis, which is a fundamental tool in the examination of test dimensionality. We present its logic, and we discuss the information that it provides to address each of the three core questions of test dimensionality.

Factor Analysis: Examining the Dimensionality of a Test

Test developers can use a variety of statistical procedures to evaluate a test's dimensionality. Although procedures such as cluster analysis and multidimensional scaling are available, factor analysis is the most common method of examination. By using factor analysis, researchers can address the core questions outlined in the section above, and this provides important insight into the potential scoring, evaluation, and use of psychological tests.

There are, in fact, two broad types of factor analysis: exploratory factor analysis (EFA) and confirmatory factor analysis (CFA). EFA is the more common type, and it is relatively easy to conduct with basic statistical software such as SPSS or SAS. In addition, EFA is often used in early stages of psychometric analysis and development. Considering these issues, the remainder of this chapter focuses primarily on EFA. We will revisit CFA briefly at the end of this chapter, and we will dedicate an entire chapter to it later in this book (Chapter 12).

The Logic and Purpose of Exploratory Factor Analysis: A Conceptual Overview

At the beginning of this chapter, we asked you to consider a six-item personality questionnaire that includes the following adjectives: *talkative, assertive, imaginative, creative, outgoing,* and *intellectual.* Furthermore, we asked you to consider the number of different attributes that are reflected in these adjectives. As we mentioned, reasonable people might disagree about this question. Based on one's particular interpretation of the adjectives and one's understanding of personality, one might argue that the six adjectives reflect one single dimension, two dimensions, or perhaps three or more dimensions.

An important difficulty with this approach—an approach based only on our interpretations of the meaning of items—is that it is not easy to evaluate which perspective is the best. That is, if you believe that there is a two-factor structure to the questionnaire but your colleague believes that there is a three-factor structure, then how could you determine who is correct or if either one of you is correct?

Rather than relying on idiosyncratic interpretations of the meaning of items, test developers and users often prefer to base their arguments on empirical data. Therefore, we might give the six-item questionnaire to a sample of 100 respondents, asking each respondent to rate each item in terms of the following response options (circling the number for the appropriate option):

1	2	3	4	5
Completely unlike me	Somewhat unlike me	Neither like me nor unlike me	Somewhat like me	Completely like me

We then enter their data into a statistical software computer program and compute the correlations among the six items. We would then use the correlations to help us identify and interpret the dimensions reflected in the items.

For example, take a moment to examine the hypothetical correlation matrix presented in Table 4.1. Note that three of the items—"talkative," "assertive," and "outgoing"—are all strongly correlated with each other. An individual who rates herself as relatively high on one of these three items is likely to rate herself as relatively high on the other two items. We also see that the other three items—"imaginative," "creative," and "intellectual"—are strongly correlated with each other. Importantly, we also see that these two clusters of items are independent. For example, the correlation between "talkative" and "creative" is 0, as is the correlation between talkative and imaginative, between outgoing and intellectual, and so on. That is, the fact that an individual rates himself as assertive, talkative, and outgoing says nothing about that person's likely level of creativity, imagination, or intellect. This pattern of correlations begins to reveal the dimensionality of the six-item personality test.

By scanning an interitem correlation matrix in this way, we could begin to understand a test's dimensionality. Essentially, we try to identify sets of items that go together—sets of items that are relatively strongly correlated with each other but weakly correlated with other items. Each set of relatively highly correlated items represents a psychological dimension or "factor."

Indeed, we can begin to address the three dimensionality questions in Figure 4.1. To determine the number of factors within a scale, we count the number of sets that we identify. If all scale items are well correlated with each other at approximately equal levels, then there is only a single set (i.e., factor) and the scale is unidimensional. If, however, there are two or more sets, then the scale is multidimensional. We identified two sets of items in the hypothetical correlation matrix in Table 4.1—these findings suggest that the six-item personality questionnaire has a two-dimensional structure (i.e., it is multidimensional). That is, three items cluster together into one dimension, and the other three cluster into a second dimension.

To determine whether the factors are correlated with each other, we would examine the pattern of correlations between the sets. That is, the potential correlations between factors are based on the correlations between items in different sets. In the example in Table 4.1, we found that the items from one set were uncorrelated with the items in the other set. This suggests that the two factors are, themselves, uncorrelated with each other—the factor represented by the items in one set is unrelated to the factor represented by the items in the other set. Thus, this six-item test appears to be a multidimensional test with uncorrelated dimensions. However, if items from one set are, in fact, correlated with items from another set, then the factors are correlated with each other. For example, we might have found a correlation of .30 between talkative and creative, a correlation of .25 between talkative and imaginative, a correlation of .32 between outgoing and intellectual, and so on. Such a pattern of moderately sized cross-factor correlations would suggest that the factors are correlated with each other—that we were working with a test that was multidimensional with correlated dimensions.

Finally, to understand the potential psychological meaning of the factor, we examine the content of the items constituting that factor. That is, a factor's potential meaning arises, in part, from the psychological concept or theme that its items share. Consider, for example, the items "talkative," "assertive," and "outgoing." What do they have in common? What is a common psychological concept that they share? Many personality psychologists would likely suggest that these items reflect an extraversion factor and that the other three items (i.e., "imaginative," "creative," and "intellectual") reflect openness to experience. The answer to this question is, of course, based on interpretation, judgment, and preference. Indeed, one person's answer might differ from another's. The interpretation of "extraversion" and "openness to experience" is based on familiarity with "the five-factor model" of personality, which is widely known in personality psychology and which includes the traits of extraversion and openness to experience. People with other perspectives and backgrounds might choose to label the factors differently.

By examining the pattern of correlations in this way, we have performed a very basic factor analysis. Unfortunately, such a simplistic "eyeballing" approach rarely works with real data. Real data usually include many more items. In the current example, we examined only six items, but many measures include considerably more than six items. For example, the Conscientiousness scale of the NEO Personality Inventory–Revised (NEO-PI–R) questionnaire (Costa & McCrae, 1992) includes 48 items. Difficulty arises because a larger number of items produces a much larger number of correlations to examine. For example, if we examined a correlation matrix for 48 items, we would have to inspect more than 1,100 correlations! Obviously, visually inspecting such a large correlation matrix is a nearly impossible task. In addition to the large number of correlations in most real data, the pattern of correlations in real data is never as clear as it appears to be

Table 4.1   (Hypothetical) Correlation Matrix for a Two-Factor Set of Items

	Talkative	Assertive	Outgoing	Creative	Imaginative	Intellectual
Talkative	1.00					
Assertive	.66	1.00				
Outgoing	.54	.59	1.00			
Creative	.00	.00	.00	1.00		
Imaginative	.00	.00	.00	.46	1.00	
Intellectual	.00	.00	.00	.57	.72	1.00

in Table 4.1. The hypothetical correlations in Table 4.1 include a few very strong positive correlations and a few zero correlations, but nothing else. In real data, correlations often are closer to .18 or −.32 than to .70. Therefore, the clusters of items in real data are much more ambiguous than the ones in Table 4.1, and this ambiguity complicates the process of evaluating dimensionality.

EFA is a statistical procedure that simplifies this process. Rather than visually inspecting a matrix of dozens or even hundreds of correlations, we can use EFA to process a large set of correlations. Because the analysis of dimensionality typically is "messier" than the example in Table 4.1, researchers often rely on EFA to examine the dimensionality of psychological measures.

Conducting and Interpreting an Exploratory Factor Analysis

Factor analysis can be conducted by using participants' raw data—their responses to each individual item in a test. However, some statistical software packages allow factor analysis to be conducted on a correlation matrix that summarizes the associations among test items. Thus, if you have access to the appropriate software, you could replicate the example analyses that we report and interpret below.

Figure 4.5 is a flowchart of the process of conducting an EFA. As this figure illustrates, EFA is often an iterative process, as the results of one step often lead researchers to reevaluate previous steps.

Choosing an Extraction Method.   In the first step of an EFA, we choose an "extraction method." This refers to the specific statistical technique to be implemented, and options include principal axis factoring (PAF), maximum likelihood factor analysis, and principal components analysis (PCA), among others.

PAF and PCA are the common choices in most applications of EFA. Although PCA is not technically a "factor" analysis, it is essentially the same thing and is the default method for several popular statistical software packages' factor analysis procedure. Although the results obtained from PAF are often quite similar to those obtained from PCA, many experts recommend PAF over PCA. For example, Fabrigar, Wegener, MacCallum, and Strahan (1999) conclude that PCA is not recommended "when the goal of the analysis is to identify latent constructs underlying measured variables" (p. 276), as is typically the case in psychometric evaluation.

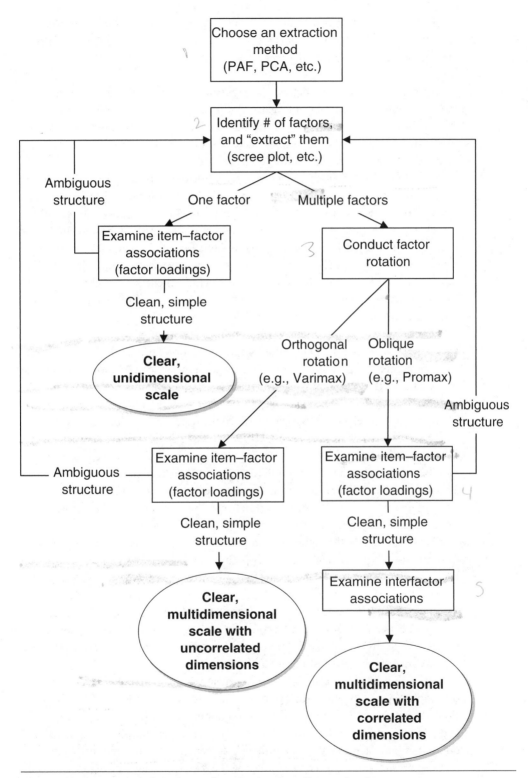

Figure 4.5 Process Flowchart of an Exploratory Factor Analysis

NOTE: PAF = principal axis factoring; PCA = principal components analysis.

To illustrate the EFA process, we will use a PAF extraction method to analyze the data illustrated in Table 4.1. Note that responses should be reverse scored, if necessary, before conducting the EFA (see Chapter 10).

Identifying the Number of Factors and Extracting Them. In the second step of an EFA, we identify the number of factors within our set of items, and we direct the statistical software to "extract" that number of factors. Unfortunately, we have no single, simple rule that we can use to make this identification. Instead, we must rely on rough guidelines and subjective judgment.

To address the "number of factors" issue, test developers and test users often refer to statistics called *eigenvalues*. In Figure 4.6, this information is presented in the "Total Variance Explained" box—specifically, the six eigenvalues are in the "Total" column under the "Initial Eigenvalues" heading. Although there are highly technical definitions of eigenvalues, what matters for our current discussion is how eigenvalues are used, not what they are. There are many ways in which this information can be used (e.g., parallel analysis; see Hayton, Allen, & Scarpello, 2004), but we will focus on the three ways that are the most common and that are integrated into most popular statistical software options.

One way of using eigenvalues is to examine the relative sizes of the eigenvalues themselves. Note that the eigenvalue output in Figure 4.6 includes six rows. Each row represents the potential number of dimensions reflected among the six test items. That is, this output will always include a number of rows that is equal to the number of items on the test, and each item might reflect a different dimension.

Examining the eigenvalues, we scan down the descending values in this column, and we hope to find a point at which all subsequent differences between values become relatively small. For example, in our output, we see a relatively large difference between the second eigenvalue (2.173) and the third eigenvalue (0.563). We also note that this difference is much larger than all the subsequent other row-by-row differences. That is, the difference between the third and fourth eigenvalues is small, as is the difference between the fourth and fifth, and so on.

The "location" of this point has implications for the answer to the "number of dimensions" question. We find this point, and we conclude that the test has a number of dimensions equal to the row with the larger eigenvalue. In Figure 4.6, the point is located between Rows 2 and 3, so we would conclude that the test has two dimensions. If the large difference was located between Rows 1 and 2, then we would conclude that the test has one dimension (i.e., that the test is unidimensional). Similarly, if the large difference was located between Rows 4 and 5, then we would conclude that the test has four dimensions.

Although it has been criticized, the "eigenvalue greater than 1.0" rule is the second common way in which eigenvalues are used to evaluate the number of dimensions. As represented by the fact that several popular statistical packages (e.g., SPSS and SAS) use this as a default option for answering the "number of dimensions" question, many factor analysts base their judgments on the number of eigenvalues that are greater than 1.0. For example, of the six eigenvalues in Figure 4.6, only two are above 1.0. Therefore, we might conclude that the test items reflect two dimensions. If our analysis had revealed three eigenvalues greater than 1.0, then we might conclude that the test items reflect three dimensions.

Total Variance Explained

Factor	Initial Eigenvalues			Extraction Sums of Squared Loadings			Rotation Sums of Squared Loadings [a]
	Total	% of Variance	Cumulative %	Total	% of Variance	Cumulative %	Total
1	2.195	36.578	36.578	1.836	30.599	30.599	1.836
2	2.173	36.222	72.800	1.808	30.131	60.730	1.808
3	.563	9.382	82.183				
4	.472	7.867	90.050				
5	.333	5.554	95.604				
6	.264	4.396	100.000				

Extraction Method: Principal Axis Factoring.

a. When factors are correlated, sums of squared loadings cannot be added to obtain a total variance.

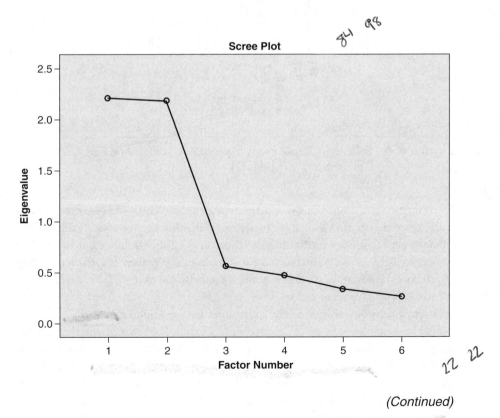

(Continued)

(Continued)

Factor Matrix[a]

	Factor	
	1	2
Intellectual	.942	.000
Imaginative	.764	.000
Creative	.604	.000
Assertive	.000	.849
Talkative	.000	.777
Outgoing	.000	.695

Extraction Method:
  Principal
  Axis Factoring.

[a.] 2 factors extracted. 19 iterations required.

Pattern Matrix[b]

	Factor	
	1	2
Intellectual	.942	.000
Imaginative	.764	.000
Creative	.604	.000
Assertive	.000	.849
Talkative	.000	.777
Outgoing	.000	.695

Extraction Method:
  Principal
  Axis Factoring.
  Rotation Method: Promax
  with Kaiser Normalization.

[b.] Rotation converged in 2 iterations.

Structure Matrix

	Factor	
	1	2
Intellectual	.942	.000
Imaginative	.764	.000
Creative	.604	.000
Assertive	.000	.849
Talkative	.000	.777
Outgoing	.000	.695

Extraction Method:
  Principal
  Axis Factoring.
  Rotation Method:
  Promax with Kaiser
  Normalization.

Factor Correlation Matrix

Factor	1	2
1	1.000	.000
2	.000	1.000

Extraction Method:
  Principal Axis Factoring.

Rotation Method: Promax
  with Kaiser Normalization.

Figure 4.6 Selected Output From Exploratory Factor Analysis of the Correlations in Table 4.1

Again, we should note that, despite its popularity, the "eigenvalue greater than 1.0" rule has been criticized as inappropriate for evaluating the number of dimensions in many applications of factor analysis (Fabrigar et al., 1999). Indeed, this guideline "is *among the least accurate methods* for selecting the number of factors to retain" (Costello & Osborne, p. 2), and it should generally *not* be used as a guideline for identifying the number of factors.

A third common way of using eigenvalues is to examine a *scree plot,* and it is probably the best of the three most common methods of identifying the number of factors. As illustrated by Figure 4.6's presentation of the scree plot resulting from our EFA, a scree plot is a graphical presentation of eigenvalues. Similar to the examination of eigenvalues discussed above, we look for a relatively large difference or drop in the plotted values. More specifically, we hope to find an obvious "leveling-off point" in the plot (as we move from left to right along the x-axis).

For example, the scree plot in Figure 4.6 shows an obvious flattening beginning at Factor 3. An obvious flattening point suggests that the number of factors is one less than the factor number of the flattening point. That is, if there is a flattening point beginning at the second eigenvalue, then this indicates the presence of only one factor. In contrast, if a flattening point begins at the third eigenvalue (as in our scree plot), then this indicates the presence of two factors, and so on.

If we do obtain a clear answer to the "number of factors" question, then we extract that number of factors. In most software programs, this simply means that we tell the program to proceed to the next step (see the flowchart in Figure 4.5) using the number of factors that we have identified. In the case of the data in Table 4.1 and Figure 4.6, we directed the program to proceed with two factors. We will return to the EFA of these data shortly.

Unfortunately, scree plots are not always clear—certainly rarely as clear as the one in Figure 4.6, which was based on hypothetical data constructed to be as obvious as possible. Providing more realistic examples, Figures 4.7 and 4.8 show selected results of two additional EFAs based on hypothetical data from two different six-item scales. Figure 4.7 is more realistic than the results in Figure 4.6, but it is still fairly clear—we see a relatively clear flattening point at the third eigenvalue, again indicating a two-dimensional structure to the items. In contrast, the scree plot in Figure 4.8 is extremely ambiguous—there is no clear flattening point that would guide our decision about the number of factors. In ambiguous cases like this, we use additional information to guide our understanding of the scale's number of dimensions.

One type of additional information is the clarity with which the scale's items are associated with its factors. For example, the ambiguous scree plot in Figure 4.8 might lead us to (somewhat arbitrarily) extract two factors and examine the item–factor associations in the next step of the EFA. As we will discuss shortly, our results from that later step might motivate us to revisit the present step, extract a different number of factors, and proceed again to the next steps. This is the iterative back-and-forth nature of EFA that was mentioned earlier.

Occasionally, we never obtain a clear answer to the "How many dimensions?" question, suggesting that the scale has no clear dimensionality. If we did encounter that situation, then we might conclude that the scale needs revision—for example, in terms of clarifying the construct(s) that it is intended to assess or in terms of revising the items themselves (see Furr, 2011, chaps. 2 and 3).

In a typical EFA, researchers make an initial decision about the scale's number of factors and then move on to one of two subsequent steps. As illustrated in the flowchart in Figure 4.5, if the scree plot (or another good guideline) suggests a single dimension, then researchers proceed directly to examining the associations between the items and that factor. We will discuss this later. However, if there is evidence of more than one dimension, then researchers next make decisions about rotating the factors.

Rotating the Factors. If the evidence suggests that a scale is multidimensional, then we usually "rotate" the factors. The purpose of this step is to clarify the psychological meaning of the factors.

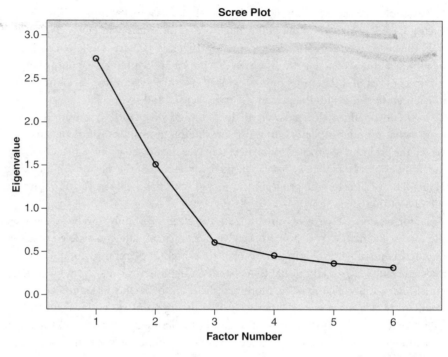

Factor Matrix[a]

	Factor	
	1	2
item6	.754	−.457
item2	.667	.536
item5	.620	−.399
item4	.589	−.339
item1	.561	.417
item3	.513	.391

Extraction Method:
  Principal Axis Factoring.

[a.] 2 factors extracted. 15 iterations required.

Pattern Matrix[a]

	Factor	
	1	2
item6	.880	.004
item5	.743	−.017
item4	.672	−.021
item2	−.015	.861
item1	.016	.694
item3	.007	.642

Extraction Method:
  Principal Axis Factoring.
Rotation Method:
  Promax with Kaiser
  Normalization.

[a.] Rotation converged in 3 iterations.

Structure Matrix

	Factor	
	1	2
item6	.882	.314
item5	.737	.245
item4	.679	.257
item2	.288	.855
item1	.260	.699
item3	.233	.644

Extraction Method:
  Principal Axis Factoring.
Rotation Method:
  Promax with Kaiser
  Normalization.

Factor Correlation Matrix

Factor	1	2
1	1.000	.352
2	.352	1.000

Extraction Method: Principal Axis Factoring.
Rotation Method: Promax with Kaiser Normalization.

Figure 4.7 Selected Output From Exploratory Factor Analysis of "More Realistic" Data From a Six-Item Questionnaire

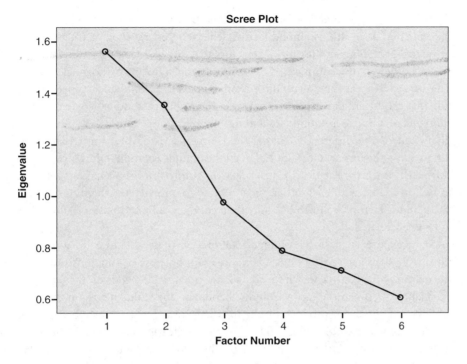

Scree Plot

	Factor Matrix[a]	
	Factor	
	1	**2**
item5	.959	−.138
item4	.359	.022
item1	.069	−.564
item3	.098	−.471
item2	.032	.368
item6	.164	.266

Extraction Method:
Principal Axis Factoring.

[a.] 2 factors extracted. 206
iterations required.

	Pattern Matrix[a]	
	Factor	
	1	**2**
item5	.969	−.004
item4	.358	.028
item1	−.024	.568
item3	.020	.480
item2	−.029	.368
item6	.118	.286

Extraction Method:
Principal Axis Factoring.
Rotation Method:
Promax with Kaiser
Normalization.

[a.] Rotation converged in
3 iterations.

	Structure Matrix	
	Factor	
	1	**2**
item5	.969	.021
item4	.359	.037
item1	−.010	.568
item3	.032	.481
item2	−.020	.368
item6	.126	.289

Extraction Method:
Principal Axis Factoring.
Rotation Method:
Promax with Kaiser
Normalization.

Factor Correlation Matrix

Factor	1	2
1	1.000	.026
2	.026	1.000

Extraction Method: Principal Axis Factoring.
Rotation Method: Promax with Kaiser Normalization.

Figure 4.8 Selected Output From Exploratory Factor Analysis of
Ambiguously Structured Data From a Six-Item Questionnaire

There are two general types of rotation, and they have differing implications for the potential associations among factors. The first general type of rotation is an orthogonal rotation, and it generates factors that are uncorrelated or "orthogonal" to each other. A procedure called "varimax" is the standard orthogonal rotation. The second general type of rotation is an oblique rotation, which generates factors that can be either correlated or uncorrelated with each other. There are many subtypes of oblique rotations, including "promax" and "direct oblimin." A full discussion of the differences among these subtypes is beyond the scope of our discussion—the important point is that all the oblique rotations allow factors to be correlated or uncorrelated with each other. To anthropomorphize, if factors "want to be" correlated with each other, then oblique rotations allow them to be correlated; and if factors "want to be" uncorrelated, then oblique rotations allow them to be uncorrelated.

Many experts suggest that oblique rotations are preferable to orthogonal rotations (e.g., Fabrigar et al., 1999). Again, the main purpose of rotation is to clarify the nature of the factors, which (as we will discuss next) depends on the pattern of associations between the factors, on one hand, and the scale's items, on the other. Oblique rotations can produce results in which these associations are as clear as possible, allowing us to understand our scales as clearly as possible. With this in mind, there is often little conceptual or psychometric reason to force a scale's factors to be orthogonal (i.e., uncorrelated)—doing so can create less clarity about the scale as compared with oblique rotations. After rotating factors, we next examine the associations between the items and the factors.

Examining Item–Factor Associations. Although a full understanding of a scale's dimensions emerges from many kinds of information (as discussed in later chapters on reliability and validity), the associations between items and factors can be an important piece of the puzzle. EFA presents these associations in terms of "factor loadings," and each item has a loading on each factor. By examining the loadings and identifying the items that are most strongly linked to each factor, we can begin to understand the factors' psychological meaning.

Generally, factor loadings range between –1 and +1, and they are interpreted as correlations or as standardized regression weights. When using an orthogonal rotation (or when a scale has only one factor), we obtain loadings that can be seen as correlations between each item and each factor. In contrast, when using oblique rotations, we obtain several kinds of factor loadings. For example, if we use the statistical program SPSS and we choose an oblique rotation, then we obtain both "pattern coefficients" and "structure coefficients." Pattern coefficients reflect the "unique association" between an item and a factor. That is, a pattern coefficient reflects the degree to which an item is associated with a factor, controlling for the correlation between the factors. For readers who are familiar with multiple regression, pattern coefficients are the standardized regression weights produced by a regression analysis in which respondents' item responses are predicted from their levels of the underlying factors. In contrast, structure coefficients are simply correlations between respondents' item responses and their levels of the underlying factors. By controlling for any correlation between factors, pattern coefficients can provide sharper clarity about the unique associations between items and factors as compared with structure coefficients.

When interpreting factor loadings, two pieces of information are important (see our discussion of interpreting correlations and covariances in Chapter 3). First, the *size* of the loading indicates the degree of association between an item and a factor—larger loadings (i.e., loadings farther from 0, closer to –1 or +1) indicate stronger associations between an item and a factor. More specifically, loadings above .30 or .40 are often seen as reasonably strong, with loadings of .70 or .80 being seen as very strong. The second important piece of information is the direction of a loading—positive or negative. A positive loading indicates that people who respond with a "high score" on the item have a high level of the underlying factor. In contrast, a negative loading indicates that people who respond with a high score on the item have a low level of the underlying factor.

For example, recall that the scree plot in Figure 4.6 strongly indicated the presence of two factors. With this in mind, we continued our EFA of these data by extracting two factors and using an oblique rotation (i.e., "Promax"). We obtained the loadings also shown in 4.6; in fact, there are three sets of loadings. The "Factor Matrix" presents the factor loadings that would be obtained before rotating the factors. Given the usefulness of factor rotations, we generally ignore these loadings. As the "Pattern Matrix" label implies, the second set of loadings is the pattern coefficients. And, of course, the "Structure Matrix" presents the structure coefficients.

Examining all three matrices reveals a very clear pattern of item–factor associations. Indeed, these results are highly consistent with our earlier "eyeball" factor analysis of the correlations in Table 4.1. Specifically, the items "intellectual," "imaginative," and "creative" load positively and strongly on Factor 1—the lowest loading being .604. Similarly, the items "assertive," "talkative," and "outgoing" load strongly and positively on Factor 2. Importantly, the first set of items (i.e., "intellectual," etc.) do not load on Factor 2, and the second set of items do not load on Factor 1.

Note that the three sets of loadings in Figure 4.6 are identical. That is, the Factor Matrix, Pattern Matrix, and Structure Matrix have identical values. This is a very atypical finding that, again, results from the fact that the correlations in Table 4.1 were created to be as clear and simple as possible. Thus, these results are rather artificial—in real analyses of oblique rotations, these matrices will differ from each other. We will illustrate this shortly.

The factor loadings in Figure 4.6 are an ideal example of "simple structure." Simple structure occurs when each item is strongly linked to one and only one factor. Again, in Figure 4.6, each item loads robustly on one factor but has a loading of .000 on the other factor. Thus, each item clearly belongs on one and only one factor.

Simple structure is important in psychometrics and scale usage. Generally, we sum or average a respondent's responses to the items that load together on a factor. For example, if we used the six-item questionnaire analyzed in Figure 4.6, we would create two scores for each person. Recall that for our six-item questionnaire, we asked each hypothetical respondent to rate himself or herself on each item, using a 5-point set of response options (i.e., 1 = *Completely unlike me*, 5 = *Completely like me*). First, we would sum (or average) a person's responses to intellectual, imaginative, and creative, producing an "openness to experience" score for each person (based only on those three items). Second, we would combine each person's responses to "assertive," "talkative," and "outgoing," producing an "extraversion" score for each person. Note that if an item does not load on a factor, then it is not included in scoring of that dimension/factor. Thus, simple structure is important because it reveals which items should be scored together. Because rotation makes it more likely that we will obtain simple structure, rotation is usually a key part of EFA.

For a more realistic example, consider the EFA results in Figure 4.7, conducted on a different (hypothetical) set of six items. As noted earlier, this scree plot indicates two factors; thus, we extracted two factors, used an oblique rotation, and obtained factor loadings. There are several important points to note. First, note that the three matrices differ from each other. Again, as noted earlier, this is typical—the Factor Matrix will differ from the Pattern Matrix, which will differ from the Structure Matrix. Second, note that the loadings in the Factor Matrix do not show simple structure. That is, each item loads fairly robustly on *both* factors. In this case, the lack of simple structure occurs because the Factor Matrix includes factor loadings that are obtained before rotation has taken place. Thus, as mentioned earlier, we typically ignore these results, even though they are often provided by the statistical package. Third, the Pattern Matrix does show very good simple structure—each item loads robustly on one and only one item. Fourth, the loadings in the Structure Matrix have a somewhat less clear simple structure than the loadings in the Pattern Matrix. This result is pretty typical, and it arises from the difference (discussed earlier) between pattern coefficients and structure coefficients. Fifth, we now see negative factor loadings, although none of the negative loadings in the Pattern Matrix are large enough to be very meaningful. As compared with the highly artificial results in Figure 4.6, the results in Figure 4.7 are a much more realistic illustration of a clear two-factor scale with very good simple structure.

For a full understanding of item–factor associations, it is important to realize that factor loadings can violate simple structure in two ways. First, an item might not load strongly on any factor, and second, an item might load strongly on more than one factor.

For example, consider again the results in Figure 4.8, illustrating a dimensionality that appears quite unclear. Based on another hypothetical six-item questionnaire, the scree plot is highly ambiguous (as discussed earlier). Because of this ambiguity, we rather arbitrarily tried a two-factor extraction, and we used an oblique rotation. Concentrating on the Pattern Matrix, we see one clear problem—Item 6 does not load very strongly on either factor (i.e., loadings below .30 on both). Two other slight problems are that the strongest factor loadings for Items 4 and 2 are below .40—ideally, an item would have an even stronger factor loading. Such results create ambiguity with regard to this scale. Do all of these items belong on the questionnaire? How should the questionnaire be scored? Are there really two factors, perhaps more, perhaps less?

As shown in the EFA flowchart (Figure 4.5), when faced with such ambiguity, one option is to revisit our initial decision about the number of factors to extract. We noted earlier that scree plots sometimes fail to provide clear information about this issue, but the item–factor associations might help shape our decision about the number of factors. Revisiting again the unclear structure in Figure 4.8, we examined factor loadings based on several different factor structures. Our hope was to find a number of factors that produces factor loadings with a clear simple structure. If we find loadings that are relatively clear and meaningful, then we might decide that the "correct" number of factors is the one producing that pattern of factor loadings. In our analysis of the ambiguous data represented in Figure 4.8, we also examined one-factor and three-factor extractions. Unfortunately, neither analysis produced clearer results.

Failing to find a clearer solution by revisiting the number of factors, there is at least one additional option for dealing with factorial ambiguity. Specifically, we might drop items that have poor structure. If an item is not strongly associated with any factor, then we conclude that it simply is not coherently related to the other items on the test or questionnaire. This might suggest that the item reflects a psychological construct that differs from the one(s) reflected by the other items on the scale (e.g., having a single math item on a vocabulary test). Alternatively, it might suggest that the item is strongly affected by random measurement error (see the later chapters on reliability). Either way, the item, as it is, likely does not belong on the scale. We noted that another problem is when an item loads robustly on more than one factor. In such cases, the item reflects more than one psychological construct. That is, responses to the item are affected by several psychological traits, abilities, or states (or what have you). Such an item does not uniquely reflect any construct, and thus we might drop it or revise it to reflect only one construct.

With this option in mind, we revisited the data reflected in Figure 4.8's ambiguous results. Noting that Item 6 seemed to load weakly on both factors (in the two-factor solution), we removed this item from the analysis and reconducted the EFA. Essentially, this addresses the dimensionality of a questionnaire that would include only Items 1 through 5. Figure 4.9 presents the results of this analysis, showing that this adjustment produces a questionnaire that now has a clearer dimensionality. Indeed, the scree plot now clearly suggests two factors, and the factor loadings have good simple structure—each of the five remaining items loads on one and only one factor. Apparently the inclusion of Item 6 created ambiguity in the questionnaire as a whole. Thus, by dropping that item from the questionnaire, we are left with a five-item questionnaire that clearly includes two dimensions.

Examining the Associations Among Factors. Finally, as shown in the EFA flowchart (Figure 4.5) when using oblique rotations, we should examine the correlations among the factors. Recall that oblique rotations allow factors to be either correlated or uncorrelated with each other, whereas orthogonal rotations force the factors to be uncorrelated. The results of oblique rotations thus include a correlation for each pair of factors, revealing the higher-order associations among factors. This information has implications for our understanding of the nature of the factors and for the scoring of the test or questionnaire. As mentioned earlier (Figure 4.1), we should create "total scores" from a multidimensional scale only when the dimensions are correlated with each other to a meaningful degree.

Returning to our first and main example (see Table 4.1 and Figure 4.6), the factor correlation is presented in the "Factor Correlation Matrix" box. This small matrix presents the correlation between the two factors that we extracted and

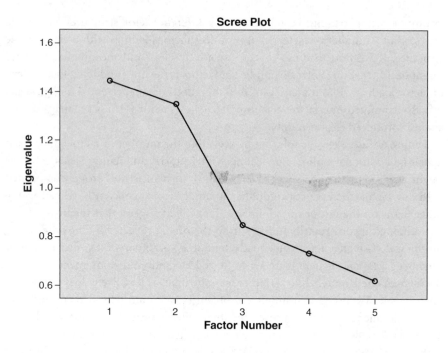

Factor Matrix[a]

	Factor	
	1	2
item4	.846	−.117
item5	.401	−.082
item1	.137	.651
item2	.030	.394
item3	.084	.368

Extraction Method:
  Principal Axis Factoring.

[a] 2 factors extracted.
279 iterations required.

Pattern Matrix[a]

	Factor	
	1	2
item4	.854	.006
item5	.410	−.024
item1	.009	.665
item2	−.046	.395
item3	.011	.376

Extraction Method:
  Principal Axis Factoring.
Rotation Method:
  Promax with Kaiser
  Normalization.

[a] Rotation converged in
3 iterations.

Structure Matrix

	Factor	
	1	2
item4	.854	.048
item5	.409	−.003
item1	.042	.665
item2	−.026	−.362
item3	.030	.377

Extraction Method:
  Principal Axis Factoring.
Rotation Method:
  Promax with Kaiser
  Normalization.

Factor Correlation Matrix

Factor	1	2
1	1.000	.050
2	.050	1.000

Extraction Method: Principal Axis Factoring.
Rotation Method: Promax with Kaiser Normalization.

Figure 4.9 Selected Output From Exploratory Factor Analysis of Data
From a Five-Item Version of the Questionnaire Originally
Analyzed in Figure 4.8

rotated earlier in the analysis. This output reveals a zero correlation between the two dimensions, indicating that the two dimensions are not associated with each other. That is, people who have a high level of openness to experience are not particularly likely (or particularly unlikely) to have a high level of extraversion.

Again, it is important to note that different data will produce different results—it is quite possible that an oblique rotation will produce dimensions that are more highly correlated with each other. For example, Figure 4.7 presents a two-factor structure in which the two factors are indeed more highly correlated, at .35. This suggests that people who have a relatively high level of the first psychological dimension are likely to have a relatively high level of the second dimension.

In sum, oblique rotations allow factors to be correlated "however they want to be." For the questionnaire represented in Figure 4.6, the factors "wanted" to be uncorrelated, and the oblique rotation allowed them to be uncorrelated (i.e., the interfactor correlation was .00). In contrast, for the questionnaire represented in Figure 4.7, the factors "wanted" to be correlated, and the oblique rotation allowed them to be correlated.

For some final insights into the links between rotations, factor correlations, and factor loadings, consider what happens if we use an orthogonal rotation for these EFAs. In the case of the data from Figure 4.6 (the original, highly artificial data), varimax rotation produces the factor loadings shown in Figure 4.10a. Note that these loadings are identical to those obtained in the original analysis based on an oblique rotation (see Figure 4.6). In the case of the data from Figure 4.7 (the more realistic data in which the factors were moderately correlated with each other), varimax rotation produces the loadings given in Figure 4.10b. Note that these loadings differ from those obtained in the analysis based on an oblique rotation (see Figure 4.7).

Take a moment to consider why this might be—why in one case orthogonal and oblique rotations produce the same result, whereas in the other case they produce different results. The answer is that for the data in Figure 4.6, the factors "want" to be uncorrelated. That is, the oblique rotation (Figure 4.6) allowed the factors to be either correlated or uncorrelated, and the results showed that the factors were "naturally" uncorrelated. Because the oblique rotation produced results in which the factors were uncorrelated, the orthogonal rotation (which forces the factors to be uncorrelated) produced the exact same results in terms of factor loadings. In contrast, the questionnaire reflected in Figure 4.7 includes factors that "want" to be correlated—the oblique rotation allowed them to be correlated, and they were, in fact, correlated at .35. When we then conducted an orthogonal rotation, which forced the factors to be uncorrelated, this changed the nature of the factors, which then changed the associations between the items and the factors (i.e., it changed the factor loadings).

Also, notice the way the factor loadings changed—compare the pattern coefficients in Figure 4.7 with the factor loadings in Figure 4.10b. This comparison reveals that the orthogonal rotation produced factor loadings that are somewhat less clear—they have worse simple structure. For example, examine the loadings for Item 6 (the top item in the matrix). In the oblique rotation, its loading on Factor 1 was .880, and its loading on Factor 2 was .004. In the orthogonal rotation, its

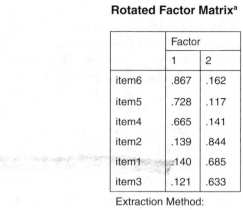

(a)

Rotated Factor Matrix[a]

	Factor	
	1	2
Intellectual	.942	.000
Imaginative	.764	.000
Creative	.604	.000
Assertive	.000	.849
Talkative	.000	.777
Outgoing	.000	.695

Extraction Method:
  Principal Axis Factoring.
Rotation Method: Varimax
  with Kaiser Normalization.

[a.] Rotation converged in
2 iterations.

(b)

Rotated Factor Matrix[a]

	Factor	
	1	2
item6	.867	.162
item5	.728	.117
item4	.665	.141
item2	.139	.844
item1	.140	.685
item3	.121	.633

Extraction Method:
  Principal Axis Factoring.
Rotation Method:
  Varimax with Kaiser
  Normalization.

[a.] Rotation converged in
2 iterations.

Figure 4.10   Factor Loadings From Orthogonal Rotation of Data From (a) Figure 4.6 and (b) Figure 4.7

loading on Factor 1 is weaker, at .867 (though still quite strong), and its loading on Factor 2 is somewhat stronger, at .162 (though still relatively weak). All the items show this pattern—in the orthogonal rotation, their main or "on-factor" loadings are somewhat weaker, and their other or "off-factor" loadings are somewhat stronger. Thus, orthogonal rotation can produce a somewhat less simple structure within the factor loadings.

A Quick Look at Confirmatory Factor Analysis

As noted earlier, there are two types of factor analysis: exploratory factor analysis (EFA) and confirmatory factor analysis (CFA). Our discussion so far has focused on EFA because it has been used more frequently than CFA, because it is relatively easy to conduct with basic statistical software, and because it is often used in early phases of the development and evaluation of psychological tests. However, a brief discussion of CFA and how it differs from EFA is potentially useful at this point.

Although both EFA and CFA are approaches to factor analysis, they have somewhat different purposes or roles. As its label implies, EFA is as an exploratory procedure—it is designed for situations in which there are few, if any, ideas about a test's dimensionality. Again, test developers and evaluators might use EFA in the early phases, while conducting basic exploratory analyses of a set of items.

In contrast, CFA is a confirmatory procedure—it is designed for situations in which there are very clear ideas about a test's dimensionality. For example, we might wish to evaluate the dimensionality of a 16-item test that has been developed specifically to have 8 questions reflecting one factor and another 8 questions reflecting a different factor. In this case, we would have a fairly clear idea about the intended dimensionality of the test. That is, we would know exactly which items were intended to load on which factor. After collecting a large number of responses to this 16-item test, we could use CFA to directly test these ideas; or perhaps more accurately, we could test whether the responses to the test items match or fit with these ideas (i.e., whether the test shows the dimensionality that it is intended to have). In this way, CFA is used to confirm, or potentially disconfirm, our hypotheses about a test's dimensionality.

There are important similarities between CFA and EFA, but the process of conducting a CFA is substantially different from the process of conducting an EFA. Indeed, CFA includes new concepts and statistics, such as inferential tests of parameter estimates and "goodness-of-fit" indices. Moreover, although most of the common statistical software packages can now be used to conduct a CFA, the way this is done differs rather dramatically from the way those packages conduct an EFA.

Given the differences between EFA and CFA, and given the additional complexity of CFA, we will return to CFA later in the book, in Chapter 12. In that chapter, we will describe the information provided by a CFA of a test, the procedures for conducting a CFA, and the application of CFA to several important psychometric questions.

Summary

In this chapter, we have discussed the concept of test dimensionality and the way in which it is examined. We have discussed three core issues regarding test dimensionality: (1) the number of dimensions reflected in a set of test items, (2) the degree of association among a test's dimensions, and (3) the psychological meaning of a test dimension. These issues serve to differentiate three types of tests, which has important implications for the way a test is scored, evaluated, and used.

This chapter provided an overview of factor analysis—what it is and how it is used to examine test dimensionality. Although factor analysis is a highly advanced statistical procedure, we have provided a general discussion and illustration of the procedures. Interested readers can obtain more details from many available sources (e.g., Gorsuch, 1983; Meyers, Gamst, & Guarino, 2006).

The first four chapters of this book have provided the conceptual and statistical foundations for the remaining chapters. In the remaining chapters, we focus on core psychometric properties. Specifically, issues such as reliability and validity require familiarity with basic concepts and procedures such as variability, correlations, and dimensionality. We will turn next to reliability.

Suggested Readings

For a more extensive introduction to factor analysis:

Meyers, L. S., Gamst, G., & Guarino, A. (2006). *Applied multivariate research: Design and interpretation* (chaps. 12A–13B). Thousand Oaks, CA: Sage.

Thompson, B. (2004). *Exploratory and confirmatory factor analysis: Understanding concepts and applications.* Washington, DC: American Psychological Association.

For a detailed technical discussion of the procedures:

Gorsuch, R. L. (1983). *Factor analysis.* Hillsdale, NJ: Lawrence Erlbaum.

For commentary and recommendations on common tendencies in the use of factor analysis:

Fabrigar, L. R., Wegener, D. T., MacCallum, R. C., & Strahan, E. J. (1999). Evaluating the use of exploratory factor analysis in psychological research. *Psychological Methods, 4,* 272–299.

For a detailed but concise discussion of the use of factor analysis in determining test score dimensionality:

Netemeyer, R. G., Bearden, W. O., & Sharma, S. (2003). *Scaling procedures.* Thousand Oaks, CA: Sage.

For recommendations on the use of factor analysis in scale development:

Floyd, F. J., & Widaman, K. F. (1995). Factor analysis in the development and refinement of clinical assessment instruments. *Psychological Assessment, 7,* 286–299.

PART II

Reliability

CHAPTER 5

Reliability

Conceptual Basis

Nurses attempt to measure the length of babies at birth and at regular intervals thereafter. If you have ever watched an attempt to measure the length of a baby, you will not be surprised to learn that it's a difficult task. Babies squirm around erratically, and they resist attempts to stretch them out to their full length. Such squirming creates difficulties for nurses who are attempting to obtain accurate measurements of babies' lengths. Furthermore, some babies are more compliant than others, which means that some are less likely to squirm around than others. Again, this creates differences among babies in that some babies may be more likely to be measured accurately than others. These kinds of problems have led researchers (e.g., Johnson, Engstrom, & Gelhar, 1997; Johnson, Engstrom, Haney, & Mulcrone, 1999) to ask questions about the reliability of these measurements.

Imagine that a nurse is asked to measure the lengths of 10 different babies, and imagine that there was some way to know beforehand (but unknown to the nurse) each baby's true length. You could, in theory, compare each baby's measured length with his or her true length. Moreover, you could examine the differences among babies' measured lengths and compare them with the differences among babies' true lengths. Ideally, you would find good consistency between these two sets of differences. That is, you would hope to find that differences among the babies' measured lengths were consistent with differences in their actual lengths—that the babies who were measured (by the nurse) as relatively long were truly relatively long. If this was the case, then you would conclude that the measurement procedure produced length "scores" that were reliable.

Throughout this book, we have emphasized the importance of understanding psychological variability—psychological tests are useful only to the degree that they accurately reflect true psychological differences. Again, in a research context, behavioral science strives to quantify the degree to which differences in one variable (e.g., intelligence) are associated with differences in other variables (e.g., parenting styles,

101

preschool experience, age, academic performance, aggression, gender, etc.). Test and other types of measures are used to assess and represent these behavioral differences. In an applied context, practitioners strive to make decisions about people, and they use behavioral tests and diagnostic procedures to inform those decisions. Such decisions rest on the assumption that behavioral differences among people exist, that the differences have important implications, and that they can be measured with some precision. Thus, psychological measurement always hinges on the ability to reflect real psychological differences accurately. This ability is at the heart of reliability.

This chapter introduces classical test theory (CTT), which is a measurement theory that defines the conceptual basis of reliability and outlines procedures for estimating the reliability of psychological measures (Gulliksen, 1950; Magnusson, 1967). For example, suppose that we give a burnout questionnaire to a group of people, and we found that people differ in their scores on the questionnaire. We would like to assume that the differences in their questionnaire scores accurately reflect the differences in their true levels of burnout. According to CTT, a test's reliability reflects the extent to which the differences in respondents' test scores are a function of their true psychological differences, as opposed to measurement error. Whether using a measure for research purposes or for applied purposes, we hope that all of our measures are highly reliable.

Although it is somewhat imprecise to speak in this way, sometimes behavioral scientists speak as if reliability is an all-or-none issue. For example, someone might ask us whether a particular test is reliable, and we are likely to answer "Yes" or "No." Such an answer seems to treat reliability as if it is a binary issue, with a test either being reliable or unreliable. Despite this common way of speaking and thinking about reliability, reliability is, in fact, on a continuum. That is, a procedure for measuring something will be more or less reliable.

One useful insight to begin with is that reliability is itself a theoretical notion. Reliability is a feature, presumably, of the results of procedures for measuring characteristics of objects or psychological characteristics of people. Just as a psychological attribute such as intelligence is an unobserved feature of a person, reliability is an unobserved feature of test scores. Furthermore, just as we must estimate a person's level of intelligence, we must estimate a test's reliability.

In this chapter, we will describe the theoretical basis of reliability from the perspective of CTT. In Chapter 6, we will describe procedures for estimating a test's reliability. We will show that it is possible, given certain assumptions of CTT, to calculate numerical values that estimate the *degree* to which scores from a measure are or are not reliable. In Chapter 7, we discuss the importance of reliability—why it matters and what its implications are for psychological testing, practice, and research. As we will detail in that chapter, reliability is a crucial issue that can have powerful implications on psychological research and practice.

Overview of Reliability and Classical Test Theory

According to CTT, reliability derives from observed scores, true scores, and measurement error. We refer to values that are obtained from the measurement of some *observed scores*

true scores

characteristic of a person as *observed scores*. In contrast, the real amounts of that characteristic are referred to as *true scores*. In our length example, a baby's length as determined by the nurse would be an observed score, and a baby's real length would be a true score. We should note that some experts would object to this relatively simple definition of true score, preferring instead to define true scores more technically as the average score that a participant would obtain if he or she completed the scale an infinite number of times. Alternatively, true scores can be seen as the scores that would be obtained if the test or measurement was perfectly precise—that is, if it was unaffected by measurement error. At a practical level, all of these definitions are essentially identical. Thus, we prefer, for current purposes, to describe true scores as noted first—as the actual or real level of the psychological attribute being measured by a test. Ideally, test users would like to interpret individuals' observed scores as good estimates of their true scores because most behavioral research and decision making are intended to reflect respondents' true psychological characteristics.

reliability

Considering the concepts of observed scores and true scores, *reliability* is the extent to which differences in respondents' observed scores are consistent with differences in their true scores. More specifically, the reliability for a measurement procedure depends on the extent to which differences in respondents' observed scores can be attributed to differences in their true scores, as opposed to other, often unknown, test administration characteristics. The extent to which these "other" characteristics contribute to differences in observed scores is referred to as *measurement error*, or just error, because they create inconsistency between observed scores and true scores. When measuring the quantity of anything, including features of physical objects or psychological characteristics of people, the results of the measurement will always be unreliable to some extent. There is no such thing as a perfectly reliable measure.

measurement error

It is usually impossible to know all of the sources of measurement error affecting test scores. In the case of measuring the length of babies, we can imagine that some error might be related to how much each baby squirms while being measured. That is, it is likely that some babies squirm more than others. If this is true, then the accuracy of the length "scores" will be affected by the amount each baby squirms. Some babies' squirming might cause their nurses to underestimate their true length, but other babies' squirming might cause their nurses to overestimate their true length. The effects of squirming are considered measurement error because they create imprecision in the measurement of babies' true lengths. Other sources of error in the babies' measurement might include the fact that different nurses might record the measurements. If each baby is measured by a different nurse and if some nurses are more careful in taking their measurements, then some babies will be more accurately measured than others. The differences in nurses' "measurement care" will obscure the differences among babies' true lengths. There are many possible sources of error that might affect the observed measurements, thereby obscuring the true differences among babies. Some of these sources of error might be subtle (e.g., nurses' carefulness), and some might be more obvious (e.g., squirming). There is no way to account for all of the possibly subtle factors that might affect observed scores.

Of course, such errors also influence the measurement of psychological attributes. Consider what might happen if a class of schoolchildren takes a mathematics achievement test. We would like to think that a child's score accurately reflects his or her true knowledge of mathematics; however, factors other than "math knowledge" are likely to influence children's test performance. Some children who are taking the test might have a cold on the day they take the test. The cold might make them groggy, which in turn causes them to perform worse on the test than they "truly" could perform, given their true mathematical ability. Some children might have eaten a nutritious breakfast, which helps them feel alert and energetic, thereby causing them to perform quite well on the test. Some children might happen to make many "lucky guesses" on the test, which makes their test score higher than it should really be, given their true mathematical ability. Some children might compute the math answers correctly but, by mistake, circle the wrong choice on an answer sheet, producing test scores that artificially underestimate their "true" mathematical ability. Such temporary and transient factors—amount of sleep, emotional state, physical well-being, guessing, misrecording answers, and so on—could artificially inflate or deflate the children's test scores relative to their true scores. Each of these factors might be a source of measurement error, compromising the quality of the test scores. To evaluate the reliability of scores from any measure, we must estimate the extent to which individual differences in observed scores are a function of measurement error versus the extent to which they are a function of true or real score differences among respondents.

One useful way to think about reliability is in terms of signal and noise—that is, in terms of our ability to detect a signal in the presence of noise. In this framework, true scores are the signal that we would like to detect, and measurement error is the noise that is obscuring the signal and making it difficult to detect. Reliability then can be seen as a ratio of signal and noise:

$$\text{Reliability} = \frac{\text{Signal}}{\text{Signal} + \text{Noise}}.$$

From this perspective, reliability is clearest when there is a strong signal and/or little noise. We will return to this conceptual framework later in this chapter.

Observed Scores, True Scores, and Measurement Error

Reliability depends on two things: (1) the extent to which differences in test scores can be attributed to real inter- or intra-individual differences and (2) the extent to which differences in test scores are a function of measurement error. In CTT, a person's observed score on a test is a function of that person's true score, plus error. If X_o represents an individual's observed test score, if X_t is the individual's true score on psychological characteristics, and if X_e is the amount of error affecting the individual's responses, then we can write the following formula to represent this assumption:

$$X_o = X_t + X_e. \tag{5.1}$$

To illustrate this point, we have constructed an artificial data set representing six people's responses to a self-esteem questionnaire (see Table 5.1a). For the sake of this example, we will pretend that we know each person's true level of self-esteem (i.e., each person's true score, X_t). Of course, we would never actually know an individual's true score—this example is intended solely to explain the theoretical basis of reliability. From this "omniscient" perspective, we see that Ashley truly has the highest level of self-esteem in this sample ($X_t = 130$), that Bob has the next highest level ($X_t = 120$), and so on.

In addition, we will also pretend that we know the degree to which each individual's questionnaire score is affected by measurement error. For example, Ashley happened to take the self-esteem questionnaire only an hour after learning that she had earned a D on a biology test. Because of this disappointing grade, she felt unusually bad about herself when she took the self-esteem questionnaire. Notice that Ashley's error score (X_e) is –10, reflecting the fact that her disappointment temporarily lowered her apparent self-esteem score. In contrast, Bob happened to take the test an hour after learning that he had been accepted into law school. Although Bob generally has a relatively high level of self-esteem (i.e., his true self-esteem score is relatively high compared with the rest of the sample), the good news about law school makes him feel even better about himself than he usually does. Notice that Bob's error score (X_e) is 25, reflecting the fact that this good news is temporarily raising his apparent self-esteem score.

As Table 5.1a shows, the respondents' observed scores on the self-esteem questionnaire are determined by their true levels of self-esteem and by the "error" effect of random events or states. For example, Ashley's observed score is as follows:

$$X_o = X_t + X_e ,$$
$$= 130 + (-10),$$
$$= 120.$$

Table 5.1   Responses to an Original Self-Esteem Questionnaire and a Revised Self-Esteem Questionnaire

Respondent	Observed Score (X_o)		True Score (X_t)		Error (X_e)
(a) Responses to original self-esteem questionnaire					
Ashley	120	=	130	+	−10
Bob	145	=	120	+	25
Carl	95	=	110	+	−15
Denise	85	=	100	+	−15
Eric	115	=	90	+	25
Felicia	70	=	80	+	−10
Mean	105.00		105		0
Variance	608.33		291.67		316.67

(Continued)

Table 5.1   (Continued)

Respondent	Observed Score (X_o)		True Score (X_t)		Error (X_e)
Standard deviation	24.66		17.08		17.80
Reliability = R_{XX} =	.48	r_{ot} =	.69	r_{oe} =	.72
r_{te} =	.00	r_{ot}^2 =	.48	r_{oe}^2 =	.52

(b) Responses to revised self-esteem questionnaire

Respondent	Observed Score (X_o)		True Score (X_t)		Error (X_e)
Ashley	135	=	130	+	5
Bob	130	=	120	+	10
Carl	95	=	110	+	−15
Denise	85	=	100	+	−15
Eric	100	=	90	+	10
Felicia	85	=	80	+	5
Mean	105		105		0
Variance	408.33		291.67		116.67
Standard deviation	20.21		17.08		10.80
Reliability = R_{XX} =	.71	r_{ot} =	.84	r_{oe} =	.53
r_{te} =	.00	r_{ot}^2 =	.71	r_{oe}^2 =	.29

Again, this "omniscient" example illustrates the first simple but fundamental theoretical assumption of CTT—that *observed scores on a psychological measure are determined by respondents' true scores and by measurement error.*

CTT makes a very important *assumption about measurement error.* Specifically, it assumes that error occurs as if it is random. In part, this means that measurement error is just as likely to inflate any particular score as it is to decrease any particular score. We assume that peoples' responses to a psychological test are affected in unpredictable ways that might make their observed scores artificially high or artificially low. Consider Ashley and Bob. It was simply chance that Ashley took the self-esteem questionnaire only an hour after hearing bad news, thereby lowering her observed score as compared with her true, stable level of self-esteem. Similarly, it was simply chance that Bob took the questionnaire after hearing good news, thereby raising his observed score as compared with his true, stable level of self-esteem. Across the entire sample of respondents, random measurement error artificially inflates some people's scores, and it artificially deflates other people's scores.

Because error affects scores as if it is random, the inflation and deflation caused by error is independent of the individuals' true levels of self-esteem. That is, measurement error can affect someone with a high true level of self-esteem in the same way (and to the same degree) as it affects someone with a low true level of self-esteem. Again, consider Ashley and Bob. The events that are temporarily affecting their responses have nothing to do with their true level of self-esteem. The timing of Ashley's grade on her biology test and the timing of Bob's news about law school are completely unrelated to how high or low their true levels of self-esteem are. The artificial data in Table 5.1a illustrate this general point. Notice that the size and direction (positive or negative) of the error effects are spread equally for respondents across the entire range of true scores. For each "high-esteem" person whose observed score is artificially deflated by measurement error, there is a high-esteem person whose observed score is artificially inflated. The same is true for people with low true levels of self-esteem.

There are two important consequences of this assumption about error. First, error tends to cancel itself out across respondents. That is, error inflates the scores of some respondents and deflates the scores of other respondents in such a way that the average effect of error across respondents is zero. Indeed, Table 5.1a shows that the mean of the six error scores is exactly 0 (i.e., $\overline{X}_e = 0$). The second consequence of the apparent randomness of error is that error scores are uncorrelated with true scores. As described above, error affects observed scores in ways that are independent of the respondents' true levels of self-esteem. Therefore, if we compute the correlation between the individuals' true scores and their error scores in Table 5.1a, we find that the correlation is exactly 0 (i.e., $r_{te} = 0$). These two consequences have important implications for reliability, as we shall soon see.

[handwritten marginal notes: "1) error cancels itself out b/c as some scores inflate, others deflate (avg. effect of error = 0)"]

[handwritten note: "2) randomness of error is that error scores are uncorrelated w/ true scores"]

[handwritten: "$r_{te} = 0$"]

Variances in Observed Scores, True Scores, and Error Scores

As mentioned earlier, reliability reflects the degree to which *differences* in observed scores are consistent with *differences* in true scores. Put another way, reliability depends on the links among observed score variability, true score variability, and error score variability. Given the importance of variability for interpreting and evaluating psychological measurement, we need to understand how the first assumption of CTT (i.e., that, for each individual, $X_o = X_t + X_e$) extends to the differences among people.

[handwritten: "$X_o = X_t + X_e$"]

This extension might make the most sense if we begin by illustrating how the true differences between people can be obscured by differences in measurement error. Take a moment to examine the individuals' true scores in Table 5.1a and focus on the difference between Ashley and Bob. Notice that Ashley's true score ($X_t = 130$) is 10 points higher than Bob's ($X_t = 120$). That is, her self-esteem is, in reality, 10 points higher than Bob's. However, notice that Ashley's observed score on the questionnaire ($X_o = 120$) is 25 points lower than Bob's observed score ($X_o = 145$). Obviously, the difference between Ashley's and Bob's true scores is inconsistent with the difference between their observed scores—Ashley's true score is higher than Bob's true score, but her observed score is lower than Bob's observed score:

$$\text{Ashley's } X_t - \text{Bob's } X_t = 130 - 120 = +10.$$

$$\text{Ashley's } X_o - \text{Bob's } X_o = 120 - 145 = -25.$$

This inconsistency is created by the measurement error that artificially deflated Ashley's observed score but artificially inflated Bob's observed sore. Of course, this inconsistency means that the apparent 25-point difference between Ashley and Bob (on the self-esteem questionnaire) is a very poor reflection of the real difference between Ashley and Bob (in their true, stable levels of self-esteem).

Because such inconsistencies potentially affect the differences among all the respondents, let us consider the relevant variances across all the participants. Variances for this hypothetical data set are computed in the standard way. For example, variance among the error scores (s_e^2) is based on using error scores (X_e) in the computations:

$$s_e^2 = \frac{\sum (X_e - \overline{X}_e)^2}{N}. \tag{5.2}$$

$$s_e^2 = \frac{(-10-0)^2 + (25-0)^2 + (-15-0)^2 + (-15-0)^2 + (25-0)^2 + (-10-0)^2}{6},$$

$$= \frac{(-10)^2 + (25)^2 + (-15)^2 + (-15)^2 + (25)^2 + (-10)^2}{6},$$

$$= \frac{100 + 625 + 225 + 225 + 625 + 100}{6},$$

$$= \frac{1900}{6}$$

$$= 316.67.$$

This value represents the degree to which error affected different people in different ways. Again, the fact that error affects people differently—artificially inflating some people's scores and artificially deflating other people's scores—is what obscures the true differences among people. Thus, a high degree of error variance indicates the potential for poor measurement. Using the standard formula for variance (see Chapter 3), we can also compute a variance for the observed scores (s_o^2) and a variance for the true scores (s_t^2), as shown in Table 5.1a.

Assuming that an individual's observed score is the sum of the individual's true score and error score (i.e., $X_o = X_t + X_e$) and that measurement error is random, it follows that the total variance of the observed scores from a group of individuals equals the sum of their true score and error score variances:

$$s_o^2 = s_t^2 + s_e^2. \tag{5.3}$$

If you examine the observed score variance (s_o^2) in Table 5.1a, you will see that it is indeed the sum of the true score variance and error score variance:

$$s_o^2 = 291.67 + 316.67,$$

$$= 608.34.$$

You may have noticed that Equation 5.3 seems inconsistent with the formula for the variance of a composite variable that was introduced in Chapter 3 (Equation 3.6). Recall that we originally described a composite score as a score that is the sum of two or more items. More generally, a composite variable is a variable (i.e., a set of scores) that is the sum of two components. Thus, observed scores can be seen as composite scores that are simply the sum of two components—true scores and measurement error. In Chapter 3, we stated that the variance for a composite score is equal to the sum of variances of the items (or components) *plus* a term that represents the extent to which the items (or components) are correlated with each other. Thus, you might expect that the variance of observed scores should be

$$s_o^2 = s_t^2 + s_e^2 + 2r_{te}s_t s_e. \tag{5.4}$$

In other words, you might expect that observed score variance should be equal to true score variance plus error variance *plus* the covariance of true scores and error scores ($c_{te} = r_{te}s_t s_e$). However, as described above, we assume that error is independent of true scores, which implies that the correlation between error score and true scores is 0 ($r_{te} = 0$). Therefore, the far-right term of the above expression, the covariance, will equal 0 and will drop out of the equation, leaving us with

$$s_o^2 = s_t^2 + s_e^2.$$

Equation 5.3 is a critically important formula in the classical theory of reliability. As we will discuss below, reliability will be defined in various ways in terms of the relationship between observed score, true score, and error score variance.

Four Ways to Think of Reliability

In CTT, there are at least four ways to think about reliability. In one way or another, each one arises from the associations among observed scores, true scores, and measurement error. At one level, the approaches differ only with respect to the methods used to algebraically manipulate the terms associated with these variances. At another level, they represent different ways of conceptualizing or characterizing the concept of reliability.

As shown in Table 5.2, these four approaches reflect two distinctions in the conceptualization of reliability. One distinction is whether an approach conceptualizes reliability in terms of "proportion of variance" or in terms of correlations. A second distinction is whether an approach conceptualizes reliability in terms of observed scores as related to true scores or to measurement error.

There are at least three reasons to become familiar with these different ways of thinking about reliability. First, it is possible that one way of conceptualizing reliability will seem clearer and more straightforward to you than any of the other ways. For example, you might find that correlations, for whatever reason, simply make more sense to you than does variance. Thus, you might find one of the

Table 5.2 A 2 x 2 Framework for Conceptualizing Reliability

		Conceptual Basis of Reliability: Observed Scores in Relation to. . .	
		True scores	Measurement error
Statistical basis of reliability in terms of . . .	Proportions of variance	Reliability is the ratio of true score variance to observed score variance $$R_{xx} = \frac{s_t^2}{s_o^2}$$	Reliability is the lack of error variance $$R_{xx} = 1 - \frac{s_e^2}{s_o^2}$$
	Correlations	Reliability is the (squared) correlation between observed scores and true scores $$R_{xx} = r_{ot}^2$$	Reliability is the lack of correlation between observed scores and error scores $$R_{xx} = 1 - r_{oe}^2$$

"correlation-based" definitions of reliability to be particularly clear. By presenting a variety of conceptualizations of reliability, we hope that each reader finds at least one that seems relatively clear. Second, an appreciation of the concepts expressed through the different approaches should help you develop a deeper understanding of the general meaning of reliability. That is, if you understand reliability from more than one perspective, then you can gain greater insights into this important aspect of psychometric theory. Third, in your readings and discussions about tests and their reliabilities, you might find that different people discuss reliability in different ways. For example, some books, articles, websites, and teachers might present only one conceptualization of reliability. Being familiar with a variety of different perspectives and knowing how they are related to each other might help you avoid confusion when confronted with them in these discussions.

Reliability as the Ratio of True Score Variance to Observed Score Variance

Probably the most common expression of reliability is the proportion of observed score variance that is attributable to true score variance:

$$R_{xx} = \frac{s_t^2}{s_o^2}, \tag{5.5}$$

where R_{xx} is the reliability coefficient. For example, for the responses presented in Table 5.1a,

$$R_{xx} = \frac{291.67}{608.33} = .48 .$$

true trait levels
attribute to differences

This value tells us that about 48% of the differences that we see among respondents' observed scores can be attributed to differences among their true trait levels.

The size of the reliability coefficient indicates a test's reliability. Reliability ranges between 0 and 1, and larger R_{xx} values indicate greater psychometric quality. This is the case because, as R_{xx} increases, a greater proportion of the differences among observed scores can be attributed to differences among true scores. Notice that if true score variance is 0, then reliability is 0. That is, an R_{xx} of 0 means that everyone has the same true score. This underscores the fact that reliability is intrinsically tied to differences among people—if respondents do not differ in the characteristic being assessed by a test (i.e., if $s_t^2 = 0$), then the test's reliability is 0 for those respondents. In contrast, if true score variance is equal to observed score variance, then $R_{xx} = 1.0$. This would indicate that there is absolutely no measurement error affecting observed scores. In reality, measurement error always occurs to some degree.

R_{xx} = reliability

Although there is no clear cutoff value separating good reliability from poor reliability, the reliability of .48 for the data in Table 5.1a is rather low. A perfect reliability ($R_{xx} = 1.0$) will not occur, but we would be much more satisfied with a reliability of .70 or .80 for research purposes and even higher for applied purposes. We would be very worried if less than half of the variance in observed scores could be attributed to true scores.

Therefore, the test user who used the self-esteem questionnaire for the data in Table 5.1a might wish to improve the questionnaire's reliability. Imagine that she revised the questionnaire by rewriting some of its items—for example, by clarifying potentially ambiguous wording and making sure to refer to the way that people "generally" feel about themselves. She hopes that such revisions will improve the reliability of the questionnaire. Furthermore, imagine that she asked the same six respondents to complete the revised version of the questionnaire. These hypothetical responses are presented in Table 5.1b. Did her revisions improve the psychometric quality of the self-esteem questionnaire?

Take a moment to contrast the data in Table 5.1a (the original questionnaire) and 5.1b (the revised questionnaire). First, note that the individuals' true scores are the same for the revised test as they were in the original test. This occurs because the questionnaire is a measure of self-esteem, and we assume that individuals' true levels of self-esteem are stable across the two testing occasions. That is, self-esteem is a trait that is generally quite stable. Although people might experience temporary fluctuations in their self-esteem, we assume that each person has an overall level that reflects his or her typical level of self-regard. The self-esteem questionnaire is intended to measure these stable levels of self-esteem.

Second, observe the differences among the respondents. Again, let us focus on Ashley and Bob. As we have already pointed out in the original questionnaire data, there was a clear inconsistency between Ashley's and Bob's true score difference and their observed score difference. Specifically, Ashley's true score is 10 points higher than Bob's true score, but her observed score was 25 points *lower* than Bob's observed score. This reflects a substantial effect of measurement error. In contrast, their observed scores on the revised questionnaire seem to be much more consistent with their true scores. Specifically, Ashley's observed score is 5 points higher than Bob's observed score. Although this 5-point difference is still somewhat inconsistent with the full 10-point difference in their true scores, it is a relatively small inconsistency. Furthermore, the observed score difference on the revised questionnaire is at least consistent with the *direction* of the difference in their true scores. That is, the revised test produced scores in which Ashley scored higher than Bob, which is consistent with their true score difference.

Thus, we begin to get a sense that the revised test does a better job of reflecting the true differences among respondents than the original test. This sense is confirmed when we compute the reliability for the revised test:

$$R_{xx} = \frac{291.67}{408.33} = .71 \,.$$

For the revised questionnaire, 71% of the observed score variance can be attributed to variance in the true scores. The reliability of the revised questionnaire is much better than the reliability of the original questionnaire. This suggests that the item revisions paid off and that future test users should probably work with the revised test.

Lack of Error Variance

A second way of conceptualizing reliability is in terms of a lack of measurement error. We have already seen that error variance (s_e^2) represents the degree to which error affects different people in different ways—artificially inflating some people's scores and artificially deflating other people's scores. These effects obscure the true differences among people, as shown in our comparisons of Ashley and Bob. Therefore, reliability can be seen as the degree to which error variance is minimal in comparison with the variance of observed scores.

In the previous section, we stated that reliability can be seen as the proportion of observed score variance that is attributable to true score variance:

$$R_{xx} = \frac{S_t^2}{S_o^2} \,. \tag{5.6}$$

We have also stated that observed score variance is the sum of true score variance and error variance (Equation 5.3):

$$s_o^2 = s_t^2 + s_e^2.$$

Rearranging the terms algebraically,

$$s_t^2 = s_o^2 - s_e^2.$$

Substituting this into the numerator of Equation 5.6, we obtain

$$R_{xx} = \frac{S_o^2 - S_e^2}{S_o^2}.$$

Again rearranging,

$$R_{xx} = \frac{S_o^2}{S_o^2} - \frac{S_e^2}{S_o^2}.$$

And simplifying,

$$R_{xx} = 1 - \frac{S_e^2}{S_o^2}. \qquad (5.7)$$

Note that

$$\frac{S_e^2}{S_o^2}$$

represents the proportion of observed score variance that is a function of error variance. Reliability is relatively high when this proportion is relatively small. That is, reliability is high when error variance is small in comparison with observed score variance.

For the data from the original self-esteem questionnaire,

$$R_{xx} = 1 - \frac{316.67}{608.33} = 1 - .52 = .48.$$

Thus, 52% of the variance in respondents' observed scores on the original questionnaire is produced by measurement error, leaving only 48% attributable to true score differences among the respondents.

What would a small degree of error variance indicate? It would indicate that the respondents' scores are being affected only slightly by measurement error. More precisely, it would indicate that the error affecting one person's score is not very different from the error affecting another person's score. We see this in the data for the revised self-esteem questionnaire, where the error scores range only from −15 to +10.

In addition, the standard deviation of error scores on the revised questionnaire is 10.80, indicating that the average person's error score is only about 11 points. In fact, measurement error accounts for only 29% of the variance in observed scores on the revised questionnaire. Contrast this with the data for the original self-esteem questionnaire, where error scores ranged from −15 to 25—a noticeably wider range of scores. In addition, the standard deviation of error scores on the original questionnaire is 17.80, indicating that the average error score is about 18 points. These facts reflect the greater effects of error in the original questionnaire, accounting for fully 52% of the variance in observed scores. Of course, if there is no error variance, then 100% of the observed variance in test scores will be associated with true score variance, and the test will be perfectly reliable.

The (Squared) Correlation Between Observed Scores and True Scores

This chapter began by stating that reliability is the degree to which differences in observed scores are consistent with differences in true scores. In Chapter 3, we saw that the correlation coefficient tells us the degree to which differences in one variable are consistent (i.e., correspond with) with differences in another variable. Thus, reliability can be seen in terms of the (squared) correlation between observed scores and true scores:

$$R_{xx} = r_{ot}^2 .$$ (5.8)

Again, looking at the data in Table 5.1a, we have calculated the correlation between the observed scores and the true score, $r_{ot} = .69$. If we square this value, we get R_{XX}, as demonstrated earlier. The (unsquared) correlation between observed scores and true scores is sometimes called the "index of reliability" (Ghiselli et al., 1981). Please do not let this confuse you. If you square the *index* of reliability, you obtain the *coefficient* of reliability. When people refer to reliability, they typically are referring to the coefficient of reliability (R_{XX}). Only rarely will you hear people refer to the index of reliability (r_{ot}); however, an understanding of their connections should provide deeper insight into the concept of reliability.

For curious readers, we will take a moment to prove algebraically that the squared correlation between observed scores and true scores (r_{ot}^2) equals the ratio of true score variance to observed score variance:

$$\frac{S_t^2}{S_o^2} ,$$

which is the most common way of conceptualizing the reliability coefficient. Recall from Chapter 3 that a correlation can be seen as a covariance divided by the product of 2 standard deviations:

$$r_{XY} = \frac{c_{XY}}{s_X s_Y} .$$

Thus, the correlation between observed scores and true scores is

$$r_{ot} = \frac{c_{ot}}{s_o s_t}.$$ (5.9)

Again, going back to the ideas raised in Chapter 3, the covariance between observed scores and true scores is

$$c_{ot} = \frac{\sum (X_o - \overline{X}_o)(X_t - \overline{X}_t)}{N}.$$ (5.10)

From Equation 5.1, we assume that $X_o = X_t + X_e$. And because the mean error score is assumed to be 0 (i.e., $\overline{X}_e = 0$ as explained above), the mean observed score is equal to the mean true score (i.e., $\overline{X}_o = \overline{X}_t$).

Inserting this and Equation 5.1 into the covariance (Equation 5.10):

$$c_{ot} = \frac{\sum (X_t + X_e - \overline{X}_t)(X_t - \overline{X}_t)}{N}.$$

Algebraically simplifying this equation, we find that the covariance between observed scores and true scores is equal to the sum of (a) the variance in true scores and (b) the covariance between true scores and error scores:

$$c_{ot} = s_t^2 + c_{et}.$$

However, as we explained earlier, we also assume that error scores and true scores are independent, which means that they are not correlated with each other (i.e., $r_{te} = 0$, and therefore $c_{te} = 0$). So the covariance between observed scores and true scores is simply equal to the variance in true scores:

$$c_{ot} = s_t^2.$$ (5.11)

Returning to the correlation between true scores and observed scores (Equation 5.9), we insert Equation 5.11 into the numerator:

$$r_{ot} = \frac{s_t^2}{s_o s_t}.$$

Simplifying this, we find

$$r_{ot} = \frac{s_t}{s_o}.$$

Squaring this, we find that that the squared correlation between observed scores and true scores is exactly equal to the ratio of true score variance to observed score variance:

$$r_{ot}^2 = \frac{s_t^2}{s_o^2}.$$

Thus, reliability can be seen as the squared correlation between observed scores and true scores. A reliability of 1.0 would indicate that the differences among respondents' observed test scores are perfectly consistent with the differences among their true scores. A reliability of .0 would indicate that the differences among respondents' observed test scores are totally inconsistent with the differences among their true scores. In such a case, the test is completely useless as a measure of a psychological characteristic. In practice, reliability is usually in between these two extremes.

Lack of (Squared) Correlation Between Observed Scores and Error Scores

Paralleling the previous ways of conceptualizing reliability, reliability can also be seen as the degree to which observed scores are uncorrelated with error scores. To the degree that differences in observed test scores reflect differences in the effects of error (instead of true scores), the test is unreliable. Thus,

$$R_{xx} = 1 - r_{oe}^2, \tag{5.12}$$

where r_{oe}^2 is the squared correlation between observed scores and error scores.

Once again, the data in Table 5.1a demonstrate this equivalence. We have calculated the correlation between observed scores and error scores ($r_{oe} = .72$). The square of this value is .52, which is equal to the ratio of error variance to observed score variance:

$$\frac{S_e^2}{S_o^2}.$$

As shown earlier, 1 minus this value is equal to the reliability: $R_{XX} = 1 - r_{oe}^2$. Thus, $R_{XX} = 1 - (.72)^2 = 1 - .52 = .48$.

Again for interested readers, we will algebraically show that the squared correlation between observed scores and error scores (r_{oe}^2) equals the ratio of error score variance to observed score variance:

$$\frac{S_e^2}{S_o^2}.$$

The correlation between observed scores and error scores is

$$r_{oe} = \frac{c_{oe}}{s_o s_e} \,.$$ (5.13)

The covariance between observed scores and error scores is

$$c_{oe} = \frac{\sum (X_o - \overline{X}_o)(X_e - \overline{X}_e)}{N} \,.$$ (5.14)

Once again, from Equation 5.1, we assume that $X_o = X_t + X_e$.

And because the mean error score is assumed to be 0 (i.e., $\overline{X}_e = 0$), the mean observed score is equal to the mean true score ($\overline{X}_o = \overline{X}_t$).

Inserting this and Equation 5.1 into the covariance (Equation 5.14):

$$c_{oe} = \frac{\sum (X_t + X_e - \overline{X}_t)(X_e - \overline{X}_e)}{N} \,.$$

Algebraically simplifying this equation, we find that the covariance between observed scores and error scores is equal to the variance of error scores:

$$c_{oe} = s_e^2 \,.$$ (5.15)

Returning to the correlation between error scores and observed scores (Equation 5.13), we insert Equation 5.15 into the numerator of Equation 5.13 to obtain the following:

$$r_{oe} = \frac{s_e^2}{s_o s_e} \,.$$

Simplifying this, we find that

$$r_{oe} = \frac{s_e}{s_o} \,.$$

Squaring this, we find that that the squared correlation between observed scores and error scores is exactly equal to the ratio of error score variance to observed score variance:

$$r_{oe}^2 = \frac{s_e^2}{s_o^2} \,.$$

Thus,

$$R_{xx} = 1 - r_{oe}^2 = 1 - \frac{s_e^2}{s_o^2} \,.$$

Perhaps the best way to think about this is to realize that if the correlation (r_{oe}) between observed scores and error scores is 0, then R_{XX} will equal 1.0. As the correlation of observed scores with error scores increases, the size of R_{XX} will decrease. For example, compare the data in Table 5.1a (the original self-esteem questionnaire) with the data in Table 5.1b (the revised self-esteem questionnaire). For the original questionnaire, the correlation between observed scores and error scores was relatively large ($r_{oe} = .72$), resulting in a relatively low reliability ($R_{XX} = .48$). In contrast, the revised questionnaire produced responses with a smaller correlation between observed scores and error scores ($r_{oe} = .53$), resulting in a higher reliability ($R_{XX} = .71$). Thus, reliability will be relatively strong when observed scores have relatively low correlations with error scores.

Reliability and the Standard Error of Measurement

Although the reliability coefficient is an extremely important piece of psychometric information (for reasons that will become even more apparent in Chapter 7), it does not directly reflect the size of measurement error associated with a test. That is, reliability does not tell us, in test score units, the average size of error scores that we can expect to find when a test is administered to a group of people. As we will see later, the size of measurement error has important applications for interpreting the accuracy of test scores and for computing probabilities of scores in testing and research settings.

Going back to an earlier section in this chapter, we see that the standard deviation of error scores could be a useful way of expressing the amount of error affecting responses to a test. Let us take a moment to think about the error score standard deviations for the two versions of the self-esteem questionnaire represented in Table 5.1. For the original version (Table 5.1a), the error score standard deviation (s_e) is 17.80, which represents the average size of the absolute values of the error scores. In this case, 17.80 tells us that, on average, the respondents' observed scores deviated from their true scores by nearly 18 points. In contrast, the error standard deviation for the revised questionnaire (Table 5.1b) is much smaller. Specifically, it is 10.80, indicating that the respondents' observed scores on the revised questionnaire deviated from their true scores by only about 11 points. Thus, the observed scores on the revised questionnaire are more accurate than the observed scores on the original questionnaire. That is, they suffer weaker effects of error, and thus they are closer to true scores.

The standard deviation of error scores has a special name—the *standard error of measurement* (se_m)—and it is one of the most important concepts in measurement theory. The standard error of measurement represents the average size of the error scores. The larger the standard error of measurement, the greater the average difference between observed scores and true scores and the less reliable the test.

As you might imagine, a test's standard error of measurement is closely linked to its reliability. In fact, as we will see later, we will need to estimate the se_m from an estimate of reliability. We can use reliability (R_{XX}) to find the standard error of measurement (se_m):

$$se_m = s_o\sqrt{1 - R_{xx}}, \qquad (5.16)$$

where s_o is the standard deviation of the observed scores. Looking at the data from Table 5.1a, we see that the standard deviation of the observed scores is 24.66 and the reliability is .48. Thus, the se_m is 17.80:

$$se_m = s_o\sqrt{1 - R_{xx}} = 24.66\sqrt{1 - .48} = 24.66(.72) = 17.80.$$

This value (17.80) is exactly equal to the standard deviation that is computed directly from the error scores (s_e).

For curious readers, we will verify that Equation 5.16 is valid and that our particular example is not by chance. Recall that reliability can be seen as the lack of error variance (see Equation 5.7):

$$R_{xx} = 1 - \frac{s_e^2}{s_o^2}.$$

Rearranging this,

$$\frac{s_e^2}{s_o^2} = 1 - R_{xx},$$

and multiplying by s_o^2,

$$s_e^2 = s_o^2(1 - R_{xx}).$$

Because $s_e^2 = se_m$ and taking the square root, we obtain

$$se_m = s_o\sqrt{1 - R_{xx}}.$$

This shows how the standard error of measurement is related to R_{XX}. Notice that if $R_{XX} = 1$, then $se_m = 0$. That is, if there is no measurement error, then reliability will be perfect. Also, notice that se_m can never be larger than s_o. That is, the standard deviation of error scores will always be less than or equal to the standard deviation of observed scores. To reiterate the more general point, we will soon see that the standard error of measurement is an important psychometric value with implications for applied measurement.

Parallel Tests

If you have been paying close attention, you might be aware of an unpleasant fact. So far, reliability theory has been framed in terms of true scores, error scores, and observed scores. In contrast to the elegant theory of reliability, the practical reality of measurement is (of course) that we have no way of knowing people's true scores on a psychological variable or the error associated with their test responses. Thus, it may appear that there is no way to translate reliability theory into the actual practice of measurement. It may appear that we cannot actually evaluate a test's reliability or its standard error of measurement.

Classical test theorists deal with this problem by making one more assumption. *They assume that two psychological tests can be constructed in such a way that they are "parallel."* Two tests can be considered parallel if all of the previous assumptions from CTT are true for each test and if the following two additional assumptions hold true:

1. Participants' true scores for one test are exactly equal to their true scores on the other test. That is, the two tests measure the same psychological construct (this condition is known as "tau equivalence").

2. The tests have the same level of error variance.

A consequence of these fundamental assumptions is that the observed scores on the tests will have the same mean and the observed scores on the tests will have the same standard deviation.

The idea of parallel tests is important because it begins to transition from theoretic concepts such as true scores and measurement error to the practical need to estimate a test's reliability. If two tests are parallel, then we will be able to compute a reliability coefficient and a standard error of measurement from their observed scores.

Imagine that you have two questionnaires that you think are measures of self-esteem—call them X and Y—and that you ask a group of people to take both tests. If the questionnaires both measure the same psychological construct (presumably self-esteem in this case) and if they have the same error variance (i.e., $s_{Xe} = s_{Ye}$), then X and Y are parallel tests. Notice that the hypothetical self-esteem questionnaires presented in Tables 5.1a and b are *not* parallel. Although their true scores are the same (i.e., they are measuring the same construct) and their observed means are identical, they have different error variances, which creates differences in the standard deviations of their observed scores. Thus, they fail to meet one of the assumptions for parallel tests.

However, if two tests—X and Y—are parallel, then we can compute the correlation in the usual way between the scores on the two tests. For example, if 100 people take tests X and Y, then each person will have two scores, and we can calculate the correlation between the observed test scores using the correlation coefficient described in Chapter 3 (r_{XY}).

According to CTT, *the correlation between parallel tests is equal to reliability.* That is, if we can reasonably assume that the two tests are parallel, then their correlation is, in fact, equal to the reliability of both tests.

Again to demonstrate the validity of this assertion, we can show that r_{XY} equals R_{XX} given the assumptions of CTT. First, based on the definition of a correlation (see Equation 3.5 in Chapter 3), the correlation between the observed scores on the two tests is the covariance between the tests divided by the product of the standard deviations of their observed scores:

$$r_{XoYo} = \frac{c_{XoYo}}{s_{Xo}s_{Yo}}.$$

If the two tests are parallel, then by definition, their observed scores have equal standard deviations (i.e., if $s_{Xe} = s_{Ye}$, then $s_{Xo} = s_{Yo}$, which we simply call s_o). Thus,

$$r_{XoYo} = \frac{c_{XoYo}}{s_o s_o} = \frac{c_{XoYo}}{s_o^2}.$$

Recalling that the definition of an observed score is $X_o = X_t + X_e$ (see Equation 5.1), the observed scores can be seen as composite variables. As described in Chapter 3, a composite score (or composite variable) is a score that's obtained by summing or averaging more than one component (e.g., by summing responses to multiple items on a questionnaire). Therefore, the covariance between the tests' observed scores is a covariance between composite variables. Furthermore, the covariance between two composite variables is the sum of the covariances between the components within the composite variables (see Equation 3.7). In the context of observed scores from the two tests, the correlation is as follows:

$$r_{XoYo} = \frac{c_{XtYt} + c_{XtYe} + c_{XeYt} + c_{XYe}}{s_o^2},$$

where c_{XtYt} is the covariance between true scores on Test X and true scores on Test Y, c_{XtYe} is the covariance between true scores on Test X and error scores on Test Y, c_{XeYt} is the covariance between error scores on Test X and true scores on Test Y, and c_{XeYe} is the covariance between error scores on Test X and error scores on Test Y.

As discussed earlier in this chapter, CTT assumes that error scores occur as if they are random. Therefore, error scores are uncorrelated with true scores. In addition, error scores on Test X are uncorrelated with error scores on Test Y. Consequently, the three covariances that include error scores (c_{XtYe}, c_{XeYt}, and c_{XeYe}) are all equal to 0, so that the correlation between parallel tests is simply

$$r_{XoYo} = \frac{c_{XtYt}}{s_o^2}.$$

Finally, recall that tests are parallel only if respondents' true scores are equal across the tests (i.e., each respondent's $X_t = Y_t$). If this assumption is valid, then the covariance between the true scores equals the variance of true scores (i.e., $c_{XtYt} = s_t^2$). This derives from the fact that a variance can be seen as the covariance between a variable and itself. Therefore, replacing the numerator in the previous equation, the correlation between parallel tests is

$$r_{XoYo} = \frac{s_t^2}{s_o^2}.$$

That is, the correlation between scores on parallel tests is equal to the ratio of true score variance to observed score variance, which is a definition of reliability (R_{XX}; see Equation 5.5).

Our discussion of parallel tests has important implications for the real world of testing. Specifically, the parallel test assumption will be crucial in Chapter 6, where we discuss the procedures used to estimate the reliability in real-life testing situations.

Domain Sampling Theory

Domain sampling theory of reliability was developed in the 1950s as an alternative to CTT (Ghiselli et al., 1981), in that both approaches arrive at the same place regarding procedures for calculating reliability, but they arrive there from different directions. For example, in CTT, the practical examination of reliability rests on the assumption that it would be possible to create two tests that are at a minimum parallel to each other. In domain sampling theory, you do not have to make this assumption, but if you follow the logic of the theory, you will end up with parallel tests by *fiat*.

Domain sampling theory rests on the assumption that items on any particular test represent a sample from a large indefinite number or domain of potential test items. Responses to each of these items are thought to be a function of the same psychological attribute. For example, suppose you had a test of self-esteem with 10 questions. Differences in responses to each of these 10 questions should be related to differences in self-esteem among the people taking the test. Up until this point, these ideas are consistent with CTT. However, domain sampling theory adds the view that the particular items on the test can be seen as a random sample from a "population" or "domain" of similar items, each of which is an equally good measure of self-esteem.

From this perspective, imagine that you created a test by selecting a set of N items at random from a domain of items. You then created a second test by selecting another set of N items (the same number of items but different items) at random from the same domain. In the long run, these two tests should have the same mean and standard deviation. In other words, on average, all test pairs selected in this fashion should be parallel to each other. If you have two parallel tests, then the test scores should correlate strongly with each other. Moreover, the extent to which the two parallel tests do not correlate strongly with each other is due to item sampling error. From this perspective, reliability is the average size of the correlations among all possible pairs of tests with N items selected from a domain of test items. The logic of domain sampling theory is the basis for a contemporary approach to reliability called generalizability theory. We will explore this in greater detail in Chapter 13.

Summary

In this chapter, we have examined the theory of reliability from the perspective of CTT. Although there are other perspectives on reliability, CTT is the most well-known, and it serves as the basis for many psychometric evaluations of psychological measures.

CTT rests on a few fundamental assumptions about test scores and the factors that affect them. As we have described, CTT is based on the assumption that observed scores on a test are a simple additive function of true scores and measurement error (i.e., $X_o = X_t + X_e$). In addition, CTT rests on the assumption that measurement error occurs as if it is random. The randomness assumption has several implications—for example, error is uncorrelated with true scores, error averages to 0, and error on one test is uncorrelated with error on another test.

These assumptions have important implications for the nature of variability among test scores. As this book has emphasized, the meaning of psychological measurements is tied closely to the need to detect and quantify differences among people. Thus, variability among observed scores is the sum of true score variability and error variability. That is, the differences among people's observed scores arise from differences in their true scores and differences in the degree to which error affects their responses.

From this perspective, reliability reflects the links between observed scores, true scores, and error. As we have discussed, there are at least four ways to conceptualize reliability. Reliability can be seen in terms of variance. It is the ratio of true score variance to observed score variance, and it can also be seen as a lack of error variance. That is, reliability is high when the differences among participants' observed scores primarily reflect the differences among their true scores. Reliability can also be seen in terms of consistency and correlations. It is the degree to which observed scores are correlated with true scores, and it can be seen as the degree to which observed scores are uncorrelated with error scores. That is, reliability is high when the differences among participants' observed scores are consistent with the differences among their true scores.

This chapter also discussed the standard error of measurement and the notion of parallel tests. These two concepts, which emerge from CTT, will be important tools when we translate the theory of reliability into the practice of psychometric evaluation of real-test data.

Indeed, this chapter has focused on the theoretical basis of reliability. To illustrate the rather technical concepts, we have pretended to be omniscient, knowing respondents' true scores and the nature of error that affected each score. Of course, we will not know such things when we work with real test responses. Therefore, we can never really know the reliability of a test (just as we can never really know an individual's level of self-esteem). However, the notion of parallel tests will allow us to actually estimate test reliability with real data. Chapter 6 describes these estimation processes.

Suggested Readings

The classic in the development of classical test theory:

Gulliksen, H. (1950). *Theory of mental tests.* New York, NY: Wiley.

For a detailed discussion of domain sampling theory:

Ghiselli, E. E., Campbell, J. P., & Zedeck, S. (1981). *Measurement theory for the behavioral sciences.* San Francisco, CA: W. H. Freeman.

Empirical Estimates of Reliability

In Chapter 5, we described the conceptual basis of reliability. As we acknowledged, though, there is a gap between the theory of reliability and the practical examination of reliability in behavioral measurement. Indeed, as we had discussed, reliability is a theoretical property of a test and cannot be computed directly. It is defined in terms of true scores and measurement error, which we cannot ever actually know. Thus, it can only be estimated from real data. In this chapter, we will show that, given the assumptions of classical test theory (CTT), observed (empirical) test scores can be used to *estimate* score reliabilities and measurement error.

There are at least three methods for estimating reliability. All three methods emerge from the notion of parallel tests, as discussed in the previous chapter. The estimates that these methods provide can be interpreted as described in the discussion of reliability in the previous chapter (e.g., as the proportion of observed score variance that is attributable to true score variance). However, the three methods differ in terms of the kind of data that are available and in the assumptions on which they rest.

In this chapter, we outline these methods, providing examples and interpretations of each. This information is important because it allows test developers and test users to examine the reliability of their tests. This is a "practical" chapter, in that it presents a "how-to" for the real-world examination of reliability. In the next chapter, we extend this discussion by detailing the implications of reliability for behavioral research, applied behavioral practice, and test development.

An important initial observation is that there is no single method that provides completely accurate estimates of reliability under all conditions. As we will discuss, the accuracy of these methods depends heavily on a variety of assumptions about the participants and the testing procedures. If these assumptions are not valid, then the reliability estimates will not be totally accurate. Indeed, data sometimes clearly imply that one or more assumptions are, in fact, not valid. In such cases, we might need to consider an alternate method for estimating reliability, or we might simply need to acknowledge the fact that our estimate of the test's reliability might not be very accurate.

In addition to discussing basic methods of estimating the reliability of test scores, we examine the reliability of "difference scores," which can be used to study phenomena such as cognitive growth, symptom reduction, personality change, person–environment fit, overconfidence, and the accuracy of first impressions. Despite their intuitive appeal, difference scores are notorious for poor psychometric quality—although this reputation might be a bit undeserved (Rogosa, 1995).

Alternate Forms Reliability

Alternate forms reliability (sometimes called parallel forms reliability) is one of the methods for estimating the reliability of test scores. By obtaining scores from two different forms of a test, test users can compute the correlation between the two forms and may be able to interpret the correlation as an estimate of the test's reliability. To the degree that differences in the observed scores from one form are consistent with differences in the observed scores from another form, the test is reliable.

The ability to interpret the correlation between alternate forms as an estimate of reliability is appropriate *only if the two test forms are parallel* (see Chapter 5). You might recall that two tests are considered parallel only if (a) they are measuring the same set of true scores and (b) they have the same amount of error variance. In addition, you should recall that the correlation between two parallel tests is exactly equal to the reliability of the test scores.

Despite the theoretical logic of parallel tests and the statistical foundations linking parallel tests to reliability, there is a serious practical problem. Specifically, we can never be entirely confident that alternate forms of a test are truly parallel in the theoretical sense. This lack of confidence occurs because we can never truly know whether two forms of a test meet the very strict assumptions of CTT and of parallel tests.

The main problem is that, in reality, we can never be certain that scores on alternate forms of a test are measures of the same psychological attribute. More specifically, we can never be sure that the true scores as measured by the first form of a test are equal to the true scores as measured by the second form of the test. This problem arises in part because different forms will, by definition, include different content. Because of differing content, the different forms might not assess the same psychological construct. For example, we might generate two forms of a self-esteem test, and we would like to assume that they are parallel. However, the content of the first form includes several items regarding self-esteem in relation to other people, but the second form includes only one such item. In such a case, the two forms of the test might actually be assessing slightly different psychological constructs (i.e., a socially derived self-esteem vs. a nonsocial self-esteem). Therefore, the respondents' true scores on the first form are not strictly equal to their true scores on the second form, and the two forms are not truly parallel. It follows that if two forms are not parallel, then the correlation between the two is not a good estimate of reliability.

A more subtle problem with alternate forms of tests is the potential for carryover or contamination effects due to repeated testing. It is possible that the act of taking one form of a test has an effect on performance on the second form of a test— respondents' memory for test content, their attitudes, or their immediate mood states might affect test performance across both forms of the test. Such effects could mean that error scores on one form are correlated with error scores on the second form. Recall that a fundamental assumption of CTT is that the error affecting any test is random. An implication of the randomness assumption is that error scores on one test are uncorrelated with error scores on a second test. However, if two forms of a test are completed simultaneously, then some of the error affecting responses to one form might carry over and also affect responses to the other form. This would violate a fundamental assumption of CTT, and it would mean that the two forms are not truly parallel tests.

Table 6.1 presents a hypothetical example illustrating the carryover problem. Imagine that six people respond to two forms of a test. Table 6.1 presents their observed scores on the two forms, along with their true scores and their error scores (as always, we must pretend to be omniscient when we imagine that we know participants' true scores and error). Notice first that the two forms meet several assumptions of CTT, in general, and of parallel tests, in particular. For example, each observed score is an additive function of true scores and error scores (i.e., $X_o = X_t + X_e$). In addition, the true scores are completely identical across the two forms, the error scores sum to 0 for each form, the true scores are uncorrelated with error scores, and the error variances are equal for the two forms (i.e., $s_e^2 = 4.67$ for both forms). As shown in Table 6.1, these qualities ensure that the two forms are equally reliable—for both forms, the ratio of true score variance to observed score variance is $R_{XX} = .38$. Thus, in our omniscient state, we know that the reliability of both tests is in fact .38, which is considerably lower than we would like it to be. If all of the assumptions of CTT and parallel tests hold true for these data, then the correlation between the two forms' observed scores should be exactly equal to .38.

Unfortunately, the data in Table 6.1 violate a fundamental assumption about the nature of error scores. Again, error scores are assumed to affect tests as if they are random, which implies that the error scores from the two forms should be uncorrelated with each other. In fact, the two sets of error scores in Table 6.1 are very strongly correlated ($r_{e1e2} = .93$). As mentioned earlier, this correlation could emerge from carryover effects, such as mood state or memory. If any such element of measurement error remains relatively stable across the two forms, then it will ensure that the two sets of error scores are positively correlated with each other. The fact that the two sets of error scores are correlated with each other, in turn, influences the correlation between the two sets of observed scores. Indeed, note that the correlation between the observed scores from the two forms is quite strong ($r_{o1o2} = .96$). Thus, the correlation between the alternate forms in this example is grossly inaccurate as an estimate of the reliability of the test, which our omniscience reveals to be .38. The test user in this example, who is unaware of

Table 6.1 Example of Carryover Effects on Alternate Forms Estimate of Reliability

	Form 1			Form 2		
Participant	Observed Score (X_{o1})	True Score $= (X_{t1})$	Error $+ (X_{e1})$	Observed Score (X_{o2})	True Score $= (X_{t2})$	Error $+ (X_{e2})$
1	14	= 15	+ −1	13	= 15	+ −2
2	17	= 14	+ 3	17	= 14	+ 3
3	11	= 13	+ −2	12	= 13	+ −1
4	10	= 12	+ −2	11	= 12	+ −1
5	14	= 11	+ 3	14	= 11	+ 3
6	9	= 10	+ −1	8	= 10	+ −2
Mean	12.5	= 12.5	0	12.5	= 12.5	0
Variance	7.58	= 2.92	4.67	7.58 =	2.92	4.67

Reliability for Form 1 　　　　　 Reliability for Form 2

$$R_{XX} = \frac{2.92}{7.58} = .38 \qquad\qquad R_{XX} = \frac{2.92}{7.58} = .38$$

$$r_{t1e1} = .00$$
$$r_{t2e2} = .00$$
$$r_{t1e2} = .00$$
$$r_{t2e1} = .00$$
$$r_{e1e2} = .93$$

Alternate forms correlation

$$r_{o1o2} = .96$$

[handwritten margin note: Assumptions of parallel test: − true scores are = − error variance are =]

the potential problems with alternate forms, could dramatically overestimate the reliability of the test.

Although we can never be certain that two test forms are truly parallel, it is sometimes possible to have two test forms that seem to fit several criteria for being parallel. As described in Chapter 5, a consequence of two assumptions of parallel tests (i.e., the true scores are the same, and the error variance is the same) is that parallel tests will have identical observed score means and standard deviations. If we have two test forms that have similar means and standard deviations, and if we feel fairly confident in assuming that they are measuring the same construct, then we might feel that the forms are "close enough" to meeting the criteria for being parallel. If we feel that the two forms are close enough to being parallel, then we might feel comfortable computing the correlation between the test forms and using it as an estimate of reliability. Under these circumstances, we would have a form of reliability known as *alternate forms* reliability.

[handwritten margin note: − same construct − similar means − similar standard deviations]

Test–Retest Reliability

The test–retest method of estimating reliability avoids some problems with the alternate forms method, and it is potentially quite useful for measures of stable psychological constructs, such as intelligence or extraversion. As mentioned, an important concern about the alternate forms method of estimating reliability is that alternate forms of a test have different content and therefore might actually measure different constructs. This would violate an important assumption about parallel tests, thereby invalidating the use of the correlation between forms as an estimate of reliability. Another approach is to have the same people take the same test on more than one occasion (i.e., a first test occasion and a "retest" occasion). If you can safely make several assumptions, then the correlation between the first test scores and the retest scores can be interpreted as an estimate of the test's reliability.

The test–retest method is similar to the alternate forms method in that its applicability rests on many of the same assumptions. As was discussed earlier in the context of alternate forms of reliability, the first assumption is that the participants' true scores are stable across the two testing occasions. That is, you must be confident that the respondents' true scores do not change from the first time they take the test to the second time. We must be able to assume that the participants who had the highest true scores at the first assessment are the same participants with the highest true trait levels at the second assessment. The second assumption that must be made is that the error variance of the first test is equal to the error variance of the second test. Among other implications, these two assumptions essentially mean that the two testing occasions produce scores that are equally reliable. If these assumptions are legitimate, then the correlation between scores from the two test administrations is an estimate of the score's reliability.

Let us consider the confidence that we might have in these two assumptions. Beginning with the second assumption (i.e., the equality of error variances), it is likely that this assumption is not unreasonable, if care is taken in the testing process. Recall that measurement error (and thus error variance) is strongly affected by temporary elements within the immediate testing situation—noise, distractions, the presence or absence of other people, and so on. Such elements of the testing situation can affect responses in apparently random ways that might mask the differences among respondents' true scores. However, under the right circumstances, you could create two testing situations that are reasonably comparable with each other. If you carefully set up the testing situations, controlling for the many extraneous variables that might affect test scores, then you might have confidence that the two testing situations are identical. For example, you could have participants complete both tests in the same room, during approximately the same time of day, and in the same interpersonal context (i.e., in a large group, a small group, or alone). By holding such elements constant across testing occasions, you might have reasonable confidence that responses are affected by error to the same degree.

It might be more difficult, however, to be confident in the first assumption—that the true scores of people taking your test are stable during the time interval between the first and second tests. Although the test–retest procedure avoids the problem of differing content that arises with the alternate forms procedure, another problem arises. Specifically, we must assume that participants' true scores have remained completely stable across the two testings, but it is quite possible that there have been changes in the respondents' levels of the psychological attribute (and thus changes in their true scores). In fact, there are at least three factors affecting our confidence in the stability assumption.

First, some psychological attributes are likely to be less stable than others. Attributes that reflect more transient or statelike characteristics are less stable than constructs that reflect more traitlike characteristics. For example, assume that you have a test of mood states—an individual's level of mood at an exact moment in time. Generally, mood state is considered to be a psychological attribute that can fluctuate from day to day, hour to hour, or even moment to moment. Thus, it would probably not make sense to assume that a person's true score on a mood state test is stable during a test–retest interval of any significant length. Furthermore, changes in mood state are likely to result from various factors affecting mood swings in different ways for different people. For example, during the test–retest interval, one person might experience physical distress of some kind, which depresses that person's mood. In contrast, another person might learn that he or she has won an award, which elevates that person's mood. As a result, the individuals' mood states during the first assessment might be quite different from their mood states during the second assessment. That is, the differences among their true construct levels are not stable across the two testings. For such statelike constructs, the test–retest method provides a poor estimate of test reliability. Notice that the mood test might be quite reliable in the sense that differences in observed test scores at any single testing occasion accurately reflect differences in true score at that occasion. However, the test–retest method might provide a very low estimate of reliability because moods have changed across the two testing occasions.

On the other hand, the test–retest procedure is likely to provide reasonable estimates of reliability for a measure of traitlike psychological attributes. For example, intelligence is generally conceived as a stable psychological characteristic. There is good theoretical rationale and strong empirical evidence suggesting that intelligence is highly stable from middle childhood through adulthood. In this case, it might be reasonable to assume that true scores do not change during a test–retest interval. If this assumption is correct, then changes in observed scores across two testings will represent measurement error, which will be reflected by the size of the test–retest reliability coefficient.

A second factor affecting our confidence in the stability assumption is the length of the test–retest interval. Longer intervals are likely to open the door to greater psychological change. True scores are more likely to change across a period of years than across a period of weeks or days. Although test–retest analyses have been conducted across periods that span years, such analyses run the risk of confounding changes in true scores with measurement error. On the other hand, short intervals might suffer from carryover effects or contamination effects, as described in the section "Alternate Forms Reliability." In our experience, many test–retest analyses of traitlike measures seem to be conducted over a period of 2 to 8 weeks.

A third factor that might affect our confidence in the stability assumption is the period at which the interval occurs. It is possible that change is more likely to occur at some periods in an individual's life than at other periods. For example, change in cognitive skills and knowledge might be more likely to occur during the school-age period than at a later period in one's life. In children, constructs such as reading skill, math skill, and knowledge in some area are likely to change as a result of schooling during a test–retest interval. Some children increase their skills and knowledge to a greater degree than others. These kinds of changes—where people's true scores change at different rates—violate an important assumption of parallel tests (and they violate the assumptions of other theoretical models that are even less restrictive than the parallel test model). Consequently, such changes impair the use of the test–retest correlation as an estimate of reliability.

To summarize, the test–retest approach to reliability depends heavily on the assumption that true scores remain stable across the test–retest interval. For this reason, a test–retest correlation coefficient is sometimes referred to as a stability coefficient. If true scores are completely stable during the test–retest interval (or at least if the differences among participants' true scores remain stable), then the test–retest correlation reflects only one thing: the degree to which measurement error affects test scores. That is, if true scores are perfectly stable, then an imperfect correlation between observed scores (i.e., a correlation that is less than 1.0) indicates the degree to which measurement error affects the observed scores. The lower the test–retest correlation, the greater the effect of measurement error and the lower the reliability of the test.

The difficulty is that we can never know the degree to which true scores actually remain stable. The three issues discussed above can make us more or less confident that true scores remain stable, but we can never be sure that true scores are in fact stable between testings.

Moreover, if true scores change during the test–retest interval, then the test–retest correlation reflects two independent factors: (1) the degree to which measurement error affects the test and (2) the amount of change in true scores. Using a simple correlational approach, these two factors cannot be separated. In such a case, an imperfect correlation between observed scores (i.e., a correlation that is less than 1.0) indicates the combined effect of measurement error *and* true score instability. In fact, it is theoretically possible (though not very realistic) that a test could be perfectly reliable but have a low test–retest correlation. This would occur if true scores are unstable across the test–retest interval. Obviously, in such a case, the test–retest correlation would be a poor estimate of the test's reliability. The bottom line is that test–retest correlations should be interpreted carefully, with regard to reliability and to the likely stability of the underlying construct.

Although the alternate forms and test–retest approaches have solid theoretical foundations as methods for estimating reliability, they suffer from several practical difficulties, as we have seen. For example, they require that at least two tests be given to the people being tested, but such repeated testings can be expensive, time-consuming, and difficult or even impossible to conduct. In addition, as we just pointed out, several assumptions must be made if you are to interpret the correlation between tests obtained from these procedures as good estimates of test reliability. Unfortunately, these assumptions might not be valid in some, or perhaps many, cases. Therefore, the alternate forms method and the test–retest method have somewhat limited applicability.

Internal Consistency Reliability

A third approach to estimating reliability is through *internal consistency*, which offers a useful practical alternative to the alternate forms procedure and the test–retest procedure. The internal consistency approach has the practical advantage of requiring respondents to complete only one test at only one point in time. There is no need to create more than one form of a test, and there is no need to require that participants complete a test on more than one occasion. Obviously, this can simplify the process of evaluating reliability considerably, and it might avoid some thorny issues regarding the validity of various assumptions.

The internal consistency approach to estimated reliability can be used for composite test scores. As we mentioned in Chapter 3, if a test includes multiple items and if the test's scores are computed from the responses to those items, then the test score is called a composite score. We mentioned also that most psychological tests are of this kind and most test scores are composite scores. Internal consistency approaches are applicable for estimating the reliability of such multiple-item tests.

The fundamental idea behind the internal consistency approach is that the different "parts" of a test (i.e., items or groups of items) can be treated as different forms of a test. In many areas of behavioral science, the internal consistency approach is the most widely used method for estimating reliability. In this section, we review several ways of estimating reliability by using an internal consistency approach.

From the perspective of internal consistency, there are two fundamental factors that affect the reliability of test scores. The first is the consistency among the parts of a test. As we shall see, if a test's parts are strongly correlated with each other, then the test is likely to be reliable. That is, if the observed differences on one part of the test (e.g., an item) are consistent with the observed differences on the other parts of the test (e.g., other items), then we are likely to conclude that the observed scores on the test as a whole are consistent with the true scores. The second factor that affects a test's reliability is the test's length—a long test is likely to be more reliable than a short test. As we shall see, this arises from the nature of measurement error and its link to reliability. We will discuss three well-known approaches to the internal consistency method of estimating reliability—(1) the split-half approach, (2) the "raw alpha" approach, and (3) the "standardized alpha" approach.

Split-Half Estimates of Reliability

If you could sort a test's items into two parallel subtests of equal size, then you could compute a score for each subtest and correlate those two scores. In effect, you would have created two parallel tests from the items within a single test. It is possible to use these subtest scores to compute an estimate of total test reliability. Because it is based on splitting a test into two separate parts, this type of reliability is known as *split-half reliability*.

Consider the small data set shown in Table 6.2, reflecting the hypothetical responses of four persons to a four-item test. Although these data do not conform to all the relevant assumptions (which we will discuss later), they should provide an

Table 6.2   Example for Internal Consistency Method of Estimating Reliability

Subtest Persons	Items 1	2	3	4	Total Score	Split-Half 1 "Odd" Subtest	"Even" Subtest	Split-Half 2 Subtest 1 and 4	Subtest 2 and 3
1	4	4	5	4	17	9	8	8	9
2	5	2	4	2	13	9	4	7	6
3	5	4	2	2	13	7	6	7	6
4	2	3	1	2	8	3	5	4	4
Mean	4	3.25	3	2.5	12.75	7	5.75	6.5	6.25
Variance	1.5	0.6875	2.5	.75	10.1875	6	2.1875	2.25	3.1875

intuitive example of the split-half method. This procedure can be seen as a three-step process.

In the first step, we create two subtest scores. For example, we might create one subtest by summing the odd items and another subtest by summing the even items. The two subtest scores are presented in Table 6.2 in the column labeled "Split-Half 1."

In the second step of the process, we compute the correlation between the two subtests. If the test is reliable, then we should find that respondents' scores on the "odd" half of the test are consistent with their scores on the "even" half of the test. In these data, the correlation between these halves is $r_{hh} = .276$ (we will call this the "split-half correlation"). The split-half correlation reflects the degree to which the two parts of the test are consistent with each other.

In the third step of the process, we enter the split-half correlation into a specialized formula to compute the reliability estimate. Many formulas for computing internal consistency estimates of reliability were developed by Charles Spearman (the father of the true score theory of reliability) and William Brown. The formulas go by different names—the Spearman-Brown split-half formula, the Spearman-Brown prophecy formula, and the Spearman-Brown formula—and are expressed in different forms. The most common form used to estimate reliability in the split-half procedure is

$$R_{XX} = \frac{2r_{hh}}{1+r_{hh}} . \tag{6.1}$$

For our example, we enter the split-half correlation into the equation, which gives us a reliability estimate of $R_{XX} = .43$:

$$R_{XX} = \frac{2(.276)}{1+.276} = \frac{.552}{1.276} = .433 .$$

Take a moment to consider why we cannot simply use the split-half correlation itself as the estimate of reliability. After all, according to the alternate forms approach and the test–retest approach, the correlation itself (i.e., between two forms or between two testings) is used as the estimate of reliability. However, for the split-half approach, we must enter the split-half correlation into a special formula to obtain the estimate of reliability. The difference between the approaches is that the split-half correlation represents the reliability of only "half" of our test. Recall that the alternate forms approach and the test–retest approach required that the full test be completed twice—respondents either complete two forms of the full test or they complete the full test itself twice. Thus, the alternate forms correlation and the test–retest correlation are correlations between two versions of the complete test. In contrast, the split-half correlation is the correlation between two halves of the test. Equation 6.1 is designed to take the correlation between the two halves of a test and "step up" to an estimate of the reliability of the complete test.

Because it is based on a correlation derived from within the test itself, the split-half reliability estimate is called an internal consistency estimate of reliability. The premise is that if items on a test are similar to each other, then splitting the test into two parts in an appropriate way (this usually involves a procedure that is thought to produce a random assortment of items) should produce two parallel subtests.

Unfortunately, the adequacy of the split-half approach once again rests on the assumption that the two halves are parallel tests. That is, the halves must have equal true scores and equal error variance. As we have discussed, if the assumptions of CTT and parallel tests are all true, then the two halves should have equal means and equal variances. You will note that the odd and even halves that we computed for the data in Table 6.2 do not seem to meet the assumption that they are parallel to each other (i.e., they clearly have different means and standard deviations). Because these two halves are not parallel tests, the split-half reliability estimate that we computed ($R_{XX} = .43$) might be an inaccurate estimate of reliability.

Indeed, we could split the data in Table 6.2 in a different way and obtain a dramatically different estimate of reliability. For example, we could create the two halves by summing Item 1 and Item 4 and by summing Item 2 and Item 3. These two halves are presented in Table 6.2 in the column labeled "Split-Half 2." Computing the correlation between these two halves, we obtain a much larger split-half correlation ($r_{hh} = .89$) than we did with the odd and even halves. Entering this value into Equation 6.1, we obtain a reliability estimate of $R_{XX} = .94$:

$$R_{XX} = \frac{2(.89)}{1+.89} = .94 \ .$$

Obviously, when the halves of a test do not meet the criteria for being "parallel," our estimate of reliability can differ substantially depending on the way we have formed the halves. In our example, one "split" led to a very low estimate of reliability for the test ($R_{XX} = .43$), but another split led to a very high estimate of reliability for the test ($R_{XX} = .94$). The problem is even more extreme for long tests, for which there are many ways in which a test could be split into halves, with each way potentially producing a different estimate of reliability. Furthermore, there is no single way of splitting a test that will produce the most accurate estimate of reliability. For these reasons, split-half reliability is not used frequently in contemporary psychometrics.

Although it is not used often in contemporary psychometric analysis, split-half reliability is easily obtained from some statistical software. For example, SPSS has a "Reliability Analysis" procedure that will quickly conduct a split-half analysis of a test's items. Using the drop-down menus, the Reliability Analysis can be found under the Scale option in the Analyze menu. You can select the test's items, putting them in the order that you would like them to be split into halves. For example, to examine the first split-half analysis discussed earlier, we first selected Items 1 and 3 and then selected Items 2 and 4. We then chose "Split Half" from among the "Model" options, and we obtained the results in Figure 6.1. For our immediate purposes, the "Correlation Between Forms" value (.276) and the "Spearman-Brown Coefficient" values (.433) reflect the split-half correlation and estimated reliability values, respectively.

One problem associated with all internal consistency measures of reliability, such as split-half reliability, has to do with the distinction between power tests and speeded tests that we discussed in Chapter 1. You will recall that a power test will include a variety of questions with different levels of difficulty. In most cases, people taking these types of tests will have adequate time to try to answer each of the questions on the test. Each person taking such a test will have a test score that reflects the number of correct responses made on the test. Most multiple-choice tests given in classroom situations are of this sort. Speeded tests, on the other hand, are usually composed of a series of *equally difficult questions*. Respondents are given a limited period of time to answer as many of the test questions as possible. It is generally assumed that each attempted answer will be correct. A score on a speeded test will reflect the number of items answered correctly during the allotted period

Reliability Statistics

Cronbach's Alpha	Part 1	Value	.667
		N of Items	2[a]
	Part 2	Value	.686
		N of Items	2[b]
	Total N of Items		4
Correlation Between Forms			.276
Spearman-Brown Coefficient	Equal Length		.433
	Unequal Length		.433
Guttman Split-Half Coefficient			.393

[a.] The items are: Item 1, Item 3.
[b.] The items are: Item 4, Item 2.

Figure 6.1 SPSS Output From Split-Half Reliability Analysis of the Data in Table 6.2

of time for taking the test. If you split a speeded test in half and calculate the number of correct responses for each respondent on each half, the test reliability would be close to perfect. In this case, the reliability of the test would reflect the reliability of respondents' response speeds; that is, there is no reason to imagine that respondents' response speed to any one question should differ from their correct response speed to any other question. By way of illustration, suppose that a person takes a speeded test and is able to answer correctly 10 questions during the test period. If you were to split the test in half in such a way that any test item had an equally likely chance of ending up in either half, then 5 of the 10 items that the person answered correctly should end up in each half. Given that each of these questions is of equal difficulty, the amount of time it takes the respondent to answer the 5 questions on one half of the test should be about the same as the amount of time it takes that person to answer the 5 questions on the other half of the test. Because split-half reliabilities calculated for speeded tests are almost always near 1.0, other types of reliability measures, such as alternate forms reliability, are generally used to assess the reliability of speeded tests.

Even though the split-half procedure might not be widely used, we believe that students of psychometrics should be familiar with the procedure. This is because the procedure is historically important, because you are likely to hear people make reference to it, and because it sets the stage for our discussion of an approach that is much more commonly used.

Although split-half reliabilities are sometimes still reported (e.g., Wechsler, 2003a, 2003b), other methods for computing internal consistency estimates of reliability have been developed. As we shall see, the other methods have at least two advantages over the split-half method. First, they use more information about the test than is used by the split-half method. Second, they require fewer assumptions about the statistical properties of the items than do split-half methods.

"Raw" Coefficient Alpha

The split-half approach is based on the perspective that the two halves within a test represent parallel subtests, with a reliability estimate emerging from the associations between the two subtests. In contrast, "item-level" approaches take the logic of internal consistency a step further by conceiving of each item as a subtest. Consequently, the associations among all of the items can be used to estimate the reliability of the complete test.

From the item-level perspective, a variety of approaches can be used to compute reliability estimates. These approaches differ in their applicability to different response formats (i.e., binary items vs. nonbinary items), in their applicability to data that meet different assumptions (i.e., parallel tests vs. a more relaxed set of assumptions), and in the use of different forms of data (i.e., item variances, interitem covariances, or interitem correlations).

The item-level internal consistency approaches can all be seen as two-step processes. In the first step, item-level and/or test-level statistics are calculated. As mentioned earlier, different approaches use different kinds of information. Some approaches are based primarily on the associations among the items, but others use both item-level information and information about scores on the complete test. In the second step, the item-level and/or test-level information is entered into specialized equations to estimate the reliability of the complete test.

We will begin with "raw" coefficient alpha (often called Cronbach's α), which is the most widely used method for estimating reliability. The first step in computing α is to obtain a set of item-level statistics. We first calculate the variance of scores on the complete test (s_X^2) Using the hypothetical data for the four-item test discussed in the split-half reliability section (see Table 6.2), (s_X^2) = 10.1875. Next, we calculate the covariance between each pair of items (recall that a covariance reflects the degree of association between two variables). Here is the matrix of covariances among the four items:

	Item 1	Item 2	Item 3	Item 4
Item 1		0.00	1.00	0.00
Item 2	0.00		0.00	0.38
Item 3	1.00	0.00		1.00
Item 4	0.00	0.38	1.00	

If we take a moment to examine these covariances, we see a potential problem for the internal consistency of the test—several covariances are 0. For example, scores for Item 1 are unrelated to scores on Item 2, indicating an inconsistency. That is, the differences among participants' responses to Item 1 are inconsistent with the differences among their responses to Item 2. If these two items were good measures of the same construct, then they should have a positive covariance. So either the items do not measure the same construct or at least one of them is heavily affected by measurement error (e.g., perhaps Item 1 has very ambiguous phrasing, which leads people to respond in ways that are unrelated to their true scores). For a test that is supposed to be measuring a single construct, we would hope to find that all of the items within the test positively covary with each other (i.e., are correlated with each other) to some degree. Thus, the covariances in Table 6.2 are somewhat disappointing, indicating that the four-item test has some problems.

After computing the covariances among all pairs of items (i.e., all "pairwise" covariances), we sum them. The sum of the interitem covariances reflects the degree to which responses to all of the items are *generally* consistent with each other. All else being equal, the larger this sum is, the more consistent the items are with each other. The sum of these covariances can be denoted as $\Sigma c_{ii'}$, which is intended to indicate that it is the sum (thus the sigma notation) of covariances between any particular item (denoted as i) and any other item (denoted as i').

The second step in this approach is to calculate the estimate of reliability by entering the variance of the scores on the complete test and the sum of the covariances into the following equation:

$\left(\dfrac{K}{K-1}\right)\left(\dfrac{\Sigma c}{\overline{S_X^2}}\right)$

$$\alpha = \text{estimated } R_{XX} = \left(\frac{k}{k-1}\right)\left(\frac{\sum c_{ii'}}{s_X^2}\right), \tag{6.2}$$

where k is the number of items in the test. For our example data,

$$\alpha = \text{estimated } R_{XX} = \left(\frac{4}{4-1}\right)\left(\frac{4.75}{10.1875}\right) = (1.333)(4.663) = .62.$$

Thus, we would estimate that the reliability of our four-item test in Table 6.2 is .62. Although a reliability of .62 is not very low, it is lower than we would like it to be. In Chapter 7, we will discuss how reliability information can be used to develop and improve psychological measures.

Many statistical programs compute reliability estimates by using raw alpha. For example, SPSS's Reliability Analysis procedure labels this value as "Cronbach's Alpha" (the RELIABILITY procedure, available under the Scale menu option). Using this procedure, selecting all of the items on the test, and choosing "Alpha" from among the "Model" options, we obtain output like that presented in Figure 6.2. These results are based on the data in Table 6.2, and the "Cronbach's Alpha" value (.62) corresponds to the value we obtained above. Similarly, the statistical package SAS has a procedure that labels this value as "Cronbach Coefficient Alpha for Raw Variables" (within the CORRELATION procedure).

If you read other presentations of reliability, you are likely to encounter another form of the equation for computing *alpha*:

$$\alpha = \text{estimated } R_{XX} = \left(\frac{k}{k-1}\right)\left(1 - \frac{\sum s_i^2}{s_X^2}\right). \tag{6.3}$$

Equation 6.3 produces the same alpha value as Equation 6.2, but we present it so that (hopefully) you can avoid any future confusion that might arise from the fact that there are differing forms of the equation. Equation 6.3 uses the variance of the total scores (s_X^2), along with item variances (s_i^2) values), instead of the interitem covariances equation (Equation 6.2). Note that the sum of the item variances in Table 6.2 is as follows:

$$\sum s_i^2 = s_1^2 + s_2^2 + s_3^2 + s_4^2$$
$$= 1.50 + .6875 + 25 + .75,$$
$$= 5.4375.$$

Reliability Statistics

Cronbach's Alpha	Cronbach's Alpha Based on Standardized Items	N of Items
.622	.626	4

Figure 6.2 SPSS Output Presenting Raw Alpha and Standardized Alpha From Reliability Analysis of the Data in Table 6.2

Entering this value into Equation 6.3, we obtain the same alpha estimate of reliability that we obtained earlier:

$$\alpha = \text{estimated } R_{XX} = \left(\frac{4}{4-1}\right)\left(1-\frac{5.4375}{10.1875}\right) = (1.333)(1-.5337) = (1.333)(.4663) = .62.$$

Again, Equations 6.2 and 6.3 lead to the same value for alpha; they differ only with regard to the information that is required (i.e., item variances or interitem covariances).

"Standardized" Coefficient Alpha   *Standardized Alpha Estimate*

Another method of estimating reliability is often called the *generalized Spearman-Brown formula* or the *standardized alpha* estimate. As its name implies, this method is highly related to raw alpha, but there is an important difference that might make it more appropriate for some tests.

The "standardized alpha" is appropriate if a test score is created by aggregating (e.g., summing or averaging) standardized responses to test items. That is, if test users standardize or *z*-score (see Chapter 3) the responses to each item before summing or averaging them, then the standardized alpha provides the more appropriate estimate of reliability.

Why would a test user decide to standardize the responses? A test's items might need to be standardized if their variances are dramatically different from each other. If this situation arises, then the score will heavily reflect those items that have the largest variabilities. Consider the hypothetical four-item test in Table 6.2, in which the total test score is obtained by summing across all four items. Notice that the items have differing variances; specifically, Item 3 has the largest variance ($s_3^2 = 2.5$), while Item 2 has the smallest variance ($s_2^2 = 0.6875$). In this type of case, it is likely that the total test score will be more highly correlated with Item 3 than with Item 2. Indeed, based on the data in Table 6.2, we can find that Item 3 and Item 2 are correlated with the total score at $r = .89$ and $r = .40$, respectively. Thus, the test is more heavily weighted to reflect the content and meaning of Item 3 than of Item 2.

Although such a differential weighting of items is not a concern for many tests, it could be a problem and could be extreme in some cases. For example, it would be a concern if items had different response scales (e.g., if some items were on a 5-point scale and others were on a 7-point scale). Similarly, it would be a major concern if scores from different measures were combined to form a new composite measure. For example, educational researchers might wish to obtain a general measure of academic ability by combining grade point average (GPA) and SAT scores. Because these two components are on such dramatically different metrics, any combination (e.g., summing or averaging) of unstandardized scores will essentially only reflect the SAT scores. Thus, researchers would likely decide to standardize the two sets of scores before creating the composite index of academic ability. In such cases, standardization is appropriate, and thus, standardized alpha would be the more appropriate estimate of reliability (as compared with raw alpha) of the "two-item" composite.

Apart from its importance as an alternative to raw alpha, we present the standardized alpha method also because it provides a perspective on reliability that is, in some ways, the most straightforward. Nunnally and Bernstein (1994) state that "it is hard to overestimate the importance of [this approach] to the theory of measurement error" (p. 232), and it is likely that they make such a claim, in part, because of its apparent simplicity. That is, this approach presents reliability estimates in terms that are, in some ways, the most fundamental and intuitive. As discussed earlier, the raw alpha procedure relies on variances and covariances, which might not be highly intuitive concepts for many people. In contrast, the standardized alpha procedure relies only on correlations, which may be more familiar and straightforward. Thus, a presentation of this method might help convey important general points about reliability and the factors that affect it. We will return to this issue later in the chapter.

The first step in the standardized alpha approach is to obtain a set of item-level statistics. We first calculate the correlations between each pair of items. Similar to the first equation for raw alpha (Equation 6.2), these values reflect the degree to which differences among the participants' response to the items are consistent with each other. Returning to the example data in Table 6.2, we compute six correlation coefficients:

Item Pair	Correlation
1 and 2	$r_{12} = .00$
1 and 3	$r_{13} = .52$
1 and 4	$r_{14} = .00$
2 and 3	$r_{23} = .00$
2 and 4	$r_{24} = .52$
3 and 4	$r_{34} = .73$

After we compute the correlations among all pairs of items (i.e., all "pairwise" correlations), we compute the average of those correlations. This average interitem correlation reflects the degree to which responses to all of the items are generally consistent with each other. For example, the average of our six correlations is .295, which indicates that, on average, the responses to the items are moderately associated with each other. This correlation is sometimes denoted as $\bar{r}_{ii'}$, which is intended to indicate that it is the average (thus the bar above the r) of the correlations between any particular item (denoted as i) and any other item (denoted as i').

The second step in this approach is to calculate the estimate of reliability by entering the average interitem correlation into the following equation, which is a generalization of the Spearman-Brown formula:

$$R_{XX} = \frac{k\bar{r}_{ii'}}{1+(k-1)\bar{r}_{ii'}},$$

(6.4)

where k is the number of items in the test. For our example data,

$$R_{xx} = \frac{4(.295)}{1+(4-1)(.295)}$$
$$= \frac{1.180}{1.885}$$
$$= .63.$$

Thus, this procedure suggests that, if we standardized the four items, then the reliability of our test in Table 6.2 is .63. This estimate is only slightly different from the raw alpha estimates that we obtained above ($\alpha = .62$). In fact, the standardized alpha procedure and the raw alpha procedure often produce similar (though not identical) estimates in real data.

Many popular statistical packages present standardized alpha alongside the raw alpha estimate. For example, SPSS's Reliability Analysis procedure labels this value "Cronbach's Alpha Based on Standardized Items." Indeed, this is apparent in Figure 6.2. Similarly, SAS labels this value "Cronbach Coefficient Alpha for Standardized Variables."

Raw Alpha for Binary Items: KR_{20} *Binary Items*

Many psychological measures include binary items (see Chapter 3). For example, the Minnesota Multiphasic Personality Inventory–2 (MMPI-2) is the most widely used measure of psychopathology, and it consists of 567 true/false items that assess a wide variety of psychopathological characteristics. Each of the 567 items produces only two possible responses, and thus they are binary items. Similarly, multiple-choice tests are generally scored in a way that provides binary responses, with each answer typically scored as either correct or incorrect.

The raw alpha equations can be used to compute the reliability estimates for a test consisting of binary items, but you are also likely to encounter a more specialized formula framed in terms of binary responses—the Kuder-Richardson 20 (KR_{20}) formula. The KR_{20} formula is algebraically identical to Equation 6.3 for raw coefficient alpha; however, it is expressed in a way that reflects a special characteristic of binary items.

As with the raw alpha methods for estimating reliability, the procedure for binary items is a two-step process. As an example, we will use the hypothetical data in Table 6.3, which includes four persons' responses to a test composed of four binary items. The first step in the process is to obtain a set of item-level and test-level statistics. For each item, we compute the proportions for each of the two possible answers. For example, for a multiple-choice test in class, we compute the proportion of respondents who answered each item correctly (we will call this proportion p for each item, consistent with our discussion of binary items in Chapter 3), and we compute the proportion of respondents who answered each item incorrectly (we will call this proportion q for each item). For the data in Table 6.3, we see that 75% of the sample answered Item 1 correctly ($p = .75$), which of course means that 25% of the sample answered the item incorrectly ($q = .25$). We next calculate

Table 6.3   Example for Computing Reliability From Binary Items

Person	Item 1	Item 2	Item 3	Item 4	Total Score
1	1	1	1	1	4
2	1	0	1	0	2
3	1	1	0	0	2
4	0	1	0	0	1
Sum	3	3	2	1	9
Mean	0.75	0.75	0.5	0.25	2.25
Variance	0.1875	0.1875	0.25	0.1875	1.1875
p	0.75	0.75	0.5	0.25	
q	0.25	0.25	0.5	0.75	
pq	0.1875	0.1875	0.25	0.1875	

the variance for each item, which is simply ($s_i^2 = pq$), as shown in Equation 3.9 (Chapter 3). Table 6.3 presents these values. In addition, we calculate the variance of the total test scores ($s_X^2 = 1.1875$), based on Equation 3.2 in Chapter 3, where the total test score is obtained by summing the responses to the items.

The second step in this approach is to calculate the estimate of reliability by entering the variance of the total test scores and the sum of the item variances into the following KR_{20} equation:

$$R_{XX} = \left(\frac{k}{k-1} \right) \left(1 - \frac{\sum pq}{s_X^2} \right). \tag{6.5}$$

For the data in Table 6.3, the sum of the item variances is

$$\Sigma pq = 0.1875 + 0.1875 + 0.25 + 0.1875 = 0.8125.$$

Entering our values into Equation 6.5, we get the following:

$$R_{XX} = \left(\frac{4}{4-1} \right) \left(1 - \frac{.8125}{1.1875} \right) = (1.333)(.316) = .42.$$

If you compare the second formula for raw alpha (Equation 6.3) with the KR_{20} formula, you will see that it differs only with respect to the way in which the item variance term is expressed.

Accuracy and Use of Internal Consistency Estimates of Reliability: Theory and Reality

In our discussion of coefficient alpha, we have not yet addressed the relevance of various theoretical assumptions. As we discussed for the alternate forms approach, the test–retest approach, and the split-half approach, reliability estimates are accurate only if certain assumptions hold true. In this brief section, we will address this issue for alpha, but let us begin by acknowledging the reality of measurement in "day-to-day" practice and research.

Despite the fundamental importance of the assumptions underlying reliability estimation, most test users seem to ignore the issue completely. In research-based uses of reliability estimates, most researchers calculate and report an alpha estimate of reliability and report it, probably with no consideration of any relevant assumptions. This standard "choice" of alpha as the method for estimating reliability is most likely based on two very practical factors. First, as we have mentioned, most of the popular statistical packages report alpha coefficients as a default part of any reliability analyses that they provide. Thus, alpha is easy to obtain from a set of data. Second, as we have also mentioned, alpha requires relatively little effort, as compared with other methods for estimating reliability. There is no need to create multiple forms of the test, as would be required for the alternate forms method. In addition, there is no need to require participants to complete the test on more than one occasion, as would be required for the test–retest method. Finally, there is no need to worry about how a test might be split into halves, as would be required for the split-half method. Thus, alpha is based on data that are relatively easy to obtain and use.

Although most test users choose the alpha method of estimating reliability without much (if any) thought about the assumptions underlying its use, it is probably a reasonable choice most of the time. This is because the assumptions underlying the use of the alpha method are somewhat more liberal (i.e., less strict and thus more easily satisfied) than the assumptions underlying the use of other methods. Trying not to get bogged down in what can be a very technical set of issues, let us take a moment to consider the assumptions underlying the use of the alpha method. The alpha method provides accurate estimates of reliability when test items are *essentially tau equivalent* (Feldt & Brennan, 1989). The notion of items being essentially tau equivalent is different from the notion that items are "parallel" to each other. The notion of essential tau equivalence rests on more liberal assumptions than the notion of parallel tests—that is, the assumption of equal error variances is not required. Therefore, the estimates from alpha are likely to be accurate more often than those that would have been obtained from methods such as the split-half approach.

In the unlikely case that test items actually do meet the strict assumptions of parallel tests, the raw alpha estimate, KR_{20}, and the split-half estimate will all give you identical and accurate estimates of reliability. If test items are essentially tau equivalent but not parallel, KR_{20} and coefficient alpha will give accurate estimates of reliability, but the split-half method will not. If test items are neither tau equivalent nor parallel, then KR_{20} and alpha will underestimate reliability (Feldt & Brennan, 1989; Osburn, 2000). Thus, it is commonly said that KR_{20} and coefficient alpha place a lower limit on the size of the estimated reliability of tests scores. In general, KR_{20} and coefficient alpha will underestimate the actual reliability of test scores (for a proof of this claim, see Crocker & Algina, 1986, pp. 120–122).

Although it is commonly said that the alpha method will underestimate reliability, we should also acknowledge that all internal consistency methods might overestimate reliability to some degree. For example, because internal consistency methods are based on responses from only one measurement occasion, they fail to account for measurement error that transcends a single measurement occasion. As stated by Feldt and Brennan (1989), "When behavioral observations are gathered in an hour or less, certain sources of error 'stand still' for each examinee. Their effects obscure the true difference among persons but are not reflected in the estimate of test error variance" (p. 110). That is, some sources of error (e.g., fatigue) might become apparent only when respondents are measured on more than one occasion. Thus, the internal consistency approach might underestimate error variance, thereby overestimating reliability.

More generally, there are several indices that have been proposed as ways of estimating reliability from an internal consistency perspective. Indeed, psychometricians have criticized the use of alpha and debated the relative meanings, strengths, and weaknesses of a variety of indices including alpha, beta, and omega, among others (e.g., Revelle & Zinbarg, 2009; Sijtsma, 2009). Partly because this debate has been highly technical and partly because alpha remains highly accessible from popular software packages, many test developers and test users continue to compute and report alpha. In sum, there are many methods for estimating the reliability of test scores. In fact, the methods that we have discussed in this chapter are merely the most popular (for a more extensive discussion, see Feldt & Brennan, 1989; Osburn, 2000; Revelle & Zinbarg, 2009). The accuracy of each method rests on a set of assumptions, and some methods rest on assumptions that are more easily satisfied than others. In practice, most test users seem to depend on the internal consistency method for estimating reliability. More specifically, they rely heavily on the coefficient alpha, most likely the raw alpha, as we have described above. This choice is at least partly driven by the convenience and practical advantages of the alpha method. However, the choice is probably reasonable because alpha rests on less restrictive assumptions than many other methods, and it seems to be fairly accurate in comparison with many other methods (Osburn, 2000).

Internal Consistency Versus Dimensionality

Some test users are very tempted to interpret a high level of internal consistency reliability as an indication that a test measures a single attribute (i.e., that it is unidimensional or conceptually homogeneous). Unfortunately, such an interpretation is tenuous at best, and it is often invalid (Cronbach & Shavelson, 2004).

It is important to separate the idea of internal consistency from the idea that items on a test are unidimensional or *conceptually* homogeneous. Each item in a conceptually homogeneous test will reflect a single psychological attribute or dimension. Measurements of internal consistency such as alpha should be thought of with caution, if at all, as measures of the conceptual homogeneity of test items (Cortina, 1993; Netemeyer, Bearden, & Sharma, 2003).

Caution is required because a test's internal consistency could be high (e.g., $\alpha = .75$) even if the test is multidimensional or conceptually heterogeneous. For example, a composite test might include two sets of items for which (a) the items within each set correlate highly with each other but (b) the items from different sets correlate weakly with each other. In such a case, the test is multidimensional—a low correlation between different sets of items suggests that the sets measure different psychological attributes (Schmitt, 1996). Although McDonald (1999) argues that this distinction is more important in theory than in practice, it is probably not a good idea to treat an internal consistency estimate of reliability (e.g., alpha) as a measure of the conceptual homogeneity or dimensionality of the test. As discussed in Chapter 4 and later in Chapter 12, statistical procedures such as factor analysis are much more appropriate methods for evaluating the dimensionality or conceptual homogeneity of test items.

Factors Affecting the Reliability of Test Scores

As mentioned earlier in this chapter, the internal consistency approach highlights two fundamental factors that affect the reliability of test scores. In this section, we explore the meaning of these factors and illustrate their influence on reliability.

This issue is important because it lays the foundation for creating tests that have strong psychometric quality. If we understand the factors that influence the reliability of test scores, then we can consider these factors when creating tests, when trying to improve tests, and when using tests in research or in practice. Knowledge of these factors can thus increase the quality of behavioral tests and enhance the quality of inferences and decisions that are based on these tests.

The first factor affecting an internal consistency reliability estimate is the *consistency among the parts of a test*. As we have seen, the consistency among the parts of a test has a direct effect on reliability estimates. All else being equal, a test with greater internal consistency—as reflected by a split-half correlation, by an average interitem covariance, or by an average interitem correlation—will have a greater estimated reliability. For an example, let us revisit the four-item example in Table 6.2. In these data, we have seen that the average interitem correlation is $\bar{r}_{ii'} = .29$, and we calculated the standardized alpha to be .63.

$$R_{XX} = \frac{k\bar{r}_{ii'}}{1+(k-1)\bar{r}_{ii'}} = \frac{4(.29)}{1+(4-1)(.29)} = .63.$$

The average interitem correlation of .29 is small to moderate, telling us that, in general, the four items are positively related to each other. That is, it tells us that the items are at least somewhat consistent with each other—if an individual has a relatively high response (i.e., 4 or 5) on one item, then he or she is likely to have a relatively high response on other items. We interpret a high level of consistency among the items as an indication of a high level of consistency between observed test scores and true test scores.

Although we are glad that the average interitem correlation is positive, the test might be improved by increasing this value. A reliability estimate of .63 is on the low end of what we would deem acceptable, and so we might wish to improve the test. For example, some of the items might be rewritten to make them clearer.

Alternatively, we might choose to replace one or two items altogether—take them out of the test and replace them with items that are more clearly relevant to the construct being measured. Imagine that we implemented either of these solutions, retained the same length of the test (four items), asked a new sample of respondents to take the revised test, and recalculated the average interitem correlation. Let us imagine that the average interitem correlation for the revised test is indeed higher—say, $\bar{r}_{ii} = .40$—which indicates that our revised test is more internally consistent than was the original. The fact that the items are more consistent with each other suggests that, as a set, they do a better job of reflecting the construct being measured. Calculating the standardized alpha reliability estimate of the scores on the revised test, we find a reliability of .73:

$$R_{XX} = \frac{4(.40)}{1+(4-1)(.40)} = \frac{1.60}{2.20} = .73 .$$

Thus, our revised test seems to produce scores that are more reliable than the original test. If our average interitem correlation on the revised test had been even higher than $\bar{r}_{ii} = .40$, then the estimated reliability would increase even more. In sum, if a test is made of parts (be they items or halves) that are highly consistent with each other, then it is likely to have better reliability than a test made of parts that are not highly consistent with each other. Thus, all else being equal, greater internal consistency produces greater reliability.

The second factor that affects a test's reliability is the *length of the test*. All else being equal, a long test is more reliable than a short test. This effect occurs because of the nature of true scores and measurement error, as well as their link to reliability. Specifically, as test length increases, true score variance will increase at a faster rate than error score variance. To understand why this happens, remember that, according to CTT, reliability can be seen as the ratio of true score variance to observed score variance (Equation 5.5):

$$R_{XX} = \frac{s_t^2}{s_o^2} .$$

In addition, recall that total observed score variance is determined by true score variance and error variance (Equation 5.3):

$$s_o^2 = s_t^2 + s_e^2 .$$

Therefore, reliability can be seen as

$$R_{XX} = \frac{s_t^2}{s_t^2 + s_e^2} . \tag{6.6}$$

So anything that increases true score variance more than error variance will increase reliability. Assuming that we lengthen the test by adding new "parts" that are parallel tests of the construct being assessed, then adding parts will have this exact effect—it will increase true score variance to a greater degree than observed score variance, thereby increasing reliability.

Let us demonstrate why this is true. Imagine that we begin with a one-part test. The true score variance for the part is s_{t1}^2. If we double the length of the test by adding a second part (of equal length to the first part) that has a true score variance of s_{t2}^2, then the *true score variance of the lengthened test* ($s_{t\text{-doubled}}^2$) will equal (based on our discussion of the variance of a composite variable; see Equation 3.6)

$$s_{t\text{-doubled}}^2 = s_{t1}^2 + s_{t2}^2 + 2r_{t1}s_{t1}s_{t2}.$$

However, if the parts are parallel tests, then the two parts have identical true scores. Thus, the correlation between the two parts' true scores is perfect (i.e., $r_{t1t2} = 1$), and the variabilities of the two parts are equal to each other (i.e., $s_{t1} = s_{t2}$ and $s_{t1}^2 = s_{t2}^2$). Because the true score variance for one part is exactly equal to the true score variance for the other part, we can simply use $s_{t\text{-one part}}^2$ to refer to the true score variance of "one part." Therefore, $s_{t1}^2 = s_{t2}^2 = s_{t\text{-one part}}^2$, and the formula reduces to

$$s_{t\text{-doubled}}^2 = 2s_{t\text{-one part}}^2 + 2s_{t\text{-one part}}^2.$$

Collecting the terms on the right, we get

$$s_{t\text{-doubled}}^2 = 4s_{t\text{-one part}}^2.$$

Thus, by doubling the length of the test, we quadruple the original true score variance.

You can easily confirm this somewhat counterintuitive result by using a software package such as Excel to (a) create a set of numbers (representing the true scores of one part of a test); (b) compute the variance of this set (obtaining $s_{t\text{-one part}}^2$—the true score variance of one part of the test); (c) multiply each number in the set by two, producing a new "doubled" set of numbers (representing the true scores that result from a doubling of the test length); and (d) compute the variance of the doubled set (obtaining $s_{t\text{-doubled}}^2$—the true score variance of a doubled test). You will find that the variance of your "doubled" values is four times greater than the variance of the original set of values.

Now we can examine the effect that doubling the test has on *error score variance*. Again, let the error variance on the first part be s_{e1}^2, the error variance on the second part be s_{e2}^2, and the error variance on the lengthened test be $s_{e\text{-doubled}}^2$. According to our discussion, the error variance of the doubled test will be (again, based on Equation 3.6)

$$s_{e\text{-doubled}}^2 = s_{e1}^2 + s_{e2}^2 + 2r_{e1e2}s_{e1}s_{e2}.$$

However, according to CTT, $r_{e1e2} = 0$ because errors are thought to be random. Therefore, the error variance of the doubled test reduces to

$$s_{e\text{-doubled}}^2 = s_{e1}^2 + s_{e2}^2.$$

In addition, if the two parts are parallel tests, then they will have equal error variances (i.e., $s_{e1}^2 = s_{e2}^2$, as part of the definition of parallel tests). Because the error variance for one part is exactly equal to the error variance for other part, we can simply use $s^2_{\text{e-one part}}$ to refer to the error variance of "one part." Therefore, $s^2_{e1} = s^2_{e2} = s^2_{\text{e-one part}}$, and the formula reduces to

$$s^2_{\text{e-doubled}} = 2s^2_{\text{e-one Part}}.$$

Thus, by doubling the length of the test, we double the error variance.

In other words, these analyses show that if the parts meet the assumptions of parallel tests, then increasing a test's length will increase true score variance to a greater degree than error variance. In our example of doubling a test, true score variance quadrupled while error variance only doubled.

Let us now consider how reliability is affected by these changes. Let $R_{XX\text{-original}}$ represent the reliability of the original test, which, if you recall, includes only a single "part" (note that this is simply a re-expression of Equation 6.6 above):

$$R_{xx-\text{orginal}} = \frac{s^2_{\text{t-one part}}}{s^2_{\text{t-one part}} + s^2_{\text{e-one part}}}.$$

In addition, let $R_{XX\text{-doubled}}$ represent the reliability of the doubled test, which is the sum of two parallel parts. Based on the demonstration above, the reliability of the doubled test can be expressed in terms of the true score variance and error variance of a single part:

$$R_{xx-\text{doubled}} = \frac{4(s^2_{\text{t-one part}})}{4(s^2_{\text{t-one part}}) + 2(s^2_{\text{e-one part}})}.$$

After several algebraic steps, which we will not present here, it can be shown that the reliability of the doubled test is a simple function of the reliability of the original test:

$$R_{xx-\text{doubled}} = \frac{2R_{xx-\text{orginal}}}{1 + R_{xx-\text{orginal}}}.$$

For example, the original test that is illustrated in Table 6.2 has an estimated reliability of .62 (from our earlier calculations of raw alpha). If we double the length of the test by adding four items that, as a set, are exactly parallel to the original four items, then the estimated reliability of the doubled test would be as follows:

$$R_{xx-\text{doubled}} = \frac{2(.63)}{1 + .63} = .77.$$

Some of you might notice that the equation above is similar to the equation of split-half reliability that was presented earlier (Equation 6.1). Indeed, in a sense, the split-half reliability equation works by estimating the reliability of a "doubled" test, where each part is half of the test.

A more general formula for estimating the reliability of a revised test (i.e., a test that has been lengthened or shortened) is a version of the Spearman-Brown prophecy formula:

$$R_{xx\text{-revised}} = \frac{nR_{xx\text{-orginal}}}{1+(n-1)R_{xx\text{-orginal}}}. \qquad (6.7)$$

In this equation, $R_{XX\text{-revised}}$ is the estimated reliability of a revised test, n is the factor by which the test is lengthened or shortened, and $R_{XX\text{-original}}$ is the reliability estimate for the original version of the test.

For example, if we tripled the length of the 4-item test in Table 6.2 (by adding two 4-item parallel sets), we would have a 12-item test with a likely reliability of .84:

$$R_{xx\text{-revised}} = \frac{3(.63)}{1+(3-1)(.63)} = .84.$$

Equation 6.7 is called a "prophecy" formula because it can be used to forecast what would happen if a test was revised in a particular way. This can be very useful in the test development process. For example, we might design a test of a given length but find that it has a low reliability. Before taking the time to collect additional data on a revised test, we can forecast the reliability of a test that is lengthened by a specific amount. For example, we might use the prophecy formula to find that doubling the length is sufficient to obtain adequate reliability. This kind of information allows a more efficient use of time and effort in the test development and evaluation process.

You might encounter another version of the Spearman-Brown prophecy formula. The equation for the standardized alpha can also be used to forecast changes in reliability. Recall Equation 6.4:

$$R_{xx} = \frac{k\bar{r}_{ii'}}{1+(k-1)\bar{r}_{ii'}}.$$

Whereas the first version of a prophecy formula requires us to think in terms of "the factor by which the test is revised" (i.e., n), the second version (Equation 6.4) simply requires us to think in terms of the number of items on a revised test (i.e., k). For example, we know that the average interitem correlation for the four-item test in Table 6.2 is $\bar{r}_{ii'} = .29$. If we are considering the possibility of adding three items to the test, and if we assume that the three new items will be just as good as the original four items, then we can assume that the average interitem correlation will remain $\bar{r}_{ii'} = .29$. We can then forecast the standardized alpha reliability of a seven-item version of the test:

$$R_{xx} = \frac{7(.29)}{1+(7-1)(.29)} = .74.$$

Thus, there are two versions of a prophecy formula, both of which illustrate the effect of test length on reliability estimates. Again, these equations can be used to forecast the reliability of tests that are changed in various ways.

As a side note, it is sometimes labor intensive to calculate the average interitem correlation among a large set of items. Most statistical packages will calculate the standardized alpha value, and they will calculate all of the interitem correlations; however, most will *not* calculate the average of these correlations. Some of us may wish to use the standardized alpha formula as a prophecy formula, but we may be too lazy to calculate the average of a large set of interitem correlations. Luckily, we can obtain the average interitem correlation by algebraically rearranging the equation for the standardized alpha (Equation 6.4). Doing so, we find that the average interitem correlation can be easily calculated if we know the standardized alpha and the number of items in the test:

$$\bar{r}_{ii'} = \frac{R_{xx}}{k - (k-1)R_{xx}} \, . \tag{6.8}$$

The idea that the reliability of a test increases as test length increases has important practical implications for test construction. For those who are in the business of constructing tests (e.g., teachers and professors), the lesson might be that longer tests will be more reliable than shorter tests. Indeed, this is true: If everything else remains the same, longer tests will be more reliable than short tests.

However, it is important to recognize that "everything else" might not remain the same. For example, the link between length and reliability is true only when the additional items are parallel to the original items. This means, for example, that the average interitem correlation would remain the same, which we assumed in the example above. In fact, the additional items might not be parallel to the existing items. If the new items are not perfectly consistent with the original items (at least on average), then the average interitem correlation might be reduced. This would hurt the reliability of the test.

Thus, the addition of new items to a test is a double-edged sword. On one hand, longer tests are more reliable than short tests, all else being equal. On the other hand, it might not be safe to assume that "all else" is in fact equal. In fact, if the average interitem correlation of a lengthened test is small enough, then the lengthened test can actually be less reliable than the original test! That is, if we add "bad" items to a test, then the lengthened test will be worse than the shorter test.

In addition, there are practical limits on the number of items that can be included in a test. Time constraints and test-taker fatigue are among these practical concerns. Furthermore, all else being equal, the benefit of lengthening a test is small for tests that are already fairly long. Technically speaking, the size of the increase in reliability will be a negatively increasing function of original test length. For example, adding 10 items to a short test will have a bigger effect on the estimated reliability of the revised test than adding 10 items to a long test. In other words, the benefit of adding items to a test decreases with the number of items that are added. The effect is illustrated in Figure 6.3.

In this figure, we have computed and plotted the standardized alpha values for tests with an average interitem correlation of .30 (which we chose arbitrarily), and the line represents the reliability for tests of different lengths. For example, we see that the estimated reliability of a 2-item version of the test is only about $R_{xx} = .33$. By adding 5 items, the reliability is increased to approximately $R_{xx} = .64$. Note that this 5-item increase in length produces a substantial .31 increase in reliability (.64 − .33 = .31)—nearly doubling the reliability of the test. If we added another

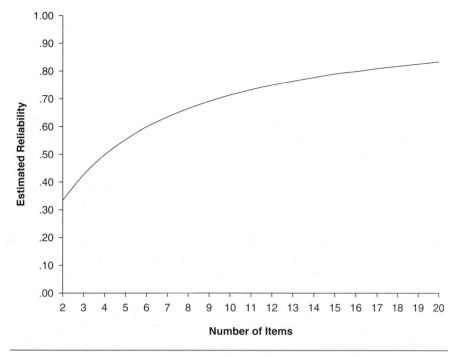

Figure 6.3 The Association Between Number of Items and Reliability (for a Test With an Average Interitem Correlation of .30)

5 items (for a total of 12 items), then the reliability of the test would be R_{XX} = .75. Although these 5 new items do increase the reliability of the test, the benefit of going from 7 to 12 items is clearly less substantial than the benefit of going from 2 to 7 items. Adding another 5 items would produce an even smaller increment in reliability. Thus, there are practical limits to the benefit of adding more and more items to a test.

Sample Homogeneity and Reliability Generalization

Another factor that has subtle but important effects on the size of reliability coefficients is the heterogeneity of the people taking the test or, more precisely, the heterogeneity of their true scores. All else being equal, the greater the variability among people in a group with respect to the psychological attribute that is being measured, the larger the reliability coefficient. You can see why this is by revisiting the definitional formula for reliability, which again can be seen as

$$R_{xx} = \frac{s_t^2}{s_t^2 + s_e^2}.$$

Therefore, anything that increases s_t^2 relative to s_e^2 will increase the size of R_{XX}. Recall that s_t^2 represents true score heterogeneity; the more heterogeneous the true scores, the larger the s_t^2.

The issue of true score heterogeneity is important partly because it highlights the fact that the reliability of a test's scores depends to some degree on the nature of the sample that is being measured. If a test is administered to a sample that is very heterogeneous (i.e., in terms of their levels of the psychological construct being measured by the test), then the reliability estimate is likely to be higher than an estimate that would be obtained from a sample that was less heterogeneous. This fact has at least two important implications. First, it underscores the important conceptual point that reliability is a characteristic of test scores; it is not a characteristic of the test itself. That is, a test might produce scores that are highly reliable in one sample (i.e., a relatively heterogeneous sample), but it might produce scores that are less reliable in another sample (i.e., a relatively homogeneous sample).

A second and related implication is that sample heterogeneity highlights the utility of *reliability generalization* studies. A reliability generalization study is intended to reveal the degree to which a test produces differing reliability estimates across different kinds of research uses and populations (Vacha-Haase, 1998). In a reliability generalization study, a researcher focuses on a specific test and gathers information from previously published research that used the test. In this process, he or she records information about the reliability of the test's scores as estimated in all the previously published research. This information can provide insight into several important psychometric questions. For example, Vacha-Haase, Kogan, Tani, and Woodall (2001) conducted a reliability generalization study of the MMPI to discover the typical reliability of MMPI clinical scale scores, the degree to which the reliability of the MMPI scale scores differs across studies, and the factors that seem to affect the reliability of the scale scores. In their study, Vacha-Haase and her colleagues examined more than 150 studies that had used the MMPI clinical scales and had reported reliability estimates based on the data. Results revealed that most of the MMPI clinical scales generally produced scores with acceptable reliability, but that reliability did vary across studies. In addition, results revealed that, for many of the MMPI clinical scales, scale scores were more reliable for adult samples (as opposed to adolescent samples) and for clinical samples (as opposed to nonclinical samples). Thus, reliability generalization studies can be used to identify and understand the ways in which sample characteristics affect the reliability of test scores.

Reliability of Difference Scores

So far, we have discussed the psychometric quality of scores on a single test. For example, we have been concerned with understanding and estimating the reliability of tests to measure intelligence, ability, self-esteem, job satisfaction, depression, and so on. However, there are times when we might also be interested in the difference between two scores.

Indeed, examinations of the difference between scores might be relevant to many behavioral questions. For example, suppose that you were interested in evaluating whether a reading program leads to improved reading skills among children. To examine this issue, you might ask a sample of children to take a reading test of some kind before they are exposed to the program and then ask them to take the same test following the program. You would be interested in studying the *change* in students' test scores, and you might be interested in a variety of questions: What is the average degree of change? Do children differ in the degree of change that they experienced? Are there characteristics that differentiate which children changed more and which changed less? Many of the most important questions about difference scores concern *variability*—you want to evaluate the degree to which the children vary in the amount of change in reading ability and whether there are any psychological variables that are associated with "amount of change." As another example, we might be interested in studying romantic couples to determine whether relationship satisfaction is associated with personality similarity. Thus, in each couple, we might be tempted to measure each partner's open-mindedness, measure how much the partners argue, and see whether couples who share similar levels of open-mindedness argue less than couples who have large disparities in their open-mindedness.

In this section, we present an overview of some fundamental issues that are important in the analysis of these types of questions. This issue is important for several reasons. First, questions such as change, similarity, disparity, inaccuracy, and improvement are important and widely studied in behavioral science. Second, when studying such questions, test users often seem to forget that reliability has fundamental implications for their ability to draw meaningful answers to their questions. That is, test users often fail to examine, report, and interpret reliability in this context. Third, the special nature of these questions raises special psychometric challenges that make reliability particularly poor in many attempts to answer the questions. Fourth, many test users might not be aware of the challenges raised by these questions. Considering all of these issues, we hope that this section helps current and future behavioral scientists understand and appreciate the importance of reliability in this context, and we hope that it provides some tools that can be used to address these challenges.

What is a *difference score*? One popular method for studying change or differences is by using difference scores. For example, after obtaining two reading test scores for each child, you could compute a difference score by subtracting a child's initial reading test score from his or her final test score. You might want to interpret a child's difference score as the degree to which his or her reading ability has improved. Note that, when subtracting the initial score from the final score, a positive difference indicates improvement—the final score was higher than the initial score. In addition, a difference score of 0 indicates no change, and a negative difference score would suggest that the child's reading skill actually declined. Thus, if a person takes the same test on two different occasions, then you can subtract one of the test scores from the other score, creating a difference score. In general terms, a difference score that is created by computing the difference between a score on test x and a score on test y is straightforwardly defined as follows:

$$D_i = X_i - Y_i, \tag{6.9}$$

where the values represent a given individual's score on the x test and the y test, and the difference between them is interpreted as a measure of the child's level of a psychological attribute—for example, reading skill improvement.

Although all difference scores are some variation of the general Equation 6.9, there are in fact several more specific varieties. The type of difference scores that we have focused on is by far the most common type of difference score. They are intra-individual change scores, in which each person has two scores on the same test or measure, with each person thus having a difference score based on the difference between the two test scores. A second type of difference score is sometimes called an intraindividual discrepancy score, in which each person again has scores on two measures but in which the two measures are from different tests. For example, an educational psychologist might be interested in the discrepancy between types of intelligence (e.g., what are the psychological implications if a child has an unusu-ally large discrepancy between her verbal intelligence and her perceptual reasoning intelligence?). In such a case, the psychologist might determine a child's relative performance on two subscales of a widely used intelligence test—for example, by computing the difference between the child's score on the WISC-IV's (Wechsler, 2003a, 2003b) Verbal Comprehension Index and the WISC-IV's Perceptual Reasoning Index. Because these are measures of two different attributes, the differ-ence reflects a discrepancy between attributes rather than a change in a single attri-bute. A third type of difference score is an interindividual difference score, which can be computed by giving two *different* people the same test and then subtracting one person's test score from the other person's score. Our earlier example of the link between personality similarity and relationship satisfaction is an example of this. Each couple has two test scores, but each person (e.g., wife and husband) has only one test score. In this case, the difference score might be computed to reflect the degree of similarity (or perhaps more appropriately, the degree of personality dissimilarity) within the couple.

For either type of difference score, it will be used and interpreted as a measure of some psychological phenomenon—for example, a child's level of reading improve-ment or a couple's level of personality dissimilarity. Because the difference score is itself a measure (albeit derived from two other measures), it will be unreliable to some extent. Therefore, a psychometrically savvy researcher would like to know the reliability of the difference scores for the same reasons that he or she would like to know the reliability of scores from any measure. Specifically, he or she would want to know the degree to which the observed difference scores reflect true psychologi-cal differences or discrepancies.

Estimating the Reliability of Difference Scores

The question then becomes how to estimate the reliability of difference scores. How might we estimate the reliability of scores that represent the *difference* between two scores that are obtained from tests that are themselves unreliable to some degree?

It can be shown that the reliability of the difference scores (R_d) can be estimated on the basis of three sets of information: (1) the estimated reliability of each of the two tests used to compute the difference scores (R_{XX} and R_{YY}), (2) the variability of the tests' observed scores ($s_{X_o}^2$, $s_{Y_o}^2$, s_{X_o}, and s_{Y_o}), and (3) the correlation between the observed test scores ($r_{X_o Y_o}$):[1]

$$R_d = \frac{s_{X_o}^2 R_{XX} + s_{Y_o}^2 R_{YY} - 2r_{X_oY_o} s_{X_o} s_{Y_o}}{s_{X_o}^2 + s_{Y_o}^2 - 2r_{X_oY_o} s_{X_o} s_{Y_o}}. \tag{6.10}$$

To illustrate this, consider an example based on the situation described earlier, in which a researcher wants to examine improvements in reading skill by using the difference score based on two reading tests. That is, an individual child's reading improvement (D_i) is computed as the difference between his or her score on the reading test at one point in time (R_{i1}) and his or her score on the reading test at a second point in time (R_{i2}):

$$D_i = R_{i2} - R_{i1}.$$

Imagine that the researcher carried out this project, administering the tests to a large number of children and obtaining the following information: The variance of the first test scores and second test scores is 30.4 and 36.2, respectively; the estimated reliability of the first test scores (say, based on raw alpha) and second test scores is .90 and .85, respectively; and the correlation between observed test scores is .50. Based on this information, the estimated reliability of the reading improvement scores is ($R_d = .75$):

$$R_d = \frac{30.4(.90) + 36.2(.85) - 2(.50)\sqrt{30.4}\sqrt{36.2}}{30.4 + 36.2 - 2(.50)\sqrt{30.4}\sqrt{36.2}} = \frac{24.96}{33.43} = .75$$

Some of you might notice something that might strike you as odd about this result. Specifically, the reliability of the difference score is poorer than the reliability of either of its two components. That is, the two tests have reliabilities of .85 or greater, but the reliability of the difference score was only .75. It might seem odd that the combination of two measures produces a score that is less reliable than either of those measures individually. To understand this potentially counterintuitive effect, you need some insights into the factors affecting the reliability of difference scores.

Factors Affecting the Reliability of Difference Scores

There are two primary factors that determine whether a set of difference scores will have good reliability. One factor is the correlation between the tests' observed scores (i.e., $r_{X_oY_o}$). Although this may seem somewhat counterintuitive at first, two tests that are highly correlated with each other will produce difference scores that have low reliability. That is, all else being equal, as the size of $r_{X_oY_o}$ *increases*, the size of R_d *decreases*. Consider two examples. Above, we illustrated Equation 6.9 (i.e., the equation for estimating the reliability of a difference score) based on an example in which the two tests were moderately correlated with each other (i.e., $r_{X_oY_o} = .50$). Based on this correlation, along with the good individual reliabilities and along with the other relevant values (i.e., variabilities, R_{XX} and R_{YY} values), we obtained a respectable reliability of .75 for the difference scores. Now, consider a case in which we have the same variabilities and R_{XX} and R_{YY} values but the two tests are even more strongly correlated with each other—say $r_{X_o Y_o} = .70$. In this case, the reliability of the difference score is noticeably lower, at only $R_d = .58$.

$$R_d = \frac{30.4(.90) + 36.2(.85) - 2(.70)\sqrt{30.4}\sqrt{36.2}}{30.4 + 36.2 - 2(.70)\sqrt{30.4}\sqrt{36.2}} = \frac{11.69}{20.16} = .58.$$

Figure 6.4 illustrates this effect more generally. Consider the solid line beginning at .90 on the y-axis. This line plots the reliabilities of the difference scores (R_d) in relation to the correlation between the two tests, across different levels of correlation. To avoid unnecessary complexity, we computed R_d values assuming that the tests were equally reliable, with both R_{XX} and R_{YY} equaling .90 (we also assumed that the tests had equal variance). As this line illustrates, the reliability of difference scores is highest when the tests are uncorrelated with each other. As the correlation between tests increases (moving along the x-axis from left to right), the reliability of the difference score decreases. To illustrate the generality of this effect even more broadly, we computed similar R_d values under several different conditions. Specifically, we computed sets of values to illustrate the effect when the individual tests have various degrees of reliability (i.e., when R_{XX} and $R_{YY} = .70, .50,$ and $.30$). In each set, the same pattern emerges—as the correlation between the tests increases, the reliability of the difference scores decreases.

A second factor that affects the reliability of difference scores is the reliability of the two tests used to compute the difference scores (i.e., R_{XX} and R_{YY}). All else being equal, tests that have high reliabilities will produce difference scores that have relatively high reliability. Thus, generally speaking, difference scores will be relatively reliable when the two individual tests are highly reliable.

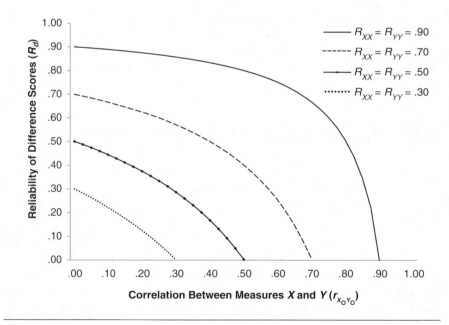

Figure 6.4 The Effect of Test (Observed Score) Correlation and Individual Test Reliabilty on the Reliability of Difference Scores

Again, consider the original example and a new one. In the original example, the two tests had relatively high reliabilities ($R_{XX} = .90$ and $R_{YY} = .85$). Based on these good individual reliabilities and the other relevant values (i.e., variabilities and $r_{X_o Y_o}$), we obtained an $R_d = .75$ for the difference scores. Consider a different case—one in which we have the same variabilities and $r_{X_o Y_o}$ values but where the two tests are estimated to have lower reliabilities—say, $R_{XX} = .50$ and $R_{YY} = .55$. For this situation, the difference scores would likely have very poor reliability:

$$R_d = \frac{30.4(.60) + 36.2(.50) - 2(.50)\sqrt{30.4}\sqrt{36.2}}{30.4 + 36.2 - 2(.50)\sqrt{30.4}\sqrt{36.2}} = \frac{3.17}{33.43} = .38 \cdot$$

Thus, the tests that were relatively reliable produced difference scores that were more reliable than those produced by tests that were relatively unreliable ($R_d = .75$ and $R_d = .38$, respectively).

Figure 6.4 again illustrates this more generally. Note the differences between the lines—at any given point on the x-axis, the lines associated with tests that have high reliability (e.g., the line for $R_{XX} = R_{YY} = .90$) are always higher than the lines associated with tests that have lower reliability. For example, let's look at the situation when two individual tests are correlated with each other at, say, .20 (on the x-axis). Looking at lines above this point, we see that when the individual tests have extremely poor reliability ($R_{XX} = R_{YY} = .30$), the difference score has a reliability of only (approximately) $R_d = .13$. As the tests increase in reliability from .30 to .50 to .70 to .90 (going from one line up to the next), the difference scores increase in reliability from (approximately) 13 to .38 to .63 to .88.

In sum, Figure 6.4 illustrates several important points about the reliability of difference scores. One is that, all else being equal, difference scores will be relatively reliable when the two individual tests are relatively uncorrelated. A second is that, all else being equal, difference scores will be relatively reliable when the two individual tests are themselves highly reliable. A third, more subtle, point is that the reliability of difference scores will not be higher than (roughly) the average reliability of the two individual test scores. Finally, the reliability of difference scores actually can be *much* smaller than the reliability of the two individual test scores. For example, it is possible that two tests might have extremely good reliabilities (say .90) but that their difference scores have a reliability of .50 or lower.

The Problem of Unequal Variability

Perhaps because of their apparent simplicity, difference scores are intuitively appealing; however, the apparent simplicity masks several serious problems. A full discussion of these problems is beyond the scope of this section, but one important psychometric issue is the fact that in some cases, difference scores simply might not be a clear reflection of psychological reality.

More specifically, in some cases, difference scores will essentially reflect only one of the two variables that are used to compute them. Somewhat technically, difference scores can be heavily confounded with one of their components. Thus, psychological inferences that emphasize change, dissimilarity, or discrepancy can be misleading, if not simply incorrect.

For example, we might be interested in examining discrepancies between classroom performance and standardized testing performance (i.e., identifying some students with a large discrepancy in these performances and other students with small discrepancies). To study this issue, we might be tempted to create discrepancy scores by subtracting a student's GPA from his or her SAT score. Unfortunately, such a score would not be psychologically meaningful as a discrepancy score. To illustrate the problem, consider four students from a school:

Student	SAT	GPA	Difference
Emily	1000	2.5	997.5
John	1000	1.0	999
Sarah	1003	4.0	999
Mark	1006	2.5	1003.5

For these students, their difference scores reflect the discrepancy between their standardized test performance and their classroom performance. More specifically, the difference score is computed by subtracting their GPA from their SAT scores, producing a value that we might wish to interpret as the degree to which each student performs better on standardized tests than his or her classroom performance. One problem should be obvious—everyone has an apparently large positive difference score. Without some careful thought, we might be tempted to interpret this as meaning that all three students are better on standardized tests than in the classroom. Obviously, this would be an invalid interpretation of these data, arising from the differing scales of measurement between SAT and GPA scores. That is, since the scoring of the two "tests" is arbitrary (see earlier chapters), the difference between them is arbitrary. For example, we could arbitrarily divide the SAT scores by 1,000—although the variability among the three SAT scores remains relationally constant, the difference scores would change dramatically.

Two more subtle and far-reaching problems lie in the variability among the difference scores. Note that John and Sarah have the same difference score, which might imply that they have the same degree of superiority on standardized tests (as compared with their classroom performance). But, given your knowledge about the meaning of SAT and GPA scores, you will probably recognize that this apparent similarity between John and Sarah is somehow incorrect. Second, if we were to examine the association between the difference scores and another variable (e.g., intelligence, achievement motivation, etc.), then the correlation would essentially reflect the correlation between SAT scores and the other variable. That is, the difference scores are almost perfectly correlated with the SAT scores—indeed, the correlation between the two sets of scores is $r = .90$! Thus, the difference scores essentially reflect SAT scores, and consequently, anything that is associated with the difference scores is, in actuality, simply associated with SAT scores. With these issues in mind, it is not clearly psychologically accurate to interpret the difference scores as indicating the "discrepancy between classroom performance and standardized test ability." It would be more accurate to interpret the difference scores simply as SAT scores.

We will not delve too deeply into the sources of this issue, other than to say that it arises when the two tests have unequal variabilities. In the current example, the SAT scores have a variance of 6.2, whereas the GPA scores have a variance of only 1.1. That is, one variable has nearly six times more variance than the other. In such cases, the difference score will be strongly linked to the variable with higher variance, and it will be weakly linked to the variable with lower variance. Interested readers can explore these sources of the problem more in Chapter 7 of Furr (2011), but we will discuss one way of dealing with the problem. If scores on two tests have very different variabilities, one solution is to standardize the test scores (see Chapter 3) prior to calculating difference scores. Recall that a variable that has been standardized has a mean of 0 and a standard deviation of 1.0. If two scales are standardized, then they will have the same mean and standard deviation, and thus they will be on the same metric. Let us revisit our four students, Emily, John, Sarah, and Mark. For a more appropriate examination of the discrepancies between their standardized test performance and their classroom performance, we would standardize their scores. Here are their standard scores (i.e., z scores), along with the differences between them:

Student	ZSAT	ZGPA	Difference
Emily	−.90	.00	−.90
John	−.90	−1.41	.51
Sarah	.30	1.41	−1.11
Mark	1.51	.00	1.51

NOTE: ZSAT = z score for SAT; ZGPA = z score for GPA.

Again, a positive difference score should indicate superiority of standardized test performance over classroom performance. However, the meaning of the scores themselves has changed in an important way. As discussed in Chapter 3, standardized scores represent the individual's score as compared with the other people in the group. For example, John's standardized SAT score is −.90, indicating that he has a below-average performance on standardized testing. But note that his standardized GPA is −1.41, indicating that he is even more below average in terms of classroom performance. Because his standardized testing score is not as bad as his classroom performance, his difference score is positive (i.e., he has higher standardized test performance than class performance, relative to others). In contrast, Sarah's difference score is negative, indicating that her standardized test performance (relative to others) is quite a bit lower than her classroom performance (relative to others). If we now compare John's difference score (1.51) with Sarah's (−1.11), then we might feel that the scores are a more accurate reflection of the real psychological issue under examination. Their two scores differ by nearly two units derived from a standardized metric, and a difference of this size is substantial. Again, if we return to their difference scores (i.e., 999) obtained from the "raw" SAT and GPA scores, we see that John and Emily inaccurately appear to be the same.

Keep in mind, however, that although it is possible to transform test scores so that they share a common metric, it does not necessarily mean that it makes sense to subtract one of these scores from the other. Presumably, difference scores are most meaningful if two test scores are thought to have some psychological attribute in common. For example, it might make sense to create difference scores as a way to examine the difference between SAT and GPA scores because both are thought to be related to academic achievement. It probably might not make as much sense, however, to create difference scores based on scores from an intelligence test and scores from a self-esteem test. The meaning of the difference scores in this case would be less clear.

In sum, the meaningfulness of difference scores depends on the degree to which the two tests have similar variabilities. This is not usually a problem for "change scores," which are derived from administering the same test on different occasions. By using the same test, we usually obtain two sets of scores with reasonably similar metrics. However, researchers and other test users should always examine the variances, even when working with change scores, to detect whether there is a problem. The variability issue is likely to be even more problematic for "discrepancy scores," which are derived from two tests that might have very different metrics. For the analysis of discrepancy scores, we need to standardize the two tests before computing difference scores. Note that the standardization subtly reconceptualizes the issue as the discrepancy between relative levels of two variables (i.e., relative standardized test performance vs. relative classroom performance).

Difference Scores: Summary and Caution

Our treatment of the difference scores is consistent with most psychometric evaluations of difference scores. Following Lord (1956, 1962), it seems that most psychometricians and researchers perceive difference scores as very problematic, partly because they tend to be less reliable than the test scores used in their computation. Indeed, it seems that many behavioral scientists are trained to mistrust difference scores inherently. Thus, if you are a researcher, you might be wary of using difference scores in your work—you are likely to be told that you have committed an egregious error.

Indeed there are reasons to be concerned about the use of difference scores in many cases. That is, our impression is that difference scores do indeed suffer from potential problems in many applications. Whether due to high intercorrelations between the component tests, poor reliability of the component tests, or unequal variances in the component tests, we worry that difference scores often have poor psychometric quality and lead to questionable psychological conclusions. Perhaps even more important, researchers often seem to ignore these problems. That is, many researchers either seem to be unaware of the problems or unsure how to detect and address them. Considering both of these issues, we believe that difference scores are particularly likely to have psychometric flaws and that researchers seem particularly unlikely to recognize or appreciate these flaws. With this in mind, we worry that the use of difference scores in many applications produces information that is of unknown psychological meaning at best and that is psychologically misleading at worst.

For example, the inverse relationship between the reliability of difference scores and the correlation between test scores can create a dilemma in certain situations. Consider an example that commonly occurs in primary schools. In many school districts, learning disability is defined in terms of a discrepancy between a child's score on a standard intelligence test and his or her score on an academic achievement test. If a child has a relatively large discrepancy between these two tests, then he or she might be classified as having some type of learning disability. Thus, the difference between the two scores is used as a measure to establish learning disability. Although standard intelligence tests and well-designed academic achievement tests have strong reliabilities (i.e., R_{XX} and R_{YY} are high), IQ scores are also likely to be highly correlated with academic achievement scores (i.e., r_{XY} is high). Furthermore, it would probably be impossible to find intelligence tests that are not highly correlated with academic achievement tests because the two psychological attributes should share many common psychological features. As illustrated in Figure 6.2, a high correlation between two tests creates a low reliability for the difference between the two tests. Thus, it is possible that the "discrepancy" procedure for defining and identifying learning disabilities is inherently unreliable, leading to questionable decisions in practice.

There is, however, a controversy regarding the quality and reliability of difference scores. Rogosa (1995) and Zimmerman and Williams (1982) provide succinct discussions of factors that contribute to the size of such reliabilities, and they show that, under some special circumstances, difference score reliabilities can be larger than the average of the test reliabilities contributing to the difference scores. The analysis of the reliability of difference scores presented in the current chapter is typical in that it depends on a variety of simplifying assumptions (e.g., regarding the correlation between true scores and the differences as well as regarding the equality of variances across the two testings). As Rogosa shows, if such simplifying assumptions do not hold true, then it is possible that difference scores are quite reliable. Rogosa summarizes his point, noting that "the difference score is reliable when individual differences in true change do exist" (p. 13).

Considering all of this, we recommend caution if and when difference scores are used. In our own work, we usually try to avoid them, opting for alternative procedures such as partial correlations or multiple regression. Indeed, Furr (2011) outlines the concerns and alternatives in much more depth, and interested readers are encouraged to consider that discussion before deciding to work with difference scores.

Summary

This chapter has taken the theory of reliability and translated it into practice. Although test users can never truly know the reliability of a set of test scores, they can use a variety of procedures to estimate the reliability. In this chapter, we have described several of the most familiar and widely used methods for estimating reliability. These three general methods include alternate forms, test–retest, and internal consistency. The accuracy of each method (in terms of providing correct estimates of reliability) depends heavily on a number of assumptions regarding the nature of true scores and error variance.

For a variety of theoretical and practical reasons, internal consistency is the most popular method for estimating reliability. More specifically, coefficient alpha (either raw or standardized) is probably the most commonly reported estimate of reliability, and it is computed by many of the most widely used statistical packages.

From the perspective of internal consistency, there are two core factors that affect reliability. All else being equal, reliability estimates are high for tests in which different parts (i.e., halves or items) are highly correlated with each other. That is, reliability is high for tests that are internally consistent. In addition, reliability estimates are higher for longer tests than for shorter tests (all else being equal). As we demonstrated, the Spearman-Brown "prophecy" formulas can be used to forecast the reliability of tests of specific lengths with specific levels of internal consistency. Such forecasts are useful in the test development and refinement process.

This chapter has also discussed the reliability of difference scores, which are tempting ways of measuring phenomena such as psychological change. Difference scores are more reliable if they are based on tests that are themselves highly reliable. However, they are less reliable if they are based on tests that are highly correlated with each other.

Thus far, we have presented the theoretical basis of reliability, which is one of the most fundamental concepts in measurement theory. In addition, we have presented the method through which reliability is actually estimated for real data. In Chapter 7, we highlight the importance of reliability—why it commands so much attention from psychometricians and test users. As you will see, the reliability of test scores has important implications for test development, for applied uses of psychological tests, and for research uses of psychological tests.

Note

1. Equation 6.10 is a very general statement of the reliability of difference scores. It is based on the basic assumptions of classical test theory, with no additional assumptions or constraints. In some sources (including a previous edition of this book), you might see a different equation for the reliability of difference scores:

$$R_d = \frac{.5(R_{XX} + R_{YY}) - r_{XY}}{1 + r_{XY}}.$$

This alternative equation is indeed accurate, but only if the two tests have equal observed-score variabilities (i.e., only if ($S^2_{X_o} = S^2_{Y_o}$). When the variabilities are not equal, this equation provides an inaccurate estimate of reliability. Thus, Equation 6.10 is the more generally accurate equation.

Suggested Readings

An extensive presentation of many different methods for estimating reliability, in addition to discussions of the required assumptions, can be found in:

Feldt, L. S., & Brennan, R. L. (1989). Reliability. In R. L. Linn (Ed.), *Educational measurement* (3rd ed., pp. 105–146). Washington, DC: American Council on Education.

An evaluation of the adequacy of various estimates of reliability is presented by:

Osburn, H. G. (2000). Coefficient alpha and related internal consistency reliability coefficients. *Psychological Methods, 5,* 343–355.

An introduction to reliability generalization is presented in:

Vacha-Haase, T. (1998). Reliability generalization: Exploring variance in measurement error affecting score reliability across studies. *Educational and Psychological Measurement, 58,* 6–20.

A short, compete, and relatively easy to follow discussion of the reliability of differences scores can be found in:

Zimmerman, D. W., & Williams, R. H. (1982). Gain scores in research can be highly reliable. *Journal of Educational Measurement, 19,* 1982.

CHAPTER 7

The Importance of Reliability

Throughout this book, we have emphasized the fact that psychological measurement is crucial for research in behavioral science and for the application of behavioral science. As a cornerstone of a test's psychometric quality, reliability is a fundamental issue in understanding and evaluating the quality of psychological measurement. The previous two chapters detailed the conceptual basis of reliability and the procedures used to estimate a test's reliability. In this chapter, we articulate the important roles that reliability plays in the applied practice of behavioral science, in behavioral research, and in test construction and refinement.

Applied Behavioral Practice: Evaluation of an Individual's Test Score

Psychological test scores are often used by psychologists and others to make decisions that have important effects on people's lives. For example, intelligence test scores can be used by courts to determine eligibility for the death sentence for convicted murderers. This may be an extreme example of how test scores can affect our lives, but it illustrates the importance of having reliable scores. It would be tragic, to say the least, if someone were sentenced to death based on an unreliable intelligence test score. There are uncounted other, albeit less dramatic, instances in which the reliability of scores on psychological tests can have an impact on the lives of ordinary people. Children are often removed from standard academic classrooms and assigned to special classes based on intelligence and achievement test scores. Similarly, tests such as the SAT and Graduate Record Examination (GRE) are used to make decisions about college admissions, and employers often use tests to make hiring and promotion decisions. Classroom instructors may not give the problem of test reliability much thought when they give their class examinations, but scores on those examinations can have an influence on students' futures.

A test's reliability has crucial implications for the quality of decisions that are made on the basis of their test scores. Recall that we can never know an individual's "true" level on an unobservable psychological construct. For example, we can never know a person's true level of intelligence or capacity for college achievement. Thus, we use psychological test scores to indicate or estimate an individual's true level of some psychological attribute. Because test scores are only estimates of people's actual psychological characteristics and because decisions about persons' lives are often based partly on these scores, we must be able to evaluate not only the quality of test scores in general but also the quality of the score obtained by any particular individual on a test. That is, we would like to be able to gauge the precision or accuracy of an individual's test score as an estimate of the individual's psychological attribute. As we will see, the reliability of test scores can be used to calculate information that will help us evaluate the quality of particular test scores.

Two important sources of information can help us evaluate an individual's test score. First, a *point estimate* is a specific value that is interpreted as a "best estimate" of an individual's standing on a particular psychological attribute. As we will discuss, there are two ways of obtaining a point estimate for an individual. The second source of information that helps us evaluate an individual's test scores is a *confidence interval*. A confidence interval reflects a *range* of values that is often interpreted as a range in which the true score is likely to fall. The logic of a confidence interval is based on the understanding that an observed score is simply an estimate of a true score. Because of measurement error, the observed score may not be exactly equal to the true score. The confidence interval around a particular observed score gives us an idea of its accuracy or precision as an estimate of a true score. If we find that an individual's observed score is associated with a wide confidence interval, then we know that the observed score is an imprecise or inaccurate point estimate of the individual's true score. We will see that these values—point estimates and confidence intervals—are directly affected by test score reliability.

Point Estimates of True Scores

Two kinds of point estimates can be derived from an individual's observed test score, representing the best single estimate of the individual's true score. One point estimate is based solely on an individual's observed test score. When an individual takes a test at a given point in time, his or her observed score is itself a point estimate. In fact, it is the single best estimate of the quantity of an underlying psychological attribute at the moment that the individual took the test. For example, if you give someone a self-esteem test, his or her score on the test is a point estimate of his or her true self-esteem score.

The second point estimate, sometimes called an adjusted true score estimate, takes measurement error into account. Once again, recall that an individual's observed score on any given test is affected by measurement error. Because testing is never perfect, an individual's test score may be somewhat inflated or deflated by momentary factors, such as fatigue, distraction, and so on. Therefore, an individual's test score at one point is artificially high or low compared with the score that the individual would likely obtain if he or she took the test a second time. As a matter of fact, if an individual took the same test on two occasions, then he or she would likely obtain two observed scores that are at least slightly different from each other. Both of those observed test scores could be considered point estimates of the individual's true score. With an understanding of reliability and the nature of measurement error, we can use an individual's observed score from one testing occasion to estimate the results of the second testing occasion. This produces an adjusted true score estimate, which reflects an effect called regression to the mean.

Regression to the mean refers to the likelihood that on a second testing an individual's score is likely to be closer to the group mean than was his or her first score. That is, if an individual's observed score is above the mean on the first testing occasion, then he or she is likely to score somewhat lower (i.e., closer to the mean) on the second testing occasion. Similarly, if an individual's observed score is *below* the mean on the first testing occasion, then he or she is likely to score somewhat *higher* (i.e., closer to the mean) on the second testing occasion. This prediction is again based on the logic of classical test theory (CTT) and random measurement error. In Chapter 5, we learned that measurement error is random and likely to affect all test scores to some degree—artificially inflating some scores (that end up relatively high) and artificially deflating some scores (that end up relatively low).

The adjusted true score estimate is intended to reflect the discrepancy in an individual's observed scores that is likely to arise between two testing occasions. The size and direction of this discrepancy will be a function of three factors: (1) the reliability of the test scores, (2) the size of the difference between the individual's original observed test score and the mean of the test scores, and (3) the direction of the difference between the original score and the mean of the test scores These factors can be used to calculate the adjusted true score estimate through the following equation:

$$X_{est} = \overline{X} + R_{xx}(X_o - \overline{X}), \quad (7.1)$$

where X_{est} is the adjusted true score estimate (i.e., an estimated result from a second testing occasion), $\overline{X}$ is the test score mean, R_{XX} is the reliability of the test, and X_o is the individual's observed score. Imagine that you have scores from a multiple-choice exam given to a class. There are 40 questions on the exam, and the exam mean is 30. Assume that the exam has an estimated reliability of .90 (this would be a very high reliability for most class examinations). If a student had a score of 38 on the exam, then his or her estimated true score would be

$$X_{est} = 30 + .90(38 - 30),$$
$$= 37.2.$$

Notice that the estimated true score (37.2) is closer to the mean (30) than was the initial observed score (38). Thus, the adjusted true score attempts to account for the likely occurrence of regression to the mean.

There are at least two important points to note about the adjusted true score estimate, in relation to the observed score. First, test reliability influences the difference between the estimated true score and the observed score. Specifically, as reliability decreases, the difference between the adjusted true score estimate and the observed score increases. That is, poorer reliability produces bigger discrepancies between the estimated true score and the observed score. This reflects the fact that regression to the mean is more likely to occur (or is likely to be more substantial) when a test's scores are affected heavily by measurement error. For example, assume that the class test's reliability is .50 and we computed the adjusted true score estimate for an individual with an observed score of 38:

$$X_{est} = 30 + .50(38 - 30),$$
$$= 34.$$

Thus, for an individual with a test score of 38, the predicted effect of regression to the mean is 4 points (38–34 = 4) for a test with poor reliability but less than 1 point (38–37.2 = .8) for a test with strong reliability.

A second important implication of the adjusted true score estimate is that the observed score's extremity influences the difference between the estimated true score and the observed score. Specifically, the difference will be larger for relatively extreme observed scores (high or low) than for relatively moderate scores. For example, let us compute the adjusted true score estimate for an individual with an observed score of 22 (i.e., an observed score that is 8 points below the mean of 30) on a test with a reliability of .90:

$$X_{est} = 30 + .90(22 - 30),$$
$$= 22.8.$$

Note that the adjusted true score estimate is 0.8 points closer to the mean than the observed score in this case. Now, let us compute the adjusted true score estimate for an individual with an observed score of 27 (i.e., a less extreme observed score that is only 3 points below the mean of 30):

$$X_{est} = 30 + .90(27 - 30),$$
$$= 27.3.$$

Note that this adjusted true score estimate is only 0.3 points closer to the mean than the observed score. Thus, the adjustment was more substantial for the relatively extreme observed score, (i.e., 22) than it was for the less extreme observed score (i.e., 27).

You might be wondering which score, X_{est} or X_o, is the best estimate of the true score. The observed score is an unbiased estimate of the true score and as such represents the best estimate of the true score, but the adjusted true score estimate is the best estimate of a predicted true score. If you gave a class exam and someone does really well on it, and you use that information to predict his or her score on the next examination, a regressed score would be, in all likelihood, a better guess than his or her observed score on the first examination.

Although the ideas of an adjusted true score estimate and regression to the mean are pervasive features of most attempts to evaluate individual scores on a test (e.g., see Wechsler, 2003a, 2003b), there are reasons to approach these ideas with caution. First, as we mentioned, an observed score on a test is the best estimate of the psychological attribute that we are trying to measure. Except in the case where we intend to predict a person's score on a subsequent test, there seems to be little reason to correct observed scores by adjusting them for regression to the mean. Second, although most psychologists seem to think that regression to the mean is, in the long run, a mathematical certainty, Rogosa (1995) has shown that there are circumstances in which it will not occur. Nevertheless, as we will see when we discuss true score confidence intervals, it is common practice to convert observed scores to adjusted true score estimates.

True Score Confidence Intervals

In applied testing situations, point estimates of an individual's true score are usually reported along with *true score confidence intervals*. Roughly speaking, confidence intervals reflect the accuracy or precision of the point estimate as reflective of an individual's true score. For example, we might administer the Wecshler Intelligence Scale for Children (WISC) to a child and find that the child obtains a score of 106. Taking this observed score as an estimate of the child's true score, we might calculate a confidence interval and conclude that we are "95% confident that the individual's true IQ score falls in the range of 100–112" (Wechsler, 2003b, p. 37). The width of a confidence interval (e.g., a 12-point range) reflects the precision of the point estimate. You will probably not be surprised to learn that this precision is closely related to reliability—tests with high reliability provide estimates that are relatively precise.

The link between reliability and the precision of confidence intervals is made through the standard error of measurement (se_m). As discussed in Chapter 5, the se_m represents the average size of the error scores that affect observed scores. The larger the se_m, the greater the average difference between observed scores and true scores. Thus, the se_m can be seen as an index of measurement error, and it is closely linked to reliability. In fact, Equation 5.16 presented the exact link between the standard error of measurement (se_m), reliability (R_{XX}), and the standard deviation of a test's observed scores (s_o):

$$se_m = s_o\sqrt{1 - R_{XX}} \ .$$

For our classroom test, we might find that the estimated reliability is .90 and the standard deviation of observed scores is $s_o = 6$. From this, we can estimate the standard error of measurement as

$$se_m = 6\sqrt{1 - .90},$$
$$= 1.90.$$

Once we have estimated the standard error of measurement for a set of test scores, we can compute a confidence interval around an individual's estimated true score. For example, if someone scored 32 on our class examination, we might wish to report a 95% confidence interval around that score. To do this, we would use the following equation:

$$95\% \text{ confidence interval} = X_o \pm (1.96)(se_m), \qquad (7.2)$$

where X_o is the observed test score (i.e., a point estimate of the individual's true score) and se_m is the standard error of measurement of the test scores. The final component of this equation (1.96) reflects the fact that we are interested in a 95% confidence interval rather than a 90% interval or any other "degree of confidence" (we will address alternate "degrees of confidence" later). Some readers—particularly those who have a background in statistical significance testing—might recognize this value as being associated with a probability of .95 from the standard normal distribution. Based on Equation 7.2, for our test, the 95% confidence interval around a score of 32 is 28.3 to 35.7:

$$95\% \text{ confidence interval} = 32 \pm (1.96)(1.90),$$
$$= 32 \pm 3.7,$$
$$= 28.3 \text{ to } 35.7.$$

Using the logic expressed by the above quote from Wechsler, we might interpret this result as indicating that we are 95% confident that the individual's true score falls in the range of 28.3 to 35.7.

Unfortunately, the exact interpretation of the true score confidence intervals is somewhat controversial. According to true score theory, observed scores are distributed normally around true scores. Because an observed score is the best estimate of a true score, the observed score represents the mean of this distribution. In our example, a score of 32 is within a 95% confidence interval that ranges from 28.3 to 35.7, but what does it mean to say that the score is in this confidence interval? Perhaps the most widely offered answer to this question is that "there is a 95% chance that the true score falls within the confidence interval." Another way to say the same thing is "The probability is .95 that the confidence interval contains the true score." These statements might be interpreted in two different ways. They might mean that there is a 95% chance that a person's true score will fall in the interval on repeated testing with the same or parallel tests, or it might mean that if you had many people with the same true score take the same test, 95% of their observed scores would fall in the interval. However, disagreement exists over such interpretations. For example, Knapp (2005) objects to the use of answers such as "There is a 95% chance that the true score falls within the confidence interval" because answers of this type imply that true scores are deviating around an observed score when it is clear that this cannot be the case. We have sympathy for Knapp's view, but in most cases, when confidence intervals are reported, they are interpreted in a way that suggests that true scores are falling somewhere in the confidence interval.

As mentioned earlier, the precision of a true score estimate is closely related to reliability. Briefly put, highly reliable tests will produce narrower confidence intervals than less reliable tests. We just saw that for our highly reliable test (R_{xx} = .90), the se_m was 1.90 and the confidence interval had a range of 7.4 points (35.7 − 28.3 = 7.4). The size of this range reflects the precision of the confidence interval—the smaller or narrower the interval, the more precise the observed score is as an estimate of the true score. Although highly reliable tests will produce narrow intervals, less reliable tests will produce wider (i.e., larger) confidence intervals, reflecting a less precise estimate of the true score. For example, let us imagine that our test had the same observed score standard deviation as our previous example (s_o = 6) but a lower reliability (say only R_{xx} = .50). In this case of a test with poor reliability, the standard error of measurement would be 4.2:

$$se_m = 6\sqrt{1 - .50},$$
$$= 4.24.$$

Note that this se_m is larger than it was for the previous example, in which reliability was .90 and the se_m was only 1.90. As we have seen, the se_m has a direct effect on the confidence interval. So in the case of our low-reliability test, the 95% confidence interval around a score of 32 is relatively a wide range of 23.7 to 40.3:

$$95\% \text{ confidence interval} = 32 \pm (1.96)(4.24),$$
$$= 32 \pm 8.3,$$
$$= 23.7 \text{ to } 40.3.$$

Thus, the test with poor reliability produced a much less precise (i.e., wider) confidence interval than the test with high reliability. Specifically, the test with R_{xx} = .50 produced an interval of 16.6 points (40.3 − 23.7 = 16.6), but we saw that the test with R_{xx} = .90 produced an interval of only 7.4 points. It is a much stronger and more precise statement to say that "we are 95% confident that an individual's true score lies between 28.3 and 35.7" than it is to say that "we are 95% confident that the individual's true score lies anywhere all the way from 23.7 to 40.3."

For our purposes, the important message from this section is that reliability affects the confidence, accuracy, or precision with which an individual's true score is estimated. That is, reliability affects the standard error of measurement, which affects the width of a confidence interval around an individual's estimated true score. Beyond this core issue, we should acknowledge that there are variations on the ways in which confidence intervals are computed and integrated with true score estimates. Confidence intervals can be computed for various degrees of confidence (e.g., 99% or 90% instead of 95%), they can be computed by using either the standard error of measurement or a value called the standard error of estimate (which is also affected by reliability), and they can be applied to either observed score estimates of true scores or adjusted true score estimates (as described in the previous section). Although such variations emerge in some applications of psychological testing, details of these variations are well beyond the scope of our current discussion.

The issues associated with estimated true scores and true score intervals might seem abstract and esoteric, but they can have important consequences in applied settings in which test scores are used to make decisions about the lives of individual people. For example, children are often classified as having mental retardation if they have an intelligence test score below 70. We know, however, that any IQ score will have some degree of unreliability associated with it (although the reliability of scores on standard, individually administered intelligence tests is very high). The degree of test score unreliability should influence your interpretation of an observed score; to what extent does an observed score reflect a child's true scores? Imagine that a child has a tested IQ score of 69. How confident would you be that the child's true score is below 70, and how likely is it that, on a second testing, the child's tested score might be greater than 70? We know that, in all likelihood, if this child is given a second intelligence test the child's IQ score will increase because of regression to the mean. At what point do we take these factors into consideration, and how do we do so when making a decision about the child's intellectual status? It is imperative that those making these types of decisions recognize the problems associated with the interpretation of psychological test scores. Our hope is that you recognize the problem and appreciate the fact that reliability has a fundamental role in it.

Behavioral Research

Reliability has important implications for interpreting and conducting research in the behavioral sciences. The interpretability of research in areas such as psychology and education hinges on the quality of the measurement procedures used in the research. In this section, we explain how reliability and measurement error affect the results of behavioral research. Awareness of these effects is crucial for interpreting behavioral research accurately and for conducting behavioral research in a productive way.

Reliability, True Associations, and Observed Associations

Earlier in this book, we discussed the importance of understanding associations between psychological variables (see Chapter 3). That is, one of the most fundamental goals of research is to discover the ways in which important variables are related to each other. For example, researchers might want to know whether SAT scores are associated with academic performance or whether personality similarity is associated with relationship satisfaction or whether "dosage of medication" is associated with decreases in depressive affect. Thus, knowing the direction and magnitude of the associations between variables is a central part of scientific research.

Psychological scientists usually rely on several basic ways of quantifying the association between variables. In terms of psychometrics, the most common way of doing this is through a correlation coefficient (again, see Chapter 3). Thus, in the following discussion, we focus mainly on the correlation coefficient as a way of explaining the importance that reliability has on behavioral research. However, it is important to realize that researchers often use other statistics to reflect the association between variables. For example, experimental psychologists are more likely to use statistics such as Cohen's d or η^2 rather than a correlation coefficient. We will touch on these statistics briefly here.

According to CTT, the correlation between observed scores on two measures (i.e., $r_{X_oY_o}$) is determined by two factors: (1) the correlation between the true scores of the two psychological constructs being assessed by the measures (i.e., $r_{X_tY_t}$) and (b) the reliabilities of the two measures (i.e., R_{XX} R_{YY} and). Specifically,

$$r_{X_oY_o} = r_{X_tY_t} \sqrt{R_{XX}R_{YY}} \cdot$$

(7.3)

Equation 7.3 is the key element of this section, with many important implications for research and applied measurement. Before we discuss those implications, we will explain how Equation 7.3 follows logically from CTT. Recall again from Chapter 3 that the correlation between two variables (r_{XY}) is the covariance divided by two standard deviations:

$$r_{XY} = \frac{c_{XY}}{s_X s_Y} \cdot$$

We will think about the numerator of this equation for a moment. Recall from Chapter 5 that, according to CTT, observed scores are composite variables (i.e., $X_o = X_t + X_e$ and $Y_o = Y_t + Y_e$). Therefore, the covariance between two sets of observed scores (i.e., observed scores on X and observed scores on Y) can be seen as the covariance between two composite variables. Following the example outlined in Chapter 3's discussion of the covariance between composite variables, the covariance between X and Y (i.e., $c_{X_oY_o}$) is

$$c_{X_oY_o} = c_{X_tY_t} + c_{X_tY_e} + c_{X_eY_t} + c_{X_eY_e},$$

where $c_{X_tY_t}$ is the covariance between true scores on test X and true scores on test Y, $c_{X_tY_e}$ is the covariance between true scores on test X and error scores on test Y, $c_{X_eY_t}$ is the covariance between error scores on test X and true scores on test Y, and $c_{X_eY_e}$ is the covariance between error scores on test X and error scores on test Y. By definition, error scores occur as if they are random. Therefore, error scores are uncorrelated with true scores, and error scores on test X are uncorrelated with error scores on test Y. Consequently, the three covariances that include error scores are equal to 0, which means that the covariance between observed scores reduces to the covariance between true scores ($c_{XY} = c_{X_tY_t}$). Thus, returning to Equation 7.3, the correlation between two sets of observed scores is

$$r_{X_oY_o} = \frac{c_{X_tY_t}}{s_{o}s_{Y_o}} \cdot$$

(7.4)

Next, we will think about the denominator of this equation. Recall from Chapter 5 that variability in a test's observed scores (e.g., s_{X_o} and s_{Y_o}) is related to the test's reliability. Specifically, reliability can be defined as the ratio of true score variance to observed score variance:

$$R_{xx} = \frac{s_{X_t}^2}{s_{X_o}^2} \text{ and } R_{YY} = \frac{s_{Y_t}^2}{s_{Y_o}^2}.$$

Rearranging these, we can express the observed standard deviations as a function of reliability and standard deviations of true scores:

$$s_{X_o} = \frac{s_{X_t}}{\sqrt{R_{xx}}} \tag{7.5a}$$

and

$$s_{Y_o} = \frac{s_{Y_t}}{\sqrt{R_{YY}}}. \tag{7.5b}$$

Entering Equations 7.5a and 7.5b into the denominator of Equation 7.4 and then rearranging, we find that

$$r_{X_o Y_o} = \frac{c_{X_t Y_t}}{\frac{s_{X_t}}{\sqrt{R_{XX}}} \frac{s_{Y_t}}{\sqrt{R_{YY}}}},$$

$$= \frac{c_{X_t Y_t}}{s_{X_t} s_{Y_t}} \sqrt{R_{XX} R_{YY}}.$$

And again, we realize that a correlation is equal to a covariance divided by standard deviations (again, see Chapter 3's discussion of the correlation coefficient). In this case, we divide true score covariance (i.e., $c_{X_t Y_t}$) by the standard deviation of true scores (i.e., s_{X_t} and s_{Y_t}), producing the correlation between true scores ($r_{X_t Y_t}$). This simplifies the equation to

$$r_{X_o Y_o} = r_{X_t Y_t} \sqrt{R_{XX} R_{YY}}.$$

This brings us back to Equation 7.3. Thus, CTT implies directly that the correlation between two measures (i.e., between observed scores) is determined by the correlation between psychological constructs and by the reliabilities of the measures.

To illustrate this, imagine that we wish to examine the association between self-esteem and academic achievement. To investigate this issue, we conduct a study in which participants complete a self-esteem questionnaire and a measure of academic achievement. Imagine that the true correlation between the constructs is .40 (i.e., $r_{X_t Y_t} = .40$). Of course, we would not actually know this true correlation; in fact, the entire point of conducting a study is to uncover or estimate this correlation.

In addition, imagine that both measures have good reliability—say, reliability is .80 for the self-esteem questionnaire and .86 for the academic achievement test. The correlation between the two measures will be

$$r_{X_oY_o} = r_{X_tY_t} \sqrt{R_{XX}R_{YY}},$$
$$= .40\sqrt{(.80)(.86)},$$
$$= .40(.829),$$
$$= .33.$$

Note that the correlation between observed scores on the two measures is smaller than the correlation between the two constructs. Specifically, the correlation between the two constructs is .40, but the correlation that we would actually obtain in our study is only .33. This discrepancy is a result of measurement error, as we will explain next.

Measurement Error (Low Reliability) Attenuates the Observed Associations Between Measures

The discrepancy between observed associations and true associations reflects four important implications of Equation 7.3. In this section, we describe and illustrate these important implications.

First, in research, observed associations (i.e., between measures) will always be weaker than true associations (i.e., between psychological constructs). This arises from two facts of life in measurement. One fact of life in measurement is that measurement is never perfect. Although scientists might be able to develop very precise measures of their constructs, measures will always be affected by measurement error to some degree. That is, measures are not perfectly reliable. A second fact of life in measurement is that imperfect measurement weakens or "attenuates" observed associations. For example, as shown by Equation 7.3, any time that reliabilities are less than perfect, an observed correlation will be weaker (i.e., closer to 0) than the true correlation. For example, what would the observed correlation be if the true correlation is .40 and both measures were nearly perfectly reliable (say both had reliabilities of .98)?

$$r_{X_oY_o} = .40\sqrt{(.98)(.98)},$$
$$= .40(.98),$$
$$= .39.$$

Thus, even the slightest imperfections in measurement will begin to attenuate observed associations. In sum, given that measurement is never perfect and that imperfect measurement attenuates our observed associations, our observed associations will always be weaker than the true associations.

A second important implication of Equation 7.3 is that the degree of attenuation is determined by the reliabilities of the measures. Simply put, the poorer the measure, the greater the attenuation. More precisely, measures that have low reliability produce more extreme attenuation than measures that have high reliability. Consider again our example of the association between self-esteem and academic achievement, in which we assumed that the true correlation was .40. We saw earlier that, using measures with reliabilities of .86 and .80, the correlation between measures was attenuated to .33. What would the correlation be if the measures of self-esteem and academic achievement were poorer? For example, if the reliabilities were only .60 for the self-esteem measure and .50 for the academic achievement measure, then we would obtain a correlation of only .22:

$$r_{X_oY_o} = .40\sqrt{(.60)(.50)},$$
$$= .40(.548),$$
$$= .22.$$

Obviously, this is a more extreme discrepancy between the true correlation and the observed correlation than we saw in the earlier example. Furthermore, the observed correlation can be extremely attenuated even if only one of the measures has poor reliability. For example, imagine that the academic achievement measure has good reliability (say .80) but the self-esteem questionnaire has very poor reliability (say .30). In this case, the observed correlation is attenuated to .20:

$$r_{X_oY_o} = .40\sqrt{(.80)(.30)},$$
$$= .40(.490),$$
$$= .20.$$

In sum, the degree of attenuation is determined by the reliabilities of the two measures. If even one measure has poor reliability, the observed correlation can be considerably weaker than the true correlation. As we will see, such attenuation can have important effects on the accuracy with which we interpret research findings.

A third important implication of the fact that measurement error attenuates associations is that error constrains the maximum association that could be found between two measures. For example, imagine that you are interested in the association between academic motivation and academic achievement. You hypothesize that students who have relatively high levels of academic motivation will have relatively high levels of academic achievement. That is, students who care strongly about doing well in school should generally perform better than students who do not care about doing well (presumably because highly motivated students are more inclined to do homework, to pay attention in class, etc.). Although you believe that your hypothesis is reasonable, you do not know the size of the association between motivation and achievement; in fact, you do not even know if there truly is *any* association between the constructs. Therefore, you conduct a study in which your participants complete a measure of academic achievement and a measure of academic motivation.

While planning your study, you search for measures of your two constructs, and you pay careful attention to the reliabilities of the various measures that you might use. You are able to find a highly reliable measure of academic achievement (say reliability = .86), but the only measure of academic motivation that you can

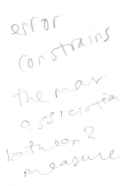
error
constrains
the max
association
between 2
measures

find has a poor reliability (say .40). Because you are familiar with Equation 7.3 and you know that measurement error attenuates the correlation between measures, you rightfully worry about the poor reliability of the motivation measure. You might even wonder about the highest possible correlation that you might obtain. That is, if your hypothesis is exactly correct and there is a perfect association between motivation and achievement, then what would your study reveal? By using Equation 7.3 and assuming a perfect association between the constructs (i.e., assuming that $r_{X_t Y_t} = 1.0$), you find that

$$r_{X_o Y_o} = 1.00\sqrt{(.86)(.40)},$$
$$= 1.00(.587),$$
$$= .59.$$

This simple analysis tells you that even if your hypothesis is completely accurate and motivation is perfectly correlated with achievement, your study would reveal a correlation of "only" .59 between the two measures. Although a correlation of .59 would probably be taken as reasonable support for your theory, you should realize that this value represents the maximum possible correlation that you could hope to obtain if you use the two measures that you have chosen. That is, given the reliabilities of your two measures, you can obtain a correlation of .59 *at best*.

This information can be useful when you interpret the correlation that you actually obtain in your study. Because motivation and achievement are probably not perfectly correlated (i.e., it is likely that $r_{X_t Y_t} < 1.0$), you will probably obtain a correlation that is quite a bit weaker than .59. In fact, you are likely to obtain a correlation much closer to .30 or even weaker, which might lead you to conclude that motivation is only moderately or even weakly associated with achievement. However, it might be very useful to interpret your results in the context of the best possible results that you could have hoped to obtain given the limits of your measures. Indeed, a correlation of .30 is much more compelling when you realize that a correlation of .59 was the best you could have hoped for considering the reliability of your measures.

A fourth important implication of Equation 7.3 is that it is possible to estimate the true association between a pair of constructs. When researchers actually conduct a study, they know or can estimate all but one component of Equation 7.3. Specifically, they do not know the true correlation between constructs; however, they can compute the observed correlation between the measures, and they can estimate the measures' reliabilities (using one of the procedures discussed in Chapter 6). By knowing all but one component of Equation 7.3, researchers can solve for the unknown component. In fact, the equation can be rearranged algebraically, producing a way of estimating the true correlation:

$$r_{X_t Y_t} = \frac{r_{X_o Y_o}}{\sqrt{R_{XX} R_{YY}}}.$$

(7.6)

Equation 7.6 is known as the *correction for attenuation* because it allows researchers to estimate the correlation that would be obtained if it were not affected by attenuation. That is, it allows researchers to estimate the true correlation—the correlation that would be obtained if perfectly reliable measures had been used in the study. If the measures were perfectly reliable, then the observed correlation would be exactly equal to the correlation between true scores.

As an illustration, assume that your study of the association between academic achievement and academic motivation revealed an observed correlation of $r_{X_o Y_o} = .26$ based on the motivation questionnaire with an estimated reliability of .40 and the achievement test with an estimated reliability of .86. Of course, you do not know the true correlation, but you can use Equation 7.6 to estimate it:

$$r_{X_t Y_t} = \frac{r_{X_o Y_o}}{\sqrt{R_{XX} R_{YY}}},$$

$$= \frac{.26}{\sqrt{(.86)(.40)}},$$

$$= \frac{.26}{.587},$$

$$= .44.$$

Thus, if all the assumptions of CTT are correct (e.g., error affects test scores as if it is random), then you estimate that the true correlation between motivation and achievement is .44.

The correction for attenuation is an important perspective within the overall connections among reliability, measurement error, observed associations, and true associations; however, the correction procedure is not used explicitly very often in real research. That is, when reading research reports, you do not often see research-ers conducting the correction for attenuation. Interestingly, recent developments in statistical analyses conduct an implicit correction for attenuation. Some of you might be familiar with a statistical procedure called structural equation modeling or latent variable modeling. Briefly, this procedure is designed (in part) to estimate the associations among unobservable psychological constructs by separating them from the effects of measurement error. In essence, the associations among psycho-logical constructs in structural equation modeling are essentially based on correla-tions that have been corrected for attenuation.

Reliability, Effect Sizes, and Statistical Significance

The fact that measurement error (i.e., low reliability) attenuates observed asso-ciations has several implications for interpreting and conducting research. First, the results of a study should always be interpreted in the context of reliability. Although we have been discussing the "results" in terms of the observed correlation between measures, there are several different kinds of results that you might see. At least two basic kinds of results should be of interest in behavioral research.

These results—effect sizes and statistical significance—are affected heavily by reliability and measurement error. People who read and/or produce research should recognize these effects and take them into account when considering the results of scientific research.

Effect Sizes. Effect sizes are descriptive statistics that represent the results of a study as a matter of *degree*. For example, some effect sizes reflect the degree of association among variables, and others reflect the size of the differences among groups or conditions. For example, the correlation coefficient is an effect size that represents the degree to which two variables are associated with each other. Indeed, the previous sections describe the way in which this particular effect size (i.e., the correlation between observed scores on two variables) is affected by reliability. In addition to correlation coefficients, effect sizes also include statistics such as regression coefficients, R^2 values, η^2 values (from analysis of variance), and Cohen's d (from t tests of means).

More and more, researchers are recognizing that effect sizes are a crucial part of their scientific results, arguably the most crucial. To fully understand the nature of their scientific findings, researchers should compute and interpret one or more effect sizes (Wilkinson & APA Task Force on Statistical Inference, 1999). In fact, some researchers have suggested that "the primary product of a research inquiry is one or more measures of effect size" (Cohen, 1990, p. 1310), and there is a clear trend for scholarly journals to require or encourage researchers to present effect sizes. Thus, it is crucially important to realize that effect sizes are affected directly by measurement error and reliability.

Although a full examination of such statistics is beyond the scope of this book, Table 7.1 summarizes the link between reliability and effect sizes (i.e., associations/differences) for three effect sizes that are very common in behavioral research—correlations, Cohen's d, and η^2. These effect sizes reflect three fundamental types of analytic contexts: (1) the correlation is usually used to represent the association between two continuous variables (e.g., Intelligence and Academic Achievement), (2) Cohen's d is usually used when examining the association between a dichotomous variable and a continuous variable (e.g., Biological Sex and Academic Achievement), and (3) η^2 is usually used when examining the association between a categorical variable with more than two levels (e.g., Dosage of Medication: 0, 10, and 20 mg) and a continuous variable (e.g., Level of Depressive Affect).

For example, researchers examining sex differences in academic achievement might compute a Cohen's d to reflect the magnitude of those observed differences:

$$d_{X_o} = \frac{\left| \overline{X}_{O1} - \overline{X}_{O2} \right|}{\sqrt{\dfrac{s_{O1}^2 + s_{O2}^2}{2}}}$$

In this particular form of the equation (which is appropriate when the two groups have equal numbers of participants), $\overline{X}_{O1}$ and $\overline{X}_{O2}$ are the two groups' observed mean levels of achievement, and s_{O1}^2 and s_{O2}^2 are the two groups' variances of observed achievement scores. The lower limit of Cohen's d is 0 (reflecting no difference between the two groups' mean levels of achievement), but its upper limit is, in theory, unlimited. Usually, the values fall between 0 and 1.5, with larger values reflecting bigger differences between the groups' means. Table 7.1 shows that the observed value for Cohen's d (d_{X_o}) depends on two things: (1) the true value of Cohen's d (i.e., d_{X_T}, the degree to which the male and female participants differ in their true average levels of Academic Achievement) and (2) the reliability of the measure of academic achievement (i.e., R_{XX}).

Table 7.1   Links Between Reliability, Effect Sizes, and Inferential
Statistics in Three Basic Analytic Contexts

Analytic Context	Effect Size	Inferential Statistic
Association between variables	Correlation $$r_{X_o Y_o} = r_{X_t Y_t} \sqrt{R_{XX} R_{YY}}$$	t test of correlation $$t = \frac{r_{X_t Y_t} \sqrt{R_{XX} R_{YY}}}{\sqrt{1 - r^2_{X_t Y_t} R_{XX} R_{YY}}} \sqrt{N-2}$$
Group differences[a] (two groups, equally sized)	Cohen's d $$d_{X_o} = d_{X_t} \sqrt{R_{XX}}$$	Independent groups t test $$t = d_{X_t} \sqrt{R_{XX}} \left(\frac{\sqrt{N-2}}{2} \right)$$
Group differences (two or more groups)	Eta squared $$\eta^2_{X_o} = \eta^2_{X_t} \sqrt{R_{XX}}$$	F test (e.g., analysis of variance) $$F = \frac{\eta^2_{X_t} R_{XX}}{1 - \eta^2_{X_t} R_{XX}} \left(\frac{df_{\text{Error}}}{df_{\text{Effect}}} \right)$$

a. The reliability values in these equations refer to reliability within each group, assuming that the groups have equal reliability.

The hypothetical data in Table 7.2 illustrate this effect for Cohen's d. This data set is much smaller than is typically found (or recommended) in behavioral research, but it reflects a hypothetical set of males and females who are measured on academic achievement (using a 0–4 scale). The "Observed Score" column presents these measured scores. If we temporarily pretend to be omniscient, then let's say we also know the participants' true levels of academic achievement and the degree to which their observed scores are affected by measurement error. Within each of these groups, the reliability of scores on the DV (i.e., Academic Achievement) is much poorer than we would typically like, being only $R_{XX} = .49$. Note that the Cohen's d value for the true scores is extremely robust ($d_{X_T} = 1.52$):

$$d_{X_t} = \frac{|3.025 - 2.375|}{\sqrt{\dfrac{0.182 + 0.182}{2}}} = \frac{0.650}{0.427} = 1.52.$$

This "true score effect size" value indicates that the "true" means are approximately 1.5 standard deviations apart—an extremely large difference, suggesting that the females truly are much more academically capable than males. In contrast, the Cohen's d value for the observed scores is noticeably less, $d_{X_o} = 1.07$. This "observed score effect size" is consistent with the equation in Table 7.2, as $1.07 = 1.52 \sqrt{.49}$. Note that measurement error creates larger variances among the observed scores ($s^2_{o1} = s^2_{o2} = 0.369$) than among true scores ($s^2_{T1} = s^2_{T2} = 0.182$). Moreover, the relatively

Table 7.2   Hypothetical Data Illustrating the Effect of Reliability on Effect Sizes and Significance Tests

Participant	Observed Score (X_O)		True Score (X_T)		Measurement Error (X_E)
Males					
1	1.6	=	2	+	−0.4
2	2.05	=	2.25	+	−0.2
3	2.3	=	2.5	+	−0.2
4	2.35	=	1.75	+	0.6
5	2.35	=	2.75	+	−0.4
6	3.6	=	3	+	0.6
Females					
7	2.25	=	2.65	+	−0.4
8	2.7	=	2.9	+	−0.2
9	2.95	=	3.15	+	−0.2
10	3	=	2.4	+	0.6
11	3	=	3.4	+	−0.4
12	4.25	=	3.65	+	0.6
Means (variance)					
Group 1	2.375 (0.369)		2.375 (0.182)		0 (0.187)
Group 2	3.025 (0.369)		3.025 (0.182)		0 (0.187)
Cohen's d	1.07		1.52		
t value	1.69		2.41		
p value	.12		.04		

large variance among the observed scores reduces (i.e., attenuates) the observed effect size compared with the true effect size. Thus, researchers who interpret only the observed effect size will fail to understand the true psychological results of their study, underestimating the effect by a robust amount.

In sum, reliability affects many kinds of effect sizes, with good reliability producing better estimates of true effect sizes. All else being equal, better reliability produces larger observed effect sizes, while poorer reliability attenuates the observed effect sizes.

Statistical Significance. A second important kind of result in behavioral research is statistical significance, which, roughly speaking, is related to a researcher's confidence in a result. That is, if a result is statistically significant, then researchers generally interpret it as being a "real" finding and not simply a fluke. As you might imagine, researchers hope that their research produces findings that are statistically significant.

Again, a full examination of such issues is beyond the scope of this book; however, it is important to realize that statistical significance is affected strongly by the size of the observed effect in a study (e.g., the size of an observed correlation or of an observed Cohen's d value). All else being equal, larger observed effect sizes make it more likely that a result will be statistically significant.

Thus, through its impact on effect sizes, reliability indirectly affects statistical significance—higher reliability allows for higher observed effect sizes, which increases the likelihood that a result will be statistically significant. Conversely, low reliability might contribute to a lack of statistical significance—lower reliability attenuates observed effect sizes, which decreases the likelihood that a result will be statistically significant.

This effect is again presented in Table 7.1 (in the "Inferential Statistic" column) and illustrated in the hypothetical data in Table 7.2. For example, Table 7.2 shows that the independent groups t test of the true scores is significant ($t_{(10)} = 2.41$, $p = .04$). That is, the true psychological "story" in Table 7.2 is that males and females differ significantly in terms of their true levels of academic achievement. However, the independent groups t test of the observed scores is not statistically significant ($t_{(10)} = 1.69$, $p = .12$). Thus, according to the observed scores, males and females do not appear to differ in terms of their academic achievement. Of course, researchers have access only to the observed data, not to true scores.

Thus, in the example in Table 7.2, the observed data would lead researchers to inaccurate conclusions about the effect of the independent variable (i.e., Sex) on the DV. As illustrated in Table 7.2, this inaccurate conclusion is driven (in part) by the poor reliability of the observed scores on the DV.

In sum, reliability is important in part because it has a clear and robust effect on two key results in a typical scientific study. By affecting effect sizes and statistical significance, reliability can have a fundamental impact on the results that researchers (and readers of research) see and interpret. If poor reliability biases these results, then researchers can be misled into making inaccurate conclusions about their work. Therefore, it is important that effect sizes and statistical significance are interpreted with close attention to the reliability of the measures used in the study. Measures with poor reliability are likely to underestimate the true effect sizes and are thus relatively likely to produce nonsignificant results.

Implications for Conducting and Interpreting Behavioral Research

The effects of reliability on effect sizes and on statistical significance are vital issues when interpreting the results of a study. There are at least three important implications of considering reliability when drawing psychological conclusions from research.

The first important implication is that researchers (and readers of research) should always consider the effects of reliability on their results when interpreting effect sizes and/or statistical significance. Imagine that you are a member of a school board that's interested in enhancing students' academic achievement. The board is considering two possible programs that are designed to enhance achievement. One is based on a theory that self-esteem affects academic achievement—students who feel good about themselves will perform better in school. Therefore, one program would be designed to increase students' self-esteem, which, in turn, could have beneficial effects on their academic achievement. The second potential program is based on a theory that academic motivation affects academic achievement—students who are properly motivated will perform better in school. This program would be designed to increase students' academic motivation, which could have beneficial effects on their achievement. Unfortunately, the school district has enough money to fund only one program, and the board wants to fund the program that might make the biggest impact on the students' achievement.

A developmental psychologist at a local university agrees to conduct a study to determine which program might be most effective. Specifically, he will recruit a sample of students and measure all three constructs—academic achievement, self-esteem, and academic motivation. To keep our example simple, let us imagine that the researcher will compute two correlations: (1) the correlation between self-esteem and academic achievement and (2) the correlation between academic motivation and academic achievement. The school board will fund the program for the variable that is most strongly associated with achievement, based on the assumption that it will have the larger impact on achievement. Therefore, if self-esteem is more strongly correlated with achievement, then the school board will fund the self-esteem program. However, if motivation is more strongly associated with achievement, then the school board will fund the motivation program.

The researcher collects the data and finds that the correlation between self-esteem and achievement ($r = .33$) is somewhat higher than the correlation between motivation and achievement ($r = .26$). Consequently, the school board begins to decide to fund the self-esteem program. However, you pause to ask the researcher about the reliability of his three measures. Although the researcher is surprised at the sophisticated level of your question, he tells you that the measure of achievement had a reliability of .86, the measure of self-esteem had an estimated reliability of .80, and the measure of motivation had an estimated reliability of .40. What do you think of this psychometric information? Does it affect your opinion about which program should be funded? It should.

Take a moment to consider the fact that the self-esteem questionnaire seems to be more reliable than the motivation questionnaire. As we have discussed, all else being equal, higher reliability will produce higher observed correlations. But notice that the correlation involving motivation ($r = .26$) was only a bit smaller than the correlation involving self-esteem ($r = .33$), even though the motivation measure was substantially less reliable (reliability = .40) than the self-esteem measure (reliability = .80). Based on our discussion of attenuation, you should have a sense that the correlation involving motivation is attenuated to a much greater extent than is the correlation involving self-esteem. That is, you should begin to think that the observed correlation involving motivation is much lower than its true correlation, in comparison to the observed correlation involving self-esteem. In fact, you could correct both correlations for attenuation by using Equation 7.6:

$$r_{X_t Y_t} = \frac{r_{X_o Y_o}}{\sqrt{R_{XX} R_{YY}}}.$$

The "corrected" correlation between motivation and achievement is

$$r_{X_t Y_t} = \frac{.26}{\sqrt{(.86)(.40)}} = .44.$$

The "corrected" correlation between self-esteem and achievement is

$$r_{X_t Y_t} = \frac{.33}{\sqrt{(.86)(.80)}} = .40.$$

These simple analyses reveal a finding with potentially important implications for the school board. Once you correct for attenuation, you see that the true (i.e., "corrected") correlation involving motivation is actually somewhat *higher* than the true correlation involving self-esteem. That is, if the assumptions of CTT are correct in this case, then motivation is somewhat more strongly related to achievement than is self-esteem. Based on this finding, the school board might reverse its initial decision and fund the motivation program instead of the self-esteem program.

Hopefully, this example illustrates the need to interpret the results of research in the context of reliability. If those of us who read research or conduct research fail to consider the effects of reliability and measurement error, then we risk misinterpreting results and reaching (or believing) faulty conclusions. This issue might be particularly important when two or more analyses are being contrasted with each other, as in the example of the school board. Two or more analyses will differ in terms of the constructs involved and in terms of the measures of those constructs. If the difference in measurement is ignored, then any observed difference in the results of the analyses might be mistakenly interpreted in terms of the difference in constructs. Thus, one important implication of our discussion of reliability is that the effects of reliability should always be considered when interpreting the results of research.

A second important research-based implication of our discussion is that researchers should try to use highly reliable measures in their work. Attenuation cannot be avoided altogether, because measurement is never perfect. However, the problem of attenuation can be minimized if researchers use highly reliable measures in their work. If researchers can use measures that are highly reliable, then they can be fairly confident that the observed associations between their measures are reasonably close approximations to the true correlations between the constructs of interest.

Despite the advantages of using highly reliable measures, there are at least two reasons why researchers might use measures with poor reliability. One reason is that there might be no highly reliable measure of the construct of interest. In such a case, a researcher must decide between proceeding with a low-reliability measure or spending time and effort attempting to develop a highly reliable measure. Of course, there is no guarantee that the time and effort will produce a highly reliable measure, so this option may seem like a risky choice. A second reason why researchers might use measures with poor reliability is that they simply have not devoted sufficient effort to finding a reliable measure. In psychology, there are thousands of measures of all kinds of constructs, and these measures are sometimes difficult to identify and obtain. Some measures are published and easily available. Other measures are published but are copyrighted and require money and specific credentials to use. Still other measures are used in the research literature but are not described in enough detail for other researchers to use. Thus, a researcher who wishes to use a highly reliable measure of a specific construct can face a daunting task of identifying which measures are available and which seem to be the most reliable. In addition, he or she will need to obtain the measure (or measures) that seem to fit his or her needs most closely. Although this can be a simple process at times, at other times it can require money, effort, and a great deal of patience. Researchers must decide if the potential costs of identifying and obtaining highly reliable measures are worth the potential benefits, as we have described in this section. In most cases they are.

A third research-based implication of the fact that reliability affects observed correlations is that researchers should report reliability estimates of their measures. Above, we argued for the importance of interpreting research results in the context of reliability. However, readers can do this only if writers provide the relevant information. Thus, if you conduct research and prepare a report such as a thesis, dissertation, or manuscript to submit for publication, then you should include reliability estimates. As discussed in the previous chapter, estimates of reliability (e.g., coefficient alpha) can be obtained easily from most of the popular statistical software packages (e.g., SPSS, SAS). In many research reports, reliability estimates are provided along with other basic descriptive statistics, such as means and standard deviations. As a writer, you should be sure to include this information. As a reader, you should expect to find and think about this information (hopefully, the writer has as well!). If you find yourself reading a research report that fails to provide reliability information, then you should feel comfortable in contacting the author of the report and requesting the relevant information.

In sum, test reliability has important effects on behavioral research. Along with the true correlation between psychological constructs, reliability affects the observed association between measures. Although researchers should strive to use the most reliable measures available, they cannot or do not always do so. Consequently, a lack of reliability weakens or attenuates the results of their statistical analyses, potentially leading to misinterpretations of their findings. Along with those who conduct research, those who read research also should consider the attenuating effects of imperfect measurement when interpreting the results of behavioral research.

Test Construction and Refinement

The previous two sections have described some of the important ways in which reliability and measurement error affect research and practice in behavioral science. It should be clear that high reliability is a desirable quality of any psychological test or measurement. Indeed, reliability is an important facet of test construction and refinement. In this section, we present some of the ways in which item information is evaluated in this process, and we highlight the role that reliability often plays.

As we saw in the previous chapter, internal consistency reliability is affected by two factors—test length and the consistency among the parts of a test. All else being equal, a longer test will be more reliable than a shorter test, and a test with greater internal consistency will be more reliable than a test with lower internal consistency.

In the test construction and refinement process, great attention is paid to the consistency among the parts of a test—typically in terms of the test items themselves. That is, test developers often examine various statistical characteristics of a test's items. They do so to identify items that should be removed from the test or to find items that should be revised to enhance their contribution to the test's psychometric quality. In general, items that enhance a test's internal consistency are preferable to items that detract from the test's internal consistency.

We will discuss three interconnected item characteristics that are important considerations in test construction and refinement: item means, item variances, and item discrimination. In terms of reliability, the overarching issue is item discrimination, which, as we shall see, is closely connected to internal consistency. Thus, our discussion will address the way in which the three item characteristics affect and reflect an item's contribution (or lack thereof) to internal consistency.

It is important to note that the procedures and concepts that we describe in this section should be conducted for *each dimension being assessed by a test*. As described in our earlier discussion of test dimensionality (Chapter 4), psychometric analysis should be conducted for each score that is produced by a test, with a score representing each psychological dimension underlying the responses to the test's items. So for a unidimensional test, we would conduct the following analyses on all of the test's items together as a single group (because all items are ostensibly combined together to create a single test score). However, for a multidimensional test, we would conduct the following analyses separately for each of the test's dimensions. For example, imagine that a self-esteem test included 20 items, with Items 1 to 10 ostensibly reflecting social self-esteem and Items 11 to 20 ostensibly reflecting academic self-esteem. At a minimum, we would conduct the following analyses once for Items 1 to 10 and then again for Items 11 to 20.

To illustrate the psychometric examination of item means, variances, and discrimination, we will use the hypothetical data presented in Table 7.3. These data represent the responses of 10 people to a unidimensional test that includes five binary items in which a correct answer is coded "1" and an incorrect answer is coded "0." Because it includes multiple items, the total test score is a composite variable, and a test developer might be concerned about evaluating and improving the psychometric quality of the test.

Using the Reliability Analysis procedure in the statistical package SPSS, we obtained a set of results that will help us evaluate the psychometric quality of the test (see the output in Table 7.4). The top section of this table reveals that the five-item test has an estimated reliability of only .59 (using coefficient alpha). For reasons discussed earlier in this chapter, we would prefer to have a test with greater reliability. Thus, we might wish to refine the test in a way that could improve its reliability for future use. The results of our SPSS analyses will help us examine the degree to which each item enhances or detracts from the test's quality, and this information can guide any test refinements.

Item Discrimination and Other Information Regarding Internal Consistency

As we have seen, one key to internal consistency reliability is the degree to which a test's items are consistent with each other. More specifically, internal consistency is the degree to which differences among persons' responses to one item are consistent with differences among their responses to other items on the test.

Thus, a test's internal consistency is intrinsically linked to the correlations among its items. For any particular item, its pattern of correlation with the other items reflects its consistency with those other items (and thus with the test as a whole). For example, if we find that an item is relatively strongly correlated with the other items on a test, then we know that the item is generally consistent with the other items. Consequently, we would know that the item enhances the internal consistency of the test. In contrast, if we find that an item is relatively weakly correlated with the other items on a test, then we know that the item is generally inconsistent with the other items. Consequently, we would suspect that the item reduces the internal consistency of the test.

With these considerations in mind, one important task is to determine which items contribute well to reliability and which detract from the test's reliability. A quick look at the correlation among a test's items might be very revealing. Indeed, a reliability-based test construction or refinement process might include an examination of the correlations among all of the items on a test.

For example, Table 7.4 presents these correlations in the "Inter-Item Correlation Matrix" output from the SPSS reliability analysis of the test responses in Table 7.3. A glance at these correlations reveals some good news and some bad news about the five-item test. The good news is that four items are relatively well correlated with each other. Specifically, Items 2 to 5 are generally intercorrelated with each other at levels of $r = .40$ or .50. Interitem correlations of this size indicate reasonable levels of internal consistency. The bad news is that one of the items is potentially problematic. Notice that Item 1 is totally uncorrelated with Item 2 and Item 3, only weakly correlated with Item 4 ($r = .25$), and *negatively* correlated with Item 5. These correlations

Table 7.3   Example Data for Test Construction and Refinement

Respondent	Item 1	2	3	4	5	Total	Total Excluding Item 1	Total Excluding Item 2
Maria	1	1	1	1	1	5	4	4
Demetrius	1	1	1	1	1	5	4	4
Rohit	1	1	0	0	1	3	2	2
James	1	0	1	1	1	4	3	4
Antonio	0	0	1	0	1	2	2	2
Esteban	0	1	0	1	1	3	3	2
Zoe	0	1	1	0	1	3	3	2
Emory	1	0	0	0	0	1	0	1
Fitz	1	0	0	0	0	1	0	1
Claudette	0	0	0	0	1	1	1	1

Table 7.4   SPSS Output From the Reliability Analysis of Data in Table 7.3

Reliability Statistics

Cronbach's Alpha	Cronbach's Alpha Based on Standardized Items	N of Items
.590	.594	5

Inter-Item Correlation Matrix

	Item 1	Item 2	Item 3	Item 4	Item 5
Item 1	1.000	.000	.000	.250	−.408
Item 2	.000	1.000	.200	.408	.500
Item 3	000	.200	1.000	.408	.500
Item 4	.250	.408	.408	1.000	.408
Item 5	−.408	.500	.500	.408	1.000

Item–Total Statistics

	Scale Mean if Item Deleted	Scale Variance if Item Deleted	Corrected Item-Total Correlation	Squared Multiple Correlation	Cronbach's Alpha if Item Deleted
Item 1	2.20	2.178	−.029	.410	.721
Item 2	2.30	1.567	.421	.337	.492
Item 3	2.30	1.567	.421	.337	.492
Item 4	2.40	1.378	.623	.410	.366
Item 5	2.00	1.778	.395	.627	.517

Table 7.4   (Continued)

Item Statistics

	Mean	Standard Deviation	N
Item 1	.60	.516	10
Item 2	.50	.527	10
Item 3	.50	.527	10
Item 4	.40	.516	10
Item 5	.80	.422	10

suggest that Item 1 is not consistent with most of the other items on the test. The overall pattern of interitem correlations suggests that Items 2 through 5 are consistent with each other but that Item 1 needs to be revised or dropped from the test.

Although the interitem correlations offer insight into the internal consistency of a test, there are more efficient ways of evaluating the consistency issue. The interitem correlations in our example are fairly straightforward—there are only a few items and the pattern of correlations is arranged in a rather clear way. In reality, most test development/refinement situations might be much more complicated, with many more items and with a more complex pattern of correlations. Thus, an examination of a matrix of interitem correlations might be somewhat impractical with real data; fortunately, alternative methods exist.

Item discrimination is a common concept for evaluating the degree to which an item might affect a test's internal consistency. Briefly stated, item discrimination is the degree to which an item differentiates people who score high on the total test from those who score low on the total test. From the perspective of reliability, we prefer to have items that have high discrimination values over those that have low discrimination values.

There are various ways of operationalizing an item's discrimination, one of which is the *item–total correlation*. We can compute the total score on a test (see Table 7.3) and then compute the correlation between an item and this total test score. The resulting correlation is called an item–total correlation, and it represents the degree to which differences among persons' responses to the item are consistent with differences in their total test scores. A high item–total correlation indicates that the item is consistent with the test as a whole (which of course is a function of all of the items within the test), which is a desirable characteristic. In contrast, a low item–total correlation indicates that the item is inconsistent with the test as a whole, which would be an undesirable characteristic from the perspective of reliability.

To illustrate this concept, the SPSS output labeled "Item-Total Statistics" in Table 7.4 presents *"corrected" item–total correlations*, which are correlations between an item and a "corrected" total test score. The corrected item–total correlation for Item 1 is the correlation between responses to Item 1 and the sum of the other four items on the test. That is, the "corrected" total test score in the analysis of Item 1 is the total that is obtained by summing all of the items except Item 1 (see the "Total

Excluding Item 1" column in Table 7.3). If we compute the correlation between the Item 1 values and the "Total Excluding Item 1" values, then we obtain a value of $r = -.029$. This value tells us that Item 1 seems to be generally inconsistent with the responses to the other four items. To compute a corrected item–total correlation for each item, SPSS computes a different corrected total test score for each item. As we have seen, the corrected item–total correlation for Item 1 requires a corrected total test score that excludes Item 1. Similarly, the corrected item–total correlation for Item 2 would require a corrected total test score that excludes Item 2, and so on. As we see in the SPSS output, all of the corrected item–total correlations are positive values of reasonable size, expect for Item 1. On the basis of these results, we should consider dropping or revising Item 1.

Another form of item discrimination is particularly applicable for items that are scored in a binary manner, as we have in Table 7.3. An item's item discrimination index (D) compares the proportion of high test scorers who answered the item correctly with the proportion of low test scorers who answered the item correctly. To do this, we begin by identifying a specific percentage of people with the highest total test scores (say all respondents who scored in the upper 30%) and the same percentage of people with the lowest total test scores (say all respondents who scored in the lowest 30%). For the data in Table 7.3, the top 30% group includes Maria, Demetrius, and James, and the bottom 30% group includes Emory, Fitz, and Claudette. To compute the item discrimination index for an item, we next calculate the proportion of people within each group who answered the item correctly (as designated by a "1" in Table 7.3). For Item 1, we see that all three people in the "top 30%" group answered the item correctly, for a proportion of $p_{high} = 1.0$. In contrast, we see that only two of the three people in the "bottom 30%" group answered the item correctly, for a proportion of $p_{low} = .66$. Finally, we compute the item discrimination index by calculating the difference between these two proportions:

$$D = p_{high} - p_{low}. \tag{7.7}$$

For Item 1, this results in an item discrimination index of .33:

$$D = 1.0 - 0.66,$$
$$= .33.$$

The result for Item 1 tells us that high-scoring people are somewhat more likely to answer Item 1 correctly than are low-scoring people. Typically, the item discrimination index ranges from 0 to 1.0, except in the unlikely case that high-scoring people are less likely to answer an item correctly than are low-scoring people. Ideally, we prefer items that have large D values, which would indicate that high scorers and low scorers differ dramatically in the likelihood of answering an item correctly. Although the SPSS output does not present the item discrimination index, the values could easily be calculated. In addition, note that the percentages chosen to form the high and low groups (e.g., 30%) are somewhat arbitrary—there is no standard percentage that is implicit in the definition of the item discrimination index.

Going further, the SPSS output in Table 7.4 provides two additional kinds of information regarding each item's contribution to the internal consistency reliability of the test. Although a full description is beyond the scope of this chapter, the "squared multiple correlation" is another index of the degree to which an item is linked to the other items. For readers who are familiar with multiple regression, these values are the R^2 values obtained when predicting "scores" on each item from the scores on all of the other items (e.g., predicting responses to Item 1 from the responses to Items 2–5). The second kind of information is potentially quite useful, although its meaning emerges directly from issues that we have already discussed. The "Cronbach's Alpha if Item Deleted" column tells us the reliability estimate that we would obtain for the test if we were to drop each item from the test. For example, the "alpha if item deleted" value for Item 1 is .721. This indicates that, if we drop Item 1 but retain the other four items, the reliability of the resulting four-item test would be estimated at .72. Note that this value is clearly larger than the reliability estimate for the entire five-item test, which is .59, as mentioned earlier. With these two reliability estimates in mind, we see that dropping Item 1 would actually improve the internal consistency of the test from .59 to .72. Thus, we would seriously consider refining the test by dropping Item 1. Also notice that reliability would *decrease* if any of the other items were dropped from the test—the other four "alpha if item deleted" values are less than .59.

In sum, we have examined several interconnected kinds of information that reveal an item's effect on test score reliability. For example, we saw that Item 1 had relatively low interitem correlations, which suggested that Item 1 is inconsistent with the other items in the test. We then saw that, although Item 1's discrimination index was greater than 0, its corrected item–total correlation was very close to 0, which suggested that Item 1 is inconsistent with total test scores in general. Finally, we saw that the test's reliability would likely increase if we removed Item 1 from the test, which is consistent with the previous results that demonstrated Item 1's inconsistency with the other four items.

Considering the results that we have discussed thus far, we have a relatively clear idea of how we might improve the five-item test. Clearly, we are likely to retain Items 2, 3, 4, and 5 in the test refinement process—they are well correlated with each other, and dropping any one of them would reduce the test's reliability. However, we are likely to either drop Item 1 altogether or examine the item (i.e., its content, its wording, its response options, etc.) to see if we can improve it. It is possible that the test could be improved substantially if we were able to revise Item 1 in a way that makes it more consistent with the other four items. If so, then we could include the revised Item 1 along with the other four items to produce a stronger five-item test.

In the next section, we address two additional item characteristics that are sometimes evaluated in a test refinement process. Our discussion will highlight the ways in which item difficulty (i.e., item means) and item variance are related to an item's effect on test reliability.

Item Difficulty (Mean) and Item Variance

An item's mean and variance are potentially important factors affecting its contribution to the psychometric quality of a test. From the perspective of reliability, an item's mean and variance are important because they may be related to the degree to which the item might be consistent with the other items on a test. Consequently, they have potential implications for an item's effect on test score reliability.

As we discussed in Chapter 3, a correlation reflects the degree to which variability within one variable is consistent with variability within another variable. Indeed, a correlation is highly dependent on variance. Specifically, the correlation between two variables is a transformation of the covariance between the two variables. In turn, the covariance between two variables hinges on the existence of variance within each variable. Simply put, if a variable (e.g., responses to a test item) has no variability, then it will not be correlated with any other variable.

Based on the intrinsic link between correlation and variance, an item's variance has potential implications for characteristics such as its interitem correlations, its item–total correlation, and its "alpha if item deleted" value. Items with limited variability are less likely to have good correlational characteristics than are items with substantial variability. Indeed, items that all respondents answer in the same way (e.g., all respondents answer correctly, or all answer incorrectly) are poor items from the perspective of reliability.

The link between an item's variability and its psychometric quality can be extended to the item's mean. In some cases, an item's mean tells us about the item's variability. Most psychological tests have practical limits on the responses that people can provide. For example, in the test presented in Table 7.3, the maximum score on each item is 1 and the minimum is 0. This "ceiling" and "floor" constrain the total test scores, and they have implications for the link between item means and item variances and, consequently, for the values of the covariances and correlations among items.

For example, imagine that Item 1 (in Table 7.3) had a mean of 1.0—what would this imply about the item's variability? Because the maximum value of an individual's response is 1, there is only one way that Item 1 can have a mean equal to 1.0. Specifically, Item 1 will have a mean of 1.0 only if every respondent answers the item correctly. Similarly, Item 1 will have a mean of 0 only if every respondent answers the item incorrectly. It should be clear that if every respondent answers an item in the same way, then the item will have no variability. And as we have discussed, if an item has no variability, then it is a poor test item from a reliability perspective. Thus, items that have "extreme" means (i.e., either very high or very low) are likely to have limited variability, and thus they are likely to have poor psychometric qualities.

An item's mean is sometimes interpreted as the item's "difficulty." For example, the mean of Item 5 is .80 (shown in Table 7.4), which tells us that 80% of the respondents answered the item correctly (because we coded a correct answer as "1" and an incorrect answer as "0"). In contrast, the mean of Item 4 is .40, which tells us that only 40% of the respondents answered the item correctly. Thus, Item 4 appears to be more difficult than Item 5. For binary response items, such as those presented in Table 7.3, CTT suggests that we would like to have items with difficulties of approximately .50. This ensures that items will have maximal variability, which avoids the difficulties associated with low variability.

Summary

In this section, we explained how reliability and measurement error affect the results of behavioral research. We showed that the correlation between the two measures is determined by the correlation between the psychological constructs being measured and by the reliabilities of the measures. These two factors will combine to influence the interpretation of the results of empirical research findings.

Test score reliability will also play a role in test score interpretation. We showed how test scores will regress to the mean of a distribution of scores and how the size of this regression will depend on score reliability. Reliability will influence the confidence intervals created around particular scores; reliable test scores will be associated with smaller intervals than will less reliable scores.

We also presented some of the ways in which test item information is evaluated, and we highlighted the role that reliability often plays in this type of evaluation. Three interconnected item characteristics that are important considerations in test construction and refinement—item means, item variances, and item discrimination—were discussed in detail.

Suggested Readings

For a discussion of regression to the mean that differs from the standard understanding of the phenomena:

Rogosa, D. R. (1995). Myths and methods: Myths about longitudinal research, plus supplemental questions. In J. M. Gottman (Ed.), *The analysis of change* (pp. 3–66). Hillsdale, NJ: Lawrence Erlbaum.

There is a short and well-crafted technical discussion of attenuation in:

McDonald, R. P. (1999). *Test theory: A unified treatment.* Mahwah, NJ: Lawrence Erlbaum. (See pp. 133–136)

PART III

Validity

CHAPTER 8

Validity

Conceptual Basis

I
magine that you have applied for your dream job. You have invested a huge amount of time, energy, and perhaps money preparing yourself to be competitive for the position. After all your preparation, you finally apply for the job for which you have been working so hard. As part of the hiring process, the company requires you to complete a personality inventory. A week or two after completing the inventory and submitting your application, the company tells you that you are not going to be hired. Although they do not say so, you suspect that their decision is partially based on the "results" of the personality inventory. Aside from disappointment and perhaps anger, what kind of reactions would you have?

You would likely have several questions. What exactly was the personality inventory supposed to measure? Is there any evidence that the inventory is in fact a good measure of whatever it is supposed to measure? Is there any logical or theoretical reason to believe that scores on the inventory are related to performance in the job that you wanted? Perhaps more important, are there any hard data showing that scores on the inventory are actually related to performance in your job?

In response to such questions, the human resources director of the company might suggest that the personality inventory is a worthwhile part of the hiring process. She might state that the company has been using it for years. In addition, she might assure you that in her experience the questionnaire is quite accurate and that it is useful for predicting who will be good employees. However, if she is going to be using the inventory to make such important decisions, then she needs to have stronger evidence than "her experience" testifying to the accuracy and utility of the questionnaire.

Your questions about the personality inventory are questions of validity, which is perhaps the most important issue in psychological measurement. In this chapter, we begin by defining validity, we discuss its meaning and implications, and we discuss the importance of validity in testing. In addition, we discuss the kinds of evidence that are necessary for establishing validity in testing, we describe the differences among several perspectives on test validity, and we contrast validity with reliability. As you will see, a test user's personal experience is inadequate as evidence for the test's validity and its use.

What Is Validity?

The concept of validity has evolved over more than 60 years, and various definitions of validity have been proposed. A rather basic definition of validity is "the degree to which a test measures what is it supposed to measure." Although this definition is relatively common and straightforward, it oversimplifies the issue a bit. A better definition, reflecting the most contemporary perspective, is that *validity* is "the degree to which evidence and theory support the interpretations of test scores entailed by the proposed uses" of a test (American Education Research Association [AERA], the American Psychological Association [APA], and the National Council on Measurement in Education [NCME], 1999, p. 9). This, more sophisticated definition has a number of important implications.

First, a measure itself is neither valid nor invalid; rather, the issue of validity concerns the interpretations and uses of a measure's scores. Consider the Conscientiousness factor on the Revised NEO-Personality Inventory (NEO-PI–R; Costa & McCrae, 1992). The NEO-PI–R is a multidimensional personality inventory, providing scores on five relatively independent domains, each of which includes six, narrower "facet" dimensions. One of the factors, or domains, included in the NEO-PI–R is labeled *Conscientiousness*. The Conscientiousness scale includes 48 items, with each item presenting a statement regarding beliefs, interests, behaviors, and so on. The test authors offer a clear interpretation of the scores derived from the items on the Conscientiousness factor. According to the authors of the NEO-PI–R, high scores on this set of items reflect the tendency toward an "active process of planning, organizing, and carrying out tasks," and they state that people with high scores on this set of items are "purposeful, strong willed, and determined" (Costa & McCrae, 1992, p. 16).

In terms of validity, the *set of items* themselves is neither valid nor invalid. Similarly, the *scores* derived from the 48 items are neither valid nor invalid. However, the authors' *interpretations* of the scores might be valid or invalid. Are the authors correct in interpreting scores on the set of 48 items in terms of planfulness, organization, and determination? Thus, validity is about the accuracy or legitimacy of one's interpretations of a test's scores.

Extending this notion beyond the interpretation of the scores, validity is related to the "proposed uses" of the scores. The NEO-PI–R Conscientiousness scale might be used by employers to screen applicants. Experts in human resources might predict that people who have relatively high scores on the Conscientiousness scale will be responsible, hardworking, motivated, and dependable employees. On the basis of this interpretation of scale scores, employers might use the Conscientiousness scale to identify people with a high level of conscientiousness and to make hiring decisions. But is there good reason to believe that scores on the Conscientiousness scale truly do provide information that differentiates potentially better and worse employees? That is, scores on the NEO-PI-R Conscientiousness scale might be interpreted validly as reflecting conscientiousness, but is conscientiousness (as measured by the scale) truly predictive of the quality of an employee's future performance?

Psychological measures are like hammers. Someone might tell you that a hammer is a useful tool, but the usefulness of a hammer depends on the job to be done. If you need to drive a nail into a surface or if you need to remove a nail from a surface, then a hammer is enormously useful. If you need to hold down a piece of paper while you are working or if you need to break through a piece of sheetrock in a wall, then a hammer might indeed be useful. However, if you need to tighten a screw, saw a piece of wood, change a light bulb, or call a contractor to fix the hole in your wall, then a hammer is completely useless. So it is somewhat simplistic and inaccurate to say that a hammer is a useful tool, *without regard to the way in which it will be used*. Similarly, it is somewhat simplistic and inaccurate to say that a particular psychological measure, such as the NEO-PI-R Conscientiousness scale, is valid, *without regard to the way in which it will be interpreted and used*. The scale's scores might be interpreted validly as indicators of conscientiousness, and they might help you select a conscientious contractor, but the scores are not validly interpreted as indicators of intelligence or extraversion.

Despite our insistence that validity is really about test score interpretation and use (and not about the test itself), test users often refer to the "validity of a test." For example, you might hear someone state that "the Conscientiousness scale of the NEO-PI-R is valid." There are at least two possible reasons why a test user might make a statement that seems to contradict our definition of validity. First, the test user might not have a sophisticated understanding of validity. Although many copyrighted psychological tests are marketed only to qualified professionals, not every professional has a deep understanding of the concept of validity. Thus, some test users might not recognize the nuances of validity, and they might believe that validity is a property of tests rather than of one's interpretations of test scores. The second reason why you might hear such a statement is that it is simply a shortcut. That is, instead of saying, "Scores on the Conscientiousness scale of the NEO-PI-R are validly interpreted *as a measure of conscientiousness*," we sometimes get a bit lazy and simply state that "the Conscientiousness scale of the NEO-PI-R is valid." Please do not let this confuse you. In measurement, validity is a property of the interpretations and uses of test scores; it is not a property of the test itself.

A second important implication of the definition of validity is that validity is a matter of degree; it is not an "all-or-none" issue. That is, the validity of a test interpretation should be conceived in terms of strong versus weak instead of simply valid or invalid. There is no magical threshold beyond which validity is established. For test users, validity should be a deciding factor in their choice of psychological tests. Although such choices are based on a number of practical, theoretical, and psychometric factors, a test should be selected only if there is *strong enough* evidence supporting the intended interpretation and use. Alternatively, test users

[handwritten margin note: 1) Validity is in regards to interpretations + use of test scores]

[handwritten margin note: 2) Validity is a matter of degree (strong-weak)]

[handwritten note at bottom: Select a test only if there is strong enough evidence supporting the intended interpretation + use]

might need to choose among a set of possible tests, and they must weigh the relative strengths of the tests being considered. For example, there are a variety of scales that an employer might use to measure the dependability, responsibility, motivation, and reliability of job applicants. The NEO-PI–R Conscientiousness scale is a reasonable choice, but employers should consider the relative strengths of alternatives that might be even better measures of the specific characteristics that they wish to assess. Tests that have garnered more good evidence of their validity are preferable to tests with less evidence of validity.

A third important facet of validity is that the validity of a test's interpretation is based on evidence and theory. In the introduction to this chapter, the hypothetical human resources director stated that *in her experience* the psychological tests were useful. This is not good enough. For a test user to be confident in an interpretation and use of test scores, there must be good empirical evidence supporting the interpretation and use. That is, there must be strong objective data derived from well-conducted psychometric studies—not simply some test users' or test developers' experience-based opinions about the test. In addition, contemporary views on validity emphasize the importance of grounding the interpretation and use of a test in a defensible psychological theory.

Although many well-developed psychological measures have strong evidence regarding the validity of their typical interpretations, many supposed psychological measures do not. For example, handwriting analysis is a popular method for "assessing" personality. Despite the popularity and historical tradition of handwriting analysis, there appears to be little peer-reviewed scientific evidence that handwriting reveals anything about personality. Similarly, many supposed psychological measures can now be found on the Internet. One example is variously known as "Color Quiz," "Colorgenics," or the "Personality Color Test." These tests are ostensibly based on "color psychology," as developed by Max Lüscher (Lüscher & Scott, 1969). When you take the Color Quiz, you are presented with eight colors, and you are asked to select the colors in the order of your preferences (see http://www.colorquiz.com/). After completing this procedure twice, you receive a series of interpretations regarding your "sources of stress," "restrained characteristics," "desired objectives," and "actual problems." The notion that your color preferences reveal something about your personality is an interesting idea, but is there any objective evidence supporting these interpretations of your color preferences? Unfortunately (but perhaps not surprisingly), a quick survey of the scientific literature reveals essentially no support for the validity of color preferences as a measure of personality characteristics (e.g., Picco & Dzindolet, 1994).

Assuming that there is indeed little scientific support for the validity of color preferences as a measure of personality, it is interesting to examine the "evidence" presented on the Color Quiz website (see http://www.colorquiz.com/about.html). The website poses this question to interested readers: "Is the test reliable?" We suspect that the authors of the website are not using the term *reliable* in the true psychometric sense outlined in previous chapters. Instead, we suspect that the authors intend to pose the question of validity: Is the test meaningful and useful as a measure of personality? Given the apparent lack of scientific evidence for color preference as a valid measure of personality, you might not be surprised by the answer provided on the website. Regarding the quality of the Color Quiz, the authors state, "We leave that to your opinion. We can only say that there are a number of corporations and colleges that use the Lüscher test as part of their hiring/admissions processes." Clearly, the website implies that the Color Quiz is a valid measure of some aspects of personality and that it is in fact used to make real decisions. However, we suggest that a human resources director using any version of the Color Quiz should be prepared to defend his or her hiring decisions in court. If the scientific evidence for the validity of "color tests" as measures of personality is as thin as it appears to be, then an applicant who is denied employment because of such a test would have legitimate reason to be angry and litigious.

The contemporary perspective on validity states that there must be psychological theory and empirical evidence supporting a particular interpretation of test scores. For example, are there strong data demonstrating that people who score relatively highly on the NEO-PI–R Conscientiousness scale are actually higher in "conscientiousness" than those who score relatively lower? Is there evidence that students who perform well on the SAT actually obtain higher grades in college than do students who perform less well on the SAT? Is there anything beyond the assertion that "there are a number of corporations and colleges that use the Lüscher test as part of their hiring/admissions processes" to support the notion that color preferences actually reflect anything about an individual's personality? Although Lüscher might offer theoretical reasons to suspect that color is somehow related to personality, such theory is not enough to argue that the Color Quiz is valid as a measure of personality. For users to have confidence in the validity of test interpretation, there must be good empirical evidence supporting the interpretations. There must be data obtained from high-quality research, and these data must provide evidence for particular interpretations of test scores.

In the sections that follow, we will examine the kinds of scientific evidence that can be used to support the validity of test interpretations. As mentioned earlier, the concept of validity has evolved over the years. For many years, the fields of psychology and education have seen validity as a three-faceted concept. From this traditional perspective, there are three types of validity—content validity, criterion validity, and construct validity. Although we will describe these concepts, we will emphasize a more contemporary perspective that highlights construct validity as the essential concept in validity (Messick, 1989). *Construct validity* refers to the degree to which test scores can be interpreted as reflecting a particular psychological construct. In 1999, three major organizations in psychology and education outlined the contemporary perspectives on testing. The AERA, APA, and NCME (1999) published a revision of the *Standards for Educational and Psychological Testing*. This publication outlined five types of evidence relevant for establishing the validity of test interpretations. As shown in Figure 8.1, the overall construct validity of test score interpretation depends on the content of the test content, the internal structure of the test, the psychological process used in test responses, the association among test scores and other variables, and the consequences of test use.

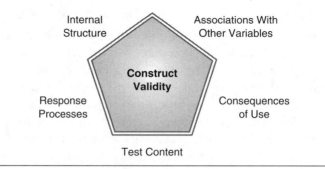

Figure 8.1 A Contemporary Perspective of Types of Information Relevant to Test Validity

However, before we discuss the types of evidence that are relevant to validity, we will highlight the reasons why validity is such an important issue in psychometrics and more broadly in testing. Although its importance might be implicitly clear from our discussion thus far, we want to be as explicit as possible about this issue. And we want to make sure that its importance is appreciated before we delve into the scientific issues and procedures related to evaluating validity.

The Importance of Validity

We suspect that the importance of validity is already apparent through our discussion thus far. Indeed, we hope that we have started to convince you that validity is perhaps the most crucial issue in a test's psychometric quality. In this section, we underscore this point by explicitly addressing the role and importance of validity in psychological research and practice. Whenever psychological measurements are conducted for any serious purpose, those measurements are meaningful and useful only if they have acceptable validity for their intended purpose. Without validity, those measurements are scientifically meaningless and potentially even hazardous.

Our ability to interpret the great bulk of behavioral research hinges on test validity. The goals of scientific research include describing, predicting, or explaining some aspect of our world—be it a physical or a psychological aspect. Accurate description, prediction, and explanation depends on the ability to manipulate or measure specific variables that are deemed important. For example, some social psychologists have examined the hypothesis that exposure to violent video games increases one's inclination to behave aggressively (e.g., Anderson & Dill, 2000; Bartholow, Sestir, & Davis, 2005). Research seems to indicate that, indeed, exposure to video violence does affect an individual's aggressive behavior. But we must remain aware that this research partially hinges on the measurement of "inclination to behave aggressively." If this key variable is measured with good validity, then we should have increased confidence in the conclusion that aggression is increased by exposure to video violence. However, if the "inclination to behave aggressively" is measured with poor validity, then we should have serious doubts about this conclusion. Without test validity, our understanding of the role of video games in aggressiveness is obscured.

Thus, validity influences the scientific process in a somewhat abstract sense, in that it affects the accuracy of our understanding of the world. Test validity can have an even more concrete impact on the outcome of the scientific process. As you know, another goal of scientific research is to guide decision making about various aspects of our social world. Such decisions can be made at the societal level or at the individual level, and test validity has important implications for both kinds of decisions.

Without test validity, decisions about societal issues could be misinformed, wasteful, or even harmful. In June 2006, the U.S. House of Representatives held hearings concerning the level of violence depicted in many popular video games. The underlying concern was that exposure to violent video games has dire consequences for those who play the video games, particularly younger players. Specifically, the hearings were based on the assumption that exposure to violent video games increases aggressive behavior. Of course, the empirical legitimacy of this assumption is a key question. To the degree that there is strong research demonstrating the legitimacy of this assumption, the congressional hearings are on a relatively solid foundation. However, if the research is based on tests with poor validity, then we should have serious doubts about the meaning of the research. Consequently, any societal decisions based on such questionable research are themselves questionable.

What would the implications be if the U.S. Congress enacted legislation on the basis of research with questionable validity? At a minimum, congressional time and attention would be wasted, and misguided laws could be passed. Furthermore, it is conceivable that public funds could be spent to "prevent" aggression by intervening against violent video games. Again, if the research is flawed by poor test validity, then such funds would be wasted. Indeed, to the degree that public funds are diverted from alternative programs that actually would be beneficial to society, wastefulness might even be harmful to people who would have benefited from those alternative programs. Let us clarify that we are not denigrating the quality of research on the effect of violent video games. Most of this research is indeed well conceived and well executed. We simply use it to provide a compelling illustration of the fundamental connections between test validity, research quality, and social decision making.

Finally, without test validity, test-based decisions about individuals could be misinformed or harmful. Decisions that are at least partially based on psychological testing include placing children in specific classes, selecting students for college admissions, hiring employees, making clinical decisions, and placing people in specific organizational roles. Such decisions have potentially life-altering implications for the individuals affected by them, and test validity can have an important impact on those decisions. To the degree that the decisions are based on well-validated measures, they hopefully benefit the test users and test takers. If decisions are based on the appropriate use of well-validated psychological tests, then (hopefully) children are more likely to be placed in appropriate classes; job applicants are more likely to be hired for jobs that fit their interests, skills, and abilities; students are more likely to be admitted to colleges that fit their academic skills; and clinical clients are diagnosed in ways that facilitate effective treatment.

However, it is possible that such decisions are based on poorly validated tests. It is even possible that these types of decisions are based on the inappropriate use of tests that have been well validated for different uses. Recall the first chapter of this book, in which we discussed the North Carolina statute that "a mentally retarded person convicted of first degree murder shall not be sentenced to death" (Criminal Procedure Act, 2007). As we mentioned in that earlier chapter, the decisions regarding a person's status as mentally retarded are based partly on the results from "an individually administered, scientifically recognized standardized intelligence quotient test administered by a licensed psychiatrist or psychologist." We hope that the term *scientifically recognized standardized* is interpreted largely as "scientifically validated," and we hope that jurors, lawyers, and judges are aware of this important issue.

Validity Evidence: Test Content

As mentioned earlier and as shown in Figure 8.1, the validity of test score interpretation hinges on five types of evidence. One type of validity evidence is the match between the actual content of a test and the content that *should be* included in the test. That is, if a test is to be interpreted as a measure of a particular construct, then the content of the test should reflect the important facets of that construct. Indeed, the supposed psychological nature of the construct should dictate the appropriate content of the test. Validity evidence of this type is sometimes referred to as content validity, but there are two ways in which content validity might be compromised.

Threats to Content Validity

One threat to content validity occurs when a test includes *construct-irrelevant content*. A test should include no content (e.g., items or questions) that is irrelevant to the construct for which the test is to be interpreted. For example, imagine that you need to develop a midterm test for a class in personality psychology and the test is intended to measure "knowledge of Freud's theories" as covered in the class lectures, discussion, and readings. In the class, three broad topics were covered—the structure of personality (i.e., id, ego, and superego), the stages of personality development, and defense mechanisms. Ideally, the content of the midterm test should include items representing a fair sample of these three topics, no more and no less. For example, biographical questions about Freud's life should not be included on the test because they were not covered in class and, thus, they are irrelevant to the construct of "knowledge of Freud's theories as covered in the class lectures, discussion, and readings." Test content that reflects issues, characteristics, or concepts that are irrelevant to the construct for which a test is to be interpreted is referred to as "construct-irrelevant" content. Such content is extraneous to the core construct for which a test is to be interpreted, and its inclusion would reduce validity.

A second threat to content validity is *construct underrepresentation*. Although a test should not include content that is beyond its core construct, it *should* include the full range of content that *is* relevant to the construct, as much as possible. Again, a test intended to assess "knowledge of Freud's theories as covered in the class lectures, discussion, and readings" should include content relevant to all three topics that were covered in class. A test that included content relevant only to personality structure and personality development would have weak validity as a measure of "knowledge of Freud's theories as covered in the class lectures, discussion, and readings" because it fails to cover the content related to defense mechanisms. Such a test would suffer from construct underrepresentation, meaning that its actual content fails to represent the full scope of the content implied by the construct that it is intended to measure. In sum, a test's content should reflect the full range of the core construct, no more and no less.

In practice, test developers and test users face a trade-off between the ideal of content validity and the reality of the testing situation. Again, a test should include items that represent an adequate sample of the construct-relevant content, no more and no less. However, there is no clear rule as to what constitutes an "adequate" sample of content. For practical reasons, a test developer might not be able to include content covering every facet or nuance of the construct to an equally thorough degree. For example, the instructor developing a test to assess "knowledge of Freud's theories as covered in the class lectures, discussion, and readings" must consider the fact that students might have only 50 minutes to complete the test. Therefore, he or she might include questions regarding details of only some of the total content. For example, he or she might include questions on only three stages of Freud's theory of personality development. So the test might not cover every conceivable facet of the construct, but hopefully the selected items reflect a reasonable range of elements relevant to the construct. In sum, practical issues, such as time, respondent fatigue, respondent attention, and so on, place constraints on the amount of content that can be included in a measure.

Content Validity Versus Face Validity

Face validity is closely related to content validity. Face validity is the degree to which a measure appears to be related to a specific construct, in the judgment of nonexperts, such as test takers and representatives of the legal system. That is, a test has face validity if its content simply looks relevant to the person taking the test. Face validity is not usually considered an important psychometric facet of validity—nonexperts' opinions have no direct bearing on the empirical and theoretical quality of a test.

Although face validity might not be a crucial facet of test validity from a psychometric perspective, it might have important implications for the test's use. The apparent meaning and relevance of a test's content might influence test takers' motivation to respond in a serious and honest manner. For example, consider a psychological inventory given to job applicants as part of the hiring process for a law enforcement agency. Applicants might assume that such a measure should include questions about problem solving, social skill, dependability, work ethics, and so on. If the inventory actually included questions about sexual attitudes or family history, then the job applicants might question the legitimacy or relevance of the entire testing procedure. Consequently, many applicants might respond randomly, respond in a way that presents a falsely positive image of themselves, or even refuse to complete the measure altogether. The utility of such a test would be almost entirely compromised. Therefore, a test with high face validity might be much better received by test takers and potential test users.

The difference between content validity and face validity is an important one. Content validity is the degree to which the content of a measure truly reflects the full domain of the construct for which it is being used, no more and no less. In a sense, content validity can be evaluated only by those who have a deep understanding of the construct in question. Experts in a field are in the best position to evaluate accurately the quality of a test of a construct within that field. Face validity is the degree to which nonexperts perceive a test to be relevant for whatever they believe it is being used to measure. Although test takers' beliefs about a test might affect their motivation and honesty in responding to a test, test takers are not often experts on the theoretical and empirical meaning of the psychological constructs being assessed by the tests. Thus, content validity, but not face validity, is an important form of evidence in the overall evaluation of construct validity.

Face validity can affect a test taker's motivation & honesty in responding

FV is a form of evidence in CV

Validity Evidence: Internal Structure of the Test

Internal Structure: way parts of a test are related to each other

A second issue related to the validity of a test interpretation concerns the internal structure of a test. A test's internal structure is the way the parts of a test are related to each other. For example, some tests include items that are highly correlated with each other, but other tests include items that fall into two or more clusters. As we will discuss, the conceptual basis of a construct has implications for the internal structure of a measure of the construct. Therefore, an important validity issue is the match between the *actual* internal structure of a test and the structure that the test *should* possess. For a test to be validly interpreted as a measure of a particular construct, the actual structure of the test should match the theoretically based structure of the construct.

Structure of test should match structure of construct

For example, we might wish to evaluate measures of self-esteem. The Rosenberg Self-Esteem Inventory (RSEI; Rosenberg, 1989) is perhaps the most commonly used measure of self-esteem in psychological research. The RSEI is often used as a measure of a single coherent construct—global self-esteem. Global self-esteem is one's overall evaluation of one's self-worth, and the RSEI includes 10 items, such as "I take a positive attitude toward myself" and "At times I think I am no good at all" (note that this item is negatively keyed). Test users who intend to interpret scores on the RSEI as a measure of global self-esteem should expect to find a particular structure among the 10 items. Specifically, if test users theorize that global self-esteem is indeed a single coherent construct and they believe that the RSEI is indeed valid as a measure of global self-esteem, then they should find that all the items on the

RSEI are highly correlated with each other, forming a single tight cluster of items. That is, if the RSEI is indeed valid as a measure of global self-esteem, then responses to the test items should exhibit a unidimensional structure that is consistent with a conceptual definition of the construct.

However, our expectations might be quite different for another measure of self-esteem. The Multidimensional Self-Esteem Inventory (MSEI; O'Brien & Epstein, 1988) was designed to measure global self-esteem along with eight components of self-esteem. The test authors state that the conceptual model underlying the MSEI

> specifies two primary levels within the hierarchy of self-esteem. The first level corresponds to global self-esteem. This level is concerned with the person's most basic, widely generalized evaluative feelings about him/herself. The second level corresponds to self-evaluations at an intermediate level of generality, which are referred to as components of self-esteem. (O'Brien & Epstein, 1988, p. 7)

Dimensions

This conceptual perspective on self-esteem was based on previous research suggesting that the components of competence, likability, lovability, personal power, moral self-approval, body appearance, and body functioning capture many of the events that affect self-esteem. Thus, the authors argue that these components reflect most of the experiences that typically affect self-esteem.

If MSEI scores are validly interpreted as measures of these components of self-esteem, then responses to the test items should exhibit a specific structure that is consistent with the multidimensional conceptual definition of the construct. That is, the items on the MSEI should form separate clusters; they should not form one large cluster. In fact, the items should more or less form one cluster for each of the components.

As discussed earlier in Chapter 4, test developers often use a statistical procedure called factor analysis to evaluate the internal structure (i.e., dimensionality) of psychological tests (see also Chapter 12, later). As described in that chapter, some items on a test might be more strongly correlated with each other than with other items, and items that are highly correlated with each other form clusters of items, called dimensions or *factors*. Factor analysis helps to identify the presence and nature of factors existing within a set of items.

Recall that factor analysis addresses several fundamental issues related to a test's internal structure. First, it helps clarify the number of factors within a set of items. As noted above, many social and personality psychologists would theorize that global self-esteem is a single coherent construct. Therefore, if the RSEI is indeed validly interpreted as a measure of global self-esteem, then responses to the 10 items on the RSEI should form only a single factor. If a factor analysis revealed that the RSEI items formed two or more factors, then we would begin to question the validity of the RSEI as a measure of global self-esteem. Thus, the number of factors is an important facet of evaluating the internal structure of a measure.

1) clarify # of Factors

To illustrate this issue in more depth, we will examine the actual RSEI responses made by 149 undergraduates. We conducted a factor analysis of these responses and examined the resulting scree plot (see Figure 8.2). Recall (from Chapter 4) that a scree plot is a graphical presentation of eigenvalues, which are often used to make judgments regarding the number of factors reflected in a set of test items. In the scree plot, we search for a relatively clear "leveling-off" point in the plot. As shown in Figure 8.2, a clear leveling-off point is at the second point. The line sharply decreases as we move from the first point (approximately an eigenvalue of 5.2) to the second point (approximately an eigenvalue of 1.1), and the remaining differences between adjacent eigenvalues are relatively small. The fact that the leveling-off point occurs at the second point provides evidence for a unidimensional structure to these RSEI responses. Because this finding is consistent with theoretically based expectations, this provides empirical evidence for the internal-structure facet of the RSEI as a valid measure of global self-esteem.

A second important use of factor analysis is to reveal the associations among the factors/dimensions within a multidimensional test. As mentioned above, the MSEI is intended to be a multidimensional test, reflecting several components of self-esteem. For such a multidimensional test, if our theory of self-esteem suggests that all the components of self-esteem are independent, then we should find that the self-esteem scales are uncorrelated with each other. However, if our theory suggests that the components are associated with each other in a particular way, then a factor analysis should reveal that particular pattern of associations.

O'Brien and Epstein (1988), the authors of the MSEI, conducted a factor analysis to investigate those associations (pp. 15–16). Their analysis revealed an interesting three-factor structure to the MSEI scales. Using an orthogonal rotation, they found

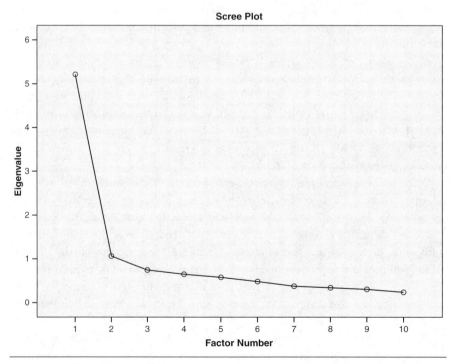

Figure 8.2 A Scree Plot From a Factor Analysis of Responses to the Rosenberg Self-Esteem Inventory

that some MSEI scales (e.g., Global Self-Esteem, Competence, Personal Power) clustered together to form an "overall self-evaluation" factor, which the authors interpreted partly as reflecting the "ability to have an active and direct impact on the world by demonstrating capabilities, leadership abilities, body agility, and self-discipline" (p. 16). Other MSEI scales (e.g., Lovability, Likability) clustered together to form a "social self-esteem" factor, which the authors suggest "is dependent on the social feedback and approval or disapproval received from significant others" (p. 16). Two scales—Moral Self-Approval and Defensive Self-Enhancement—clustered together to form a "defensiveness and private self-evaluation" factor, which the authors suggest has "little in the way of objective or tangible social feedback" (p. 16).

A third primary use of factor analysis in the context of validity is identifying which items are linked to which factors. In developing a measure, our conceptual under-standing of a construct might lead us to generate specific items that reflect particular aspects of the construct. For example, the authors of the MSEI might have written specific items to reflect each of the specific dimensions of self-esteem that they wished to measure. To evaluate the quality of the measure then, we must ensure that the items that are intended to reflect a particular factor actually are connected to that factor and to no other factors. Recall that this evaluation is made through an examination of the factor loadings, which represent the associations between items and factors.

In such an analysis, the authors of the MSEI report the results of a factor analysis of all the items on their inventory (O'Brien & Epstein, 1988, pp. 14–15). They dem-onstrated that nearly every item was connected strongly to the component that it was written to reflect and weakly connected to all other components. For example, the 10 items written for the competence component were clearly connected to that component and to no other. Similarly, the 10 items written for the moral self-approval component were clearly connected to it and to no other. The results were not perfect, though. For example, although the 10 items written for the body appearance component were connected to it and no other, two global self-esteem items and three likeability items were also connected to the body appearance component. Despite a few imperfections in the internal structure of the MSEI, the authors seem generally satisfied that the factor analysis provides adequate support for the validity of the internal structure of the MSEI.

In sum, the internal structure of a test is an important issue in construct valid-ity. A test's internal structure should correspond with the structure of the construct that the test is intended to measure. Typically, internal structure is examined through the correlations among the items in a test and among the subscales in a test (if there are any), and researchers often use factor analysis in this process. We return to this issue in Chapter 12, in which we present the logic behind confirma-tory factor analysis.

Validity Evidence: Response Processes

A third type of validity evidence is the match between the psychological processes that respondents *actually* use when completing a measure and the processes that

psychological processes test taker should use during test vs. what they use

they *should* use. Many psychological measures are based on assumptions about the psychological processes that people use when completing the measure. For example, a researcher developing a measure of extraversion might include an item such as "I often attend parties," and this researcher might assume that respondents will read the item, search their memories for the number of times they have attended parties, and then make a judgment about whether that number qualifies as "often." If participants do not use such a process, then the measure might not provide scores that are interpretable as the test developer intended.

A recent study of the effect of "control deprivation" on cognitive performance illustrates the sometimes subtle problem of response processes. Previous research has suggested that people who lack control over their outcomes in one task will show impaired performance on subsequent tasks. In the study, participants first engaged in a task in which some of them were able to exert control over a noise but others were not. In this "noise control" task, all participants were exposed to a loud buzzing noise, and they were instructed to learn a sequence of keystrokes that would temporarily suppress the noise. During this task, half of the participants were required to learn a very easy sequence, which ensured that they would eventually control the noise. The other half of the participants were required to learn an impossible sequence, which ensured that they would lack control over the noise. After the noise control task, all participants completed a series of word tasks. They were given a list of scrambled words (e.g., pynhm) and were required to identify the correct word (e.g., nymph). Participants were instructed to proceed one word at a time and to proceed to the next word only after completing the prior word. The total number of words correctly unscrambled was taken as the measure of cognitive performance. The researchers hypothesized that control deprivation on the noise task would impair attention, which would produce lower scores on the word scramble task.

Take a moment to consider the psychological process that participants were assumed to use when responding to the scrambled words. The researchers implicitly assumed that participants would need to devote cognitive attentional resources to the word task. Although cognitive factors such as intelligence and previous experience with word puzzles could also affect performance on the word task, such factors were reasonably assumed to be constant across noise control groups because participants had been randomly assigned to the groups. Thus, the researchers assumed that if they found a group difference in the mean number of words correctly unscrambled, it would be because control deprivation would impair some participants' ability to devote full attention to the word task. The impairment of cognitive resources would reduce those participants' ability to concentrate on the word task, which would in turn decrease their performance on the task.

The results did not support the predictions—the participants who had experienced control deprivation on the noise task completed just as many words (on average) as did the participants who had not experienced control deprivation. Many researchers would have taken this as evidence against the hypothesized effect of control deprivation on cognitive performance. However, the researchers who conducted this study paid careful attention to the participants' responses to the measure of cognitive performance. When examining these responses, the researchers realized that some participants had not followed the instructions to continue to the next scrambled word only after successfully unscrambling the previous word. That is, some participants either had forgotten the instructions or had consciously chosen to ignore them. Closer inspection revealed a group difference in this "cheating" behavior—more participants in the control deprivation group "cheated" as compared with the control group.

What does this group difference suggest about the psychological processes that affect the measure of cognitive performance? Although the researchers had assumed that differences in performance would primarily reflect differences in attentional processes, their inspection revealed at least one other process that affected performance. Specifically, "adherence to instructions" also had an effect on performance because the participants who "cheated" were able to unscramble more words correctly. It is possible that their hypothesis was actually correct—that control deprivation impairs attention, which reduces cognitive performance—but the participants who had experienced control deprivation also cheated, which inflated their scores on the measure of cognitive performance.

Hopefully, this example illustrates the important point that construct validity can be evaluated in part by considering the processes involved in responding to a measure. In this example, the word task did not have strong validity as a measure of attention-based cognitive performance. The researchers' laudable attention to their data revealed that the word task also might have been affected by the participants' adherence (or lack thereof) to the task instructions. In sum, their research is inconclusive regarding their original hypotheses, but their attention to response processes raises intriguing issues regarding the association between control deprivation and rule adherence.

considering process involved in responding to a measure

Validity Evidence: Associations With Other Variables

A fourth type of validity evidence involves the associations between test scores and other variables. As illustrated in Figure 8.1, the contemporary view of validity emphasizes the theoretical understanding of the construct for which test scores are to be interpreted. Based on this view, we need to consider the way in which that construct might be connected to other relevant psychological variables. If respondents' test scores are to be interpreted as reflecting the respondents' standing on a specific psychological construct, then our theoretical understanding of that construct should lead us to expect that test scores will have particular patterns of associations with other variables.

constructs relationship to other psych. variables

For example, if the RSEI is to be interpreted as a measure of global self-esteem, then we should think carefully about the nature of global self-esteem. Specifically, we should consider the way in which global self-esteem is associated with other psychological constructs such as happiness, depression, intelligence, social motivation, assertiveness, and so on. Our theoretical perspective on self-esteem might lead us to believe that people with high levels of self-esteem should be relatively happy, relatively nondepressed, and relatively highly socially motivated. In addition, our theoretical perspective might state that self-esteem is unrelated to intelligence—people with low levels of self-esteem are equally intelligent, on average, as people with high levels of self-esteem. Thus, our theoretical perspective on self-esteem suggests a particular pattern of associations between self-esteem and other psychological constructs. If RSEI scores can be validly interpreted as a measure of self-esteem (as we understand it), then we should find a particular pattern of associations between RSEI scores and measures of happiness, depression, social motivation, and intelligence.

Thus, the fourth type of validity evidence involves the match between a measure's *actual* associations with other measures and the associations that the test *should have* with the other measures. If a test's pattern of actual correlations with other tests matches the pattern of correlations that our theoretical perspective leads us to expect, then we gain evidence supporting the interpretation of the test as a measure of the construct in question. For example, imagine that we conduct a study in which respondents complete the RSEI along with measures of happiness, depression, social motivation, and intelligence. If we find that the RSEI is indeed positively correlated with happiness and social motivation, negatively correlated with depression, and uncorrelated with intelligence, then we gain confidence that RSEI scores can be interpreted validly as a measure of self-esteem. Conversely, if a test's pattern of actual correlations with other tests does *not* match the pattern of correlations that our theoretical perspective leads us to expect, then we have obtained evidence *against* the interpretation of the test as a measure of the construct in question. Indeed, if we find that RSEI scores are uncorrelated with happiness and social motivation, then we lose confidence that it should be interpreted as a measure of self-esteem.

When evaluating the pattern of validity associations between a measure and other measures, it is important to consider several types of evidence. *Convergent evidence* is the degree to which test scores are correlated with tests of related constructs. In the global self-esteem example, our theoretical perspective states that happiness and social motivation are related to self-esteem. In addition, our theoretical perspective states that depression is related to self-esteem, albeit in a negative direction. Thus, if our research reveals that the RSEI is in fact positively correlated with measures of happiness and social motivation and negatively correlated with measures of depression, then we have obtained convergent evidence.

Often in the process of evaluating the validity of test interpretations, researchers will ask respondents to complete several different measures of the same construct. For example, we might ask our respondents to complete the RSEI, along with other measures of self-esteem, such as the Coopersmith (1967/1981) Self-Esteem Inventory and MSEI. We would naturally expect to find strong positive correlations between the RSEI and other measures of self-esteem. If we failed to find this, then we would question the validity of the RSEI as a measure of self-esteem. Similarly, researchers might include responses by "informants" to evaluate a test. For example, we might ask each of our respondents to recruit a close acquaintance, and we could ask the acquaintances to rate the self-esteem of the respondents. Although we might not expect to find an extremely high correlation, we would likely expect to find a positive correlation between our respondents' self-reported RSEI scores and the RSEI ratings provided by their acquaintances. That is, we would expect to find that the respondents who described themselves as having relatively high self-esteem were described by their acquaintances as having relatively high self-esteem. In sum, convergent evidence often comes in the form of correlations among different ways of measuring the same construct.

When evaluating the pattern of correlations between a measure and other measures, we must also consider discriminant evidence. *Discriminant evidence* is the degree to which test scores are uncorrelated with tests of unrelated constructs. In the global self-esteem example, our theoretical perspective states that intelligence is unrelated to self-esteem. Thus, our research should reveal that the RSEI is in fact uncorrelated (or only weakly correlated) with measures of intelligence. If we found that RSEI scores were actually positively correlated with intelligence, then the RSEI would lack discriminant validity as a measure of self-esteem. That is, the RSEI would appear to measure more than just self-esteem.

discriminant evidence— test scores are non-correlated w/ tests of unrelated constructs

Discriminant evidence is an important but perhaps subtle concept. Whether a measure is being used for research purposes or for applied purposes, test users must be confident that they know exactly which psychological variables are being measured. Consider a study that might be conducted by a developmental psychologist. The researcher might be interested in the association between self-esteem and academic ability. The researcher might recruit a sample of high school students to complete the RSEI, and he might also obtain the students' permission to get their standardized academic achievement test scores from their academic records. He computes the correlation between RSEI scores and academic achievement scores, and he finds a correlation of .40. He interprets this as indicating that students who have relatively high self-esteem tend to perform relatively well in school. On the basis of these results, he might even suggest that schools devote resources toward increasing students' self-esteem. The conclusions might be considered to have important implications for psychological theory. They might even influence the way school systems spend money.

Before putting too much confidence in the researcher's conclusions, we should carefully consider the methods used in his study, including the discriminant validity of his supposed measure of self-esteem. Whether his conclusions are correct depends in part on the degree to which the RSEI has discriminant validity as a measure of self-esteem. If scores on the RSEI are in fact highly correlated with measures of intelligence, then the RSEI lacks discriminant validity and is at least partly a measure of intelligence. Thus, the correlation found by the researcher might be more accurately interpreted as indicating that students who have relatively high intelligence tend to perform relatively well in school. Indeed, it is possible that the trait of self-esteem is actually unrelated to academic performance and that the researcher has made a serious error in his conclusions. This error could have harmed psychological theory, and it could lead to wasteful spending of limited school resources.

Another common distinction related to this type of evidence is the distinction between concurrent validity evidence and predictive validity evidence. *Concurrent validity evidence* refers to the degree to which test scores are correlated with other relevant variables that are measured *at the same time* as the primary test of interest.

concurrent— measured @ the same time

For example, the website of the College Board, the company that administers the SAT, tells students that the SAT Reasoning Test "is a measure of the critical thinking skills you'll need for academic success in college" (College Board, 2006). How could we evaluate the validity of the SAT as a measure of the skills needed for academic success? One possibility would be to have students complete the SAT during their senior year in high school and then correlate their SAT scores with their high school grade point average (GPA). That is, we could examine the correlation between their SAT scores and the GPA scores that were obtained at more or less the same time the students responded to the SAT. *Predictive validity evidence* refers to the degree to which test scores are correlated with relevant variables that are measured *at a future point in time*. For example, another way of evaluating the validity of the SAT is to have students complete the SAT during their senior year in high school and then correlate their SAT scores with the GPA obtained during their freshman year in college. That is, we could examine the correlation between students' SAT scores and their GPA scores that were obtained a year or more after they took the SAT. Although the distinction between concurrent and predictive validity evidence is traditionally important, the larger point is that both concepts refer to the match between test scores and other relevant variables. As we discussed earlier, the match between test scores and other relevant variables is referred to as convergent validity. Therefore, concurrent validity and predictive validity are essentially varieties of convergent validity.

There are many important issues involved in evaluating convergent and discriminant evidence, and such evidence is arguably the most important facet of validity. The current description has focused mostly on their conceptual meaning and importance. Because of the importance of convergent and discriminant evidence, the next chapter will explore many additional issues in greater detail.

Validity Evidence: Consequences of Testing

As discussed earlier, one key difference between the contemporary perspective on validity and the traditional three-faceted perspective on validity is that the contemporary perspective emphasizes the primacy of construct validity over content validity and criterion validity (more will be said about this later). However, an even more radical and contentious difference may be the assertion that the social consequences of testing are a facet of validity.

The 1999 *Standards for Educational and Psychological Testing* states that validity includes "the intended and unintended consequences of test use" (AERA, APA, & NCME, 1999, p. 16). More specifically, Cronbach (1988) states that test developers, users, and evaluators "have an obligation to review whether a practice has appropriate consequences for individuals and institutions and especially to guard against adverse consequences" (p. 6). For example, if a construct and its measurement seem to benefit males more than females in the workplace, then we should be concerned about the use of the test. Are test scores equally valid for males and females as a measure of the intended construct? How large is the difference in the benefits for males and females?

This suggestion that the consequences of testing be considered an intrinsic part of construct validity has generated quite a bit of debate. Almost everyone would agree that test users, test takers, and policymakers should be concerned about the possibility that a testing program might unfairly and adversely affect some people more than others. However, not everyone agrees that the *consequences of a testing program* should be considered a facet of the *scientific evaluation of the meaning of test scores*. For example, Lees-Haley (1996) considers the assertion that validity includes an assessment of the actual and potential consequences of test use, and he poses the following questions: "But whose consequences? And who will decide? Enemy psychologists? Pacifists? Generals? Whose social values shall we use to assess the consequential validity of these tests?" (p. 982). Clearly, the infusion of value judgments into an ostensibly objective scientific process raises some interesting issues. Reflecting one perspective on this, Lees-Haley bluntly argues that "consequential validity is a dangerous intrusion of politics into science" (p. 982).

Proponents of consequential validity would respond by arguing that science can never be separated from personal and social values. The questions that scientists investigate are shaped partly by society's values and partly by their own personal values. For example, the theoretical assumptions that scientists make are partly shaped by value judgments, and even the labels that scientists attach to their theoretical concepts are partly shaped by values. As an example based on Messick's (1989) important work, consider two psychologists who are developing a theory around a personality construct. One psychologist believes that the construct should be called "flexibility versus rigidity" to differentiate people who can adapt their cognitive and behavioral tendencies in response to changing circumstances from people who tend to retain cognitive and behavioral stability. The other psychologist considers the construct and the psychological difference that it is intended to reflect, but she believes that the construct should be called "confusion versus consistency." Which labels are "scientifically" correct? Should a high level of cognitive and behavioral variability be considered flexibility, or should it be considered confusion? Should a low level of cognitive and behavioral variability be considered rigidity, or should it be considered consistency?

Similarly, consider the following personality characteristic—the tendency to experience, recognize, monitor, and understand emotional reactions. Imagine that a test developer creates a measure of this characteristic and happens to find that females score higher than males, on average. What would the test developer choose to call the test and the construct that it is intended to measure? Knowing that females tend to score higher than males, would the test developer be likely to call it "emotional sensitivity"? If results had indicated that males tended to score higher than females, would the test developer instead choose to call it "emotional intelligence"? Furthermore, imagine that a human resources director was told that you have a high level of "emotional sensitivity." Would his impression of you be different if he had been told that you have a high level of "emotional intelligence"? Which label would you prefer? Would you have been hired if the human resources director believed that you were "intelligent" instead of "sensitive"?

The point here is that value judgments have potentially subtle (and sometimes not so subtle) influences on the scientific process. Proponents of consequential validity argue that such influences should be recognized and evaluated as clearly as possible in a testing context.

The issue of test bias will be discussed in greater detail in Chapter 11; however, some brief comments are relevant here. Earlier, we suggested that consequential validity concerns the possibility that some people are unfairly and adversely affected by a testing program. It is important to recognize the difference between *fairness* in testing and the *consequences* of testing. A test can have adverse consequences for a person or a group of people, and yet the test might still be fair. For example, imagine that females tend to score higher than males on measures of conscientiousness. And imagine that a human resources director uses a conscientiousness questionnaire in the hiring process, resulting in fewer males being hired than females. Is this fair? Does it constitute "adverse consequences" for males?

In this case, fairness depends on the nature of the gender difference in test scores. Why might females and males have different scores on the test? One possibility is that the test is biased. That is, the test does not measure conscientiousness equally well for all people—for whatever reason, it is a good measure of conscientiousness for females but not for males. This is clearly an issue of validity—the test is not equally valid for all people. Therefore, hiring decisions made partly on the basis of test scores may be unfairly biased against males.

A second possibility is that the test is not biased. That is, the test does in fact measure conscientiousness equally well for females and males; it just so happens that, on average, females truly tend to have higher levels of conscientiousness than do males. In this case, hiring decisions made partly on the basis of test scores are not unfairly biased against males (assuming that there are empirical data demonstrating that conscientiousness does predict job performance).

What about the consequences of the testing program? Whether or not the test is fair or biased against males, males are "adversely affected" by the way the test scores are used. However, the test is "biased" only if the test is not equally valid for females and males. The existence of a group difference in test scores, by itself, does not tell us whether the test is biased, in terms of its validity as a measure of a psychological characteristic. In Chapter 11, we will discuss these issues in more detail, and we will present ways of evaluating whether a test is actually biased between groups.

Other Perspectives on Validity

So far, this chapter has conceptualized validity in terms of the degree to which test scores can be accurately interpreted as reflecting a particular psychological construct. This perspective assumes that test scores are linked to a construct that has a clear theoretical basis. Indeed, the types of evidence outlined above are related to the fit between various aspects of test responses and various aspects of a construct's theoretical basis. Because it ties test scores so strongly to theory-based psychological attributes, this perspective is, in essence, a theory-testing view of validity. However, there are at least three alternative perspectives on validity. You might encounter these alternative perspectives in your readings or discussions, so we briefly describe them here.

Criterion validity is an alternative perspective that de-emphasizes the conceptual meaning or interpretation of test scores. Test users might simply wish to use a test to differentiate between groups of people or to make predictions about future outcomes. For example, a human resources director might need to use a test to help predict which applicants are most likely to perform well as employees. From a very practical standpoint, she might not care about the particular psychological construct that the test might be measuring, and she might not be concerned about the theoretical implications of high and low test scores. Instead, she focuses on the test's ability to differentiate good employees from poor employees. If the test does this well, then the test is "valid" enough for her purposes.

From the traditional three-faceted view of validity mentioned earlier, criterion validity refers to the degree to which test scores can predict specific criterion variables. From this perspective, the key to validity is the empirical association between test scores and scores on the relevant criterion variable, such as "job performance." Concurrent validity and predictive validity have traditionally been viewed as two types of criterion validity because they refer to the association between test scores and specific criterion variables. According to the traditional perspective on criterion validity, the psychological meaning of test scores is relatively unimportant—all that matters is the test's ability to differentiate groups or predict specific outcomes.

Although criterion validity is a relatively common term in psychometrics and has traditionally been viewed as a separate type of validity, the contemporary perspective suggests that evidence of criterion associations should be subsumed within the larger and more important concept of construct validity (Messick, 1989). From this perspective, criterion validity is not sufficient on its own, even for purely practical or applied contexts such as employee screening. Indeed, Messick (1989) suggests that

> even for purposes of applied decision making, reliance on criterion validity or content coverage is not enough. The meaning of the measure, and hence its construct validity, must always be pursued—not only to support test interpretation but also to justify test use. (p. 17)

Another alternative perspective on validity emphasizes the need to learn what test scores mean, rather than testing specific hypotheses about test scores. That is, instead of assuming that the theoretical basis of a construct is fully formed and then testing specific hypotheses regarding that theory, test developers and users can evaluate a test by assuming that the meaning of test scores is itself an interesting and important question to be addressed. Such an "inductive" approach to validity proceeds by examining the associations between test scores and a large set of potentially important and relevant psychological variables (Gough, 1965; Ozer, 1989). In contrast, the perspective emphasized so far in this chapter has been called a "deductive" approach to validity (Ozer, 1989) because test evaluation proceeds by deducing a particular hypothesis from the theoretical basis of a construct and then empirically evaluating the accuracy of the hypotheses. Whereas the deductive perspective is a theory-testing approach, the inductive perspective is a more exploratory approach. The goal of an inductive approach is to understand the full meaning of test scores, beyond the meaning that might be constrained by reference to a specific construct. From this approach, researchers "let constructs evolve as a planned part of the test construction process itself" (Tellegen & Waller, 2008, p. 262).

The inductive approach to validity might be most relevant within a research context, and it can be seen as a back-and-forth process. In an applied context, test developers and test users will probably focus on a test for the purposes of a well-specified use, such as predicting job performance. However, in a research context, test developers and test users might be interested in tackling a new area of interest and developing a theoretical foundation for the area. In such a case, test construction and evaluation go hand-in-hand with the researcher's evolving understanding of the constructs being measured. For example, Tellegen and Waller (2008) describe the development and evaluation of the Multidimensional Personality Questionnaire (MPQ). In its current version, the MPQ consists of 11 primary personality factor scales (e.g., Social Potency, Achievement, Stress Reaction), which are clustered into four broad traits (e.g., positive emotional temperament, negative emotional temperament). The development of the MPQ was motivated by a desire "to clarify and highlight the nature of several 'focal' dimensions repeatedly emphasized or adumbrated in the personality literature" (p. 264). During the years-long development of the MPQ, items were written, administered, analyzed, and rewritten repeatedly. During this process, the researchers refined their understanding of the constructs that seemed to be emerging from the MPQ.

Although the inductive approach to test validity can be informative in terms of expanding our understanding of a measure's theoretical and practical implications, it is not commonly emphasized in the testing literature. More typically, tests are typically developed with a focus on fairly specific well-conceived constructs, and test developers usually spend their energy evaluating test score interpretation with keen regard to those specific constructs. Less often do test developers spend time and effort examining a more comprehensive view of the test's implications.

A third alternative perspective on test validity strongly emphasizes the connection between tests and psychological constructs. Borsboom, Mellenbergh, and Van Heerden (2004) suggest that the sole issue in test validity is whether test responses are affected by the construct that the test is intended to measure. That is, a test is a valid measure of a construct if and only if the intended construct truly influences respondents' performance on the test. From this perspective, Borsboom et al. reject the argument that the consequences of testing are relevant to test validity. They even argue that the correlations between test scores and measures of other attributes are not directly relevant to test validity. Instead, they suggest that "the primary objective of validation research is . . . to offer a theoretical explanation of the processes that lead up to the measurement outcome" (p. 1067).

The perspective offered by Borsboom et al. (2004) is an interesting contrast and complement to the perspectives presented in this chapter. It is clearly at odds with an approach that emphasizes criterion validity and with the inductive approach to validity. These two approaches either minimize the importance of psychological constructs altogether (criterion validity) or suggest that the test developer's understanding of a construct evolves and changes along with the test itself (inductive approach). In contrast, the perspective offered by Borsboom et al. emphasizes the importance of a test developer's well-articulated theoretical understanding of a single construct in test development and validity. That is, constructs not only exist and are a crucial part of validity, but they should be the guiding forces in the test development and validation processes. In the context of the main definition of validity offered in this chapter (based on the AERA, APA, & NCME, 1999, *Standards for Educational and Psychological Testing*), the Borsboom et al. approach would seem to reject much except for the importance of constructs and the theoretically based examination of the response processes underlying performance on the test.

Contrasting Reliability and Validity

With the concept of validity now in mind, it might be useful to contrast validity and reliability. These two concepts are fundamental to a sophisticated understanding of psychometrics, and it is important to understand the difference clearly.

Recall from previous chapters that a test's reliability is the degree to which differences in test scores reflect differences among people in their levels of the trait that affects test scores. At this point, we might add a bit to that definition and suggest that a test's reliability is the degree to which differences in test scores reflect differences among people in their levels of the trait that affects test scores, *whatever that trait might be*. That is, we can discuss the reliability of a particular test without even being aware of the potential interpretation of test scores or the nature of the trait being measured by the test.

On the other hand, validity is intrinsically tied to the interpretation of test scores and to the nature of the trait supposedly being assessed by the measure. In a sense, reliability might be considered to be a property of test responses, whereas validity is a property of the interpretation of test scores. That is, reliability is a relatively simple quantitative property of test responses, but validity is an issue more tied to psychological theory and to the implications of test scores.

Even though they are separate concepts, reliability and validity are linked both conceptually and statistically. Conceptually, for many areas of interest in the behavioral sciences, validity requires reliability. For example, intelligence is usually conceptualized as a psychological trait that is quite stable across time and situations—your true level of intelligence does not change very much from week to week or month to month. Therefore, a test that is intended to be a measure of intelligence should result in scores that are reasonably stable across time. That is, a valid test of intelligence will be reliable. Put another way, if a test's scores are not stable across time (i.e., if the test does not have test–retest reliability), then it cannot be valid as a measure of intelligence. Even though validity often requires reliability, the reverse is not true. A measure might have excellent internal consistency and very high test–retest reliability, but we might not interpret it in a valid manner. In sum, a test must be reliable if it is to be interpreted validly, but just because a test is reliable does not mean that it will be interpreted validly.

Summary

This chapter presented the conceptual basis of test validity. As defined in the *Standards for Educational and Psychological Testing*, validity is "the degree to which evidence and theory support the interpretations of test scores entailed by the proposed uses" of a test (AERA, APA, & NCME, 1999, p. 9). We described several key implications of this way of thinking about validity—validity concerns the interpretation of test scores, it is a matter of degree, and it is based on empirical evidence and theory. Because empirical evidence is a key consideration in evaluating the validity of test scores, we also described five types of evidence that are relevant to test validity—test content, internal structure, response processes, associations with other variables, and the consequences of testing. We then contrasted the contemporary view of validity with traditional perspectives that are still commonly discussed and with reliability. Finally, we reiterated the importance of validity in terms of its implications for research and for real-world decision making.

Suggested Readings

A recent classic in test validity, this is an extensive summary of the perspective of a major figure in test validity:

Messick, S. (1989). Validity. In R. L. Linn (Ed.), *Educational measurement* (3rd ed., pp. 13–103). New York, NY: Macmillan.

Another thorough summary of advances in test validity:

Shepard, L. A. (1993). Evaluating test validity. In L. Darling-Hammond (Ed.), *Review of research in education* (Vol. 19, pp. 405–450). Washington, DC: American Educational Research Association.

This is a classic article in the history of test validity, being one of the most cited articles in all of psychology:

Cronbach, L. J., & Meehl, P. E. (1955). Construct validity in psychological tests. *Psychological Bulletin, 51,* 281–302.

An interesting complement to the construct validity focus of much recent theorizing:

Schmidt, F. L. (1988). Validity generalization and the future of criterion-related validity. In H. Wainer & H. I. Braun (Eds.), *Test validity* (pp. 173–189). Hillsdale, NJ: Lawrence Erlbaum.

This is an interesting commentary on the notion of consequential validity:

Lees-Haley, P. R. (1996). Alice in validityland, or the dangerous consequences of consequential validity. *American Psychologist, 51,* 981–983.

This is the most recent view on validity from the perspective of three major organizations concerned with psychological testing:

American Educational Research Association, American Psychological Association, and National Council on Measurement in Education. (1999). *Standards for educational and psychological testing.* Washington, DC: American Educational Research Association.

CHAPTER 9

Estimating and Evaluating Convergent and Discriminant Validity Evidence

Chapter 8 presented conceptual perspectives on validity, and it summarized five types of evidence that are used to gauge construct validity. As described in that chapter, convergent and discriminant evidence reflects the degree to which test scores have the "correct" patterns of associations with other variables. In this chapter, we focus more deeply on the way in which convergent and discriminant evidence can be evaluated, and we discuss issues bearing on the interpretation of convergent and discriminant evidence.

To restate the issue briefly, psychological constructs are embedded in a theoretical context. That is, the conceptual foundation of a construct includes the connections between the construct and a variety of other psychological constructs. The interconnections between a construct and other related constructs have been called a *nomological network*, which refers to the network of "meaning" surrounding a construct (Cronbach & Meehl, 1955). For example, Baumeister and Leary (1995) introduced the concept of a "need to belong," which was defined as the "drive to form and maintain at least a minimum quantity of lasting, positive, and significant interpersonal relationships" (p. 497). Although they hypothesized that this is a fundamental human need, they also observed that people differ in the degree to which they experience this need. Some people have a relatively great need to experience frequent interactions within close and caring relationships, while other people seem to need such interactions less. Leary, Kelly, Cottrell, and Schreindorfer (2006) theorized about the nomological network surrounding the need to belong. Specifically, they suggested that the need to belong was somewhat similar to characteristics such as the need for affiliation, the need for intimacy, sociability, and extraversion. Furthermore, the need to belong was essentially unrelated to constructs such as conscientiousness, openness to experience, and self-esteem.

[handwritten margin note: measure of construct should be strongly correlated w/ some constructs & weakly w/ others]

The nomological network of associations among constructs dictates a particular pattern of associations among measures of those constructs. The nomological network surrounding a construct suggests that a measure of the construct should be strongly associated with measures of some constructs but weakly correlated with measures of other constructs. For example, Leary et al. (2006) predicted that their 10-item "Need to Belong" (NTB) measure would be weakly to moderately correlated with measures of need for affiliation, sociability, and extraversion; negatively correlated with a measure of social isolation; and essentially uncorrelated with measures of conscientiousness, openness to experience, and self-esteem. Their predictions guided their evaluation of the convergent and discriminant quality of the NTB.

[handwritten margin note: "estimating the degree to which test scores actually show the predicted pattern of association]

A crucial part of the validation process is estimating the degree to which test scores actually show the predicted pattern of associations. In this chapter, we present some methods used in this process, some important factors affecting the outcome of the process, and some key considerations in interpreting the outcomes.

Methods for Evaluating Convergent and Discriminant Validity

[handwritten margin note: 4 methods of evaluating convergent + discriminant validity evidence]

There are at least four methods used to evaluate the degree to which measures show convergent and discriminate associations. These procedures differ in several ways— some are more conceptually complex than others; some can be more statistically complex than others; some are decades old, while others are relatively new; and some require more explicit predictions than others. Despite these differences, the following methods are (or might become) common and useful ways of evaluating convergent and discriminant validity evidence.

Focused Associations

[handwritten margin note: associations btwn test scores + specific variables]

Some measures have clear relevance for a few very specific variables. Evaluating the validity of interpretations for such measures can focus on the associations between test scores and those relatively few specific variables. In a sense, these specific associations are "make-or-break" in terms of the convergent and discriminant validity evidence for such measures. Research verifying those crucial predicted associations provides strong validity evidence, but research failing to verify the associations casts serious doubts on validity.

As mentioned in Chapter 8, the SAT Reasoning Test is intended to be "a measure of the critical thinking skills [needed] for academic success in college" (College Board, 2006). This description implies that two kinds of variables might be particularly critical for evaluating the SAT Reasoning Test. First, as a measure of "critical thinking skills," the SAT should be associated with other measures of relevant critical thinking skills. Second, because it is intended to assess a construct required for "academic success in college," the SAT should be associated with measures of collegiate academic performance.

In establishing the quality of the SAT, the College Board appears to be most concerned with the latter issue. Several documents that are made available to students, educators, and prospective researchers emphasize the correlation between SAT scores and academic indicators such as first-year college grades. For example, the *SAT Program Handbook*, published by the College Board for school counselors and admissions officers, includes several references to validity (College Board, 2006). In the first section regarding validity, the *Handbook* states that a study of more than 110,000 students from more than 25 colleges revealed an average correlation of .55 between SAT scores and freshman grades. The *Handbook* goes on to mention additional studies providing predictive validity evidence for the SAT in relation to college grades. Clearly, the College Board focuses its validity argument heavily on the correlations between the SAT and a specific set of criterion variables related to academic performance in college.

Thus, one method for evaluating the validity of test interpretations is to focus on a few highly relevant criterion variables. To the degree that test scores are indeed correlated with those crucial variables, test developers and test users gain increased confidence in the test. Those correlations, sometimes called *validity coefficients*, are fundamental for establishing validity. If research reveals that a test's validity coefficients are generally large, then test developers, users, and evaluators will have increased confidence in the quality of the test as a measure of its intended construct.

Validity generalization is a process of evaluating a test's validity coefficients across a large set of studies (Schmidt, 1988; Schmidt & Hunter, 1977). Unlike the SAT, many measures used in the behavioral sciences rely on validity evidence obtained from relatively small studies. In fact, many if not most validity studies include fewer than 400 participants—particularly if those studies include anything besides self-report data. Often a researcher conducting a single validity study will recruit a sample of 50 to 400 participants, administer the measure of interest to those participants, assess additional criterion variables deemed relevant, and compute the correlation between the scores on the measure of interest and scores on the criterion measures. Such studies are the basis of many measures used for research in personality psychology, clinical psychology, developmental psychology, social psychology, organizational psychology, and educational psychology. Individual validity studies often include relatively small samples due to limits on researchers' time, funding, and other resources.

Although studies with relatively small samples are common and are conducted for many practical reasons, they do have a potentially important drawback. Specifically, a study conducted at one location with one type of population might produce results that do not generalize to another location or another type of population.

For example, the results of a study of bank employees might demonstrate that scores on the Revised NEO Personality Inventory (NEO-PI–R) Conscientiousness scale are relatively good predictors of job performance for bank tellers. Although this is potentially valuable and useful evidence for human resources directors in the banking industry, do these results offer any insight for human resources directors in the accounting industry, the real estate industry, or the sales industry? That is, is the association between

generalize to many populations?

conscientiousness scores and job performance strong only for bank tellers, or does it generalize to other groups? Perhaps the trait of conscientiousness is more relevant for some kinds of jobs than for others. If so, then we should not assume that the NEO-PI–R Conscientiousness scale is a valid predictor of job performance in all professions.

Validity generalization studies are intended to evaluate the predictive utility of a test's scores across a range of settings, times, situations, and so on. A validity generalization study is a form of meta-analysis; it combines the results of several smaller individual studies into one large analysis (Schmidt, Hunter, Pearlman, & Hirsh, 1985). For example, we might find 25 studies examining the association between the NEO-PI–R Conscientiousness scale and job performance. One of these studies might have examined the association among bank tellers, another might have examined the association within a sample of school teachers, another might have examined the association within a sample of salespersons, and so on. Each study might include a different kind of profession, but each study also might include a different way of measuring job performance. For instance, some studies might have relied on managers' ratings of employees' job performance, while other studies might have used more concrete measures of job performance, such as "dollars sold." Thus, we might find that the 25 different studies reveal apparently different results regarding the strength of association between NEO-PI–R Conscientiousness scores and job performance.

form of meta-analysis

Validity generalization studies can address at least three important issues. First, they can reveal the general level of predictive validity across all of the smaller individual studies. For example, the analysis of all 25 studies in our conscientiousness example might reveal that the average validity correlation between NEO-PI–R Conscientiousness scores and job performance is .30. Second, validity generalization studies can reveal the degree of variability among the smaller individual studies. We might find that among the 25 studies in our generalization study, some have quite strong associations between NEO-PI–R Conscientiousness scores and job performance (say correlations of .40 to .50), while others have much weaker associations (say correlations of .00 to .10). If we found this kind of variability, then we might need to conclude that the association between NEO-PI–R Conscientiousness scores and job performance does not generalize across the studies. Conversely, our validity generalization study might reveal that among the 25 studies in our generalization study, almost all have moderate associations between NEO-PI–R Conscientiousness scores and job performance (say correlations of .20 to .40). If we found this smaller amount of variability among the 25 studies, then we might conclude that the association between NEO-PI–R Conscientiousness scores and job performance does in fact generalize across the studies quite well. Either way, the finding would be important information in evaluating the validity and use of the NEO-PI–R in hiring decisions.

Validity Gen Studies address 3 issues:

1) reveal the general level of predictive validity across all of the small studies

2) Reveal the degree of variability among the smaller indiv. studies (generalization)

The third issue that can be addressed by validity generalization studies is the source of variability among studies. If initial analyses reveal a wide range of validity coefficients among the individual studies, then further analyses might explain why the studies' results differ from each other. For example, we might find a methodological difference among studies that corresponds to the validity coefficient differences among the studies. We might discover that

3) Source of variability among studies

(why do the results differ from each other)

strong validity coefficients were found in studies in which managers provided ratings of job performance but that weaker validity coefficients were found in studies in which concrete measures such as "dollars sold" were used to assess job performance. Thus, differences in the measurement of the criterion variable seem to contribute to differences in the size of the validity coefficient. This kind of methodological source of variability should be considered when evaluating the implications of the general level and variability of validity coefficients across studies.

example

In sum, some psychological tests are expected to be strongly relevant to a few specific variables. If research confirms that such a test is indeed strongly associated with its specific criterion variables, then test developers, users, and evaluators gain confidence that the test scores have good convergent validity as a measure of the intended construct. A validity generalization study evaluates the degree to which the association between a test and an important criterion variable generalizes across individual studies that cover a range of populations, settings, and so on.

strong association of criterion variables → good convergent validity

Sets of Correlations

The nomological network surrounding a construct does not always focus on a small set of extremely relevant criterion variables. Sometimes, a construct's nomological network touches on a wide variety of other constructs with differing levels of association to the main construct. In such cases, researchers evaluating convergent and discriminant validity evidence must examine a wide range of criterion variables.

examine a wide range of criterion variables

In such cases, researchers often compute the correlations between the test of interest and measures of the many criterion variables. They will then "eyeball" the correlations and make a somewhat subjective judgment about the degree to which the correlations match what would be expected on the basis of the nomological network surrounding the construct of interest.

subjective judgement about correlations

For example, Hill et al. (2004) developed a new measure of perfectionism, and they presented evidence of its convergent and discriminant validity. The Perfectionism Inventory (PI) was designed to measure eight facets of perfectionism, so it was intended to have a multidimensional structure (see the discussion on "internal structure" in Chapter 8). Specifically, the PI was designed to assess facets such as concern over mistakes, organization, planfulness, striving for excellence, and need for approval. To evaluate the convergent and discriminant validity evidence, participants were asked to complete the PI along with measures of 23 criterion variables. Criterion variables included other measures of perfectionism. In addition, because perfectionism is associated with various kinds of psychological distress, the criterion variables included measures of several psychological symptoms (e.g., obsessive-compulsive disorder, anxiety, fear of negative evaluation). The correlations between the PI scales and the 23 criterion scales were presented in a correlation matrix that included more than 200 correlations (see Table 9.1).

example

Table 9.1 Example of Sets of Correlations in the Validation of the Perfectionism Inventory: Correlations Between Perfectionism Indicator Scales and Related Measures

Scale	CM	HS	NA	OR	PP	PL	RU	SE	CP	SEP	PI–C
Perfectionism: MPS–F[a]											
Concern over mistakes	.82	.43	.58	.18	.38	.30	.70	.52	.47	.78	.72
Doubts about actions	.63	.37	.60	.24	.20	.38	.70	.43	.47	.67	.65
Parental criticism	.41	.25	.20	$-.03^{ns}$	.60	$.02^{ns}$	.32	.17	.14	.49	.36
Parental expectations	.31	.27	.18	$.07^{ns}$	.85	$.06^{ns}$	.29	.32	.23	.53	.43
Personal standards	.47	.50	.36	.45	.3	.44	.52	.72	.70	.55	.71
Organization	.12	.36	.18	.89	.11**	.49	.31	.51	.76	.23	.55
Perfectionism: MPS–HF[b]											
Self-oriented	.47	.42	.34	.47	.42	.45	.55	.79	.71	.57	.73
Other oriented	.33	.62	.14**	.29	.30	.26	.37	.42	.53	.36	.51
Socially prescribed	.65	.35	.49	.16**	.58	.21	.61	.42	.38	.74	.65
Symptoms: BSI[c]											
Somatic complaints	.35	.14*	.31	.13*	.11*	$.13^*$	.34	.17	.19	.35	.31
Depression	.46	.16**	.46	$.03^{ns}$	.15**	.18	.46	.13*	.17	.49	.39
Obsessive–compulsive	.40	.14**	.46	$.08^{ns}$	.10**	.19	.46	.18	.19	.45	.37
Anxiety	.42	.28	.42	.22	.25	.25	.49	.29	.35	.50	.49
Interpersonal sensitivity	.52	.18	.68	.17	.13*	.22	.56	.27	.28	.60	.51
Hostility	.41	.30	.31	.10*	.21	$.05^{ns}$	.39	.15**	.20	.42	.36

Phobic anxiety	.39	.14**	.39	.13*	.15**	.13*	.39	.15**	.21	.42	.37
Paranoia	.48	.28	.49	.18	.21	.21	.54	.30	.33	.55	.51
Psychoticism	.49	.19	.48	.09ns	.16**	.19	.49	.17	.22	.51	.43
Global Severity Index	.54	.24	.55	.16	.20	.21	.57	.25	.29	.59	.51
Obsessive-Compulsive Inventory[d]											
Frequency	.43	.24	.45	.39	.08ns	.34	.52	.42	.47	.47	.54
Distress	.50	.28	.49	.40	.03ns	.33	.60	.44	.48	.51	.57
Fear of negative evaluation[a]	.63	.26	.83	.16	.20	.31	.64	.33	.34	.73	.62
Social desirability: MCSDS[c]	-.15**	-.17	-.09*	-.04ns	-.14**	-.09*	-.18	-.16	-.12**	-.18	-.18

SOURCE: Hill et al. (2004). Copyright © 2004 *Journal of Personality Assessment.* Reproduced by permission of Taylor & Francis Group (http://www .taylorandfrancis.com).

NOTES: For all correlations, $p < .001$ (except as noted). CM = Concern Over Mistakes; HS = High Standards for Others; NA = Need for Approval; OR = Organization; PP = Perceived Parental Pressure; PL = Planfulness; RU = Rumination; SE = Striving for Excellence; CP = Conscientious Perfectionism; SEP = Self-Evaluative Perfectionism; PI-C = Perfectionism Indicator Composite score; MPS-F = Frost's Multidimensional Perfectionism Scale; MPS-HF = Hewitt and Flett's Multidimensional Perfectionism Scale; BSI = Brief Symptom Index; MCSDS = Marlowe-Crowne Social Desirability Scale.

a. $n = 613$.
b. $n = 355$.
c. $n = 368$.
d. $n = 207$.

$*p < .05$, one-tailed; $**p < .01$, one-tailed; $ns\ p > .05$, all one-tailed.

To evaluate the convergent and discriminant validity evidence, Hill and his colleagues (2004) carefully examined the correlations and interpreted them in terms of their conceptual logic. For example, they noted that the Concern Over Mistakes scale of the PI was strongly associated with a Concern Over Mistakes scale from a different measure of perfectionism. Similarly, they noted that the Striving for Excellence scale of the PI was strongly associated with a Personal Standards scale (i.e., indicating high expectations for one's performance and an inclination to base self-appraisal on performance) and a Self-Oriented Perfectionism scale (i.e., indicating unrealistic standards for performance and the tendency to fixate on imperfections in one's performance) from other measures of perfectionism. They also examined the associations between the PI scales and the various measures of psychological distress. For example, they noted that three of the PI scales—(1) Rumination, (2) Concern Over Mistakes, and (3) Need for Approval—were strongly associated with fear of negative evaluation and with the frequency and severity of symptoms of obsessive-compulsive disorder.

This approach to evaluating validity is common. Researchers gather a large amount of data concerning the test of interest and measures from a variety of other tests. They then examine the pattern of correlations, and they judge the degree to which the pattern generally "makes sense" given the conceptual meaning of the construct being assessed by the test.

Multitrait–Multimethod Matrices

One of the most influential papers in the history of psychological measurement was published in 1959 by Campbell and Fiske. In this paper, Campbell and Fiske built on the concept of construct validity as articulated by Cronbach and Meehl (1955). As we have already discussed, Cronbach and Meehl outlined a conceptual meaning of construct validity based on the notion of a nomological network. Although their paper was a hugely important conceptual advance, Cronbach and Meehl did not present a way to evaluate construct validity in a rigorous statistical manner. Campbell and Fiske developed the logic of a multitrait–multimethod matrix (MTMMM) as a statistical and methodological expansion of the conceptual work done by Cronbach and Meehl.

For the analysis of an MTMMM, researchers obtain measures of several traits, each of which is measured through several methods. For example, researchers evaluating a new self-report questionnaire of social skill might ask participants to complete the questionnaire along with self-report measures of several other traits, such as impulsivity, conscientiousness, and emotional stability. In addition, they might ask close acquaintances of the participants to provide ratings of the participants' social skill, impulsivity, conscientiousness, and emotional stability. Finally, they might hire psychology students to interview each participant and then provide ratings of the participants' social skill, impulsivity, conscientiousness, and emotional stability. Thus, for each participant, the researchers obtain data relevant to multiple traits (social skill, impulsivity, conscientiousness, and emotional stability), each of which is measured through multiple methods (self-report, acquaintance ratings, and interviewer ratings).

The overarching purpose of the MTMMM analysis is to set clear guidelines for evaluating convergent and discriminant validity evidence. This purpose is partially served through evaluating two importantly different sources of variance that might affect the correlations between two measures—trait variance and method variance. To understand these sources of variance, imagine that researchers examining the new self-report measure of social skill find that scores on their measure are highly correlated with scores on a self-report measure of emotional stability. What does this finding tell them?

Strictly speaking, the finding tells them that people who say that they are relatively socially skilled tend to say that they are relatively emotionally stable. But does this finding reflect a purely psychological phenomenon in terms of the associations between two constructs, or does it reflect a more methodological phenomenon separate from the two constructs? In terms of psychological phenomena, it might indicate that the trait of social skill shares something in common with the trait of emotional stability. That is, the measures might share trait variance. For example, people who are socially skilled might tend to become emotionally stable (perhaps because their social skill allows them to create social relationships that have emotional benefits). Or people who are emotionally stable might tend to become more socially skilled (perhaps because their stability allows them to be comfortable and effective in social situations). Or it might be that social skill and emotional stability are both caused by some other variable altogether (perhaps there is a genetic basis that influences both stability and social skill). Each of these explanations indicates that the two traits being assessed—social skill and emotional stability—truly overlap in some way. Because the traits share some commonality, the measures of those traits are correlated with each other.

Despite our inclination to make a psychological interpretation of the correlation between social skill and emotional stability, the result might actually have a relatively nonpsychological basis. Recall that our example was based on the correlation between self-report measures. Thus, the correlation might be produced simply by *shared method variance*. That is, the correlation is positive because it is based on two measures derived from the same source—respondents' self-reports in this case. When measures are based on the same data source, they might share properties apart from the main constructs being assessed by the measures.

For example, people might tend to see themselves in very generalized terms—either in generally "good" ways or in generally "bad" ways. Therefore, a positive correlation between self-reported social skill and self-reported emotional stability might be due solely to the fact that people who report high levels of social skill simply tend to see themselves in generally good ways; therefore, they also tend to report high levels of emotional stability. Similarly, people who report low levels of social skill simply tend to see themselves in generally bad ways; therefore, they also tend to report low levels of emotional stability. In this case, the apparent correlation between social skill and emotional stability does not reflect a commonality between the two traits being assessed by the measures. Instead, the correlation is simply a by-product of a bias inherent in the self-report method of measurement. That is, the correlation is an "artifact" of the fact that the two measures share the same method (i.e., self-report). Testing experts would say that the ratings share method variance.

ambiguous

Strong correlation can mean many things

difference in methods could make a weak correlation when it should be strong

MTMMM Organizes

Due to the potential influences of trait variance and method variance, a correlation between two measures is a somewhat ambiguous finding. On one hand, a strong correlation (positive or negative) could indicate that the two measures share trait variance—the constructs that they are intended to measure have some commonality. On the other hand, a strong correlation (again positive or negative) could indicate that the two measures share method variance—they are correlated mainly because they are based on the same method of measurement.

The ambiguity inherent in a correlation between two measures cuts both ways; it also complicates the interpretation of a *weak* correlation. A relatively weak correlation between two measures could indicate that the measures do not share trait variance—the constructs that they are intended to measure do not have any commonality. However, the weak correlation between measures could reflect differential method variance, thereby masking a true correlation between the traits that they are intended to assess. That is, the two traits actually could be associated with each other, but if one trait is assessed through one method (e.g., self-report) and the other is assessed through a different method (e.g., acquaintance report), then the resulting correlation might be fairly weak.

These ambiguities can create confusion when evaluating construct validity. Specifically, the influences of trait variance and method variance complicate the interpretation of a set of correlations as reflecting convergent and discriminant validity evidence. Each correlation represents a potential blend of trait variance and method variance. Because researchers examining construct validity do not know the true influences of trait variance and method variance, they must examine their complete set of correlations carefully. A careful examination can provide insight into trait variance, method variance, and, ultimately, construct validity. The MTMMM approach was designed to articulate these complexities, to organize the relevant information, and to guide researchers through the interpretations.

As articulated by Campbell and Fiske (1959), an MTMMM examination should be guided by attention to the various kinds of correlations that represent varying blends of trait and method variance. Recall from our example that the researchers evaluating the new measure of social skill gathered data relevant to four traits, each of which was measured through three methods. Let us focus on two correlations for a moment: (1) the correlation between the self-report measure of social skill and the acquaintance report measure of social skill and (2) the correlation between the self-report measure of social skill and the self-report measure of emotional stability. Take a moment to consider this question: If the new self-report measure can be interpreted validly as a measure of social skill, then which of the two correlations should be stronger?

Based purely on a consideration of the constructs being measured, the researchers might predict that the first correlation will be stronger than the second. They might expect the first correlation to be quite strong—after all, it is based on two measures of the same construct. In contrast, they might expect the second correlation to be relatively weak—after all, social skill and emotional stability are different constructs. However, these predictions ignore the potential influence of method variance.

Taking method variance into account, the researchers might reevaluate their prediction. Note that the first correlation is based on two different methods of assessment, but the second correlation is based on a single method (i.e., two self-report measures). Thus, based on a consideration of method variance, the researchers might expect to find that the first correlation is weaker than the second.

As this example hopefully begins to illustrate, we can identify different types of correlations, with each type representing a blend of trait variance and method variance. Campbell and Fiske (1959) point to four types of correlations derived from an MTMMM (see Table 9.2):

Table 9.2   MTMMM Basics: Types of Correlations, Trait Variance, and Method Variance

(handwritten note in margin: method vs. association)

Association Between the Two Constructs		Method Used to Measure the Two Constructs	
		Different Methods (e.g., Self-Report for One Construct and Acquaintance Report for the Other)	**Same Method (e.g., Self-Report Used for Both Constructs)**
Different constructs (not associated)	Label	Heterotrait-heteromethod correlations	Heterotrait-monomethod correlations
	Sources of variance	Nonshared trait variance and nonshared method variance	Nonshared trait variance and shared method variance
	Example	Self-report measure of social skill correlated with acquaintance report measure of emotional stability	Self-report measure of social skill correlated with self-report measure of emotional stability
	Expected correlation	Weakest	Moderate?
Same (or similar) constructs (associated)	Label	Monotrait-heteromethod correlations	Monotrait-monomethod correlations
	Sources of variance	Shared trait variance and nonshared method variance	Shared trait variance and shared method variance
	Example	Self-report measure of social skill correlated with acquaintance report measure of social skill	Self-report measure of social skill correlated with self-report measure of social skill (i.e., reliability)
	Expected correlation	Moderate?	Strongest

- *Heterotrait-heteromethod correlations* are based on measures of different constructs measured through different methods (e.g., a self-report measure of social skill correlated with an acquaintance report measure of emotional stability).
- *Heterotrait-monomethod correlations* are based on measures of different constructs measured through the same method (e.g., a self-report measure of social skill correlated with a self-report measure of emotional stability).
- *Monotrait-heteromethod correlations* are based on measures of the same construct measured through the different methods (e.g., a self-report measure of social skill correlated with an acquaintance report measure of social skill).
- *Monotrait-monomethod correlations* are based on measures of the same construct measured through the same method (e.g., a self-report measure of social skill correlated with itself). These correlations reflect reliability—the correlation of a measure with itself.

Reliability

Campbell and Fiske (1959) articulated the definitions and logic of these four types of correlations, and they tied them to construct validity. A full MTMMM of hypothetical correlations is presented in Table 9.3. The matrix includes 66 correlations among the three measures of four traits, along with 12 reliability estimates along the main diagonal. Each of these 78 values can be characterized in terms of the four types of correlations just outlined. The evaluation of construct validity, trait variance, and method variance proceeds by focusing on various types of correlations as organized in the MTMMM.

Evidence of convergent validity is represented by monotrait-heteromethod correlations, which are printed in boldface in the MTMMM. These values represent the correlations between different ways of measuring the same traits. For example, the correlation between self-report social skill and acquaintance report social skill is .40, and the correlation between self-report social skill and interviewer report social skill is .34. These correlations suggest that people who describe themselves as relatively socially skilled (on the new self-report measure) tend to be described by their acquaintances and by the interviewers as relatively socially skilled. Monotrait-heteromethod correlations that are fairly strong begin to provide convergent evidence for the new self-report measure of social skill. However, they must be interpreted in the context of the other correlations in the MTMMM.

strong validity
↓
Same trait need to be the most highly correlated

To provide strong evidence of its convergent and discriminant validity, the self-report measure of social skill should be more highly correlated with other measures of social skill than with any other measures. Illustrating this, the MTMMM in Table 9.3 shows that, as would be expected, the monotrait-heteromethod correlations are generally larger than the heterotrait-heteromethod correlations (inside the dashed-line triangles, reflecting the associations between measures of different constructs assessed through different methods). For example, the correlation between the self-report measure of social skill and the acquaintance report measure of emotional stability is only .20, and the correlation between the self-report measure of social skill and the interviewer report measure of conscientiousness is only .09. These correlations, as well as most of the other heterotrait-heteromethod correlations, are noticeably lower than the monotrait-heteromethod correlations discussed in

Table 9.3 Example of MTMMM Correlations

Methods	Traits	Self-Report				Acquaintance Report				Interviewer Report			
		Social Skill	Impulsivity	Conscien- tiousness	Emotional Stability	Social Skill	Impulsivity	Conscien- tiousness	Emotional Stability	Social Skill	Impulsivity	Conscien- tiousness	Emotional Stability
Self-report	Social skill	(.85)											
	Impulsivity	.14	(.81)										
	Conscientiousness	.20	.22	(.75)									
	Emotional stability	.35	.24	.19	(.82)								
Acquaintance	Social skill	**.40**	.14	.10	.22	(.76)							
	Impulsivity	.13	**.32**	.13	.19	.18	(.80)						
	Conscientiousness	.09	.17	**.36**	.14	.14	.26	(.68)					
	Emotional stability	.20	.23	.11	**.41**	.30	.28	.18	(.78)				
Interviewer report	Social skill	**.34**	.11	.19	.20	**.23**	.01	.11	.19	(.81)			
	Impulsivity	.03	**.25**	.12	.19	.06	**.24**	.10	.14	.22	(.77)		
	Conscientiousness	.09	.09	**.30**	.14	.09	.08	**.20**	.06	.24	.30	(.86)	
	Emotional stability	.14	.16	.08	**.33**	.13	.12	.06	**.19**	.44	.38	.29	(.78)

233

the previous paragraph (which were correlations of .40 and .34). Thus, the correlations between measures that share trait variance but do not share method variance (the monotrait-heteromethod correlations) should be larger than the correlations between measures that share neither trait variance nor method variance (the heterotrait-heteromethod correlations).

An even more stringent requirement for convergent and discriminant validity evidence is that the self-report measure of social skill should be more highly correlated with other measures of social skill than with self-report measures of other traits. The MTMMM in Table 9.3 shows that, as would be expected, the monotrait-heteromethod correlations are generally larger than the heterotrait-monomethod correlations (inside the solid-line triangles reflecting the associations between measures of different constructs assessed through the same method). The data in the MTMMM in Table 9.3 provide mixed evidence in terms of these associations. Although the correlations between the self-report measure of social skill and the self-report measures of impulsivity and conscientiousness are relatively low (.14 and .20, respectively), the correlation between the self-report measure of social skill and the self-report measure of emotional stability is relatively high, at .35. Thus, the self-report measure of social skill overlaps with the self-report measure of emotional stability. Moreover, it overlaps with this measure of a different construct to the same degree that it overlaps with other measures of social skill. This finding might raise concerns about the discriminant validity of the self-report measure that is supposed to assess social skill. Thus, the correlation between measures that share trait variance but do not share method variance (the monotrait-heteromethod correlations) should be larger than the correlations between measures that do not share trait variance but do share method variance (the heterotrait-monomethod correlations). Ideally, the researchers would like to see even larger monotrait-heteromethod correlations than those in Table 9.3 and even smaller heterotrait-monomethod correlations.

In sum, an MTMMM analysis, as developed by Campbell and Fiske (1959), provides useful guidelines for evaluating construct validity. By carefully considering the important effects of trait variance and method variance on correlations among measures, researchers can use the logic of an MTMMM analysis to gauge convergent and discriminant validity. In the decades since Campbell and Fiske published their highly influential work, researchers interested in measurement have developed even more sophisticated ways of statistically analyzing data obtained from an MTMMM study. For example, Widaman (1985) developed a strategy for using factor analysis to analyze MTMMM data. Although such procedures are beyond the scope of our discussion, readers should be aware that psychometricians continue to build on the work by Campbell and Fiske.

Despite the strong logic and widespread awareness of the approach, the MTMMM approach to evaluating convergent and discriminant validity evidence does not seem to be used very frequently. For example, we conducted a quick review of the articles published in the 2005 volume of *Psychological Assessment*, which is a research journal published by the American Psychological Association (APA). The journal is intended to present "empirical research on measurement and evaluation relevant to the broad field of clinical psychology" (APA, n.d.). In our review, we identified 13 articles claiming to present evidence related to convergent and discriminant validity, or construct validity more generally. Of these 13 articles, only 2 used an MTMMM approach. Furthermore, those 2 articles used multiple measurement occasions as the multiple "methods." That is, participants completed the same measure at different times, providing the same method of measurement at two or three different times. Although this review is admittedly limited and informal, it underscores our impressions of the (in)frequency with which MTMMM analyses are used.

Regardless of the frequency of its use, the MTMMM has been an important development in the understanding and analysis of convergent and discriminant validity evidence. It has shaped the way many people think about construct validity, and it is an important component of a full understanding of psychometrics.

Quantifying Construct Validity

[handwritten: quantifying construct validity QCV]

The final method that we will discuss for evaluating convergent and discriminant validity evidence is a more recent development. Westen and Rosenthal (2003) outlined a procedure that they called "quantifying construct validity" (QCV), in which researchers formally quantify the degree of "fit" between (a) their theoretical predictions for a set of convergent and discriminant correlations and (b) the set of correlations that are actually obtained.

[handwritten: "degree of fit" between theoretical predictions of a set of convergent + discriminant correlations & set of correlations obtained]

At one level, this should sound familiar, if not redundant! Indeed, an overriding theme in our discussion of construct validity is that the theoretical basis of a construct guides the study and interpretation of validity evidence. For example, in the previous sections, we have discussed various ways in which researchers identify the criterion variables used to evaluate convergent and discriminant validity evidence, and we have emphasized the importance of interpreting validity correlations in terms of conceptual relevance to the construct of interest.

However, in practice, evidence regarding convergent and discriminant validity often rests on rather subjective and impressionistic interpretations of validity correlations. In our earlier discussion of the "sets of correlations" approach to convergent and discriminant validity evidence, we stated that researchers often "eyeball" the correlations and make a somewhat subjective judgment about the degree to which the correlations match their expectations (as based on the nomological network surrounding the construct of interest). We also stated that researchers often judge the degree to which the pattern of convergent and discriminant correlations "makes sense" in terms of the theoretical basis of the construct being assessed by a test. But what if one researcher's judgment of what makes sense does not agree with another's judgment? And exactly how strongly do the convergent and discriminant correlations actually fit with the theoretical basis of the construct?

Similarly, when examining the MTMMM correlations, we asserted that some correlations were "generally larger" or "noticeably lower" than others. We must admit that we tried to sneak by without defining what we meant by "generally larger" and without discussing exactly *how much* lower a correlation should be to be considered "noticeably" lower than another. In sum, although the correlations themselves are precise estimates of association, the interpretation of the overall pattern of convergent and discriminant correlations often has been done in a somewhat imprecise and subjective manner.

Given the common tendency to rely on somewhat imprecise and subjective evaluations of patterns of convergent and discriminant correlations, the QCV procedure was designed to provide a precise and objective quantitative estimate of the support provided by the overall pattern of evidence. Thus, the emphasis on precision and objectivity is an important difference from the previous strategies. The QCV procedure is intended to provide an answer to a single question in an examination of the validity of a measure's interpretation: "Does this measure predict an array of other measures in a way predicted by theory?" (Westen & Rosenthal, 2003, p. 609). ✳

There are two complementary kinds of results obtained in a QCV analysis. First, researchers obtain two effect sizes representing the *degree of fit* between the actual pattern of correlations and the predicted pattern of correlations. These effect sizes, called $r_{\text{alerting-CV}}$ and $r_{\text{contrast-CV}}$, are correlations themselves, ranging between -1 and $+1$. We will discuss the nature of these effect sizes in more detail, but for both, large positive effect sizes indicate that the actual pattern of convergent and discriminant correlations closely matches the pattern of correlations predicted on the basis of the conceptual meaning of the constructs being assessed. The second kind of result obtained in a QCV analysis is a test of statistical significance. The significance test indicates whether the degree of fit between actual and predicted correlations is likely to have occurred by chance. Researchers conducting a validity study using the QCV procedure will hope to obtain large values for the two effect sizes, along with statistically significant results.

The QCV procedure can be summarized in three phases. First, researchers must generate clear predictions about the pattern of convergent and discriminant validity correlations that they would expect to find. They must think carefully about the criterion measures included in the study, and they must form predictions for each one, in terms of its correlation with the primary measure of interest. For example, Furr and his colleagues (Furr, Reimer, & Bellis, 2004; Nave & Furr, 2006) developed a measure of impression motivation, which was defined as a person's general desire to make specific impressions on other people. To evaluate the convergent and discriminant validity of the scale, participants were asked to complete the Impression Motivation scale along with 12 additional personality questionnaires. To use the QCV procedure, Furr et al. (2004) needed to generate predictions about the correlations that would be obtained between the Impression Motivation scale and the 12 additional scales. They did this by recruiting five professors of psychology to act as "expert judges." The judges read descriptions of each scale, and each one provided predictions about the correlations. The five sets of predictions were then averaged to generate a single set of predicted correlations.

The criterion scale labels and the predicted correlations are presented in Table 9.4. Thus, the conceptually guided predictions for convergent and discriminant correlations are stated concretely. For example, the judges predicted that impression motivation would be relatively strongly correlated with public self-consciousness (e.g., "I worry about what people think of me" and "I want to amount to something

[margin notes, handwritten]

precise + objective quantitative estimate of the support provided by the overall pattern of evidence

1) 2 effect sizes — degree of fit
$r_{\text{alt-CV}}$ — want large
$r_{\text{con-CV}}$

2) Test of statistical significance — does degree of fit btwn actual + predicted corr. happen by chance? wants sig

3 Phases:
1) predict pattern
2) con + dis validity corr. expected to find

Table 9.4   Example of the Quantifying Construct Validity Process

Criteria Scales	Predicted Correlations	Actual Correlations	z-Transformed Correlations
Dependence	.58	.46	.50
Machiavellianism	.24	.13	.13
Distrust	−.04	−.24	−.24
Resourcefulness	.06	−.03	−.03
Self-efficacy	−.04	.12	.12
Extraversion	.18	.03	.03
Agreeableness	.36	.39	.41
Complexity	.08	.06	.06
Public self-consciousness	.64	.51	.56
Self-monitoring	.56	.08	.08
Anxiety	.36	.24	.24
Need to belong	.56	.66	.79

special in others' eyes") and the need to belong (e.g., "I need to feel that there are people I can turn to in times of need" and "I want other people to accept me"). The judges expect that people who profess a desire to make an impression on others should report the tendency to worry about others' impressions of them and the need to be accepted by others. Conversely, the judges did not believe that impression motivation scores would be associated with variables such as distrust and complexity, reflecting predictions of discriminant validity.

In the second phase of the QCV procedure, researchers collect data and compute the actual convergent and discriminant validity correlations. Of course, these correlations reflect the degree to which the primary measure of interest is *actually* associated with each of the criterion variables. For example, Furr et al. (2004) collected data from people who responded to the Impression Motivation scale and the 12 criterion scales listed in Table 9.4, and they computed the correlations between the Impression Motivation scale and each of those other criterion scales. As shown in Table 9.4, these correlations ranged from −.24 to .51. Participants who scored high on the Impression Motivation scale tended to report relatively high levels of public self-consciousness and the need to belong. In addition, they tended to report relatively low levels of distrust, but they showed no tendency to report high or low levels of complexity or extraversion.

In the third phase, researchers quantify the degree to which the actual pattern of convergent and discriminant correlations fits the predicted pattern of correlations. A close fit provides good evidence of validity for the intended interpretation of the test being evaluated, but a weak fit would imply poor validity. As described earlier, the fit is quantified by two kinds of results—effect sizes and a significance test.

2 effect sizes reflect amount of evidence of con + dis validity as a matter of degree

r-alerting cv → corr between set of predicted corrs + actual (a large r-alt-cv means prediction were True)

The two effect sizes reflect the amount of evidence of convergent and discriminant validity as a matter of degree. The $r_{\text{alerting-CV}}$ effect size is the correlation between the set of predicted correlations and the set of actual correlations. A large positive $r_{\text{alerting-CV}}$ would indicate that the correlations that the judges predicted to be relatively large were indeed the ones that actually were relatively large, and it indicates that the correlations that the judges predicted to be relatively small were indeed the ones that actually were relatively small. Take a moment to examine the correlations in Table 9.4. Note, for example, that the judges predicted that dependence, public self-consciousness, self-monitoring, and the need to belong would have the largest correlations with social motivation. In fact, three of these four scales did have the largest correlations. Similarly, the judges predicted that distrust, resourcefulness, self-efficacy, and complexity would have the smallest correlations with social motivation. Indeed, three of these four scales did have the smallest correlations (relative to the others). Thus, the actual correlations generally matched the predictions made by the judges. Consequently, the $r_{\text{alerting-CV}}$ value for the data in Table 9.4 is .79, a large positive correlation. In actuality, the $r_{\text{alerting-CV}}$ value is computed as the correlation between the predicted set of correlations and the set of "z-transformed" actual correlations. The z transformation is done for technical reasons regarding the distribution of the underlying correlation coefficients. For all practical purposes, though, the $r_{\text{alerting-CV}}$ effect size simply represents the degree to which the correlations that are predicted to be relatively high (or low) are the correlations that actually turn out to be relatively high (or low).

r-contrast-cv (large # = more validity) adjusts for inter-corrs among criterion variables + for the absolute level of correlations btwn main test + criterion var

Although its computation is more complex, the $r_{\text{contrast-CV}}$ effect size is similar to the $r_{\text{alerting-CV}}$ effect size in that large positive values indicate greater evidence of convergent and discriminant validity. Specifically, the computation of $r_{\text{contrast-CV}}$ adjusts for the intercorrelations among the criterion variables and for the absolute level of correlations between the main test and the criterion variables. For the data collected by Furr et al. (2004), the $r_{\text{contrast-CV}}$ value was approximately .68, again indicating a high degree of convergent and discriminant validity. As the QCV procedure is a relatively recent development, there are no clear guidelines about how large the effect sizes should be to be interpreted as providing evidence of adequate validity. At this point, we can say simply that higher effect sizes offer greater evidence of validity.

Statistical test

In addition to the two effect sizes, the QCV procedure provides a test of statistical significance. Based on a number of factors, including the size of the sample and the amount of support for convergent and discriminant validity, a z test of significance indicates whether the results are likely to have been obtained by chance.

Problem - predictions could be poor, not validity → poor choice of criterion variables

Although the QCV approach is a potentially useful approach to estimating convergent and discriminant evidence, it is not perfect. For example, low effect sizes (i.e., low values for $r_{\text{alerting-CV}}$ and $r_{\text{contrast-CV}}$) might not indicate poor evidence of validity. Low effect sizes could result from an inappropriate set of predicted correlations. If the predicted correlations are poor reflections of the nomological network surrounding a construct, then a good measure of the construct will produce actual correlations that do not match the predictions. Similarly, a poor choice of criterion variables could result in low effect sizes. If few of the criterion variables used in the validity study are associated with the main test of interest, then they do not represent the nomological network well. Thus, the criterion variables selected for a QCV analysis should represent a range of strong and weak associations, reflecting a clear pattern of convergent and discriminant evidence. Indeed, Westen and Rosenthal (2005) point out that "one of the most important limitations of all fit indices is that they cannot address whether the choice of items, indicators, observers, and so forth was adequate to the task" (p. 410).

In addition, the QCV procedure has been criticized for resulting in "high correlations in cases where there is little agreement between predictions and observations" (Smith, 2005, p. 404). That is, researchers might obtain apparently large values for $r_{\text{alerting-CV}}$ and $r_{\text{contrast-CV}}$ even when the observed pattern of convergent and discriminant validity correlations does not match closely the actual pattern of convergent and discriminant validity correlations. Westen and Rosenthal (2005) acknowledge that this might be true in some cases; however, they suggest that the QCV procedures are "aids to understanding" and should be carefully scrutinized in the context of many conceptual, methodological, and statistical factors (p. 411).

We have outlined several strategies that can be useful in many areas of test evaluation, but there is no single perfect method or statistic for estimating the overall convergent and discriminant validity of test interpretations. Although it is not perfect, the QCV does offer several advantages over some other strategies. First, it forces researchers to consider carefully the pattern of convergent and discriminant associations that would make theoretical sense, on the basis of the construct in question. Second, it forces researchers to make explicit predictions about the pattern of associations. Third, it retains the focus on the measure of primary interest. Fourth, it provides a single interpretable value reflecting the overall degree to which the pattern of predicted associations matches the pattern of associations that is actually obtained, and finally, it provides a test of statistical significance. Used with care, the QCV is an important addition to the toolbox of validation.

Factors Affecting a Validity Coefficient

The strategies outlined above are used to accumulate and interpret evidence of convergent and discriminant validity. To some extent, all the strategies rest on the size of validity coefficients—statistical results that represent the degree of association between a test of interest and one or more criterion variables. In this section, we address some important factors that affect validity coefficients.

When conducting or reading studies regarding validity, it is important to be aware of these factors. For a truly informed understanding of validity research, it is important to understand why a test's scores might be strongly or, more problematic, weakly associated with key criterion variables. Indeed, there are a many reasons why a test's scores might not be strongly associated with key criterion variables. Although weak convergent associations might reflect flaws in the test, we shall see that such a failure might not actually be due to shortcomings in the test itself. By considering the factors that can affect these associations, people who produce and interpret validity studies will reach conclusions that are more well-informed and accurate.

Thus far, we have emphasized the correlation as a coefficient of validity because of its interpretability as a standardized measure of association. Although other statistical values can be used to represent associations between tests and criterion variables (e.g., regression coefficients), most such values are built on correlation coefficients. Thus, our discussion centers on some of the key psychological, methodological, psychometric, and statistical factors affecting correlations between tests and criterion variables.

Associations Between Constructs

One factor affecting the correlation between measures of two constructs is the "true" association between those constructs. If two constructs are strongly associated with each other, then measures of those constructs will likely be highly correlated with each other. Conversely, if two constructs are unrelated to each other, then measures of those constructs will probably be weakly correlated with each other. Indeed, when we conduct research in general, we intend to interpret the observed associations that we obtain (e.g., the correlations between the measured variables in our study) as approximations of the true associations between the constructs in which we are interested. When we conduct validity research, we predict that two measures will be correlated because we believe that the two constructs are associated with each other.

Measurement Error and Reliability

In earlier chapters (Chapters 5–7), you learned about the conceptual basis, the estimation, and the importance of reliability as an index of (the lack of) measurement error. As we discussed in those chapters, one important implication of measurement error is its effect on correlations between variables—measurement error reduces, or attenuates, the correlation between measures. Therefore, measurement error affects validity coefficients, just like any other correlation.

As we saw in earlier chapters, the correlation between tests (say X and Y) of two constructs is a function of the true correlation between the two constructs and the reliabilities of the two tests:

$$r_{X_o Y_o} = r_{X_t Y_t} \sqrt{R_{XX} R_{YY}}. \tag{9.1}$$

In this equation, $r_{X_o Y_o}$ is the correlation between the two tests (i.e., the correlation between the observed scores). More specifically, it is the validity correlation between the primary test of interest (say the "X" test) and the test of a criterion variable (the "Y" test). In addition, $r_{X_t Y_t}$ is the true correlation between the two constructs, R_{XX} is the reliability of the test of interest, and R_{YY} is the reliability of the test of the criterion variable.

For example, in their examination of the convergent validity evidence for their measure of impression motivation, Furr et al. (2004; Nave & Furr, 2006) were interested in the correlation between impression motivation and public self-consciousness. Imagine that the true correlation between the constructs is .60. What would the actual validity correlation be if the two tests had poor reliability? If the impression motivation test had a reliability of .63 and the public self-consciousness test had a reliability of .58, then the actual validity coefficient obtained would be only .36:

$$r_{X_o Y_o} = .60\sqrt{.63}\sqrt{.58},$$
$$= .60(.604),$$
$$= .36.$$

Recall that to evaluate convergent validity, researchers should compare their correlations with the correlations that they would expect based on the constructs being measured. In this case, if Furr et al. (2004) were expecting to find a correlation close to .60, then they might be relatively disappointed with a validity coefficient of "only" .36. Therefore, they might conclude that their test has poor validity as a measure of impression motivation.

Note that the validity coefficient is affected by two reliabilities: (1) the reliability of the test of interest and (2) the reliability of the criterion test. Thus, the primary test of interest could be a good measure of the intended construct, but the validity coefficient could appear to be poor. For example, if the impression motivation test had a good reliability of, say, .84 but the public self-consciousness test had a very poor reliability of .40, then the actual validity coefficient obtained would be only .35:

$$r_{X_o Y_o} = .60\sqrt{.84}\sqrt{.40},$$
$$= .60(.580),$$
$$= .35.$$

So even if the primary test is psychometrically strong and interpreted validly, the use of a psychometrically weak criterion measure will produce poor validity coefficients. Therefore, when evaluating the size of a validity correlation, it is important to consider both the reliability of the primary test of interest and the reliability of the criterion test. If either one or both is relatively weak, then the resulting validity correlation is likely to appear relatively weak. This might be a particularly subtle consideration for the criterion variable. Even if the primary test of interest is a good measure of its intended construct, we might find poor validity correlations. That is, if the criterion measures that we use are poor, then we are unlikely to find evidence supporting the validity of the primary test! This important issue is easy to forget.

There are rough guidelines for identifying problematic levels of reliability and for handling those problems. As mentioned in Chapter 5, researchers are generally satisfied if a test's reliability is above .70 or .80, with higher levels being even better. If a test's or a criterion variable's reliability is much lower than this, then we would have concerns about its effect on validity coefficients. Of course, the lower one or more of the reliabilities are, the greater our concern would be.

In terms of handling the problem, there are at least two possibilities. One is to simply discount a validity coefficient that is based on poor reliability, or at least to reduce the weight that one would give it in one's consideration of validity evidence.

The other possibility is to use the logic of the correction for attenuation discussed in Chapter 7, to adjust the validity coefficient. However, it might make sense to adjust only for the criterion variable's reliability. That is, if the purpose of a validation analysis is to evaluate the psychometric quality of a particular test, then it seems inadvisable to adjust for that test's lack of psychometric quality. Thus, to adjust for only one test's reliability, researchers can use the following variation on the correction for attenuation:

$$r_{XY-adjusted} = \frac{r_{XY-orginal}}{\sqrt{R_{YY}}},$$

(9.2)

where $r_{XY-original}$ is the original validity correlation, R_{YY} is the estimated reliability of the criterion variable (i.e., not the test of interest being validated), and $r_{XY-adjusted}$ is the adjusted validity correlation. This equation adjusts a validity correlation by assuming that the criterion variable is measured without any measurement error.

Restricted Range

Recall from Chapter 3 that a correlation coefficient reflects covariability between two distributions of scores. That is, it represents the degree to which variability in one distribution of scores (e.g., scores on a test to be validated) corresponds with variability in another distribution of scores (e.g., scores on a test of a criterion variable). From this perspective, it is important to realize that the amount of variability in one or both distributions of scores can affect the correlation between the two sets of scores. Specifically, a correlation between two variables can be reduced if the range of scores in one or both variables is artificially limited or restricted.

A classic example of this is the association between SAT scores and academic performance. Earlier, we discussed the fact that much of the evidence for the quality of the SAT scores rests on the correlation between SAT scores and academic performance as measured by college grade point average (GPA). The marketers of the SAT would like to demonstrate that people who score relatively high on the SAT tend to have relatively good performance in college. Implicitly, this demonstration requires that people who score relatively low on the SAT tend to have relatively poor performance in college. To demonstrate this kind of association, researchers would need to demonstrate that variability in the distribution of SAT scores corresponds with variability in the distribution of college GPAs. However, the ability to demonstrate this association is minimized by restricted range in two ways.

First, range restriction exists in GPA as a measure of academic performance. In most colleges, GPA can range only between 0.0 and 4.0. The worst that any student can do is a GPA of 0.0, and the best that any student can do is 4.0. But does this 4-point range in GPA really reflect the full range of possible academic performance? Consider two students, Leo and Mary, who do well in classes and earn As in all of their courses. Although Leo did perform well, he barely earned an A in each of his courses. So he "squeaked by" with a 4.0, and the 4.0 in a sense represents the upper limit of his academic performance. Mary also performs well, earning As in all of her courses. But Mary outperformed every other student in each of her courses. In each course, she was the only one to earn an A on any test, and she had clearly mastered all the material on each and every assignment that her professors graded. So Mary also received a 4.0, but her 4.0 in a sense underestimates her academic ability. She had mastered all the material so well that her professors wished that they could give her grades higher than an A. Although Leo and Mary received the same "score" on the measure of academic performance (i.e., they both have 4.0 GPAs), they actually differ in the quality of their performance. Leo fully earned his 4.0 and should be proud of it, but the professors would probably agree that Mary outperformed him. Thus, the 4-point GPA scale restricts the range of measurement of academic performance.

Note that GPA is restricted in both directions—on the high end and on the low end. Consider Jenny and Bruce. Although both Jenny and Bruce failed all of their classes, Bruce nearly passed each class. On the other hand, Jenny wasn't even close to passing any classes. So both Bruce and Jenny earned a GPA of 0.0, but in a sense, Bruce had better academic performance than Jenny. In terms of test grades, homework grades, and paper grades, Bruce outperformed Jenny (i.e., he received 59 on each assignment, while she received scores in the 30s on each assignment). Despite the difference in their performance during the semester, Jenny could not receive a lower GPA than Bruce, because the GPA scale "bottoms out" at 0.0.

The scatterplot in Figure 9.1 shows a hypothetical data set for 5,000 students. This scatterplot presents the idealized association between SAT scores and "unrestricted" college GPA. That is, it presents scores for students whose academic performance is not restricted by a 4-point GPA scale. Notice that some unrestricted GPA scores fall below 0.0 on the plot, reflecting differences between students like Jenny and Bruce. Notice also that some GPA scores fall above 4.0, reflecting differences between students like Leo and Mary. For the data displayed in Figure 9.1,

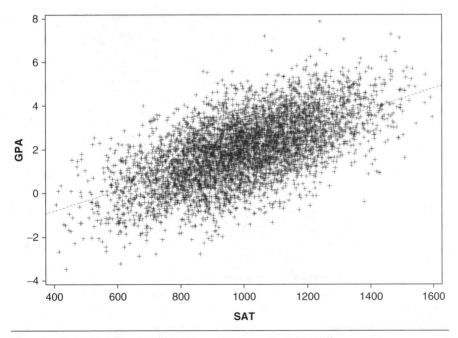

Figure 9.1 Scatterplot of SAT and "Unrestricted" College GPA

the correlation between SAT and GPA was .61. This indicates that students who received relatively low SAT scores tended to have relatively low "unrestricted" GPAs.

But of course, GPA actually is restricted, as just discussed. Therefore, students whose academic performance might, theoretically, merit a 5.0 or a 6.0 can earn only a 4.0 in practice. Similarly, students whose academic performance might merit a GPA below 0 cannot actually receive less than 0. So all those students who might, in an abstract sense, deserve GPAs above 4.0 (or below 0) will in reality receive a GPA of 4.0 (or 0).

The scatterplot in Figure 9.2 shows the data for the same 5,000 students, based on the "restricted" GPA scores. Note that there are no GPA scores above 4.0—the scores are "maxed out" at 4.0. And note that there are no GPA scores below 0.0—the scores are bottomed out at 0. This scatterplot appears to be more compressed, and the association between SAT and GPA is not as clear as it was in the first scatterplot. Consequently, for the data displayed in Figure 9.2, the correlation between SAT and GPA was reduced, a bit, to .60. Thus, the restriction of range in GPA scores has a slightly diminishing effect on the correlation.

A second way in which range restriction minimizes the ability to demonstrate the association between SAT scores and academic performance is in the number of people who actually obtain college GPAs. That is, students with very low SAT scores are much less likely to be admitted to college than are students with higher SAT scores. If we were to conduct a real study of the association between SAT scores and academic performance, we would probably be limited to a subsample of all the students who have SAT scores. This is because we would be limited to only those students who took the SAT and who were admitted to college. For better or

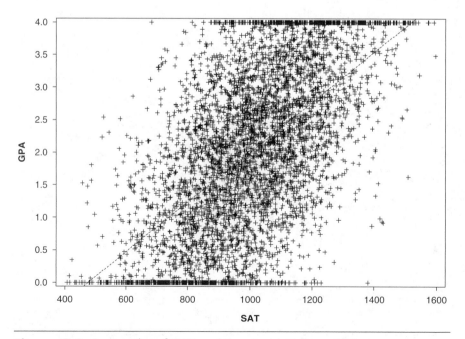

Figure 9.2 Scatterplot of SAT and Restricted College GPA

for worse, not all students who take the SAT are admitted to college. In our hypothetical data set, nearly 400 "students" had SAT scores below 700. In reality, these students might not be admitted to college; therefore, they would never actually have a college GPA score.

The scatterplot in Figure 9.3 shows the data for the remaining 4,600 students, with SAT scores greater than 700. Note that there are no people with SAT scores below 700. That is, we are assuming that most if not all of those people would not be admitted to college, and thus they would not be included in an analysis of the association between SAT scores and college GPAs. This scatterplot is even more compressed than the previous two. Consequently, for the data displayed in Figure 9.3, the correlation between SAT and GPA was reduced even more, to .55.

In sum, the SAT and GPA example illustrates range restriction and its effect on validity correlations. Specifically, range restriction can shrink the correlation, thereby appearing to provide relatively poorer evidence of validity. When evaluating the quality of a psychological measure, we often depend on correlations (or other statistical values that are based on correlations) to reflect the degree of convergent and discriminant validity. And as we've discussed, when searching for convergent evidence, we expect to find strong correlations. However, we need to be aware that restricted range can reduce the correlations that are actually obtained in a validity study. In the current example, the correlation between SAT and GPA was affected by restriction in two ways, and it was somewhat smaller than an "unrestricted" correlation between SAT scores and academic performance. Although the effect of range restriction might not be dramatic in the current example, being aware of the phenomenon improves our ability to interpret validity coefficients.

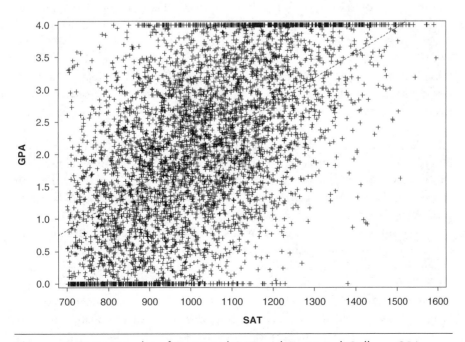

Figure 9.3 Scatterplot of Restricted SAT and Restricted College GPA

Unfortunately, there are no clear, simple guidelines about detecting range restriction; rather, it requires careful thought and attention from researchers. For example, it would require knowledge about the relevant tests or variables (e.g., knowing that GPA scores range from 0 to 4 and that SAT scores range from 400 to 1,600). In addition, it would require examination of the scores obtained in a given study in comparison with the range of possible scores on the relevant tests. For example, it would require a researcher to examine the actual range of SAT scores in a given analysis and to compare this range with the possible range of 400 to 1,600. If the range of obtained scores is dramatically different form the range of possible scores, then there might be reason for concern about range restriction. Perhaps more subtly, if the range of obtained scores falls within a certain "side" of the distribution of possible scores, then there might be particularly serious concerns about range restrictions. For example, the SAT scores in our analysis were mainly weighted toward the high end of possible SAT scores, with none in the range of 400 to 700.

Although there are no easy tricks to detect range restriction, careful attention to this issue can be an important part of validation evidence. Indeed, there are procedures for adjusting or correcting correlations to account for range restriction (Sackett & Yang, 2000; Schmidt, Oh, & Le, 2006). A discussion of these procedures is beyond the scope of this section, but we encourage interested readers to explore them on their own.

Skew and Relative Proportions

Another factor that affects the size of a validity coefficient is the "skew" of the distributions of scores being examined. In Chapter 3, we mentioned that some distributions of scores might be "normal" or symmetric, having just as many high scores as low scores. However, other distributions might be skewed, with an imbalance of high scores relative to low scores (see Figure 3.2). Although this factor might not be as widely known as some of the other factors affecting validity coefficients, the skew of a variable can have a robust impact on correlations (Dunlap, Burke, & Greer, 1995). Specifically, if the two variables being correlated have different "skews", then the correlation between those variables will be reduced. For example, imagine a case where one variable is normally distributed (i.e., unskewed; see Figure 3.1) but the other is heavily skewed in some way (e.g., Figure 3.2a). In this case, the correlation between those two variables cannot be 1.0; indeed, it might be capped at some relatively small value. In contrast, imagine that neither variable is skewed and that both are normally distributed. In this case, the correlation between the two variables can reach 1.0, and all else being equal, it will be larger than the correlation in the first case (where one variable was skewed). Thus, if a validation study is conducted on a variable that is heavily skewed, then we might obtain a relatively small validity coefficient.

For a demonstration and discussion of this effect, it might be most straightforward to consider the association between a continuous variable and a dichotomous variable. Imagine that we developed a self-report inventory to measure depression. And imagine that we would like to evaluate its convergent quality by correlating its scores with diagnoses made by trained clinical psychologists. To do this, we recruit a sample of participants who complete our inventory and who are interviewed by clinicians. The clinicians then provide a diagnosis for each participant, labeling each participant as either depressed or nondepressed. Thus, our main test of interest (i.e., the new self-report inventory) is on a continuous scale, and the criterion variable (i.e., diagnosis) is a dichotomous categorical variable representing two groups of participants—those diagnosed with depression and those without depression. To evaluate the validity of our new scale as a measure of depression, we might compute a validity correlation between these two variables.[1] Indeed, we would hope to find that participants' scores on our new inventory are strongly correlated with clinicians' ratings.

In this case, the relative proportion of participants in the two groups is akin to the skew of the diagnosis variable. That is, if the groups are equally sized, then the variable is unskewed; however, if the groups are not equally sized, then the variable is skewed in some way. For example, if only a small proportion of participants are diagnosed as depressed, then the "diagnosis" variable will be heavily skewed in a way that is somewhat similar to the scatterplot in Figure 3.2a.

Thus, as implied earlier, the validity correlation between the two variables would be affected by the relative proportion of participants in each of the two groups. More precisely, the size of the validity correlation between inventory scores and clinicians' diagnoses is influenced by the proportion of participants who are diagnosed as having depression (vs. not having depression). If the group sizes are equal, then the validity correlation is likely to be larger than when the group sizes are unequal. Following from this, if our validation study is conducted on groups having heavily unequal numbers of participants, then we might obtain a relatively small validity coefficient.

Let us examine and demonstrate this influence concretely. If we were computing the validity correlation in this example, each participant would have scores on two variables—depression inventory score and diagnostic category—as illustrated by the hypothetical data in Table 9.5. Obviously, the depression inventory scores are already on a quantitative scale (let us say that scores can range from 0 to 30). However, the diagnostic category variable must be quantified so that we can compute the validity. To do this, we assign one value to all participants diagnosed as nondepressed and another value to all participants diagnosed as depressed. These values could be 1 and 2, 1 and 10, −1,000 and +1,000, or any other pair of numbers (as long as all the people in each group receive the same value). For our purposes, we will code the "nondepressed" group as "1" and the depressed group as "2" (see Table 9.5).

Table 9.5 Data Illustrating the Effect of Relative Proportions on Validity Coefficients

Participant	Depression Inventory	Diagnosis	Diagnosis Code
1	6	Nondepressed	1
2	5	Nondepressed	1
3	7	Nondepressed	1
4	1	Nondepressed	1
5	11	Nondepressed	1

(Continued)

Table 9.5 (Continued)

Participant	Depression Inventory	Diagnosis	Diagnosis Code
6	9	Nondepressed	1
7	3	Nondepressed	1
8	6	Nondepressed	1
9	4	Nondepressed	1
10	8	Nondepressed	1
11	10	Nondepressed	1
12	2	Nondepressed	1
13	5	Nondepressed	1
14	7	Nondepressed	1
15	6	Nondepressed	1
16	10	Depressed	2
17	15	Depressed	2
18	5	Depressed	2
19	8	Depressed	2
20	12	Depressed	2
Mean	7.00		.25
Standard deviation	3.39		.43
Covariance		.75	
Correlation		.51	

Recall from Chapter 3 that the correlation between two variables is the covariance between the two variables divided by the product of their two standard deviations (see Equation 3.5). For a correlation between one continuous variable (C) and one dichotomous variable (D), the correlation (r_{CD}) is

$$r_{CD} = \frac{c_{CD}}{s_C s_D},$$

(9.3)

where c_{CD} is the covariance between the two variables, s_C is the standard deviation of the continuous variable, and s_D is the standard deviation of the dichotomous variable.

Two of these terms are directly affected by the proportion of observations in the two groups, as defined by the dichotomous variable. Assuming that the groups are coded "1" (for Group 1) and "2" (for Group 2), then the covariance is

$$c_{CD} = p_1 p_2 (\overline{C}_2 - \overline{C}_1),$$

(9.4)

where p_1 and p_2 are the proportion of participants in Groups 1 and 2, respectively, $\overline{C}_1$ is the mean of the continuous variable for the participants in Group 1, $\overline{C}_2$ and is the mean of the continuous variable for the participants in Group 2. In our data set, 15 of the 20 participants are in the nondepressed diagnostic group (Group 1), and 5 are in the depressed group (Group 2). Thus, the two proportions are .75 (15/20= .75) and .25 (5/20= .25). In addition, the average score on the depression inventory is 6 for the nondepressed group and 10 for the depressed group. Thus, the covariance is

$$
\begin{aligned}
c_{CD} &= (.75)(.25)(10-6), \\
&= (.1875)(4), \\
&= .75.
\end{aligned}
$$

The standard deviation of the dichotomous variable is the second term affected by the proportion of observations in the two groups defined by the dichotomous variable. Again, assuming that the groups are coded "1" (for Group 1) and "2" (for Group 2), then based on our discussion of binary (i.e., dichotomous items) in Chapter 3 and Equation 3.9, we know that this standard deviation is

$$
s_D = \sqrt{p_1 p_2}. \tag{9.5}
$$

For the data in Table 9.5, the standard deviation of the dichotomous "diagnosis" variable is

$$
\begin{aligned}
s_D &= \sqrt{(.75)(.25)}, \\
&= .433
\end{aligned}
$$

Taking these terms into account, the equation for the correlation can be reframed and simplified to show the direct influence of the relative proportions:

$$
\begin{aligned}
r_{CD} &= \frac{p_1 p_2 (\overline{C}_2 - \overline{C}_1)}{s_C \sqrt{p_1 p_2}}, \\
r_{CD} &= \frac{\sqrt{p_1 p_2} (\overline{C}_2 - \overline{C}_1)}{s_C}.
\end{aligned} \tag{9.6}
$$

For the example data in Table 9.5, the validity correlation is

$$
\begin{aligned}
r_{CD} &= \frac{\sqrt{(.75)(.25)}(10-6)}{3.39}, \\
&= \frac{1.72}{3.39}, \\
&= .51.
\end{aligned}
$$

This correlation is positive and fairly strong, indicating good convergence between our new scale and clinicians' diagnoses. More specifically, it reveals that that those participants who had relatively "high scores" on the diagnosis variable also tended to have higher scores on the depression inventory than did those participants who had relatively "low scores" on the diagnosis variable. It might seem odd to think of "high scores" or "low scores" on a diagnosis, but recall the way we coded the diagnoses (Table 9.5). That is, we coded the diagnosis variable so that the participants who were diagnosed as depressed had "higher" diagnosis scores (i.e., a score of 2) than the participants who were diagnosed as nondepressed (who were given a score of 1). Therefore, we can interpret the correlation as showing that the participants diagnosed as depressed (i.e., those with relatively high scores on the diagnosis variable) tended to obtain high scores on the depression inventory as compared with the participants diagnosed as nondepressed (i.e., those with relatively low scores on the diagnosis variable).

Equation 9.6 reveals the influence of group proportions on validity correlations. All else being equal, equally sized groups will allow larger correlations than will unequal groups. If two groups are equally sized, then the two proportions are .5 and .5. The product of these two proportions (.5 x .5 = .25) is the maximum of any two proportions. That is, any other pair of proportions will produce a product less than .25, and the greater the disparity in group sizes, the lower the product (e.g., .40 x .60 = .24, .10 x .90 = .09). And as shown in Equation 9.6, all else being equal, lower products will produce lower correlations.

In sum, a subtle factor that might affect some validity coefficients is the skew of the variables being examined. As illustrated in the relative proportions of people in two groups, if a validity coefficient is based on a skewed variable (e.g., a dichotomous variable in which the relative proportion of participants is highly unequal), then the resulting validity coefficient might be lower than expected. This issue should be kept in mind when interpreting validity coefficients.

Again, there are no rules of thumb for concluding that a variable is so skewed as to cause concern. Rather, researchers and readers should be attentive to this possibility; they should examine the skew of variables in a validity study and adjust their expectations accordingly. In any analysis of a highly skewed variable, more specifically when one variable is skewed and the other is not (or when the other is skewed in a different way), we should expect a relatively small validity coefficient.

Method Variance ↓ reduces correlation

We discussed method variance in our earlier presentation of the MTMMM. We will not say much more about it here; however, method variance is an important consideration beyond its role in an MTMMM analysis. Any time a researcher correlates test scores with scores from a different method of assessment, method variance is likely to reduce the correlation. Or perhaps more precisely stated, correlations between two different methods of assessment are likely to be smaller than correlations between measures from a single method of assessment.

This issue has an important implication for validity coefficients. When evaluating validity coefficients, we are more impressed with evidence from correlations between different methods of assessment than with evidence from a single method of assessment. For example, if we were evaluating a new self-report measure of social skill, we might correlate scores on the new measure with scores on self-report measures of charisma, based on the notion that social skill is associated with charisma. We might be happy to find a correlation of .40 between the measures, and we might interpret these results as evidence of convergent validity. After all, these results suggest that people who report having high social skill (based on our new measure) also report being relatively charismatic. Despite our satisfaction at finding these results, we would probably be even more enthusiastic if we had found a correlation of .40 between our self-report measure of social skill and an *acquaintance report* measure of charisma. That is, the result would be more compelling if we could say that people with high scores on our new measure of social skill are described as charismatic by their acquaintances. When two variables are measured through different methods of assessment, they tend to be less strongly correlated with each other than when two variables are measured through the same method.

Validity studies based solely on self-report are informative and common, but they are not perfect. Again, self-report data are relatively easy, inexpensive, and generally quite good, so we do not intend to imply that self-report data are inferior to data derived from other forms of measurement. However, correlations based solely on self-report questionnaires are potentially inflated due to shared method variance. In contrast, correlations that are based on data from two different assessment methods are less likely to be artificially inflated. Thus, they provide an important complement to the more common reliance on self-report data. When interpreting correlations based on different methods, it is important to realize that they are likely to be smaller than correlations based solely on self-report data as a result of method variance.

Time

diff point in time = ↓ corr.

We have seen that construct validity is sometimes evaluated by examining the correlation between a test given at one point in time (e.g., SAT) and a criterion variable measured at a later point in time (e.g., college GPA). All else being equal, validity coefficients based on correlations between variables measured at different points in time (i.e., predictive validity correlations) are likely to be smaller than coefficients based on correlations between variables measured at a single point in time (i.e., concurrent validity correlations). Furthermore, it is likely that longer periods between two points in time will produce smaller predictive validity correlations.

longer period of time : ↓ corr

Predictions of Single Events

An important factor that can affect validity coefficients is whether the criterion variable is based on an observation of a single event or on an aggregation or accumulation of events. For example, imagine that you developed a questionnaire that you intend to interpret as a measure of extraversion. And imagine that you wished to gather convergent validity evidence by correlating its scores with observations of "talkativeness" in social interaction. Your understanding of the extraversion construct suggests that extraverted people should be relatively talkative in a social interaction, so you expect to find a moderate to large positive correlation between scores on your questionnaire and observations of talkativeness.

To test this validity prediction, let us say that you recruited a sample of 50 participants, who completed your questionnaire and then engaged in a 5-minute social interaction with a stranger "partner" of the other sex. The partners then rated the participants on talkativeness, using a 1 to 10 scale, with high scores indicating greater talkativeness. You compute the correlation between your questionnaire and the talkativeness ratings, and you find only a small positive correlation. You are disappointed, and you feel compelled to conclude that your questionnaire is a poor measure of extraversion.

Before you decide to revise your measure or discard it entirely, you should consider the nature of your criterion variable. Specifically, you should remember that it was based on an observation of a single behavior (i.e., talkativeness) in a single social situation (i.e., a 5-minute interaction with an other-sex stranger). Even beyond the issue of method variance, you should consider that there are many factors that could influence an individual's talkativeness in any one moment. What kind of mood was the individual in? How was the partner acting? Was there a task or a topic of conversation that inhibited the individual's talkativeness?

Chances are that your validity correlation could have been larger if you had gathered observations of your participants from several different interactions or over a longer period of time. For a variety of reasons, including issues of poorer reliability, single events are less predictable than are aggregations of events or accumulations of observations (Epstein, 1979).

A particularly compelling example of the difficulty of predicting single events was provided by Abelson (1985). Some baseball players are paid tens of millions of dollars, partly because they have batting averages that are much higher than the average player. Obviously, owners and managers of baseball teams believe that players with high batting averages will be much more successful than players with low batting averages. That is, in any single at bat, the player with a high batting average should have a much greater chance of hitting the ball than a player with a low batting average. But is this actually true? How much variability in at-bat success is actually explained by batting average? Abelson examined baseball statistics to evaluate the association between batting average (scored from 0 to 1.0) and the chances of success at any single at bat.

Abelson's (1985) analysis revealed what he interpreted as a "pitifully small" (p. 132) association between batting skill (as reflected in batting average) and success in a single at bat. In light of such a small statistical association, he considered why he, other statistical experts, other baseball fans, and even baseball managers believed that batting average is such an important issue. He concludes that "the individual batter's success is appropriately measured over a long season, not by the individual at bat" (p. 132). That is, although the ability to predict a single event (i.e., an individual at bat) is perhaps meager, what matters are the cumulative effects of many such events. Even a meager level of predictability for any single event can produce a much more substantial level of predictability as those events accumulate.

In sum, single events—whether they are baseball at bats or a specific social behavior in a specific social situation—might be inherently difficult to predict. In terms of validity coefficients, one must consider this issue in relation to the criterion variable. Is the criterion to be predicted a single event, such as a single observation of social behavior? Or is the criterion a cumulative variable, such as the average level of social behavior across many observations? Large validity coefficients are more likely to be obtained when the criterion variable is based on the accumulation or aggregation of several events than when it is based on only a single event.

↑ coefficients when it's an accumulation of events

Interpreting a Validity Coefficient

After a validity coefficient is obtained, it must be interpreted. Test developers, evaluators, and users must decide whether validity coefficients are large enough to provide compelling evidence of convergence or if they are small enough to provide assurance of discriminant validity. Although it is a precise way of quantifying the degree of association between two measures, the correlation coefficient might not be highly intuitive. Particularly for newcomers to a field of study, the knowledge that a correlation is, for example, .40 is not always very informative. In our experience, the tendency seems to be for people to note that .40 seems far from a perfect correlation of 1.0, and thus they interpret it as quite small. For people who are not used to interpreting correlations in behavioral science, anything less than perfect is often seen as a somewhat weak association.

anything less than perf is weak

This tendency could be problematic when evaluating a validity coefficient, particularly when discussing validity with someone who is not experienced with interpreting correlations. For example, the human resources director for a company might need to convince employers, test takers, or lawyers that a particular test is a valid predictor of job performance. To make her case, she cites research evidence showing a .40 correlation between test scores and job performance. As we know, this suggests that people who score relatively high on the test tend to exhibit relatively high job performance. However, her audience of employers, test takers, or lawyers might interpret this evidence quite differently. In fact, they might argue that a correlation of .40 is far from perfect, and they might even interpret it as evidence of the invalidity of the test! How could the human resources director convince others that the test is actually a useful and valid predictor?

As discussed above, issues such as the true correlation between constructs, method variance, relative proportions, and reliability are some key factors affecting the size of a validity coefficient. Several additional important issues become relevant in the overall interpretation of the size and meaning of a validity coefficient.

Squared Correlations and "Variance Explained"

Squared corr = proportion of variance

In psychological research, a common practice is to interpret a squared correlation. Specifically, a squared correlation between two variables is often interpreted as the proportion of variance in one variable that is explained or "accounted for" by the other. For example, if we found a correlation of .30 between social skill and self-esteem, we might interpret this as showing that 9% of the variance in self-esteem is explained by social skill (because .30 squared is .09). Actually, we could also interpret this result as showing that 9% of the variance in social skill is explained by self-esteem.

The "variance explained" interpretation is appealing, given our earlier assertion that research in general (and psychometrics in particular) is concerned with measuring and understanding variability. Indeed, the more variability in a phenomenon that we can explain or account for, the more we feel like we understand the phenomenon. Furthermore, the "variance explained" interpretation fits various statistical procedures such as regression and analysis of variance (ANOVA), which rely on partitioning or predicting variability. Thus, you will frequently read or hear researchers interpreting associations in terms of squared correlations and the amount of variance explained.

Despite the appeal of this approach, the "squared correlation" approach to interpreting associations has been criticized for at least three reasons. First, it is technically incorrect in some cases. Although the statistical basis of this argument is beyond the scope of our current discussion, Ozer (1985) argues that in some cases, the correlation itself, and not the squared correlation, is interpretable as the proportion of variation explained. Second, some experts point out that variance itself is on a nonintuitive metric. Recall from an earlier chapter that, as a measure of differences among a set of scores, variance is based on *squared* deviations from the mean. The variance has some nice statistical properties, but how are we to interpret squared differences from a mean? D'Andrade and Dart (1990) point out that thinking in terms of squared differences or distance is not usually meaningful—do you provide directions to your house by telling friends that it is 9 squared miles from the interstate? The squared correlation approach might be seen as a nonintuitive and, therefore, nonuseful perspective on the association between variables.

The third criticism of the squared correlation approach is the least technical but perhaps the most powerful of the three. Simply put, squaring a correlation makes the association between two variables seem too small. It is not uncommon to hear researchers bemoaning the fact that they have explained "only" 9% or 12% of the variance in a phenomenon. Or you might read criticism of a research finding that explains "only" 16% of the variance. Indeed, 9%, 12%, and 16% do not sound like great amounts of anything. After all, this implies that nearly 90% of the variance is unexplained, and that sounds like a lot! However, as we will discuss in a later section, 9%, 12%, or 16% of the variance in a phenomenon might be a meaningful and important amount of variance. This is particularly true if we are talking about the association between only two variables. For example, if we can use a single variable, such as social skill, to explain nearly 10% of the variability in an important and complex phenomenon such as self-esteem, then perhaps that is a pretty important association.

The baseball example provided by Abelson (1985) is also relevant here. Recall that Abelson's examination led him to conclude that the association between batting average and the chances of success at any single at bat was very small. In fact, his conclusion was based on analyses revealing that only *one third of 1%* of the variance in any single batting performance was explained by batting skill (as reflected in batting average). As discussed earlier, Abelson pointed out that the cumulative effect of many at bats could account for the general belief that batting average was an important indicator of batting skill. D'Andrade and Dart (1990) offer a different perspective in explaining the discrepancy between Abelson's effect size (an apparently very small percentage of variance) and the conventional wisdom that batting average is an important statistic. They suggest that the discrepancy partly results from the fact that percentage of variance is a poor measure of association. Commenting on a table provided by Abelson, they point out that his results could be legitimately interpreted as showing that the difference between a .220 batter and a .320 batter results in a 10% difference in their likelihood of getting a hit in any single at bat. D'Andrade and Dart acknowledge that "10% may not be huge," but they suggest that "those who bet to win like 10% edges. So do baseball managers" (p. 58).

The "squared correlation" or "variance explained" interpretation of validity coefficients is a common but potentially misleading approach. Although it fits the view of research and measurement as tied to variability, it has several technical and logical problems. Perhaps most critically, a "variance explained" approach tends to cast associations in a way that seems to minimize their size and importance.

For example, one notable organization has criticized the SAT for, among other things, having poor validity in terms of predicting college GPA. Indeed, the National Center for Fair and Open Testing (NCFOT, 2007) notes that the correlation between SAT scores and college freshman GPA is about .48. They assert that

> this number is deceptive, however. To determine how much of the difference in first-year grades between students the SAT I really predicts, the correlation coefficient must be multiplied by itself. The result, called r squared, describes the difference (or variation) among college freshman grades. Thus, the predictive ability (or r squared) of the SAT I is just .22, meaning the test explains only 22% of the variation in freshman grades.

Obviously, the intended point of this assertion is that the SAT is, in fact, a poor predictor of college academic performance and is thus invalid and useless.

Unfortunately, this assertion is misguided in at least two important ways. First, contrary to the assertion's argument, there is no need to square a correlation in order to interpret it. Indeed, researchers from many areas of psychology and other sciences report correlations regularly without squaring them. The correlation itself is a meaningful and reasonable index of association, as we have discussed throughout this book. Going further, it makes no sense to imply that a given value is deceptive or inappropriate but that squaring it makes it clear and interpretable. Second, the suggestion that the ability to account for 22% of the variance in freshman GPA is poor is itself off the mark. Indeed, in many areas of behavioral science, an association of this magnitude is, in fact, very robust. As researchers ourselves, we would be quite happy if we could account for "only" 22% of the variance in an important and complex variable like freshman GPA. Indeed, for us, as psychological scientists trained in the study of individual differences and predictive validity, these results provide compelling evidence *in support of* the SAT as a measure of capacity for academic achievement. Thus, this example shows the dangers of a misguided interpretation of "squared correlations" as a way of interpreting validity correlations.

In the remainder of this section, we present better ways of interpreting the magnitude of a validity coefficient. The next two subsections put validity correlations in specific contexts that are themselves ways of understanding the meaning of a given association.

Estimating Practical Effects: Binomial Effect Size Display, Taylor-Russell Tables, Utility Analysis, and Sensitivity/Specificity

One useful way of interpreting a correlation is by estimating its impact on "real-life" decision making and predictions. The larger a correlation is between a test and a criterion variable, the more successful we will be in using the test to make predictions or decisions about the criterion variable. This interpretive approach casts the associative strength of a test in terms that are closely tied to the "practice" of testing and test use.

Returning to the SAT, we can frame the issue in terms of using it as a tool to predict academic performance. That is, we can frame the issue in a way that university administrators, faculty members, student applicants, high school counselors, and parents are likely to find relatively intuitive. More specifically, we can frame the question in terms of the percentage of times that SAT-based predictions about students' college GPAs are likely to be accurate. How often will SAT scores lead to accurate predictions, and how often will they lead to inaccurate predictions?

There are at least four procedures that have been developed to present the implications of a correlation in terms of our ability to use the correlation to make successful predictions. These procedures include the binomial effect size display (BESD; Rosenthal & Rubin, 1982), the Taylor-Russell tables (Taylor & Russell, 1939), utility analysis (Brogden & Taylor, 1950), and an analysis of test sensitivity and specificity (Loong, 2003). We will discuss each of these in turn.

The BESD is designed to illustrate the practical consequences of using a correlation to make decisions. Specifically, it is usually formatted to make predictions or decisions for a group of 200 people—100 of whom have relatively high scores on the test of interest and 100 who have relatively low scores on the test. How many of the high scorers are likely to perform well on a criterion variable, and how many low scorers are likely to perform poorly? In terms of the SAT example, how many people who have above-average SAT scores will earn above-average GPAs, and how many people who have below-average SAT scores will earn below-average GPAs? See Table 9.6a for a 2 x 2 table that reflects this issue. We can use the BESD procedure to show how many successful and unsuccessful predictions will be made on the basis of a correlation.

Table 9.6   Example of the Binomial Effect Size Display

College GPA		
(a) For a correlation of *r* = .00		
Test Score	*Below Average*	*Above Average*
Below average	50	50
Above average	50	50
(b) For a correlation of *r* = .48		
Test Score	*Below Average*	*Above Average*
Below average	A	B
	74	26
Above average	C	D
	26	74

NOTE: GPA = grade point average.

To illustrate this, let us start with a worst-case scenario of zero correlation between SAT scores and college GPA. If SAT scores are uncorrelated with GPA, then we would have only a 50:50 success rate (see Table 9.6a) in using SAT scores to predict whether students' GPAs are relatively high or low. That is, among 100 people with below-average SAT scores, 50 would earn below-average GPAs, and 50 would earn above-average GPAs. Similarly, among the 100 people with above-average SAT scores, 50 would earn below-average GPAs, and 50 would earn above-average GPAs. As this example illustrates, if a test is uncorrelated with a criterion variable, then using the test to make predictions is no better than flipping a coin. Certainly, college admissions officers would reject a test that had a validity coefficient that produced a success rate no better than flipping a coin would.

But what about a scenario in which there is a nonzero correlation between test and criterion? If test scores are correlated with job performance, then we would be more successful than 50:50. Rosenthal and Rubin (1982) provide a way of illustrating exactly how much more successful we would be. Note that the 2 x 2 table presented in Table 9.6b is formatted so that Cell A corresponds to the number of people who have relatively low SAT scores and who will likely earn below-average GPAs. To determine this value, we use the following formula:

$$\text{Cell A} = 50 + 100(r/2),$$

Binomial effect size

where *r* is the correlation between test and criterion. If test scores are correlated with job performance at *r* = .48 (e.g., as suggested by the NCFOT, 2007), then 74 people with below-average SAT scores would have below-average SATs:

$$Cell\ A = 50 + 100(.48/2),$$
$$= 50 + 24,$$
$$= 74.$$

Our prediction for Cell B (the number of people with relatively low SAT scores who are predicted to earn relatively high GPAs) is

$$Cell\ B = 50 - 100(r/2),$$
$$= 50 - 100(.48/2),$$
$$= 50 - 24,$$
$$= 26.$$

The predicted success rates for Cells C and D parallel those for Cells A and B:

$$Cell\ C = Cell\ B = 50 - 100(r/2) = 26,$$
$$Cell\ D = Cell\ A = 50 + 100(r/2) = 74.$$

Now, based on the data presented in the BESD, let us consider the importance or utility of a correlation that is "only" .48. If a college admissions committee accepted only applicants with relatively high SAT scores, then 74% of those applicants will turn out to earn high GPAs in college and only 26% will turn out to earn poor GPAs. A 74% success rate is not perfect, but it seems quite good for complex phenomena such as academic achievement. Depending on a variety of factors, college administrators and faculty might view a 74% success rate as very good indeed.

Take a moment to compare the potential interpretations of the finding that SAT scores are correlated at approximately .48 with college GPA. First, some people might square the correlation and be disappointed that the SAT "explains only 22% of the variation in freshman grades." But what does 22% of the variation mean in real-life, practical terms? Is it truly as bad as the NCFOT (2007) would have us believe? A second interpretation would suggest not—indeed, the BESD approach provides rather compelling evidence in support of the validity and practical utility of the SAT as a tool for predicting college performance. That is, the finding that SAT-based admission decisions would be correct nearly 75% of the time is quite impressive, considering the huge number of factors that affect each student's performance in college. Based on these results, practically speaking, the SAT seems to offer meaningful information about a test taker's likelihood of achieving classroom success. In sum, the BESD can be used to translate a validity correlation into a framework that is relatively intuitive. By framing the association as the rate of successful predictions, the BESD presents the association between a test and a criterion in terms that most people are familiar with and can understand easily.

Despite the intuitive appeal of the BESD, it has been criticized as an estimate of the practical effects of a correlation (Hsu, 2004). One key criticism is that it automatically frames the illustration in terms of an "equal proportions" situation. That is, it is intended for a situation in which the number of people with low test scores is equal number to the number of people with high test scores. In addition, it is cast for a situation in which half the sample are "successful" on the criterion variable and half are unsuccessful. As described earlier in this chapter, the relative proportion of scores on a variable (i.e., its skew) can affect the size of a correlation. Although the BESD's assumption of equal relative proportions might be reasonable in some cases, it might not be representative of many real-life situations. For example, a college admissions committee might accept only 25% of the applicants, not 50%. In addition, high GPAs might be rather difficult to achieve, perhaps only a 30% chance.

For situations in which the equal proportions assumption is untenable, we can examine the tables prepared by Taylor and Russell (1939). These tables were designed to inform selection decisions, and they provide the probability that a prediction (e.g., a selection decision) based on an "acceptable" test score will result in successful performance on the criterion. As with the BESD, the Taylor-Russell tables cast the predictor (test) and outcome scores as dichotomous variables. For example, a human resources director might use an integrity test or an ability assessment to help make hiring decisions. Thus, she might conceive of test scores as either passing or failing, in terms of meeting the standards for a hiring decision. In addition, she will conceive of the job performance criterion as either successful performance or unsuccessful performance. The key difference between the BESD and the Taylor-Russell tables is that the Taylor-Russell tables can accommodate decisions that are based on various proportions both for passing/failing on the test and for successful/unsuccessful performance.

To use the Taylor-Russell tables, we need to identify several pieces of information. First, what is the size of the validity coefficient? Second, what is the selection proportion—the proportion of people who are going to be hired? That is, are 10% of applicants going to be hired (leaving 90% not hired), or will 30% be hired? Third, what is the proportion of people who would have "successful" criterion scores if the selection was made without the test? That is, assuming that hires were made without regard to the test scores, how many employees would achieve successful job performance?

With these three pieces of information, we can check the Taylor-Russell tables to estimate the proportion of people with acceptable scores who go on to have successful performance. For example, if we knew that 10% of a sample would be hired (a selection proportion of .10) and that the general rate of successful performance was 60% (a success proportion of .60), then we could estimate the benefit of using a test to make the selection decisions. If the applicant-screening test has a validity coefficient of .30, then the Taylor and Russell tables tell the human resources director that 79% of the applicants selected on the basis of the test would show successful job performance. Note that this percentage is greater than the general success rate of 60%, which is the success rate that is estimated to occur if hires were made without the use of test scores. So the human resources director concludes that the test improves successful hiring by 19%.

The Taylor-Russell tables have been popular in industrial/organizational psychology in terms of hiring decisions. Our goal in describing them is to alert you to their existence (see Taylor & Russell, 1939) and to put their importance in the context of evaluating the meaning of a validity coefficient.

[Handwritten margin notes: "Taylor Russel"; "selection decisions"; "Useful when you know who are going to be higher"]

Utility analysis

↓

Cost vs. benefit

Test sensitivity

↓ people have something)

test specificity

↓ don't have something

Utility analysis is a third method of interpreting the meaning of a validity coefficient, and it can be seen as expanding on the logic of the BESD and the Taylor-Russell tables. Utility analysis frames validity in terms of a cost-versus-benefit analysis of test use. That is, "is a test worth using, do the gains from using it outweigh the costs?" (Vance & Colella, 1990, p. 124). Although a full discussion of utility analysis is beyond the scope of this section, we will provide a brief overview.

For a utility analysis, researchers assign monetary values to various aspects of the testing and decision-making process. First, they must estimate the monetary benefit of using the test to make decisions, as opposed to alternative decision-making tools. For example, they might gauge the monetary benefit of hiring employees based partly on test scores as opposed to hiring employees without the aid of the test scores. Note that the logic of the Taylor-Russell tables provides some insight into this issue. For example, those tables show the proportion of applicants selected on the basis of the test who would show successful job performance, which researchers might then use to estimate the monetary impact of hiring a specific number of people who show successful job performance. Second, researchers must estimate the monetary costs of implementing the testing procedure as part of the decision-making process, such as the costs incurred by purchasing and scoring the test(s), training decision makers in the interpretation and use of test scores, and the time spent by test takers and decision makers in using the test(s). As an outcome of a utility analysis, researchers can evaluate whether the monetary benefits of test use (which, again, are affected by the ability of the test to predict important outcomes) outweigh the potential costs associated with test use.

An analysis of test sensitivity and test specificity is a fourth approach to evaluating the practical effects of using a specific test. Particularly useful for tests that are designed to detect a categorical difference, a test can be evaluated in terms of its ability to produce correct identifications of the categorical difference. For example, a test might be intended to help diagnose the presence versus absence of a specific psychological disorder. In such a case, there are four possible outcomes of the diagnosis, as shown in Table 9.7:

1. *True positive:* The test leads test users to a correct identification of a test taker who truly has the disorder.

2. *True negative:* The test leads test users to a correct identification of a test taker who truly does not have the disorder.

3. *False positive:* The test leads test users to mistakenly identify a test taker as having the disorder (when the individual truly does not have the disorder).

4. *False negative:* The test leads test users to mistakenly identify a test taker as not having the disorder (when the individual truly does have the disorder).

Obviously, test users would like a test to produce many correct identifications and very few incorrect identifications.

Sensitivity and specificity are values that summarize the proportion of identifications that are correct. As shown in Table 9.7, sensitivity reflects the ability of a test to identify individuals who have the disorder, and specificity reflects the ability of a

Table 9.7   Example of Sensitivity and Specificity

		In Reality, Disorder Is			
		Present	**Absent**		
Test Results Indicate That Disorder Is	**Present**	80 True positive	120 False positive	All with positive test 200	Positive predictive value 80/200 = .40
	Absent	20 False negative	780 True negative	All with negative test 800	Negative predictive value 780/800 = .975
		All with disorder 100 Sensitivity 80/100 = .80	All without disorder 900 Specificity 780/900 = .87	Everyone = 1,000 Base rate (prevalence, pretest probability) = 100/1,000 = .10	

test to identify individuals who do not have the disorder. More technically, sensitivity reflects the probability that someone who has the disorder will be identified correctly by the test, and specificity reflects the probability that someone who does not have the disorder will be identified correctly by the test. In practice, researchers and test users can never truly know who has the disorder, but sensitivity and specificity are estimated to be high in research that uses a highly trusted standard for gauging whether an individual has the disorder.

In sum, tools such as the BESD, the Taylor-Russell tables, utility analysis, and sensitivity/specificity allow test users and test evaluators to illustrate more concretely the implications of a particular validity coefficient and the use of a given test. Such procedures are clearly important and useful when a test is tied closely to a specific outcome, characteristic, or decision.

Guidelines or Norms for a Field

Yet another way in which validity correlations should be evaluated is in the context of a particular area of research or application. Different areas of science might have different norms for the size of the associations that are typically found. Some areas have greater experimental control over their variables than other areas. Some areas have more precise measurement techniques than others. Some areas may have more complex phenomena, in terms of multidetermination, than others. Such differences affect the magnitude of results obtained in research.

Researchers in the physical sciences might commonly discover associations that most psychologists and other behavioral scientists would consider incredibly strong. For example, a 2000 study examined the association between the mass of black holes at the center of a galaxy and the average velocity of stars at the edge of the galaxies (Gebhardt et al., 2000). This study included approximately 26 galaxies (the "subjects" in this study), and two variables were measured for each galaxy. One variable was the size of the black hole at the center of the galaxy, and the other was the velocity of the stars that orbit on the edge of the galaxy. Analyses revealed a correlation of .93 between the two variables. Such a high correlation is rarely, if ever, found with real data in psychology. Similarly, Cohen (1988) notes that researchers in the field of classical mechanics often account for 99% of the variance in their dependent variables.

In psychology, Jacob Cohen is often cited as providing rough guidelines for interpreting correlations as small, medium, or large associations. According to Cohen's (1988) guidelines for the interpretation of correlations, correlations of .10 are considered small, correlations of .30 are considered medium, and correlations of .50 are considered large (note that Cohen provides different guidelines for interpreting other effect sizes, such as d). More recently, Hemphill (2003) conducted a review of several large studies and suggests that a more appropriate set of guidelines would cite correlations below .20 as small, correlations between .20 and .30 as medium, and correlations greater than .30 as large.

Even within the field of psychology, different areas of research are likely to have different expectations for their effect sizes. For example, Hemphill's (2003) guidelines are derived from studies of psychological assessment and treatment. The degree to which his guidelines are appropriate for other areas of psychology or the behavioral sciences in general has not yet been examined. Similarly, Cohen (1988) acknowledges that his guidelines "may be biased in a 'soft' direction—i.e., towards personality-social psychology, sociology, and cultural anthropology and away from experimental and physiological psychology" (p. 79).

Sometimes, there are clear comparison standards for a particular validity coefficient. That is, there might be a well-established body of literature regarding the various factors that are correlated with a particular criterion of interest. In such a case, it is simple to evaluate the validity coefficient for a new test in the context of the existing body of literature.

For example, there is a large body of literature regarding the correlates of college academic performance, and this can be used to evaluate the predictive power of SAT scores. We can return again to critics of the SAT, who state that "the SAT is not a good predictor of academic performance" and that "insofar as any academic measure [is the gold standard for predicting college performance], it is High School GPA" (Soares, 2008). Such an endorsement would suggest that high school GPA would be the best comparison for the predictive power of the SAT. As it turns out, despite the critics' implications to the contrary, there is very little difference between the predictive power of the SAT and the predictive power of HSGPA. For example, the website of the NCFOT (2007), which cited the predictive power of the SAT at .48, states that HSGPA is correlated with college GPA at a minimally larger .54. Similarly, a well-known study of nearly 80,000 college applicants in California revealed predictive correlations of .36 and .39 for the SAT and high school grades, respectively[2] (Geiser & Studley, 2001). People who are familiar with correlational results will realize that such modest differences are a very weak basis for concluding that there is a meaningful difference in the predictive power of two variables, and those differences certainly do not justify the conclusion that HSGPA is "the gold standard" for predicting college performance while at the same time concluding that the SAT "is not a good predictor." Indeed, such findings provide an important context for understanding the predictive validity of the SAT—if you believe that high school grades are meaningful predictors of college academic performance, then you must also believe that SAT scores are meaningful predictors of college academic performance.

In sum, the interpretation of validity coefficients, as with any measure of association, needs to be done with regard to the particular field. Careful and well-informed attention to the existing empirical work in a field can provide an important context for interpreting the magnitude of a specific validity coefficient.

[handwritten margin note: regards to particular field]

Statistical Significance

[handwritten margin note: Confidence that our results were not due to chance]

If you read a study that revealed a predictive validity coefficient of .55 for the SAT, would you interpret the result as providing evidence of convergent validity? Using the BESD procedure, a correlation of this size would produce a success rate of nearly 80%, in terms of admitting students with high SAT scores into college. However, what if you found out that the study included only 20 participants? Would this change your opinion of the study? If so, how? What if you found out that the study included 200 participants? Would this improve your opinion of the study? In what way would it be a better study?

Earlier in this chapter, we mentioned a real study of the predictive validity of the SAT. This was a large study, including more than 100,000 students from 25 colleges. What is the benefit of such a large study? Is it necessary to have such a large study? As you might know, most studies in psychology, including most validation studies, include much smaller samples—typically a few 100 participants at the most. What, if anything, is lost by having samples of this size?

Statistical significance is the final consideration we will discuss in evaluating evidence of convergent and discriminant quality. Statistical significance is an important part of what is called *inferential statistics*, which are procedures designed to help us make inferences about populations. Either from previous experience or from our brief discussion in Chapter 7, some of you might already be familiar with inferential statistics such as *t* tests (e.g., for correlations or for comparing two means), *F* tests (e.g., from ANOVA or from multiple regression), or χ^2 (e.g., from an analysis of frequencies). We will take a moment to explain a few basic issues in inferential statistics, and then we will consider their role in interpreting validity evidence.

Most studies include a relatively small sample of participants. These participants provide the data that are analyzed and serve as the basis for interpretations and conclusions. But researchers usually want to make conclusions about people beyond the few who happened to participate in their particular study. Indeed, researchers usually assume that the participants in their studies represent a random sample from a larger population of people. For example, the 20, 200, or 100,000 people who happen to be included in a SAT study are assumed to represent all students who might take the SAT and attend college.

Because the sample of participants in a study is assumed to represent a larger population, researchers further assume that the participants' data represent (more or less) data that would be collected from the entire population. Thus, they use the data from the sample to make inferences about the population that the sample represents. For example, researchers who find a predictive validity coefficient of .55 for the SAT would like to believe that their results apply to more than the 20, 200, or 100,000 people who participated in their study.

However, researchers are aware that making inferences from a relatively small sample to a larger population is an uncertain exercise. For example, just because data from 20 participants might reveal a predictive validity correlation of .55 for the SAT, should we have great confidence that the SAT has predictive validity in the entire population of participants who might take the SAT? In fact, it is quite possible that the sample of 20 people does not represent the entire population of students who might take the SAT. Therefore, it is possible that the predictive validity results found in the sample do not represent the actual predictive validity in the entire population.

Researchers use inferential statistics to help gauge the confidence that they should have when making inferences from a sample to a population. Researchers compute inferential statistics alongside statistics such as correlations to help them gauge the representativeness of the correlation found in the sample's data. Roughly stated, if a result is deemed "statistically significant," then researchers are fairly confident that the sample's result is representative of the population. For example, if a study reports a statistically significant positive predictive validity correlation for the SAT, then researchers feel confident in concluding that SAT scores are in fact positively associated with college GPAs in the population from which the study's sample was drawn. On the other hand, if a result is deemed to be statistically nonsignificant, then researchers are not confident that the sample's result represents the population. For example, if a study reports a statistically nonsignificant positive predictive validity correlation for the SAT, then researchers will likely conclude that the positive correlation in the sample might have been a fluke finding caused purely by chance. That is, they are not willing to conclude that SAT scores are in fact positively associated with college GPAs in the population from which the study's sample was drawn.

With this background in mind, you are probably not surprised to learn that many researchers place great emphasis on statistical significance. Many researchers tend to view statistically significant results as "real" and worth paying attention to, and they view nonsignificant results either as meaningless or as indicating a lack of association in the population. Although these views are not entirely accurate, they seem to be common.

Thus, the size of a validity coefficient is only part of the picture in evaluating the evidence for or against construct validity. In addition to knowing and interpreting the validity coefficient itself (e.g., is it small, medium, or large?), test developers, test users, and test evaluators usually want to know whether the validity coefficient is statistically significant. When evaluating convergent validity evidence, researchers expect to find validity coefficients that are statistically significant. In contrast, when evaluating discriminant validity evidence, researchers expect to find validity coefficients that are nonsignificant (i.e., indicating that the test might not be correlated with the criterion in the population).

Because statistical significance is often such an important part of the interpretative process, we believe that you should have a basic understanding of the issue being addressed and the factors affecting statistical significance. As applied to the typical case of a validity coefficient, statistical significance addresses a single question—do we believe that there is a nonzero validity correlation in the population from which the sample was drawn?

Note that this is a "yes or no" question. The statistical significance process leads to a dichotomous decision—researchers conclude either that there probably is an association between a test and a criterion in the population or that there might not be an association between the test and the criterion in the population. Again, when evaluating convergent validity, researchers would like to conclude that there is an association between a test and a criterion in the population, so they hope to find results that are statistically significant. When evaluating discriminant validity, researchers would like to conclude that there is no (or a small) association between a test and a criterion, so they hope to find results that are nonsignificant. In fact, Campbell and Fiske (1959) included statistical significance as a key part of interpreting the results of an MTMMM analysis.

A more sophisticated version of the basic question is this: *Are the results in the sample compelling enough to make us confident that there is a nonzero correlation in the population from which the sample was drawn?* This highlights the notion of confidence, and it generates two subquestions outlining the factors affecting statistical significance. One question is this: *How confident are we* that there is a nonzero validity correlation in the population from which the sample was drawn? The second question is this: *Are we confident enough* to actually conclude that there is a nonzero correlation in the population from which the sample was drawn?

There are two factors affecting the amount of confidence that there is a nonzero correlation in the population—the size of the correlation in the sample's data and the size of the sample. First, consider the fact that larger correlations increase the confidence that the population correlation is not 0. If the correlation between SAT scores and GPA is literally 0 in a population, then what correlation would we be likely to find in a sample of people drawn from that population? Even if the correlation in the population is exactly .00, we might not be very surprised to find a small correlation of .07 in a sample. Such a small correlation is only slightly different from the population correlation. We might not even be too surprised to find a correlation of .15 in a sample. Going further, we might not be shocked to find a somewhat larger correlation of, say, .30 in a sample, even if the sample comes from a population in which the correlation is 0. Such a result (a correlation of .30) is not likely, but it is not impossible. In fact, it is possible that a very strong correlation (e.g., a correlation of .89) could occur in a sample, even if the sample comes from a population in which the correlation is actually 0.

In short, relatively large correlations are unlikely to occur (though not impossible) in a sample's data if the sample is drawn from a population in which the correlation is 0. Indeed, if we find a large correlation in a sample, then it is much more likely that the population's correlation is in fact something larger than 0. For example, if we find a correlation of .30 in our sample, then it's more likely that the population's correlation is something like .20, .30, or .40, rather than .00. Therefore, larger correlations in the sample's data increase our confidence that the population correlation is not 0. Consequently, larger correlations in the sample data increase the likelihood that the correlation will be considered statistically significant.

Sample size is the second factor affecting the amount of confidence that there is a nonzero correlation in the population. All else being equal, larger samples increase confidence when making inferences about the population. Imagine that you hear about a study reporting a correlation of .30 between SAT scores and college GPA. If you knew that this study included only 20 participants, then how confident would you be in concluding that there is a positive correlation between SAT scores and college GPA among *all* students who could take the SAT? What if you knew that this study included 200 participants or 100,000 participants? Obviously, larger sample sizes should make us more confident when making conclusions about a population.

In sum, the size of the correlation and the size of the sample affect our confidence in concluding that there is a nonzero correlation in the population. The precise statistical equations are beyond the scope of this discussion, but in general, larger correlations and larger samples increase our confidence that the correlation in the population is not 0 (for a brief presentation of such equations, see Table 7.1 in Chapter 7). Thus, larger correlations and larger samples increase the likelihood that the results of the validity study will be statistically significant. An equation (based on Rosenthal, Rosnow, & Rubin, 2000) summarizes the issue:

Confidence that a test is correlated with a criterion *in the population*	=	Size of the validity coefficient in the sample	x	Size of the sample

However, for results to be deemed statistically significant, we must have a specific level of confidence that the population correlation is not 0.

Thus, the second question regarding statistical significance is this: *Are we confident enough* to actually conclude that there is a nonzero correlation in the population from which the sample was drawn? Large correlations and large sample sizes increase our confidence, but we must ask if the results of a particular study make us confident *enough* to deem the results statistically significant.

To answer this question, researchers set a specific level of confidence as a cutoff point that must be met before they conclude that the population correlation is not 0. By tradition, most behavioral researchers use a 95% confidence level as the cutoff point for declaring results to be statistically significant. Put another way, most behavioral researchers are willing to declare results statistically significant if they find that there is only a 5% chance of being wrong (i.e., a probability of .05). This cutoff is the "alpha level" of a study (please note that this is a different "alpha" from the one introduced in Chapter 6). If our inferential statistics surpass the alpha level, then we are confident enough to conclude that there is a nonzero validity correlation in the population from which the sample was drawn.

As mentioned earlier, statistical significance is an important issue in interpreting evidence for convergent and discriminant validity. The fact that statistical significance is affected by sample size, effect size (i.e., the size of the validity coefficient in the sample), and alpha level is an extremely important point. These issues should be considered when interpreting inferential statistics. For example, the results of a validity study can be statistically significant even if the validity correlation is quite small. This could occur if the size of the sample in the validity study was sufficiently large. Similarly, the results of a validity study can be nonsignificant even if the validity correlation is quite large. This could occur if the size of the sample in the validity study was quite small.

How should this information be interpreted when gauging the results of a validity study? We mentioned earlier that most researchers would hope to find convergent correlations that are statistically significant and they would hope to find discriminant correlations that are nonsignificant. But what are the implications of finding a convergent validity correlation that is nonsignificant? The typical interpretation would be that the test in question has weak convergent validity (i.e., the convergent correlation might well be 0 in the population). However, such a result should be interpreted with regard to the size of the correlation and the size of the sample. A nonsignificant convergent validity correlation could occur because the correlation is small or because the sample is small. If the correlation is small, then this is certainly evidence against the convergent validity of the test. However, if the correlation is moderate to large in size but the sample is small, then the results might not indicate poor convergent validity. Instead, the results could indicate a poorly conceived study in that its sample was inappropriately small. If a study included a sample that was too small, then perhaps a larger study should be conducted before making any conclusions about construct validity.

Similarly, what are the implications of finding a discriminant validity correlation that is statistically significant? The typical interpretation would be that the test in question has weak discriminant validity (i.e., the discriminant correlation is probably not 0 in the population). Again, such a result should be interpreted with regard to the size of the correlation and the size of the sample. A significant discriminant validity correlation could occur because the correlation is large or because the sample is large. If the correlation is large, then this is certainly evidence against the discriminant validity of the test. However, if the correlation is small but the sample is quite large, then the results might not indicate poor discriminant validity. For example, it is possible that small correlations of only .10, .06, or even smaller could be statistically significant if the sample were large enough (say in the thousands of participants). In such cases, the statistical significance is almost meaningless and should probably be ignored.

In sum, statistical significance is an important but tricky concept as it is applied to validity evidence. Although it plays a legitimate role in the interpretation of convergent and discriminant validity coefficients, it should be treated with some caution. As a rule, convergent correlations should be statistically significant, and discriminant validity correlation should be nonsignificant. However, this general rule should be applied with an awareness of other factors. A sophisticated understanding of statistical significance reveals that the size of the sample and the size of the convergent and discriminant validity correlations both determine significance. Thus, a nonsignificant convergent correlation could reflect the fact that the study had an inadequate sample size, and a significant discriminant correlation could reflect the fact that the study had an extremely large sample size.

Summary

Convergent and discriminant evidence is key to the empirical evaluation of test validity, and this chapter presents issues related to the estimation and evaluation of these important forms of validity evidence. We began by describing four methods that have been used to estimate and gauge the degree of convergence and discrimination among tests (e.g., MTMMM). We then discussed seven factors that can affect the size of validity coefficients (e.g., measurement error, relative proportions, method variance). Finally, we presented four important issues that should be considered when judging the meaning and implications of validity coefficients (e.g., variance explained, statistical significance, practical importance). Awareness of the issues described in this chapter can provide a more sophisticated and informed perspective on the meaning and evaluation of test validity.

Notes

1. We might instead conduct an independent groups t test to compare the mean depression scores of the two groups, hypothesizing that the depressed group of participants will have a higher mean on our new scale than the nondepressed group. Indeed, this is a very common way to examine the association between a dichotomous variable and a continuous variable. However, it rests entirely on the same issues described in the text. Indeed, the t test is simply a function of the correlation, as described here, along with the group sizes (see Chapter 7, especially Table 7.1). Thus, the relative proportion of participants in the two groups will have a direct effect on the magnitude of the t test, which will affect the likelihood that we will conclude that the group means are, in fact, different from each other.

2. These values (.39 and .36) are not reported directly by Geiser and Studley (2001), but they are easily obtained by taking the square roots of the relevant "Percent of Variance" values in their Table 1. The values in this table can be converted to r^2 values as indicators of the percentage of variance in GPA that is explained by high school GPA and by SAT scores. For the one-predictor models in this table, the square roots of the r^2 values are simple correlations. Specifically, .39 is the square root of .154, and .36 is the square root of .133.

Suggested Readings

This is a discussion of the interpretation of effect sizes:

Abelson, R. P. (1985). A variance explanation paradox: When a little is a lot. *Psychological Bulletin, 97,* 129–133.

This is a classic article, in which the multitrait–multimethod matrix is presented for the first time:

Campbell, D. T., & Fiske, D. W. (1959). Convergent and discriminant validation by the multitrait multimethod matrix. *Psychological Bulletin, 56,* 81–104.

This presents the Taylor-Russell tables:

Taylor, H. C., & Russell, J. T. (1939). The relationship of validity coefficients to the practical effectiveness of tests in selection: Discussion and tables. *Journal of Applied Psychology, 23,* 565–578.

This article presents the logic and computation details of the quantifying construct validity procedure:

Westen, D., & Rosenthal, R. (2003). Quantifying construct validity: Two simple measures. *Journal of Personality and Social Psychology, 84,* 608–618.

This presents an overview of the concept of statistical power, which is an important issue in evaluating the statistical significance of validity coefficients:

Cohen, J. (1992). A power primer. *Psychological Bulletin, 112,* 155–159.

This article presents a factor-analytic approach to the examination of MTMMM data:

Widaman, K. F. (1985). Hierarchically nested covariance structure models for multitrait multimethod data. *Applied Psychological Measurement, 9,* 1–26.

PART IV

Threats to Psychometric Quality

CHAPTER 10

Response Biases

At the beginning of our discussion of validity, we asked you to imagine that you had taken a personality questionnaire as part of a job application process. Let's revisit that example and ask you to imagine yourself completing the questionnaire. You arrive at a question that asks, "Have you ever stolen anything from an employer?" and another that asks, "Do you always tell the truth to others?" As you think about these questions, you recall the time when you "borrowed" a very nice pen from a previous workplace but "forgot" to return it. In addition, you think about the fact that you told your best friend that you needed to work last weekend, when in fact you just wanted to relax at home by yourself. However, you also think about the fact that you would like to get the job, and you consider the answers that might make the employer more likely to hire you. Thus, despite the fact that your truthful answer to the first question should be "Yes" and your truthful answer to the other question should be "No," you, like most of us, might be quite tempted to provide, let's say, "alternative" responses to both of the questions.

How does your desire to be hired affect the quality of the personality questionnaire? The employer might wish to interpret your responses as indicative of honesty or integrity. However, if you chose to make the alternative responses, then your responses are no longer validly interpreted as indicative of integrity. Instead, they are biased by your motivation to impress the employer, and they do not reflect your true level of integrity, slightly imperfect though it might be.

In this chapter, we address the problem of response biases, and we describe some solutions that psychologists have developed to cope with the problem. As much as we might hope that responses to psychological measures are perfectly accurate reflections of individuals' true psychological characteristics, we know that such responses can be systematically biased for a variety of reasons.

These biases are important because they can harm the psychometric quality of many types of tests, scales, and inventories. More specifically, they can diminish test reliability and the validity with which we interpret psychological measures such as personality inventories, attitude surveys, ability tests, achievement tests, and

Biases harm psychometric quality of tests, scales, + inventories

[margin handwritten note: diminished validity compromises decisions about individuals]

neuropsychological tests. Diminished validity can in turn compromise the decisions that are made about individuals, and it can cause problems for interpreting research based on those measures. That is, the psychometric damage done by response biases can, in turn, do serious damage to our ability to use psychological measures in a meaningful way.

Whether they are conscious or unconscious, malicious or cooperative, self-enhancing or self-effacing, response biases are a constant concern in psychological measurement. Indeed, response biases are a fundamental problem for those of us who study or work with human behavior. Furthermore, they are a problem that may be unique to the study of human behavior. Scientists who study rocks, planets, insects, chemicals, hurricanes, or flowers rarely have concerns that their subjects are motivated to appear particularly intelligent or unintelligent, healthy or unhealthy, friendly or powerful, competent or needy, honest or virtuous. Psychologists must worry about all such problems, and more.

Aware of such problems, psychologists have dedicated themselves to identifying, understanding, detecting, and handling biases affecting responses to psychological tests and measures (e.g., Cronbach, 1946, 1950; Schwarz, 1999). We first describe some response biases that have been of greatest concern to behavioral scientists. We then turn to insights and solutions—some simple and some complex—that are used to understand, detect, minimize, and cope with those biases.

Types of Response Biases

The quality of psychological measurement can be affected by a variety of response biases. In this section, we describe a number of biases that have concerned the developers and users of psychological measures. Some of these biases are affected by the content or format of a test, some are affected by factors of the testing context, others reflect respondents' conscious efforts to respond in invalid ways, and still others reflect unconscious factors that bias responses. Whatever their differences, all the biases reviewed in this section have the potential to compromise the quality of psychological measurement.

Acquiescence Bias ("Yea-Saying and Nay-Saying")

[margin handwritten note: Acquiescence Bias → agrees w/ statements w/o regard for the meaning of those statements]

Psychologists and other behavioral scientists have been concerned with acquiescence bias for more than 80 years (e.g., Block, 1965; Cady, 1923; Cloud & Vaughn, 1970; Cronbach, 1942; Lentz, 1938; Ray, 1983; Smith, 2004). *Acquiescence bias* occurs when an individual agrees with statements without regard for the meaning of those statements. Many psychological inventories include statements that might be true for an individual (e.g., "I enjoy my job"), and individuals are asked to respond by agreeing or disagreeing with the statements. Acquiescence bias can affect responses to such items, which are often found on personality trait inventories, attitude questionnaires, interest inventories, clinical inventories, and marketing surveys.

The acquiescence bias and its effects are illustrated in Table 10.1a. Imagine an industrial/organizational psychologist who is interested in the association between job satisfaction and perceived prestige. She hypothesizes that people with relatively high job satisfaction will be those who perceive their jobs as relatively prestigious. She asks employees of a business to complete a job satisfaction questionnaire that includes the following four items:

1. I really enjoy my work.

2. I find my work personally fulfilling.

3. In general, I am satisfied with the day-to-day aspects of my job.

4. There is very little that I would change about my job.

Furthermore, imagine that responses are made on a 7-point scale (1 = *strongly disagree*, 2 = *moderately disagree*, 3 = *slightly disagree*, 4 = *neutral*, 5 = *slightly agree*, 6 = *moderately agree*, 7 = *strongly agree*). The scoring "key" to this hypothetical questionnaire is such that an individual's responses to the items are simply summed to form a total job satisfaction score, with high scores reflecting high levels of satisfaction. Table 10.1a presents the responses to these items and the total score for the satisfaction questionnaire. Examining these data, we see that Respondents 1, 2, and 4 have the highest scores on the job satisfaction questionnaire, and we would like to interpret this as indicating that they have the highest levels of job satisfaction.

The items' phrasing is an important issue in this hypothetical questionnaire. Note that each item is phrased so that an "agreement" response (i.e., a response of 5, 6, or 7) is interpreted as meaning that the respondent is at least somewhat satisfied with his or her job. Psychometricians might say that items are all "keyed in the positive direction" because a positive (i.e., agreement) response to each item reflects a relatively high level of the construct being assessed.

The fact that all items are keyed in the same direction is important because it makes the questionnaire particularly susceptible to the effects of an acquiescence response bias. Let us once again imagine that we are omniscient and we know that two participants (Participants 1 and 4, as noted in Column 2 of Table 10.1a) exhibited an acquiescence bias but that the other four participants were responding validly. Note that the acquiescent responders agreed to all four items, even though they honestly might not be satisfied with their jobs. The difficulty is compounded by the fact that at least one additional participant (Participant 2) also agreed with all four items because he is genuinely satisfied with his job. If we were not omniscient—if we did not know that Participants 1 and 4 were responding invalidly—then we would not be able to distinguish the acquiescent responders from those who were genuinely satisfied with their job.

Acquiescent responding has straightforward implications for test users in applied psychology. Specifically, if some people engage in acquiescent responding while others do not, then test users might not be able to use test scores effectively to identify which people have a high level of the construct being assessed. That is, test users might not be able to detect which respondents have a high level of the construct and which respondents are simply responding with an acquiescent bias.

all items keyed in same direction ⟶ susceptible to effects of acquiescence response bias.

Cannot use test scores effectively to identify which people have a high level of assessed construct vs acquiescent bias.

Table 10.1   Acquiescent Response Bias Can Create a Spurious Correlation

(a) Responses to original tests

Participant	Acquiescence	JS Items				JS Total	PP Items				PP Total	Valid Responders JS	PP
		1	2	3	4		1	2	3	4			
1	Y	6	5	7	6	24	5	5	4	5	19	—	—
2	N	7	5	6	7	25	2	2	2	1	7	25	7
3	N	3	4	5	4	16	5	4	5	4	18	16	18
4	Y	6	6	6	7	25	5	5	5	5	20	—	—
5	N	1	4	2	3	10	1	2	1	2	6	10	6
6	N	3	2	4	3	12	3	3	3	3	12	12	12

Correlation between JS and PP = −.43   −.09

(b) Raw responses to balanced tests

Participant	Acquiescence	JS Items				PP Items			
		1	2	3	4	1	2	3	4
1	Y	6	5	7	6	5	5	4	5
2	N	7	3	6	1	2	4	2	5
3	N	3	4	5	4	5	2	5	2
4	Y	6	6	6	7	5	5	5	5
5	N	1	4	2	5	1	4	1	4
6	N	3	6	4	5	3	3	3	3

(c) Reverse-scored responses to balanced tests

Participant	Acquiescence	JS Items				JS Total	PP Items				PP Total	Valid Responders JS	PP
		1	2	3	4		1	2	3	4			
1	Y	6	3	7	2	18	5	1	4	1	11	—	—
2	N	7	5	6	7	25	2	2	2	1	7	25	7
3	N	3	4	5	4	16	5	4	5	4	18	16	18
4	Y	6	2	6	1	15	5	1	5	1	12	—	—
5	N	1	4	2	3	10	1	2	1	2	6	10	6
6	N	3	2	4	3	12	3	3	3	3	12	12	12

Correlation between JS and PP = −.10   −.09

NOTE: JS = job satisfaction; PP = perceived prestige.

For example, a human resource manager might administer a Conscientiousness scale to a set of job applicants but might not be able to identify which applicants truly have high levels of Conscientiousness. If this problem is ignored, then any decisions that are based on such test scores might be misinformed and misguided. The human resources director, for example, might end up hiring several applicants who are simply acquiescent responders rather than truly conscientious workers.

Acquiescent responding also has serious implications for behavioral research, compromising researchers' ability to answer their research question accurately. Returning to our job satisfaction example, let's say that, along with the job satisfaction questionnaire, participants complete a four-item measure of perceived prestige that is answered on 5-point scale of agreement (1 = *strongly disagree*, 2 = *disagree*, 3 = *neutral*, 4 = *agree*, 5 = *strongly agree*). As shown in Table 10.1a, those participants who were acquiescent while responding to the Job Satisfaction (JS) scale were also acquiescent while responding to the Perceived Prestige scale. Participants 1 and 4 once again respond to all questions by using the "agreement" options (4 and 5).

Across all six participants (including the valid responders as well as the acquiescent responders), the correlation between job satisfaction and perceived prestige is $r = .43$ (see Table 10.1a). This "total sample" correlation suggests that the two constructs are related to each other, which is consistent with the researcher's hypothesis.

However, because we are temporarily omniscient, we can examine the correlation between job satisfaction and perceived prestige among *only those four participants who responded validly*. We see that this "valid responder" correlation is quite weak, $r = -.09$. Thus, according to valid responses, satisfaction and prestige are *not* associated with each other. We see that the inclusion of acquiescent participants created an artificially (i.e., spuriously) high correlation between the two measures. Because the researcher is not omniscient, she has access only to the original correlation. Based on this, she would reach an incorrect conclusion about the link between job satisfaction and perceived prestige.

Thus, acquiescent responders present a subtle but potentially important threat to the psychometric quality of the psychological measurement, which can compromise behavioral practice and research. Briefly stated, test users might not be able to differentiate acquiescent responders from valid responders who happen to have a high level of the construct being assessed. If a measure's items are all scored in the same direction, then a set of "positive" responses could reflect a valid set of responses, or it could reflect an acquiescent response bias. An important consequence of acquiescence bias is that if multiple tests are "contaminated" by the bias, then the tests will be more strongly correlated with each other than are the underlying constructs. This consequence occurs because respondents who are acquiescent on one test are likely to be acquiescent on the other, which ensures that they will obtain relatively high scores on both tests. As discussed in Chapter 3, a positive correlation occurs when people who have relatively high scores on one variable tend to have relatively high scores on another variable.

Although we have focused on the acquiescence or "yea-saying" bias, it can also take the form of "nay-saying," where an individual disagrees with statements

Acquiescence - can be negative too

regardless of their meaning. A nay-saying bias can have similar effects as the yea-saying bias. By ensuring that people who obtain relatively low scores on one test will also obtain relatively low scores on another test, the nay-saying bias creates correlations that are artificially more positive than they should be.

In sum, acquiescence response bias (including nay-saying) is a threat to psychometric quality that has long concerned psychologists and other behavioral scientists. Although some researchers question the existence or impact of response biases (Rorer, 1965), much evidence suggests that acquiescence bias does exist and affects various forms of psychological measurement (Knowles & Nathan, 1997; Van Herk, Poortinga, & Verhallen, 2004). The bias seems to occur most often when respondents do not easily understand test items—because the items are complex or ambiguous, because the testing situation presents distractions, or because the respondent naturally tends to have difficulty understanding the material. As our examples have illustrated, the bias can create artificially high (or low for the nay-saying bias) test scores for tests in which all items are keyed in the same direction. Consequently, the bias can affect research by creating correlations that are artificially more positive than they should be.

Occurs when respondents do not understand test items, distractions in test situation, difficulty understanding material

Extreme and Moderate Responding

Extreme + Moderate Responding

As we have seen, many questionnaires include statements or questions that require people to respond in terms of intensity, endorsement, or occurrence. For example, the State-Trait Anxiety Inventory (STAI; Spielberger, 1983) is a widely used questionnaire designed to assess respondents' levels of state anxiety and trait anxiety. The STAI's Trait Anxiety subscale consists of 10 statements about one's general level of psychological distress. Items on this scale include statements such as "I lack self-confidence" and "I am a steady person" (note that this item is negatively keyed). For each statement, respondents have four response options: *almost never*, *sometimes*, *often*, and *almost always*.

On many such questionnaires, the response options reflect different degrees of intensity, endorsement, or occurrence, with some reflecting an extreme degree and other options reflecting more moderate degrees. For example, on the STAI, the *almost always* option is a more extreme choice (reflecting a more extreme degree of occurrence) than the *often* option. Other scales include response options referring to the degree of accuracy of statements or the degree to which a respondent agrees with statements. For example, the International Personality Item Pool (Goldberg et al., 2006) includes a Spirituality/Religiousness (S/R) scale with items such as "I am a spiritual person," and responses can be made on a 5-point scale: *very inaccurate*, *moderately inaccurate*, *neither inaccurate nor accurate*, *moderately accurate*, and *very accurate*. On the S/R scale, the *very accurate* option is a more extreme choice than the *moderately accurate* option (reflecting a more extreme degree of accuracy), and the *very inaccurate option* is a more extreme choice than the *moderately inaccurate* option.

degrees of intensity, endorsement, or occurance in response options

degree of accuracy

The problem of extreme and moderate response biases (or "extreme response style") refers to differences in the tendency to use or avoid extreme response options. On the STAI, one respondent might be much more willing to make an

differences in tendencies to use/avoid extreme response options

"extreme" response choice (e.g., answering *almost always* to the statement "I lack self-confidence") than another respondent, *even if those two respondents have the same level of anxiety.* Similarly, on the S/R scale, one respondent might be much more willing to respond with *very accurate* to the statement "I am a spiritual person" than another respondent, even if the two respondents have the same level of spirituality. Simply put, people might differ in their willingness to use extreme response options, and this can obscure differences in true construct levels.

The ambiguities created by differences in participants' use of extreme response options have important implications for applied psychological practice and for research results. As noted earlier for acquiescence bias, extremity bias can create ambiguity in respondents' scores, which can lead decision makers to make inappropriate decisions on the basis of those scores.

In terms of behavioral research, extremity bias can produce results that lead to inaccurate conclusions. As an example, consider the data in Table 10.2. Imagine that a researcher is studying the association between spirituality and emotional distress and he hypothesizes that the correlation will be positive—people with higher levels of spirituality will tend to have relatively high levels of distress. To examine this association, he asks participants to complete a four-item version of the STAI (high scores should indicate greater anxiety and distress), along with a four-item version of the S/R scale (high scores should indicate greater spirituality).

Once again, we will pretend to be omniscient. In Table 10.2, the "True Anxiety" column presents the participants' true levels of trait anxiety. We see, for example, that Participants 1 and 2 have the same trait level (i.e., both true scores are 14) as do Participants 4 and 5 (i.e., both true scores are 6). Computing the correlation between true anxiety levels and true spirituality levels (see Table 10.2), we find essentially no association ($r = -.04$). Thus, our omniscience allows us to realize that there is truly no tendency for people with relatively high spirituality to have any more or less anxiety than people with relatively low spirituality. This contradicts the researcher's hypothesis that high spirituality is associated with high levels of distress.

Of course, the researcher would not know participants' true trait levels, having access only to test responses. So let us examine the participants' actual responses

Table 10.2 Extremity Bias

Participant	Bias	True Anxiety	STAI Items 1	2	3	4	Total STAI	True Spirituality	S/R Items 1	2	3	4	Total S/R
1	Extreme	14	4	4	4	4	16	11	4	4	4	4	16
2	Moderate	14	3	3	3	3	12	12	2	2	2	2	8
3	No	12	3	4	3	2	12	4	1	1	1	1	4
4	Moderate	6	2	2	2	2	8	9	2	2	3	3	10
5	Extreme	6	1	1	1	1	4	8	1	1	1	1	4
6	No	7	1	3	2	1	7	15	3	5	4	3	15

NOTE: STAI = State-Trait Anxiety Inventory; S/R = Spirituality/Religiousness scale.

to the four-item version of the STAI and compare them with their true trait levels. For this version of the STAI, the researcher used the following scoring: 1 = *almost never*, 2 = *sometimes*, 3 = *often*, and 4 = *almost always*. Note that Participant 1 responded *almost always* to all four items, for a total score of 16. Also note that Participant 2 responded *often* to all four items, for a total score of 12. Thus, these two participants obtain different scores on the measure of anxiety, even though they have the same trait level of anxiety. This discrepancy arises because Participant 1 was willing to use a more extreme response option than Participant 2. As this discrepancy illustrates, the extremity bias can generate artificial differences among respondents' test scores. Note that this tendency is stable in that it also affects participants' responses to the S/R scale.

In addition to generating artificial differences among respondents' test scores, the extremity bias can obscure true differences among respondents' construct levels. Consider Participants 2 and 3. These participants have different true trait levels of anxiety, but their test scores are identical. Because Participant 2 is reluctant to use a more extreme response option, her test score is not as high as her trait level warrants. Thus, her test score is identical to that of a participant with a lower trait level.

Ultimately, these types of problems can produce results that lead to inaccurate research conclusions. Earlier, in our omniscient state, we calculated the correlation between participants' true anxiety levels and their true spirituality levels (see Table 10.2), finding essentially a zero correlation. Now, let's compute the correlation between participants' measured anxiety scores (STAI trait scores) and their measured spirituality scores (S/R scale scores). Based on the data in Table 10.2, this correlation is $r = .36$, which would lead the researcher to conclude that spirituality is *positively* associated with anxiety. Obviously, the correlation based on the measured scores (which are affected by the extremity problem) is meaningfully different from the correlation based on true scores (which we know only through omniscience). Therefore, the psychological conclusions derived from the statistical analyses of the measured scores are incorrect, in comparison with the conclusion that would be derived if the researcher had direct knowledge of the participants' true trait levels. In this way, the extremity problem can contribute to incorrect research conclusions. In the current example, the researcher would incorrectly conclude that spirituality is associated with emotional distress.

Note that the use of extreme response options is itself not a bias or a problem, nor is the use of more moderate response options. Indeed, test users hope that the use of response options reflects an individual's trait level—people with more extreme trait levels (i.e., either particularly high or particularly low) *should* use more extreme response options, and people with more moderate trait levels *should* use more moderate response options. However, problems arise when (a) people with identical construct levels differ in their tendency to use moderate and extreme response options or (b) when people with different construct levels do not differ in their willingness to use moderate and extreme response options.

Psychologists and other behavioral scientists have studied the extent and the sources of the extremity problem—is it actually true that some people are more willing to use extreme response options than others, and if so, then why? Research suggests that there is indeed reason to be concerned about the extremity bias. Studies

[handwritten margin notes: artificial differences among respondents' test scores; obscure true differences among respondents' construct levels; false correlations]

have shown that differences in the tendency to use extreme response options are fairly stable across measures and across time (e.g., Bachman & O'Malley, 1984; Jain & Agarwal, 1977; Merrens, 1970), although some studies have failed to replicate this effect. One example of research indicating the stability of the effect was conducted by Bachman and O'Malley (1984), who found "substantial and rather consistent individual differences in the tendency to use—or to avoid—extreme response categories" (p. 506), with these consistencies lasting for intervals of up to 4 years.

In sum, the extremity bias can diminish the quality of psychological measures. Some respondents are willing to use extreme response options, but others tend to avoid extreme response options. The difference in response styles can obscure differences in the respondents' true trait levels. Such effects can, in turn, compromise psychological practice and can diminish the accuracy of research conclusions.

Social Desirability

The social desirability problem has garnered perhaps the greatest attention among psychologists concerned with response biases. The *social desirability response bias* is the tendency for a person to respond in a way that seems socially appealing, regardless of his or her true characteristics. At the beginning of this chapter, we asked you to imagine yourself completing a questionnaire as part of a hiring process. In that scenario, we highlighted the possibility that you would be tempted to provide responses that would appeal to the employer. You might be tempted to respond in a way that enhances desirable qualities such as honesty, integrity, conscientiousness, and emotional stability. If responses are caused by a motivation to appear socially desirable, then they fail to reflect the respondents' true levels of the constructs being assessed. This can diminish the reliability and validity of the measurement process.

Social desirability bias can be affected by at least three sources. First, it can be affected by a test's content. Some psychological constructs have greater implications for social appeal than do others, and thus tests that focus on those constructs might be more adversely affected by social desirability than tests of other constructs. For example, personality characteristics such as psychological well-being (vs. psychological distress) or honesty (vs. deceitfulness) might be closely linked to social desirability, with well-being and honesty clearly more desirable than distress and deceitfulness. On the other hand, characteristics such as extraversion (vs. introversion) might be less affected by such motivations (John & Robins, 1993). Second, the social desirability bias might be affected by the testing context. Socially desirable responding might be more likely to occur in contexts in which respondents can be identified than in contexts in which they are anonymous. When respondents can be linked to their responses, they might be more likely to provide responses that are socially appealing. In addition, socially desirable responding might be more likely to occur in contexts in which important consequences hinge on the testing outcomes. The hiring example represents a context in which test responses can have important implications—the possibility that individuals are hired partially depends on their scores on the psychological measures. Socially desirable responding is

3) personality of respondent (personal pref)

probably less of a concern if there are no important consequences of the testing (although it is still a potential problem, as we will see below).

A third potential source of socially desirable responding is the personality of the respondents. As demonstrated by research dating back at least to the 1950s, some people are more likely to provide socially desirable responses than others. Again, the difficulty arises because differences in participants' tendency to provide socially desirable responses can obscure differences in participants' true levels of the traits being assessed.

Obviously, there is serious concern about the impact that social desirability can have in some areas of applied psychology. Indeed, many personality tests are fairly "transparent" in terms of being obvious about the types of qualities that are being assessed, and in such tests it is easy to "fake" having desirable qualities (Alliger & Dwight, 2000; Baer, Wetter, & Berry, 1992; Viswesvaran, & Ones, 1999). Unfortunately, some evidence suggests that such faking occurs quite commonly, at least in the context of job applications (Donovan, Dwight, & Hurtz, 2003). Such faking can, in turn, affect decision making in psychological practice. For example, if job applicants exaggerate their positive qualities and minimize their negative qualities, then hiring decisions can be compromised severely. Indeed, it has been suggested that "when faking occurs, those hired under a [testing based] selection strategy are likely to be fakers" (Alliger & Dwight, 2000, p. 62).

affects decisions in psychological practice

In addition, social desirability is a serious concern for behavioral researchers as well. To understand the social desirability response bias and its effect on research results, imagine that a researcher examines the association between emotionality and relationship quality. She hypothesizes that people who tend to experience high levels of positive emotions (or who tend to experience low levels of negative emotions) also tend to develop high-quality relationships. More technically, she expects to find a positive correlation between positive emotionality and relationship quality, and she expects to find a negative correlation between negative emotionality and relationship quality. To examine this issue, she asks participants to complete the Positive and Negative Affect Schedule (PANAS; Watson, Clark, & Tellegen, 1988). The PANAS is a very widely used measure of affectivity, and it can be used to measure trait-level (i.e., stable) differences in respondents' general tendencies to experience positive emotions and negative emotions. The PANAS includes two scales—Positive Affect (PA) and Negative Affect (NA)—each of which includes 10 emotions (e.g., strong, proud, excited, nervous, guilty, distressed). Although researchers use the PANAS in many different ways, let us imagine that our researcher asked participants to read each item and rate the extent to which they generally feel each emotion, with responses made on a 5-point scale. The PA and NA scales were scored by computing the mean of the 10 responses for each scale, so scores range between 1 and 5, with higher scores reflecting a greater tendency to experience each type of affect. Finally, the researcher asks participants to rate the overall quality of their social relationships on a scale of 1 to 100, with higher levels representing better relationship quality.

Note that these three constructs—positive affect, negative affect, and relationship quality—are potentially affected by social desirability biases. At least in Western cultures, high positive affect is culturally preferable to low positive affect, and low negative affect is preferable to high positive affect. That is, people who express strength, pride, and enthusiasm are generally seen as socially appealing and admirable, whereas people who express nervousness, guilt, and distress are generally seen as socially unappealing and not admirable. Finally, most cultures would perceive high-quality relationships as valuable and desirable. Thus, an individual who wishes to appear socially appealing is likely to claim high levels of positive affect, to claim low levels of negative affect, and to report high-quality relationships.

Let us again imagine that we are omniscient, knowing participants' true levels of positive affect, negative affect, and relationship quality. For example, Table 10.3 shows that Participant 1 has the highest true level (4.5) of positive affect (PA) and that Participant 2 has the next highest level (4). Also, note that Participant 4 truly has the highest level of relationship quality (RQ). Computing the correlation between these true levels of PA and the true levels of RQ, we find mild support for the researcher's hypothesis—a weak positive correlation (i.e., $r = .23$). Similarly, the association between true negative affect (NA) and true RQ provides additional mild support for the researcher's hypothesis—a weak negative correlation (i.e., $r = -.21$). Thus, our omniscience allows us to observe a weak tendency for people with relatively high PA levels or low NA levels to also have relatively high-quality relationships.

False correlations

Let us also imagine that, in our omniscient state, we know the degree to which each participant is motivated to provide socially desirable answers. As shown in the column labeled "SD Motive" in Table 10.3, Participant 2 is highly motivated to provide socially desirable responses, Participants 3 and 5 are somewhat motivated to do so, but the remaining participants have no particular motivation to appear more desirable than they "truly" are.

We can see how social desirability affects the measurement of the three constructs. Specifically, for participants motivated by a social desirability bias, measured scores are more toward the "desirable" direction than are their true levels.

Table 10.3 Example of the Effect of the Social Desirability Response Bias on Research Findings

Participant	True Scores PA	NA	RQ	SD Motive	Measured Scores PA	NA	RQ
1	4.5	5	60	None	4.5	5	60
2	4	2	55	High	5	1	95
3	3	1.5	65	Low	3.375	1.125	80
4	2.25	3	85	None	2.25	3	85
5	1.5	4	45	Moderate	2	3.5	65
6	1.75	3.25	40	None	1.75	3.25	40
Correlation with RQ	.23	−.21			.51	−.65	

NOTE: SD = socially desirable; PA = Positive Affect scale; NA = Negative Affect scale; RQ = relationship quality.

For example, note Participant 2, who has a high level of social desirability motivation. This participant's measured score on the PA scale (i.e., 5) is higher than his true level of PA (i.e., 4), reflecting a desire to claim an artificially high level of PA. Thus, this participant's high motivation to appear socially desirable has influenced his responses to some of the PA items, resulting in an inflated score on the measure of PA. Similarly, his score on the NA scale (i.e., 1) is lower than his true level of NA (i.e., 2), reflecting a desire to claim an artificially low level of NA. Thus, measured scores on desirable constructs such as PA and RQ are artificially inflated for those participants with a social desirability motivation, and scores on "undesirable" constructs such as NA are artificially deflated. In contrast, for participants who are not motivated by a social desirability bias, their measured scores are equivalent to their true values, regardless of the "desirability" of the construct.

An important consequence of social desirability bias is that research results can be compromised. Of most concern is the possibility that individual differences in social desirability bias can create spurious or artificially strong correlations between measures that are "contaminated" by the bias. The data in Table 10.3 illustrate this effect. As we have discussed, there are at least two problems in the data. First, participants differ in terms of their motivation to appear socially desirable—some have moderate or strong motivation, but others have weak or no motivation. Second, the three variables are linked to social desirability, and thus their measurement is potentially contaminated by social desirability motivation (indeed, the measures in Table 10.3 are contaminated by the bias, as we have seen). The effect of these two problems is that the participants with social desirability motivation tend to have higher scores on PA and RQ (and lower scores on NA) than the participants with no social desirability motivation. Therefore, the social desirability bias inflates the degree to which people who tend to score high on one measure also tend to score high on the other measures. This in turn affects the correlations among the measures.

The effect of the social desirability bias is apparent in the artificially inflated correlations among the three measures. Note that the correlations among the true scores are much weaker than the correlations among the three *measures*. Earlier, our omniscience allowed us to know that the "true" correlation between PA and RQ was only .23 and that the "true" correlation between NA and RQ was only −.21. As Table 10.3 shows, the correlations among the measures are much stronger—the correlation between the PA measure and the RQ measure is .51, and the correlation between the NA measure and the RQ measure is −.65. Thus, the social desirability bias can artificially inflate the correlation among measures. In our example, the researcher might interpret the artificially inflated correlations between measures (i.e., $r = .51$ and $r = −.65$) as evidence of very strong associations between emotionality and relationship quality. Again, our temporary omniscience revealed that such interpretations are incorrect—the correlations among the constructs are actually much weaker than the researcher realizes. The researcher is severely overestimating the size of the associations because of measurement invalidity caused by the social desirability bias. Such overestimations can, in turn, produce misleading inferences about theories and could produce inappropriate decisions in applied settings.

As mentioned earlier in this section, psychologists have studied extensively the social desirability response bias. One of the most active researchers in this area has been Del Paulhus, a personality psychologist who has been interested in socially desirable responding as an aspect of personality. One important outcome from Paulhus's work has been the finding that there may be multiple forms of social desirability bias. Paulhus points to two processes through which socially desirable responding occurs. One process is a conscious *impression management*, where test takers intentionally attempt to appear socially desirable. For example, a job applicant might feel motivated to artificially exaggerate desirable characteristics and artificially minimize undesirable characteristics while completing a personnel selection test. In a clinical context, impression management is sometimes called "faking good," as it refers to underreporting of clinical symptoms. That is, a respondent might attempt to appear less pathological by falsely denying various pathological symptoms. A second process is an unconscious *self-deception*, where test takers hold unrealistically positive views of themselves, firmly believing their overestimation of their psychological characteristics.

Paulhus (2002) argues that impression management and self-deception biases differ in terms of being statelike versus traitlike. He suggests that impression management biases are relatively statelike, occurring in response to immediate situational demands. In other words, the tendency to *consciously* respond in an overly desirable manner is usually a reaction to particular measurement contexts, such as completing a personnel selection inventory. In contrast, Paulhus suggests that self-deception biases reflect traitlike differences among people. That is, some people are more predisposed toward self-deception than others, and this difference can affect their responses across many different measurement contexts.

Despite the long-standing concern over social desirability bias and its potential effects on the quality of psychological test scores, some researchers argue that such concerns are at least somewhat exaggerated. Some of the most compelling arguments for this arise from data suggesting that "in most applications, attempts to correct scores for defensiveness or SD [social desirability] do not enhance validity" (McCrae & Costa, 1983, p. 886). Such conclusions are partly based on findings that measures of social desirability are uncorrelated with important outcomes such as job performance (Viswesvaran, Ones, & Hough, 2001), that repeated testing after failure to be hired does not produce meaningful changes in scores (Hogan, Barrett, & Hogan, 2007), and that statistically controlling for individual differences in social desirability does not improve the criterion-related validities of personality trait measures (McCrae & Costa, 1983; Ones, Viswesvaran, & Reiss, 1996). Despite such findings, many psychologists remain concerned about the potential effect of social desirability on psychological tests and their use.

Malingering

Although many psychologists have been concerned about respondents' artificial enhancement of their social desirability, other psychologists are very concerned about the opposite problem. Specifically, in some extremely important testing contexts, respondents might attempt to exaggerate their psychological problems. Particularly in some applied testing contexts, respondents might be strongly motivated to appear more cognitively impaired, emotionally distressed, physically challenged, or psychologically disturbed than they truly are. This phenomenon is called *malingering* or *faking bad*, and it is recognized by the American Psychiatric Association's *Diagnostic and Statistical Manual of Mental Disorders*, 4th edition (*DSM-IV*, 1994) as a serious problem in psychological assessment and diagnosis.

Take a moment to consider why individuals might attempt to exaggerate the presence or severity of their psychological problems. Consider some of the testing contexts in which malingering is most likely to occur—criminal competence hearings, disability evaluations, workers' compensation claims, and personal injury examinations (Berry, Baer, Rinaldo, & Wetter, 2002; Mittenberg, Patton, Canyock, & Condit, 2002). In all such contexts, examinees potentially benefit from being diagnosed with some kind of psychological or neuropsychological disorder. Criminals might receive relatively mild sentences if they are diagnosed with a mental disorder, workers might receive monetary settlements if they are judged to have suffered an impairment at work, and accident victims might receive monetary benefits if they are deemed to suffer from neuropsychological problems resulting from their accidents. In sum, malingering is a serious concern in applied testing situations in which the test taker has an incentive to appear impaired.

It is probably obvious that malingering potentially compromises the quality of psychological assessment. For example, cognitive abilities such as attention and memory can be affected by traumatic brain injury. Consequently, a person involved in an automobile accident might reap great financial benefits from insurance settlements if he or she can convince the courts that he or she has suffered brain injury that compromises cognitive ability. Indeed, many neuropsychological assessments include tests of attention and memory, and the person might intentionally perform poorly (or at least attempt to) to be diagnosed with a cognitive impairment. Malingering can have clear consequences for the accuracy and fairness of diagnoses, judgments, and decisions that are based on the compromised measures.

Malingering is more than a theoretical possibility in applied testing contexts. Researchers (e.g., Berry et al., 2002; Mittenberg et al., 2002) estimate that malingering occurs in 7.3% to 27% of general psychological evaluations and as much as 31% to 45% of forensic evaluations (i.e., criminal competence, disability hearings, etc.). In fact, there is evidence that attorneys intentionally coach clients in the methods used to detect malingering, as we will discuss later (Wetter & Corrigan, 1995; Youngjohn, 1995). Thus, malingering is a legitimate concern in psychological assessment, and experts conclude that the failure to consider its influence "potentially carries high costs for insurers, disability systems, and ultimate society at large" (Berry et al., 2002, p. 275).

Careless or Random Responding

Sometimes test takers provide responses that are truly random or somewhat random. Whether due to carelessness or to a lack of motivation to respond meaningfully, some respondents might choose answers in a completely random or semirandom fashion that is unrelated to item content. For example, an individual taking a test in which items are answered on a 5-point scale of agreement (1 = *strongly disagree*, 5 = *strongly agree*) might simply compete the test by "cycling through" the response scale—marking *strongly disagree* (1) for Item 1, *disagree*

(2) for Item 2, *neutral* (3) for Item 3, *agree* (4) for Item 4, and *strongly agree* (5) for Item 5 and returning to *strongly disagree* (1) at Item 6 to begin the cycle again. Obviously, this produces scores that are meaningless with regard to the construct that is intended to be assessed.

Guessing

guessing

Some psychological tests are designed so that specific responses are correct and others are incorrect. For example, achievement tests such as the SAT or the Graduate Record Exam (GRE) include items evaluating a respondent's verbal or mathematical skills. Each item on these tests has a single correct answer, and respondents obtain high scores by answering many items correctly. Such tests are often used in situations in which important consequences (e.g., college admission) are partly contingent on test scores.

For these kinds of tests used in these kinds of consequential situations, respondents might be motivated to guess. Particularly for tests that have a limited set of response options (e.g., multiple-choice questions), respondents may guess at an answer in an attempt to raise their scores. Indeed, guessing is such a likely occurrence that some achievement tests are scored in a way that accounts for the effect of guessing (as we will discuss later in this chapter).

Where answering is better than leaving blank

For cases in which a respondent truly does not know which response option is likely to be correct, guessing can compromise the quality and meaningfulness of test scores. That is, a correct guess increases a respondent's test score, artificially inflating it in comparison with the respondent's true score. Thus, decisions that are based on test scores might be affected by guessing. Similarly, differential guessing could be a source of random measurement error. If some respondents are "luckier" than others (i.e., some respondents randomly produce more correct guesses than other respondents) or if some respondents guess while others do not, then guessing produces test scores that are inconsistent with the true differences among respondents.

artificial inflation of test score

inconsistent w/ the true differences among respondents

Methods for Coping With Response Biases

As we have discussed, several response biases can compromise the reliability and validity of psychological measures. In turn, compromised reliability and validity have important consequences for research and application of psychological measures. As we have seen, various response biases can lead to inappropriate decisions for individuals in applied measurement contexts. In addition, response biases can obscure the associations among psychological constructs, leading to inappropriate conclusions in behavioral research contexts.

Aware of these threats to psychometric quality and applied testing, psychologists use a variety of strategies for coping with response biases. In the remainder of this chapter, we will discuss some of these strategies in relation to the specific goals for which they are used, as summarized in Figure 10.1. As this figure illustrates,

		Goals		
		Prevent or Minimize the Existence of Bias	**Minimize the Effects of Bias**	**Detect Bias and Intervene**
Strategies	**Manage Testing Context**	Anonymity Minimize Frustration Warnings		
	Manage Test Content or Scoring	Simple items Neutral items Forced choice Minimal choice	Balanced scales Corrections for guessing	Embedded validity scales
	Specialized Tests			Desirability tests Extremity tests Acquiescence tests

Figure 10.1   Examples of Methods for Coping With Response Bias

there are at least three general kinds of strategies—managing the testing context, managing the test content and/or scoring, and using specially designed "bias" tests. In addition, there are at least three general goals that these strategies are intended to accomplish. Some solutions are intended to minimize the existence of response biases, some are intended to minimize the effects of response biases, and some are designed to detect biased responses, allowing test users to intervene in some way (which we will discuss later).

Minimizing the Existence of Bias by Managing the Testing Context

Perhaps the best way to cope with response biases is to prevent them from occurring. Although a test user might never be sure that he or she has prevented response biases, there are strategies that might reduce the likelihood of various biases. Some strategies focus on the way in which a respondent experiences the testing context. That is, the occurrence of response biases might be minimized by managing the way in which the test is presented to respondents and by managing the demands placed on the respondent within the testing situation.

For example, Paulhus (1991) suggests that social desirability bias might be minimized by reducing the situational factors that could elicit socially desirable responding. In many research contexts, test users can assure participants that their responses will be anonymous. Knowing that there is no way for their responses to be identified personally, participants might be quite willing to provide honest responses. This suggestion is based on the rationale that anonymity allows respondents to feel comfortable in honestly admitting to undesirable attitudes, thoughts, behaviors, feelings, or traits. Although anonymity might increase honest responding, there is a potential drawback. Specifically, anonymity might also increase the possibility of random responding. Many participants in behavioral research, particularly in psychological research, are undergraduate students taking classes in introductory psychology. Although students are not forced to participate, some of them might *feel* coerced into participating. The anonymity of a research context might interact with any feelings of coercion, producing very low motivation to be honest and conscientious (Lelkes, Krosnick, Marx, Judd, & Park, 2012). Thus, some participants might take advantage of the anonymity, responding carelessly, quickly, and perhaps even totally randomly. As we will discuss in a later section, it might be possible to identify such responses and exclude them from any analyses.

Another method for managing the testing context is to create a testing situation that minimizes respondent fatigue, stress, distraction, or frustration. Such cognitive-emotional states can increase the potential for response biases (Paulhus, 1991). By decreasing a respondent's ability to concentrate or by increasing the likelihood that a respondent's motivation will wane, such states could elicit random responding, social desirability, or other biases. In both applied and research testing contexts, it might be advisable to limit testing periods to a time frame that will not fatigue respondents (e.g., in our experience, we avoid requesting more than an hour of objective testing from our research participants). In addition, it is probably advisable to conduct measurement procedures in environments that are fairly quiet, with few potential distractions.

A final example of managing the testing context is to tell respondents that the validity of their responses can be evaluated. Some research indicates that respondents who are told that false responding can be detected are relatively likely to admit to socially undesirable attitudes, behaviors, or traits that might otherwise remain hidden (Paulhus, 1991). This strategy is of particular interest as a solution to malingering. Some research (e.g., Butcher, Morfitt, Rouse, & Holden, 1997; Fink & Butcher, 1972) shows that valid responses on the Minnesota Multiphasic Personality Inventory (MMPI) scales are increased when respondents are informed that random responses or dishonesty can be detected (although some research shows no effects of such warnings, e.g., Butcher, Atlis, & Fang, 2000). In fact, validity can be increased if participants merely *believe* that biased responding can be detected. Research suggests that even if test users actually cannot detect biased responses, the mere possibility of detection can convince some respondents to be more honest and unbiased.

Minimizing the Existence of Bias by Managing Test Content

In their attempts to cope with the problem of response biases, test users and test developers will often use specific kinds of test content to minimize the existence of response biases. By choosing specific kinds of items or specific kinds of response formats, test developers might be able to nullify or reduce some biases.

Simple items

As mentioned earlier, respondent frustration might lead to biased responding. Thus, test developers might write test items that are as straightforward and simple as possible. If a test is easy for respondents to understand and complete, then respondents are less likely to become frustrated or distracted. The avoidance of frustration and distraction might, in turn, reduce the tendency toward carelessness, low motivation, and, ultimately, biased responding.

write SD items in a neutral way

Another strategy is to write items that are neutral in terms of social desirability. For example, a measure of "friendliness" might have a strong pull toward social desirability—many people might perceive friendliness as a desirable characteristic, and they might be tempted (consciously or otherwise) to exaggerate their friendliness. However, it is possible that items might be written in a way that underemphasizes the desirable quality of being friendly and the potentially undesirable quality of being unfriendly. For example, the item "I am a surly and hostile person" might be used to reflect the unfriendly end of the dimension—this item might elicit relatively few "true" or "agree" responses because it is so clearly undesirable. An alternative might be "I am sometimes less friendly than other people." Although it is not "perfect," it expresses unfriendliness in a way that might make respondents more willing to admit to it. Similarly, moral behavior is often viewed as admirable and therefore socially desirable. A recent study relied on participants' self-reports of morality, but the researchers were concerned about social desirability bias and the possibility that some participants might artificially inflate their reports of moral behavior or artificially minimize reports of their immoral tendencies (Meindl, Jayawickreme, Furr, & Fleeson, 2012). To handle this, they asked questions in three ways—an "undisguised" way, a euphemistic way, and a dysphemistic way. In each case, they presented a description of a person and asked participants to rate how much they were like those people. For example, to assess dishonesty, they presented an "undisguised" description of a dishonest person ("A person who intentionally says things that include falsehoods") as well as a euphemistic description ("A 'linguistically creative' person who intentionally says things that include falsehoods"). The logic behind this strategy is that the euphemistic description will be perceived as relatively positive, in that being "linguistically creative" might be interpreted as a desirable quality. Thus, the positive connotations of linguistic creativity might offset the more negative connotations of telling "falsehoods," thereby composing an item that, on balance, was relatively neutral (i.e., less socially undesirable) than the undisguised item. Indeed, analyses showed that the euphemistic and dysphemistic items were rated as being more neutral, in terms of desirability, than the undisguised items.

Forced-choice items

↓ SD effects

In addition to managing the content of the items, test developers might consider using certain kinds of response formats as a way of minimizing the presence of response bias. Test developers have used "forced-choice" items to minimize the existence of social desirability bias. Forced-choice items are items that present two characteristics and require that respondents endorse one and only one of them. For example, an item on a personality test might present the characteristics "friendly" and "assertive," and respondents would be asked to identify the characteristic that is *more* descriptive of their personalities. Note that, in this example, both characteristics are approximately equally socially desirable. Similarly, an item might include characteristics that are equally undesirable (e.g., "timid" and "argumentative"), again requiring respondents to identify which one is more descriptive of them. Because each pair of choices is equated in terms of desirability, the forced-choice format prevents respondents from simply picking the more desirable choice. Test developers can also design test formats to minimize the existence of the extremity problem. For example, they can provide only two choices for each item. Again, using a personality test for an example, they might present a characteristic such as "friendly" along with only two response options—"Yes" and "No." In a sense, such a format prevents extremity bias by eliminating any "extreme" response options altogether. The downside of this strategy is that it prevents valid differences in trait extremity from manifesting themselves in responses to the item.

Minimizing the Effects of Bias by Managing Test Content or Scoring

↓ extremity effects

↓ effects = managing test content or scoring

Despite our best efforts to prevent or minimize the occurrence of response biases, they are likely to occur to some degree. Thus, test content can be designed in a way that reduces the effect of some response biases that do occur, in terms of their impact on test scores. Similarly, test users might be able to use specialized scoring procedures in order to reduce the effect of biases on some tests.

The best example of managing test content to reduce the effect of bias might be the use of balanced scales to cope with acquiescence bias. As described earlier, acquiescence bias occurs when a person agrees to a statement without regard for the meaning of the statement. As we illustrated, this bias is a particular problem when all the items in a questionnaire are keyed in the same direction. In addition, we demonstrated how the bias can play havoc with the analysis of questionnaire data—respondents with an acquiescent bias are indistinguishable from respondents who truly have high trait levels (assuming that items are keyed in a positive direction), which can create artificially strong correlations between questionnaires. A common solution to this problem is to create a test such that the effect of the bias is reduced, in terms of its influence on the analysis of questionnaire data. The solution is to use "balanced" scales.

↓ acquiescence by using balanced scales

+ + - keyed items

A *balanced scale* is a test or questionnaire that includes some items that are positively keyed and some that are negatively keyed. In our earlier example (see Table 10.1a), we imagined that a researcher asks six employees to respond to the following four "job satisfaction" items (each on a 7-point scale, with 1 = *strongly disagree* and 7 = *strongly agree*):

1. I really enjoy my work.

2. I find my work personally fulfilling.

3. In general, I am satisfied with the day-to-day aspects of my job.

4. There is very little that I would change about my job.

We noted that all four items are positively keyed because a positive response (some level of agreement) indicates a greater level of job satisfaction. To minimize the potential effects of acquiescence bias, the researcher might use the following revised set of items:

1. I really enjoy my work.

2. I do not find my work personally fulfilling.

3. In general, I am satisfied with the day-to-day aspects of my job.

4. There is much that I would change about my job.

Note that the revised questionnaire includes two items that are negatively keyed (or "reverse keyed"). Specifically, Items 2 and 4 are revised so that a negative response (some level of denial or disagreement with the statement) indicates a greater level of job satisfaction. The revised scale is balanced because it includes two items that are positively keyed (i.e., where agreement with the statement indicates high satisfaction) and two items that are negatively keyed (i.e., where disagreement with the statement indicates high satisfaction).

Table 10.1b presents the employees' responses to the balanced scale. The key difference between these responses and the original responses (Table 10.1a) is that valid responders conform to the balanced item format, but acquiescent responders do not. For example, consider Participant 2, a valid responder with a high level of job satisfaction. This participant agrees with the positively keyed items (i.e., Items 1 and 3) and disagrees with the negatively keyed items (i.e., Items 2 and 4), as would be expected from someone with a high level of satisfaction who is paying attention to item content. In contrast, consider Participant 1, an acquiescent responder. This participant agrees with all four items, ignoring the fact that some agreements indicate a high level of satisfaction but others indicate a low level. This suggests that the person is simply agreeing to the items without regard for their content.

For a balanced scale to be useful, it must be scored appropriately. The scoring key must accommodate the fact that the scale includes positively keyed items and negatively keyed items. Usually, test users prefer that a high "total" score on a test or questionnaire represents high levels of the construct being measured. For example, they would like a high score on the JS scale to represent a high level of job satisfaction.

To accomplish this, the test user must "reverse score" the negatively keyed items. To reverse score a negatively keyed item, the test user recodes individuals' responses so that a relatively large value represents a high level of the construct being measured. For example, the JS scale is a 7-point scale. Therefore, the researcher recodes an answer of "7" (*strongly agree*) to an answer of "1" (*strongly disagree*), an answer of "6" (*moderately agree*) to a "2" (*moderately disagree*), and a "5" (*slightly agree*) to a "3" (*slightly disagree*). Similarly, the test user recodes responses so that a relatively small value represents a low level of the construct being measured. Therefore, the researcher recodes an original answer of "1" (*strongly disagree*) to an answer of "7" (*strongly agree*), an answer of "2" to a "6," and a "3" to a "5." This reverse-scoring process logically recalibrates responses so that relatively large values for all items (i.e., a 7, 6, or 5) represent high levels of the construct being measured and relatively small values (i.e., a 1, 2, or 3) represent low levels. Table 10.1c presents the reverse-scored responses to the balanced scale.

Let us consider how balanced scales minimize the effects of acquiescence response bias. The most immediate benefit of balanced scales is that they differentiate acquiescent responders from valid responders who have high levels of the construct being assessed (as a side note, balanced scales also differentiate nay-saying responders from valid responders who have low levels of the construct).

Take a moment to examine the acquiescent responders in Table 10.1c, and notice how their scores on the balanced scales differ from their scores on the original scales (Table 10.1a). For example, note that Participant 1's score on the balanced JS scale is only 18, whereas his score on the original JS scale was 24. Similarly, note that Participant 4's score on the balanced JS scale is 15, whereas his score on the original scale was 26. Thus, balanced scales ensure that acquiescent responders obtain scores that are close to the sample average (i.e., not extremely high or low).

Now take a moment to examine the valid responders in Table 10.1c. For example, Participant 2's score remains high—the same as it was on the original scale (i.e., 25). Valid responders who had high scores on the original scale still have high scores on the balanced scale, and valid responders who had low scores on the original scale still have low scores on the balanced scale.

moderate trait levels due to balanced scale

Thus, test users can be fairly confident that valid responders are the only responders who will obtain extreme (i.e., particularly high or low) scores on the test. Consequently, there is a small chance of mistakenly believing that an acquiescent responder has a relatively high (or low) level of the construct being assessed by the trait.

Although balanced scales allow test users to avoid mistaking acquiescent responders for valid responders who have high trait levels, you might suspect that this simply creates a new problem. You probably noticed in Table 10.1c that we now cannot differentiate acquiescent responders from valid responders who have moderate trait levels. In a sense, we have indeed traded one problem for another. However, we have avoided a very serious problem by creating a problem that is much less serious, at least for research purposes. For research purposes, the use of balanced scales has important implications for the accuracy of research findings.

some people truly have moderate levels of the trait

The research implications of using balanced scales can be seen in the correlation between job satisfaction and perceived prestige, which was the goal of the original research question. Returning to the original scales in which all items were positively keyed (see Table 10.1a), note that the correlation across all six responders was $r = .43$. Relying on the original scale, the researcher would conclude that there is a moderate to strong association between job satisfaction and perceived prestige. However, we will again pretend to be omniscient—knowing which responders were valid and which were acquiescent. Examining the data from the four valid responders, we find a very weak negative correlation between satisfaction and prestige (i.e., $r = -.09$). Thus, the fact that two participants responded with an acquiescence bias compromised the results of the analyses, causing the researcher to make an incorrect conclusion about the link between the constructs.

Now, let us consider the correlation computed from the balanced scale (Table 10.1c). Note that the correlation across all six responders is $r = -.10$. This is much closer to the "valid responder" correlation (i.e., $r = -.09$) than was the correlation obtained from the six responses to the original scale. Therefore, if the researcher

Still more accurate than an unbalanced scale

uses the balanced scale, her conclusions will be much more accurate than if she uses the original (unbalanced) scale.

In sum, balanced scales have potentially important benefits for behavioral research. Although they do not prevent acquiescence response bias or always completely eliminate its effects, they do reduce its effects on research results. By using balanced scales, test users can be fairly confident that their research results are not heavily compromised by acquiescence bias. As illustrated in Table 10.1, balanced scales can avoid a spurious (i.e., a bogus) correlation that could result from acquiescence response bias. The potentially important benefits of using balanced scales more than outweigh their meager cost (incurred by generating negatively keyed items and reverse scoring those items).

Correction for guessing

As mentioned earlier, test users might also use specialized scoring procedures to minimize the effect of bias on test scores and test use. We have discussed guessing as a problem that might affect ability tests or achievement tests such as the SAT and GRE. Indeed, such tests use scoring procedures that are intended to adjust test scores for the potential effects of guessing. For example, the SAT has a scoring procedure that weights incorrectly answered items differently than items that are simply left unanswered. Specifically, an item that is answered correctly earns 1 point, an item that is answered incorrectly results in a subtraction of ¼ point, and an item that is omitted results in no points. Without going into great detail, the effect of this scoring procedure is that the benefit of random guessing is minimized. Interestingly, educated guessing can still be beneficial for SAT test takers. That is, if a respondent can eliminate one or more response options, then he or she is likely to benefit from guessing among the remaining response options.

No answer is better than a wrong answer = ↓ benefits of random guessing

Managing Test Content to Detect Bias and Intervene

Managing test content: detect bias & intervene

Response biases can remain a concern even after test developers and test users attempt to minimize their existence and their effects on test scores. Despite the best efforts to prevent or minimize the degree to which biases affect test scores, such biases may continue to affect responses, decisions, and analyses.

As another defense against response biases, test users might be able to detect responses that are potentially biased in a variety of ways. In this section and the next, we will discuss methods that have been designed to identify participants who seem to be manifesting some form of response bias. After those participants have been identified, test users have several options for handling their responses, including discarding and statistical control.

Several well-known measures of psychopathology and personality include *validity scales*. Validity scales are sets of items that are embedded within a large inventory, and they are intended to quantify the degree to which a respondent is manifesting specific response biases. Using these scales, test users can examine a participant's pattern of responses across the set of items and evaluate the degree to which the response pattern seems to reflect random responses, acquiescent responses, artificially "good" responses, artificially "bad" responses, and so on. A great deal of psychometric attention has been devoted to creating and evaluating validity scales for widely used measures such as the MMPI, the Millon Clinical Multiaxial

Validity scales = set of items embedded in a large inventory) quantify the degree to which a respondent is manifesting specific response biases

Inventory (MCMI), the NEO Personality Inventory (NEO-PI), and the California Psychological Inventory (CPI).

Perhaps the most widely known validity scales are those on the MMPI. The most recent edition of the MMPI (the MMPI-2) includes at least seven scales intended to provide information about the likelihood that a respondent manifested a variety of biases. For example, the L scale is intended to reflect a respondent's attempt to present an overly positive impression. According to Graham (1990), the L scale (sometimes called the "Lie scale") consists of 15 items that describe "minor flaws and weaknesses to which most people are willing to admit" (p. 23). People who deny these very common characteristics will obtain high scores on the L scale. Thus, the L scale is seen as a measure of social desirability bias. The F scale (sometimes called the "Infrequency scale") is another MMPI validity scale, consisting of 64 items that are endorsed (i.e., admitted to or agreed with) by very few respondents. A high score on the F scale represents some form of deviant responding, indicative of random responding, malingering, an "all-true" response pattern, an "all-false" response pattern, or possibly a genuinely disturbed psychological state. Additional MMPI validity scales include the K scale (to detect "faking good"), the VRIN scale ("Variable Response Inconsistency," to detect random responding), and the TRIN scale ("True Response Inconsistency," to detect yea-saying or nay-saying).

One of our earlier examples can help illustrate the way in which a response pattern can be used to detect the presence of a particular response bias. If we again examine the hypothetical responses presented in Table 10.1c, then we can see how acquiescence bias will produce a very specific pattern of responses on a balanced scale. Returning to those responses, our temporary omniscience allowed us to know that Participant 1 was responding with an acquiescence bias. A careful examination of that person's responses reveals that he or she is inconsistent in a very specific way. Recall that the four-item scale was balanced, with two positively keyed items (Items 1 and 3) and two negatively keyed items (Items 2 and 4) that were reverse scored.

Based on the reverse-scoring process, we would expect a participant who is responding validly to produce a fairly consistent set of responses. For example, a participant with a genuinely high level of job satisfaction should select responses that primarily lie above the scale midpoint. Participant 2 illustrates this consistency—all of this person's responses (i.e., 7, 5, 6, and 7) are above the scale midpoint of 4. Therefore, this person's responses are consistently in the direction of high job satisfaction. Similarly, we see that Participant 6's responses are consistently at or below the scale midpoint, and this response pattern indicates a relatively low level of job satisfaction.

In contrast, a participant with an acquiescence bias will select responses that, when scored appropriately, are inconsistently above and below the scale midpoint. For example, Participant 1 provided responses that, after the reverse-scoring process, are scattered around the midpoint. This contradicts what is expected from a participant with a truly high trait level or a truly low trait level. A test user who is not omniscient might see this kind of inconsistent response pattern and reasonably suspect that the respondent was manifesting an acquiescence response bias.

A test user who detects that an individual might be manifesting one or more response biases has at least three options for using this information to intervene in the assessment or research process. First, he or she might exclude the individual's test scores from further consideration or analysis. In an applied context, the test user might ask the individual to take the test again or might simply disregard the test scores. According to one applied testing expert, if an individual's responses are deemed to be dishonest or made without due consideration, then the individual's scores "should be considered invalid and should not be interpreted further" (Graham, 1990, p. 22). In a research context, the test user might drop the individual's data from any statistical analysis. A second option for handling suspect test scores is to retain the scores but use them cautiously. In an applied context, a test user might consider the test scores but place little weight on them in the overall assessment or diagnosis of an individual. In a research context, a test user might retain the data and simply accept the fact that various response biases might be affecting his or her results in various ways. A third option for researchers is to retain any potentially invalid data but use statistical procedures to account for the fact that some respondents might have provided invalid responses. Procedures such as partial correlations or multiple regression allow researchers to use scores on validity scales to "statistically control" for potentially invalid responses. For example, such procedures can allow a researcher to examine the association between job satisfaction and perceived prestige separately for those participants who appear to be valid respondents and those who appear to be invalid respondents.

Although validity scales might *appear to be* very useful, psychometricians and test users demand evidence that actually demonstrates their utility. Some studies fail to support the utility of validity scales (e.g., Piedmont, McCrae, Riemann, & Angleitner, 2000), but many studies attest to the "validity of validity scales." An example of a typical study is reported by Hahn (2005). This study used an "analog" design in which participants represented several groups. One group was a sample of hospitalized psychiatric patients. Because none of these patients had sought any form of compensation, they were assumed to be representative of valid responders with high levels of psychopathology. A second group included college students who were instructed to provide invalid responses. They were told to "fake bad" by presenting themselves as severely disturbed, and they were intended to be "analogs" for respondents who are attempting to malinger. All participants completed the MMPI-2, and analyses examined the ability of the validity scales to detect any differences among the groups. Results showed that, as would be expected, the analog malingerers scored higher on validity scales that are intended to signal that a respondent is providing deviant responses and is possibly malingering (e.g., the F scale). Although there are reasonable concerns about overgeneralization from results that are based on students who are pretending to be disturbed (or who are pretending to be overly desirable), much of this research provides evidence that validity scales do indeed differentiate such groups (Baer & Miller, 2002; Rogers, Sewell, Martin, & Vitacco, 2003).

In sum, embedded validity scales are a potentially useful method of detecting some kinds of response bias. By including such scales within a much larger set of scales that measure personality and psychopathology, test developers give test users the opportunity to detect potentially invalid test scores and to intervene in some way. Although there are some concerns about their real-world applicability, a substantial body of research suggests that validity scales work well when used to differentiate "known fakers" from presumably genuine respondents.

Using Specialized Tests to Detect Bias and Intervene

The final method that we will discuss for managing response biases is closely related to the previous method. Along with validity scales embedded within long measures of personality and psychopathology, psychologists have developed separate scales to measure a variety of response biases. As with the embedded validity scales, separate measures of response biases can be used in a variety of ways—they allow test users to identify and eliminate potentially invalid responses, and they allow researchers to statistically control the effects of response biases.

These scales have been used in at least two additional ways. First, in an effort to better understand response biases, psychologists have also used these measures of response biases to study their potential psychological causes and implications. By measuring a response bias and correlating its scores with measures of other psychological, behavioral, or demographic variables, psychologists can attain a deeper understanding of the possible cognitive, emotional, or motivational factors that produce the response bias. Second, test developers and test evaluators can use these scales to gauge the degree to which a test's scores might be affected by response biases. That is, they might find that a score on a new test is highly correlated with a particular response bias, and they might be able to use this information to guide test improvements or alert test users to potential problems.

Scales that are intended to measure individual differences in the tendency to provide socially desirable responses are a widely used method for detecting response biases. The Marlowe-Crowne Social Desirability Scale (Crowne & Marlowe, 1960) has been a widely used measure of social desirability. The scale is intended to reveal the degree to which an individual claims uncommon virtues and denies common flaws. It includes 33 statements, such as "Before voting I thoroughly investigate the qualifications of all the candidates" (an uncommon virtue) and "On occasion I have had doubts about my ability to succeed in life" (a common flaw). Respondents rate each item on a binary true/false scale. If a respondent claims many uncommon virtues and denies many common flaws, then his or her score is interpreted as revealing an attempt to appear socially desirable.

As mentioned in our earlier discussion of the social desirability response bias, recent work indicates that the bias is more complex than was originally conceived in the 1940s, 1950s, and 1960s (Paulhus, 2002). As part of the evolution of their research on the process and content of social desirability response biases, Paulhus and his colleagues developed the Brief Inventory of Desirable Responding (BIDR). The most recent research version of the BIDR (Paulhus, 1991) includes two main scales—a 20-item Self-Deceptive Enhancement scale and a 20-item

Impression Management scale (in addition, a 20-item Self-Deceptive Denial scale is available through the author's website). The items include self-relevant statements (e.g., "I am a completely rational person") that are answered on a 7-point scale ranging from *not true* to *very true*. High scores on the scales reflect tendencies toward socially desirable responding. Research indicates that the BIDR scales can be internally consistent, stable across at least a 5-week period, and reasonably good measures of the intended constructs (Paulhus, 1991).

Additional tests are intended to detect malingering in terms of cognitive impairment. For example, the Dot Counting Test (DCT; Lezak, 1995) includes 12 cards on which various numbers of dots are printed. Half of the cards present the dots in a grouped format, and the other half present the dots in a random arrangement. Test takers are asked to count the dots on each card as quickly as possible, with the responses and response times recorded by the test administrator. Presumably, test takers should require more time to count dots that are randomly arranged than dots that are grouped in a systematic manner. Therefore, malingering is suspected when a test taker requires as much time to count the dots on the grouped cards as on the random arrangement cards. Although the evidence is mixed, some research indicates that the DCT is a potentially useful method of detecting malingered cognitive impairment (Binks, Gouvier, & Waters, 1997; Boone et al., 2002).

Although measures of social desirability and malingering are much more widely used than measures of other response biases, such measures do exist. For example, a measure of acquiescence was developed by Couch and Keniston (1960); however, in his review of the measures of various response biases, Paulhus (1991) concludes that "none of the instruments claiming to measure general acquiescence tendencies can be recommended to the researcher" (p. 48). Similarly, Greenleaf (1992) criticized the literature examining extreme response style for inadequate concern about a standardized measure of the bias. Indeed, Greenleaf cites the conflicting results that have emerged from examinations of the correlates of extremity, and he points out that such ambiguity could be explained partially by the fact that each researcher tended to use a different (and unvalidated) measure of extremity. Although Greenleaf presents a 16-item measure of extremity bias, he concludes that additional "improved measures of [the extremity bias] are worth developing" (p. 347).

Response Biases, Response Sets, and Response Styles

This brief section is intended to clarify terminology that you might encounter. In this chapter's discussion of response biases, we have addressed a variety of tendencies to respond to questionnaires on the basis of factors apart from the actual content of the questionnaire. In this discussion, we have pointed to a variety of factors that contribute to these biases. Some factors might be temporary, reflecting aspects of the testing situation (e.g., the consequences of the testing) or the test itself (e.g., the test format or ambiguity of items). Such factors are often called *response sets* (Paulhus, 1991). Other factors are more tied to stable characteristics of individuals (e.g., some individuals are more concerned in general about appearing socially desirable than others), and such factors are often called *response styles*. Thus, response biases can arise from response sets (i.e., something about the testing situation produces biases) and from response styles (i.e., something about a person being tested produces biases). Note, however, that psychologists are not consistent in their use of these terms.

[handwritten margin note: Response Styles = tied to stable characteristics of individuals; concern to be SD]

[handwritten note: RB can arise from Response Sets and styles]

Summary

As this chapter has illustrated, a variety of biases can affect responses to psychological measures, and such biases have the potential to reduce the psychometric quality of those measures and the psychological meaning of their scores. As we have described, these biases can arise from aspects of the tests (e.g., confusing items or ambiguous scale anchors), from the nature of the testing context (e.g., serious consequences are partially contingent on test scores), and from personality characteristics of test takers (e.g., a stable tendency toward self-deception, acquiescence, or minimal self-disclosure).

Behavioral scientists are well aware of these biases and their consequences for applied decisions and for research conclusions that are based on psychological measurement. To cope with the problems that can arise from response biases, psychologists have developed many strategies for minimizing their existence, for minimizing their effects on test scores, or for detecting them and handling responses that appear to be contaminated.

Suggested Readings

This is a solid overview of issues in malingering, with particular relevance to psychopathological testing:

> Berry, D. T. R., Baer, R. A., Rinaldo, J. C., & Wetter, M. W. (2002). Assessment of malingering. In J. N. Butcher (Ed.), *Clinical personality assessment* (2nd ed., pp. 269–302). New York, NY: Oxford University Press.

This is a classic analysis of social desirability and acquiescence, with regard to MMPI responses:

> Block, J. (1965). *The challenge of response sets: Unconfounding meaning, acquiescence, and social desirability in the MMPI.* New York, NY: Appleton-Century-Crofts.

This is another classic article in the history of the psychometric awareness and evaluation of response biases:

> Cronbach, L. J. (1946). Response sets and test validity. *Educational and Psychological Measurement, 6,* 475–494.

This is a recent summary of decades of research and theorizing regarding the nature and assessment of social desirability:

> Paulhus, D. L. (2002). Socially desirable responding: The evolution of a construct. In H. Braun, D. N. Jackson, & D. E. Wiley (Eds.), *The role of constructs in psychological and educational measurement* (pp. 67–88). Hillsdale, NJ: Lawrence Erlbaum.

This is an analysis of a method for assessing extremity bias:

Greenleaf, E. A. (1992). Measuring extreme response style. *Public Opinion Quarterly, 56,* 328–351.

This is an empirical examination of a theory of the basis of acquiescence bias:

Knowles, E. S., & Condon, C. A. (1999). Why people say "yes": A dual-process theory of acquiescence. *Journal of Personality and Social Psychology, 77,* 379–386.

This is an accessible discussion of the processes that respondents go through when taking self-report tests, and it addresses the way test formats can affect these processes:

Schwarz, N. (1999). Self-reports: How the questions shape the answers. *American Psychologist, 54,* 93–105.

CHAPTER 11

Test Bias

As we have seen, psychological tests can be well conceived and well constructed, but none are perfect. The reliability of test scores can be compromised by measurement error, and the validity of test score interpretations can be compromised by response biases that systematically obscure the psychological differences among respondents.

In this chapter, we will examine the possibility that the validity of test score interpretations can be compromised further by test biases that systematically obscure the differences (or lack thereof) among *groups* of respondents. Psychological tests are often used to make important decisions that affect the lives of real people: Which colleges (if any) will decide to accept you? In which class will your child be enrolled? Will an employer decide to hire you? To the degree that such decisions are based on tests that are biased in favor of, or against, specific groups of people, such biases have extremely important personal and societal implications.

Seen in groups of respondents

Suppose you are interested in knowing whether gender differences exist in mathematical ability. You give a reasonably reliable mathematics test to a representative group of males and females, and you find that, on average, males have higher math scores than females. As a researcher, you would be tempted to interpret your test scores in terms of the psychological construct that they are intended to reflect—that males tend to have greater mathematical ability than females. However, it is possible that the participants' test scores should not be interpreted as reflecting purely their mathematical ability. That is, it is possible that the test is biased in some way. For example, *if* the males' test scores overestimated their true mathematical ability and the females' test scores underestimated their true ability, then the test is biased. In this case, the difference between the test scores for males and females might be due to test score bias, not due to a difference in their true mathematical abilities.

Test biases over estimates or under estimates

In this chapter, we discuss two important forms of test bias, and we discuss the methods that are used to detect those biases. Roughly speaking, the two types of test bias reflect *biases in the meaning of a test* and *biases in the use of a test*. Construct

meaning of test → Bias in use of a test

301

1)
Construct Bias:
test has diff meanings
for 2 groups in
terms of the construct
being measured
~ Biases in meaning of
test ~

2) Predictive Bias:
Tests use has diff.
implications for 2
groups
~ Biases in use of test~
• Relationship between
scores on 2 diff tests
• predictor test + criterion
measure

independent

How to identify:
1) internal methods
to identify construct bias
2) external methods
to identify predictive
bias

Existence of differences
in groups does not
always mean the
test scores are biased.

bias (also known as measurement bias or internal bias) occurs when a test has different meanings for two groups, in terms of the precise construct that the test is intended to measure. Construct bias concerns the relationship of observed scores to true scores on a psychological test. If this relationship is systematically different for different groups, then we might conclude that the test is biased. Construct bias can lead to situations in which two groups have the same average true score but different averages on observed scores on a test of the construct.

The second type of bias is predictive bias, which occurs when a test's use has different implications for two groups. Predictive bias (also known as differential validity or external bias) has to do with the relationship between scores on two different tests. One of these tests (the predictor test) is thought to provide values that can be used to predict scores on the other test (the outcome test or criterion measure). For example, college admissions officers might use SAT scores to predict freshman college GPAs. SAT would be the predictor test, and GPAs would be the outcome measure. In this context, test bias concerns the extent to which the link between predictor test *true* scores and outcome test observed scores differs for the two groups. If the SAT is more strongly predictive of GPA for one group than for another, then the SAT suffers from predictive bias, in terms of its use as a predictor of GPA.

The two types of bias—construct and predictive—are independent. Indeed, a test might have no construct bias but might suffer from predictive bias, or vice versa. For example, the SAT might accurately reflect true "academic aptitude" differences among groups of people (and thus have no construct bias), but academic aptitude might not be associated with freshman GPA equally for two groups of people (and thus predictive bias would exist).

In this chapter, we will discuss several ways to operationally define and identify test score bias. At least two categories of procedures can be used to identify test score bias: (1) internal methods to identify construct bias and (2) external methods to identify predictive bias. We emphasize the operational nature of this task to remind you that test score bias in both of its forms is a theoretical concept, in part because both types of bias depend on the theoretical notion of a true score. There is no single way to detect test score bias any more than there is a single way to calculate directly psychometric test score properties such as reliability or validity. There are, however, various generally accepted ways to estimate the degree to which test bias exists.

An overarching issue in the definition and detection of test bias is that the existence of a group difference in test scores *does not* necessarily mean that the test scores are biased. Suppose you find that females have higher scores than males on a test of optimism. This difference is *not* prima facie evidence that the test is biased (Jensen, 1980, 1998; Thorndike, 1971). Indeed, the participants' test scores might in fact be good estimates of their true levels of optimism. In such a case, the test is not biased, and the group difference in the test scores reflects a real difference in average optimism. Consider doing a study in which you weigh representative groups of males and females. You would doubtless find that the average weight of females is lower than the average weight of males. You would not take this difference to mean that the scale you used to measure weight produced scores that were biased.

Why Worry About Test Score Bias?

It is likely that everyone reading this book has taken a psychological test of some kind. Virtually all children schooled in the United States or other industrialized countries are exposed on a regular basis to academic achievement tests. In the United States, most students who plan to attend an institution of higher education have taken the SAT or American College Testing (ACT) test. Most graduate schools in the United States require student applicants to take the Graduate Record Exam (GRE). Applicants for most federal government jobs are required to take a civil service examination, and corporations regularly screen job applicants and sometimes evaluate employees by using psychological tests.

Scores on these and other types of psychological tests are often used to make important decisions about people. In educational settings, intelligence tests scores are used to place children in special programs. Intelligence test scores are used by law courts to make decisions about who can and who cannot be sentenced to death following a murder conviction. Educational institutions use scores on standardized tests to make admission decisions. Corporations and governments often make job decisions about people based, at least in part, on test scores. In the United States, most public school teachers have to take and pass standardized tests to become certified school teachers. The use of psychological tests in our society is pervasive, and scores on these tests can have an important impact on people's lives and on our public and private institutions.

Because testing is a pervasive feature of our society and because test scores have important consequences for people, we would like to develop tests that produce scores that allow us to differentiate among people based on real psychological differences and not on group membership. For example, if we have a test of optimism, then we would like to be sure that scores are determined only by levels of optimism and not contaminated by some other extraneous factor, such as the biological sex of the person taking the test. In other words, we want unbiased tests.

Our desire for unbiased test scores is rooted in our belief that we should not discriminate for or against a person because of his or her biological sex, ethnicity, race, religious preference, or age. In some cases, the list of groups that should be protected from test score bias has been expanded to include factors such as sexual preference, pregnancy, marital status, linguistic background, and various disabilities. In each of these cases, we should be confident that any observed score differences on psychological tests are a function of true score differences. It is especially important to be able to show that test scores are not biased in those instances in which average observed scores on some type of psychological test differ between groups.

Detecting Construct Bias: Internal Evaluation of a Test

Construct bias is related to the meaning of test scores. If a test suffers from construct bias, then the scores on a test might have different meanings for different groups of people. And if that is true, then it does not make psychological sense to compare test scores across those two groups. Given that the primary goal of test-ing is to detect psychological variability—usually in terms of differences between people—an inability to compare people from different groups is a serious problem. If test users ignore this problem, then any decisions, interpretations, predictions, or conclusions drawn from such comparisons are potentially flawed and psychologi-cally unfounded.

Imagine that we obtain evidence suggesting that the scores on our mechanical aptitude test suffered from construct bias related to biological sex. Such a finding should make us consider the possibility that test scores reflect different psychologi-cal attributes in the two groups. For example, the males' responses to the test might be determined primarily by a single construct—mechanical aptitude—but the females' responses might be determined by two constructs—mechanical aptitude and stereotype threat (the tendency to behave in ways that confirm stereotypes about one's group) (Spencer, Steele, & Quinn, 1999). Thus, the mechanical aptitude test does not measure the same psychological attributes for the two sexes, and it would be inappropriate to compare a male's test score with a female's test score and conclude that the male has greater mechanical aptitude. For example, it would be inappropriate for us to use the test as the basis for hiring a particular male rather than a particular female.

Construct bias is often evaluated by examining responses to individual items on a test. An item on a test is biased (a) if people belonging to different groups responded in different ways to the item *and* (b) if it could be shown that these differing responses were not related to group differences associated with the psy-chological attribute measured by the test. For example, suppose you had a 100-item mechanical aptitude test. If you selected one item from the test and found that males' responses were similar to females' responses, then the item would not appear to be biased (assuming that the males and females had the same level of mechanical aptitude). On the other hand, if males and females with the *same level of aptitude* responded in different ways to the item, then you would suspect some type of bias in the item. Again, note that bias exists only if both facts are true—there are group differences in the responses to an item *and* those differences are not due to group differences in the primary construct of interest. The fact that two groups have dif-ferent responses to an item is, by itself, not evidence of bias.

As we have discussed, most psychological tests are composite tests—they contain multiple items or questions. For such composite tests, the overall test score bias is a function of the bias associated with each of the items or questions in the test. If we examine all of the items on a test and find none that seem to be biased, then we would assume that the total test score is unbiased. However, if one or more items do seem to be biased, then we would suspect that the total test score might also be biased.

Remember that test bias concerns the relationship between group differences in true scores and group differences in observed test scores. In the case of construct bias, a test item would be biased if responses to the item for people who belong to one group reflect their true scores on the relevant psychological attribute but responses to the item for people who belong to another group do not (we are assuming some minimum degree of reliability for the test of interest). Of course, we can never know a person's true score with respect to any attribute. Therefore, the procedures that we are going to discuss are *estimates* of the existence and degree of construct bias.

We will describe several specific procedures that can be used to estimate the existence and degree of construct bias. These procedures focus on the internal structure of the test, as described in the discussion of validity in Chapter 8. In that chapter, we defined internal structure as "the way the parts of a test are related to each other." Most simply, internal structure refers to the pattern of correlations among items and/or the correlations between each item and the total test score. To evaluate the presence of construct bias, we examine the internal structure of a test separately for two groups. If the two groups exhibit the same internal structure to their test responses, then we conclude that the test is unlikely to suffer from construct bias. However, if the two groups exhibit different internal structures to their test responses, then we conclude that the test is likely to suffer from construct bias.

There are at least four methods for detecting construct bias. Most of these are quite manageable within popular statistical software packages such as SPSS or SAS. However, one of them—differential item functioning—is currently possible only with specialized software such as BILOG or PARSCALE.

Item Discrimination Index

One method of detecting construct bias is by computing item discrimination indexes separately for two groups. As described in Chapter 7, an item's discrimination index reflects the degree to which the item is related to the total test score (i.e., that people who answer an item correctly tend to do better on the test as a whole than people who answer that item incorrectly). By implication, a strong discrimination indicates that an item is highly similar conceptually to most of the other items on a test. In this way, item discrimination indexes reflect, in part, the structure of associations among test items.

Historically, the item discrimination index was developed in association with classical test theory. The index is an important measure of the extent to which responses to test items can be used to differentiate among people on the basis of the amount of their knowledge of some topic or on the amount of some other type of psychological attribute.

Again, imagine that we give a mechanical aptitude test to a group of people. Now, consider two groups of people—a group that has high scores on the test and a group that has low scores. Also consider the probability that one of the test items will be answered correctly by someone from each group (i.e., the proportion of people in each group who will answer the items correctly). That is, what proportion of people in the high-scoring group will answer the item correctly, and what proportion of people in the low-scoring group will answer the item correctly? Your answer should depend on the degree to which the item is in fact related to the construct being assessed by the test. That is, if the item does indeed reflect mechanical aptitude, then you'd expect a relatively high proportion of "high scorers" to answer it correctly and a relatively low proportion of "low scorers" to answer it correctly. Indeed, the "high scorers" presumably have a lot of mechanical aptitude, so they should be more likely to answer a specific question correctly than the "low scorers," who presumably have less aptitude—as long as the question is indeed clearly related to mechanical aptitude. Obviously, if the item is not clearly related to mechanical aptitude, then we would not expect to find a difference between the groups. For example, we would note the high mechanical aptitude test scorers to be more likely to answer a psychometrics question correctly than the low mechanical aptitude scorers.

The proportion of people answering a question correctly can be used to compute an item discrimination index. If people who have high mechanical aptitude have a high probability of answering a particular aptitude question correctly while people who have low mechanical aptitude have a low probability of answering the question correctly, then the question would have a high item discrimination index value (e.g., .90). This would indicate that the item strongly discriminates (i.e., differentiates) among people with varying levels of aptitude. This would, in turn, suggest that it is a good reflection of the construct being assessed by the test. In contrast, if people who have low aptitude answered the question correctly nearly as often as people who have high aptitude, then the question would have a low item discrimination index value (e.g., .10). In such a situation, the item does not clearly discriminate among people with varying levels of the construct being measured. Obviously, such an item is not a good reflection of the construct.

The item discrimination index can be used to estimate construct bias. Specifically, we would select an item, compute its discrimination index separately for two groups of people, and then compare the groups' indexes. For example, we might wish to know whether an item on our mechanical aptitude test is biased in terms of gender. Thus, we compute an item discrimination index for males and for females. That is, we would determine the proportion of high-scoring males who answer the item correctly and the proportion of low-scoring males who answer the item correctly, and then we would use these proportions to determine the discrimination index for males. We would do the same for females, and then we would compare the two discrimination indexes. If the two discrimination index values are approximately equal, then this would indicate that the item reflects the construct in the same way for both genders. Thus, we would likely conclude that the item is probably not biased. However, if the two discrimination index values are not approximately equal, then this would suggest that the item does not reflect the construct equally well for both genders (or that the item reflects somewhat different constructs in males and in females). Such results would lead us to conclude that the item is probably biased in some way. That is, we would conclude that the item seems to belong on the test for one group but not for the other group. If this were the case but we kept the item on the test, then the test would be somewhat different for the two groups. Thus, the test scores would not be exactly comparable between the two groups, which creates a problem when our goal is to interpret test scores with regard to a particular psychological construct. To solve this problem, we would revise the item or remove it from the test. This analysis would be conducted for each of the items on the test.

[handwritten margin note: Revise or remove item]

An important feature of the item discrimination index as a measure of construct bias is that it is independent of the number of people in the groups that are being compared who answer an item correctly. For example, we might find that one of our mechanical aptitude items was answered correctly by only 40% of the males but by 60% of the females. Even so, the item discrimination index for the question could be the same for both groups. In this case, we would assume that the item is functioning as a measure of mechanical aptitude in the same way for both groups but that females know more about the material than males (i.e., more of them answered the item correctly).

[handwritten margin note: independent of # of people in group who answer correctly]

Factor Analysis *[handwritten: — examines construct bias]*

A second method for examining construct bias is by conducting a factor analysis of items separately for two or more groups of people. As we have discussed in previous chapters, factor analysis is an important tool for evaluating the internal structure of a test. Factor analysis is a statistical procedure for partitioning the variance or covariance among test items into clusters or "factors" that in some sense "hang together" (see Chapters 4 and 12 for detailed descriptions of exploratory factor analysis and confirmatory factor analysis, respectively).

Recall from Chapter 4 that when items are highly correlated with each other, they are believed to reflect a factor. For a multidimensional test, responses to some items on a test are more highly positively correlated with each other than they are to responses to other items on the test. In contrast, if all of the items on a test have similar correlations with each other (i.e., there is no evidence of more than one cluster of items), then we say that the test is unidimensional or that all of the test score variance, other than error variance, is accounted for by a single factor.

Factor analysis can be used to evaluate the internal structure of a test separately for two groups of people. For example, we might find that among males, the mechanical aptitude test has a clear unidimensional structure—all of the items seem to be highly correlated with each other, suggesting that test scores reflect one and only one construct. To evaluate the potential presence of construct bias, we would examine the factor structure for females' responses to the test items as well. If we found a single factor among females' responses, then we might conclude that the aptitude test has the same internal structure for males and females. Consequently, we might conclude that the test does not suffer from construct bias. However, if we conducted a factor analysis of females' responses and found two factors or more, then we might conclude that the test has a different internal structure for males and for females. We might then conclude that the test does indeed suffer from construct bias. That is, we would conclude that the total test scores reflect different psychological constructs for males and for females.

[handwritten margin note: evaluates internal structure of a test]

Differential Item Functioning Analyses

[margin note: evaluate - construct bias]

[margin note: IRT]

Perhaps the best way to evaluate construct bias is a procedure called differential item functioning analysis. Differential item functioning analysis is a feature of a psychometric approach called item response theory (IRT; a detailed discussion of IRT will be presented in Chapter 14). An important aspect of IRT is the assumption that it is possible to estimate respondents' trait levels directly from test data. The trait levels are, in essence, participants' true scores for the psychological attribute that is being measured. If we assume that we can estimate the trait levels for all the people in two groups and if we have their responses to a test item, then we can see if the trait levels and the item responses match up in the same way for both groups. If they do not, then it is possible that the item is biased.

[margin note: estimate respondents' trait levels based on test data]

[margin note: trait levels to item responses match up in same way for both groups]

IRT is based on the idea that there is a mathematical function relating a participant's trait level to the probability that he or she will answer a test question in a certain way (e.g., correctly). For example, you might find that an individual with a trait level that is 1 standard deviation above the mean has a .80 probability of answering a particular item correctly, and you might find that an individual with a trait level that is 1 standard deviation below the mean has only a .20 probability of answering the item correctly.

If you have a group of people take a test and you know their respective trait levels (based on their test scores), then you can use specialized statistical software to generate an item characteristic curve (ICC) illustrating this function for each item. Furthermore, if you have two groups of people, then you can draw ICCs separately for each group.

[margin note: Similar ICC's for groups]

To evaluate the presence of construct bias, you would compare the ICCs of the two groups. If an item is not biased, then the two groups' ICCs should be very similar. That is, the probability that two people will answer an item correctly should be the same if the two people have the same trait level. However, if the item is biased, then the two groups' ICCs will be dissimilar. That is, the probability that two people (e.g., a male and a female) will answer an item correctly might be different even if the two people have the same trait level. Such a situation would clearly reflect the presence of construct bias.

For example, you could use IRT to evaluate whether an item on a mechanical aptitude test was biased with respect to biological sex. Using concepts that are more fully described in Chapter 14, you could compute mechanical aptitude knowledge scores for each person in a study (these represent their trait levels), and you could compute the probability that the item is answered correctly for each person. You use this information to draw an ICC (see Figure 11.1). Now, you sort the people in your study into two groups (i.e., a group of males and a group of females) and draw ICC curves separately for each group. If the curves overlap, then you would probably conclude that the item is not biased. Suppose, however, you obtained the results illustrated in Figures 11.2 or 11.3. Results such as these would lead you to suspect item bias, and they illustrate two types of bias.

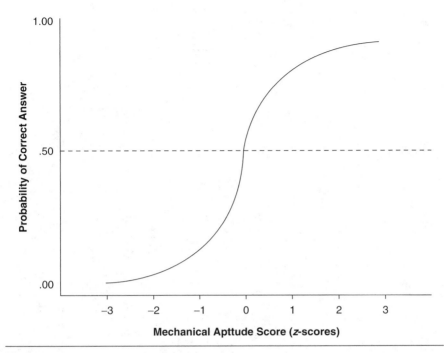

Figure 11.1   ICC Curve for a Test Item

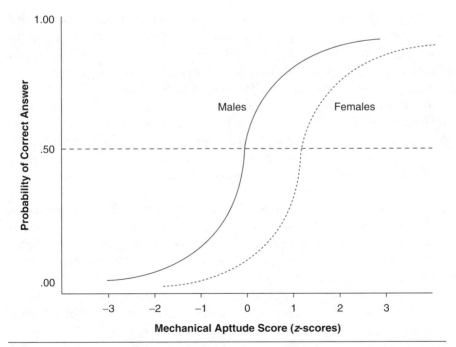

Figure 11.2   ICC Curves for Males and Females Illustrating Possible Uniform Bias

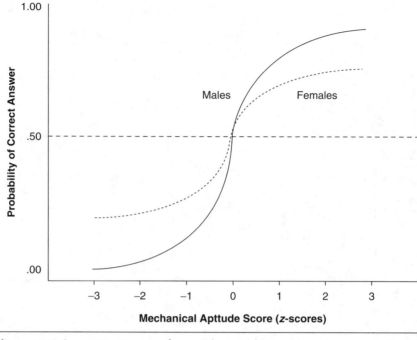

Figure 11.3   ICC Curves for Males and Females Illustrating Possible Nonuniform Bias

Figure 11.2 is an example of *uniform bias*. In this example, it appears that females, with the same mechanical knowledge as males, find the item more difficult to answer than the males. For example, imagine that Fiona and Mark have the same true level of mechanical aptitude—say they are 1 standard deviation above the mean (+1 z score in the figure). If the test is unbiased, then they should have the same probability of answering the item correctly (i.e., the item should be equally difficult or easy for both of them). However, if our analyses suggested something like Figure 11.2, then this would imply that the item is, for some reason, easier for Mark than it is for Fiona. Looking at Figure 11.2, we see that for a male whose mechanical aptitude is 1 standard deviation above the mean, he has approximately an 80% chance of answering the item correctly (i.e., a probability of about .80). However, we also see that for a female who is 1 standard deviation above the mean, she has only about a 25% chance of answering correctly. This should be an obvious source of concern—if two people have the same level of ability but are not equally likely to answer the item correctly, then there is something wrong with the item. There is something producing a bias.

Figure 11.3 illustrates *nonuniform bias*, a situation in which the ICCs differ in shape as well as location. In this case, at some levels of aptitude, females find the item easier than males who have the aptitude; however, at other levels of aptitude, females find the item more difficult than males who have the same aptitude. That is, the exact consequence of bias differs, depending on one's level of aptitude.

In both cases, it appears that the item is measuring different traits for males and females. The ICC approach is a visual method for detecting construct bias, but there are IRT methods that are even more precise ways of evaluating the presence of construct bias (e.g., L. L. Smith & Reise, 1998).

Although IRT's differential item functioning analysis is a strong method for identifying construct bias, it has a downside. IRT analyses are quite complex in a variety of ways—there are issues regarding the appropriate model to use, the procedures for determining whether parameter differences between groups are really different or simply due to measurement error, the need for very large sample sizes, the need for item samples and samples of people that are heterogeneous enough to represent the complete range of traits the test is designed to measure, and the need for specialized statistical software to conduct the analyses. These complexities are such that IRT is still only emerging as a widely appreciated and understood method of detecting construct bias. Again, Chapter 14 provides much deeper discussion of the basics of IRT.

Rank Order

If test items can be ranked in order of difficulty, then there is another quick and computationally easy way to estimate construct bias. Using our 100-item aptitude test as an example, some test questions will probably be easier to answer than others, and they can be ranked in order of difficulty. The rankings can be done separately for different groups (e.g., males and females).

If the items' difficulty ranks differ across groups, then we would suspect that test score construct bias exists. We would suspect this because each item does not appear to be a measure of the same thing for both groups. You can use the ranks to compute Spearman's rank-order correlation coefficient (rho, interpreted in the same way as r_{XY}) to index rank-order consistency across groups. If rho is low (e.g., < .90), we might suspect construct bias. If you found evidence of construct bias, you would probably want to follow up on the finding with additional analyses to identify the particular source of the low correlation coefficient (see Jensen, 1980).

Notice that the correlation between the ranks can be high even if the proportion of correct responses to each item differs across groups. Using our aptitude test as an example, males might be less likely than females to give correct answers to the test questions, but the rank ordering of questions according to difficulty might be the same across groups. Again, as with the item discrimination index, group differences in correct responding are not by themselves an indication of test score bias.

Summary

In summary, construct bias occurs when test scores represent different constructs for different groups or when they represent the same construct to differing degrees in different groups. There are several methods for estimating whether construct bias exists and for identifying specific items that might be most problematic. Using this information, test developers can revise the test to reduce the bias. For example, they might drop, revise, or replace the items that seem most biased. We turn next to a different type of bias that can plague psychological testing—predictive bias.

Detecting Predictive Bias: External Evaluation of a Test

As mentioned earlier, predictive bias concerns the degree to which a test's scores are equally predictive of an outcome for two groups. Ideally, if a test is going to be used to make decisions or predictions about people, then it does so equally well for all groups of people. If this is not the case—that is, if a test seems to be more predictive for some groups than for others—then the test suffers from predictive bias.

For example, scores on the SAT are thought to measure academic achievement. On the assumption that academic achievement measured during secondary school years might be related to academic achievement during the freshman year in college (e.g., as measured by freshman GPA), institutions of higher education often use SAT scores to make admission decisions. The idea is that it is possible to predict, at least with some degree of accuracy, student freshman-year academic performance based on SAT scores. If the SAT predicts freshman GPA equally well for various groups of students, then we would have no concerns about predictive bias. However, if the SAT predicts GPA better from some groups of students than for others, then we might suspect that the SAT suffers from predictive test score bias.

Predictive bias is examined by obtaining scores on two variables or measures. Analyses are then conducted to examine the degree to which scores on the main test of interest (the predictor test) can be used to predict people's scores on another psychological measure (the outcome measure) that is thought to be related to scores on the main test of interest.

Detection of predictive bias begins with the assumption that "one size fits all"— that the test is equally predictive for all groups. As we will illustrate, analyses are conducted to evaluate this assumption formally. If those analyses confirm that the test is equally predictive for both groups, then we conclude that the test probably does not suffer from predictive bias (at least with regard to the specific outcome in question and the specific groups in question). However, if those analyses indicate that one size does not fit all—that predictor test scores are not equally predictive for both groups—then we conclude that the test might suffer from predictive bias.

Imagine that you are a training program selection officer working for a corporation that spends large sums of money training employees to develop the mechanical skills needed by the corporation to run its operations. Your job is to select the most promising candidates for this training program. Because of the cost of the program, it is essential that you select only those people who are most likely to perform well in the training program. Indeed, your job depends on how well you make these selections. In an attempt to improve your selection success rate, you develop a mechanical aptitude test that you administer to all trainee candidates. Furthermore, you assume that scores on the test are going to be related to some outcome measure of posttraining performance. For example, following training, each trainee might be rated by a supervisor in terms of the trainee's level of mechanical competency. Finally, you suspect that there is a positive linear relationship between the pretraining aptitude test scores and the posttraining supervisor ratings of competence. That is, candidates with high aptitude scores (i.e., predictor scores) should have better ratings (i.e., outcome scores) than candidates with lower aptitude scores.

In your development and evaluation of the aptitude test, you might be concerned about predictive test bias. Formally speaking, predictive bias has to do with the use of test scores to predict a relevant outcome (e.g., behavior, competency, or performance) in situations other than the testing situation in which the predictor test was administered. Thus, if you had reason to believe that the aptitude test was strongly predictive of supervisor ratings for males but not for females, then you would suspect that the test was biased.

To evaluate the efficacy of your new aptitude test and to evaluate any potential predictive bias, you will need at least three pieces of information from participants in the training program. First, you need to get test scores by testing all trainees before they enter the program. Second, you obtain their scores on the outcome measure (i.e., supervisor ratings) at the end of the training program. Third, you need to know each participant's gender.

Using this information, you will then need to examine two issues: (1) Does your test actually help you predict the outcome of training? (2) Does your test predict the outcome of training equally well for various groups of trainees? The two issues are often addressed by using correlations or a statistical procedure called regression, with which you use the pretraining mechanical aptitude test scores to calculate *predicted* posttraining supervisor rating scores.

Basics of Regression Analysis

Regression analysis is based on the assumption that there is a linear relationship between test scores and outcome scores. If there is such a relationship, then the formula for a straight line can be used to predict outcome scores from aptitude scores:

$$\hat{Y} = a + b(X),$$

where $\hat{Y}$ is the predicted training outcome score for an individual training candidate, a is the intercept (i.e., the predicted value of a person's outcome score if that person had an aptitude test score of 0), b is the regression coefficient or slope (i.e., a number that tells you how much of a difference you would expect to see in $\hat{Y}$ for a 1-point difference in aptitude test scores), and X is an individual's aptitude test score. Many popular statistical software packages can be used to conduct the regression analysis (e.g., SPSS, SAS), which produces values of a and b.

Once you have obtained the values for the intercept and slope of the regression equation, you can evaluate the predictive ability of the test. For example, you can take any individual's score on the aptitude test (X), plug it into the regression equation, and calculate a predicted score on the supervisor ratings ($\hat{Y}$) for that individual.

To illustrate this process, we will use the data in Table 11.1. In this table, we have aptitude scores for four trainees, along with each trainee's outcome score (note that an analysis of this kind would involve many more than four trainees). Based on a regression analysis conducted using SPSS, we obtain estimates of the intercept and slope. As shown in the "B" column of Figure 11.4 (under the "Unstandardized Coefficients" heading), the intercept (a, labeled "Constant" in Figure 11.4) is 56.03, and the slope (b, labeled "AptTest" in Figure 11.4) is .58. These results tell us that a trainee with an aptitude score of 0 is predicted to obtain an outcome rating of 56.03 and that a 1-point difference in aptitude scores is associated with a .58 difference in outcome scores.

As mentioned earlier, these values can be used to obtain predicted scores for all trainees by plugging their aptitude scores into the following regression equation:

$$\hat{Y} = 56.03 + .58(X)$$

Predicted supervisor rating = 56.03 + .58(Aptitude score).

For example, a trainee with an aptitude score of 69 is predicted to earn a supervisor rating of 96.05:

$$\hat{Y} = 56.03 + .58(69),$$
$$\hat{Y} = 96.05.$$

Similarly, a trainee with an aptitude score of 70 is predicted to earn a supervisor rating of 96.63:

$$\hat{Y} = 56.03 + .58(70),$$
$$\hat{Y} = 96.63.$$

Note that the difference between these two predictions is .58 (96.63 − 96.05 = .58), which reflects the slope in the regression equation. That is, a 1-point difference in aptitude test score (70 − 69 = 1) is associated with a .58 difference in outcome scores.

Table 11.1   Data Illustrating Regression Analysis

Trainee	Aptitude Test Score	Supervisor Rating	Predicted Supervisor Rating
1	32	75	74.59
2	40	80	79.23
3	57	81	89.09
4	60	98	90.83

Coefficients[a]

Model	Unstandardized Coefficients		Standardized Coefficients		
	B	Std. Error	Beta	t	Sig.
1 (constant)	56.034	16.018		3.498	.073
AptTest	.581	.329	.781	1.766	.219

[a] Dependent Variable: Suprating

Figure 11.4   Results of Regression Analysis of the Data in Table 11.1

If we calculate predicted rating scores for a wide range of aptitude test scores, then we can generate a regression line or a "line of best fit." Each point on a regression line is associated with the most likely (predicted) Y value for each possible X value. The line is used to illustrate the association between predictor test scores and outcome scores. In Table 11.1, we have computed predicted scores ($\hat{Y}$) for each trainee. In Figure 11.5, we have plotted each of our four candidates' observed outcome score against his or her observed predictor test score, and we have drawn a regression line that reflects each candidate's predicted outcome score.

One Size Fits All: The Common Regression Equation

one equation = applicable to all = no biases

The estimation of predictive bias usually begins by establishing what would happen if no bias exists. If a test is not biased, then one regression equation should be equally applicable to different groups of people. The assumption that different groups share a common regression equation is based on the idea that "one size fits all"—regardless of biological sex, ethnicity, culture, or whichever group difference is being considered, a single regression equation adequately reflects the predictive ability of the test in question.

Imagine that you give your aptitude test to a large number of trainee candidates (e.g., 100). Let's say that there are an equal number of male and female candidates

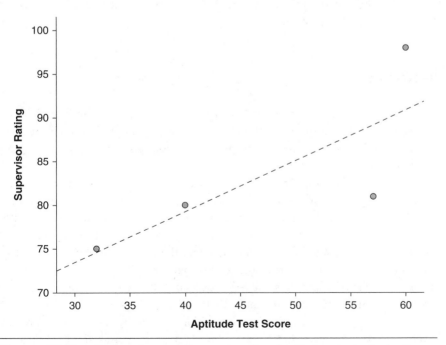

Figure 11.5   Scatterplot and Regression Line for Trainee's Aptitude Scores and Supervisor Ratings

and you want to make sure that your aptitude test is not biased with respect to biological sex.

To begin your examination of this issue, you could compute the regression equation based on the data from the entire sample, regardless of sex. Imagine that you found that the intercept from this regression equation is $a = 56.03$ and that the slope is $b = .58$. These values represent the common regression equation, and they will be called the common intercept and the common slope. Again, if your aptitude test is unbiased in terms of gender, then the common regression equation (calculated from males and females together) should be equally applicable to males and females, when each gender is examined separately.

To evaluate the presence of predictive bias, additional regression analyses must be conducted. To determine whether the common regression equation is indeed equally applicable to males and females, we must calculate one regression equation for males and one for females. We must then compare these group-level regression equations with the common regression equation. If the group-level values do not match the common regression equation, then you might suspect that your aptitude test scores are biased.

In practice, a variety of sophisticated statistical analyses can be conducted on these values to precisely estimate the presence of predictive test bias, but our discussion will focus on the more conceptual level. To elucidate the meaning of various patterns of results, we first focus on the meaning of biased intercepts, then on the meaning of biased slopes. However, in practice, it may be more likely that groups would differ on both of these elements of prediction rather than being exactly equal on one but differing on the other. Thus, we will also illustrate the effect of bias in terms of intercepts and slopes.

Intercept Bias   -always 7 pts higher at all levels

Suppose that group-level regression analyses reveal that males and females have slopes that are similar to the common regression equation but that their intercept values differ from the common intercept. In this case, you would suspect that your test suffers from intercept bias.

For example, imagine that in your evaluation of scores from our mechanical aptitude test, you conduct regression analyses separately for the 50 males and the 50 females. You find that, for both groups, the slope is $b = .58$, which is equal to the common slope. However, you find that the intercept for males is $a = 58.03$, and the intercept for females is $a = 54.03$. Note that these group-level intercept values differ from the common intercept, indicating that "one size does *not* fit all," at least in terms of the intercept. Thus, the test appears to suffer from intercept bias.

What exactly is intercept bias, and what are its implications? The fact that the males' intercept is higher than the females' intercept indicates that males at any given level of aptitude will tend to receive higher supervisor ratings (outcome scores) than females at the same level of aptitude. To illustrate this, let us compute the predicted outcome score for a male with an aptitude score of 70 and for a female with an aptitude score of 70:

Predicted outcome score for male = 58.03 + .58(70),

Predicted outcome score for male = 98.63;

Predicted outcome score for female = 54.03 + .58(70),

Predicted outcome score for female = 94.63.

These computations show that for a male and a female who have the same level of aptitude, the male is predicted to obtain a supervisor rating that is 4 points higher than the female's.

If we assume that the outcome variable (i.e., supervisor ratings) is itself unbiased, then this intercept bias indicates that the aptitude test does not "work" the same for males and for females. As we saw earlier, the common regression equation resulted in a predicted supervisor rating of 96.63 for a trainee who had an aptitude score of 70. Comparing this result with the results of our group-level predictions, the common regression equation appears to underestimate the prediction for males and to overestimate the prediction for females. That is, the common regression equation would lead us to predict that a male would score 2 points lower on the supervisor ratings (as compared with the "male" regression line) and a female would score 2 points higher (as compared with the "female" regression line). Thus, one size does *not* fit all, and the test appears to be predictively biased.

If a test suffers only from intercept bias, then the size of the group discrepancy is constant across all aptitude scores. For example, our regression analyses show a 4-point discrepancy for a male and a female who both had an aptitude score of 70, and if the aptitude test suffers only from intercept bias, then the sex difference will be 4 points *at every level of aptitude*. This is illustrated in Figure 11.6, which presents a common regression line (dashed) and two group-level regression lines. As this figure illustrates, the lines are parallel, suggesting that a male trainee of a given aptitude level will obtain a predicted rating that is always 4 points higher than a female who has the same level of aptitude.

at every level of aptitude

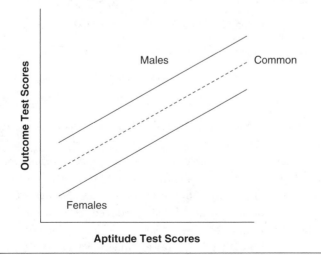

Figure 11.6   Regression Lines for Males and Females in Relation to the Common Regression Line Illustrating Possible Intercept Bias

Slope Bias

[handwritten: both higher @ one level 1st @ another]

A second way in which a test can be predictively biased is through slope bias. It is possible that group-level regression analyses reveal that males and females have intercept values that are similar to the common regression equation but that their slope values differ from the common slope. This would indicate that (the connection between predictor scores and outcome scores differs between the two groups.)

For example, imagine that your analyses reveal that, for both groups, the intercept is $a = 56.03$, which is equal to the common intercept. However, you find that the slope for males is $b = .53$, while the slope for females is $b = .63$. Note that these group-level slope values differ from the common slope (i.e., .58), indicating that one size does *not* fit all, in terms of the connection between predictor test scores and outcome scores.

Slope bias has important implications for the degree of discrepancy between the groups' predicted outcome scores. The fact that the two groups have different slopes indicates that the amount of bias is not constant across aptitude levels. To illustrate this, let us compute the predicted outcome score for a male with an aptitude score of 70 and for a female with an aptitude score of 70:

[handwritten left margin: bias is not constant across aptitude levels]

$$\text{Predicted male outcome score} = 56.03 + .53(70),$$

$$\text{Predicted male outcome score} = 93.13;$$

$$\text{Predicted female outcome score} = 56.03 + .63(70),$$

$$\text{Predicted female outcome score} = 100.13.$$

As summarized in Table 11.2, this shows that for a male and a female with an aptitude of 70, the female will be predicted to have an outcome score that is 7.0 points higher than the male. Now, let us compute the predicted outcome score for a male and a female who have aptitude scores of 60:

[handwritten left margin: degree to which the predicted outcome score differs for males + female w/ same level of predictive scores]

$$\text{Predicted male outcome score} = 56.03 + .53(60),$$

$$\text{Predicted male outcome score} = 87.83;$$

$$\text{Predicted female outcome score} = 56.03 + .63(60),$$

$$\text{Predicted female outcome score} = 93.83.$$

In this case, the female will be predicted to have an outcome score that is only 6.0 points higher than the male's.

Thus, the bias (i.e., the degree to which the predicted outcome score differs for males and females who have the same level of aptitude) is relatively small for relatively low levels of aptitude, but it is larger for higher levels of aptitude. That is, the discrepancy between male and female predicted scores will tend to increase as scores on the aptitude test increase. This type of "pure" slope bias is illustrated in Figure 11.7, which shows that the regression lines for males and for females gradually move apart.

Table 11.2 Predicted Outcome Scores, Based on Aptitude Scores

Aptitude Test Score	Predicted Outcome Score		Difference in Predicted Outcome Scores
	Male	*Female*	
70	93.13	100.13	Female predicted to score 7 points higher
60	87.83	93.83	Female predicted to score 6 points higher

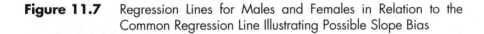

Figure 11.7   Regression Lines for Males and Females in Relation to the Common Regression Line Illustrating Possible Slope Bias

Intercept and Slope Bias

So far, we have illustrated "pure" intercept bias and "pure" slope bias—cases in which either the intercept is biased or the slope is biased, but not both. To summarize, pure intercept bias indicates that there is a discrepancy between groups' predicted scores and that the size of this discrepancy does *not* change as aptitude scores increase or decease in size. In contrast, pure slope bias indicates that the size of this discrepancy does change as aptitude scores increase or decease in size.

It is also possible (perhaps even more so than either form of "pure" bias) for intercept and slope biases to exist simultaneously. In this case, there will be a complex relationship between the size of aptitude scores and the outcome scores for the different groups. For example, we might find that for people who have low levels of aptitude, the predicted outcome scores for males might be higher than the predicted outcome scores for females. But our analyses might also reveal that for people who have *high* levels of aptitude, the predicted outcome scores for males might be lower than the predicted outcome scores for females. Although there are many patterns of discrepancy that might occur, one possible outcome of this type is illustrated in Figure 11.8.

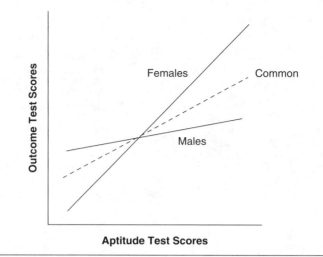

Figure 11.8   Regression Lines for Males and Females in Relation to the Common Regression Line Illustrating Possible Slope and Intercept Bias

Outcome Score Bias

Our discussion of predictive bias has focused on the possibility that the scores on the predictor test are biased. However, it is also possible that the scores on the outcome variable could be biased. For example, it is possible that the supervisor who provides the posttraining ratings of competence is biased in favor of one group; the test we use to measure outcomes, such as our 100-item mechanical competency test, could also be biased. We have been assuming that the outcome measure is not biased, but of course, it could be.

The Effect of Reliability

We should acknowledge that both the regression coefficient and the intercept are sensitive to test score reliability. In our discussion of predictive bias, we have been assuming high predictor test and outcome test score reliabilities (e.g., R_{xx} greater than .90). A drop in test score reliability can have a profound effect on these parameters and thereby, at least potentially, affect predictive bias. These effects are complex and beyond the scope of our discussion, but for interested readers, we recommend Jensen (1980, chap. 9).

Other Statistical Procedures

We also want to point out that there are additional statistical procedures, which we have not mentioned here, that are used to detect test score bias. For example, structural equation modeling is a statistical procedure that, under the right circumstances, can yield data related both to construct bias and to predictive bias. We mentioned the use of regression as a statistical tool to uncover predictive bias. There are complex regression procedures, such as hierarchical regression, that extend the power of regression analyses, allowing researchers to test specific hypotheses about the sources of predictive bias. Structural equation modeling and regression tools such as hierarchical regression are very complex statistical procedures and beyond the scope of this book.

Test Fairness

Finally, we want to mention briefly a controversial issue in *psychological testing*, test fairness. When psychological test scores are used to make decisions that affect the lives of people, it is possible that people who belong to a particular group (e.g., individuals affiliated with specific ethnic or racial minorities) might feel that the scores are being used unfairly to disadvantage those members in that group. For example, suppose an employer uses a psychological test to screen potential employees. Also suppose that, on average, males do better on the test than females and, as a result, males are more likely than females to be hired. Females, for various reasons, might feel that the use of the test is not fair.

It is important to distinguish test fairness from test score bias. As we have seen, test bias is a psychometric concept embedded in theories of test score validity. It is defined within psychometric theories, and it is detectable through specific statistical and research methods that allow researchers to make informed decisions regarding test bias.

Test score bias — science

Test fairness, on the other hand, does *not* refer to a psychometric property of a test. Test fairness has to do with the appropriate use of test scores, and it is a social, philosophical, or perhaps legal term that represents someone's value judgment (Ghiselli et al., 1981; Jensen, 1980; Thorndike, 2005). The old adage that fairness is in the eye of the beholder applies here. We could ask people if they think that the use of a particular test is fair or not, but their answers might have absolutely nothing to do with the psychometric properties of the test. For example, we might have convincing evidence that the scores on a particular test are not biased in the ways that we have described in this chapter, but some people might still believe that the test scores are not being used in a fair manner. Furthermore, *they could be right* because fairness and bias are two different concepts existing in two different realms of knowledge, the realm of science and the social-political realm.

Test fairness — appropriate use of test scores (social, philosophical)

Although it is not a psychometric concept, test fairness is an important issue in psychological testing. Psychological testing has to do with procedures for selecting, administering, and interpreting test scores in an applied setting. Presumably, individuals who give and use psychological tests are familiar with the psychometric properties of those tests. What those individuals who are giving the test do with the test scores might influence someone's judgment concerning the fairness of the test. Furthermore, a test with stellar psychometric properties might be used to make judgments that are not fair. The psychometric properties of tests, including information about potential test score biases, should always be *one* factor that informs the use of tests in applied settings, but people's beliefs about the fairness of the use of test scores might or might not be influenced by those psychometric properties.

Example: Is the SAT Biased in Terms of Race or Socioeconomic Status?

In this section, we provide a real-life example of a psychometric examination of bias in a widely used psychological test. Because the SAT is so widely used as a decision-making tool, this examination focuses on predictive bias rather than construct bias. In addition, the examination is based on regression procedures, though not exactly as we have described them in this chapter.

We present this example for several reasons. First, we want to show concretely how this work might be conducted and presented in a real-life examination of test bias. The "idealized" hypothetical examples and procedures that we've provided lay the foundation for this real-life example, but not all real-life examples follow the exact procedures that we have described. Thus, it might be useful for readers to be able to think more flexibly about the ways you might encounter analyses of test bias. Second, we want to illustrate how difficult and confusing this work can be. The examination that we discuss in this section has been cited in heated debates about the validity and bias of the SAT. Unfortunately, as you shall see, there does indeed seem to be confusion about what these results truly imply. We hope that our discussion stimulates your ability to think carefully and appropriately about the complexities of test bias.

In 2001, the University of California (UC) published an in-depth analysis of the SAT's predictive validity and potential bias (Geiser & Studley, 2001). This report was based on nearly 80,000 students who had entered the eight campuses of the UC system over a 4-year period in the mid- to late 1990s. The report covers many psychometric and practical issues, including the SAT's potential predictive bias. More specifically, it examines potential bias in terms of race/ethnicity and socioeconomic status. We will take these two issues in turn.

Race/Ethnicity

In the UC report, race/ethnicity was examined in terms of five groups: African Americans, Native Americans (referred to as American Indians in the report), Asian Americans, Chicanos/Latinos, and Whites. The report presented average SAT scores for each group, revealing differences that are potentially significant. For example, two of the groups had average SAT scores that were greater than 1,200, and two of the groups had averages less than 1,100. Considering the implications that SAT scores can have for students' admission to college, differences of this size certainly raise legitimate concerns about the nature and use of the SAT. However, recall from our earlier discussion that the existence of group differences in test scores is not, in itself, evidence of test bias. Thus, an in-depth psychometric examination is warranted.

Conducting analyses closely related to the procedures outlined above, the authors used regression to examine potential predictive bias. They computed the predictive validity of the SAT in terms of its ability to predict college freshman GPA. However, rather than presenting regression slopes, as we illustrated above, the researchers presented "variance-explained" values. Like regression slopes or correlations, these values can be used to reflect the degree to which variability in one variable (e.g., GPA) is predictable from variability in another variable (e.g., SAT scores). When expressed in percentages, these values can range from 0 to 100, with higher values reflecting greater predictive power. Thus, you can roughly think of these as "percent predictability"—a 0 means that the SAT is totally unrelated to college GPA, and a 100 means that the SAT can be used to predict GPA perfectly. As described in Chapter 9's discussion of validity coefficients, it is not uncommon to find values below 20% when attempting to predict complex psychological outcomes such a college GPA.

Using this analytic strategy, the researchers presented variance-explained values for each race/ethnicity. That is, for each race/ethnicity, they conducted a regression analysis with GPA as the outcome and SAT scores as the predictor:

$$GPA = a + b(SAT).$$

Each such analysis produced a variance-explained value, as summarized in Table 11.3. As shown in the leftmost numeric column, these values ranged from a low of 8.5% to a high of 12.6% (note that Table 11.3 also includes correlations between SAT scores and GPA for each group, which can be obtained simply by taking the square root of the variance explained values from one-predictor regression equations). These values suggest some differential predictive power—the SAT seems to be more predictive for some races/ethnicities (e.g., Asian Americans) than for others (e.g., American Indians), with some groups coming between those extremes (e.g., African Americans and Whites).

Do the values in Table 11.3 suggest the existence of predictive bias? The answer is not entirely clear.

Table 11.3 Summary of SAT Scores and High School GPA as Predictors of College GPA in Geiser and Studley's (2001) Report of the University of California

| | Predictor | | | |
| | SAT | | HSGPA | |
Race/ Ethnicity	Variance Explained (%)	Correlation	Variance Explained (%)	Correlation
African American	10.0	.32	9.5	.31
American Indian	8.5	.29	8.8	.30
Asian American	12.6	.35	15.9	.40
Chicano/ Latino	10.9	.33	12.0	.35
White	10.1	.32	15.6	.39

NOTE: HSGPA, High School grade point average.

On one hand, there are indeed differences in the values, which might suggest the presence of bias. That is, the fact that the SAT is somewhat more predictively powerful for some groups than for others might be taken as evidence of predictive bias (i.e., akin to slope bias).

On the other hand, it's not clear that these differences are large enough to warrant substantial concern. For example, using the Binomial Effect Size Display (BESD; see Chapter 9), we can translate these values into the "percentage of predictions that would be correct." This reveals that 64.5% of the predictions (based on the SAT) would be correct for the American Indian group, whereas the predictions for Asian Americans would be only slightly better, at 67.5%.

To gauge the magnitude of the differences in Table 11.3, we can also compare the differences in the SAT's predictive power with differences in the predictive power of high school GPA (HSGPA). The UC report included results from regression analyses in which college GPA scores were predicted by HSGPA, and these results are presented in Table 11.3. Interestingly, with a low of 8.8% and a high of 15.9%, these predictive values actually range *wider* than the values for the SAT. That is, there are bigger racial/ethnic disparities in the predictive power of HSGPA than in the SAT. Thus, the UC report seems to suggest that the HSGPA suffers from *more* predictive bias than does the SAT. Also interestingly, this fact seems to have been ignored or deemed unimportant by those who criticize the SAT and promote the use of HSGPA in the admission process. If the predictive differences of HSGPA are not large enough to warrant concern, then the (smaller) predictive differences of the SAT should not. In sum, these results do not provide clear evidence of predictive bias for the SAT in terms of race/ethnicity.

Socioeconomic Status

The UC report also examines potential biases related to socioeconomic status (SES). For this, the authors examined two pieces of information—family income and parent's educational status. Higher levels of family income and parental education were interpreted as indicators of high SES. Based on the same basic data set of nearly 80,000 students, a different report (Geiser & Santilices, 2007) showed that SAT scores are indeed associated with these markers of SES. Specifically, analyses revealed correlations of .32 and .39 between SAT Verbal scores and family income and parents' education, respectively (with correlations of .24 and .32 for SAT Math). Again, these values are cause for legitimate concern, as they indicate that students who come from higher-SES background tend to have higher SAT scores than do students coming from lower-SES backgrounds.

Again using a regression-based procedure, the researchers examined the possibility that the predictive power of the SAT was compromised by SES. That is, they examined the possibility that the SAT's predictive power was solely due to its link to SES. Although this is not exactly an examination of predictive bias, as outlined above, it does touch on an important issue related to the SAT's use in the admission process. It has been argued that, if the SAT's predictive power derives solely from its connection to SES, then its use in admissions creates an unfair disadvantage for students coming from a low-SES background.

Thus, the researchers examined the predictive power of the SAT while controlling for SES. To determine whether the SAT has any predictive power above and beyond its connection to SES, the researchers used "multiple regression" procedures. Specifically, they conducted a regression analysis in which college GPA was the outcome and in which there were several predictors, including SAT scores, family income, and parental education. When multiple predictors are entered into a regression analysis, the results tell us about each predictor's "unique" predictive power. That is, we can determine whether a predictor provides any useful information above and beyond the information that's provided by the other predictors in the analysis.

Initial analyses revealed that, across all students, the SAT's correlation with college GPA was .36. If the SAT carries any useful predictive information beyond the other predictors in the regression analysis, then its predictive power will not drop much from this value. That is, statistically controlling for the other predictors should not have much effect on the SAT's predictive power. However, if the SAT's predictive information is heavily connected to the other predictors in the analysis, then its predictive power will drop substantially.

What were the results? Was there evidence that the predictive power of the SAT is compromised by SES? The answer to this question is clear, though it has been misinterpreted greatly.

When examining the following regression equation (Equation 1), there was essentially no evidence of a compromised predictive power:

$$\text{College GPA} = a + b(\text{SAT}) + b(\text{Family income}) + b(\text{Parental education}). \qquad (1)$$

That is, when "controlling for" only the two SES variables, the predictive power of the SAT changed only slightly from its simple correlation of .36. As shown in the "Equation 1" column of Table 11.4, the SAT's predictive power remained high, at .345, after controlling for any overlap with SES (note that this value is a standardized regression coefficient, which is very closely related to correlations, typically ranging from −1 to +1, like correlations). Again, the fact that the SAT's predictive power remained very close to its original correlational value clearly suggests that its predictive power is *not* meaningfully compromised by a link to SES in these data.

Unfortunately, the official UC report did not present the results of this crucial analysis. That is, the report did not include any analysis in which the predictive power of the SAT was examined while controlling only for the two SES variables. Indeed, the results for Equation 1 are available only from raw statistical output available through the UC system's website (UC Office of the President, n.d.), not in the official report that has been circulated and read widely.

The official report, unfortunately, provided a different analysis—one that offers no clear insight into the possibility that SES compromises the SAT's predictive power. Specifically, it presents the result of a regression equation that included SAT and the two SES variables as predictors of college GPA, along with HSGPA and SAT-II as two additional predictors (note that the SAT-II is an achievement test designed to assess knowledge of specific topic areas, but scores on it are extremely highly correlated with scores on the original SAT). Thus, it was of the form

Table 11.4   Regression Results (Standardized Regression Coefficients) for Three Analyses Linking SAT Scores to College GPA

Predictors	Equation 1	Equation 2	Equation 3
SAT	.345	.02	.10
Family income	.01	.03	
Parental education	.04	.06	
HSGPA		.28	
SAT-II		.24	.32

NOTE: HSGPA, High School grade point average.

$$\text{College GPA} = a + b(\text{SAT}) + b(\text{Family income}) + b(\text{Parental education}) + b(\text{HSGPA}) + b(\text{SAT-II}). \qquad (2)$$

The results of this equation are presented in the "Equation 2" column of Table 11.4, and they do indeed show that the SAT's predictive power is dramatically reduced. In fact, it has dropped from .36 (i.e., its original correlation with college GPA) to essentially 0. The fact that its predictive power has dropped so much has led some critics to conclude that the SAT is indeed compromised by its link with SES. For example, Soares (2008) cited these exact results as support for the conclusions that "SES differences . . . reduce SATI effects to an extent not worth noticing" and that "when one statistically controls for SES, the weak contribution of the SAT in a regression model drops down to near zero." Ultimately, these results contributed to the assertion that "the cost of adding the SAT to [the admission process as reflected in the regression equation] is to stack the odds against underprivileged youths" and to the decision to remove the SAT from the required part of a university's admission process.

For a sophisticated understanding, it is useful to recognize why Equation 2 fails to justify the conclusion that the predictive power of the SAT is compromised by SES. This recognition hinges on a clear understanding of what we get when we conduct a multiple regression analysis (i.e., an analysis in which more than one predictor is in the equation).

In such an analysis, the results for one predictor reflect its predictive power after controlling for *all* other predictors in the equation. Thus, in Equation 2, the predictive value for SAT reflects its predictive power after controlling for SES *and* HSGPA *and* SAT-II. Indeed, the SAT's small predictive value in Equation 2 is not truly due to SES. Rather, the primary reason why the SAT's predictive value is so small is that SAT-II is also included as a predictor in the equation. That is, the SAT is extremely highly correlated with the SAT-II. Therefore, when controlling for SAT-II scores, there is very little predictive power left for the SAT. Indeed, the "Equation 3" column in Table 11.4 shows the results of a regression equation in which SAT and SAT-II are the only two predictors:

$$\text{College GPA} = a + b(\text{SAT}) + b(\text{SAT-II}).$$

As the results show, controlling for the SAT-II alone severely reduces the predictive power of the SAT, all the way from .36 to .10. Controlling for additional variables (i.e., SES and HSGPA) has relatively modest effects on the predictive power of the SAT. Thus, the small predictive value of the SAT in Equation 2 is due to its overlap with SAT-II rather than to any links to SES.

So what are the more appropriate interpretations of the overall pattern of findings, including Equation 1? The main conclusions should be that SES differences have minimal effect on the SAT's predictive power, because when one statistically controls for SES alone, the contribution of the SAT in a regression model is essentially unchanged. Thus, these results provide no meaningful evidence that the SAT's predictive power is compromised by a link with SES. Instead, the results (Equations 2 and 3) show that the SAT is highly redundant with SAT-II—so much that if you know students' SAT-II scores, then their SAT scores provide no new information. If we move beyond these particular analyses, the issue of SAT's predictive bias has mixed support—some research suggests there is bias, whereas other research suggests not. Overall, these particular results provide no support for the suggestion that the SAT unfairly acts "to stack the odds against underprivileged youths".

In sum, the UC's analysis of the SAT provides a useful and important example of a real-life examination of test bias. Not only does it illustrate some of the ways in which researchers attempt to investigate predictive bias, but it also illustrates the need for a solid understanding of certain statistical procedures and for careful consideration of their results.

Summary

In the past few chapters, we have discussed a variety of issues that are fundamental to the concepts of reliability and validity. In Chapter 8, we introduced the conceptual foundations of validity as it relates to the interpretation and use of test scores. That chapter presented several kinds of evidence that have implications for validity (e.g., the internal structure of a test, the test's association with other variables). In Chapter 9, we presented an in-depth coverage of the methods that are used to evaluate the "nomological network" of test scores. That is, procedures such as the multitrait–multimethod matrix and the quantifying construct validity process can be used to gauge the degree to which test scores manifest the associations from which they are predicted on the basis of a particular construct.

The current chapter and the previous chapter discussed important considerations that threaten the reliability and validity of test score interpretation and use. In Chapter 10, we discussed response biases (e.g., acquiescence bias, social desirability bias) that systematically obscure the true differences among individuals. In the current chapter, we focused on test bias, which traditionally refers to the possibility that the true differences among groups are systematically obscured (or artificially created) Although there are widely used methods for coping with response biases, the methods that have been proposed for coping with test bias tend to be somewhat controversial and beyond the scope of our current discussion. For a recent survey of the issues, interested readers are directed to Sackett, Schmitt, and Ellingson (2001).

In sum, the validity of test score interpretation and use is a fundamental concern to behavioral scientists who are interested in psychological measurement. Through decades of conceptual and methodological development, psychometricians, test users, and test developers have articulated the meaning and evaluation of validity. Although threats to validity do exist, psychologists and others interested in psychological measurement have made great strides in identifying such threats and in developing strategies for detecting, preventing, or minimizing them. Nevertheless, psychological tests should always be used and interpreted with close regard for the theoretical and evidential basis of their meaning and application, as described in the previous chapters.

Suggested Readings

One of the most informative and complete discussions of test bias and test fairness can be found in:

Jensen, A. R. (1980). *Bias in mental testing.* New York, NY: Free Press.

This is an accessible and thoughtful discussion of the issues and evidence related to validity and potential bias in "high-stakes" testing in several important domains of applied psychological testing.

Sackett, P. R., Schmitt, N., Ellingson, J. E., & Kablin, M. B. (2001). High-stakes testing in employment, credentialing, and higher education: Prospects in a post-affirmative-action world. *American Psychologist, 56,* 302–318.

PART V

Advanced Psychometric Approaches

CHAPTER 12

Confirmatory Factor Analysis

In Chapters 4 and 8, we discussed the internal structure, or dimensionality, of a psychological test. Recall that a test's internal structure and dimensionality have to do with the number and nature of psychological constructs that are assessed by a test's items. For example, in Chapter 4, we presented a hypothetical 6-item personality test, and we discussed the possibility that those 6 items (talkative, assertive, outgoing, creative, imaginative, and intellectual) might reflect two psychological traits—extraversion and openness to experience. Similarly, in Chapter 8, we described the 10-item Rosenberg Self-Esteem Inventory (RSEI), and we noted that its items are usually seen as reflecting only one psychological trait—global self-esteem. Thus, dimensionality and internal structure refer to the way a test's items cohere together and thereby represent one or more psychological constructs.

As a quick refresher, take a moment to recall the importance of a test's dimensionality. As we have discussed in earlier chapters, a test's dimensionality has fundamental implications for the test's development, reliability, validity, and use. In terms of test development, internal structure should be a major consideration when constructing a new test or scale. For example, a test might be designed to match a specific dimensionality (e.g., to reflect five uncorrelated personality traits or a single dimension of self-esteem), and examinations of internal structure can reveal the degree to which the test being developed actually corresponds to this dimensionality. In terms of reliability, a test's dimensionality or internal structure reflects the test's internal consistency. That is, evaluation of a test's dimensionality reveals which items are consistent with which other items (e.g., are all items roughly equally consistent with each other, or are there sets of items that are particularly consistent with each other?). In terms of validity, a test's internal structure is important because the appropriate interpretation of a test's scores depends on the match between its actual internal structure and the internal structure of its intended construct(s). For example, if we discovered that the RSEI included two uncorrelated dimensions, then it would be invalid to interpret the RSEI solely in terms of a unitary global self-esteem trait. Following from its implications for test development, reliability, and validity, a test's internal structure has robust implications for its use. That is, internal structure should guide the way a test is scored, producing one or more scores that are meaningful, both psychologically and quantitatively (see Figure 4.1).

In our earlier discussions of dimensionality, we highlighted exploratory factor analysis (EFA) as a statistical tool that is often used to evaluate a test's dimensionality. As we noted, EFA is most appropriate when one has few, if any, hypotheses about a scale's internal structure. Again, for example, we began our discussion of the six personality items in Chapter 4 began by assuming that we had no idea about the number of dimensions reflected in those items.

In contrast, confirmatory factor analysis (CFA) is useful when there are clear hypotheses about a test's dimensionality. That is, CFA is designed to examine a test's dimensionality when a test developer or test evaluator has clear expectations about the number of factors or dimensions underlying a test's items, the links between the items and factors, and the association between the factors.

In this chapter, we introduce several important issues in CFA. Specifically, we discuss basic issues in the logic of CFA, the process of conducting a CFA, and the key results that are obtained from a CFA. In addition, we discuss the way CFA can be used to examine fundamental psychometric issues—dimensionality (of course), reliability, and validity. Although the information obtained from CFA is most directly relevant to a test's internal structure, it also can be used to examine a test's internal consistency, and it can be used to evaluate convergent and discriminant evidence.

Our presentation, like the two chapters that follow, is intended to be relatively nontechnical and intuitive—we emphasize the basic logic of CFA and the psychological interpretation of its key results. However, CFA is a complex multivariate statistical procedure, with many technical considerations and problems. We cannot address many such issues in this chapter, and we recommend that interested readers consult other specialized sources for a more focused coverage (e.g., Brown, 2006; Hoyle, 2011; Thompson, 2004).

On the Use of EFA and CFA

The Frequency and Roles of EFA and CFA

Our emphasis on EFA in the earlier chapters reflects two facts about the typical use of factor analysis in psychometric evaluation. First, EFA has been used much more frequently than CFA. This discrepancy is at least partly due to the fact that EFA has been integrated much more seamlessly into statistical packages that are user-friendly and widely used. For example, EFA has long been integrated into the popular SPSS statistical package, but the ability to conduct CFA in SPSS is only recently becoming available and even now still requires additional software components.

Despite this long-standing difference in the frequency with which EFA and CFA have been used, CFA seems to be enjoying emerging interest and application.

This emergence is likely due to the increasing availability and user-friendliness of statistical software that is capable of conducting CFA. For example, the popular statistical packages SAS and SPSS now include modules that are capable of conducting CFA (though again, these might not be included in all versions of either package). Moreover, when using some software (e.g., the AMOS package in SPSS), one can conduct CFA without doing much more than creating figures to represent hypotheses about a test's dimensionality (e.g., Figures 4.2, 4.3, or 4.4).

A second issue in the use of factor analysis is that EFA and CFA are most appropriate for different phases of the test development and evaluation process. EFA is perhaps most appropriate for the early phases of test use. That is, EFA is most useful when test developers might still be clarifying their understanding of the constructs and of the test itself. In contrast, CFA is more appropriate in later phases of test development—after the initial evaluations of item properties and dimensionality and after any significant revisions of test content. Some psychologists have suggested a more integrated approach, pointing out that EFA can, in fact, be used in a somewhat hypothesis-driven way and that CFA is often, in fact, used in a way that is somewhat exploratory. Interested readers are directed to other sources for in-depth discussion of these points (e.g., Hopwood & Donnellan, 2010).

Using CFA to Evaluate Measurement Models

As noted earlier, when using CFA, we evaluate hypotheses about specific "measurement models" regarding the dimensionality or internal structure of a test. That is, CFA allows test developers and test evaluators to understand the degree to which their hypothesized measurement models are consistent with actual data produced by respondents. For example, based on previous research and theory, we might hypothesize that the RSEI has a unidimensional structure (i.e., we might hypothesize a one-factor measurement model). Using CFA, we can test this "model" formally—we can collect responses to the RSEI items and examine the degree to which those actual responses produce data in which the RSEI items cohere into a single factor.

Moreover, we can—if necessary and appropriate—alter our hypothesized model in a way that makes it more consistent with the actual structure of responses to the test. For example, some information produced by our CFA of the RSEI might indicate that the actual responses are, in fact, not consistent with a unidimensional model. Thus, we might examine other information from our CFA and discover that a two-dimensional structure is much more consistent with the data. In this way, we might modify our hypothesis regarding the true structure of the RSEI.

Furthermore, we can examine several measurement models in a series of CFAs, using the results to discover the one that best matches participants' actual responses. For example, we could formally test the RSEI's "fit" with both a unidimensional model and a two-dimensional model, and we could formally test which model is in fact more consistent with the actual test responses that we have obtained.

The Process of CFA for Analysis of a Scale's Internal Structure

In this section, we describe the process of conducting a CFA and interpreting its main results. Our goal is to provide a conceptual perspective on the logic, process, and meaning of CFA. With this goal in mind, we do not provide details about the way to conduct CFA in any particular statistical package. Rather, we lay a conceptual foundation that helps readers become informed consumers of CFA-based psychometric analysis. This conceptual foundation should also be valuable for readers who also wish to be producers of CFA-based psychometric information; indeed we hope that our conceptual coverage provides a solid foundation for additional training in the "how to" of CFA with respect to a variety of specific statistical packages (e.g., Byrne, 2001, 2006; Diamantopoulos & Siguaw, 2000; Hatcher, 1994).

Overview of CFA and Example

The typical process of conducting a CFA is summarized in Figure 12.1. In the following discussion, we present the steps in this process, and we discuss the logic of each step and the psychometric information that is obtained and usually reported. We describe the steps in which test developers and test evaluators have active roles (the unshaded boxes in Figure 12.1) and the steps that are carried out by statistical software (in the shaded boxes). As illustrated in Figure 12.1, CFA can be an iterative, back-and-forth process. The process begins when we articulate and evaluate a specific measurement model, but the process often does not end there. Often, after initially evaluating a specific measurement model, we revise the model and then evaluate the revised model. In fact, this revision and reevaluation can occur multiple times as we learn more and more from the CFA process.

After carrying out a CFA of a test, test developers and test evaluators usually report key information about the model-testing process. This information includes any revisions that have been made to the model(s). Usually, the information highlights the measurement model that is most consistent with the test's actual internal structure, as discovered via the CFA.

To illustrate and explain this process, we discuss a CFA of the Authenticity Scale (Wood, Linley, Maltby, Baliousis, & Joseph, 2008). The Authenticity Scale was intended to measure the degree to which a person "knows himself or herself" and "acts accordingly," and it was based on a conceptual model that identifies three dimensions of authenticity (with example items):

1. *Self-alienation* was defined (roughly) as the degree to which a person really understands himself or herself (e.g., "I don't know how I really feel inside").

2. *Authentic living* was defined as the degree to which a person behaves and expresses emotion in a way that is an honest reflection of his or

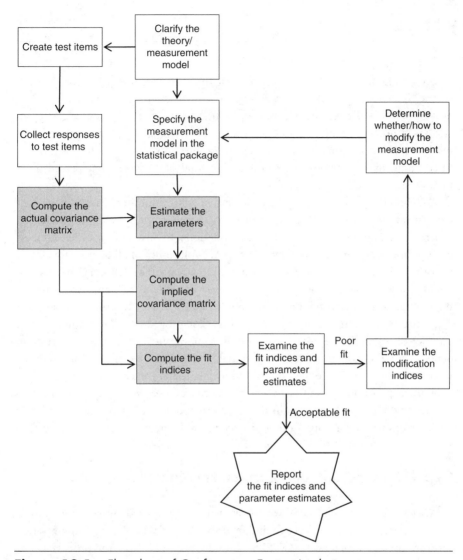

Figure 12.1   Flowchart of Confirmatory Factor Analysis

her self-perception (e.g., "I think it is better to be yourself than to be popular").

3. *Accepting external influence* was defined as the degree to which a person understands that other people can influence one's life and conforms to these influences (e.g., "I am strongly influenced by the opinions of others").

Considering this conceptual basis, the Authenticity Scale was intended to have a three-dimensional structure, with a subscale for each of the three dimensions. Each item is phrased as a self-relevant statement, and respondents are asked to rate their level of agreement with each item, using response options ranging from 1 ("Does not describe me at all") to 7 ("Describes me very well").

Preliminary Steps

Before conducting a CFA, there are at least three key preliminary steps. First, of course, is clarification of the psychological construct to be assessed and initial development of the test items. Indeed, Wood et al. (2008) describe a conceptually based process of writing a large number of items, an initial analysis of some responses to those items (e.g., an EFA), and a selection of 4 items for each of the three intended dimensions. This produced a total of 12 items that passed some initial tests of psychometric quality.

A second preliminary step is the collection of a large number of responses to the test. The appropriate sample size for a CFA is an important but complex issue, and experts have offered a variety of recommendations. In terms of absolute numbers of respondents, recommendations range from a minimum of 50 people (for simple measurement models and "clean" conditions) to 400 people or more. Other recommendations are made in terms of the ratio of respondents to items, with suggestions ranging from 5 respondents per item to 20 (or more) respondents per item. The bottom line is that, as a complex multivariate procedure, CFA requires a large number of responses—it is not uncommon to have much more than 200 respondents in a CFA. For example, Wood and his colleagues recruited three samples totaling more than 550 people to respond to the 12-item test.

A third preliminary step is to reverse score any negatively keyed items. This ensures that all items are keyed in the same direction, and it avoids any confusion arising from items that might otherwise seem highly inconsistent with each other.

Step 1: Specification of Measurement Model

After these preliminary steps, we translate our hypothesized measurement model into a statistical software package designed to conduct CFA. Using contemporary software packages such as AMOS/SPSS, SAS, EQS, and LISREL, the process can be quite straightforward. Such packages allow us simply to draw a figure to represent or "specify" the measurement model. The packages translate these drawings into statistical equations, which it uses to conduct the CFA. Of course, these packages also allow us to create those equations ourselves, rather than by drawing a figure. However, it is likely that most people opt to begin with the drawing capabilities.

For example, Figure 12.2 illustrates two measurement models evaluated in the CFA of the Authenticity Scale (Wood et al., 2008), and it shows at least three elements of a measurement model that need to be specified—as summarized in Table 12.1. First, we must specify the number of dimensions, factors, or latent variables (represented by ovals) that are hypothesized to underlie the test's items (represented by rectangles). For example, Figure 12.2a presents a unidimensional measurement model in which the scale's 12 items load on a single Authenticity factor. Note that this unidimensional model does not correspond to the three-factor structure for which the Authenticity Scale was designed. However, Wood and his colleagues tested this model as a comparison with their main hypothesized model, which is presented in Figure 12.2b. This figure presents a "hierarchical" multidimensional measurement model in which the scale's items load on three "lower-level" factors (i.e., Self-Alienation, Authentic Living, Accepting External Influence), all of which load on a single, more fundamental "higher-order" general Authenticity factor.

A second element of the measurement model to be specified is the links between items and factors. That is, we must specify which items are linked to (i.e., load on) each factor. In the typical factor-analytic figure (e.g., Figures 12.2a and 12.2b), a pathway (i.e., arrow) between an item and a factor indicates that the item is hypothesized to load on a factor. There are two general guidelines that are generally followed when specifying these links. First, in most measurement models, at least one item is linked to each factor. For example, in Figure 12.2a, all items are hypothesized to load on the sole factor. Similarly, there are four items loading on each of the three lower-level factors in Figure 12.2b. Note that there are no items loading on the general Authenticity factor in Figure 12.2b. This is typical for such higher-level factors (i.e., factors on which other factors load)—we will return to this later.

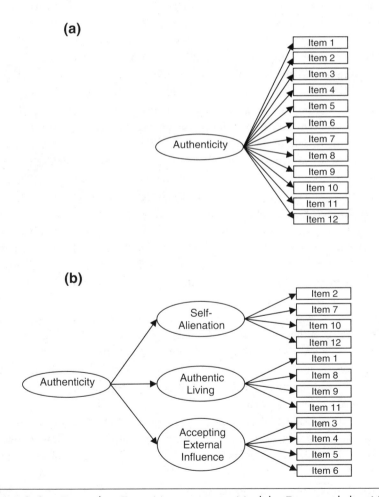

Figure 12.2   Example: Two Measurement Models Examined by Wood et al. (2008)

Table 12.1   Facets of the Measurement Model to be Specified

Facets

Required specifications:

1. Number of factors
2. The associations between items and factors
3. The potential associations between factors (if more than one factor is hypothesized)

Examples of some additional specification options:

4. Exact values of one or more parameters (e.g., specific factor-loading values)
5. Equality of parameters (e.g., two factor loadings constrained to be equal)

A second general guideline is that each item is typically linked to only one latent variable. Typically, we create each test item to reflect one and only one psychological characteristic, though different items might reflect different characteristics. With this in mind, we generally hypothesize that each item loads on one and only one factor. For example, the second item in the Authenticity Scale was written to reflect Self-Alienation, and the first item was written to reflect Authentic Living. Thus, Figure 12.2b hypothesizes that Item 2 should load only on the Self-Alienation factor, and Item 1 should load only on the Authentic Living factor.

If a measurement model is multidimensional (e.g., Figure 12.2b), then we must specify a third element of the model—the possible associations between factors. We have two possible ways of indicating that factors are associated with each other. First, we can specify that the factors load on a higher-order factor. Indeed, Figure 12.2b is a hierarchical measurement model in which three lower-order factors load on a higher-order factor. This suggests that a person's levels of Self-Alienation, Authentic Living, and Acceptance of External Influence are hypothesized to be affected by his or her level of general Authenticity. This hierarchical relationship suggests that the three lower-order factors are associated with each other. That is, if two or more lower-order factors load on a higher-order factor, then by extension, those lower-order factors should be associated with each other. For example, Figure 12.2b indicates that people who have a high level of Authentic Living will also tend to have a high level of Acceptance of External Influence. A second way in which we can indicate that factors are associated with each other is by having them simply be correlated with each other, as represented by a two-way arrow between them. In contrast to one-way arrows (which indicate that one thing affects another thing), two-way arrows simply indicate that two things are associated with each other, without any implication of causality. With this in mind, we might choose to omit the general Authenticity factor in Figure 12.2b and instead draw three two-way arrows—one arrow for each pair of the remaining factors (e.g., between Self-Alienation and Authentic Living).

When thinking about the associations between factors, we might also hypothesize that factors are *not* associated with each other. Consider the multidimensional test with uncorrelated factors that we discussed in Chapter 4 (e.g., Figure 4.4).

To indicate the hypothesis that two factors are not correlated with each other, we simply omit any connection between those factors. That is, we would not include a higher-order factor that connects them, and we would not include a two-way arrow between them.

Typically, when specifying the hypothesized item–factor links and any factor–factor associations, our hypotheses are fairly simple—we simply hypothesize that a link/association exists or not. That is, we hypothesize either that an item is associated with a particular factor or not and we hypothesize that factors are associated with each other or not. The statistical software will then estimate the precise associations. In other words, we simply hypothesize that peoples' responses to particular items are affected by their levels of particular psychological characteristics. We then rely on the statistical software to estimate the actual magnitude of those effects. Essentially, the presence of a pathway between an item and a factor (or between two factors) indicates a hypothesized nonzero association; in contrast, the absence of a pathway indicates a hypothesized zero association. In sum, we generally specify the model in a way that the associations are "freely estimated"; that is, we essentially state that "these parameters are probably not zero" and allow the software to estimate the parameters' precise values.

It is worth noting that the models in Figure 12.2 are somewhat simplified and that you might encounter more complex representations. Specifically, sometimes figures are drawn so that each item also has a unique random error term associated with it. However, such complexity is not always included in published psychometric work. Thus, we will keep the description as simple as possible for our immediate purposes, and we will return to this additional complexity in the "Reliability" section of this chapter.

Step 2: Computations

After we have specified the hypothesized measurement model, we then ask our statistical software to conduct the CFA based on those specifications and on the data that we have collected (i.e., actual responses to the test). Although the statistical computations are conducted "behind the scenes" by the software, a quick overview of the statistical process can enhance insight into CFA and its main results. At a rather simplified level, the basic CFA computations have four phases.

Phase 1: Actual Variances and Covariances. In the first phase of the CFA computations, the collected data are used to compute the items' variances and the covariances among the items. That is, the software computes the actual degree of variance for each item and the actual level of covariance between each pair of items. For example, in the analysis of the Authenticity Scale, the software computes 12 variances and 66 covariances (i.e., $66 = 12(12 - 1)/2$). These values are used in subsequent phases.

Phase 2: Parameter Estimates (and Inferential Tests). Indeed, in the second phase of computations, the items' actual variances and covariances are used to estimate values for the "parameters" as specified by the researcher. Parameters are quantitative values that are related to specific elements of the measurement model, and they are an important part of the results produced by CFA. There are several key types of parameters to be estimated. One type of parameter is the factor loading(s) for each item. As discussed earlier, when we hypothesize that an item loads on a factor, we usually do not hypothesize a specific value for that loading (i.e., we do not usually hypothesize that the item loads on the factor to any specific degree). Instead, we usually rely on the statistical software to compute a value for that parameter. For example, in the analysis of the model presented in Figure 12.2b, the software will compute 12 parameter estimates for the factor loadings—one for each item. A second type of parameter that often occurs in multidimensional tests are those that connect factors to each other—either correlations between factors or the loading of lower-order factors on higher-order factors. Again, when we hypothesize that one factor loads on another or that two factors are correlated, we usually do not hypothesize specific values. Thus, for example, in a CFA of the model in Figure 12.2b, the software will compute three parameter estimates for the loadings of the three lower-order factors on the higher-order factor. There are other types of parameters that can be estimated (e.g., error variances), but the item–factor parameters and the factor–factor parameters are typically of most interest.

To compute the parameter estimates, the software begins with the actual variances and covariances from the first phase of computations. For example, in the analysis of the model in Figure 12.2b, it would use, in part, the actual covariance (i.e., association) between Item 2 and Item 7 to estimate the loadings that those items might have on the Self-Alienation factor. Indeed, if the two items are strongly associated with each other (i.e., if they have a robust covariance—if people who endorse Item 2 are very likely to endorse Item 7), then they might have something strongly in common with each other. Thus, the statistical software might compute strong loadings for both items on the Self-Alienation factor, which they would have in common (i.e., the Self-Alienation factor is the "thing" that the items have in common). The actual variances and covariances are thus used to compute values for all factor loadings, interfactor correlations, error variances, and so on.

Importantly, CFA software also computes an inferential statistic (i.e., significance test) for each parameter estimate. We will return to this later—for now we will note that the typical null hypothesis for a given parameter is that the parameter's estimated value is 0 in the population from which the sample was drawn.

Phase 3: Implied Variances and Covariances. In the third phase of computations, the software uses its estimated parameter values (from Phase 2) to compute "implied" item variances and covariances. That is, the software computes item variances and covariances, as implied by the estimated parameters. For example, if both Item 2 and Item 7 have very strong loadings on the Self-Alienation factor, then this implies that they will be strongly correlated with each other (i.e., they will have a relatively large covariance). However, if both items have very weak loadings on the Self-Alienation factor, then this implies that they are weakly correlated with each other.

This third phase might seem circular—indeed, you might suspect that the implied variances and covariance should exactly match the actual variances and covariances; after all, the implied variances and covariances are based on parameter estimates, which are themselves computed from the actual variances and covariances! In fact, there will not be exact matches (except under very specific conditions), and moreover, there can be substantial mismatches between actual and implied variances/covariances. The mismatches can happen because the parameter estimates are based on the software's attempt to account for a great amount of information when computing each parameter estimate. For example, we noted earlier that software would use, in part, the actual covariance (i.e., association) between Item 2 and Item 7 to estimate the loadings that those items might have on the Self-Alienation factor. This is true, but it oversimplifies the process. In fact, the software's estimate of Item 2's factor loading is based on the variances and covariances of *all* the items. After all, the Self-Alienation factor directly involves four items (see Figure 12.2b), which means that there are at least 6 covariances to be considered and balanced in computations related to Self-Alienation. Actually, it is even more complicated, because Self-Alienation is hypothesized to load on Authenticity, which in turn is hypothesized to affect the other two factors. Thus, the model implies that the Self-Alienation factor will be correlated with the other two factors. This in turn implies that the four Self-Alienation items will be correlated with the other eight items on the scale (i.e., 32 additional covariances). So when computing each and every parameter estimate, the software must balance and weigh a huge amount of information. Sometimes, when attempting to find solutions to the problem of balancing all of this information, the CFA produces parameter estimates that are not good representations of each single piece of information.

Thus, it is important to consider the degree of match or mismatch between the actual variances/covariances and the implied variances/covariances. If the hypothesized model is good (i.e., if it is a good approximation of the true model underlying the scale's items), then the implied variances and covariances will match closely the actual variances and covariances computed in the first phase of analysis. However, if the model is poor, then the implied values will differ greatly from the actual values. This important issue is the focus of the next computational phase.

Phase 4: Indices of Model Fit. In the fourth phase, the software produces information regarding the general adequacy or "fit" of the hypothesized model. To do this, it compares the implied variances/covariances to the actual variances/covariances, and it computes indices of "model fit" and modification. If the comparison between implied and actual values reveals only minor discrepancies or mismatch, then the software produces indices of "good fit." This would indicate that the hypothesized measurement model adequately reflects the actual pattern of responses to the test. In contrast, if the comparison between implied and actual values reveals large discrepancies or mismatches, then the software produces indices of "poor fit." This, of course, would indicate that the hypothesized measurement model does not adequately reflect the actual pattern of responses to the test. In the next section, we will discuss the interpretation of these values in more depth.

Going further, CFA software can compute "modification indices" that indicate specific ways in which the measurement model could be improved. These values reveal potential modifications that would bring the model closer to the factor structure that truly may be underlying the test's items (as they were responded to in the sample). For example, a modification index derived from analysis of Figure 12.2b might indicate that Item 2 loads on the Authentic Living factor in addition to the Self-Alienation factor. Because the original hypothesized model in Figure 12.2b does not hypothesize that Item 2 loads on Authentic Living, we might consider modifying our hypothesis to fit this suggestion.

Step 3: Interpreting and Reporting Output

After collecting responses to the test, specifying a measurement model that we believe underlies those responses, and computing parameter estimates and fit indices, we interpret the results. CFA produces many types of output addressing a variety of psychometric and statistical issues, and this section describes some of the most important and commonly reported results.

As shown in Figure 12.1, the particulars of this step and the next depend on the results that are obtained. Depending on some of the results, we might examine other results. Moreover, depending on what we find, we might conclude our analysis and report our findings, or we might modify our hypothesized model and rerun the analysis. Ideally, we will find that our hypothesized measurement model is a good match to the actual responses to the test. In that case, we might examine only two sets of results.

Fit Indices. Typically, we first examine the fit indices that address the overall adequacy of our hypothesized measurement model. As described earlier, "good fit" indicates that the hypothesized measurement model is consistent with the actual responses to the test, and this supports the validity of the model. That is, if the fit indices are good, then we can have initial confidence in interpreting the test's dimensionality as we had hypothesized. However, "poor fit" indicates that the hypothesized dimensionality is not consistent with the actual responses to the test. This is usually seen as evidence against the validity of the hypothesized measurement model, and we should not interpret the test's dimensionality as we had initially hypothesized.

Most CFA programs will compute and present many fit indices. For example, the statistical package SAS computes approximately 20 fit indices as part of its "calis" procedure, which is used to conduct CFA. Although many fit indices are available, most published reports of a CFA present only a few. Unfortunately, there is no clear consensus regarding best fit indices to interpret and report, thus different reports will present different sets of fit indices.

That said, there are a few that you might be most likely to encounter in reports of CFA. The computational details for these indices are beyond the scope of our current discussion; the important goal at this point is to be familiar with some of these indices and with their general interpretations. The chi-square statistic is probably the most commonly reported fit index, and it actually indicates the degree of "poorness of fit" or "misfit" of the model. That is, large, significant chi-square values are evidence of poor fit, whereas small, nonsignificant chi-square values indicate good fit, providing support for a hypothesized measurement model. Note that this "significant is bad" interpretation of chi-square is quite the opposite of the typical perspective on statistical significance, in which we generally hope to find that a test is statistically significant. Although chi-square values are usually included in reports of CFA, it is important to note that sample size affects the chi-square values: All else being equal, large samples will produce large chi-square values, which produce statistical significance.

Interestingly, this is a bit of a paradox for CFA. On one hand, we want to have large samples so that we can obtain robust, reliable parameter estimates. On the other hand, large samples increase the chance that we will obtain significant chi-square values, which would seem to indicate that our hypothesized model is invalid.

Partly because of this paradox, reports of CFA usually include additional fit indices. These alternative indices include the goodness-of-fit index (GFI), the incremental fit index (IFI), the normed fit index (NFI), the comparative fit index (CFI), the nonnormed fit index (NNFI, also known as the Tucker-Lewis Index, or TLI), the root mean square of approximation (RMSEA), the root mean square residual (RMR), the standardized root mean square residual (SRMR), and the Akaike information criterion (AIC), to name but a few. Note that these indices, unlike the chi-square index, do not include a formal test of statistical significance.

Importantly, these fit indices have different scales and norms for indicating model fit. For example, the CFI ranges from 0 to 1.0, with larger values indicating a good fit. In contrast, the RMR has a lower bound of 0 but an upper bound that depends on the test's scale of measurement, with smaller values indicating good fit. As another example, the SRMR ranges from 0 to 1.0 (like the CFI), but lower values indicate good fit (like the RMR). Many sources are available for guidance in interpreting indices (e.g., Hu & Bentler, 1999; Kline, 2010).

For example, in an article describing the CFA of the Authenticity Scale (Wood et al., 2008), fit indices are the first results that are presented. In that report, the researchers present four fit indices—chi-square, SRMR, CFI, and RMSEA—related to their analysis of the model in Figure 12.2b (their primary model of interest). Considering the possibility that some readers might not be familiar with these particular indices, the researchers note specific values that have been recommended by experts as indicative of "good fit" as represented by these indices (i.e., SRMR values ≤ .08, CFI values ≥ .95, and RMSEA values ≤ .06), although they also noted that these recommendations are a bit more conservative than what is often taken as indicating an adequate fit. Based on a CFA of responses from 213 students, the fit indices are presented in the "12.2b" column of Table 12.2. On finding CFI, SRMR, and RMSEA values very close to the conservative recommendations, the researchers concluded that the model (as shown in Figure 12.2b) "provided a good fit" (p. 393) to the Authenticity Scale's responses. They also reported a significant chi-square but reminded readers of the link between large sample sizes and statistical significance, and they ignored the chi-square's apparent indication of misfit. Such dismissal of a significant chi-square value is common in CFA reports.

To more fully evaluate the adequacy of their main model of interest, Wood et al. (2008) compared this model with the alternative, unidimensional measurement

Table 12.2   Fit Indices for Two Measurement Models Examined by Wood et al. (2008): Sample 3 (N = 213)

| | Measurement Model | | |
Fit Index	Figure 12.2b	Figure 12.2a	Cited Benchmark
Chi-squared	90.06*[a]	353.45*[b]	NA
SRMR	.08	.16	<.08
CFI	.94	.53	>.95
RMSEA	.06	.16	<.06

NOTE. Benchmarks are those cited by Wood et al. (2008). SRMR = standardized root mean square residual; CFI = comparative fit index; RMSEA = root mean square of approximation.
[a] $df = 51$.
[b] $df = 54$.
*$p < .05$.

model in Figure 12.2a. The results indicated a much poorer fit for this alternative model—see the "Figure 12.2a" column in Table 12.2. Specifically, poor fit is indicated by a CFI value well below the .95 benchmark cited by Wood and colleagues, by SRMR and RMSEA values well above their benchmarks, and by a large, significant chi-square value. The comparison of this model with the three-dimensional model (in Figure 12.2b) strengthened the researchers' confidence that the Authenticity Scale's internal structure is indeed well represented by the model in Figure 12.2b.

As shown in Figure 12.1, the examination of fit indices can lead in two possible directions. First, if the fit indices suggest that the model is adequate, then we will examine parameter estimates to evaluate the more specific psychometric qualities of the test. Second and alternatively, if the fit indices instead suggest that the model is inadequate, then we will likely examine the modification indices and consider ways in which the model could be revised.

Parameter Estimates and Significance Tests. After deciding that a measurement model has an adequate overall fit, we then examine a variety of parameter estimates. We obtain an estimated value for each parameter, including values for the items' factor loadings and the interfactor associations. Parameter estimates are an important facet of a test's overall dimensionality and, as we shall see, other psychometric properties.

As described earlier, an item's loading on a factor represents the degree to which differences among peoples' responses to an item are determined by differences among their levels of the underlying psychological construct that is assessed by that item. If an item is hypothesized to load on a particular factor, then we expect to discover a large, positive, and statistically significantly factor loading. If we do indeed find such results, then we are likely to conclude that the item is a good reflection of the underlying psychological dimension. Thus, we are likely to keep that item on the test. However, if we find that the item's factor loading is small and/or nonsignificant, then we are likely to conclude that the item is unrelated to the psychological dimension. In this case, we are likely to remove the item from the test. We then might respecify the model to accommodate this change (i.e., eliminating the item from the model) and rerun the computations to evaluate the revised test. We realize that this scenario might seem paradoxical—how could we have a generally well-fitting model (as indicated by the fit indices) but a weak factor loading? The answer is that fit indices represent the overall adequacy or fit of the entire measurement model and that a model can have generally good support despite having some weak specific aspects.

Once again turning to the CFA of the Authenticity Scale (Wood et al., 2008), Figure 12.3 presents some key parameter estimates obtained in the analysis of the three-dimensional measurement model. Recall that the fit indices indicated good support for this model (Table 12.2), so the researchers interpreted and reported the parameter estimates for this model. Figure 12.3 presents standardized factor loadings and interfactor associations. Note that as standardized factor loadings, these values are interpretable like factor loadings from an EFA. That is, they are interpreted in terms of correlations or standardized regression weights—generally ranging between −1 and +1. As these values indicate, all 12 items loaded robustly on their hypothesized factors—the weakest factor loading was Item 1's loading of .60 on the Authentic Living factor. Figure 12.3 also indicates that each lower-order factor loads strongly on the higher-order factor—the weakest loading being the −.58 loading of Accepting External Influence on the higher-order Authenticity factor. Finally, although the researchers do not explicitly state this, the magnitudes of these 15 parameter estimates lead us to assume that all of them are statistically significant.

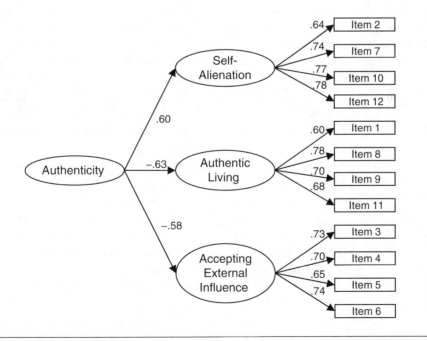

Figure 12.3   Measurement Model in Figure 12.2b With Parameter Estimates Reported by Wood et al. (2008)

As done in the report of the Authenticity Scale's CFA, researchers usually high-light these particular parameters—the items' factor loadings and any interfactor associations (Wood et al., 2008). They sometimes also present parameters reflecting items' error variances or items' variance-explained values. However, because these values are implied by the factor loadings themselves, researchers usually choose not to include this extra information. Indeed, the report of the Authenticity Scale's CFA did not report present these values.

In sum, as Figure 12.1 suggests, CFA interpretation and the subsequent steps depend on several important issues. The most important issue is perhaps the over-all adequacy of an initial hypothesized measurement model, as indicated by the fit indices. If the fit indices suggest that the model fits well, then we generally move to an examination of the parameter estimates. If we find that those parameter esti-mates provide further support for the model (e.g., there are no weak, nonsignificant factor loadings), then we will likely finish the CFA by concluding that the model is a good representation of the test's internal structure. However, things do not always proceed so smoothly. Indeed, if the fit indices indicate that the model fits poorly, then we will likely revise our hypothesis about the model's internal structure. This brings us to the next potential step in a CFA—model modification and reanalysis, with the goal of improving our understanding of the test's true dimensionality.

Step 4: Model Modification and Reanalysis (If Necessary)

As Figure 12.1 illustrates, the results of a CFA sometimes, perhaps often, force us to consider modifying a hypothesized measurement model. If we obtain fit indices suggesting that a model is inconsistent with the actual responses to the test items, then we will likely examine modification indices to find hints about the revisions that we can make to the model.

When conducting a CFA, we obtain a large number of modification indices; indeed, each one represents a parameter that was left out of (i.e., set to zero in) the initial measurement model. For example, the model in Figure 12.2b implies that Item 2 loads on the Self-Alienation factor but not on the Authentic Living factor. Thus, Wood et al. (2008) initially allowed the software to estimate Item 2's loading on Self-Alienation (see Figure 12.3), but they set or "fixed" the loading of Item 2 on the Authentic Living factor to 0, indicating that Item 2 has no direct association with Authentic Living. When we examine modification indices for this model, we thus would find a value referring to this "fixed" parameter—the "fixed-to-zero" factor loading of Item 2 on Authentic Living. Indeed, we would find modifica-tion values for every parameter that was initially set to zero—for example, the association between Item 2 and Authentic Living, the association between Item 2 and Acceptance of External Influence, the association between Item 1 and Self-Alienation, the association between Item 1 and Acceptance of External Influence, and so on.

The magnitude of a modification index reflects the potential impact of revising the relevant parameter. For example, a CFA of the model in Figure 12.2b might pro-duce a relatively large modification index related to Item 2's potential loading on the Authentic Living factor. To anthropomorphize a bit, this would indicate that Item 2 "wants" to load on the Authentic Living factor in addition to the Self-Alienation factor. That is, it would indicate that peoples' responses to Item 2 are affected by both their degree of Self-Alienation and their degree of Authentic Living. More statistically, it would indicate that if we allowed Item 2 to load on both factors, then the fit indices would be improved. Thus, by examining the modification indices and making changes based on the largest indices, we learn about the real dimensionality of the test, and our measurement model becomes a better reflection of this reality.

With this in mind, as Figure 12.1 indicates, after examining modification indices, we might change one or more parameters and then rerun the analysis. Analysis of the revised model will produce new output—new fit indices, new parameter estimates, and so on. We then evaluate the adequacy of the revised model, and we either examine parameter estimates (if the revised model fits well) or examine the new modification indices (if the model still fits poorly).

We should note a few cautions regarding modification in a CFA. First, modification begins to obscure the difference between confirmatory analysis and exploratory analysis. This reiterates our earlier comment that CFA can be used in a semi-exploratory manner. Second, a test developer or test evaluator should be hesitant to perform many modifications in a CFA, with particular hesitancy about modifications that lack a clear conceptual basis. Such modifications might arise from response patterns that are idiosyncratic or unique to that sample of people, and not be representative of other test takers more generally. Thus, if more than one or two modifications are made to a model, then test developers and test evaluators should strongly consider evaluating the revised model in a different sample of test takers (i.e., a "cross-validation sample") before drawing strong inferences about the "true" internal structure of the test in a way that generalizes to a broad range of people.

Comparing Models

Earlier, we noted that the analysis of the Authenticity Scale included a comparison of the two models in Figure 12.2. Although the three-dimensional model was the main one of interest, the researchers contrasted it against the unidimensional model (Wood et al., 2008).

Indeed, when conducting a CFA of a test, test developers and test evaluators often evaluate competing measurement models. The point of such comparisons is to identify which model is the best representation of the test's true internal structure. Rather than evaluating a single possible model's fit, test developers and test evaluators can learn even more by evaluating and comparing several reasonable potential measurement models. All else being equal (e.g., in terms of theoretical basis), we would prefer measurement models with a relatively good fit. That is, we would identify the model having the most supportive fit indices and conclude that it reflects the test's true dimensionality. This can provide strong insight into the test's actual properties.

A full discussion of strategies for comparing models is beyond the scope of this chapter. However, interested readers can find such a discussion in other sources (e.g., Brown, 2006; Hoyle, 2011).

Summary

As a psychometric tool, CFA can provide great insight into the internal structure of psychological tests. By allowing us to test hypotheses about specific measurement models, CFA is an important complement to EFA. However, the value of CFA goes beyond the evaluation of dimensionality, and the following sections describe the way in which it can be extended to the evaluation of test reliability and validity.

CFA and Reliability

Coefficient alpha is the most widely used method of estimating reliability (see Chapter 4), but its accuracy depends on psychometric assumptions that may not be valid in some applications of behavioral research (Miller, 1995; Zinbarg, Revelle, Yovel, & Li, 2005). Indeed, alpha's accuracy as an estimate of reliability is determined by the pattern and nature of items' psychometric properties (e.g., do the items have correlated errors, do they have equal factor loadings?).

These issues have led psychometricians to use factor analysis (or principal components analysis) for estimating reliability (e.g., Armor, 1974). Although CFA is not currently used widely in this way, experts have recently developed CFA-based procedures for this purpose. In this section, we describe a CFA-based procedure for estimating the reliability of unidimensional scales; additional details, examples, and alternatives can be found in several sources (e.g., Brown, 2006, pp. 337–351; Raykov, 2004; Zinbarg et al., 2005).

When using CFA, we can estimate reliability through a two- or three-step process, depending on the need to modify the initial measurement model. First, we use CFA to evaluate the test's basic measurement model. Consider, for example, the Interaction Anxiousness scale (IAS; Leary, 1983). The IAS is a 15-item personality scale designed to reflect the tendency to experience social anxiety in interactions in which an "individual's responses are contingent on the responses of other interactants" (e.g., a one-on one conversation, as opposed to a speech delivered to an audience; Leary, 1983, p. 68). Each item presents a self-relevant statement (e.g., "I often feel nervous even in casual get-togethers"), and respondents are asked to rate their level of agreement/endorsement of each.

Figure 12.4a presents a simple unidimensional model hypothesized to reflect the dimensionality of the IAS—all 15 items load on a single Interaction Anxiousness factor, with no additional links among items. Note that this figure is a bit more complex than Figure 12.2a, discussed earlier. Specifically, in this figure, each item is affected by a unique error term that represents the effect of random measurement error on responses to each item. These error terms are part of all CFA models, but they are often omitted from graphical presentations of CFA models (e.g., see Figures 12.2 and 12.3). We collected responses to the IAS from a relatively small sample of respondents ($n = 107$, smaller than is ideal), and a CFA indicated that the

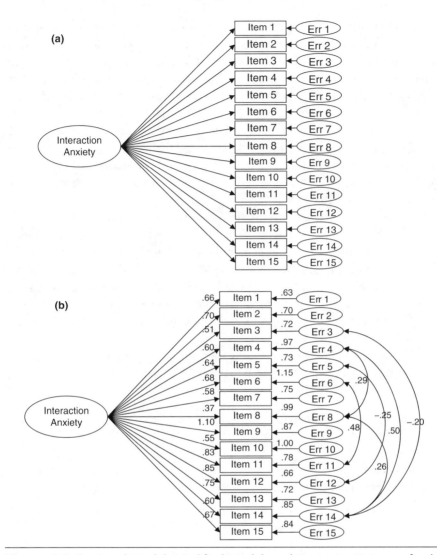

Figure 12.4   Initial Model, Modified Model, and Parameter Estimates for the Interaction Anxiousness Scale

unidimensional model did not fit the IAS well in these respondents—$X^2_{(90)} = 224.30$, $p < .05$; NNFI = .74, CFI = .78; RMSEA = .12, and SRMR = .09.

In the second step of the process, we modify and reanalyze the measurement model if necessary. As in the case of our CFA of the IAS, if the initial hypothesized model fits poorly, then we identify useful revisions to the model (via the modification indices). Specifically, we focus mainly on potential associations among the items' error terms. For example, we examined modification indices from the poorly fitting model in Figure 12.4a, and we identified six useful modifications. Not only did the modification indices provide statistical support for these changes but the changes largely were psychologically reasonable as well. For example, the modification indices suggested that Items 4 and 14 "wanted to be correlated with each other." Indeed, both items refer to interactions with people in positions of authority (i.e., "I get nervous when I must talk to a teacher or boss" and "I get nervous when I speak to someone in a position of authority"). Thus, these two items shared something that was a bit different from the remaining items, none of which refer explicitly to authority figures. Similarly, the results suggested that Items 6 and 11 were statistically linked, and indeed, these are the only two items that explicitly include the word *shy*. Thus, Items 4 and 14 share an "authority" commonality, whereas Items 6 and 11 share a "shyness" commonality.

Considering the relative magnitudes of several modification indices and the conceptual connections between pairs of items, we modified the model by adding six parameters—the pairwise associations between items' error terms. Our reanalysis revealed a much improved fit for the modified model ($X^2_{(84)} = 122.76$, $p < .05$; NNFI = .92, CFI = .94; RMSEA = .07, and SRMR = .07). Figure 12.4b presents the modified model and unstandardized parameter estimates, including each item's factor loading, the error variance of each item, and the six covariances between error terms.

In the final step of the process, we use these unstandardized parameter estimates to estimate the test's reliability. Recall that reliability is defined as

$$\text{Reliability} = \frac{\text{True variance}}{\text{True variance} + \text{Error variance}}.$$

The parameter estimates obtained via CFA can be used to estimate the true variance and error variance, and thus they can be used to estimate reliability (Brown, 2006):

$$\text{Estimated reliability} = \frac{\left(\sum \lambda_i\right)^2}{\left(\sum \lambda_i\right)^2 + \sum \theta_{ii} + 2\sum \theta_{ij}}. \qquad (12.1)$$

In this equation, λ_i refers to an item's factor loading, θ_{ii} refers to an item's error variance, and θ_{ij} refers to the covariance between the error terms of two items (this is zero for models without correlated error terms). In terms of our earlier discussion of reliability, $\left(\sum \lambda_i\right)^2$ reflects the variance of true scores (i.e., signal), because the factor loadings reflect the links between the items and the "true" psychological attribute. Similarly, the sum $\sum \theta_{ii} + 2\sum \theta_{ij}$ reflects random error variance (i.e., noise), because these terms reflect the unique aspects that affect each item but that are not related to the underlying psychological attribute of interest. Thus, Equation 12.1 represents the theoretical definition of reliability as the ratio of true score variance to total observed score variance (with observed variance being the sum of true score variance and error variance; see Chapter 5). For the results in Figure 12.4, true score variance is estimated as 101.81:

Similarly, error variance is estimated as 14.52:

$$\left(\sum \lambda_i\right)^2 = (0.66+0.70+0.51+0.60+0.64+0.68+0.58+0.37$$
$$+1.10+0.55+0.83+0.85+0.75+0.60+0.67)^2 = 101.81.$$

$$\sum \theta_{ii} = (0.63+0.70+0.72+0.97+0.73+1.15+0.75+0.99+0.87$$
$$+1.00+0.78+0.66+0.72+0.85+0.84) = 12.36,$$
$$\sum \theta_{ij} = (0.29+0.48+(-0.25)+(-0.20)+0.50+0.26) = 1.08,$$
$$\sum \theta_{ii} + 2\sum \theta_{ij} = 12.36 + 2(1.08) = 14.52.$$

Thus, the estimated reliability of the IAS is

$$\frac{101.81}{101.81+14.52} = .87.$$

For these responses to the IAS, the CFA-based reliability estimate is only somewhat smaller than the reliability estimate obtained via coefficient alpha, which is $\alpha = .89$. Although the difference between the two estimates is not large in this case, it can be much more dramatic, and it reflects the alpha's tendency to misestimate reliability (Miller, 1995).

CFA is a very flexible tool for examining reliability, going well beyond the relatively simple analysis of a unidimensional test such as the IAS. For example, it can be used to estimate reliability for multidimensional scales, to estimate group differences in reliability, and to obtain confidence intervals around estimates of reliability (e.g., Raykov, 2004).

CFA and Validity

Going even further, CFA can be a useful tool for evaluating validity in several ways. First, as implied by our relatively in-depth discussion of CFA's ability to test a specific hypothesis about a test's internal structure, CFA offers insight into the "internal-structure" aspect of validity (i.e., does the actual structure of responses to the test items fit the structure that is implied by the theoretical basis of the intended construct?).

Second, if test responses are collected along with measures of related constructs or criteria, then we can evaluate the test's association with those variables. Whether we view this associative evidence in terms of convergent/discriminant validity, concurrent validity, criterion validity, predictive validity, or external validity, it provides important information about the psychological meaning of test scores. There are at least two ways in which we can use CFA to examine these facets of validity.

One way in which we use CFA for evaluating convergent and discriminant validity is by applying it to multitrait–multimethod (MTMM) matrices. As discussed in Chapter 5, an MTMM study includes multiple traits/constructs (e.g., social skill, impulsivity, conscientiousness, and emotional stability), each of which is assessed through multiple methods (e.g., self-report, acquaintance ratings, and interviewer ratings). When we examine the associations among the entire set of scores, we can evaluate convergent validity, discriminant validity, method effects, and other important validity information. There are several CFA-based methods for evaluating an MTMM matrix, though a full discussion is beyond the scope of this chapter. Interested readers can consult other good sources for this information (e.g., Brown, 2006, chap. 6; Marsh & Grayson, 1995).

A second way to use CFA to examine convergent validity (and potentially discriminant validity) is through the focused examination of a test along with one or more criterion variables. For example, we could examine the construct validity of the IAS by collecting individuals' responses to the IAS along with other measures of their tendency to experience social anxiety. Indeed, the people who completed the IAS, as described in the previous section, also completed a measure of "situational social anxiety." That is, they completed a survey that described 11 different social situations and asked the participants to rate the level of anxiety that they would likely experience in each of those situations. Presumably, people who rate themselves as likely to experience a high level of social anxiety, on average, across the 11 situations will also have high scores on the IAS.

With such information, we can address several important psychometric questions: Does the IAS have a unidimensional structure as hypothesized? To what degree do participants' anxiety ratings from the 11 situations reflect a single "situational social anxiety" factor? To what degree is the IAS factor associated with a potential "situational anxiety" factor? Using CFA, we can evaluate all of these issues.

For example, we used CFA (actually, structural equation modeling, or SEM) to examine the model illustrated in Figure 12.5. First, as described earlier, we evaluated the internal structure of the IAS, to properly represent its internal structure. Second, we similarly evaluated the internal structure of the situational anxiety questionnaire, discovering that two of the situations did not load on a core "situational anxiety" factor. Thus, we dropped those two items, and we discovered some correlated error terms among the remaining nine items. Third, after clarifying

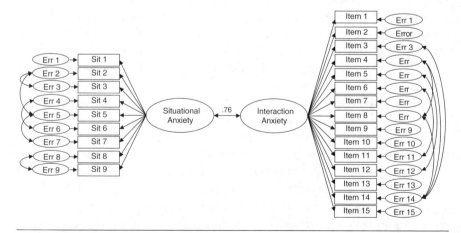

Figure 12.5   A Model to Evaluate the Convergent Validity of the Interaction Anxiousness Scale

the measurement models for the two questionnaires, we examined the model in Figure 12.5. As shown in this figure, we were primarily interested in the correlation between the two factors. And as shown in the figure, the correlation was extremely strong, and it was statistically significant. (Note that we include only this parameter estimate in the figure, for the sake of simplicity.)

By conducting such an analysis, we can evaluate validity evidence in terms of the association between a test and a relevant criterion, while also accounting for measurement error in both the test and the criterion. This is an important advantage of CFA over many alternative analytic strategies (e.g., the zero-order correlation between scale scores and criterion scores). Such models and similar ones (e.g., Figure 2 in McArdle, 1996) extend CFA to SEM, but the basic principles described in this chapter apply to SEM as well as to CFA. Again, readers interested in additional details on SEM are directed to a variety of useful sources (e.g., Hoyle, 2011).

Summary

CFA is a useful and increasingly accessible tool that we can use in the development and/or evaluation of psychological tests. It provides power and flexibility when evaluating a test's dimensionality, reliability, and validity, and it has important advantages over other statistical techniques (e.g., EFA and regression) and indices (e.g., coefficient alpha). To be sure, it requires more thought and careful attention than do some other psychometric tools; however, its important advantages and its increasing accessibility make it a very useful tool for the examination of psychometric quality.

CHAPTER 13

Generalizability Theory

D r. Johnson is a developmental psychologist interested in studying aggressiveness in adolescents. For her research, she has a number of options for measuring aggressiveness. She might ask "target" participants to complete a self-report inventory designed to assess their aggressiveness, or she might ask the participants to recruit friends who could provide ratings of the participants' aggressiveness. Alternatively, she might wish to avoid relying on questionnaires and instead measure aggressiveness by observing the target participants' behavior.

For example, Dr. Johnson might ask participants to spend 5 minutes being videotaped while chatting with a stranger of the opposite sex. She could then recruit her research assistant, Doris, to watch the videotapes, and she could ask Doris to judge each target's level of behavioral aggression. Understanding the importance of including multiple items, she might ask Doris to rate each target on three items that she believes are related to aggression: hostile, angry, and belligerent. Dr. Johnson's goal is to quantify the differences among the target participants in terms of the aggressiveness that they exhibit.

This measurement strategy fits well with the classical test theory (CTT) approach to psychometrics described in our chapters on reliability. Dr. Johnson's strategy is relatively simple, where only one potential source of measurement error could be evaluated. With this design, Dr. Johnson can use CTT to evaluate the degree to which item differences contribute to measurement error. As discussed in Chapter 6, she could evaluate the degree to which differences among the three items were related to measurement error, and she could compute coefficient alpha to estimate the reliability of the three-item measure of aggression. Furthermore, as discussed in Chapter 7, she could use tools such as the Spearman-Brown prophecy formula to estimate the reliability of a measure with more or fewer similar items.

But Dr. Johnson might have concerns about this relatively simple measurement strategy. In particular, she might worry about relying on only one observer to provide the behavioral ratings. As a unique individual, Doris has her own way of thinking about and interpreting behavior, including behavior that might be related to aggression. For example, Doris might tend to perceive sarcasm as quite aggressive. If a target participant makes a sarcastic remark, then Doris might interpret the remark as aggressive, but many others might interpret it as humorous rather than aggressive.

To deal with this potential limitation, Dr. Johnson might decide to recruit Ken and Tim to be additional observers to watch the videotapes and rate the targets' behavior. In this design, each observer would independently rate each target participant on each item. Dr. Johnson will then combine the ratings provided by all three observers to form overall aggression scores for her participants, hoping that each observer's unique interpretations of the behaviors are offset by the other observers' interpretations.

Although CTT is useful for conceptualizing and evaluating the quality of some measurement strategies, it cannot efficiently handle Dr. Johnson's improved strategy. The improved strategy is more complex than her original strategy because it includes multiple "facets" that could be evaluated as sources of measurement error—items and observers. Whereas her original strategy included multiple items, her improved strategy includes multiple items *and* multiple observers as two facets of the measurement process.

It is possible that different facets have different effects on the quality of measurement. For example, it is possible that the three items work well as measures of aggressiveness but that the different observers disagree dramatically in their ratings.

Despite the potential importance of such differences, CTT cannot tease apart multiple facets of the measurement process. An approach called generalizability theory (G theory) allows us to separate the effects of multiple facets and to adjust measurement strategies accordingly.

In this chapter, we present the logic and process of a psychometric analysis based on generalizability theory (Cronbach, Gleser, Nanda, & Rajaratnam, 1972). First, we outline some of the basic concepts in G theory, and we distinguish them from CTT. Second, we present two examples of a G theory analysis, explaining the rationale, calculation, and interpretation of the process. The first example is relatively simple, and it is intended to introduce the process of G theory analysis and to illustrate its parallels with CTT. The second example is more complex, and it illustrates the greater flexibility of G theory. Finally, we will describe several issues that affect the process and interpretation of analysis based on G theory.

Multiple Facets of Measurement

As a psychometric framework, G theory is well suited for complex measurement strategies in which multiple facets might affect measurement quality. This is a fundamental and potentially valuable difference between G theory and CTT.

Variability in psychological measurements might be created by many different facets of the measurement strategy, and these facets might in turn affect the measure's quality. For example, Dr. Johnson might be concerned about the number of items, the number of observers, and the way in which these two facets combine to affect measurement quality.

Recall from Chapter 5 that, from the perspective of CTT, total variance in a measure's observed scores is decomposed into only two components: true score variance and error variance (see Equation 5.3). In CTT, error variance is viewed as undifferentiated, amorphous, and monolithic (Brennan, 2001; Cronbach et al., 1972). That is, CTT cannot differentiate the effects of multiple facets, such as items and observers—they are all pooled into a single "measurement error." Thus, Dr. Johnson's improved measurement strategy will produce nine ratings of each target participant—three observers each rating three items. From the perspective of CTT, these nine ratings can only be treated as nine "tests" of aggression.

In contrast, from the perspective of G theory, total variance in a measure's observed scores can be decomposed into many components or facets, depending on the design of the measurement strategy. Perhaps most crucially, measurement error can be differentiated into many facets. That is, G theory can be used to investigate the effects that different aspects of a measurement strategy have on the overall quality of the measure. There are many theoretical and practical reasons why we might wish to differentiate among various sources of measurement error. For example, Dr. Johnson might wish to distinguish and understand differences among observers and differences among items as separable but potentially synergistic sources of measurement error in her improved strategy.

For theoretical reasons, Dr. Johnson might be interested in teachers' perceptions of students' aggressive behavior. Therefore, she might conduct a study in which several adult observers watch adolescents interact with each other and rate their aggression. For this study, she is interested in observers' differential perceptions of aggression, and she might wish to disentangle this from the differences among the items.

Alternatively, Dr. Johnson might have practical reasons for disentangling items and observers as separate facets of the measurement process. For instance, she might be planning a large-scale study of aggression, and she may need to prepare an efficient but reliable method for measuring aggressive behavior. In terms of the time and money required, relying on multiple observers might be more expensive than relying on multiple items—the inclusion of each additional observer (e.g., going from three to five observers) is probably more expensive and time consuming than simply asking each observer to rate additional items (e.g., going from three to five items). However, she does not yet know the psychometric impact of adding (or removing) observers or items. Perhaps the overall measure of aggression would be improved greatly by adding more observers but might be improved only slightly by adding more items.

To estimate the potential benefits of various measurement strategies for her large-scale study, Dr. Johnson conducts a small-scale pilot study consisting of three items and three observers. By using the G theory framework to examine the pilot data, Dr. Johnson can evaluate the psychometric quality of various combinations of numbers of observers and numbers of items (e.g., two observers each rating four items or three observers each rating two items). That is, she can use the information from her pilot study to estimate the psychometric quality that would likely be obtained from alternative combinations. This information, considered along with the practical costs of adding observers and/or items, can help optimize the efficiency and quality of the measurement strategy for her large-scale study.

In the language of G theory, each element of the measurement strategy is called a *facet*, and different measurement strategies are partly defined by their number of facets. Consider Dr. Johnson's original strategy, which included three items rated by one observer in one situation at one point in time. Because the strategy systematically included more than one item, "item" is considered the only "facet" of the measurement strategy. That is, each item might have its own unique way of being rated, and a G theory analysis can be conducted to evaluate the effect of differences among items. There were no other characteristics of the measurement strategy that were systematically designed to have more than one level or form—there were three different items, but there was only one observer (i.e., Doris) and only one situation (i.e., conversation with an opposite-sex stranger), at only one point in time. Because there was only one observer in the original design, G theory cannot be used to evaluate differences among observers. Similarly, because there was only one situation in the original design, G theory cannot be used to evaluate differences among situations. However, because there were three different items included in the design, G theory can be used to evaluate differences among items. With only one characteristic of the measurement strategy (i.e., items) that has more than one level, Dr. Johnson's original design is considered a one-facet design.

More complex measurement strategies have multiple facets. Dr. Johnson's improved strategy included several different items and several different observers (i.e., Doris, Ken, and Tim). This improved strategy is a two-facet design, and Dr. Johnson can evaluate the differences among observers as well the differences among items. This improved strategy would allow several interesting and potentially important psychometric questions, as we will illustrate later. For an even more complex design, Dr. Johnson might observe participants in two situations: (1) a conversation with an opposite-sex stranger and (2) a conversation with a same-sex stranger. For this study, she might ask the three observers to rate participants on each of the three items in each of the two situations. This, more complex design would have three facets—items, observers, and situations. Again, this three-facet design would allow an even greater number of interesting and potentially important questions, beyond those allowed by a two-facet design.

Generalizability, Universes, and Variance Components

As the name implies, the concept of *generalizability* is at the heart of G theory. Briefly, measurement quality is evaluated in terms of the ability to make inferences from (a) scores based on a limited number of observations to (b) scores based on a nearly unlimited number of observations.

When a psychological or behavioral variable is measured, only a limited number of observations are made. For example, Dr. Johnson's original measurement strategy included only three items—hostile, belligerent, and angry. From the typical perspective of G theory, the important issue is the degree to which the scores obtained from the limited number of observations included in a measure represent the scores that *would be* obtained from a large "universe" of observations. In a sense,

Dr. Johnson's three aggression items are a sample from the entire set or universe of items that reflect aggressive behavior. There are many other behavioral items (e.g., confrontational, antagonistic, combative, etc.) that could have been included in her "aggression" measure, and it is possible that different items would work somewhat differently for her study. Thus, she needs to be concerned about the degree to which the specific items included in her study might be representative of the many other items that could be used to measure aggression. Although Dr. Johnson used only three items, she would like to assume that these three items will produce scores that are representative of or generalizable to or consistent with the scores that would be obtained if all possible "aggression" items had been used.

In this way, G theory can be seen as an extension of domain-sampling theory, as discussed in Chapter 5. That discussion described the concept of a domain of items, and reliability was derived from this concept. Similarly, G theory is based on the notion of a universe of items (or other methods of measurement), and reliability is framed in terms of our ability to generalize from a small set of items to a score that would be obtained by using an entire universe of items.

As another example, consider scores made in physical competitions such as Olympic figure skating. In the current scoring system for Olympic figure skating, ratings from only nine judges are used to score the competitors' performances (U.S. Figure Skating, 2012). The nine judges are chosen because of their qualifications, but they might be seen as a small sample from the large group of qualified judges from around the world. Furthermore, from the perspective of G theory, the scores obtained through the nine judges should represent the scores that would be obtained if all possible qualified judges were to observe and rate the performances. That is, we would like to believe that the scores generalize to something beyond the idiosyncratic perceptions of the nine people who happened to be selected as judges.

In our earlier discussion of reliability (Chapters 5–7), we emphasized the concept of consistency, which can also be seen as an important concept in G theory. Earlier, we discussed reliability as the consistency between observed scores and true scores, and we showed that reliability is estimated from the consistency among items on a test. From the perspective of G theory, Dr. Johnson is interested in the consistency between the scores on her three-item measure of aggression and the scores that would be obtained from a measure made of the entire universe of aggression items. More to the point, Dr. Johnson is interested in the degree to which the variability in individuals' test scores is consistent with the variability in their "universe" scores.

In a G theory analysis, estimates of generalizability are based on *variance components* representing the degree to which differences exist in the "universe" for each element of the design (Shavelson & Webb, 1991). For example, one variance component represents the variability among the large set (i.e., the population) of people from which the observed target participants were drawn. For an even deeper understanding of variance components, imagine that a participant receives a score on every aggression item from the entire universe of aggression items. This hypothetical score is the participant's "universe score" because it is based on the entire universe of items. Now imagine that each person in the population received a universe score (again, based on the entire universe of aggression items). A variance component is the variance of universe scores within the population of individuals.

The sizes of variance components have important implications for measurement design and quality. More specifically, the size of a facet's variance component indicates the degree to which it has an impact on observed scores. If a variance component is relatively large, then that facet has a relatively large impact on scores. That is, if a facet has a large variance component, then the different levels of that facet tend to produce different scores on the measure. For example, if Dr. Johnson's analysis shows that "item" facet in her pilot study has a relatively large variance component, then she would infer that different items are interpreted differently—that is, that the items tend to differ substantially in the ratings that they elicit. It might be the case that "hostile" simply tends to be rated lower than "belligerent" for some reason. Thus, the items seem to be working somewhat differently as indicators of aggression. Moreover, this would imply that a different set of items might elicit dramatically different ratings of aggression.

Going further, variance components can have important implications for the psychometric quality of a measurement strategy. For example, if Dr. Johnson's analysis reveals a relatively large estimated variance component for the item facet, then she might have concerns about using only three items in her measurement design. That is, a large variance component would mean that items differ robustly. Thus, if she uses only a small number of items in her measurement design, then she might obtain scores that have poor generalizability. In other words, she might obtain scores that would differ substantially from scores that would be obtained if she used a different set of items, or from the "universe" scores that would be obtained if she used all possible items (which is, of course, only a theoretical possibility). Of course, this raises question such as "If the three original items are poor as a set, then which three items could be used instead? And is three even enough?" Perhaps she needs to use a larger number of items in order to get a closer approximation to the universe of possible items.

As we mention below, we are primarily interested in the relative sizes of the variance components in an analysis. That is, when estimating generalizability and psychometric quality, our results are affected most heavily when some variance components are much larger than others. As we noted earlier in the book (Chapter 3) the absolute size of a variance term is inherently ambiguous because it depends on the magnitude of the effect and on the scale of measurement. What we mentioned with regard to the simple variance statistic in Chapter 3 also applies to "variance components" in G theory.

G Studies and D Studies

G theory can be used for many kinds of analyses, but a basic G theory analysis is a two-phase process. In the first phase, variance components are estimated from data collected through a measurement strategy of interest. In this phase, the factors affecting observed score variance (and thus affecting generalizability) are identified, and their effects can be estimated. For example, Dr. Johnson can estimate the degree to which the ratings of targets' aggressiveness are affected by differences among target participants, differences among items, and differences among observers, and the ways in which these facets interact with each other (e.g., the degree to which the observers use the items differently). This phase is often known as a *G study* because it is used to identify the degree to which the various facets might affect the generalizability of the ratings (Marcoulides, 1996).

In the second step of a G theory analysis, the results of the first step can be used to estimate the generalizability of various combinations of the facets. Because these estimations are the basis for making decisions about future measurement strategies, this second step is often known as a *D study* (Marcoulides, 1996). For example, Dr. Johnson can conduct a D study to estimate the number of items and observers that would be needed to obtain a generalizability of .80 for judgments of aggressiveness based on observations of behavior. It might be difficult or expensive for Dr. Johnson to increase the number of observers that can contribute ratings. Therefore, she might be very interested in estimating the number of items that would be required to obtain a particular generalizability, based on a design with a small number of observers. On the basis of these estimates, she can make a well-informed decision about the optimal measurement strategy to adopt.

Conducting and Interpreting Generalizability Theory Analysis: A One-Facet Design

Our first example illustrates the logic, computations, and interpretation of a G theory analysis of a relatively simple measurement strategy. For this example, we will focus on Dr. Johnson's original design, in which participants are rated by an observer using three items. As described above, this is a one-facet design because there is only one element with multiple levels that differ in a systematic way. That is, "item" is a facet because the design includes several items. Again, there are no other elements of the measurement strategy that vary systematically—there is only one observer, only one situation, only one point in time, and so on. Although we will use this simple measurement strategy to begin illustrating G theory, it could also be examined through CTT. Thus, we will use this example to show how G theory parallels CTT in the simple case of a one-facet design.

Imagine that Dr. Johnson collected the data in Table 13.1. In this example, five target participants are observed by Doris, who rates each participant on three items associated with aggression. Ratings are made on 10-point scale in which high scores indicate greater aggressiveness. To obtain an overall aggressiveness score for each target, Dr. Johnson plans to average across the three ratings for each target. Again, Dr. Johnson hopes that the differences in the overall aggressiveness scores can be generalized to the "universe scores" that would be obtained if participants were rated on the entire universe of aggressiveness items. As described earlier, a key goal of the G theory analysis is to estimate this generalizability. A high level of generalizability would mean, roughly speaking, that the scores based on three items are likely to be similar to the scores that would be based on all possible aggression items. Moreover, it would mean that there are minimal differences among her three items, and those differences do not produce much measurement error. To begin the analysis, we must examine the factors affecting the ratings and, consequently, the psychometric quality of the scores.

Table 13.1   Example Data for One-Facet Generalizability Theory: Ratings of Five Targets on Three Items

Target	Item			Target Mean
	Hostile	**Angry**	**Belligerent**	
Ann	3	3	3	3
Bob	1	1	2	1.3
Carolyn	3	3	4	3.3
Drew	3	5	5	4.3
Eleanor	3	7	6	5.3
Item mean	2.60	3.80	4.00	

Phase 1: G Study

For the first phase of a G theory analysis (the G study phase), researchers generate estimates of variance components for each of the factors affecting the ratings. Typically, researchers can use analysis of variance (ANOVA), which is available in all popular statistical software packages (alternative variance decomposition procedures, such as SAS's VARCOMP procedure, will also produce these values). As you may know, ANOVA is a statistical procedure that is commonly used in experimental research. The purpose of ANOVA is to examine the variability within a distribution of scores (e.g., ratings of participants' behavior) and to tease apart or "decompose" the degree to which the variability is associated with various factors of the measurement process (e.g., target participants, items).

Dr. Johnson conducts an ANOVA to examine the variability within the 15 ratings—ratings of the five participants on three items—and the results are shown in Table 13.2. The ANOVA allows Dr. Johnson to partition the rating data into the relevant effects and to estimate the variance component for each effect.

In the case of a one-facet design, there are three factors that might affect the variability in the distribution of ratings. One factor is, of course, the extent to which

Table 13.2   Analysis of Variance and Generalizability Results for Behavioral Observation: Example Data

Effect	df	Sum of Squares	Mean Squares	Variance Component	Proportion of Variance
Target	4	27.067	6.767	1.967	.608
Item	2	5.733	2.867	0.400	.124
Residual	8	6.933	0.867	0.867	.268
Total	14	39.733		3.233	1.000

targets differ in their average level of aggressiveness. Notice in Table 13.1 that, averaged across the three items, Ann's average aggressiveness score (3.0) is lower than Drew's (4.3). This suggests that Ann generally behaved less aggressively than Drew did. The variability among targets' average aggressiveness scores reflects the degree to which target participants differ in aggressiveness. All else being equal, measurement quality will be best when the target participants differ from each other. As discussed in the earlier chapters on correlations and reliability, variability among participants is a key part of the measurement process. In essence, this factor is what Dr. Johnson hopes to capture with her measurement strategy.

The second factor is the extent to which items differ in their average level of aggressiveness. Notice in Table 13.1 that, averaged across target participants, "hostile" has a lower average rating (2.60) than "belligerent" (4.00). The variability among the item averages reflects the degree to which the items elicited different ratings across target participants. Thus, part of the reason why the 15 ratings differ from each other is because the items elicited different average ratings.

Measurement error is the third factor affecting differences among the 15 ratings in Table 13.1. Recall that Dr. Johnson's goal is to detect clear and consistent differences among her participants, but the ratings suggest that the differences are somewhat inconsistent across the items. Note in Table 13.1 that Ann is rated as equally hostile as Drew, but she is rated as less angry than Drew. So which person is more aggressive? Are Ann and Drew equally aggressive, as suggested by their same hostility ratings? Or is Ann less aggressive than Drew, as suggested by the fact that her anger rating is lower than his? The inconsistency between the two items partially obscures the difference between Ann and Drew, so it is considered measurement error.

For the one-facet measurement design, ANOVA produces two main effects and a residual (or error) term. In most experimental applications of ANOVA, we would conduct significance tests of the effects; however, a G theory application of ANOVA does not require significance tests. In fact, the results of the ANOVA, primarily the mean squares, are useful for G theory only because they allow us to estimate variance components.

Table 13.2 presents the results of the ANOVA, and Table 13.3 presents the equations for estimating the variance components in this design. In addition, Table 13.2 presents the estimates of the variance components (σ^2 values) and the proportion of variance for each effect (the variance component divided by the sum of the variance components). For example, the variance component for the target effect is

$$\sigma_t^2 = \frac{MS_t - MS_{Res}}{n_i},$$

$$= \frac{6.767 - .867}{3},$$

$$= \frac{5.9}{3},$$

$$= 1.967.$$

Results reveal the degree to which each facet affects ratings of aggressiveness. As noted earlier, the absolute size of a variance component is difficult to interpret

Table 13.3   Equations for Estimating Variance Components in the Target Item Model

Effect	Equation
Target	$$\sigma_t^2 = \frac{MS_t - MS_{Res}}{n_i}$$
Item	$$\sigma_i^2 = \frac{MS_i - MS_{Res}}{n_t}$$
Residual	$$\sigma_{Res}^2 = MS_{Res}$$

because it depends on the magnitude of the effect and on the scale of measurement. Therefore, an effect's variance component is usually most meaningful when compared with the variance components of other effects in the analysis, or when it is viewed as a proportion of total variability. We will illustrate the meaning and use of these values for each effect in the design.

The primary effect of interest is the *target effect*. This effect reflects the degree to which targets elicit different mean ratings, averaged across all items. As shown in Table 13.2, the estimated variance component for the target effect is the largest variance component of all the effects (1.967). In fact, differences among the target means account for more than 60% of all the variability in the ratings:

$$\frac{1.967}{1.967 + 400 + .867} = .608.$$

The relatively large size of this variance component (in comparison with the other variance components in this analysis) is good news for Dr. Johnson, who is interested in measuring the differences among the target participants. The target effect essentially is the "signal" that she is trying to detect, and its relatively large variance component indicates that there is a strong signal.

If the target effect is the signal that Dr. Johnson would like to detect, then we need also to consider the noise that potentially masks that signal. There are two kinds of decisions that might be made on the basis of a G theory analysis, and they treat noise or error in different ways. To keep matters somewhat straightforward, we will now focus only on "relative" decisions, which have the closest connection to measurement error and reliability as defined in CTT. Relative decisions (also known as norm-referenced decisions) concern the relative order of participants, or the participants in relation to each other. For example, if an honor society admits the top 15% of a group of students, then the society is interested in the rank order of the students, and its admissions decision is based on students' scores in relation to each other. Toward the end of this chapter, we will briefly discuss the other type of decisions, which are called "absolute" or criterion-referenced decisions.

In the one-facet design, the *residual effect* is the noise that potentially masks the signal of the target effect. If the measurement strategy is good, then the participants with high scores on one item should also have high scores on the other items. More technically, if there are clear differences among participants, if the items are all good reflections of the behavioral construct in question, and if the ratings are not affected by random states of the participants, observer, or measurement context, then the differences among participants should be consistently apparent across the items. Unfortunately, Dr. Johnson might find inconsistency in some way, which would indicate the noise that obscures a signal.

Specifically, inconsistency across the items might come from three possible sources. First, there might not be clear differences among participants (i.e., a weak signal). Second, the items might not be equally good reflections of the construct. Third, the ratings might be affected by random states or forces in the assessment context. The last two possibilities (items' relation to the construct and random effects) are captured by the residual effect's variance component. In Dr. Johnson's data, the residual effect ($\sigma_{Res}^2 = .867$) is small in comparison with the variance component for the target effect, reflecting only 27% of the variance.

For a more complete perspective on the logic of G theory, let us examine the main effect of items and consider why it is *not* considered a source of error when detecting differences among participants. The variance component for *items* indicates the degree to which some items elicited higher mean ratings than did other items. As illustrated in Table 13.1, the items' mean ratings (averaged across targets) range from 2.6 to 4.0. However, because Dr. Johnson is primarily interested in detecting the differences among the target participants, her primary psychometric concern is whether the items operated consistently with each other, in terms of the relative ordering of the targets. The fact that the items differ in the average ratings that they elicited is unrelated to the issue of whether the items operated *consistently* in terms of the relative ordering of the targets. Therefore, the main effect of items is not considered error, in terms of Dr. Johnson's ability to detect differences among targets.

Phase 2: D Study

The second phase of a G theory analysis is often a D study that informs decisions for future measurement strategies. As mentioned earlier, test users should try to maximize the quality and efficiency of their measurement strategies, but these are somewhat contradictory goals. On one hand, Dr. Johnson should include a large enough number of items to ensure a high level of generalizability for her large-scale study. On the other hand, she would like to include a small number of items, which would simplify the rating process for her observer, minimize the time needed to measure aggression, and potentially even save money. By conducting the D study phase of analysis, Dr. Johnson estimates the psychometric quality of different measurement strategies, and the results can help plan a good measurement strategy for her large-scale study.

To conduct a D study, test users estimate "coefficients of generalizability" for various measurement strategies. If Dr. Johnson is interested in obtaining a measure of individual differences among the target participants, then she is interested in "relative" generalizability coefficients. As mentioned earlier, a coefficient of generalizability is analogous to reliability as defined by CTT, in that it represents the degree to which the observed differences among target participants are consistent with the differences that would be obtained if a nearly unlimited number of observations were obtained. Like coefficient alpha, generalizability coefficients can range from 0 to 1.0. In fact, one particular kind of generalizability is equal to coefficient alpha for some measurement designs, as we will illustrate. For her one-facet design, Dr. Johnson estimates generalizability coefficients for different numbers of items.

Conceptually, a generalizability coefficient represents a ratio of signal and noise. When measuring psychological or behavioral differences among participants, the test user is essentially trying to detect a signal (i.e., differences among participants) that is potentially obscured by noise (i.e., random measurement error and other specific facets of the measurement strategy). There are two factors affecting the ability to detect a signal—the strength of the signal and the amount of noise. A generalizability coefficient can be seen as

$$\text{Generalizability coefficient} = \frac{\text{Signal}}{\text{Signal} + \text{Noise}}.$$

To estimate generalizability coefficients, test users use variance components obtained from the G study phase of analysis. As described earlier, the variance component of the target effect represents the signal that Dr. Johnson is trying to detect, and the variance component for the residual term represents the noise that could be masking the signal. More specifically, to obtain an estimate of the coefficient of generalizability (ρ^2) for a particular measurement strategy, she obtains a ratio of the appropriate variance components weighted by the number of items for the measurement strategy:

$$\rho_t^2 = \frac{\sigma_t^2}{\sigma_t^2 + \dfrac{\sigma_{Res}^2}{n'_i}}. \tag{13.1}$$

In this equation, ρ_t^2 is the relative generalizability coefficient for the differences among targets, σ_t^2 is the estimated variance component for the target effect, σ_{Res}^2 is the estimated variance component for the residual term, and n'_i is the number of items being considered. For example, Dr. Johnson can use the variance components from her G study (see Table 13.2) to estimate the relative generalizability coefficient for her three-item measure of aggression:

$$\rho_t^2 = \frac{1.967}{1.967 + \dfrac{.867}{3}},$$

$$= \frac{1.967}{1.967 + .289},$$

$$= .872.$$

The relatively large size of this coefficient (well above .80) indicates that the three-item strategy of measuring aggression seems to be adequately generalizable. In fact, the generalizability coefficient for the differences among targets in a one-facet design is exactly equal to coefficient alpha (which you can demonstrate by computing α for the data in Table 13.1).

Although the three-item strategy has good generalizability, Dr. Johnson might be interested in evaluating other measurement strategies using more or fewer items. Table 13.4 presents the relative generalizability coefficients estimated for different numbers of items. For example, her estimate of the relative generalizability coefficient that would be obtained with only two items is

$$\rho_t^2 = \frac{1.967}{1.967 + \dfrac{.867}{2}},$$

$$= \frac{1.967}{1.967 + .433},$$

$$= .819.$$

Table 13.4 and Figure 13.1 show the results of Dr. Johnson's D study. As they demonstrate, generalizability increases as more items are added; however, those increases begin to level off after three or four items. On the basis of these results, Dr. Johnson might decide that three items provide sufficient psychometric quality. Furthermore, she might decide that the potential psychometric benefit of adding a fourth or fifth item is not worth any additional time or effort on the part of her observer.

In sum, this example illustrates G theory as applied to a one-facet measurement strategy. Hopefully, it conveys a sense of the process, logic, and meaning of G theory and the information that it generates. We presented a one-facet example to illustrate some of the fundamental aspects of G theory in a relatively simple illustration and to show that G theory is equivalent to CTT for one-facet designs using relative generalizability coefficients. However, this example does not demonstrate the true strength of G theory. As discussed earlier, a key difference between G theory and CTT is that G theory can accommodate multiple facets of measurement error. We turn to this in the next example.

	Coefficient	
Items (n'_i)	Relative (ρ_t^2)	Absolute (ϕ_t^2)
1	.69	.61
2	.82	.76
3	.87	.82
4	.90	.86
5	.92	.89
6	.93	.90
7	.94	.92

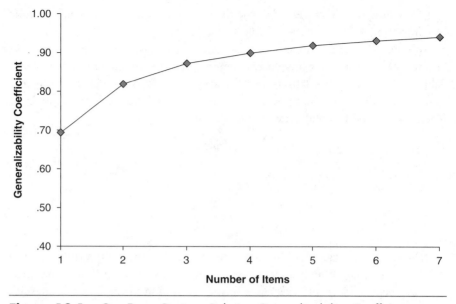

Figure 13.1   One-Facet Design: Relative Generalizability Coefficients as a Function of the Number of Items

Conducting and Interpreting Generalizability Theory Analysis: A Two-Facet Design

With the ability to examine multiple facets of the measurement design simultaneously, G theory is a very useful alternative to CTT. Many measurement designs might rely on more than one facet of measurement, and the facets might influence psychometric quality to differing degrees. G theory can tease apart these influences.

Recall that Dr. Johnson's improved strategy calls for several observers to rate the target participants on several items. This is an improvement over her original strategy because any individual observer might have unique ways of perceiving and interpreting the targets' behavior. In fact, the one-facet design described above is limited because all the ratings were produced by only one observer—Doris. Although the example above showed that Doris's ratings seem to have good generalizability, it is possible that Doris is a particularly perceptive and conscientious observer. Dr. Johnson might be concerned that most other observers would produce ratings with weaker psychometric quality. And if Doris cannot work on Dr. Johnson's large-scale study, then Dr. Johnson will need to recruit other observers. To what degree are the results of the G theory analysis of Doris's ratings (as described earlier) generalizable to other observers? With these issues in mind, Dr. Johnson recruited two additional observers to watch the same five target participants and rate their behavior on the same three aggressiveness items.

Table 13.5 presents the data that Dr. Johnson could obtain from such a study. In this example, five target participants are rated by three observers using the same three items. The observers rated each target on each item, using a 1- to 10-point

Table 13.5 Example Data for Two-Facet Generalizability Theory: Ratings of Five Targets by Three Observers Using Three Items

Target	Ken			Doris			Tim			Target Mean
	Hostile	Angry	Belligerent	Hostile	Angry	Belligerent	Hostile	Angry	Belligerent	
Ann	2	2	2	3	3	3	3	5	1	2.67
Bob	1	3	2	1	1	2	4	5	3	2.44
Carolyn	2	3	3	3	3	4	5	7	3	3.67
Drew	5	8	6	3	5	5	7	7	6	5.78
Eleanor	8	7	9	3	7	6	4	7	9	6.67

scale in which high scores indicated greater aggressiveness. Again, Dr. Johnson plans to average across all the ratings that were made for each target. And again, she hopes that the differences in the observed aggressiveness scores are generalizable.

The improved design includes two facets of the measurement strategy—items and observers. Thus, Dr. Johnson hopes to be able to generalize across two "universes." As described for the one-facet design, she hopes that the scores obtained from the three items in her study are generalizable to the scores that would be obtained from all items that could be used to measure aggression. In addition, she hopes that the scores obtained from her three observers are generalizable to the scores that would be obtained if a huge set of observers provided ratings of aggression. That is, she hopes that her averaged scores are generalizable across a universe of items and across a universe of observers.

The analysis of a multiple-facet design works much like a one-facet design. First, a G study is conducted, and variance components are estimated for each effect related to the measurement strategy. In multiple-facet designs, as in one-facet designs, ANOVA is usually used to estimate the variance components. Second, a D study is conducted, and generalizability coefficients are estimated for various measurement strategies. In multiple-facet designs, generalizability coefficients are still estimated through an analysis of signal to noise as represented by ratios of variance components.

Despite these similarities, there is an important difference between one-facet designs and multiple-facet designs. The difference lies in the complexity of the components affecting variability of the data. With each single facet added to a design, there are several components that are added. Recall that a one-facet design included 3 components—in Dr. Johnson's example, these were targets, items, and the residual. However, a two-facet design can include 7 components, a three-facet design can include 16 components, and so on. This additional complexity adds complexity to the "noise" or error element of generalizability coefficients. In this section of the chapter, we examine a two-facet design as a way of illustrating the important logic of more complex designs.

Phase 1: G Study

Again, ANOVA is used to generate estimates of variance components for each factor affecting the ratings. Dr. Johnson conducts an ANOVA to examine the variability within the 45 ratings (5 targets × 3 items × 3 observers), and the results are shown in Table 13.6. She is interested in the degree to which the ratings are affected by the three main effects (differences among target participants, differences among observers, and differences among items), the interactions among those effects, and random error. Table 13.7 presents the equations for estimating the variance components in this design, and Table 13.6 presents the estimates of the variance components and the proportion of variance for each effect.

The results reveal the degree to which each effect influences the ratings of aggressiveness, and Table 13.8 presents interpretations and examples for each effect. In evaluating the relative generalizability of the coding procedures as a measure of individual differences in targets' aggressiveness, four of the effects are of particular interest—one effect represents the signal to be detected, and three contribute to the noise masking the signal. Table 13.9 presents averages to help illustrate these effects.

The primary effect of interest is again the *main effect of the targets*. As mentioned in Table 13.8, this effect reflects the degree to which the targets elicited different mean ratings, averaged across observers and items. The main effect of the targets reflects the differences among the target participants' averages, which range from 2.44 to 6.67 (see Table 13.9). As shown in Table 13.6, the estimated variance component for the target effect is the largest of all the variance components:

$$\sigma_t^2 = \frac{MS_t - MS_{ti} - MS_{to} + MS_{Res}}{n_i n_o},$$
$$= \frac{32.133 - 1.550 - 2.900 + 1.417}{3 \times 3},$$
$$= \frac{29.1}{9},$$
$$= 3.233.$$

In fact, differences among the target means account for more than 50% of the variability in the ratings, which indicates that the signal is relatively strong. As in the one-facet design, this is good news for Dr. Johnson, who is interested in measuring the differences among the target participants. The generalizability coefficients to be computed will reflect the degree to which the differences among the target participants are consistent across items and observers.

In terms of her ability to detect differences among the target participants, measurement error (i.e., noise) includes three effects. These effects are included in the

Table 13.6 ANOVA and Generalizability Results for Behavioral Observation: Example Data

Effect	df	Sum of Squares	Mean Square	Variance Component	Proportion of Variance
Target	4	128.533	32.133	3.233	.544
Item	2	12.044	6.022	0.289	.049
Observer	2	19.244	9.622	0.439	.074
Target × Item	8	12.400	1.550	0.044	.007
Target × Observer	8	23.200	2.900	0.494	.083
Item × Observer	4	6.222	1.556	0.028	.005
Residual	16	22.667	1.417	1.4170	.238
Total	44	224.311		5.944	1.000

Table 13.7 Equations for Estimating Variance Components in the Target × Observer × Item Model

Effect	Equation
Target	$\sigma_t^2 = \dfrac{MS_t - MS_{to} - MS_{ti} + MS_{Res}}{n_o n_i}$
Item	$\sigma_i^2 = \dfrac{MS_i - MS_{ti} - MS_{oi} + MS_{Res}}{n_t n_o}$
Observer	$\sigma_o^2 = \dfrac{MS_o - MS_{to} - MS_{oi} + MS_{Res}}{n_t n_i}$
Target × Item	$\sigma_{ti}^2 = \dfrac{MS_{ti} - MS_{Res}}{n_o}$
Target × Observer	$\sigma_{to}^2 = \dfrac{MS_{to} - MS_{Res}}{n_i}$
Item × Observer	$\sigma_{oi}^2 = \dfrac{MS_{oi} - MS_{Res}}{n_t}$
Residual	$\sigma_{Res}^2 = MS_{Res}$

Table 13.8 Substantive Interpretations and Examples of the Effects in Generalizability Theory Analysis

Effect	Interpretation (the Degree to Which . . .)	Example
Target (T)	Targets elicited different mean ratings, averaged across the 3 observers and the 3 items.	Target X gets a higher average rating than Target Y.
Item (I)	Items elicited different mean ratings, averaged across the 5 targets and the 3 observers.	Item 1 has a higher average rating than Item 2.
Observer (O)	Observers provided different mean ratings, averaged across the 5 targets and the 3 items.	Observer A gives higher average ratings than Observer B.
T × I[a]	Targets were rank ordered differently across items, in terms of their ratings averaged across the observers.	On Item 1, Target X was rated higher than Target Y, but on Item 2, Target X was rated lower than Target Y.
T × O[a]	Targets were rank ordered differently across observers, in terms of their ratings averaged across the two items.	Observer A rates Target X higher than Target Y, but Observer B rates Target X lower than Target Y.
I × O	Items were rank ordered differently by the observers, in terms of the ratings averaged across the targets.	Observer A tends to rate Item 1 higher than Item 2, but Observer B tends to rate Item 1 lower than Item 2.
Residual[a]	Variance in ratings is not associated with any of the above effects.	

[a.]These terms are considered as contributing to "error" in the relative generalizability of the target effect.

Table 13.9 Means of Ratings

Main effects

Target	Mean	Observer	Mean	Item	Mean
Ann	2.67	Ken	4.20	Hostile	3.60
Bob	2.44	Doris	3.50	Angry	4.87
Carolyn	3.67	Tim	5.10	Belligerent	4.27
Drew	5.78				
Eleanor	6.67				

Interactions

	Target x Observer				Target x Item				Observer x Item		
Target	Ken	Doris	Tim	Target	Hostile	Angry	Belligerent	Observer	Hostile	Angry	Belligerent
Ann	2.00	3.00	3.00	Ann	3.00	3.33	2.00	Ken	3.60	4.60	4.40
Bob	2.00	1.33	4.00	Bob	2.00	3.00	2.33	Doris	2.60	3.80	4.00
Carolyn	2.67	3.33	5.00	Carolyn	3.00	4.33	3.33	Tim	4.60	6.20	4.40
Drew	6.33	4.33	6.67	Drew	5.00	6.67	5.67				
Eleanor	8.00	5.33	6.67	Eleanor	5.00	7.00	8.00				

numerator of the variance component for the target effect (MS_{ti}, MS_{to}, and MS_{Res}), and they will affect the generalizability coefficient for the target effect. First, the Target × Item interaction reflects the degree to which the targets were rank ordered differently across the items. A large Target × Item interaction would indicate that the items operate somewhat inconsistently across the targets, thus potentially clouding the differences among the targets. That is, a large Target × Item interaction would indicate that the difference between the targets is inconsistent across the items. Table 13.6 shows that the Target × Item interaction is relatively small in Dr. Johnson's data (accounting for less than 1% of the variance), which is reflected in the averages in Table 13.9. Note, for example, that Drew scores noticeably higher than Carolyn on all three of the items. Drew's average hostility score (averaged across all three observers) is 2 points higher than Carolyn's average hostility score (i.e., 5 − 3 = 2), his average anger score is 2.34 points higher than her average anger score, and his average belligerence score is 2.34 points higher than her average belligerence score. Thus, the difference between Drew and Carolyn is quite consistent across the three items. Put another way, the differences among the targets *do* seem generalizable across the items, and Dr. Johnson concludes that there is very little "noise" created by the small Target × Item effect.

A second source of error in this example is the Target × Observer interaction, which reflects the degree to which the observers provided different rank orderings of the targets. The Target × Observer averages in Table 13.9 illustrate this effect. For example, notice that the three observers are inconsistent with each other in their judgments of the difference between Ann and Bob. Although Doris sees Ann as more aggressive than Bob, Ken sees no difference between the two, and Tim sees Ann as *less* aggressive than Bob. Specifically, Doris's average rating of Ann is 3.00 (averaged across the three items), and her average rating of Bob is 1.33. In contrast, Ken's average rating of Ann is 2.00, as is his average rating of Bob. Finally, Tim's average rating of Ann is 3.00, and his average rating of Bob is 4.00. If Dr. Johnson's goal is to detect a difference between Ann and Bob, then the inconsistency in the observers' judgments about the difference between Ann and Bob is a problem. Again, the primary goal in this measurement example is to obtain a clear and consistent measure of the differences among the target participants on aggressiveness scores (i.e., to obtain a generalizable measure of individual differences in aggressiveness). With this goal in mind, the Target × Observer effect contributes to error because a large effect would indicate that the relative ordering of the target participants is *not* consistent or generalizable across the observers. As shown in Table 13.6, the Target × Observer interaction accounts for approximately 8% of the variability in the ratings.

A third source of error is reflected in the *residual* term, which represents two elements that might produce noise in the measurement. Because the observers provided only one rating of each target on each item (in each situation), Dr. Johnson cannot separate the three-way interaction between targets, observers, and items from pure "error" variance. Both of these components would be considered measurement error because they would contribute to ambiguity/inconsistency in terms of the rank ordering of targets across the observers and items. As Table 13.6 indicates, the residual accounts for 24% of the variance in the ratings.

For an even more complete understanding, a discussion of the three remaining effects is useful. These effects are *not* considered to be measurement error because they do not compromise the rank ordering of the targets. The *main effect of observer* indicates the degree to which some observers provided higher average ratings than other observers—the degree to which some observers tend to see people as generally more or less aggressive than do other observers. As illustrated in Table 13.9, the observers' average ratings (averaged across targets and items) range from 3.5 to 5.1. This suggests that Doris tended to view the target participants as less aggressive in general than did Tim. Importantly, the fact that the observers differed in their ratings of aggressiveness in general is unrelated to the issue of whether the observers were *consistent with each other* in terms of the relative ordering of the targets. Therefore, the main effect of observers is not considered error, in terms of Dr. Johnson's ability to detect differences among the targets. Note that the Target × Observer interaction discussed earlier indicates the degree to which target differences are inconsistent across the observers (which would be considered measurement error), but this is statistically and conceptually separate from the possibility that some observers provided higher ratings than others, in general, across all the targets.

As described for the one-facet design, the *main effect of item* indicates the degree to which some items elicited higher mean ratings than did other items. As illustrated in Table 13.9, the items' mean ratings (averaged across targets and observers) range from 3.6 to 4.9. Again, the fact that the items differed in the ratings of aggressiveness that they elicited is unrelated to the issue of whether the items operated consistently in terms of the relative ordering of the targets. Therefore, the main effect of items is not considered error, in terms of Dr. Johnson's ability to detect differences among the targets.

Finally, the Item × Observer interaction indicates the degree to which the observers differed in their average rank orderings of the items, as averaged across the targets. Note that Doris's average rating for angry (3.80) is lower than her average rating for belligerent (4.00), but Ken's ratings are in the opposite direction—his average rating for angry (4.60) is higher than his average rating for belligerent (4.40; see Table 13.9). Thus, the observers seem to be interpreting and using these items in different ways. Although Doris and Ken seem to have used these two items differently in general, this difference should not affect the specific differences among the target participants. Therefore, the item-by-observer interaction is not considered to be measurement error, in terms of Dr. Johnson's ability to detect a clear and consistent rank ordering of the targets.

G theory's differentiation of measurement error allows Dr. Johnson to understand the degree to which the targets' mean scores (i.e., the measure of individual differences in aggressiveness) are affected by each facet of the measurement strategy—observers and items. She can then use the variance components in Table 13.6 to make decisions about the number of observers and the number of items that might be used in future research.

Phase 2: D Study

As described for the one-facet design, the relative generalizability coefficient is analogous to reliability in CTT. And again, it can be seen as a ratio of signal and noise:

$$\text{Generalizability coefficient} = \frac{\text{Signal}}{\text{Signal} + \text{Noise}}.$$

The only difference between the one-facet and two-facet designs is the makeup of noise. More specifically, the relative generalizability coefficient for a particular measurement strategy is

$$\rho_t^2 = \frac{\sigma_t^2}{\sigma_t^2 + \dfrac{\sigma_{ti}^2}{n'_i} + \dfrac{\sigma_{ti}^2}{n'_o} + \dfrac{\sigma_{ti}^2}{n'_i n'_o}}. \tag{13.2}$$

In this equation, ρ_t^2 is the relative generalizability coefficient for the differences among targets, and σ_t^2 is the estimated variance component for the target effect (i.e., the "signal" to be detected). The remaining elements of the equation constitute the "noise" that is potentially obscuring the signal. Specifically, σ_{ti}^2 is the estimated variance component for the Target × Item effect, σ_{to}^2 is the estimated variance component for the Target × Observer effect, σ_{Res}^2 is the estimated variance component for the residual term, n'_i is the number of items being considered, and n'_o is the number of observers being considered.

For example, Dr. Johnson can use the variance components to estimate the generalizability for a measurement strategy in which two observers use only one item:

$$\rho_t^2 = \frac{3.233}{3.233 + \dfrac{0.044}{1} + \dfrac{0.494}{2} + \dfrac{1.417}{1 \times 2}},$$

$$= \frac{3.233}{3.233 + 0.999},$$

$$= .764.$$

This indicates that she would likely obtain a moderate level of generalizability, but she might consider increasing the number of observers and/or the number of items. For example, her estimate of the generalizability coefficient that would be obtained with two observers and two items is approximately .84:

$$\rho_t^2 = \frac{3.233}{3.233 + \dfrac{0.044}{2} + \dfrac{0.494}{2} + \dfrac{1.417}{2 \times 2}},$$

$$= \frac{3.233}{3.233 + 0.623},$$

$$= .838.$$

Equation 13.2 reveals the core advantage of a generalizability approach over a CTT approach to measurement. From the CTT perspective in which error is undifferentiated, there is no ability to gauge the separate effects of observers and items and thus no ability to evaluate different combinations of numbers of observers and items as separate facets of the measurement strategy. However, the G theory perspective (i.e., Equation 13.2 along with estimated variance components) allows Dr. Johnson to estimate the psychometric quality of various combinations of observers and items. By systematically testing various combinations of numbers of observers and numbers of items, she can estimate the generalizability for various measurement strategies. This information, considered along with the practical costs and benefits of adding observers and/or items, can help optimize the efficiency and quality of a measurement strategy.

To illustrate the results of such a process, Table 13.10 and Figure 13.2 present generalizability coefficients estimated for various combinations of observers and items. These estimates are derived from Equation 13.2, using the variance components reported in Table 13.6. The values illustrate two important points. First, Dr. Johnson could find the combinations of observers and items that would be estimated to produce a specific reliability. For example, an estimated reliability of .80 is obtained through several combinations of observers and items. Specifically, three observers using one item, one observer using five items, and two observers using two items would all be estimated to provide a reliability of approximately at least .80. So if she desires a minimum reliability of .80, then Dr. Johnson could weigh the costs and benefits of each of these three combinations. Second, Dr. Johnson can see the points at which adding more observers and/or items produces minimal increments in reliability. For example, consider the increment in reliability associated with using five observers instead of three. Figure 13.2 suggests that this increment would be relatively small, particularly considering the possible "cost" of increasing the number of observers who need to be recruited, trained, monitored, and so on. This kind of information might be useful in planning an efficient strategy for collecting behavioral observations.

Table 13.10   Generalizability Coefficients Estimated Using Variance Components

		Coefficient	
Items (n_i')	Observers (n_o')	Relative (ρ_t^2)	Absolute (ϕ_t^2)
1	1	.62	.54
1	3	.83	.74
1	5	.88	.80
3	1	.77	.68
3	3	.91	.85
3	5	.94	.89
5	1	.80	.71
5	3	.92	.87
5	5	.95	.91
7	1	.82	.73
7	3	.93	.88
7	5	.96	.92

Other Measurement Designs

The examples in this discussion have included a single-facet strategy and a two-facet strategy, but G theory is applicable to a variety of measurement situations, and there are many variations on the strategies that have been illustrated. There are at least four important ways in which G theory analyses can differ, and these differences depend on the design of the measurement strategy and the intended use of the scores.

Number of Facets

As our two examples have illustrated, measurement designs can differ in the number of facets. One-facet designs are quite common in some areas of research and practice. For example, the typical self-report personality questionnaire is a one-facet measurement strategy, with items as the only facet. Furthermore, for some one-facet designs, G theory is equivalent to CTT. However, multiple-facet designs can be very useful for a variety of theoretical or practical reasons. As illustrated in our examples, Dr. Johnson had practical reasons for including multiple observers and multiple items as two facets of her potential measurement strategy. Measurement strategies could be even more complex, with more than two or three facets.

As illustrated in this chapter, the number of facets has implications for the number of effects in the analysis. Larger, more complex designs involve more effects, which generate more variance components. The variance components can provide important

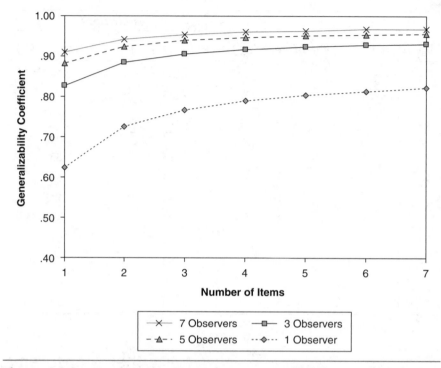

Figure 13.2   Two-Facet Design: Relative Generalizability Coefficients as a Function of Number of Items and Number of Observers

information about the factors affecting scores, and they are used to estimate generalizability coefficients. Apart from this complexity, the basic logic and process of G theory is similar across designs with fewer and greater numbers of facets.

Random Versus Fixed Facets

In a G theory analysis, each facet is considered either random or fixed. This is a somewhat subtle difference that is decided by the individual conducting the analysis, and the individual must make the decision for each facet. The logic and examples outlined in this chapter reflect *random facets*, which are common in most applications of G theory. Consider the item facet in Dr. Johnson's two-facet design. We mentioned that Dr. Johnson viewed the three items as representative of a large universe of items that could have been selected for the study. In a sense, the three items are a random sample from this universe. That is, Dr. Johnson would not care if the three items that she used were exchanged for three different aggression items (e.g., confrontational, antagonistic, combative). Because Dr. Johnson views the items as exchangeable or as a random sample from a universe of items, she considers the item facet to be random.

Other measurement designs might include *fixed facets*. A facet is considered fixed if the individual conducting the G theory analysis does *not* wish to generalize beyond the few conditions included in the analysis. For example, Dr. Johnson might truly be interested in only the three items used in her study, without conceptualizing them as being representative of some broader set of items. If she did not view these items as exchangeable for other items (i.e., if she did not view the items as being randomly selected from a universe of aggression items), then she would consider "item" to be a fixed facet. In addition, a facet is considered fixed if all conditions of a facet are included in the analysis. For example, a developmental psychologist might wish to assess children's aggressiveness through questionnaires completed by both biological parents. In this case, "biological parent" might be a facet of the measurement design, and the psychologist might be interested in generalizing across both parents. However, the mother and the father exhaust the entire set of "biological parents," and so the psychologist cannot generalize beyond the mother and the father to a larger universe of biological parents. That is, the universe of the biological parent facet includes only two conditions—mother and father. And since the psychologist's study includes the only two possible conditions, the entire universe is represented in her study, and the facet is considered fixed.

For a G theory analysis, the individual conducting the analyses must consider the fixed versus random difference for each facet in the design. For multiple-facet studies, it is possible to have a mixed design in which one or more facets are fixed and one or more facets are random. For example, the developmental psychologist obtaining aggressiveness ratings from parents might have a mixed two-facet design. As discussed, the biological parent facet should probably be considered fixed. However, if each parent rates the child on three items that were randomly selected from a universe of potential aggressiveness items, then the item facet should probably be considered random. With one fixed facet and one random facet, the psychologist has a mixed design.

Although the difference between fixed and random facets is somewhat subtle, it can have important implications for the analyses that are conducted and for the psychometric results. There are at least two ways in which the difference can have psychometric implications.

First, the distinction between random effects and fixed effects can affect the apparent psychometric quality of one's assessment. For example, we recomputed the generalizability coefficient (for the target effect) for Dr. Johnson's procedure, based on a two-observer, one-item design. Earlier, we estimated the coefficient to be $\rho_t^2 = .76$, based on the assumption that all facets were random. We reestimated this coefficient based on the assumption that the item facet is fixed while the observer facet is random. Following the terms laid out by Brennan (1992), the results showed that the target effect's generalizability coefficient in this mixed design is $\rho_t^2 = .77$. That is, the estimated generalizability in the mixed model is somewhat greater than in the fully random model. Although the difference here is small (.77 vs. .76), it can be substantial. Moreover, the direction of the difference is typical, the generalizability from the mixed model being larger than the generalizability from the random model.

Second and relatedly, the distinction between random and fixed effects has implications for test users' ability to make broad versus narrow generalizations about the quality of their measures. When treating a facet as random, test users are conceptualizing the elements of that facet as a random sample from a broad universe of elements. For example, if Dr. Johnson treats "items" as a random facet, then she is conceptualizing her particular items as being drawn from a broad universe of items that could be used to measure aggression. Thus, she is attempting to generalize broadly—that is, from her particular items to that broad universe of items. In contrast, when treating a facet as fixed, test users are conceptualizing the elements of that facet in a much more narrow way, being interested only in those facets, without regard to the larger set of items. For example, if Dr. Johnson treats "items" as fixed, then she is interested only in the particular items that she chooses to use. Thus, she is attempting to evaluate the degree to which scores from one assessment might generalize to another assessment using the same item(s).

In sum, the question of whether a given facet should be considered random or fixed needs to be answered by the individual planning to use the measurement. That is, there is no generally correct or incorrect answer to the question. Although most measurement strategies are likely to be conceptualized in terms of random effects, any particular measurement strategy might be used in a way that includes one or more fixed effects.

Crossed Versus Nested Designs

In a G theory analysis with multiple facets, pairs of facets are either crossed or nested. This is an important characteristic of the research design in a G study (and in ANOVA more generally) because it has implications for the effects that can be estimated. Our two-facet example reflects two effects that are *crossed*, which is common in many applications of G theory. In this design, each of the three observers rated each of the three items. That is, a rating was made for each possible combination of the observer facet and the item facet. When data are gathered for each possible combination of two facets, the facets are said to be crossed.

In contrast, a *nested* design occurs when all possible combinations of two facets are not included in the study. For example, Dr. Johnson could have conducted a study in which each observer used different items—Doris might have used the items mean, quarrelsome, and angry, Ken might have used the items hostile, aggressive, and belligerent, and Tim might have used the items confrontational, combative, and antagonistic. In this case, there are nine items, but each observer rates only three. Thus, all possible combinations of items and observers are not represented in the design, and we would say that items are nested in observers.

The issue of crossing and nesting is important because it determines which effects can be estimated in a G theory analysis, which affects the apparent psychometric quality of the measurement strategy. For example, in the two-facet design illustrated earlier, in which the facets are crossed, seven effects were estimated—three main effects, three two-way interactions, and a residual term. However, if items were nested in observers, then only five effects could be estimated. This design difference, in turn, creates differences in the way generalizability coefficients are computed and thus creates differences in the conclusions that can be drawn from the analyses. Again, a full discussion of this issue is beyond the scope of our presentation; however, we believe that it is important to be aware of the distinction between crossed versus nested designs and to realize that the distinction can affect G theory analyses.

Relative Versus Absolute Decisions

As mentioned earlier, G theory can be used to make two kinds of decisions. Our examples focused on "relative" decisions, which concern the relative order of participants. Again, if an honor society admits the top 15% of a group of students, then the society is interested in the rank order of the students, and their admissions decision is based on students' scores in relation to each other. When tests are used to make relative decisions, they are often called "norm-referenced tests" (Brennan, 2001).

In contrast, "absolute" decisions are based on the absolute level of an individual's score. For example, individuals attempting to enlist in the U.S. Army must take the Armed Services Vocational Aptitude Battery (ASVAB), which is described as a measure of

> knowledge and ability in ten different areas; from math to electronics. It is not an IQ test, but the ASVAB is one of the ways to help you decide what job areas in the Army would be best for you. (http://www.goarmy.com/contact/how_to_ join.jsp)

The Army's recruitment website tells potential recruits that "to be considered for enlistment in the Army, you need to score at least a 31." Presumably, a score below 31 disqualifies a recruit, but a score of 31 or greater keeps a recruit in the enlistment pool. Thus, the Army makes enlistment decisions partly based on a recruit's absolute score on the ASVAB, not by taking some percentage of recruits. When tests are used to make absolute decisions, they are often called "criterion-referenced tests" (Brennan, 2001).

In terms of estimating psychometric quality, the difference between relative and absolute decisions is important because it affects the way "noise" or error is conceived. That is, it affects the number of variance components that contribute to error when computing generalizability coefficients. In general, error consists of fewer components in relative decisions than in absolute decisions, and thus relative decisions tend to have larger generalizability coefficients.

For the one-facet example described earlier, absolute error variance (error variance for absolute decisions) includes one more component than relative error variance (error variance for relative decisions). Specifically, the generalizability coefficient for absolute decisions (ϕ^2, sometimes called an index of dependability) in the one-facet example is

$$\phi_t^2 = \frac{\sigma_t^2}{\sigma_t^2 + \dfrac{\sigma_i^2}{n_i'} + \dfrac{\sigma_{Res}^2}{n_i'}}.$$

Notice that this equation includes the variance component for the item effect, which was not included in the generalizability coefficient for relative decisions (see Equation 13.1). For a measurement strategy based on three items, the estimated absolute generalizability coefficient is .823:

$$\phi_t^2 = \frac{1.967}{1.967 + \dfrac{0.400}{3} + \dfrac{0.867}{3}}.$$

$$= \frac{1.967}{1.967 + 4.22},$$

$$= .823.$$

This coefficient is somewhat lower than the coefficient that was estimated for a relative decision ($\rho_t^2 = .87$). The final row in Table 13.4 presents absolute generalizability coefficients for various numbers of items.

For the two-facet example described earlier, absolute error variance includes three more components than relative error variance. Specifically, the generalizability coefficient for absolute decisions in the two-facet example is

$$\rho_t^2 = \frac{\sigma_t^2}{\sigma_t^2 + \dfrac{\sigma_i^2}{n'_i} + \dfrac{\sigma_o^2}{n'_o} + \dfrac{\sigma_{ti}^2}{n'_i} + \dfrac{\sigma_{to}^2}{n'_o} + \dfrac{\sigma_{io}^2}{n'_i n'_o} + \dfrac{\sigma_{Res}^2}{n'_o n'_i}}.$$

Notice that this equation includes the variance component for the item effect, the observer effect, and the Item × Observer interaction, none of which were included in the generalizability coefficient for relative decisions (see Equation 13.2). For a measurement strategy based on two items and two observers, the estimated generalizability coefficient for absolute decisions is .76:

$$\phi_t^2 = \frac{3.233}{3.233 + \dfrac{0.289}{2} + \dfrac{0.439}{2} + \dfrac{0.044}{2} + \dfrac{0.494}{2} + \dfrac{0.028}{2 \times 2} + \dfrac{1.417}{2 \times 2}},$$

$$= \frac{3.233}{3.233 + 0.944},$$

$$= 76.$$

This coefficient is somewhat lower than the coefficient that was estimated for a relative decision ($\rho_t^2 = .84$). The final row in Table 13.10 presents absolute generalizability coefficients for various numbers of items in the two-facet example.

It is worth noting that, in most research contexts, researchers are interested in the "relative" perspective rather than the absolute perspective. That is, they are interested in understanding the relative differences in participants' scores on a measure—why some people have relatively high scores and why some people have relatively low scores. Researchers are less interested in participant's absolute scores on the tests. For example, they are not interested in understanding why Ann has an average aggression score of 2.67 and why Drew has an average of 5.78 (see Table 13.5). Rather, they are more interested in understanding why Ann is approximately 3 points less aggressive than Drew—what makes her less aggressive and what are the implications of the difference in their scores. Thus, researchers will generally be interested in the "relative" perspective and in generalizability coefficients.

In sum, the difference between relative and absolute decisions can have important effects on the size of generalizability coefficients. By defining error in different ways, relative and absolute decisions include different variance components in error variance, which in turn creates differences in the resulting generalizability coefficients. Without worrying too much about why this difference exists or how the exact equations are generated, it is important to be aware of the differences and to be aware that absolute decisions are usually associated with greater error and less generalizability.

Summary

G theory expands the traditional perspective on psychometric quality in at least two ways. First, it extends our conceptualization of reliability to include the possibility that multiple facets might systematically affect the quality of a measurement strategy. Second, it provides the statistical tools to estimate the effects of each facet and to plan measurement designs that optimize quality and efficiency.

The current chapter outlined the basic logic as related to the most prototypical G theory design—relative decisions based on random facets that are crossed. However, it also briefly discussed alternative design issues that have implications for the logic, calculation, and interpretation in G theory. In sum, G theory is a flexible and powerful psychometric perspective that expands CTT in important ways.

Suggested Readings

The classic presentation of generalizability theory is:

> Cronbach, L. J., Gleser, G. C., Nanda, H., & Rajaratnam, N. (1972). *The dependability of behavioral measurements: Theory of generalizability for scores and profiles.* New York, NY: John Wiley.

The eminent psychometrician Lee Cronbach prepared a commentary on reliability theory and the widely used coefficient alpha nearly 50 years after its introduction. This commentary, as well as an argument that generalizability theory provides a more comprehensive perspective on reliability, is presented in:

> Cronbach, L. J., & Shavelson, R. J. (2004). My current thoughts on coefficient alpha and successor procedures. *Educational and Psychological Measurement, 64,* 391–418.

A rather technical but clear and thorough discussion of generalizability theory is presented in:

> Brennan, R. L. (2001). *Generalizability theory.* New York, NY: Springer-Verlag.

A widely used conceptual introduction to generalizability theory is presented in:

> Shavelson, R. J., & Webb, N. M. (1991). *Generalizability theory: A primer.* Newbury Park, CA: Sage.Four Scales of Measurement.

CHAPTER 14

Item Response Theory and Rasch Models

Item response theory (IRT) is another contemporary alternative to classical test theory (CTT). Although the roots of IRT have a long history (e.g., Lord, 1953; Rasch, 1960), IRT has emerged relatively recently as an alternative way of conceptualizing and analyzing measurement in the behavioral sciences. IRT is more computationally complex than CTT, but its proponents suggest that this complexity is offset by several important advantages.

In this chapter, we present an overview of IRT, with the goal of outlining the conceptual basis of IRT in a relatively accessible manner. In many areas of contemporary psychological testing, IRT is an increasingly central part of test development and evaluation. Thus, for readers who wish to be familiar with some of the most contemporary approaches to test development and psychometrics, IRT is an important topic. Certainly, we won't discuss IRT in all its complexity and scope; indeed, IRT can be quite technically complex, and its scope is increasing consistently. Rather, our goal is to provide a solid overview of some of the most fundamental concepts of IRT and to do so in a way that will be relatively straightforward and conceptual.

We will describe some of the most fundamental concepts in IRT, including the idea of item parameters, measurement models, and test information. We'll use examples to help clarify these concepts, hopefully enhancing readers' overall grasp of IRT. Finally, we will discuss several of the general ways in which IRT has been used in psychological testing, demonstrating the breadth and applicability of this emerging psychometric approach.

Factors Affecting Responses to Test Items

At its heart, IRT is a psychometric approach emphasizing the fact that a person's response to a particular test item is influenced by qualities of the individual and by qualities of the item. Based on this perspective, IRT provides procedures for obtaining information about individuals, items, and tests. Advocates of IRT state that these procedures produce information that is superior to the information produced by CTT. As we shall see, various forms of IRT exist, representing different degrees of complexity or different applicability to various kinds of tests. In this way, IRT is indeed flexible and broad.

Imagine that Suzy takes a five-item test of mathematical ability. According to the most basic form of IRT, the likelihood that Suzy will respond correctly to Item 1 on the test is affected by two things. If Suzy has high mathematical ability, then she will have a relatively high likelihood of answering the item correctly. In addition, if Item 1 is difficult, then Suzy will have a relatively low likelihood of answering the item correctly. Therefore, the probability that she will respond correctly to Item 1 is affected by her mathematical ability and by the difficulty of Item 1. This logic can be extended to various kinds of psychological measures, but the basic form of IRT states that a person's response to an item is affected by the individual's trait level (e.g., Suzy's mathematical ability) and the item's difficulty level. More complex forms of IRT include additional factors (or parameters) affecting a person's responses to items.

Respondent Trait Level as a Determinant of Item Responses

One factor affecting a person's probability of responding in a particular way to an item is the individual's level on the psychological trait being assessed by the item. For example, a person who has a high level of mathematical ability will be more likely to respond correctly to a math item than will a person who has a low level of mathematical ability. Similarly, a person who has a high level of extraversion will be more likely to endorse or agree with an item that measures extraversion than will a person who has a low level of extraversion. An employee who has a high level of job satisfaction will be more likely to endorse an item that measures job satisfaction than will an employee with a low level of job satisfaction.

Item Difficulty as a Determinant of Item Responses

An item's level of difficulty is another factor affecting a person's probability of responding in a particular way. A math item that has a high level of difficulty will be less likely to be answered correctly than a math item that has a low level of difficulty (i.e., an easy item). For example, the item "What is the square root of 10,000?" is less likely to be answered correctly than is the item "What is 2 + 2?" Similarly, an extraversion item that has a high level of difficulty will be less likely to be endorsed than an extraversion item that has a low level of difficulty.

At first, the notion of "difficulty" might not be intuitive in the case of some psychological attributes. For example, it might be odd to think of a personality inventory as having "difficult" items, but consider these two hypothetical items that you might find on a questionnaire to measure extraversion: "I enjoy having conversations with friends" and "I enjoy speaking before large audiences." Assuming that these two items are validly interpreted as measures of extraversion, the first item is, in a sense, easier to endorse than the second item. That is, it is likely that more people would say that it is enjoyable to have a conversation with friends than to speak in front of a large audience. Similarly, in the context of job satisfaction, the statement "My job is OK" is likely "easier" to agree with than is the statement "My job is the best thing in my life."

Although they are separate issues in an IRT analysis, trait level and item difficulty are intrinsically connected. In fact, item difficulty is conceived in terms of trait level. Specifically, a difficult item requires a relatively high trait level to be answered correctly, but an easy item requires only a low trait level to be answered correctly. Returning to the two mathematical items, students might need to have a ninth-grade mathematical ability in order to have a good chance of answering correctly a square root question. In contrast, they might need only a second-grade mathematical ability to have a good chance of answering correctly an addition question.

The connection between trait level and difficulty might be particularly useful for understanding the concept of item difficulty in personality inventories or attitude surveys. Recall the extraversion items mentioned earlier: "I enjoy having conversations with friends" and "I enjoy speaking before large audiences." We suggested that the first item is easier than the second. Put another way, the first item requires only a low level of extraversion to be endorsed, but the second would seem to require a much higher level of extraversion to be endorsed. That is, even people who are fairly introverted (i.e., people who have relatively low levels of extraversion) would be likely to agree with the statement that they enjoy having conversations with their friends. In contrast, a person would probably need to be very extraverted to agree with the statement that he or she enjoys speaking in front of a large audience.

In an IRT analysis, trait levels and item difficulties are usually scored on a standardized metric, so that their means are 0 and the standard deviations are 1. Therefore, a person who has a trait level of 0 has an average level of that trait, and a person who has a trait level of 1.5 has a trait level that is 1.5 standard deviations above the mean. Similarly, an item with a difficulty level of 0 is an average item, and an item with a difficulty level of 1.5 is a relatively difficult item.

In IRT, item difficulty is expressed in terms of trait level. Specifically, an item's difficulty is defined as the trait level required for participants to have a .50 probability of answering the item correctly. If an item has a difficulty of 0, then a person with an average trait level (i.e., a person with a trait level of 0) will have a 50:50 chance of correctly answering the item. For that same item (i.e., an item with a difficulty of 0), a person with a high trait level (i.e., a trait level greater than 0) will have a higher chance of answering the item correctly, and a person with a low trait level (i.e., a trait level less than 0) will have a lower chance of answering the item correctly. Higher difficulty levels indicate that higher trait levels are required for participants to have a 50:50 chance of answering the item correctly. For example, if an item has a difficulty of 1.5, then a person with a trait level of 1.5 (i.e., a trait level that is 1.5 standard deviations above the mean) will have a 50:50 chance of answering the item correctly. Similarly, lower difficulty levels indicate that only relatively low trait levels are required for participants to have a 50:50 chance of answering the item correctly.

Item Discrimination as a Determinant of Item Responses

Just as the items on a test might differ in terms of their difficulties (some items are more difficult than others), they might also differ in terms of the degree to which they can differentiate individuals who have high trait levels from individuals who have low trait levels. This item characteristic is called item discrimination, and it is analogous to an item–total correlation from CTT (Embretson & Reise, 2000).

An item's discrimination value indicates the relevance of the item to the trait being measured by the test. An item with a positive discrimination value is at least somewhat consistent with the underlying trait being measured, and a relatively large discrimination value (e.g., 3.5 vs. .5) indicates a relatively strong consistency between the item and the underlying trait. In contrast, an item with a discrimination value of 0 is unrelated to the underlying trait supposedly being measured, and an item with a negative discrimination value is inversely related to the underlying trait (i.e., high trait scores make it *less* likely that the item will be answered correctly). Thus, it is generally desirable for items to have a large positive discrimination value.

Why would some items have good discrimination and others have poor discrimination? Consider the following two items that might be written for a mathematics test:

1. How many pecks are in three bushels? (a) 12 (b) 24

2. What is 10 times 10? (a) 10 (b) 100

Think about the first item for a moment. What is required of a respondent to answer this item correctly? To answer the item correctly, the student needs to have enough mathematical ability to perform multiplication. However, this item also requires additional knowledge of the number of pecks in a bushel. The fact that this item requires something apart from basic mathematical ability means that it is not very closely related to mathematical ability. In other words, having a high level of mathematical ability is not enough to answer the item correctly. The student might have the ability to multiply 4 times 3, but he or she might not have a very good chance of answering the item correctly without the knowledge that there are four pecks in a bushel. Thus, this item would likely have a low discrimination value, as it is only weakly related to the underlying trait being assessed by the test of mathematical ability. In other words, this item does not do a very good job of discriminating students who have a relatively high level of mathematical ability from those who have relatively low mathematical ability. Even if Suzy answers the item correctly and Johnny answers the items incorrectly, we might not feel confident concluding that Suzy has a higher level of mathematical ability than does Johnny—perhaps Johnny has the mathematical ability, but he simply does not know the number of pecks in a bushel (see our discussion of "Construct Irrelevant Content" in Chapter 8).

Now consider the second math item. What is required of a respondent to answer it correctly? This item requires the ability to perform multiplication, but it requires no additional knowledge or ability. The only quality of the student that is relevant to answering the item correctly is mathematical ability. Therefore, it is a much more "pure" mathematical item, and it is more strongly related to the underlying trait of mathematical ability than is the first item. Consequently, it would likely have a relatively high discrimination value. In other words, this item does a better job of discriminating individuals who have a relatively high level of mathematical ability from those who have relatively low mathematical ability. That is, if Suzy answers the item correctly and Johnny answers the items incorrectly, then we feel fairly confident concluding that Suzy has a higher level of mathematical ability than does Johnny.

Guessing

Guessing is related to a third item property that might affect participants' responses to some types of test items. For tests such as multiple-choice exams or true/false exams of knowledge or ability, some test takers might resort to guessing if they do not know the correct answer to an item. When taking such tests, participants might answer some items correctly, just on the basis of guessing and chance.

Thus, IRT can include a guessing component to account for this possibility, and it is related to the probability that participants will answer an item correctly purely on the basis of chance. For example, the guessing component for true/false items accounts for the fact that guessing will produce a correct answer 50% of the time. Similarly, the guessing component for multiple-choice items depends on the number of response options that are available—if there are four response options, then the guessing component accounts for the fact that guessing will produce a correct answer 25% of the time. This property is mainly relevant to tests of knowledge, skill, ability, or achievement, rather than personality or attitudes. That is, it is relevant for items that are scored as correct or incorrect; thus, it is likely to be examined only for tests with those types of items.

IRT Measurement Models

From an IRT perspective, we can identify the components affecting the probability that a person will respond in a particular way to a particular item. A *measurement model* expresses the mathematical links between an outcome (e.g., a person's response to a particular item) and the components that affect the outcome (e.g., qualities of the person and/or qualities of the item).

A variety of models have been developed from the IRT perspective, and these models differ from each other in at least two important ways. One important difference among the measurement models is in terms of the item characteristics, or *parameters*, that are included in the models. That is, some models are designed to account for only one parameter, whereas other, more complex models account for two or more parameters. A second important difference among measurement models is in terms of the response option format. For example, some models are designed to be used for binary items, such as true/false, yes/no, or correct/incorrect items. Others are designed for items with more than two response options (i.e., polytomous items), such as Likert-type items with five options reflecting one's level of agreement.

In this section, we describe some of the more commonly used IRT measurement models. Our descriptions are intended to convey the basic logic and meaning of the models, to further illuminate the logic and nature of an IRT perspective on psychometrics.

One-Parameter Logistic Model (or Rasch Model)

The simplest IRT model is often called the *Rasch model* or the *one-parameter logistic model* (1PL). According to this model, a person's response to a binary item (i.e., right/wrong, true/false, agree/disagree) is determined by the individual's trait level and only a single item characteristic or parameter—the item's difficulty.

One way of expressing the Rasch model is in terms of the probability that a person with a particular trait level will correctly answer an item that has a particular difficulty. This is often presented as (e.g., Embretson & Reise, 2000)

$$P(X_{is} = 1 | \theta_s, \beta_i) = \frac{e^{(\theta_s - \beta_i)}}{1 + e^{(\theta_s - \beta_i)}}. \tag{14.1}$$

This equation might require some explanation:

P refers to probability. In this, case it refers to a "conditional" probability, as described below.

X_{is} refers to a particular response (*X*) made by subject *s* to item *i*. More specifically, "$X_{is} = 1$" refers to a "correct" response or an endorsement of the item.

θ_s refers to the trait level of subject *s*.

β_i refers to the difficulty of item *i*.

e is the base of the natural logarithm (i.e., *e* = 2.7182818 . . .), found on many calculators.

So $P(X_{is}=1|\theta_s, \beta_i)$ refers to the probability (*P*) that subject *s* will respond to item *i* correctly. The vertical bar in this statement indicates that this is a "conditional" probability. That is, it indicates that the probability that the subject will correctly respond to the item depends on (i.e., is conditional on) the subject's trait level (θ_s) and the item's difficulty (β_i). As mentioned earlier, in an IRT analysis, trait levels and item difficulties are usually scaled on a standardized metric, so that their means are 0 and the standard deviations are 1.

Consider two examples, in terms of a mathematics test. First, what is the probability that a person who has an above-average level of math ability (say, a level of math ability that is 1 standard deviation above the mean, $\theta_s = 1$) will correctly answer an item that has a relatively low level of difficulty (say, $\beta_i = -.5$)?

$$P(X_{is} = 1|1, -.5) = \frac{e^{(1-(-.5))}}{1+e^{(1-(-.5))}} = \frac{e^{(1.5)}}{1+e^{(1.5)}} = \frac{4.48}{1+4.48} = .82.$$

These calculations indicate that there is a .82 probability that the individual will correctly answer the item. In other words, there is a high likelihood (i.e., greater than an 80% chance) that this individual will answer correctly. This should make intuitive sense because a person with a high level of ability is responding to a relatively easy item.

Now, what is the probability that a person who has a below-average level of math ability (say, a level of math ability that is 1.39 standard deviations below the mean, $\theta_s = -1.39$) will correctly answer an item that has a relatively low level of difficulty (say, $\beta_i = -1.61$)?

$$P(X_{is} = 1|-1.39, -1.61) = \frac{e^{(-1.39-(-1.61))}}{1+e^{(-1.39-(-1.61))}} = \frac{e^{(.22)}}{1+e^{(.22)}} = \frac{1.25}{1+1.25} = .56.$$

This indicates that there is a .56 probability that the individual will correctly answer the item. In other words, there is slightly more than a 50:50 chance that this individual will answer correctly. This should make intuitive sense because the individual's trait level ($\theta = -1.39$) is only slightly higher than the item's difficulty level ($\beta = -1.61$). Recall that the item difficulty level represents the trait level at which a person will have a 50:50 chance of correctly answering the item. Because the individual's trait level is slightly higher than the item's difficulty level, the probability that the individual will correctly answer the item is slightly higher than .50.

Two-Parameter Logistic Model

A slightly more complex IRT model is called the *two-parameter logistic model* (2PL) because it includes two item parameters. According to the 2PL model, a person's response to a binary item is determined by the individual's trait level, the item difficulty, and the item discrimination. Thus, the difference between the 2PL and the 1PL, or Rasch model, is the inclusion of the item discrimination parameter. This can be presented as (e.g., Embretson & Reise, 2000)

$$P(X_{is} = 1|\theta_s, \beta_i, \alpha_i) = \frac{e^{(\alpha_i(\theta_s - \beta_i))}}{1+e^{(\alpha_i(\theta_s - \beta_i))}}, \tag{14.2}$$

where α_i refers to the discrimination of item i, with higher values representing more discriminating items (and all other terms are defined as in the 1PL model above). Thus, the 2PL model states that the probability of a respondent answering an item correctly is conditional on the respondent's trait level (θ_s), the item's difficulty (β_i), and the item's discrimination (α_i).

Consider again the items "How many pecks are in three bushels?" and "What is 10 times 10?" Let us assume that the two items have equal difficulty (say, $\beta = -.5$). However, let us also assume that they have different discrimination values, as discussed earlier (say, $\alpha_1 = .5$ and $\alpha_2 = 2$).

Consider two potential responses to the first item. What is the probability that Suzy, who has an above-average level of math ability (say, a level of math ability that is 1 standard deviation above the mean, $\theta = 1$), will correctly answer Item 1?

$$P(X_{is} = 1|1, -.5, .5) = \frac{e^{(.5(1-(-.5)))}}{1 + e^{(.5(1-(-.5)))}} = \frac{e^{(.75)}}{1 + e^{(.75)}} = \frac{2.12}{1 + 2.12} = .68.$$

Now, what is the probability that Johnny, who has an average level of math ability ($\theta = 0$), will correctly answer Item 1?

$$P(X_{is} = 1|0, -.5, .5) = \frac{e^{(.5(0-(-.5)))}}{1 + e^{(.55(0-(-.5)))}} = \frac{e^{(.25)}}{1 + e^{(.25)}} = \frac{1.28}{1 + 1.28} = .56.$$

Take a moment to note the difference. Suzy's level of mathematical ability is substantially higher than Johnny's, but her probability of answering the item correctly is only slightly higher than Johnny's (i.e, .68 vs. .56). This is a relatively large difference in trait level (1 standard deviation) but a relatively small difference in the likelihood of answering the item correctly. Thus, this item doesn't seem to reflect the difference between the two respondents very well—the people are highly different in terms of trait level, but they are not very different in terms of the likelihood that they will answer the item correctly. That is, the item does not discriminate very robustly between people at different trait levels.

Now, let us consider the second item. What are the probabilities that Suzy and Johnny will answer Item 2 correctly?

$$\text{Suzy: } P(X_{is} = 1|1, -.5, 2) = \frac{e^{(2(1-(-.5)))}}{1 + e^{(2(1-(-.5)))}} = \frac{e^{(3)}}{1 + e^{(3)}} = \frac{20.09}{1 + 20.09} = .95.$$

$$\text{Johnny: } P(X_{is} = 1|0, -.5, 2) = \frac{e^{(2(0-(-.5)))}}{1 + e^{(2(0-(-.5)))}} = \frac{e^{(1)}}{1 + e^{(1)}} = \frac{2.72}{1 + 2.72} = .73.$$

Take a moment to consider the difference for Item 2. Suzy has a .95 probability of answering the item correctly, and Johnny has only a .73 probability of answering the item correctly. Recall that the difference between the students' mathematical ability is still 1 standard deviation, but (unlike for Item 1) Suzy's probability of answering Item 2 correctly is noticeably higher than Johnny's. As compared with Item 1, we see that Item 2—the item with the higher discrimination value—draws a sharper distinction between individuals who have different trait levels.

Just as the 2PL model is an extension of the Rasch model (i.e., the 1PL model), there are other models that are extensions of the 2PL model. You might not be surprised to learn that the *three-parameter logistic model* (3PL) adds yet another item parameter. We will forgo a discussion of this model, other than to note that the third parameter is an adjustment for guessing.

In sum, the 1PL, 2PL, and 3PL models represent IRT measurement models that differ with respect to the number of item parameters that are included in the models. However, all of these models are designed for items with binary outcomes as the response option. As mentioned earlier, there is at least one additional way in which IRT measurement models differ from each other—in terms of the response option format, particularly in terms of the number of response options.

Graded Response Model

Many tests, questionnaires, and inventories in the behavioral sciences include more than two response options. For example, many personality questionnaires include self-relevant statements (e.g., "I enjoy having conversation with friends"), and respondents are given three or more response options (e.g., *strongly disagree, disagree, neutral, agree, strongly agree*). Such items are known as a *polytomous items*, and they require IRT models that are different from those required by binary items. Models such as the graded response model (GRM; Samejima, 1969), the partial credit model (Masters, 1982), and the nominal response model (Thissen, Cai, & Bock, 2010) are polytomous IRT models.

Although the models for polytomous items differ in terms of the response options that they can accommodate, they rely on the same general principles as the models designed for binary items. That is, they reflect the idea that a person's response to an item is determined by the individual's trait level and by item properties, such as difficulty and discrimination.

However, these models are also more complex than the models for binary items. For example, the GRM produces several difficulty parameters for each item, whereas (as noted earlier) the previous models include only a single difficulty parameter. Furthermore, the nominal response model includes several discrimination parameters for each item.

We will briefly present the GRM, for two reasons. First, it provides a useful example representing these more complex models, thus expanding the possible insights into IRT. That is, a well-rounded basic understanding of IRT should include some familiarity with the logic of models designed for polytomous items, and the GRM is a good vehicle for doing so. Second, the GRM might be the most commonly applied IRT model in some areas of psychology, particularly in the measurement of personality and psychopathology (Preston, Reise, Cai, & Hays, 2011). Thus, some readers might be particularly likely to encounter this model in many applications of IRT.

In a sense, the GRM initially conceptualizes a polytomous item in terms of several dichotomous response distinctions. Generally speaking, if there are m response options or categories, then there are $m - 1$ distinctions. For example, consider again a personality questionnaire item such as "I enjoy having conversation with friends," which might have five response options (e.g., *strongly disagree, disagree, neutral, agree, strongly agree*). For such an item, there are four possible distinctions: (1) the difference between *strongly disagreeing* with the item and *disagreeing*, (2) the difference between *disagreeing* and being *neutral*, (3) the difference between being *neutral* and *agreeing*, and (4) the difference between *agreeing* and *strongly agreeing*.

According to the GRM, each of these dichotomous differences can be represented as follows:

$$P(X_{is} \geq j | \theta_s, \beta_{ij}, \alpha_i) = \frac{e^{(\alpha_i(\theta_s - \beta_{ij}))}}{1 + e^{(\alpha_i(\theta_s - \beta_{ij}))}}, \tag{14.3}$$

where j refers to a particular response option, β_{ij} is a difficulty parameter for response option j on item i, and the other parameters are as defined earlier. $P(X_{is} \geq j | \theta_s, \beta_{ij}, \alpha_i)$ refers to the probability that a person with trait level s will respond to item i in response option j or higher (which is conditional on the person's trait level, the difficulty of the relevant response distinction for category j of item i, and the discrimination value of item i). Because there are $m - 1$ dichotomous response differences, there are $m - 1$ difficulty parameters (β_{ij}s) for each item. Note however that the GRM includes only a single discrimination parameter (α_i) for an item.

For example, we might use our statistical software to analyze responses to the item "I enjoy having conversations with friends" and find the following (estimated) difficulty parameters: $\beta_1 = -1.78$, $\beta_2 = -.57$, $\beta_3 = .45$, $\beta_4 = 1.53$, $\alpha = 2.32$. These parameters indicate the difficulty associated with each response dichotomy. That is, each represents the trait level (i.e., θ) required to move from one response option to the next "higher" one on the scale. For example, the first difficulty parameter (β_1) reveals that someone who has a trait level of -1.78 has a 50% chance of responding higher than *strongly disagree* (i.e., responding *disagree* or more positively). Similarly, β_4 indicates that someone with a trait level of 1.53 will have a 50% chance of responding higher than *agree* (i.e., responding *strongly agree*).

Of course, response probabilities can be computed for people with particular trait levels, representing the probability that the person will respond in each of the response categories. For example, a person with an average level of extraversion $\theta_s = 0$), which is presumably the trait that drives responses to the "I enjoy having conversations with friends" item, would have the following response probabilities:

- Responding *disagree* or higher (i.e., responding higher than *strongly disagree*):

$$P(X_{is} \geq disagree | 0, -1.78, 2.32) = \frac{e^{(2.32(0-(-1.78)))}}{1 + e^{(2.32(0-(-1.78)))}} = \frac{62.15}{1 + 62.15} = .98.$$

- Responding *neutral* or higher (i.e., responding higher than *disagree*):

$$P(X_{is} \geq neutral | 0, -.57, 2.32) = \frac{e^{(2.32(0-(.57)))}}{1 + e^{(2.32(0-(-.57)))}} = \frac{3.75}{1 + 3.75} = .79.$$

- Responding *agree* or higher (i.e., responding higher than *neutral*):

$$P(X_{is} \geq agree | 0, .45, 2.32) = \frac{e^{(2.32(0-(.45))}}{1 + e^{(2.32(0-(.45))}} = \frac{.35}{1 + .35} = .26.$$

■ Responding *strongly agree* (i.e., responding higher than *agree*):

$$P(X_{is} = Strongly\ agree\,|\,0, 1.53, 2.32) = \frac{e^{(2.32(0-1.53))}}{1 + e^{(2.32(0-1.53))}} = \frac{.03}{1 + .03} = .03.$$

Take a moment to note the pattern of these probabilities, specifically the fact that they become smaller as the response options become more extremely positive (i.e., as the options reflect more "difficult" choices). We see that a person with an average trait level is very likely to respond higher than *strongly disagree*, which should make intuitive sense. That is, a person with an average level of extraversion would be strongly expected to say something besides *strongly disagree* when asked if he or she enjoys having conversations with friends. Going further, we see that this person would have a nearly 80% chance of responding without any level of disagreement (i.e., responding *neutral* or higher). Going even further, we see that the probabilities become smaller and smaller as the options reflect greater degrees of endorsement of the item (i.e., as they reflect more extreme levels of extraversion).

Using these values, we can then estimate the probability that a person will choose a specific response option when responding to this item. That is, Equation 14.3 can be seen as reflecting a person's probability of responding in particular *ranges* of response options (e.g., *disagree or higher, agree or higher*, etc.). These values can now be used to find the likelihood that the person will make a *specific* response to the item (e.g., *disagree, agree, strongly agree*, etc.). This can be done by computing the difference between two adjacent "range" probabilities, as just discussed:

$$P(X_{is} = j\,|\,\theta_s, \beta_{ij}, \alpha_i) = P(X_{is} \geq j-1\,|\,\theta_s, \beta_{ij}, \alpha_i) - P(X_{is} \geq j\,|\,\theta_s, \beta_{ij}, \alpha_i) \quad (14.4)$$

In this equation, *j* refers to one response option (e.g., *disagree*), and *j* − 1 refers to the immediately prior option (e.g., *strongly disagree*). Thus, based on the probabilities computed from Equation 14.3, we can estimate the following probabilities for a person with an average level of extraversion ($\theta_s = 0$):

■ Probability of endorsing the *strongly disagree* option = 1 − .98 = .02 (note that the probability of responding in the range of *strongly disagree* or higher is 1.0, since that range includes the entire set of response options).
■ Probability of endorsing the *disagree* option = .98 − .79 = .19
■ Probability of endorsing the *neutral* option = .79 − .26 = .53
■ Probability of endorsing the *agree* option = .26 − .03 = .23
■ Probability of endorsing the *strongly agree* option = .03 − .00 = .03 (note that the probability of responding higher than *strongly agree* is .00, since there are no response options beyond *strongly agree*)

Of course, people who have different trait levels will have different probabilities of responding to the various options. People with low trait levels will be relatively likely to respond with the lower response options (e.g., *strongly disagree* or *disagree*), indicating low endorsement of the trait. In contrast, people with high trait levels will be relatively likely to respond with higher response options, such as *agree* or *strongly agree*. By using the equations above, we could use the GRM to estimate response probabilities for any particular trait level.

Obtaining Parameter Estimates: A 1PL Example

You might wonder how we obtain the estimates of trait level, item difficulty, and item discrimination that are entered into the equations described above. In real-world research and application, these parameters are almost always estimated by using specialized statistical software to analyze individuals' responses to sets of items. Indeed, software packages such as PARSCALE, BILOG, and MUTLTILOG allow researchers to conduct IRT-based analyses (these programs are currently available from Scientific Software International). Although early versions of these packages were not very user-friendly, more recent versions are increasingly easy to use. Nevertheless, an example of a relatively simple IRT analysis conducted "by hand" might give you a deeper sense of how the process works and thus give you a deeper understanding of IRT in general.

Table 14.1 presents the (hypothetical) responses of six individuals to five items on a test of mathematical ability. In these data, "1" represents a correct answer, and "0" represents an incorrect answer. Such a small data set is not representative of "real-world" use of IRT. Ideally, we would have a very large data set, with many respondents and many items. However, we will use a small data set to illustrate IRT analysis as simply as possible.

An important step in IRT analysis is to choose an appropriate measurement model. Note that the responses in our example represent a binary outcome—correct versus incorrect. Therefore, we would choose a model that is appropriate for binary outcomes (e.g., the 1PL, 2PL, 3PL). Having focused on this class of models, we would then choose a model that includes parameters in which we are interested. An advanced issue involves an evaluation of which model "fits" best. That is, we could conduct analyses to determine whether a particular model *should be* applied to a particular data set. At this point, however, we will use the Rasch model (the 1PL model) as the measurement model for analyzing these data because it is the simplest model.

Several kinds of information can be obtained from these data. Recall from our earlier description of the 1PL that this model includes two determinants of an item

Table 14.1   Raw Data for IRT Example: A Hypothetical Five-Item Test of Mathematical Ability

Person	Item 1	Item 2	Item 3	Item 4	Item 5
1	1	0	0	0	0
2	1	1	0	1	0
3	1	1	1	0	0
4	1	1	0	1	0
5	1	1	1	0	1
6	0	0	1	0	0

NOTE: IRT = item response theory.

response—the respondent's trait level and the items' difficulty level. We will focus first on information about the respondents, and we will estimate a trait level for each of the six individuals who have taken the test. We will then estimate the item difficulties.

The initial estimates of trait levels can be seen as a two-step process. First, we determine the proportion of items that each respondent answered correctly. For a respondent, the proportion correct is simply the number of items answered correctly divided by the total number of items that were answered. As shown in Table 14.1, Respondent 5 answered four of the five items correctly (4/5), so her proportion correct is .80. Table 14.2 presents the proportion correct for each respondent. To obtain estimates of trait levels, we next take the natural log of the ratio of proportion correct to proportion incorrect:

$$\theta_s = \ln\left(\frac{P_s}{1-P_s}\right), \tag{14.5}$$

where P_s is the proportion correct for Respondent 5. This analysis suggests that Respondent 5 has a relatively high trait level:

$$\theta_s = \ln\left(\frac{.80}{1-.80}\right) = \ln(4) = 1.39.$$

This suggests that Respondent 5's trait level is almost 1.5 standard deviations above the mean.

The initial estimates of item difficulties also can be seen as a two-step process. First, we determine the proportion of correct responses for each item. For an item, the proportion of correct responses is the number of respondents who answered the item correctly divided by the total number of respondents who answered the

Table 14.2   IRT Example: Item Difficulty Estimates and Person Trait-Level Estimates

Person	Item 1	Item 2	Item 3	Item 4	Item 5	Proportion Correct	Trait Level
1	1	0	0	0	0	0.20	−1.39
2	1	1	0	1	0	0.60	0.41
3	1	1	1	0	0	0.60	0.41
4	1	1	0	1	0	0.60	0.41
5	1	1	1	0	1	0.80	1.39
6	0	0	1	0	0	0.20	−1.39
Proportion correct	0.83	0.67	0.50	0.33	0.17		
Difficulty	−1.61	−0.69	0.00	0.69	1.61		

NOTE: IRT = item response theory.

item. For example, Item 1 was answered correctly by five of the six respondents, so Item 1's proportion of correct responses is 5/6 = .83. Table 14.2 presents the proportion of correct responses for each item. To obtain estimates of item difficulty, we compute the natural log of the ratio of the proportion of incorrect responses to the proportion of correct responses:

$$\beta_i = \ln\left(\frac{1 - P_i}{P_i}\right), \tag{14.6}$$

where P_i is the proportion of correct responses for item i. This analysis suggests that Item 1 has a relatively low difficulty level:

$$\beta_i = \ln\left(\frac{1 - .83}{.83}\right) = \ln(.20) = -1.61,$$

This value suggests that even a person with a relatively low level of mathematical ability (i.e., a trait level that is more than 1.5 standard deviations below the mean) will have a 50:50 chance of answering the item correctly. Table 14.2 presents the difficulty levels for each of the five items.

Table 14.2 provides initial estimates of ability levels and item difficulties. These results were obtained by using Microsoft Excel, rather than one of the specialized IRT software packages. When specialized IRT software is used to conduct analyses (as it should be for a complete IRT analysis), it implements additional processing to refine these initial estimates. This processing is an iterative procedure, in which estimates are made and then refined in a series of back-and-forth steps, until a prespecified mathematical criterion is reached. The details of this procedure are beyond the scope of our discussion, but such iterative processes are used in many advanced statistical techniques.

Item and Test Information

As a psychometric approach, IRT provides information about items and about tests. In an IRT analysis, item characteristics are combined to reflect characteristics of the test as a whole. In this way, item characteristics such as difficulty and discrimination can be used to evaluate the items and to maximize the overall quality of a test.

Item Characteristic Curves

Psychometricians who use IRT often examine item characteristic curves to present and evaluate characteristics of the items on a test. Item characteristic curves, such as those presented in Figure 14.1, reflect the probabilities with which individuals across a range of trait levels are likely to answer each item correctly. The item characteristic curves in Figure 14.1 are based on a 1PL analysis of the five items from the hypothetical mathematics test analyzed earlier. For item characteristic curves, the x-axis reflects a wide range of trait levels, and the y-axis reflects probabilities ranging from 0 to 1.0.

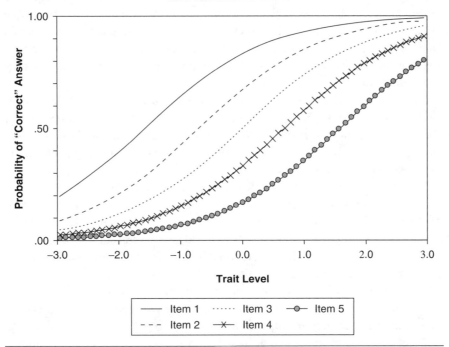

Figure 14.1 Item Characteristic Curves

Each item has a curve, and we can examine an item's curve to find the likelihood that a person with a particular trait level will answer the item correctly. Take a moment to study the curve for Item 1—what is the probability that a person with an average level of mathematical ability will answer the item correctly? We find the point on the Item 1 curve that is directly above the "0" point on the x-axis (recall that the trait level is in z score units, so zero is the average trait level), and we see that this point lies between .80 and .90 on the y-axis. Looking at the other curves, we see that a person with an average level of mathematical ability has about a .65 probability of answering Item 2 correctly, a .50 chance of answering Item 3 correctly, and a .17 probability of answering Item 5 correctly.

Thus, the item characteristic curves provide clues about the likelihoods with which individuals of any trait level would answer any item correctly. Note that the order of the curves, from left to right on the x-axis, reflects their difficulty levels. In Figure 14.1, Item 1, with the leftmost curve, is the easiest item, and Item 5, with the rightmost curve, is the most difficult item.

The item characteristic curves are drawn based on the mathematical models, as presented above (in Figure 14.1, the equation for the 1PL or Rasch model). To draw an item characteristic curve for an item, we can repeatedly use the model to compute the probabilities of correct responses for many trait levels. By entering an item's difficulty and a particular trait level (say, −3.0) into the model, we obtain the probability with which a person with that particular trait level will answer that item correctly. We can then enter a different trait level into the model (say, −2.9) and obtain the probability with which a person with the different trait level will answer the item correctly. After conducting this procedure for many different trait levels, we simply plot the probabilities that we have obtained. The line connecting these probabilities reflects the item's characteristic curve. We conducted this procedure for each of the items on the hypothetical five-item test in Table 14.1. To obtain Figure 14.1, we used the spreadsheet software package Microsoft Excel to compute 305 probabilities for the five items (61 probabilities for each item) and to plot the points onto curves.

As we have noted, the curves presented in Figure 14.1 are based on the simplest model—the 1PL model. Not only does this model include only one item parameter (i.e., difficulty), but it is also designed for items that have only two response possibilities (i.e., binary items). As discussed earlier, other models are designed for more complex measurement scenarios.

For example, recall that the GRM was designed for items with more than two response options, and it includes difficulty *and* discrimination parameters. Analyses based on this model would produce more complex characteristic curves for each of a test's items. That is, each item would have several curves—one for each of its response options. Each curve reflects the probabilities with which people of any trait level would choose a particular response option.

To illustrate this, we plotted an item characteristic curve for the item that we used earlier to illustrate the GRM ("I enjoy having conversations with friends"). Recall that it had five response options and the following parameter estimates: $\beta_1 = -1.78$, $\beta_2 = -.57$, $\beta_3 = .45$, $\beta_4 = 1.53$, $\alpha = 2.32$. Based on these values, we computed response probabilities for a wide range of trait levels, and we did this for each of the five response options. Figure 14.2 presents the curves for this item.

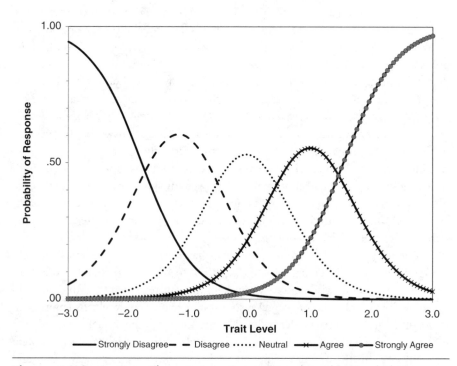

Figure 14.2 An Item Characteristic Curve, Based on the Graded Response Model

As shown in Figure 14.2, each response option has its own curve, representing the probability that people of any particular trait level will endorse that option. Note that as you move from one curve to another, from left to right in the figure, the options increase in their level of endorsement. That is, *strongly disagree* is farthest left, while *strongly agree* is farthest right. This ordering of the curves parallels, reflects, and is driven by, the four difficulty parameters (β values) produced by the analysis.

Based on the GRM, each item would have its own set of response curves like those in Figure 14.2. These item characteristic curves can convey visual information about the response tendencies associated with each item. Although test developers and users are interested in such tendencies, they are usually even more interested in the psychometric quality of each item and of the test as a whole. To examine this, they evaluate properties called item information and test information, which is closely related to reliability.

Item Information and Test Information

From the perspective of CTT, reliability is an important psychometric consideration for a test. Recall from Chapters 5 and 6 that from the perspective of CTT, we can articulate and estimate the reliability of a test. For example, we might compute coefficient alpha as an estimate of a test's reliability. An important point to note is that we would compute only *one* reliability estimate for a test and that estimate would indicate the degree to which observed test scores are correlated with true scores. The idea that there is a single reliability for a particular test is an important way in which CTT differs from IRT.

From the perspective of IRT, a test does not have a single "reliability." Instead, a test might have stronger psychometric quality for some people than for others. That is, a test might provide better information at some trait levels than at other trait levels. This is an important difference between IRT and CTT, and it might require a bit of explanation.

Imagine four people who have different trait levels—Elizabeth, Heather, Chris, and Lahnna. We can depict their relative "true" trait levels along a continuum:

Low trait level	Average trait level	High trait level
Elizabeth Heather		Chris Lahnna

In terms of the underlying psychological trait, Elizabeth and Heather are both below the mean, with a relatively small difference between them. In contrast, Chris and Lahnna are at a relatively high trait level, with a relatively small difference between them.

As we have emphasized repeatedly throughout this book, the purpose of psychological tests is to detect psychological variability. Indeed, the key goal of most psychological testing is to differentiate (i.e., discriminate) people with relatively high trait levels from people with lower trait levels. From an IRT perspective, a test provides "good information" when it can accurately detect differences between individuals at different trait levels.

Even a test that has modest psychometric quality should be able to reflect large differences in trait levels. For example, referring to the four individuals above, a test with moderate psychometric quality should be able to differentiate between the two people with below-average trait scores, on one hand, and the two people with above-average trait scores, on the other. That is, Elizabeth and Heather should score lower than Chris and Lahnna, even if the test is only a modestly good one.

However, if we want to reflect the much smaller and more subtle differences between test takers, then we would need a test with strong psychometric properties. For example, if we wanted to detect the difference between Elizabeth and Heather, or if we wanted to know whether Chris's trait level was different from Lahnna's, then the test would need to quite sensitive.

Moreover and importantly, an IRT approach allows for the possibility that a test might be better at reflecting differences at some trait levels rather than at other trait levels. For example, the test might be better at reflecting the difference between Chris and Lahnna than between Elizabeth and Heather. That is, the test might provide better information at high trait levels than at low trait levels.

How could a test provide information that differs by trait level? For example, why would a test be able to discriminate between people who have relatively high trait levels but not between people who have relatively low trait levels? Imagine a two-item test of mathematical ability:

1. What is the square root of 10,000?

2. Solve for x in this equation: $56 = 4x^2 + 3y - 14$.

Both items require a relatively high level of mathematical ability, at least compared with some potential items. If Elizabeth and Heather have low levels of mathematical ability (say, they can both add and subtract, although Heather can do this a bit better than Elizabeth), then they will answer neither item correctly. Therefore, Elizabeth and Heather will have the same score on the two-item test and the test cannot differentiate between them. In contrast, Chris and Lahnna have higher levels of mathematical ability, and each might answer at least one item correctly. Because Lahnna's ability level is a bit higher than Chris's, she might even answer both items correctly, but Chris might answer only one item correctly. Thus, Chris and Lahnna might have different scores.

Considering this pattern of responding, the test can reflect some differences but not others. That is, the test might differentiate the people with high trait levels (Chris and Lahnna) from the people with low trait levels (i.e., Elizabeth and Heather). In addition, it might differentiate the people with high trait levels (i.e., Chris from Lahnna) from each other. However, the test does not differentiate between the people with low trait levels.

In sum, if a test's items have characteristics (e.g., item difficulty levels) that are more strongly represented at some trait levels than at others, then the test's psychometric quality might differ by trait levels. The two-item mathematics test has items with only high difficulty levels, and thus it does not provide clear information discriminating among people at low trait levels.

We can use IRT to pinpoint the psychometric quality of a test across a wide range of trait levels. This can be seen as a two-step process. First, we evaluate the psychometric quality of each item across a range of trait levels. Just as we can compute the probability of a correct answer for an item at a wide range of trait levels (as illustrated in item characteristic curves, as discussed earlier), we can use the probabilities to compute information at the same range of trait levels. For the 1PL (Rasch) model, item information can be computed as (Embretson & Reise, 2000)

$$I(\theta)=P_i(\theta)(1-P_i(\theta)), \tag{14.7}$$

where $I((\theta)$ is the item's information value at a particular trait level (θ) and $P_i((\theta)$ is the probability that a respondent with a particular trait level will answer the item correctly. For example, Item 1 in Table 14.2 has an estimated difficulty level of −1.61. A person with a trait level that is, say, 3 standard deviations below the mean has a probability of only .20 of answering Item 1 correctly (see the equation for computing the probabilities for a Rasch model). Thus, for a trait level of 3 standard deviations below the mean $(\theta = -3)$, Item 1 has an information value of .16:

$$I(-3) = .20(1 - .20),$$

$$I(-3) = .16.$$

In contrast, Item 1 has an information value of .01 at a trait level of 3 standard deviations *above* the mean $(\theta = 3)$.

Higher information values indicate greater psychometric quality. Therefore, Item 1 has better psychometric quality at relatively low trait levels than at relatively high trait levels. That is, it is more capable of discriminating among people with low trait levels than among people with high trait levels (presumably because almost everyone with high trait levels will answer the item correctly). Table 14.3 includes probability values and information values that have been computed for each item at seven trait levels. If we compute information values at many more trait levels, we could display the results in a graph called an *item information curve.*

Table 14.3   IRT Example: Probability of Correct Item Responses, Item Information, and Test Information for Various Trait Levels

| Trait Level | P(X = 1\|θ) Probability of Correct Answer | | | | | Information | | | | | |
	Item 1	Item 2	Item 3	Item 4	Item 5	Item 1	Item 2	Item 3	Item 4	Item 5	Test
−3	0.20	0.09	0.05	0.02	0.01	0.16	0.08	0.05	0.02	0.01	0.32
−2	0.40	0.21	0.12	0.06	0.03	0.24	0.17	0.10	0.06	0.03	0.60
−1	0.65	0.42	0.27	0.16	0.07	0.23	0.24	0.20	0.13	0.06	0.86
0	0.83	0.67	0.50	0.33	0.17	0.14	0.22	0.25	0.22	0.14	0.97
1	0.93	0.84	0.73	0.58	0.35	0.06	0.13	0.20	0.24	0.23	0.86
2	0.97	0.94	0.88	0.79	0.60	0.03	0.06	0.10	0.17	0.24	0.60
3	0.99	0.98	0.95	0.91	0.80	0.01	0.02	0.05	0.08	0.16	0.32

NOTE: IRT = item response theory.

Figure 14.3a presents item information curves for each item in our hypothetical five-item test of mathematics. There are several important issues in interpreting these figures. First, the height of the curve indicates the amount of information that

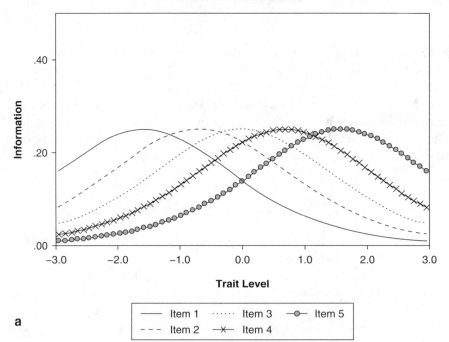

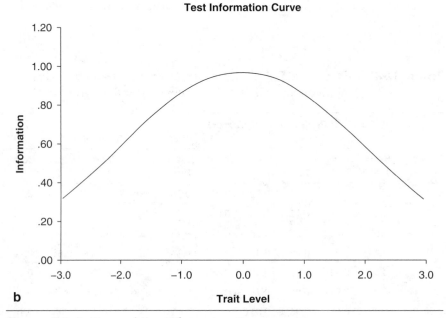

Figure 14.3 Test and Item Information Curves

the item provides—higher curves indicate greater psychometric quality. Second, the highest point on a curve represents the trait level at which the item provides the most information. In fact, an item provides the most information at a trait level that corresponds with its difficulty level, estimated earlier. For example, Item 1 (the easiest item) provides the best information at a trait level of −1.61, which is its difficulty level. In contrast, Item 1 does not provide much information at trait levels that are above average. Third, and relatedly, the items often differ in the points at which they provide good information. For example, Item 1 provides good information at relatively low trait levels, Item 3 provides good information at average trait levels, and Item 5 provides good information at relatively high trait levels.

Of course, when we actually use a psychological test, we are concerned with the quality of the test as a whole more than the qualities of individual items. Therefore, we can combine item information values to obtain test information values. Specifically, item information values at a particular trait level can be added together to obtain a test information value at that trait level. Again, Table 14.3 provides test information values for our five-item hypothetical test of mathematical ability at seven trait levels, and it shows, for example, that the test information score at an average trait level ($\theta = 0$) is simply the sum of the item information values at this trait level:

$$.97 = .14 + .22 + .25 + .22 + .14,$$

Again, if we compute test information scores at many trait levels, we can plot the results in a test information curve, as shown in Figure 14.3b.

A test information curve is useful for illustrating the degree to which a test provides a different quality of information at different trait levels. Note that our hypothetical test provides the greatest information at an average trait level and it provides less information at more extreme trait levels. That is, our test does well at differentiating among people who have trait levels within 1 or 2 standard deviations of the mean. In contrast, it is relatively poor at differentiating among people who have trait levels that are more than 2 standard deviations below the mean, and it is relatively poor at differentiating among people who have trait levels that are more than 2 standard deviations above the mean.

As we have described, Figure 14.3a presents item information curves based on the simplest IRT model—the 1PL or Rasch model. Again, this model includes only one type of item parameter—item difficulty. Thus, we see that the items can provide maximal information at different trait levels. That is, the items differ in their difficulty, and each one has its best psychometric quality at its specific difficulty level.

However, as we have also described, some IRT models include more than one item parameter. For example, the 2PL and the GRM include both difficulty and discrimination parameters for each item. Of course, item and test information can be estimated based on these models as well.

Although the logic behind item information is the same for these more complex models, its computation is more complex. Therefore, we will not delve into the complexities of those computations, but we will present and describe item information curves that are based on those models. Again, this can help expand your familiarity with IRT as a flexible psychometric approach.

For models that include both difficulty and discrimination as item parameters, item information curves can vary in two ways. First, as we have seen for the 1PL model, the curves can vary in terms of location. That is, they can vary in the trait levels at which their maximal information occurs, as reflected in the fact that the curves "top out" at different points along the x-axis. Second, item information curves can also vary in terms of height. That is, they can vary in the amount of information that they provide, as reflected in the fact that the curves "top out" at different points along the y-axis.

For example, Figure 14.4 presents three item information curves that could be obtained from models such as the 2PL or the GRM. Note that the curves differ in terms of location and height. From this figure, we see that Item 2 is the easiest item (with its greatest information occurring at approximately 1 standard deviation below the average trait level) and Item 3 is the most difficult (with its greatest information obtained at about 1 standard deviation above the average trait level). We also see that Item 2 provides the best psychometric quality by far. That is, its curve reaches much higher on the Information axis than do the other two items. In fact, Item 3 provides very little information, even at its maximal level.

Figures such as 14.4 can provide useful psychometric information for people interested in test development and evaluation. That is, they can highlight items that might merit revision or deletion from a test. For example, Figure 14.4 suggests that Item 3 provides almost no useful information at any trait level. Based

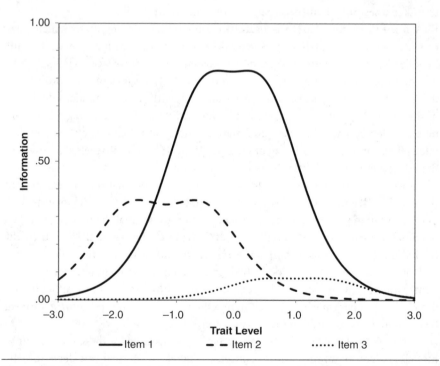

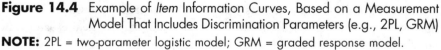

Figure 14.4 Example of *Item* Information Curves, Based on a Measurement Model That Includes Discrimination Parameters (e.g., 2PL, GRM)

NOTE: 2PL = two-parameter logistic model; GRM = graded response model.

on this finding, we might consider dropping that item, or at least examining it in more detail to determine why it performs so poorly (e.g., poor wording, inclusion of construct-irrelevant variance, etc.). In addition, if we decide to drop Item 3, we might want to replace it with an item (or items) that provides good information at high trait levels. Although Item 1 provides good information across a range of trait levels, we might want to be sure to have items that provide good information for making discriminations among people who are 1 to 3 standard deviations above the average trait level. Thus, item information curves can provide very useful insights into items, tests, and test development possibilities.

In sum, take a moment to consider again the difference between IRT and CTT with regard to test reliability. From a CTT perspective, a test has one reliability that can be estimated using an index such as coefficient alpha. From an IRT perspective, a test's psychometric quality can vary across trait levels. This is an important but perhaps underappreciated difference between the two approaches to test theory.

Applications of IRT

IRT is a theoretical perspective with tools that have many applications for measurement in a variety of psychological domains. The discussion of item difficulty and discrimination is perhaps most intuitively applied to the measurement of abilities. Indeed, the College Board has used IRT as the basis of the SAT for several years. In addition, several states use IRT as the basis of their achievement testing in public school systems. Beyond its application to ability testing, IRT has been applied to domains such as the measurement of attitudes (e.g., Strong, Breen, & Lejuez, 2004) and personality characteristics (Chernyshenko, Stark, Chan, Drasgow, & Williams, 2001; Fraley, Waller, & Brennan, 2000; Kashdan et al., 2009).

Test Development and Improvement

A fundamental application of IRT is the evaluation and improvement of the basic psychometric properties of items and tests. Using information about item properties, test developers can select items that reflect an appropriate range of trait levels and that have a strong degree of discriminative ability. Guided by IRT analyses, these selections can create a test with strong psychometric properties across a range of trait levels.

For example, Fraley et al. (2000) used IRT to examine the psychometric properties of four inventories (with a total of 12 subscales) associated with adult attachment. By computing and plotting test information curves for each subscale, Fraley and his colleagues revealed that one inventory in particular, the Experiences in Close Relationships scales (ECR; Brennan, Clark, & Shaver, 1998), provides a higher level of information than the other inventories. Even further, Fraley and his colleagues used IRT to guide and evaluate modifications to the ECR scales. These modifications produced revised ECR scales with better overall test information quality than the original ECR scales. Notably, this increase in test information was obtained without increasing the number of items.

Differential Item Functioning

Earlier in this book, we discussed test bias. From an IRT perspective, analyses can be conducted to evaluate the presence and nature of differential item functioning (DIF). Differential item functioning occurs when an item's properties in one group are different from the item's properties in another group. For example, DIF exists when a particular item has one difficulty level for males and a different difficulty level for females. Put another way, the presence of differential item functioning means that a male and a female who have the same trait level have different probabilities of answering the item correctly. The existence of DIF between groups indicates that the groups cannot be meaningfully compared on the item.

For example, Smith and Reise (1998) used IRT to examine the presence and nature of DIF for males and females on the Stress Reaction scale of the Multidimensional Personality Questionnaire (MPQ; Tellegen, 1982). The Stress Reaction scale assesses the tendency to experience negative emotions such as guilt and anxiety, and previous research has shown that males and females often have different means on such scales. Smith and Reise argued that this difference could reflect a true gender difference in such traits or that it could be produced by differential item functioning on such scales. Their analysis indicated that although females do appear to have higher trait levels of stress reaction, DIF exists for several items. Furthermore, their analyses revealed interesting psychological meaning for the items that did show DIF. Smith and Reise state that items related to "emotional vulnerability and sensitivity in situations that involve self-evaluation" were easier for females to endorse, but items related to "the general experience of nervous tensions, unexplainable moodiness, irritation, frustration, and being on-edge" (p. 1359) were easier for males to endorse. Smith and Reise conclude that inventories designed to measure negative emotionality will show a large gender difference when "female DIF-type items" are overrepresented and that such inventories will show a small gender difference when "male DIF-type items" are overrepresented. Such insights can inform the development and interpretation of important psychological measures.

Person Fit

Another interesting application of IRT is a phenomenon called *person fit* (Meijer & Sijtsma, 2001). When we administer a psychological test, we might find a person whose pattern of responses seems strange compared with typical responses. Consider two items that might be found on a measure of friendliness:

1. I like my friends.

2. I am willing to lend my friends as much money as they might ever want.

Most people would probably agree with the first statement (i.e., it is an "easy" item). In contrast, fewer people might agree with the second statement. Although most of us like our friends and would be willing to help them, not all of us would be truly willing to lend our friends "as much money as they might ever want." Certainly, those of us who would lend any amount of money to our friends also would be very likely to state that we like our friends (i.e., endorse the first item). That is, it would not be very strange to find someone who is willing to lend any amount of money to her friends if she also likes her friends, but it would be quite odd to find someone who would be willing to lend any amount of money to her friends if she does not like her friends. There are four possible response patterns for this pair of items, and three of these patterns would have a fairly straightforward interpretation.

Pattern	Item 1	Item 2	Interpretation
1	Disagree	Disagree	Unfriendly person
2	Agree	Disagree	Moderately friendly person
3	Agree	Agree	Very friendly person
4	Disagree	Agree	Unclear interpretation

The analysis of person fit is an attempt to identify individuals whose response pattern does not seem to fit any of the expected patterns of responses to a set of items. Although there are several approaches to the analysis of person fit (Meijer & Sijtsma, 2001), the general idea is that IRT can be used to estimate item characteristics and then to identify individuals whose responses to items do not adhere to those parameters. For example, IRT analysis might show that Item 1 above has low difficulty (i.e., it does not require a very high level of friendliness to be endorsed) and that Item 2 has higher difficulty. It would be odd to find a person who endorses a difficult item but who does not endorse an easy item.

The identification of individuals with poor person fit to a set of items has several possible implications. Poor person fit could indicate cheating, random responding, low motivation, cultural bias of the test, intentional misrepresentation, or even scoring or administration errors (Schmitt, Chan, Sacco, McFarland, & Jennings, 1999). Furthermore, in a personality assessment context, poor person fit might reveal that a person's personality is unique in that it produces responses that do not fit the "typically expected" pattern of responses (Reise & Waller, 1993).

Computerized Adaptive Testing

An additional application that is commonly associated with IRT is called *computerized adaptive testing* (CAT). CAT is a method of computerized test administration that is intended to provide an accurate and very efficient assessment of individuals' trait levels. Computerized adaptive testing works by using a very large item pool for which IRT has been used to obtain information about the psychometric properties of the items. For example, test administrators might assemble a pool of 300 items and conduct research to estimate the difficulty level for each item. Recall that item difficulty is linked to trait level—an item's difficulty level is the trait level that is required for a respondent to have a .50 probability of answering the item correctly. The information about item difficulties is entered into a computerized database.

As a person begins the test, the computer presents items with difficulty levels targeted at an average trait level (i.e., difficulty levels near zero). From this point, the computer adapts the test to match the individual's apparent trait level. If the individual starts the test with several correct answers, then the computer searches its database of items and selects items with difficulty levels that are a bit above average. These relatively difficult items are then presented to the individual. In contrast, if the individual starts the test with several incorrect answers, then the computer searches its database of items and selects items with difficulty levels that are a bit below average. These relatively easy items are then presented to the individual. Note that the two individuals might respond to two tests that are almost completely different.

As the individual continues taking the test, the computer continues to select items that pinpoint the individual's trait level. The computer tracks the individual's responses to specific items with known difficulty levels. By tracking this information, the computer continually reestimates the individual's trait level as the individual answers some items correctly and others incorrectly. The computer ends the test when it has presented enough items to provide a solid final estimation of the individual's trait level.

Interestingly, the accuracy and efficiency of computerized adaptive tests are obtained by giving different tests to different individuals. This might at first seem counterintuitive but consider the purpose of adaptive testing. The purpose of adaptive testing is to present items that target each individual's trait level efficiently. That is, it presents only the items that really help estimate precisely each examinee's trait level. If a person clearly has a high level of ability, then it is unnecessary to require the individual to respond to very easy questions. Similarly, if a person clearly has a lower level of ability, then we learn nothing by requiring the individual to respond to difficult items. Therefore, instead of presenting a common 300-item test to every individual, a CAT program presents each individual with only as many items as are required to pinpoint his or her trait level—probably much less than 300 items. Ideally, this method of test administration is more efficient and less aversive for respondents.

Computerized adaptive testing has been used mainly in ability, knowledge, and/or achievement testing. For example, the National Council of State Boards of Nursing (NCSBN) maintains licensure standards for nurses across the United States. Earning a license involves a testing process that uses a pool of nearly 2,000 items with known difficulty levels and a CAT administration process to present items and score respondents. The website for the NCSBN assures candidates for licensure that, as compared with a traditional pencil-and-paper test format, "CAT is able to produce test results that are more stable using fewer items by targeting items to the candidate's ability" (NCSBN, 2010, p. 46). Similarly, the Graduate Management Admissions Test (GMAT) is taken by nearly a quarter of a million people worldwide each year (Graduate Management Admission Council [GMAC], 2011), and as of this writing, it is primarily administered through computerized adaptive testing. To explain the adaptive nature of the test, the website for the GMAT informs test takers that "the GMAT adjusts to your individual ability level, which both shortens the time it takes to complete the exam and establishes a higher level of accuracy than a fixed test." (GMAC, n.d.). Clearly, CAT is a practically useful application of IRT, and its use seems to be growing.

Summary

In sum, IRT is an approach to psychometrics that is said to have several advantages over traditional CTT. IRT encompasses a variety of statistical models that represent the links between item responses, examinee trait level, and an array of item characteristics. Knowledge of item characteristics, such as item difficulty and item discrimination, can inform the development, interpretation, and improvement of psychological tests.

Although IRT-based analyses are computationally complex, specialized software has been designed to conduct the analyses, and this software is becoming more and more user-friendly. Continued research and application will reveal the nature and degree of practical advantage that IRT has over CTT.

Suggested Readings

An accessible introduction to a variety of issues in IRT, oriented toward psychologists:

> Embretson, S. E., & Reise, S. (2000). *Item response theory for psychologists*. Mahwah, NJ: Lawrence Erlbaum.

This is a classic source in the history of IRT:

> Lord, F. M. (1953). The relation of test score to the trait underlying the test. *Educational and Psychological Measurement, 13*, 517–548.

This is an accessible discussion of the issues and challenges of using IRT in personality assessment:

> Reise, S. P., & Henson, J. M. (2003). A discussion of modern versus traditional psychometrics as applied to personality assessment scales. *Journal of Personality Assessment, 81*, 93–103.

This reference provides a thorough and in-depth description of many issues involving the Rasch model (1PL):

> Bond, T. G., & Fox, C. M. (2001). *Applying the Rasch model: Fundamental measurement in the human sciences*. Mahwah, NJ: Lawrence Erlbaum.

This is a nice example of the application of IRT to psychological data:

> Fraley, R. C., Waller, N. G., & Brennan, K. A. (2000). An item-response theory analysis of self-report measures of adult attachment. *Journal of Personality and Social Psychology, 78*, 350–365.

This is a nice conceptual introduction to IRT:

> Hambleton, R. K., Swaminathan, H., & Rogers, H. J. (1991). *Fundamentals of item response theory*. Newbury Park, CA: Sage.

References

Abelson, R. P. (1985). A variance explanation paradox: When a little is a lot. *Psychological Bulletin, 97,* 129–133.

Allen, M. J., & Yen, W. M. (1979). *Introduction to measurement theory.* Monterey, CA: Brooks/Cole.

Alliger, G. M., & Dwight, S. A. (2000). A meta-analytic investigation of the susceptibility of integrity tests to coaching and faking. *Educational and Psychological Measurement, 60,* 59–72.

American Educational Research Association, American Psychological Association, and National Council on Measurement in Education. (1999). *Standards for educational and psychological testing.* Washington, DC: American Educational Research Association.

American Psychiatric Association. (1994). *Diagnostic and statistical manual of mental disorders* (4th ed.). Washington, DC: Author.

American Psychological Association. (n.d.). *Psychological assessment: Journal description.* Retrieved from http://www.apa.org/journals/pas/description.html

Anderson, C. A., & Dill, K. E. (2000). Video games and aggressive thoughts, feelings, and behavior in the laboratory and in life. *Journal of Personality and Social Psychology, 78,* 772–790.

Armor, D. J. (1974). Theta reliability and factor scaling. In H. L. Costner (Ed.), *Sociological methodology* (pp. 17–50). San Francisco, CA: Jossey-Bass.

Bachman, J. G., & O'Malley, P. M. (1984). Yea-saying, nay-saying, and going to extremes: Black–White differences in response style. *Public Opinion Quarterly, 48,* 491–509.

Baer, R. A., & Miller, J. (2002). Underreporting of psychopathology on the MMPI-2: A meta-analytic review. *Psychological Assessment, 14,* 16–26.

Baer, R. A., Wetter, M. W., & Berry, D. T. R. (1992). Detection of underreporting of psychopathology on the MMPI: A meta-analysis. *Clinical Psychology Review, 12,* 509–525.

Bartholomew, D. J. (1996). *The statistical approach to social measurement.* New York, NY: Academic Press.

Bartholow, B. D., Sestir, M. A., & Davis, E. B. (2005). Correlates and consequences of exposure to video game violence: Hostile personality, empathy, and aggressive behavior. *Personality and Social Psychology Bulletin, 31,* 1573–1586.

Baumeister, R. F., & Leary, M. R. (1995). The need to belong: Desire for interpersonal attachments as a fundamental human motivation. *Psychological Bulletin, 117,* 497–529.

Beck, A. T., Steer, R. A., & Brown, G. K. (1996). *Beck Depression Inventory–II (BDI-II).* San Antonio, TX: Harcourt Assessment.

Beck, A. T., Ward, C. H., Mendelson, M., Mock, J., & Erbaugh, J. (1961). An inventory for measuring depression. *Archives of General Psychiatry, 4,* 561–571.

Berry, D. T. R., Baer, R. A., Rinaldo, J. C., & Wetter, M. W. (2002). Assessment of malingering. In J. N. Butcher (Ed.), *Clinical personality assessment* (2nd ed., pp. 269–302). New York, NY: Oxford University Press.

Binks, P. G., Gouvier, W. D., & Waters, W. F. (1997). Malingering detection with the dot counting test. *Archives of Clinical Neuropsychology, 12,* 41–46.

Blanton, H., & Jaccard, J. (2006). Arbitrary metrics in psychology. *American Psychologist, 61,* 27–41.

Block, J. (1965). *The challenge of response sets: Unconfounding meaning, acquiescence and social desirability in the MMPI.* New York, NY: Appleton-Century-Crofts.

Boone, K. B., Lu, P., Back, C., King, C., Lee, A., Philpott, L., . . . Warner-Chacon, K. (2002). Sensitivity and specificity of the Rey Dot Counting Test in patients with suspect effort and various clinical samples. *Archives of Clinical Neuropsychology, 17,* 625–642.

Borsboom, D., Mellenbergh, G. J., & Van Heerden, J. (2004). The concept of validity. *Psychological Review, 111,* 1061–1071.

Brennan, K. A., Clark, C. L., & Shaver, P. R. (1998). Self-report measurement of adult attachment: An integrative overview. In J. A. Simpson & W. S. Rholes (Eds.), *Attachment theory and close relationships* (pp. 46–76). Reading, MA: Addison-Wesley.

Brennan, R. L. (1992). Generalizability theory. *Educational Measurement: Issues and Practice, 11,* 27–34.

Brennan, R. L. (2001). *Generalizability theory.* New York, NY: Springer-Verlag.

Brogden, H. E., & Taylor, E. K. (1950). The dollar criterion: Applying cost accounting concepts to criterion selection. *Personnel Psychology, 3,* 133–154.

Brown, T. A. (2006). *Confirmatory factor analysis for applied research.* New York, NY: Guilford Press.

Burns, R. C. (1987). *Kinetic house-tree-person drawings (K-H-T-P): An interpretative manual.* New York, NY: Brunner-Routledge.

Butcher, J. N., Atlis, M., & Fang, L. (2000). The effects of altered instructions on the MMPI-2 profiles of college students who are not motivated to distort their responses. *Journal of Personality Assessment, 74,* 492–501.

Butcher, J. N., Dahlstrom, W. G., Graham, J. R., Tellegen, A., & Kaemmer, B. (1989). *Minnesota Multiphasic Personality Inventory–2 (MMPI-2): Manual for administration and scoring.* Minneapolis: University of Minnesota Press.

Butcher, J. N., Morfitt, R. C., Rouse, S. V., & Holden, R. R. (1997). Reducing MMPI–2 defensiveness: The effect of specialized instructions on retest validity in a job applicant sample. *Journal of Personality Assessment, 68,* 385–401.

Byrne, B. (2001). *Structural equation modeling with AMOS: Basic concepts, applications, and programming.* Mahwah, NJ: Lawrence Erlbaum.

Byrne, B. (2006). *Structural equation modeling with EQS* (2nd ed.). Mahwah, NJ: Lawrence Erlbaum.

Cady, V. M. (1923). *The estimation of juvenile incorrigibility* (Journal of Delinquency Monograph Series, No. 2). Whitter, CA: California Bureau of Juvenile Research, Whittier State School.

Campbell, D. T., & Fiske, D. W. (1959). Convergent and discriminant validation by the multitrait-multimethod matrix. *Psychological Bulletin, 56,* 81–104.

Chernyshenko, O. S., Stark, S., Chan, K. Y., Drasgow, F., & Williams, B. A. (2001). Examining the fit of IRT models to personality items. *Multivariate Behavioral Research, 36,* 523–562.

Cloud, J., & Vaughn, G. M. (1970). Using balanced scales to control acquiescence. *Sociometry, 33,* 193–202.

Cohen, B. H. (2001). *Explaining psychological statistics* (2nd ed.). New York, NY: Wiley.

Cohen, J. (1988). *Statistical power analysis for the behavioral sciences* (2nd ed.). Hillsdale, NJ: Lawrence Erlbaum.

Cohen, J. (1990). Things I have learned (so far). *American Psychologist, 45,* 1304–1312.

College Board. (2006). *SAT Reasoning Test.* Retrieved from http://www.collegeboard.com/student/testing/sat/about/SATI.html

Coombs, C. H. (1950). Psychological scaling without a unit of measurement. *Psychological Review, 57,* 15–158.

Coopersmith, S. (1981). *The antecedents of self-esteem.* Palo Alto, CA: Consulting Psychologists Press. (Original work published 1967)

Cortina, J. M. (1993). What is coefficient alpha? An examination of theory and applications. *Journal of Applied Psychology, 78,* 98–104.

Costa, P. T., & McCrae, R. R. (1992). *Revised NEO Personality Inventory (NEO-PI–R) and NEO Five-Factor Inventory (NEO-FFI) professional manual.* Odessa, FL: Psychological Assessment Resources.

Costello, A. B., & Osborne, J. W (2005). Best practices in exploratory factor analysis: Four recommendations for getting the most from your analysis. *Practical Assessment, Research & Evaluation, 10*(7), 1–9.

Couch, A., & Keniston, K. (1960). Yea-sayers and nay-sayers: Agreeing response set as a personality variable. *Journal of Abnormal and Social Psychology, 20,* 151–174.

Criminal Procedure Act, N.C. Gen. Stat. & 15A-2005 (2007).

Crocker, L., & Algina, J. (1986). *Introduction to classical and modern test theory.* New York, NY: Holt, Rinehart & Winston.

Cronbach, L. J. (1942). Studies of acquiescence as a factor in the true-false test. *Journal of Educational Psychology, 33,* 410–415.

Cronbach, L. J. (1946). Response sets and test validity. *Educational and Psychological Measurement, 6,* 475–494.

Cronbach, L. J. (1950). Further evidence on response sets and test design. *Educational and Psychological Measurement, 10,* 3–31.

Cronbach, L. J. (1960). *Essentials of psychological testing* (2nd ed.). New York, NY: Harper & Row.

Cronbach, L. J. (1988). Five perspectives on the validity argument. In H. Wainer & H. I. Braun (Eds.), *Test validity* (pp. 3–18). Hillsdale, NJ: Lawrence Erlbaum.

Cronbach, L. J., Gleser, G. C., Nanda, H., & Rajaratnam, N. (1972). *The dependability of behavioral measurements: Theory of generalizability for scores and profiles.* New York, NY: Wiley.

Cronbach, L. J., & Meehl, P. E. (1955). Construct validity in psychological tests. *Psychological Bulletin, 51,* 281–302.

Cronbach, L. J., & Shavelson, R. J. (2004). My current thoughts on coefficient alpha and successor procedures. *Educational and Psychological Measurement, 64,* 391–418.

Crowne, D. P., & Marlowe, D. (1960). A new scale of social desirability independent of psychopathology. *Journal of Consulting Psychology, 24,* 349–354.

D'Andrade, R., & Dart, J. (1990). The interpretation of *r* versus r^2 or why percent of variance accounted for is a poor measure of size of effect. *Journal of Quantitative Anthropology, 2,* 47–59.

Diamantopoulos, A., & Siguaw, J. A. (2000). *Introducing LISREL: A guide for the uninitiated.* London, England: Sage.

Donovan, J. J., Dwight, S. A., & Hurtz, G. M. (2003). An assessment of the prevalence, severity, and verifiability of entry-level applicant faking using the randomized response technique. *Human Performance, 16,* 81–106.

Dunlap, W. P., Burke, M. J., & Greer, T. (1995). The effect of skew on the magnitude of product–moment correlations. *Journal of General Psychology, 122,* 365–377.

Educational Testing Service. (2011). *About the test collection at ETS.* Retrieved from http://www.ets.org/test_link/about

Ekman, P., & Friesen, W. V. (1978). *Facial action coding system: A technique for the measurement of facial movement.* Palo Alto, CA: Consulting Psychologists Press.

Embretson, S. E., & Reise, S. (2000). *Item response theory for psychologists.* Mahwah, NJ: Lawrence Erlbaum.

Epstein, S. (1979). The stability of behavior: I. On predicting most of the people much of the time. *Journal of Personality and Social Psychology, 7,* 1097–1126.

Fabrigar, L. R., Wegener, D. T., MacCallum, R. C., & Strahan, E. J. (1999). Evaluating the use of exploratory factor analysis in psychological research. *Psychological Methods, 4,* 272–299.

Feldt, L. S., & Brennan, R. L. (1989). Reliability. In R. L. Linn (Ed.), *Educational measurement* (3rd ed., pp. 105–146). New York, NY: Macmillan.

Fink, A. M., & Butcher, J. M. (1972). Reducing objections to personality inventories with special instructions. *Educational and Psychological Measurement, 32,* 631–639.

Fraley, R. C., Waller, N. G., & Brennan, K. A. (2000). An item-response theory analysis of self-report measures of adult attachment. *Journal of Personality and Social Psychology, 78,* 350–365.

Furr, R. M. (2011). *Scale construction and psychometrics for social and personality psychology.* London, England: Sage.

Furr, R. M., Reimer, B., & Bellis, F. A. (2004). *Development and validation of the Impression Motivation and Efficacy Scale (IME)* (Unpublished technical report). Wake Forest University.

Galton, F. (1863). *Metreorographica, or methods of mapping the weather.* New York, NY: Macmillan.

Galton, F. (1869). *Hereditary genius.* London, England: Macmillan.

Galton, F. (1879). Psychometric experiments. *Brain, 2,* 149–162.

Galton, F. (1883). *Inquires into human faculty and its development.* London, England: Macmillan.

Galton, F. (1885). The measure of fidget. *Nature, 32,* 174–175.

Galton, F. (1889). Correlations and their measurement, chiefly from anthropometric data. *Nature, 39,* 238.

Galton, F. (1902). The most suitable proportion between the values of first and second prizes. *Biometrika, 1,* 385–399.

Galton, F. (1907). Grades and deviates. *Biometrika, 5,* 400–406.

Gebhardt, K., Bender, R., Bower, G., Dressler, A., Faber, S. M., Filippenko, A. V., . . . Tremaine, S. (2000). A relationship between nuclear black hole mass and galaxy velocity dispersion. *Astrophysical Journal, 539,* L13–L16.

Geiser, S., & Santilices, M. (2007). *Validity of high-school grades in predicting student success beyond the freshman year.* Berkeley: University of California, Center for Studies in Higher Education.

Geiser, S., & Studley, R. (2001, October). *UC and the SAT: Predictive validity and differential impact of the SAT I and SAT II at the University of California.* Oakland, CA: University of California Office of the President. (Available at http://www.ucop.edu/sas/research/researchandplanning/)

Ghiselli, E. E., Campbell, J. P., & Zedeck, S. (1981). *Measurement theory for the behavioral sciences.* San Francisco: W. H. Freeman.

Goldberg, L. R., Johnson, J. A., Eber, H. W., Hogan, R., Ashton, M. C., Cloninger, C. R., & Gough, H. C. (2006). The International Personality Item Pool and the future of public-domain personality measures. *Journal of Research in Personality, 40,* 84–96.

Gorsuch, R. L. (1983). *Factor analysis.* Hillsdale, NJ: Lawrence Erlbaum.

Gough, H. G. (1965). Conceptual analysis of psychological test scores and other diagnostic variables. *Journal of Abnormal Psychology, 70,* 294–302.

Graduate Management Admission Council. (n.d.). *Format and timing.* Retrieved from http://www.mba.com/the-gmat/test-structure-and-overview/format-and-timing.aspx

Graduate Management Admission Council. (2011). *2011 World Geographic Trend Report for GMAT examinees.* Retrieved from http://www.gmac.com/market-intelligence-and-research/research-library/geographic-trends/world-geographic-trends-report-ty11.aspx

Graham, J. R. (1990). *MMPI-2: Assessing personality and psychopathology.* New York, NY: Oxford University Press.

Green, P. E., & Rao, V. R. (1971). Conjoint measurement for quantifying judgmental data. *Journal of Marketing Research, 8,* 355–363.

Greenleaf, E. A. (1992). Measuring extreme response style. *Public Opinion Quarterly, 56,* 328–351.

Guilford, J. P. (1954). *Psychometric methods.* New York, NY: McGraw-Hill.

Gulliksen, H. (1950). *Theory of mental tests.* New York, NY: Wiley.

Hahn, J. (2005). Faking bad and faking good by college students on the Korean MMPI-2. *Journal of Personality Assessment, 85,* 65–73.

Hatcher, L. (1994). *A step-by-step approach to using the SAS system for factor analysis and structural equation modeling.* Cary, NC: SAS Institute.

Hayton, J. C, Allen, D. G., & Scarpello, V. G. (2004). Factor retention decisions in exploratory factor analysis: A tutorial on parallel analysis. *Organizational Research Methods, 7,* 191–205.

Hemphill, J. F. (2003). Interpreting the magnitude of correlation coefficients. *American Psychologist, 58,* 78–79.

Herszenhorn, D. M. (2006, May 5). As test-taking grows, test-makers grow rarer. *The New York Times.* Retrieved from http://www.nytimes.com/2006/05/05/education/05testers.html?pagewanted=1&_r=2.

Hill, R. W., Huelsman, T. J., Furr, R. M., Kibler, J., Vicente, B. B., & Kennedy, C. (2004). A new measure of perfectionism: The Perfectionism Inventory (PI). *Journal of Personality Assessment, 82,* 80–91.

Hogan, J., Barrett, P., & Hogan, R. (2007). Personality measurement, faking, and employment selection. *Journal of Applied Psychology, 92*(5), 1270–1285.

Hopwood, C. J., & Donnellan, M. B. (2010). How should the internal structure of personality inventories be evaluated? *Personality and Social Psychology Review, 14,* 332–346.

Howell, D. C. (1997). *Statistical methods for psychology* (4th ed.). Belmont, CA: Duxbury.

Hoyle, R. H. (2011). *Structural equation modeling for social and personality psychology.* London, England: Sage.

Hsu, L. M. (2004). Biases of success rate differences shown in binomial effect size displays. *Psychological Methods, 9,* 183–197.

Hu, L. T., & Bentler, P. M. (1999). Cutoff criteria for fit indexes in covariance structure analysis: Conventional criteria versus new alternatives. *Structural Equation Modeling, 6,* 1–55.

Jain, U., & Agrawal, L. (1977). Generality of extreme response style. *Journal of Psychological Researches, 21,* 67–72.

Jensen, A. R. (1980). *Bias in mental testing.* New York, NY: Free Press.

Jensen, A. R. (1998). *The g factor.* Westport, CT: Praeger.

Jensen, A. R. (2005). Mental chronometry and the unification of differential psychology. In R. J. Sternberg & J. E. Pretz (Eds.), *Cognition and intelligence: Identifying the mechanisms of the mind* (pp. 26–50). Cambridge, England: Cambridge University Press.

John, O. P., & Robins, R. W. (1993). Determinants of interjudge agreement on personality traits: The Big Five domains, observability, evaluativeness, and the unique perspective of the self. *Journal of Personality, 61,* 521–551.

Johnson, T. S., Engstrom, J. L., & Gelhar, D. K. (1997). Intra- and interexaminer reliability of anthropometric measurements of term infants. *Journal of Pediatric Gastroenterology & Nutrition, 24,* 497–505.

Johnson, T. S., Engstrom, J. L., Haney, S. L., & Mulcrone, S. L. (1999). Reliability of three length measurement techniques in term infants. *Pediatric Nursing, 25,* 13–17.

Kashdan, T. B., Gallagher, M. W., Silvia, P., Breen, W. E., Terhar, D., & Steger, M. F. (2009). The Curiosity and Exploration Inventory-II: Development, factor structure, and initial psychometrics. *Journal of Research in Personality, 43,* 987–998.

Kline, R. B. (2010). Principles and practice of structural equation modeling (3rd ed.). New York, NY: Guilford Press.

Knapp, T. R. (2005). *The reliability of measuring instruments* (3rd ed.). Retrieved from http://www.tomswebpage.net/images/reliability.doc

Knowles, E. S., & Nathan, K. (1997). Acquiescent responding in self-reports: Social concern or cognitive style. *Journal of Research in Personality, 31,* 293–301.

Leary, M. R. (1983). Social anxiousness: The construct and its measurement. *Journal of Personality Assessment, 47,* 66–75.

Leary, M. R., Kelly, K. M., Cottrell, C. A., & Schreindorfer, L. S. (2006). *Individual differences in the need to belong: Mapping the nomological network* (Unpublished manuscript). Wake Forest University.

Lees-Haley, P. R. (1996). Alice in validityland, or the dangerous consequences of consequential validity. *American Psychologist, 51,* 981–983.

Lelkes, Y., Krosnick, J. A., Marx, D. M., Judd, C. M., & Park, B. (2012). Complete anonymity compromises the accuracy of self-reports. *Journal of Experimental Social Psychology, 48,* 1291–1299.

Lentz, T. F. (1938). Acquiescence as a factor in the measurement of personality. *Psychological Bulletin, 35,* 659.

Lezak, M. D. (1995). *Neuropsychological assessment* (3rd ed.). New York, NY: Oxford University Press.

Loong, T.-W. (2003). Understanding sensitivity and specificity with the right side of the brain. *British Medical Journal, 327,* 716–719.

Lord, F. M. (1953). On the statistical treatment of football numbers. *American Psychologist, 8,* 750–751.

Lord, F. M. (1956). The measurement of growth. *Educational and Psychological Measurement, 46,* 421–437.

Lord, F. M. (1962). Elementary models for measuring change. In C. W. Harris (Ed.), *Problems in measuring change* (pp. 21–38). Madison: University of Wisconsin Press.

Lord, F. M., & Novick, M. R. (1968). *Statistical theories of mental test scores.* Reading, MA: Addison-Wesley.

Luce, R. D., & Tukey, J. W. (1964). Simultaneous conjoint measurement: A new type of fundamental measurement. *Journal of Mathematical Psychology, 1,* 1–27.

Lüscher, M., & Scott, I. (1969). *The Lüscher Color Test.* New York, NY: Washington Square Press.

Magnusson, D. (1967). *Test theory.* Reading, MA: Addison-Wesley.

Marcoulides, G. A. (1996). Estimating variance components in generalizability theory: The covariance structure analysis approach. *Structural Equation Modeling, 3,* 290–299.

Marsh, H. W., & Grayson, D. (1995). Latent variable models of multitrait-multimethod data. In R. H. Hoyle (Ed.), *Structural equation modeling: Concepts, issues, and applications* (pp. 177–198). Thousand Oaks, CA: Sage.

Masters, G. N. (1982). A Rasch model for partial credit scoring. *Psychometrika, 47,* 149–174.

Maxwell, S. E., & Delaney, H. D. (2000). *Designing experiments and analyzing data: A model comparison perspective.* Mahwah, NJ: Lawrence Erlbaum.

McArdle, J. J. (1996). Current directions in structural factor analysis. *Current Directions in Psychological Science, 5,* 10–17.

McCrae, R. R., & Costa, P. T., Jr. (1983). Social desirability scales: More substance than style. *Journal of Consulting and Clinical Psychology, 51,* 882–888.

McDonald, R. P. (1999). *Test theory: A unified treatment.* Mahwah, NJ: Lawrence Erlbaum.

Meijer, R. R., & Sijtsma, K. (2001). Methodology review: Evaluating person fit. *Applied Psychological Measurement, 25,* 107–135.

Meindl, P., Jayawickreme, E., Furr, R. M., & Fleeson, W. (2012). *Examining the consistency of moral behaviors and thoughts.* Unpublished Manuscript. Wake Forest University.

Merrens, M. (1970). Generality and stability of extreme response style. *Psychological Reports, 27,* 802.

Messick, S. (1989). Validity. In R. L. Linn (Ed.), *Educational measurement* (3rd ed., pp. 13–103). New York, NY: Macmillan.

Meyers, L. S., Gamst, G., & Guarino, A. (2006). *Applied multivariate research: Design and interpretation.* Thousand Oaks, CA: Sage.

Michell, J. (1990). *An introduction to the logic of psychological measurement.* Hillsdale, NJ: Lawrence Erlbaum.

Miller, M. B. (1995). Coefficient alpha: A basic introduction from the perspectives of classical test theory and structural equation modeling. *Structural Equation Modeling, 2,* 255–273.

Mittenberg, W., Patton, C., Canyock, E. M., & Condit, D. C. (2002). Base rates of malingering and symptom exaggeration. *Journal of Clinical and Experimental Neuropsychology, 24,* 1094–1102.

National Center for Fair & Open Testing (2007, August 20). *SAT I: A faulty instrument for predicting college success.* Retrieved from http://www.fairtest.org/satvalidity.html

National Council of State Boards of Nursing. (2010). *2010 NCLEX-RN detailed test plan.* Retrieved from https://www.ncsbn.org/2010_NCLEX_RN_Detailed_Test_Plan_Candidate.pdf

Nave, C. S., & Furr, R. M. (2006, January). *Development and validation of a social motivation/social efficacy scale.* Poster presented at the 7th annual meeting of the Society for Personality and Social Psychology, Palm Springs, CA.

Netemeyer, R. G., Bearden, W. O., & Sharma, S. (2003). *Scaling procedures: Issues and applications.* Thousand Oaks, CA: Sage.

Nunnally, J. C., & Bernstein, I. H. (1994). *Psychometric theory* (3rd ed.). New York, NY: McGraw-Hill.

O'Brien, E. J., & Epstein, S. (1988). *MSEI: Multidimensional Self-Esteem Inventory.* Odessa, FL: Psychological Assessment Resources.

Ones, D. S., Viswesvaran, C., & Reiss, A. D. (1996). The role of social desirability in personality testing for personnel selection: The red herring. *Journal of Applied Psychology, 81,* 660–679.

Osburn, H. G. (2000). Coefficient alpha and related internal consistency reliability coefficients. *Psychological Methods, 5,* 343–355.

Ozer, D. J. (1985). Correlation and the coefficient of determination. *Psychological Bulletin, 97,* 307–315.

Ozer, D. J. (1989). Construct validity in personality assessment. In D. Buss & N. Cantor (Eds.), *Personality psychology: Recent trends and emerging directions* (pp. 225–234). New York, NY: Springer-Verlag.

Paulhus, D. L. (1991). Measurement and control of response bias. In J. P. Robinson, P. R. Shaver, & L. S. Wrightsman (Eds.), *Measures of personality and social psychological attitudes* (pp. 17–59). New York, NY: Academic Press.

Paulhus, D. L. (2002). Socially desirable responding: The evolution of a construct. In H. Braun, D. N. Jackson, & D. E. Wiley (Eds.), *The role of constructs in psychological and educational measurement* (pp. 67–88). Hillsdale, NJ: Lawrence Erlbaum.

Picco, R. D., & Dzindolet, M. T. (1994). Examining the Lüscher Color Test. *Perceptual and Motor Skills, 79,* 1555–1558.

Piedmont, R. L., McCrae, R. R., Riemann, R., & Angleitner, A. (2000). On the invalidity of validity scales: Evidence from self-reports and observer ratings in volunteer samples. *Journal of Personality and Social Psychology, 78,* 582–593.

Preston, K., Reise, S., Cai, L., & Hays, R. D. (2011). Using the nominal response model to evaluate response category discrimination in the PROMIS emotional distress item pools. *Educational and Psychological Measurement, 71,* 523–550.

Rasch, G. (1960). *Probabilistic models for some intelligence and attainment tests.* Copenhagen, Denmark: Danish Institute for Educational Research.

Ray, J. J. (1983). Reviving the problem of acquiescent response bias. *Journal of Social Psychology, 121,* 81–96.

Raykov, T. (2004). Behavioral scale reliability and measurement invariance evaluation using latent variable modeling. *Behavior Therapy, 35,* 299–331.

Reise, S. P., & Waller, N. G. (1993). Traitedness and the assessment of response pattern scalability. *Journal of Personality and Social Psychology, 65,* 143–151.

Revelle, W., & Zinbarg, R. E. (2009). Coefficients alpha, beta, omega and the glb: Comments on Sijtsma. *Psychometrika, 74*(1), 145–154.

Rogers, R., Sewell, K. W., Martin, M. A., & Vitacco, M. (2003). Detection of feigned mental disorders: A meta-analysis of the MMPI-2 and malingering. *Assessment, 10,* 160–177.

Rogosa, D. R. (1995). Myths and methods: Myths about longitudinal research, plus supplemental questions. In J. M. Gottman (Ed.), *The analysis of change* (pp. 3–65). Hillsdale, NJ: Lawrence Erlbaum.

Roid, G. (2003). *Stanford-Binet Intelligence Scales* (5th ed., Technical Manual). Itasca, IL: Riverside.

Rorer, L. G. (1965). The great response-style myth. *Psychological Bulletin, 63,* 129–156.

Rosenberg, M. (1989). *Society and the adolescent self-image* (Rev. ed.). Middletown, CT: Wesleyan University Press.

Rosenthal, R., Rosnow, R. L., & Rubin, D. B. (2000). *Contrasts and effect sizes in behavioral research: A correlational approach.* New York, NY: Cambridge University Press.

Rosenthal, R., & Rubin, D. B. (1982). A simple, general purpose display of magnitude of experimental effect. *Journal of Educational Psychology, 74,* 166–169.

Sackett, P. R., Schmitt, N., & Ellingson, J. E. (2001). High-stakes testing in employment, credentialing, and higher education: Prospects in a post-affirmative-action world. *American Psychologist, 56,* 302–318.

Sackett, P. R., & Yang, H. (2000). Correction for range restriction: An expanded typology. *Journal of Applied Psychology, 85,* 112–118.

Samejima, F. (1969). Estimation of latent ability using a response pattern of graded scores. *Psychometric Monograph, 34*(4, Pt. 2, No. 17).

Schmidt, F. L. (1988). Validity generalization and the future of criterion-related validity. In H. Wainer & H. Braun (Eds.), *Test validity* (pp. 173–189). Hillsdale, NJ: Lawrence Erlbaum.

Schmidt, F. L., & Hunter, J. E. (1977). Development of a general solution to the problem of validity generalization. *Journal of Applied Psychology, 62,* 529–540.

Schmidt, F. L., Hunter, J. E., Pearlman, K., & Hirsh, H. R. (1985). Forty questions about validity generalization and meta-analysis. *Personnel Psychology, 38,* 697–798.

Schmidt, F. L., Oh, I.-S., & Le, H. (2006). Increasing the accuracy of corrections for range restriction: Implications for selection procedure validities and other research results. *Personnel Psychology, 59,* 281–305.

Schmitt, N. (1996). Uses and abuses of coefficient alpha. *Psychological Assessment, 8,* 350–353.

Schmitt, N., Chan, D., Sacco, J. M., McFarland, L. A., & Jennings, D. (1999). Correlates of person fit and effect of person fit on test validity. *Applied Psychological Measurement, 23,* 41–53.

Schwarz, N. (1999). Self-reports: How the questions shape the answers. *American Psychologist, 54,* 93–105.

Shavelson, R. J., & Webb, N. M. (1991). *Generalizability theory: A primer.* Newbury Park, CA: Sage.

Sijtsma, K. (2009). On the use, the misuse, and the very limited usefulness of Cronbach's alpha. *Psychometrika, 74,* 107–120.

Smith, G. T. (2005). On construct validity: Issues of method and measurement. *Psychological Assessment, 17,* 396–408.

Smith, L. L., & Reise, S. P. (1998). Gender differences on negative affectivity: An IRT study of differential item functioning on the Multidimensional Personality Questionnaire Stress Reaction Scale. *Journal of Personality and Social Psychology, 75,* 1350–1362.

Smith, P. B. (2004). Acquiescence response bias as an aspect of cultural communication style. *Journal of Cross-Cultural Psychology, 35,* 50–61.

Soares, J. (2008, September 24). *Open letter to faculty on Wake Forest's new admissions policy with annotated bibliography.* Retrieved from http://www.wfu.edu/wowf/2008/sat-act/soares/

Spencer, S. J., Steele, C. M., & Quinn, D. M. (1999). Stereotype threat and women's math performance. *Journal of Experimental Social Psychology, 35,* 4–28.

Spielberger, C. D. (1983). *Manual for the State-Trait Anxiety Inventory (STAI).* Palo Alto, CA: Consulting Psychologists Press.

Stevens, S. S. (1946). On the theory of scales of measurement. *Science, 1103,* 677–680.

Stevens, S. S. (1951). Mathematics, measurement, and psychophysics. In S. S. Stevens (Ed.), *Handbook of experimental psychology* (pp. 1–49). New York, NY: Wiley.

Strong, D. R., Breen, R., & Lejuez, C. W. (2004). Using item response theory to examine gambling affinity as an underlying vulnerability across a continuum of gambling involvement. *Personality and Individual Differences, 36,* 1515–1529.

Taylor, H. C., & Russell, J. T. (1939). The relationship of validity coefficients to the practical effectiveness of tests in selection: Discussion and tables. *Journal of Applied Psychology, 23,* 565–578.

Tellegen, A. (1982). *Brief manual of the Multidimensional Personality Questionnaire* (Unpublished manuscript). University of Minnesota.

Tellegen, A., & Waller, N. G. (2008). Exploring personality through test construction: Development of the Multidimensional Personality Questionnaire. In G. J. Boyle, G. Matthews, & D. H. Saklofske (Eds.), *The SAGE handbook of personality theory and assessment: Vol. 2. Personality measurement and testing* (pp. 261–292). London, England: Sage.

Thissen, D., Cai, L., & Bock, R. D. (2010). The nominal categories item response model. In M. L. Nering & R. Ostini (Eds.), *Handbook of polytomous item response theory models: Development and applications* (pp. 43–75). New York, NY: Taylor & Francis.

Thompson, B. (2004). *Exploratory and confirmatory factor analysis: Understanding concepts and applications.* Washington, DC: American Psychological Association.

Thorndike, E. L. (1918). The nature, purpose, and general methods of measurements of educational products. In *The seventeenth yearbook of the National Society for the Study of Education* (pp. 16–24). Bloomington, IL: Public School.

Thorndike, R. L. (1971). Concepts of cultural fairness. *Journal of Educational Measurement, 8,* 63–70.

Thorndike, R. M. (2005). *Measurement and evaluation in psychology and education* (7th ed.). Upper Saddle River, NJ: Pearson Education.

UC Office of the President. (n.d.). *Supporting documents for UC and the SAT: Predictive validity and differential impact of the SAT I and SAT II at the University of California* (Regressions.rtf). Retrieved from http://www.ucop.edu/sas/research/researchandplanning/supporting.htm

U.S. Figure Skating (2012). *International Judging System (IJS).* Retrieved from http://www.usfsa.org/New_Judging.asp?id=289

Vacha-Haase, T. (1998). Reliability generalization: Exploring variance in measurement error affecting score reliability across studies. *Educational and Psychological Measurement, 58,* 6–20.

Vacha-Haase, T., Kogan, L., Tani, C. R., & Woodall, R. A. (2001). Reliability generalization: Exploring reliability coefficients of MMPI clinical scales scores. *Educational and Psychological Measurement, 61,* 45–59.

Vance, R. J., & Colella, A. (1990). The utility of utility analysis. *Human Performance, 3,* 123–139.

Van Herk, H., Poortinga, Y. H., & Verhallen, T. M. M. (2004). Response styles in rating scales: Evidence of method bias in data from six EU countries. *Journal of Cross-Cultural Psychology, 35,* 346–360.

Viswesvaran, C., & Ones, D. S. (1999). Meta-analysis of fakability estimates: Implications for personality measurement. *Educational and Psychological Measurement, 59,* 197–210.

Viswesvaran, C., Ones, D. S., & Hough, L. M. (2001). Do impression management scales in personality inventories predict managerial job performance ratings? *International Journal of Selection and Assessment, 9,* 277–289.

Watson, D., Clark, L., & Tellegen, A. (1988). Development and validation of brief measures of positive and negative affect: The PANAS scales. *Journal of Personality and Social Psychology, 54,* 1063–1070.

Wechsler, D. (2003a). *WISC-IV administrative and scoring manual.* San Antonio, TX: Psychological Corporation.

Wechsler, D. (2003b). *WISC-IV technical and interpretive manual.* San Antonio, TX: Psychological Corporation.

Westen, D., & Rosenthal, R. (2003). Quantifying construct validity: Two simple measures. *Journal of Personality and Social Psychology, 84,* 608–618.

Westen, D., & Rosenthal, R. (2005). Improving construct validity: Cronbach, Meehl, and Neurath's ship. *Psychological Assessment, 17,* 409–412.

Wetter, M. W., & Corrigan, S. K. (1995). Providing information to clients about psychological tests: A survey of attorneys' and law students' attitudes. *Professional Psychology: Research and Practice, 26,* 474–477.

Widaman, K. F. (1985). Hierarchically nested covariance structure models for multitrait-multimethod data. *Applied Psychological Measurement, 9,* 1–26.

Wilkinson, L., & APA Task Force on Statistical Inference. (1999). Statistical methods in psychology journals: Guidelines and explanations. *American Psychologist, 54,* 594–604.

Wood, A. M., Linley, P. A., Maltby, J., Baliousis, M., & Joseph, S. (2008). The authentic personality: A theoretical and empirical conceptualization, and the development of the Authenticity Scale. *Journal of Counseling Psychology, 55,* 385–399.

Wright, B. D. (1997). A history of social science measurement. *Educational Measurement: Issues and Practice, 16,* 33–45.

Youngjohn, J. R. (1995). Confirmed attorney coaching prior to neuropsychological evaluation. *Assessment, 2,* 279–283.

Zimmerman, D. W., & Williams, R. H. (1982). Gain scores in research can be highly reliable. *Journal of Educational Measurement, 19,* 149–154.

Zinbarg, R. E., Revelle, W., Yovel, I., & Li, W. (2005). Cronbach's alpha, Revelle's beta, McDonald's omega: Their relations with each and two alternative conceptualizations of reliability. *Psychometrika, 70,* 123–133.

Subject Index

Author Index

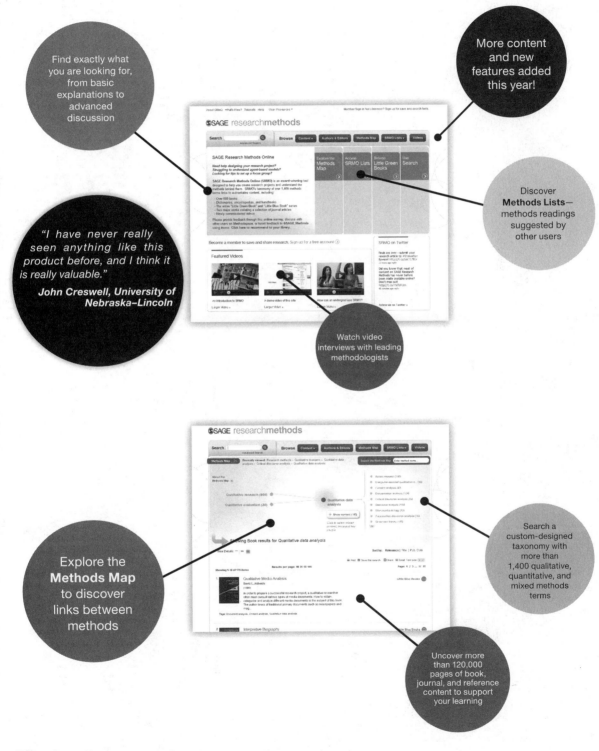

SAGE research methods

The essential online tool for researchers from the world's leading methods publisher

Find exactly what you are looking for, from basic explanations to advanced discussion

More content and new features added this year!

"I have never really seen anything like this product before, and I think it is really valuable."

John Creswell, University of Nebraska–Lincoln

Discover **Methods Lists**— methods readings suggested by other users

Watch video interviews with leading methodologists

Explore the **Methods Map** to discover links between methods

Search a custom-designed taxonomy with more than 1,400 qualitative, quantitative, and mixed methods terms

Uncover more than 120,000 pages of book, journal, and reference content to support your learning

Find out more at
www.sageresearchmethods.com